LECTURES
on
NATURAL RIGHT
and
POLITICAL SCIENCE

GEORG WILHELM FRIEDRICH HEGEL

LECTURES ON NATURAL RIGHT AND POLITICAL SCIENCE

THE FIRST PHILOSOPHY OF RIGHT

Heidelberg 1817–1818
with Additions from the Lectures of 1818–1819

Transcribed by
PETER WANNENMANN

Edited by the
STAFF OF THE HEGEL ARCHIVES

with an Introduction by
OTTO PÖGGELER

Translated by
J. MICHAEL STEWART and PETER C. HODGSON

UNIVERSITY OF CALIFORNIA PRESS
Berkeley Los Angeles London

University of California Press
Berkeley and Los Angeles, California

University of California Press
London, England

This volume is a translation of Georg Wilhelm Friedrich Hegel, *Vorlesungen über Naturrecht und Staatswissenschaft*, Heidelberg 1817/18 (vol. 1 of *G. W. F. Hegel: Vorlesungen: Ausgewählte Nachschriften und Manuskripte*), edited by C. Becker, W. Bonsiepen, A. Gethmann-Siefert, F. Hogemann, W. Jaeschke, Ch. Jamme, H.-Ch. Lucas, K. R. Meist, and H. Schneider, with an introduction by O. Pöggeler, copyright © 1983 by Felix Meiner Verlag GmbH, Hamburg.

Library of Congress Cataloging-in-Publication Data
Hegel, Georg Wilhelm Friedrich, 1770–1831.
    [Vorlesungen über Naturrecht und Staatswissenschaft. English]
    Lectures on natural right and political science: the first philosophy of right: Heidelberg, 1817–1818, with additions from the lectures of 1818–1819 / Georg Wilhelm Friedrich Hegel; transcribed by Peter Wannenmann; edited by the staff of the Hegel Archives; with an introduction by Otto Pöggeler; translated by J. Michael Stewart and Peter C. Hodgson.
    p.   cm.
    Includes bibliographical references and index.
    ISBN 0–520–20104–3 (alk. paper)
    1. Natural law.   2. Political science.   3. State, The.   I. Wannenmann, P. (Peter)   II. Ruhr-Universität Bochum. Hegel-Archiv.   III. Title.
JC233.H44613   1996
323'.01—dc20
                                       95–31238
                                         CIP

Printed in the United States of America

1 2 3 4 5 6 7 8 9

CONTENTS

PREFACE

We are pleased to offer this translation of the earliest version of Hegel's *Philosophy of Right*, namely the lectures on "Natural Right and Political Science" delivered in Heidelberg in 1817–18. The manuscript containing law student Peter Wannenmann's transcription of the lectures was discovered in 1982 and published a year later by the editorial staff of the Hegel Archives at the Ruhr University in Bochum. Plans for an English translation have been under way for a decade but have been delayed by various circumstances.

The annotations to the text provided by the German editors are limited to indications of sources for quotations and references to other works occurring in the text as well as to cross-references to other passages in the text. They are not a commentary and also do not seek to comment on parallel passages in Hegel's writings. As far as possible, references are to those editions that it is certain Hegel used; in other cases first editions are cited wherever possible. References are also given to modern standard editions in the original languages, but not to English translations except in the case of works by Hegel. The translators have added a few notes that call attention to significant differences between these lectures and the published version of 1821, *Elements of the Philosophy of Right*. For an excellent commentary see the editorial notes to the recent translation of the latter, edited by Allen W. Wood and translated by H. B. Nisbet (Cambridge University Press, 1991).

The textual apparatus of the German edition identifies all variations between Wannenmann's manuscript and the edited text. We retain only those variations that have a bearing on meaning. We have reproduced the emphasized words in the dictated paragraphs; presumably the emphasis is attributable to Hegel. The expository passages following the dictation are printed in the German without breaks; we have added paragraph breaks at appropriate points.

The translation principles guiding our work are similar to those established for other volumes in this series of Hegel Lectures; see the Editorial Introduction to *Lectures on the Philosophy of Religion*, vol. 1 (University of California Press, 1984), pp. 52–58. In particular it should be noted that we have avoided gender-specific language as much as possible. The glossary prepared for this work draws upon the one used for the philosophy of religion and has been greatly assisted by the glossary provided in the Wood and Nisbet edition of the philosophy of right. The translation of a few specific terms is discussed in the translators' notes, and the German of key terms or of difficult-to-translate terms is often given in brackets in the text. We have slightly modified and updated the bibliography; and we have added a few references to the editorial introduction by Otto Pöggeler.

Note: J. Michael Stewart died in December 1994 before this book could be published. The translation is largely his work, occupying much of his attention during his last two years. It is a fitting culmination to his contribution to Hegel studies through the new translations published by the University of California Press.

PETER C. HODGSON

ABBREVIATIONS

FREQUENTLY CITED WORKS

Fichte, *Beitrag*   Johann Gottlieb Fichte. *Beitrag zur Be-*
                         richtigung der Urtheile des Publikums
                         über die französische Revolution. Part 1,
                         Zur Beurtheilung ihrer Rechtmässigkeit.
                         N.p., 1793.

Fichte, *Gesamtausgabe*   Johann Gottlieb Fichte. *Gesamtausgabe.*
                         Published by the Bavarian Academy of
                         Sciences. Edited by R. Lauth, H. Jacob,
                         and H. Gliwitzky. Division I. Stuttgart–
                         Bad Cannstatt, 1964 ff.

Hegel, *Gesammelte*   Georg Wilhelm Friedrich Hegel. *Gesam-*
Werke   *melte Werke.* Edited by the Academy of
                         Sciences of Rhineland-Westphalia in as-
                         sociation with the Deutsche Forschungs-
                         gemeinschaft. 40 vols. projected. Ham-
                         burg, 1968 ff.

Hegel, *Werke*   Georg Wilhelm Friedrich Hegel. *Werke.*
                         Complete edition edited by an Associa-
                         tion of Friends. 18 vols. Berlin, 1832 ff.
                         Some volumes issued in second editions.

Kant, *Rechtslehre*   Immanuel Kant. *Metaphysische Anfangs-*
                         gründe der Rechtslehre. Königsberg,
                         1797. (Part 1 of the *Metaphysik der*
                         Sitten.)

Kant, *Schriften*	Immanuel Kant. *Gesammelte Schriften.* Edited by the Royal Prussian Academy of Sciences. Berlin, 1900 ff.
Montesquieu, *De l'esprit des lois*	(Charles Louis de Secondat, Baron de) Montesquieu. *Œuvres.* New edition, revised and supplemented by the author. Vol. 1 contains *Les XXI premiers livres de l'esprit des lois.* Vol. 2 contains *Les X derniers livres de l'esprit des lois.* London, 1757.
Montesquieu, *Œuvres complètes*	Montesquieu. *Œuvres complètes.* Vol. 2 contains *De l'esprit des lois,* pp. 225–995. N.p., 1951.

SIGNS AND SYMBOLS

[. . .]	= Insertions in the text by the editors and translators.
34 |	= Page numbers of the German edition, on the outer margin with page breaks marked by vertical slash in text. *Vorlesungen über Naturrecht und Staatswissenschaft* (Hamburg: Felix Meiner Verlag, 1983).
[*Ed.*]	= Editorial annotations.
[*Tr.*]	= Translators' notes.
Ms. reads:	= Readings of the manuscript that have been altered in the edited text for purposes of meaning.
Non-indented passages	= Hegel's dictated paragraphs.
Indented passages	= Hegel's expositions as recorded by Wannenmann.

INTRODUCTION

Otto Pöggeler

When Karl Marx published in 1844 an article in the *Deutsch-Französische Jahrbücher* intended as the introduction to his forthcoming *Critique of Hegel's Philosophy of Right*, he claimed that "German philosophy of right and of the state" was "the only form of German history standing on a par with the official present." Marx acknowledged that through Hegel (whose *Philosophy of Right* it was indeed his intention to criticize) "German philosophy of right and of the state" had received its "most consistent, richest, and final version." The actual political conditions in Germany were, in Marx's view, an anachronism; even those who rejected them had barely, by French chronology, reached the level of 1789. In Germany Luther had thrown off external religious authority in order to establish an inner religious authority—and make theology a contributing factor in the failure of the Peasant Wars. But philosophy had already taken the further steps needed to revolutionize the legacy of the past, with the Hegelian Left's critique of religion providing the final push in this direction.

Forming the counterpart to the dim view Marx took of German conditions by comparison with those in France were the equally bright prospects he sensed to be resulting from the contrast between political backwardness and the advances made by philosophy. Could discontent with existing conditions not combine with thought in such a way that prevailing conditions would be revolutionized once and for all? In thus looking for a final, conclusive revolution and the emancipation of "the" human being as such, the young Marx—before he turned to the analysis of English economic conditions and economic theories, and before the more strongly marked empiricism of his *German Ideology*—can be said to have been, in a bad sense, "more monkish" than Luther and "more philosophical" than Hegel. In any event by 1843, when he began to develop his critique of Hegel's political thought during his stay in Kreuznach, Marx had come to reject the idea of a representative constitution with which Hegel had sought to bind civil society (even as it was in process of emancipating itself) to the state once again and thus reconcile old European and revolutionary tendencies. Opposing historical forces must, in Marx's view, fight it out, and there was no logical artifice that could mediate between them. But this was to reject the basic idea that had underlain Hegel's concern with the questions posed by a "practical philosophy" from the time he had first begun writing political pamphlets. After Oriental despotism and classical republicanism, the system of representation, so we are told in his critique of the German constitution,[1] is a "third universal form" to which "world spirit" has attained in the political field.

The young Hegel had initially accepted the view that classical republicanism could be recovered for his own time through the French Revolution and by guiding the German spirit in the light of the shining example afforded by Greece. He had then seen, however, that in the political domain (as also in the religious) European history was being led by new motifs. The attachment of the Germanic peoples to the freedom of the individual, and the bond of loyalty of individuals, had continued to operate under feudalism. When in the fourteenth century new economic conditions gave rise to the emergence of strong guilds among the corporations set up by the estates, and the new municipalities developed auton-

1. [Tr.] The so-called *Verfassungsschrift*, composed between 1799 and 1803 (see Hegel, *Gesammelte Werke* 5:1–219); translated as "The German Constitution" in *Hegel's Political Writings*, trans. T. M. Knox with an introductory essay by Z. A. Pelczynski (Oxford, 1964), pp. 143–242.

omous forms of administration, the resulting territorial state had used the representation of these corporations and councils to place its authority on a stable basis. The French Revolution, it now seemed to Hegel, had swept away a system in which the rights of the estates no longer made possible the assumption of duties but had become mere privileges. Even where, instead of outmoded forms being swept away by revolutionary action, a reform sought to reintroduce reason to the legacy of tradition, the historically new was in Hegel's view at work, a process beginning with the rise of the middle classes during medieval times.

In opposition to Sieyes, Hegel insisted that representation and consequently the parliamentary system, under which in the large and complex states of the modern age the few speak for the many, had their roots in the Middle Ages. What had to be done was to reanchor the representatives to their proper sphere, to the sphere of the estates or classes (using that term [*Stände*] in a new sense). The problem that now arose was how to combine a parliamentary system of this kind, drawing the political consequences from the emancipation of civil society, with the state's traditional regulatory function. It was not only Karl Marx who saw in this the central problem of Hegel's philosophy of right but also Lassalle, who maintained in stronger terms the significance of the state, and also Lorenz von Stein, who carried the discussion over into the field of social science. Conversely, Hegel's view that civil society has emerged as a relatively independent form of the ethical in relation to the house or family and the polis or state was the point that proved unacceptable to a historian like Dahlmann or a Hegelian such as Johann Eduard Erdmann.

To begin with, Hegel was discussed primarily on the basis of his political options. It was left out of account that the young Hegel had been an enthusiastic supporter of the French Revolution, but that after bitter disappointment his hopes had then turned to Austria as trustee for a renewal of the German Empire. The question was whether Hegel, who since the battle of Jena had had an abiding enthusiasm for Napoleon, carried on the heritage of the Revolution or rather was to be claimed as the philosopher of the reestablished Prussian state. Was he not thus in fact the German national philosopher in the same way that Schiller and Goethe were regarded as the great national poets? Could he be claimed even for Bismarck's Germany?

When the wars and civil wars of the twentieth century had destroyed the old Europe and removed it from the center of the world, the question remained as to what contribution Hegel had made to consideration of the new direction taken by history since 1800. Was Hegel the philosopher who had recognized the emancipatory tendencies of civil society but, faced with the contradictions of development, had sought refuge in once more affirming the positive role of the state? Or had he appealed to the regulatory function of the state in a conservative or rather pro-governmental frame of mind? With his recourse to metaphysical solutions had he helped to pave the way for the most diverse varieties of totalitarianism? Or could not on the contrary the young Hegel at least be ranged on the side of those protesting against the senselessness of the present-day world, or at all events calling for a new experience of history and historicity? The main question in regard to Hegel now concerned less the changing options to which he subscribed than the guiding conception underlying his entire political philosophy.

When in the autumn of 1820 Hegel submitted his compendium *Naturrecht und Staatswissenschaft im Grundrisse* for publication, he attached to the book a preface[2] which adopted a harshly and one-sidedly polemical attitude toward current political affairs. However, in this preface Hegel does not deal only with contemporary events; instead he is mainly concerned to give vent to his awareness that there has been a break in world history. The traditions of practical philosophy or of political science extending from Aris-

---

2. [Tr.] See G. W. F. Hegel, *Elements of the Philosophy of Right*, ed. Allen W. Wood, trans. H. B. Nisbet (Cambridge: Cambridge University Press, 1991), pp. 9–23. The complete German title is *Naturrecht und Staatswissenschaft im Grundrisse: Grundlinien der Philosophie des Rechts* (Natural right and political science in outline: Elements of the philosophy of right). The work has come to be known by its subtitle.

totle to Christian Wolff have been given up along with the former pattern of Europe. This type of philosophizing, "which like an exercise in Scholasticism might have continued to spin its web in seclusion," has now, so he affirms, been brought into a closer relationship with actuality, "in which the principles of rights and duties are a serious matter." In this way it had come to an "open break." Hegel sees the danger of the time in the fact that the attempt to understand rights and duties on the basis of the self-determining activity of freedom turns into doubt as to whether this task is not in fact beyond the powers of reason. An "atheism of the ethical world" in his view sees the spiritual universe deserted by reason and merely repeats the confused protests of youth. When Hegel rebukes Fries on the occasion of his Wartburg oration for making the articulated fabric of ethical life into a mishmash of "heart," "friendship," and "enthusiasm," he is to be sure retracting key words that had been valid for him in his own youth, above all during the time of his association with Hölderlin in Frankfurt.

However, these motifs from Hegel's youth come to the surface again in 1844 when Ruge, Marx, Bakunin, and Feuerbach open their *Deutsch-Französische Jahrbücher* with an exchange of correspondence. Writing on the "Rousseau Island" in the Lake of Biel, Bakunin speaks of the silver tones of freedom and in this way alludes to lines in Klopstock's "Ode to the Revolution," which in the days of enthusiasm for the French Revolution were on everyone's lips (and so also occur in Hegel's student scrapbook). In a letter to Marx, Ruge quotes Hölderlin's lament for "this disjointed age" in his *Hyperion,* the work on which he was engaged when he and Hegel began to see each other again in Frankfurt. As Hegel's early writings were at that time still unknown, Marx hoped to find at least a pointer to Schelling's first published works. What was involved here, however, was not a question of reference to texts but the resurfacing of motifs that operated from within history itself as an actuating force on thought.

Today Hegel's 1820 *Philosophy of Right* stands beside Plato's *Republic* and Aristotle's *Politics,* beside Hobbes's *Leviathan* and Rousseau's *Contrat social.* Admittedly some are of the opinion that

Hegel's compendium lacks the literary merit and representative function of these other works. Was Hegel at all successful in giving full weight, in a mature and valid presentation, to the motifs that shaped his thought? Did he achieve for what was presented the demonstrative value he does after all claim for it? The work is seen as molded by a spirit of servility and accommodation, and it is feared that the tightened censorship resulting from the Carlsbad Decrees (1819) may have caused Hegel to pass over certain thoughts in silence. Heinrich Heine had already at an early stage characterized German philosophy (even if not that of Hegel in particular) as the "dream" of the French Revolution. After meeting Hegel's distant disciple Karl Marx he also attributed this role specifically to Hegelian philosophy. Heine spoke too of the fear of censorship, which in the form of self-censorship becomes "fear of one's own words." To be sure, imputations of this kind fail to take into account the way in which Hegel contrasted constitutional development in France and Germany in an all-embracing European comparison. They disregard what historical knowledge we may possess regarding censorship practice at that time and Hegel's relaxed reaction to it.

Hegel's *Philosophy of Right* cannot be discredited with this type of criticism; and it therefore remains incumbent on us to study the decisively new approaches made to the problem in the work of 1820—such as the redefinition of the role of society or the application of concepts of Aristotelian theology to the idea of the good as an end in itself. As a compendium, however, the *Philosophy of Right* was intended to be expounded in lectures and revision courses; moreover, it grew out of the actual business of lecturing. It may therefore be useful to make available in a study edition Hegel's first attempt at this subject—the dictated paragraphs and the transcript of his expositions from the lectures given at Heidelberg in the winter of 1817–18. The aim of this edition must not only be to add to the continuous stream of new variants and reconstructions of variants for the formulation of Hegel's thought, to which authentic texts afford us better access; it must also serve to orient us toward the study of his authorized publications, not away from them. The transcript published here indeed embodies Hegel's "original philosophy of right" and so makes it possible to identify with more certainty the starting point for that part of the definitive Hegelian system which presents the philosophy of objective spirit as a philosophy of right.

Hegel's lectures on "Natural Right and Political Science" were delivered in Heidelberg during the winter of 1817–18 six times a week from 10:00 to 11:00 A.M. "on the basis of dictated passages." They were given at a time when the restored Bourbon regime in France had acquired a constitutional basis in the Charter, and when the German *Länder*—especially the southwestern German states of Baden and Württemberg whose boundaries had been redefined— were seeking to give themselves a constitution in accord with the directives of the Congress of Vienna. Thus conversations everywhere were marked by discussions on constitutional matters. It was at this point that Hegel first emerged as a political author with a review of the constitutional negotiations in his native state of Württemberg.[3] So it is not surprising that the formulation of part of his system for delivery as lectures lays stress, in a manner not encountered again, on questions of constitutional development as well as on institutions such as trial by jury, and that it harshly criticizes possible cases of arbitrary action by officials (not without reference to the clique of bureaucrats in Württemberg).

The transcript was compiled by the law student Peter Wannenmann. Wannenmann followed Hegel to Berlin and tried to supplement his Heidelberg transcript with notes from the lectures Hegel gave on the philosophy of right in the winter of 1818–19. But in doing so he ran into difficulties because Hegel inserted a large number of paragraphs into the first part of his lectures, and thus the new presentation no longer fitted into the framework of the Heidelberg lectures. Consequently Wannenmann broke off the Berlin notes on 10 November 1818, at the end of the introduction. He returned to Heidelberg for the following term, as can be seen from the Heidelberg matriculation register.

Hegel lectured on the basis of dictated passages; that is, he dictated the individual paragraphs and then expounded them. Another

3. [*Tr.*] "Proceedings of the Estates Assembly in the Kingdom of Württemberg, 1815–16," translated in *Hegel's Political Writings*, pp. 246–294.

of his pupils, Friedrich Wilhelm Carové, writing anonymously as "Rheinpreusse" in the *Hallische Jahrbücher* of March 1841, quoted (in a review of a work by Ogienski entitled *Hegel, Schubarth und die Idee der Persönlichkeit in ihrem Verhältnis zur preussischen Monarchie*) two short extracts from his transcript of the same lecture series as evidence for the fact that in Heidelberg Hegel espoused the cause of "constitutional monarchy" even more decisively. These passages from §§ 137 and 170 agree word for word with Wannenmann's text, thus confirming that the latter's record of the dictated passages is reliable. As for Hegel's expositions of the dictated paragraphs, what we have is naturally only a selective record, as can be seen by comparing the expositions recorded by Wannenmann in 1818–19 (to be sure as a supplement to his Heidelberg transcript) with the transcript of these expositions compiled by Homeyer from the same lectures.

The subsequent fate of Wannenmann's transcript is unknown. In the 1950s it was unearthed by the Mannheim geographer Plewe in an antiquarian bookstore in Heidelberg in a pile of old papers and unsalable books that were awaiting removal. Plewe got permission to take the worthless manuscript away with him and gave it to his colleague Brecht, who taught philosophy in Mannheim and Heidelberg. Brecht in turn passed on the manuscript (annexed to transcripts of lectures given by Heidegger) to the Deutsches Literaturarchiv, Marbach am Neckar. Sincere thanks are due to the Literaturarchiv and its Director, Prof. Dr. Bernhard Zeller, for permission to make available this valuable transcript of one of Hegel's lecture series in this study edition.

In what follows we shall endeavor first to place these lectures in the history of the development of practical philosophy as Hegel saw it, and then to outline the newly elaborated system.

I

By March 1818, when Hegel completed his lectures on the philosophy of right at Heidelberg, he had long since decided to accept the post of professor in Berlin. This restless movement, from

Bavaria to Baden and then directly on to Berlin, was Hegel's response to a restless time. Only a few years had elapsed since the wars of liberation, the fall of Napoleon, and the reorganization of Europe by the Congress of Vienna; and the new states were now endeavoring to place themselves on a stable footing. When Hegel dealt with world history in the seven closing sections of his lectures, he also invoked, in the exposition to § 164, the sadness aroused by the ruins of Palmyra, Persepolis, and Egypt; memories going back to his youth obviously merged here with present-day experiences. Returning from travels in the East, the Comte de Volney had in 1791 published his book *Les ruines; ou, Méditations sur les révolutions des empires*, in which he laid bare the secrets of mythologies and international conflicts from the standpoint of the Enlightenment. Georg Forster had brought out a German translation one year later, but Hegel had in his library the French original. In his Heidelberg lectures (and also later in his Berlin lectures on the philosophy of history) Hegel urges the need to go beyond mourning: "But what is laid low, *has* been laid low and *had* to be laid low. World spirit is unsparing and pitiless" (§ 164). It is not only the empires of the East that had necessarily to be laid low; Hegel's own times had eliminated something great, the old Europe, in favor of what was new. For Hegel, taking leave of the old gave heart for welcoming the new. Like a leitmotiv running through these lectures is the proposition "What is rational must happen" (cf. §§ 122, 134). This formula is even more dynamic and historically affirmative than the later, hotly debated passage on the actuality of the rational and the rationality of the actual.[4] But the Heidelberg version was later passed on by Gans when he lectured on Hegel's *Philosophy of Right* (Heinrich Heine characteristically recounted the Heidelberg version as if he had heard it from Hegel himself).

In his Heidelberg lectures (as also in supplementary notes to the relevant paragraphs of the Heidelberg *Encyclopaedia*) Hegel, living at a time of great historical upheaval, adduces the doctrine of history as a succession of empires, the best-known expression of

---

4. [*Tr.*] See below, § 122, n. 53.

which is in the Book of Daniel. When the feared Assyrian Empire suddenly collapsed in 612 B.C.E., and the victors, the kingdom of the Medes and the new Babylonian Empire, were ousted by the Persians a few decades later, people discovered this doctrine in a moment of trauma they never forgot. Later apocalyptic writers also made use of the doctrine when they sought a vision of history as a whole. To be sure, the successive empires pointed here to the coming of God's kingdom, and the four beasts to the Son of Man.

When in the turmoil of his own period of upheaval Hegel divided history as a whole into the four world-historical empires—the Oriental, the Greek, the Roman, and the Germanic—he altered the ancient model fundamentally. Above all he did not make the four empires subject to the coming judgment of the kingdom of God, but saw the judgment itself in the history of these empires. Thus he quotes, as the most profound thing that can be said about the rise and fall of peoples, Schiller's saying that world history is the court of world judgment (§ 164). It is true that in his poem "Resignation" Schiller had not said that world history *is* the court of world judgment; rather he had seen in world history (and not in some transcendent, postulated event) the locus in which world judgment is accomplished. But Hegel also stresses that this judgment is not the mere "might" of spirit or naked being as destiny. "To be sure, one must harden one's heart when contemplating the destinies of peoples, but they are not [what they are] merely because they are"—such are the terms in which Hegel expounds § 164. What are actualized in the destinies of peoples are the principles of reason, and these can ultimately be grasped by free thought in their necessary connectedness. So the stress on reason in actuality is emphatically not an affirmation of the merely factual, and above all not a simple acceptance of the status quo.

There can, however, be no doubt that Hegel believes himself capable of enduring his own age of turmoil only if he understands the path leading up to it as a necessary one, which essentially could not have been different from what it was. So those peoples who were defeated and did not become world-historical are given to understand even in their graves that they were not bearers of a justified principle either. The concluding § 170 views the contemporary constitutional form, namely constitutional monarchy, as "both image and actuality of developed reason," the idea being that through its religious representations and concepts self-consciousness attains freedom in this actuality. Hegel takes up the tradition of classical philosophy, which as early as Plato's *Timaeus* had seen time as the image of eternity, and which then brought together in ordered coherence, in eternity as *aeternitas*, what in time appeared in random order. With Hegel, however, eternity is the accomplishment of time as history-in-movement.

Hegel sees his own age in the light of the French Revolution. With the Napoleonic Wars, the Revolution had spread over all Europe, had borne fruit in the reforms carried out in the Rhenish Confederation of Bavaria (where Hegel had held the post of Gymnasium director) and also in Prussia, and now following the fall of Napoleon had to be brought to an end in the countries of Europe. Hegel reverts to this guiding theme in his lectures in a wide variety of contexts. For example as early as § 26 the exposition stresses the importance of studying the "history of how ownership became free." When states first arose, property had not belonged to individuals; rather a field, for example, had been owned by the family. Roman law had been defective because of its many limitations; Christianity had viewed human beings as free, but feudalism had made ownership unfree (thus helping to bring about the French Revolution!). The exposition to § 33 attributes to the belief that the state is a social contract a "great influence" on the French Revolution. The purpose is to show that the principle of contract cannot rightly be carried over from the sphere of private law to that of constitutional law. When Hegel takes up the question of constitutional law and speaks in more detail of the founding of states, he adduces arguments in § 125 that are directly related to his current disagreement with the constitutional battle being waged in Württemberg, but at the same time hark back to his earliest views on questions of constitutional policy. "Our day," so he maintains, "has seen a step taken toward the rational existence of the state that has not been taken for a thousand years past: the right of reason has been asserted over against the form of private right." The founders of states not only impose their will but intervene on behalf of the still-hidden universal will.

Another feature in the evolution of the state is that in the Middle Ages corporations of burghers were established by analogy with the corporations of feudalism. Alongside the self-administration of the towns, these associations sought to provide a system of legal protection for the various types of labor and economic activity that were emerging from political tutelage. Privileges that could have been guaranteed only by the state as a whole were upheld against the state, even if the state was one that in manifold ways ceded the right of the state to princes or corporations as the private rights of individuals. Hegel refers to Johann Jakob Moser (§ 125), the Württemberg estates member and scholar who wrote a compendium setting out the rights of the state and private rights in the former German Empire. The Revolution had been an assault on privileges, but the émigrés in France and the gentrified members of estates (*Standesherren*) in Germany were wrongfully demanding their privileges back. If compensation were to be claimed for the fact that the nobility had lost the right of appointment to officers' posts, then it was conversely more appropriate for the state to "present this class with a bill for its enjoyment" of these privileges in earlier days. After surveying the countries of Europe with regard to the fight against privileges, Hegel says: "Here belong the revolutions of modern times." To his mind the revolutionary process embraces the entire civilized world of his day and reaches back in varying degrees far into the history of the individual countries. While in France and England the state had at an early stage gained sway over the forces of particularism, things were different in Germany and Italy.

But the dismantling of privileges is only one side of the great upheaval; the other side consists in the legal protection conferred on the new developments by the state as a whole, so that the state is built up from below. It was the religious conviction of Christendom that what mattered was the salvation of each and every individual. When a thousand years ago this encountered the sense of freedom of the newly emerging European peoples, the result was a lengthy process in which freedom was also gained for the capacity of individuals to earn their living by labor and their own achievement, and through education to carve out for themselves a place in a society based on the division of labor. The aim is to provide a legal system guaranteeing the mode of life of the "middle class," and above all to draw it into the administration of state power by means of the representational system or constitutional monarchy.

In the thirty years since Hegel had begun his studies in Tübingen the face of Europe had been radically changed; and those engaged in formulating new constitutions were seeking to take into account the effects of the inner changes that had transformed the different states. The smaller states whose boundaries had been redefined fitted in between the five major powers of Britain, France, Russia, Austria, and Prussia. And it was in southwest Germany, where Hegel came from and to which he had returned, that the map had been transformed in particularly radical fashion. The patchwork of secular and ecclesiastical princedoms, knightly domains, free imperial cities, and imperial abbacies had been essentially reduced to the two states of Baden and Württemberg. At the time Hegel was being educated in the spirit of the late Enlightenment at the Stuttgart Gymnasium, it still seemed as if the old Duchy of Württemberg was capable of renewing itself and achieving stability at the last hour by drawing on the efforts marking the Enlightenment. In the last decades of his long reign Duke Karl Eugen sought to let his absolutism work for the benefit of the realm (e.g., by founding the Karlsschule). But the young Hegel had only just begun to attend the University of Tübingen as a student when the French Revolution broke out; this showed unmistakably that the old Europe could no longer be saved by reformist compromises. Even if some reports of student agitation in the Evangelical Seminary are overgrown with legends, there is no doubt that Hegel like his friends came out decidedly in favor of the Revolution. When as a professor in Berlin he traveled to Paris in 1827 and on the way passed through Valmy, where artillery fire had sealed the fate of the coalition army, he wrote to his wife of the "immense interest" that places like Valmy and the events associated with it had once had for him in his youth.

After completing his studies Hegel went as a private tutor first south to Switzerland, then north to Frankfurt. The years in Switzerland were marked by the attempt to justify the republicanism of the Revolution in philosophical terms too, as a renewal of classical republicanism. However, as Hegel was very concretely concerned, as a pamphleteer, with Bern's wrongful domination of the canton of Vaud, as well as with the constitutional reform in his homeland Württemberg, he inevitably came to inquire more and more into the conditions characterizing European history and consequently the contemporary era. In his renewed association with Hölderlin in Frankfurt, Hegel eventually came to take up a position against French plans for conquest and to opt for Austria as trustee of the old empire. This option was open to him because, as he saw it, all France had done was to replace the centralism of royal authority by an artificial and no less centralized national representation, while countries like Austria had retained the participation of the estates in the administration of power in the form of a corporate representation, and were building up the state from below.

When Hegel was a student in Tübingen we are told that he was a keen reader of Rousseau's writings, in order to have done with the rules and fetters of the understanding. As far as political science is concerned, however, Hegel is influenced less by the constructions of rational law than by the historically exemplified intuitions of a Montesquieu, for whom the spirit of a people results from the interplay of many spheres. The time he spent in Bern gave Hegel a passionate concern for human rights. A sharp line must be drawn between legality and morality, so that the state may no longer, as in Hegel's homeland Württemberg, interfere in matters of faith and link civil rights with religion. Religion and politics seem to go hand in glove insofar as theology denies sinful humanity the capacity for freedom and self-determination and so paves the way for despotism. But can one at the same time take the rights of the individual as one's starting point and follow the Greeks, in whose city-states the individual was encompassed by the whole fabric of ethical life? Is it possible strictly to separate church and state if one seeks the whole human being in the entirety of political, religious, and ethical life?

Renewing his association with Hölderlin in Frankfurt, Hegel comes to see the divine itself as the union brought about by love or the "friendship of souls." What is experienced in love is to be depicted in a new mythology in such a way that this mode of religion underpins relationships based on freedom. The so-called "Earliest Systematic Program of German Idealism" (1796)[5] opposes to the "pitiful human work" of the state, which seeks to prevent need by protecting "liberty" and "property,"[6] the work of humanity wherein a new religion makes possible the freedom and equality of all. In a commentary on Kant's *Metaphysics of Morals*, Hegel not only lays stress on the relationship of church and state; he also makes use of the concept of life—a life that raises itself within the finite to the eternal and feels a unity in love with all that lives, yet continually differentiates itself into new configurations and thus comes under the sway of destiny. What was separated as legality and morality is now understood from the standpoint of the unity of life. Another feature of the differentiations into which life enters is that it seeks to prevent need by labor and provides a system of legal protection for the effective division of labor. It was in the great commercial city of Frankfurt that Hegel first began to study the British economic system, writing a commentary on Steuart's *Principles*. The fact that direct democracy is no longer possible in large modern states makes a representative constitution appear inevitable.

Having studied theology in Württemberg and been subsequently

5. [Tr.] Published in *Das älteste Systemprogram: Studien zur Frühgeschichte des deutschen Idealismus*, ed. Rüdiger Bubner, *Hegel-Studien*, Beiheft 9 (Bonn, 1973), pp. 261–265; translated in H. S. Harris, *Hegel's Development: Toward the Sunlight, 1770–1801* (Oxford, 1972), pp. 510–512.

6. [Tr.] The words "liberty" and "property" are in English in the original, and the reference is to Hegel's studies in Adam Smith, James Steuart (see below), and other classical British economists.

engaged as a private tutor in Frankfurt, Hegel in May 1800 received permission from the Stuttgart Consistory Court "to visit a few universities outside Württemberg." After a few days in Mainz he left the city for good and moved to Jena. The separate peace concluded at Basel, whereby Prussia left the first coalition against France, had brought northern Germany several years of quiet, fostering the development of German classicism in Weimar and romanticism and the idealist philosophy in Jena. Hegel attached himself to Schelling, his former friend from student days, and found himself plunged into the thick of the dispute about the right way to arrive at an adequate philosophical system. Rudolf Abeken, a student in Jena who attended lectures by Schelling and also Hegel, wrote in his memoirs that compared with Schelling's new philosophy of the absolute, even Napoleon's great deeds and victories had become as nothing. Admittedly it was not Hegel's way to turn aside from politics in this manner. However, his article on the reorganization of the German Empire under Austrian leadership was overtaken by political events before publication. The *Reichsdeputationshauptschluss*[7] helped to restructure the German *Länder* in its own fashion; Austria was increasingly forced to turn its back on the policy associated with Joseph II and Leopold II, moving closer to Russia, where freedom was an unfamiliar idea; and the empire passed away. In Hegel's eyes Prussia was a parvenu, compelled to move toward centralized control of all political life, though not in the same way as postrevolutionary France. On seeing the Prussian troops, Hegel (whose brother served as a Württemberg officer in Napoleon's army and was at the time in Jena) had predicted their defeat and the consequent collapse of Frederick the Great's Prussia. At all events he finally opted for Napoleon's policy based on the Rhenish Confederation, which stimulated middle-class activity by means of a new legal system and gave the new states representative constitutions. As editor of a Bamberg newspaper Hegel reported faithfully how the historian Johannes von Müller, as minis-

7. [Tr.] The final decisions of the special commission set up by the Great Powers in 1801 to compensate the German princes for loss of territory on the west bank of the Rhine by apportioning among them the majority of ecclesiastical states and imperial cities still in existence.

ter and director of educational establishments in the kingdom of Westphalia, was preparing a model constitution.

In his first formulations of a system, Hegel initially seeks to show how the absolute is to be grasped and how it actualizes itself under the conditions of the first, or physical, and the second, or ethical, nature. Ethical life too is "nature," i.e., the ethics of a people in their substantive entirety. So natural law cannot be based in atomistic fashion on the individual; rather it must show how in various ways nature attains to its right (and so alone makes possible the rights of the individuals). By dint of activity this second nature must make itself what it is, and so it is a "work." In the same way as Aristotle in book 1 of his *Politics*, Hegel in these preliminary drafts indicates what is necessary before a people can exist as an "ethical work," namely that people must communicate through language, ward off material need through labor, and reproduce themselves within the family. These "potentialities" (*Potenzen*) make possible the systems of life to which the management of communal concerns by the state then relates: industry and commerce as a system of needs, private law as the means of regulating this system, and finally the education of children and cultivation of ethics—or, to order them differently, family, the economy, and right as modes in which "coercive law" mediates the universal and the individual will.

In order to be able to define more precisely the separate spheres that make up a people, Hegel draws on the old doctrine of estates or classes (*Stände*). Classical Greek philosophy seems to raise its head again when Hegel assigns to the class made up of the (ruling and war-waging) nobility the function of engaging in politics and the necessary leisure for philosophizing, while he attributes to the other classes, engaged as they are in agriculture, industry, and commerce, only a "relative" ethicality. However, Hegel does seek to do justice to the insight that contemporary human beings are "citoyens" as well as "bourgeois." The absolute, so it is argued in the essay on "Natural Law,"[8] sacrifices part of itself in the

8. [Tr.] Published in the *Kritisches Journal der Philosophie*, 1802–3 (see *Gesammelte Werke* 4:415–485); translated as *Natural Law* by T. M. Knox (Philadelphia, 1975).

classes of relative ethicality in order to set itself free for its highest actualization.

During the latter part of his Jena period, Hegel poses the question as to the uniform basis from which it might be possible to develop the "potentialities" that enable a people to become an ethical work. The *Realphilosophie* of 1805–6[9] gives as this basis the ego, which is intelligence and will; this makes it possible to think of ethical spirit no longer as mere nature but as the other of nature, which takes shape in the reciprocal recognition of one self by another. This confers a new meaning on motifs of modern natural-law theory and the philosophy of Kant and Fichte. In the doctrine of estates or classes the basic features of the classical ethic of the city-state are lost. Confronting the lower classes (those engaged in agriculture, industry, and commerce) is the universal class, in which the man of affairs (i.e., primarily the administrative official) stands alongside the scholar and the officer. The classes are defined functionally, according to the tasks that have to be performed in the people as a whole. Hegel shows how history is carried forward by creative labor rather than by relations of authority. With these well-known reflections Hegel disposes of the classical writers' disparagement of honest toil, which denied labor any properly human worth and made the productive activity of *poiesis* part of the business of social interaction. In the complex modern state we cannot rest content with the beautiful ethical life of ancient times, in which the citizens sustained the *polis* in a system of direct democracy and all individuals displayed in their virtues the substantive concerns of the whole. The new forms of differentiation call for their own "node" wherein they are brought together again, and this Hegel sees in constitutional monarchy. Here he formulates an idea that will characterize his philosophy from then on: society based on the division of labor is accepted, but the transference of the notion of contract to the state is rejected because it is

---

9. [*Tr.*] The third of the Jena system-outlines, treating the philosophies of nature and spirit (see *Gesammelte Werke* 8:1–287). *Realphilosophie* designates the philosophy of the "real" (the second and third parts of Hegel's philosophical system) as opposed to the philosophy of the "ideal," or logic and metaphysics (the first part).

only by means of a detour through history that an emergent state attains legality. In their inmost moral and religious life human beings are referred beyond the nation to which they belong to the whole of history and what is eternal in it.

To this corresponds a new view of religion in which the ethical spirit acquires knowledge of itself. Religion no longer unfolds historically from the religion of the Greeks, which comprehends the powers of nature in the immediacy of art, through the Christian religion of anguish and division, to a people's intuition of itself in its deity. Alongside the religion of nature, which is now assigned to the East, is set instead the Greek religion of art and a rationally interpreted Christianity as the ultimate religion integrating all that has gone before. In this way Hegel opposes to the conviction that antiquity can be restored by the Revolution a view of the inner articulation of history with which he had already, in his article on the German constitution, distinguished Oriental despotism from ancient republicanism and the modern representative system. The *Phenomenology of Spirit* (1807) shows how the basic political and religious forms themselves grow out of the historical process.

As director of the Nuremberg Gymnasium, Hegel worked for eight years in a Rhenish Confederation state in which his friend Niethammer had the task of introducing a new educational policy, principally for the newly acquired Protestant territories. During these years Hegel's views on education took shape, but the period was marked by something of a pause in the further development of the philosophy of right. Under his contract Hegel had to give instruction in law, morals, and religion, following on, we may say, from Kant's *Metaphysics of Morals* and his philosophy of religion. Hegel followed the prescribed path, alien as it was, distinguishing between practical and theoretical consciousness and introducing the state as the actuality of right after dealing with civil law and criminal law. In discussing morality Hegel also spoke of constitutional duties and of the state as the unity binding together ethics, education, and modes of thinking and acting—since the introduction of legality must not result in the state's becoming a "machine."

Undoubtedly the reconfiguration of speculative philosophy

played a part in the way this component of the system was ultimately incorporated into the system as a whole. According to the
closing sections of the *Realphilosophie* of 1805–6, logic or speculative philosophy was designed to include six chapters: being, relationship, life and cognition, knowing knowledge, spirit, spirit's
knowledge of itself. It was therefore the intention that one of these
chapters should elaborate the structural elements of (ethical) spirit
(in line with this the *Phenomenology* also contains a lengthy chapter on spirit). In the *Science of Logic*, the last part of which was
published in 1816, all that remains of this treatment is a brief indication of the idea of the good, in which the good is not even interpreted in the manner of the subsequent *Philosophy of Right* as an
end in itself. In contrast, the idea of life is developed at disproportionate length, and so the danger arises that in terms of its structure the idea of the good is not sufficiently distinguished from the
teleology of life, and the actuality of the ethical in history is understood to an undue extent from the standpoint of the process of
life, as a self-contained process. This inevitably results in the transformation of practical philosophy, for which the normative problem is of prime concern, into a philosophy of objective spirit, by
which spirit is led through history to its consummation in model
institutions.

Hegel's last years in Nuremberg saw the fall of Napoleon and
reestablishment of the community of European states by the Congress of Vienna. Hegel's letters to his friend Niethammer show that
Napoleon's defeat was a bitter pill for him to swallow. He sees in
it the epitome of the tragic: as the executor of world spirit, the
hero is dragged down by the masses, who play the role of the classical chorus. But Hegel also points out that he had already predicted in the *Phenomenology* that spirit would migrate from the
land of revolution to the land of self-consciousness. Napoleon had
reintroduced the old structures on the foundations laid by the Revolution without providing an intellectual justification for what had
been introduced anew and differently. He had disregarded the traditions of individual peoples and set insufficient store by the work
of free universities.

Once Hegel was able to return to university life in Heidelberg, he wanted to provide philosophical support for the new political and religious life in the European states. Thus he adopted a very positive attitude to the newly formed student fraternities whose hope it was to see the promises of the wars of liberation redeemed in a *constitutional* monarchy and a more united Germany. And it is specifically these Heidelberg lectures on the philosophy of right that show the extent to which political and educational considerations were involved in Hegel's work. At the same time, Hegel came into public view as a political writer with his review of the documents recording the constitutional struggle in Württemberg. That his lectures influenced the political debates of the students is evident from the fact that F. W. Carové went over them with "some" of his fellow students in the winter of 1818–19. This law student and romantic author from the Rhineland received his degree under Hegel with a dissertation devoted to the statutes of the student fraternities, and Hegel also saw to it that he did not have to submit the compulsory piece in Latin. In this way Hegel supported the political aspirations of Carové, who opposed the exaggerated and anachronistic concept of dueling honor and sought the admission of Jewish students to the student fraternities. In his memoirs Theodor von Kobbe, who played a leading part in these fraternities, maintained that the effect of Hegel's lectures had been that he won over few students but that these were the best ones, and that these then persuaded the others "that one must learn a great deal before one can improve the world."

A good half-year after his arrival in Heidelberg, Hegel published an *Encyclopedia of the Philosophical Sciences* (1817) as a basis for his teaching activity. This outline of his system places what had formerly been "natural right" between the parts dealing with subjective and absolute spirit, as the doctrine of "objective spirit," and distinguishes the theories of right, of morality, and of ethical life. When, in the theory of right, before defining ownership and contract, and before showing how right is infringed by legal disputes and crime, Hegel introduces the self-knowledge of spirit in the freedom of the individual as "person," he could draw on material he had used for dictation when he was teaching at the Nuremberg Gymnasium, and also on the *Realphilosophie* of the Jena period. In the chapter on morality the theory of manifold duties is formalized into a theory of action for which the good is duty; but the theory of the various stages of action does not yet figure prominently. Ethical life is understood within the context of the people, which produces its actuality through activity and so makes itself, as universal work, what it is. The various spheres of this actuality are the universal class or estate (primarily made up of rulers and civil servants), the particular estate (those engaged in agriculture, industry, and commerce), and the estate of individuality or the family. As the natural ethical substantiality the family can also be placed before the estates, in which case the constitutional character of the people derives from the universal estate. As work the people expresses its universality in laws, whose actuality is the living ethos. In contrast with the aggregate of the many, which it is a misnomer to call a "people," universality properly subsists in the government, at whose head stands the prince or sovereign. The fact that the individual ethical spirit of one people comes up against other peoples means that consideration must be given to the state and its external right. Then, thirdly, the spirits of the different peoples have to be given their place in history as a whole. The extent to which Hegel now grasps history and the works accomplished in it by the different peoples as a self-enclosed process is clear from a marginal comment on § 465, dealing with the revealed or revelatory (Christian) religion: "Everything must be brought *out of the enclosed God* [Alles heraus *aus dem verschlossenen Gotte*]." The philosophy of subjective spirit in itself replaces the uncertainty attaching to action and belief by a final transparency, which gives preponderance to the theoretical aspect.

Hegel had the option of coupling lectures on the encyclopaedia as a whole—on logic and metaphysics as well as anthropology and psychology—with the preparation of his textbook, or taking the textbook itself as a basis once it was ready. He had to lecture on history of philosophy and (in his last semester at Heidelberg) on aesthetics "following his own outline" or "on the basis of dictated passages"—for absolute spirit was presented only in schematic fashion in the textbook. It is surprising that immediately after the textbook appeared, Hegel also lectured on "Natural Right and Political Science" on the basis of dictated passages; but this series of lectures in the winter of 1817–18 marked a further modification of approach as a result of which the philosophy of right attained its definitive structure. "Right" was grasped in more consistent fashion as "abstract right"; the theory of morality was finally formalized as a doctrine of the stages of action; and ethical life was from now on articulated in the three exemplary forms of family, civil society, and the state.

Thereafter Hegel continued to work uninterruptedly on the final elaboration of the philosophy of right. The following winter—1818–19 in Berlin—he expanded the first part of the lectures by inserting further sections, so that for reasons of time the last part had to remain more schematic. The ensuing winter (1819–20) brought simultaneously another reading of the lectures and the final revision of the compendium. Here too Hegel further modified his system; for example, both this winter's lectures and the compendium reflect a new understanding of the state on the basis of inner and outer "sovereignty." A surviving fragment on the power of the sovereign, written on a degree certificate dated 30 December 1819, shows Hegel working intensively on § 286 of the compendium. On 30 October 1819 he had informed his friend Creuzer that he had wanted to reciprocate the latter's gift of a book, albeit "inadequately," by sending him "a few folio sections dealing with philosophy of right," in other words the first printed installment of his compendium; but had been unable to do so, for not everyone could be "as diligent and quick in their work" as Creuzer. "I was just going to have a start made on printing when I learned of the decrees of the Diet [at Carlsbad]. Now that we [know] where we stand in regard to freedom from censorship, I will very shortly be submitting the text for printing." So, as was the case with his other publications, Hegel made only slow progress with the preparation of his manuscript, and was thus also able to take the new censorship provisions into account for the printing process. In June 1820 he submitted the first half of the manuscript to the censor, but the remainder followed swiftly, and by October 1820 he was able to present his book to the minister von Altenstein as evidence of his activity.

While still halfway through his lectures, at the beginning of January 1818, Hegel was again invited to move to Berlin. He was to be sure in Stuttgart in the spring for negotiations about a post in Tübingen (evidently to succeed von Wangenheim as curator or chancellor of the University of Tübingen); but Hegel had long since decided in favor of Berlin. The idea of combining the German states of the South and Southwest in a triadic structure forming an independent force alongside Austria and Prussia—an idea that von Wangenheim continued to promote after he entered politics—was one that Hegel probably now viewed as an illusion. It was Prussia that claimed his attention because Prussia, now substantially enlarged, was seeking to attain inner unity not merely by building up the government but also by educational reform. At the close of the Heidelberg lectures on philosophy of right (§ 170), Hegel affirms that rationality is to be found in the "middle class," whose task it is as the "intellectual estate" to present the wishes of the people as the "material extreme" to the sovereign. At some point Hegel jotted down in connection with his inaugural lecture in Heidelberg: "Prussia founded on intellectuals."

The minister von Altenstein had thought of offering Hegel in addition a post at the Academy of Sciences, and in this way Hegel hoped to be relieved in Berlin of the "precarious function of teaching philosophy at a university," and to play an active role, possibly as president of the academy, in educational and academic policy. But the murder of Kotzebue by Karl Sand, member of a student fraternity, provoked the Restauration establishment into the reactionary Carlsbad Decrees; and Hegel had been little more than a year in Berlin when the constitutional struggle in Prussia ended in failure. His services were not required for the function he desired. When he saw that educational reform too was becoming a matter for the government, he delegated most of the work to his disciple Johannes Schulze; and he himself abandoned the plan to write a work on national education policy (a *Staatspädagogik*) as a sequel to the publication of the *Philosophy of Right* (as he informed Niethammer on 9 June 1821). It was, however, possible for Hegel to continue to elaborate his philosophy and spread its influence through a school. Unfortunately we do not as yet have any transcripts of the lectures on philosophy of right in the winter of 1821–22. The lectures recorded in the winter semesters of 1822–23 and 1824–25 show that the philosophy of history had already been removed and made the subject of a separate series of lectures. Thereafter Hegel left the lectures on philosophy of right to his pupils and further elaborated the philosophy of history.

Hegel's lectures show the extent to which he reacted to current changes in the political situation. Thus he warned his students against impatience when Prussia as an integral state had not acquired a constitution, or not yet a representative one. In the winter of 1824–25 he expounded § 272 in the following terms: "Every state has a constitution; even if it has no estates it has a constitution, which may be more explicit or more implicit." The revolutions of 1830 profoundly disturbed Hegel; he was horrified to see the United Provinces fall apart again, and on confessional grounds. He had regarded the confessional problem as solved; and now in his last years in Berlin, when religious renewal was being overlaid with political overtones, he declared emphatically that only the Protestant religion could be reconciled with a rational political order, while in Catholic states, which had not had the benefit of the Reformation, revolutions must continue to occur. Shortly before his death Hegel was again at work as a political writer, penning an article on the constitutional reform in England.[10] Despite much clear-sightedness he shows here the uncertainty of an old man, regarding the reforms as necessary and yet fearing them. When Hegel's former pupil Gans took an unduly liberal line in his lectures, Hegel's intervention was again enlisted, probably by the crown prince himself. But after giving two lectures of a new course

---

10. [*Tr.*] "The English Reform Bill" (1831), translated in *Hegel's Political Writings*, pp. 295–330.

on philosophy of right—and an unedifying dispute with Gans—
Hegel died in November 1831. In these two lectures Hegel pro-
tested against the notion that right, which was created from reason, was opposed as mere "human handiwork" to a "divine right."
The last words of these lectures, as recorded by David Friedrich
Strauss, are as follows: "Freedom is the innermost element, and it
is from it that the whole edifice of the spiritual world arises."

II

If we may trust Wannenmann's transcript on this point, in his
winter course of 1817–18 Hegel plunged without further prefa-
tory remarks directly into the subject matter, namely the definition
of the concept of right and exposition of the different aspects of
natural right and political science. This subject matter embraces
both jurisprudence and economics and also history. Hegel had been
trained as a theologian, even if as a student he had occasionally
wanted to switch over to law. As the son of a Württemberg civil
servant he had, however, taken an interest in problems of constitutional history and from then on had constantly extended his
knowledge of legal science. While employed as private tutor he had
taken an interest in social development in Britain, where in 1795
Whitbread had proposed a minimum wage and in 1796 Pitt had
introduced a Poor Law in Parliament. Hegel began his study of
British economists in Frankfurt and continued it later. While still
at the Gymnasium he had become interested in the Enlightenment's attempts to construct a scientifically based picture of history. As Hegel became ever more strongly conscious of the fact that
he was living in a time of upheaval, he inevitably came to see his
own age too in a historical light. Whereas nowadays in a faculty
of law a student of criminal law will hardly venture to express an
opinion to a student of constitutional law concerning the latter's
specialty, Hegel in his compendium spoke for the disciplines of
three faculties.

In § 69 of his lectures, after considering abstract right and morality, Hegel goes on to discuss ethical life. In so doing he casts a glance backward and forward over his whole system: right as the "unmediated concrete existence" of freedom and morality as the "reflection of the free subject into itself" are merely "ideal moments"; whereas ethical life *is* idea and consequently, as rational actuality, *both* being and reflection, both reality and concept. Abstract right and morality are only enabling moments that sublate themselves, while ethical life is something whole and actual, which exists in the forms made possible by these moments. This whole consists in family, civil society, and state, the last-named being one of the succession of states in history. If this whole represents itself according to its substantive inner content, it comprises religion. And in the Christian era religion takes cognizance not merely of the "spirit of the particular people" but of the spirit of the historical whole in which the peoples are "limited spirits" (as we are told in the exposition to § 71).

In giving the chapter on "law" (*Recht*) (Part I) the title "abstract right" (*das abstrakte Recht*), Hegel shows that it is not a question of the sphere of legality nor even solely a question of private right (which we first encounter, as actually practiced, in the administration of justice on the part of civil society). All we are here concerned with are "ideal moments," namely the way in which ethical life is "person" in the abstract culmination of its unmediated being. In ethical life the individual person opens up in three directions: vis-à-vis the thing, which can be owned: vis-à-vis other persons, with whom contracts can be concluded and articles exchanged; and vis-à-vis oneself, inasmuch as right must defend itself against wrong. Morality too is treated solely as "ideal moment": as subject, the person gains the possibility of reflection and develops differing forms of action (from the ethicality of conditions prior to the emergence of right to a morally reflected system of right). In this way duty can relate to the good and so to institutions as forms of the living good. This means that the traditional doctrine of concrete duties and virtues falls away since duties are now understood on the basis of institutions. By means of this doctrine of abstract right and of (equally abstract) morality as action, it becomes possible for Hegel to elaborate the doctrine of ethical life in a form strictly governed by right. Naturally Hegel knows that human beings live in many forms of community; but in his philosophy of right he confines himself to the essential by distinguishing the natural ethical life of the family (which is subject to right primarily in its dissolution) first from civil society and then from the state as the locus, properly speaking, of right.

In Jena, Hegel had spoken of *ius naturae civitatis et gentium* or simply of "natural right"; but from now on he couples natural right (*Naturrecht*) and political science (*Staatswissenschaft*). In speaking of political science he is taking up the old title of the "Politics." When the state was in process of breaking free from traditional forms, it was possible to oppose to political science a new natural right as a binding force. Hegel on the contrary sees natural right as the ordering element in all positive and historical happenings, and so can combine the opposing natural right and political science in a philosophy of right. It is true that in so doing he stretches the concept of right to include also the right of world spirit to transcend the limited spirits of the individual peoples. In any event the exposition to § 2 of his lectures constitutes Hegel's justification for the new title he employs, that of a "philosophical doctrine of right."

Since Hegel incorporates his philosophical doctrine of right into the system as a whole and takes over from the system presuppositions of crucial importance, the introduction to the lectures develops the concept of right from that of the self-realizing free will, at least in a summary and schematic manner. Abstract right is no longer divided (as was still the case with Kant's *Metaphysics of Morals*) on the basis of the distinction between the right of things and of persons. That to which one can have a right under the right of persons (e.g., the labor of an employee) is according to Hegel also only a limited "thing." As persons, human beings have the right to appropriate things in accord with the principle of "property." It is true that the *Phenomenology of Spirit* still uses the distinction between the system of personal and material right, but in an analysis of the unmediated or beautiful ethical life of the

Greeks. Since his Jena days it was clear to Hegel that it was in Roman law that the categorization of everything as persons was worked out. However, Hegel views Roman law in the light of its later accommodation to natural law; in this way he fails to see that Roman law is primarily public law (not, as he stresses, private law). When Hegel portrays and criticizes Roman family law on account of the unethical privileges and rights of possession devolving on the man, he disregards the fact that this system stemmed from kinship structures.

During his lectures in Heidelberg, Hegel returned to the bookseller Winter on 1 February 1818 those volumes of Savigny's *Geschichte des römischen Rechts im Mittelalter* he had previously asked for, explaining that "I had been mistaken regarding the purpose of this work and had had something quite different in mind." Instead of Savigny's work Hegel asked for Ritter von Hugo's textbook on Roman law, which he then went on to use in his compendium, with the result that he came into dispute with the famous jurist. He does not seem to have paid attention to the disagreement between Thibaut and Savigny concerning the possibility of a national codification of law until he reached Berlin; in Heidelberg he did, however, attack Savigny's seminal work *Das Recht des Besitzes* in the exposition to § 27.

Hegel assigns to the person a sphere of ownership as it were in terms of natural right. But he gives the existence of property a temporal connotation: property can be acquired by occupancy and lost by prescription. Hegel also assigns value to mere possession, while in his view something owned and not used is not fully owned. Savigny on the contrary had shown that possession was not originally protected in Roman law but only as the latter was further elaborated in the Pandects. His work *Das Recht des Besitzes* says specifically in regard to possession that it is a fact but not a right. If in contrast possession is infringed, forcible infringement can be rescinded. Possession can thus involve legal consequences, so that it is indirectly a right, or fact and right simultaneously. Where possession has been infringed, remedial action admittedly does not fall under the law of things but under the law of obligations, as one of the *obligationes ex maleficiis*. While Hegel too now stresses there can be no ownership without possession, he criticizes Savigny for being one-sided: in his view the more important aspect is the relationship of possession to property, the fact that possession can give rise to property because it confers a right to property.

At this time, when reforms were in the air, these "abstract" questions of right had great political significance. Since a dual system of ownership—*dominium directum et utile*—had been inherited from feudalism, it was possible in given cases to claim a right of ownership for peasants who were "in possession" and were now to be emancipated. Savigny with his stress on possession as a fact takes the side of the nobility, Hegel that of the middle classes, for whom everything that could be possessed became capable of becoming private property. Above all, this dispute bore on the question of what constitutes the foundation of legal science. Is it to be based on a search for the rational in history? We see here the germ of a disagreement that persisted over the years. The Berlin law faculty was shaken to the core when Hegel's pupil Gans was admitted to it against Savigny's wishes. Gans then carried on the dispute with Savigny over the right of possession in such a way that public opinion throughout Germany followed the argument. It was one of Hegel's pupils from the Nuremberg Gymnasium, Georg Friedrich Puchta, starting from Savigny's standpoint, who sought to bring about a settlement that even today influences debates on the subject.

Instead of speaking of right vis-à-vis a person, which can never be acquired by my own power from my side alone, Hegel develops the principle of contract (and in so doing, though he is here presenting "abstract" rights in principle, classifies the different types of contract). When Hegel later treats of the family, he at once emphasizes that in the immediate, natural unity of the family neither is the principle of individual ownership valid nor can the family itself be comprehended solely as a contract. When Kant speaks of personal rights to things (e.g., to the use of the sexual organs of one's spouse), Hegel rejects this way of viewing the matter as unethical. In drawing up the list of abstract rights, the right of inheritance is left out of account, to be dealt with later in relation to the dissolution of families. Constitutional law or public right is also disregarded for the structure of abstract right.

The state, maintains Hegel in opposition to modern natural-law theory, is not a contract. Since contract consists for him in the exchange of goods between individuals, he is bound to criticize Rousseau's "social contract." This criticism may be determined by a shift in the meaning of contract and so be unjust to Rousseau's contention. In the case in point Hegel rightly points out that it is necessary to determine who is to be included among the citizens regarded as entering into a free association. The question who is accounted a citizen is also considered for example by Kant on the basis of historical origin (since not only women but also the itinerant barber who travels around with his shaving bowl are denied citizen status). But also in Hegel's philosophy of right, is it not determined in advance, namely from the system as a whole, that the principles of ownership and contract take full effect in civil society, yet for various reasons are subject to limitations in family and state?

In a third section Hegel deals with the infringement of abstract right and the ensuing remedial action under the principles of "ownership" and "contract," taking into account disputes in civil law and criminal law or crime and punishment. When in this connection in his theory of punishment he vehemently attacks Feuerbach's theory of deterrence, it is clear what a contentious issue in the debates of his own time and the present day Hegel here tackles.

Under the heading "morality" (Part II) Hegel analyzes differing forms of action—from deeds of the heroes of antiquity, which still do not presuppose any developed ethic or condition of right, to the actualization of the good by means of a decision of conscience. This unusual approach is based on a firmly held position. In explaining what will be included in the "sphere of morality," Hegel notes in § 10 that "we here leave aside the doctrine of virtue." In his youth Hegel had been at one with Rousseau, Schiller, and Hölderlin in complaining that one no longer saw human beings (i.e., "whole" human beings with the "totality" of their character) but only a people, torn apart into a multitude of specialists—craftsmen, thinkers, priests, etc. The Jena essay on natural law seeks to reflect this contemporary criticism.[11] Natural law, so it is argued there, shows how nature (as second or ethical nature) attains its right, while morals shows how right is mirrored in the virtues of the individual. Aristotle had taken ethics as the fundamental discipline of practical philosophy and so developed it as the theory of sound moral conduct or the theory of virtue. In his essay Hegel reserves virtue as such to a particular political estate, which in bravery possesses the virtue of virtues; as for the second estate, that of industry and commerce, it is only in the complex relationships of the emancipated economic sphere that it exhibits the reflected image of the process wherein nature attains its right. This reflected image belongs for Hegel not to ethics but to the science of morality, viewed in a narrower, more strongly privatistic sense.

In his Heidelberg lectures Hegel draws the consequences of the position he had reached at the end of his time in Jena, namely that all estates or classes are to be understood on the basis of the way in which a people's "labor" is divided; life in the modern state has become so complex that the ethical whole no longer ever appears in its proper shape in the virtue of an individual. The models of antiquity can indeed be used to awaken political consciousness among the young; but when as adults they enter a society based on the division of labor, they all—including the officers, officials, and scholars of the "universal" class—become to a certain degree "bourgeois." Only in the partial form peculiar to the sphere to which they belong can they participate in the administration of the political whole. "Uprightness" is no longer seen as the distinctive ethical life of the bourgeois as against the virtue of the citizen; in the multilayered fabric of a constitutional monarchy it is "virtue," or what remains of the virtue of former times (as Hegel explains with a major historical retrospect in the exposition to § 135).

If one considers how action seeks to realize the rational in the actual, one can follow Kant in making morality purely a matter of

11. [Tr.] See above, n. 8.

the disposition and leaving aside everything natural—what is given and what ensues. Hegel opposes this position, without falling into an ethics of results; action is viewed in its various configurations, such as the one in which the intention is not yet directed to the organically good but to welfare, which remains tied to the particularity of individuals. Hegel directly attacks Kant, Fichte, and the Romantics, who separate the "ought" or the inner disposition of a beautiful soul from what happens in actuality and make it the affair of an infinite striving or longing. For Hegel it is not only that the conscience that actualizes the good is the culmination of successive stages of ethical consciousness; this good that is to be actualized also progressively takes shape in history in differing modes of concreteness. If Hegel after considering abstract right and morality as "ideal moments" presents as ethical life the organically good that is apprehended by the conscience, can he be sure that he is not merely contemplating a transitional stage in history? In the very last year of his life, in his essay on the constitutional conflict in England, Hegel will revert to his former call for justice as the criterion for judging existing or desirable institutions. But where is this justice to be found in Hegel's system? He assumes that history has led to rational institutions, which are also to be understood systematically as a necessarily coherent mode of concreteness of the good. But is this not to combine metaphysics and history in a way that undervalues the openness of history and the risk of human action?

In Part III of his philosophical doctrine of right, Hegel identifies as the paradigmatic forms of existing ethical actuality the family, civil society, and the state. In so doing he finds the definitive systematic expression for the break he had already made in Jena with traditional practical philosophy. Classical tradition opposes the household to the *polis*; this household, the *oikos*, is not only the family in the narrower sense but the family also as an economic unit with servants and dependent laborers. Only the head of a household can be a member of *societas civilis*. (While still a Gymnasium student Hegel copied down an excerpt from Sulzer's *Übersicht über die Praktische Philosophie* that similarly contrasts the state as civil society with the household.) In recent historical times, under the protection of monarchy, the sphere of industry and trade had broken away from the household and achieved a degree of emancipation making it largely independent of the state. Hegel pays due regard to this process by henceforth giving this sphere the name of civil society and so distinguishing it from the state.

The structure of civil society is sketched, in a spirit of economic liberalism, on the basis of the economy and the protection it enjoys under private law. The nobility, which was previously the determining factor, is drawn into the orbit of this sphere and characterized negatively in contrast with it. The particular function of the nobility whose landed property is held together by primogeniture is to provide a class of office bearers for a first house [of parliament]. On the one hand this new form of nobility provides an intermediary between people and monarchy; on the other hand it ensures an incorruptible, balanced policy thanks to its economic independence. Even if the land-tenure system of the nobility and peasants still favors living and working in the family, at least in negative terms these classes too are understood in the light of the differentiation of civil society, i.e., on the basis of the division of labor. In the French Revolution the third estate seized power for itself by an uprising, but in Hegel's view those states that were not directly affected by the Revolution are also affected, through its repercussions and the ensuing reforms, by the principle that individuals achieve their status in society through the occupation they freely choose and the way they are trained for it.

In calling for district courts, publicity in legal proceedings, and even jury courts (as in the Rhenish legal system, which was imposed by the French), Hegel seeks to make the citizen aware of an independence that can only be judged by other no less independent "associates." Hegel speaks explicitly of "associations" and so calls to mind the origins of the Germanic legal tradition. He is thus unable to accept the view of the jurists (as epitomized by Savigny) that Roman law alone provides the formal training required for the future development of a system of German law. In his view the link between the constitutional monarchy he advocates and the Roman and Byzantine Empire and its administration of justice is not unbroken. The further development of Roman law had presupposed despotism, and ever since its adoption by the School of Bologna recent history has been alienated from its own traditions. (Such are the terms in which Hegel expresses his views in the expositions to §§ 109–116 as a supplement to the arguments he had developed earlier.)

Hegel links civil society to the state by means of the "police," using that word in its former sense, referring to the state's supervision of industry and commerce. Hegel's Heidelberg lectures do not yet couple the word "police" with the word "corporations" in the title; but in the text itself, in postulating the self-organization of civil society in the autonomous administration of the municipalities and the organization of the workers in corporations, he is calling for a second source of the ethical alongside the family. (The latter can now be only the organizational form of agricultural labor as well as the mere natural base for the office-bearing and educated nobility, who are now coupled with the scholars, civil servants, and officers.) The preference Hegel accorded for a while to Austria and then to Napoleon's Rhenish Confederation had been motivated by the fact that he still thought he could find in Austria this organization of the state from below and saw Napoleon as the teacher of constitutional law who combined representative constitutions with the *Code civil*. The so-called *System of Ethical Life* of the first Jena years (1802–3)[12] saw ethical life as the Briareus of Greek legend, who with "myriads of eyes, arms, and other limbs, each of which is an absolute individual," represents the people, who in the state constitution are composed of many self-administering units. So Hegel was already urging at that time that the system of needs should organize itself inwardly through the "constitution" of the estate in question and should not merely submit to direction by the state. But it is only some fifteen years later that Hegel in his Heidelberg lectures fixes on the title "corporation" for this kind of self-organization (the parallel essay on the dispute concerning the Württemberg constitution speaks of "associations and corporations"). Hegel is evidently thinking of the

---

12. [*Tr.*] Published by Georg Lasson as *System der Sittlichkeit*, 2d ed. (Leipzig, 1923); translated into English by H. S. Harris and T. M. Knox, *System of Ethical Life and First Philosophy of Spirit* (Albany, 1979).

advanced stage the division of labor had reached in England and the attempts being made to combat the problems to which it gave rise. At the same time he seems desirous of harking back to the old guild institutions; however, by virtue of the principle of freedom of choice of occupation, the corporations differ from the prerevolutionary guilds, which rested on privilege.

For the state Hegel demands a system of government that as a constitutional monarchy does not stand opposed to democracy and aristocracy but incorporates their motifs. Thus the emancipated sphere of civil society should be integrated anew and the nobility united with the office-bearing middle classes through education and office. In the era of constitutionalism following the fall of Napoleon, Hegel reverts, often even in the very words he uses, to assessments and conceptions he had formulated in earlier years and different historical circumstances. His article on the German constitution had examined the differing course of French and German history from the point of view of comparative constitutional history, and so set the problems of the development of the representative system within the European framework. Now Hegel in turn contrasts England and France, where the state was quickly able to impose its will on the forces of particularism, with the particularism prevalent in Italy and Germany. Whereas England shows continuous development, for differing reasons both France and the German *Länder* must have new constitutions. Hegel notes that in June 1814 Louis XVIII gave France a Constitutional Charter comprising a Chamber of Peers and a Chamber of Deputies (even if the latter is elected on a high property qualification and can take no legislative initiative). The Congress of Vienna had called for constitutions for the German *Länder*. On the basis of the debates in his own state of Württemberg Hegel comes out in favor of state officials also being eligible for election. He takes issue with Kant by envisaging a division of powers in which each power includes the others within itself.

In accord with the main thrust of his philosophical doctrine of right, Hegel begins with the immediate being that the communal resolve acquires through the signature of the monarch. The executive power, which applies the laws to particular cases, is then coupled with the legislative power, which formulates the laws themselves in their universality. Hegel also regards two chambers or houses as particularly effective and balanced. He opposes the idea of a national assembly in the manner of Sieyes since he makes the self-administering machinery of the communities and corporations responsible for nominating the deputies of the one chamber. The aim is to avoid the danger of a central authority, elected in abstract fashion, standing in opposition to the unarticulated amorphous mass of the people. Hegel deems it more appropriate that in the German *Länder* the new parliamentary assemblies should join onto the old assemblies of the estates. In this way he believes it possible also to couple the self-organization of the workers with parliamentary representation (in France the measures taken against guilds and privileges in fact delayed the development of trade unions by decades). With this conception of constitutional policy Hegel seeks to build on the ideas of the French Revolution, but in a way that endeavors to correct the historically conditioned one-sidedness of the French solution (in the same way that de Tocqueville tried to do later). Hegel thus propounds a view of political science that as far as constitutional policy is concerned involves a concrete conception opposed to the guiding conception of the French Revolution.

In history, according to Hegel, the mutual relationship of the individual states is such that there is in the last resort no praetor set over them. The court of judgment is history itself, visualized in its entirety (at this time Hegel also procured a copy of Johannes von Müller's posthumous *Allgemeine Geschichte*). This hard, realistic view is tempered by its starting point, namely that in all civilized states people pursue their particular occupations, but that religion represents what is eternal for history as a whole and no longer for one limited people. In Hegel's eyes, "public spirit" and "patriotism" do not mean embracing the cause of the state in an exceptional situation, but fulfilling the limited duties deriving from one's occupation; thus it is that the "egoism" of the individual can be presented in the expository passage to § 132 as the obverse of "patriotism." The Swabian Reichsfreiherr and Prussian Colonel von Massenbach, who as officer was implicated in the military catastrophe at Jena, is cited as an example for the way in which people who have failed in one specific field come forward as "patriots"—in the case in point by writing on general political subjects in a Bonapartist, Machiavellian vein (the exposition to § 154 juxtaposes the pronouncements of von Massenbach as one of those who "shout the loudest" with his insipid, ill-conceived judgments regarding the extent to which the English were interested in parliamentary proceedings). When individuals find their place in a society based on division of labor through the free choice of their occupation, then they ought also to become politically active, as their partisan interests dictate, through the representative system, and they should play their part in the administration of communal affairs. This partisan participation in the universal is the only form of participation Hegel now recognizes.

If individuals as citizens define their particular place in society and the state as a whole by means of their work, then they must be educated and trained for the occupation they freely choose. So it is that the former Nuremberg Gymnasium director and educational counselor prescribes in §§ 85 and 86 a right of children to education. But Hegel does not ask for education to be made a separate province; it is a mistake, he says, "to do as Pestalozzi and others have done and withdraw children from the world and educate them in such a way as to give them [only] their own interests." He is at one with Montesquieu in maintaining that instruction is purveyed before, alongside, and after schooling by one's parents and also by the world. Hegel—who in Nuremberg was also responsible for extending schooling to the children of the poor—gives as horrible examples the forcible treatment of children by their fathers in ancient Rome and child labor in England in the first years of the Industrial Revolution. The state should ensure that each child receives a definite education in accord with universal criteria; it is in this sense that the text later goes on to say (in § 158) that children become "children of the state."

Participation in the service of the state must not be restricted by birth and class privileges but must essentially be open to every citizen who is qualified: "Herein lies the genesis of present-day higher education." Instead of the nepotism of the provincial universities, Hegel accordingly urges that "all universities in Germany should form a whole," that academic freedom should be restored, and that every university teacher should be appointed on the basis of objective criteria, although also as an official enjoying security of tenure (§ 144). In § 158 Hegel advocates what was later called "cultural policy": art, religion, and science are to be through and through the "life of the state," in other words portray the living principle of the state; but they are also to be regarded as an "end in and for themselves" and so have an autonomy that must be guaranteed by the state itself. If previously the fear of God had provided for religion and the prince for science and art, "the needs of these spheres are not necessarily provided for in this way." Hegel points out that the church had opposed science and neglected to raise religious truths "to the sphere of science." "Contemporary states are still a far cry from establishing universal institutions for these spheres; the universities and academies of sciences have taken the place of the monasteries."

It was during this period that the brothers Boisserée exhibited in Heidelberg their collection of Old Masters from the Lower Rhine and the Netherlands, so reminding the citizens of the new constitutional monarchies of the early links between prince and townspeople in the Flemish and Rhenish cities. The logical sequel to the activity of such private collectors was obviously the establishment of a public museum enjoying state protection. Here there were new tasks for the state to assume; how these tasks were to be performed had still to be determined. But it was inevitable that with the views he held Hegel would clash in Berlin not only with the conservatism of Savigny. It is true that in Berlin he tried to maintain friendly relations with Wilhelm von Humboldt; but educational policy as determined in its broad lines by Johannes Schulze had diverged from the basic conviction of Goethe's day that in a society based on the division of labor individuals could overcome the bias inherent in their activity by the all-around development of their energies. Already in the first works of his Jena period Hegel had attacked Schleiermacher's view of religion and the state, a view made up partly of Romanticism, partly of Enlightenment liberalism. Schleiermacher maintained in a more emphatic way than Hegel the need for a process of emancipation converting the "household" of former days into a free confraternity such as would preserve spiritual plurality in the face of all speculative claims to universal validity. To be sure, the universities and academies were also for Hegel corporations that in free collegial union pursued an intrinsic end. But Hegel, evidently in harmony with the vanishing hopes entertained by the minister von Altenstein, looked to the academies also as a means of implementing the state's cultural policy. Schleiermacher was bound to oppose any efforts in this direction.

At the very beginning of the nineteenth century, in his article on the German constitution, Hegel made fun of the fact that "during the thousand years that had elapsed since Charlemagne" the constitution of the empire did not seem to have changed one bit if it is the case that "at his coronation the newly elected emperor still wears Charlemagne's crown, scepter, orb, even his shoes, cloak, and jewels." In truth the new "giant" states and the "pygmies" between them had, in Hegel's view, diverged in a way that changed the entire picture. At that time he still wanted to reestablish the former empire in the sense that, taking the military establishment as a starting point, he envisaged alongside the college of princes a bench of municipal delegates and with it a chamber of civil deputies as a representative system. After the Congress of Vienna, in his Heidelberg lectures, Hegel assigns this system of representation as a constitutional monarchy to the constellation of states led by the Pentarchy. He points out that in the thousand years since Charlemagne the communal life of human beings has radically altered. Bearing in mind that Christianity attaches value to the salvation of each individual, and that the ethical sensibility of the Germanic peoples emphasizes freedom and the association of the free based on loyalty and solidarity, now all individuals are expected to attain their position in society through their labor and achievement and no longer to inherit it from systems of authority forged in ancient battles and disputes. The "civil society" that comes into being in this manner is given a share in the administration of power within the constitutional monarchy through a system of representation. The traditional nobility and princes too are given a function to perform in the body politic as a whole, a function determined at least in a negative sense by its being contrasted with the spirit of the middle classes. But those who determine their place in society by their work and achievement must be qualified for their work by education and must be able to visualize the meaning of their life expressly through art, religion, and science. The new state also assumes responsibility for the educational and cultural facilities that in their autonomy make possible the spiritual life of the state.

Once Hegel has elaborated his conception in this shape, the philosophical doctrine of right automatically comes within the orbit of his system as a whole. His differentiation of nature and spirit and his formulation of a distinct philosophy of subjective spirit had laid down in advance that human beings exist not only in the natural ethical life of the family but also in the state, and that the ethical whole gains a sense of its own significance through art, religion, and science. Indeed it is no longer practical philosophy but the philosophy of subjective spirit that recognizes that all individuals are persons worthy of right. In the compendium of 1820 Hegel even attempts (although he does not pursue the attempt consistently to the end) to furnish the detailed argumentation of the *Philosophy of Right* with a secure basis by drawing parallels with arguments in the *Science of Logic*. Hegel draws our attention to the fact that the ethical sphere has the form of right by prefacing his analysis of ethical life with an exposition of the ideal moments of abstract right and morality. However, the impression is unavoidable that, starting from the guiding principles of his thought, Hegel could just as well have arrived at a different structure for his philosophy of right. Whereas the philosophy of right tacks the analysis of the institutions of ethical life onto its exposition of the ideal moments and concludes with a portrayal of the course of history, the aesthetics for example begins by exploring the idea of the beautiful and only then goes on to show the configurations it assumes in history and finally the individual arts. However much of a closed circle Hegel's system may seem, it is in truth open to unresolved questions. We must also bear in mind that Hegel had to take account of a changing environment. In Heidelberg the attention he pays to the Württemberg bureaucracy is dictated by his fight against the arbitrariness of officials; in Prussia he has to take into account that this state has still to gain its unity and must do so by the administrative path. In presenting the hereditary monarchy and it alone as the institution by means of which the executive and legislature become fully effective, Hegel faces a difficult task and becomes entangled in curiosities that one must not today pursue too far if one is not to obscure the actual relevance of his philosophy of right.

In the final analysis Hegel's approach bears at every turn the imprint of wrestling with experience, and this experience forms a continuing chain. There can be no doubt that in important respects Hegel did not foresee the future course of events. His conception of the system of representation does not yet take into account that it was not only interest groups (*Fraktionen*) that formed in a national assembly but parties, which sought to organize in concrete terms the emergent will in the people as a whole. Hegel's sole aim is to seek rationality in what is actual, and he has no desire to stray beyond what is actual or is becoming actual. But when he calls for "corporations" he describes an institution that never became actual in this manner, and that on the contrary was made impossible as labor relations became progressively more extensive and more differentiated. For all his attentiveness to the development of economics, Hegel evidently remained geared to an all too traditional view of productive labor within a readily comprehensible framework. Although he saw that industrialization must give rise to a "rabble" or proletariat, he did not perceive the explosive force contained in this process. The menacing power nationalism was to attain in the nineteenth century also remained hidden from him. The Heidelberg lectures declare in § 160 that though Germany has many central points, the people's wish is directed to a "federal union of the individual central points." He hardly took the German Confederation seriously, however, and it is only in ironic terms that § 322 of the Berlin compendium can refer to this "wish." So Hegel's philosophy of right stands despite itself in a historical context of which it is not possible to form a complete picture. In endeavoring to conceptualize the upheaval that marked the end of the eighteenth and the beginning of the nineteenth centuries, Hegel hands down to us a task that, following two world wars and in the light of the catastrophes that threaten us, has become almost inconceivably more difficult.

THE MANUSCRIPT

The Editors[1]

The manuscript of the text here published is a transcript or note-book (*Nachschrift*) compiled by the law student Peter Wannen-mann[2] from Hegel's lecture series on philosophy of right delivered in 1817–18 in Heidelberg and from the start of the lectures deliv-ered in Berlin in 1818–19. It is the property of the Deutsches Lit-eraturarchiv/Schiller-Nationalmuseum in Marbach am Neckar and bears the accession number 81.1021. The manuscript originates from the posthumous papers of the late Franz-Joseph Brecht and only became known at the beginning of 1982.

It comprises 213 thick yellowish-white quarto manuscript sheets, in part slightly torn at the edges, and now showing some foxing. The script is in black ink, which is sometimes visible on the other side of the sheet in a slightly brownish color. Some pages are spat-tered with inkblots although this does not affect the intelligibility of the text. The manuscript is bound in a thick black cardboard cover, in the usual manner for lecture transcripts at that time. A brown title plate on the spine bears the slightly damaged inscription

---

1. [*Tr.*] The editors were the entire staff of the Hegel Archives (Ruhr Uni-versity, Bochum) at the time of publication (1983): C. Becker, W. Bonsiepen, A. Gethmann-Siefert, F. Hogemann, W. Jaeschke, C. Jamme, H.-C. Lucas, K. R. Meist, and H. Schneider.

2. [*Ed.*] Apart from the entries in the Heidelberg University Register recording Wannenmann's matriculation and transfer to Berlin, the University archives appar-ently contain no further information regarding his studies in Heidelberg.

Naturrecht und Staatswissenschaft von Hegel. The front cover is followed by a blank flyleaf and the unpaginated title page with the stamp SCIPIO RINECK and the verso blank. The text of the Heidelberg lectures follows with two further unpaginated pages containing the table of contents, the next unpaginated page containing the beginning of the introduction, and pages 2–401 containing the remainder of the text. On page 401 below the name Wannenmann there is an undecipherable sign and a flourish. Page 402 is blank. The introduction to the Berlin lectures follows on pages 403–422. On page 422 below the words, "End of the Introduction. Berlin, 10 November 1818," there is a flourish. The volume closes with a blank flyleaf.

Before being written on, the sheets were prepared in such a way as to leave a frame within which to write. It can be assumed that paper was obtainable in this form from the retailers since other transcripts also show this sheeting. The text is very neatly written in small German script; some shortened forms and abbreviations are used, but their sense is unambiguous and the expanded forms have been supplied by this edition without comment. There are relatively few deletions, interlinear additions, or marginal additions keyed to the body of the text. The dictated passages of text are occasionally indented (e.g., in § 121); such instances are not specifically indicated. One peculiarity of the writer is that he runs words together; here they have been separated out, again without comment. The manuscript is undoubtedly a fair copy, that is, a version compiled at home on the basis of notes taken down while the lecturer was speaking. Texts written down during actual lectures are completely different in character. The main paragraphs in each section were dictated by Hegel, and this is corroborated by comparison with a fragment relating to the philosophy of right of which F. W. Carové has preserved a record.[3] However, the transmission even of these dictated passages occasionally shows certain deficiencies due to mistakes in copying the original notes into the

---

3. [*Ed.*] See Friedhelm Nicolin, "Hegel über konstitutionelle Monarchie: Ein Splitter aus der ersten Rechtsphilosophie-Vorlesung," *Hegel-Studien* 10 (1975): 79–86.

fair copy. By contrast, the formulation of the expositions (the indented paragraphs following the dictated passages) is in all probability largely the work of Wannenmann. They contain numerous significant weaknesses and awkwardnesses in the formulation of Hegel's ideas, which Wannenmann's original notes presumably reproduced only in a very compressed form.

Some variations in the script and in the color of the ink can be easily explained by the fact that such fair copies were not all written down at once. This does not mean that Wannenmann's text could not have been compiled very soon after the lectures ended. But this cannot be proved from the dates given at the end of the Heidelberg lectures and the Berlin introduction since in accord with the practice at that time these dates probably mark the end of the whole series or (in the second case) of the specific lectures Wannenmann attended. As far as can be said at present in the absence of comparable sources, the Heidelberg lectures seem to be transmitted in full, while all we have of the Berlin series is the introduction, and not even that in full.

NATURAL RIGHT AND POLITICAL SCIENCE

Heidelberg, 1817–1818

INTRODUCTION

§ 1

Natural right [*Naturrecht*] has as its object the rational determinations of right and the actualization of this its idea. Its source—
constituting its divine, eternal origin—is thought, which grasps the
will in its free self-determination.

(a) *Positive right* [*positive Recht*] is in general that right
which has validity in a particular state and must therefore be
respected as an authority that is maintained by coercion or fear
or by confidence and faith, but that can also be upheld through
rational insight. As far as its general content is concerned, positive right may be either rational or, as is customarily the case, a
blend of rational and of contingent, arbitrary provisions; some
of these derive from violence and repression or from the inepti-
tude of the legislators, while some have been carried over from
a more imperfect state of society into a more perfect, founded
on a higher consciousness of freedom, the changes that have occurred having been decreed singly and according to the needs of
the moment, regardless of the coherence of the whole.

(b) In addition to rational right, however, a positive sphere
of right arises automatically as soon as right acquires validity
and external actuality. On the one hand the particular existence
of a people is marked by distinctive conditions that influence the
determinations of right; on the other, the empirical cases and

distinctions to which rational right must be applied are not actually expressed in it even though they are contained in it. The more developed and elaborated the state of society, the more comprehensive become the particular determinations of right (such extensions being, incidentally, merely a matter for the understanding). Furthermore, the real existence [*Existenz*] of right brings about | a comparison of wholly heterogeneous objects, one of which has to represent the value of the other, e.g., in the case of punishments, obligatory service, etc., where an absolute equivalence cannot be established.

(c) Lastly, because as actual it occurs in utterly determinate individuality, actual right requires a final decision—a decision wholly determined *as* individuality—[yet] a decision that, by virtue of the universality of reason, is not confined within these narrow limits.

§ 2

The sphere of right is not the soil of nature—certainly not of external nature, but also not of subjective human nature, insofar as human will, determined by human nature, is in the sphere of natural needs and instincts. On the contrary, the sphere of right is the spiritual sphere, the *sphere of freedom* [*Sphäre der Freiheit*]. It is true that nature also has a place in the realm of freedom, to the extent that the idea of freedom expresses itself and gives itself existence [*Existenz*], but freedom remains the foundation, and nature only enters in as something dependent.

The term "natural right" or "natural law" [*Naturrecht*] ought to be abandoned and replaced by the term "philosophical doctrine of right" [*philosophische Rechtslehre*], or (as will also emerge) "doctrine of objective spirit." The expression "nature" [*Natur*] contains the ambiguity that by it we understand [(1)] the essence [*Wesen*] and concept [*Begriff*] of something, (2) unconscious, immediate nature as such. So by "natural law" has been understood the supposed legal order valid by virtue of immediate nature; with this is connected the fiction of a "state of nature" [*Naturzustand*], in which authentic right or law supposedly exists. This state of nature is opposed to the state of society, and in particular to the [political] state [*Staat*]. There has also been a prevalent misconception in this regard, as if society were not something implicitly and explicitly in conformity with the essence of spirit, and necessary for it, but a kind of artificial evil and misfortune, and as if genuine freedom were limited in it. | Rather is it the case that a state [*Zustand*] that could be de- 7 scribed as a state of nature would be one wherein there were no such things as right and wrong because spirit had not yet attained to the thought of its freedom (and it is only with this thought that right and wrong begin); or rather, since the human being exists essentially as self-consciousness and with the concept of good and evil, the state of nature is a state of unfreedom and wrong, which must be sublated before freedom and its actuality can be attained.

§ 3

The science of right has the free will as its principle and starting point. As far as its coming to be is concerned, this concept accordingly falls outside the science of right and is thus to be accepted here as given from the sphere of philosophy. The will contains (1) the element as absolute negativity—the pure *indeterminacy* [*Unbestimmtheit*] of the ego consisting in its pure reflection into itself, having within itself no limitation, no immediately present content determined by nature, needs, desires and instincts, or in any other way. This is the boundless infinity of the absolute abstraction of pure thinking, of *universality* [*Allgemeinheit*].

§ 4

(2) As absolute negativity the ego is at the same time the *passing over to determinacy* and the positing of a determinacy or of a distinction as an inner content, a content that may be given further by nature or may be pure concept of the ego itself. Here either the ego decides to *close itself off* [*Beschliessen*], to posit one determinacy as its essence and exclude everything else, or else it decides to *open itself up* [*Entschliessen*], insofar as all determinacy [is] contained in the ego as *universal*; and it is only through positing itself | as something determinate that the ego enters into 8

determinate existence [*Dasein*]¹—the *absolute finitude* or infinitude of its *individuality* [*Einzelheit*].

§ 5

(3) The will is the unity of these two moments. It is only through its infinite self-determination that the ego is pure universality or simple identity, and it is only absolutely self-enclosed solitude when it relates itself in infinite fashion to itself or is simply identity and universality with itself. By the decision to open up, in other words the actual will, the ego also excludes from itself an other, and reflects itself into this other at the same time that it reflects itself into itself. But here in the will as such, all that can initially be concluded is that the ego in determining itself at the same time remains indifferent to this determinacy, remains universal, knowing the determinacy in which it is actual as *its own* and *merely ideal* [*ideell*],² as a mere possibility by which it is likewise not constrained but which it can immediately sublate.

§ 6

(4) This unity is the will *in itself* (the will as implicit) or *for us*. But the will is *free* insofar as it makes itself its object and content, therefore wills itself, i.e., insofar as it wills to be free. In this way it is *for itself* (explicitly) what it is *in itself* (implicitly).

---

1. [*Tr.*] Hegel uses two terms for "existence," *Dasein* and *Existenz*. *Dasein* is for Hegel a logical term, denoting a transition from immediacy to determinacy, externality, opposition, whereas *Existenz* refers to concrete, empirical, immediate existence. Depending on context, we translate *Dasein* as either "existence" or "determinate existence" in order to bring out the element of determinacy, of being-*there* (*da*), that is in it. *Existenz*, which occurs less frequently, is translated as "existence" with the German following in brackets. Despite the technical and etymological distinctions between the terms, they often appear to be used synonymously in this work. See also § 69, n. 1.

2. [*Tr.*] In this work Hegel frequently uses the expressions *ideell* and *reell*. They refer obviously to the distinction between the ideal and the real, or the subjective and the objective, or the logical and the empirical; but they designate the respective terms of this distinction in abstract, undialectical form, cut off from each other. Hence we frequently translate as "merely ideal" and "merely real." What is *truly* ideal (*ideal* in German) overreaches the distinction between the merely ideal and the merely real; it is the ideal-real or what Hegel calls the *Idee*, the unity of concept and objectivity.

§ 7

The will that has being for itself, explicitly, as well as in itself, implicitly, is *true* and absolute because it determines itself to be in its existence [*Dasein*]—i.e., as standing over against itself—what its concept is, in other words because the pure concept has the intuition of itself as its reality. It is *free* because it relates itself to nothing else, but, as infinite negativity, only to itself. It is utterly *universal* because in it all limitation and particularization of individuality is sublated, such limitation or particularization residing solely in the | antithesis between the concept or subjective side and   9 its object or content.

[3]The will that only has being *implicitly* is the *natural* will in general. As self-determining individuality it posits a difference within itself. What is thus differentiated (1) is a content in general and (2) has the form of being mine. But in the natural will this form and this content are still distinct, and what is mine is something other than the ego. This natural will is the *arbitrary will* [*Willkür*], the will in the sphere of desires, drives, and inclinations, which has for its content anything given (externally or inwardly) and therefore finite, and can renounce this finite content because it is only its own through its self-determination. But the new content that it substitutes for what it has renounced is likewise a determinate content of this kind, so that the arbitrary will can go on sublating this content *infinitely* [without] thereby escaping from finitude.

Because the will that subsists as arbitrary will has a given content to which it is opposed as something particular for itself, it is *subjective*. By contrast, the will that has itself as its determination is the will that is utterly identical with itself, the *objective* will, spirit in its objectivity.

The will in general is essentially *intelligence, knowledge* of self. Only as pure knowledge is it free will; as theoretical, however, free intelligence is, to be sure, self-active and its thoughts

---

3. [*Tr.*] The three paragraphs of the exposition to § 7 are headed by the words "Remark 1," "Remark 2," "Remark 3" in Wannenmann's transcript. This together with the considerable amount of emphasis found in these paragraphs suggests that they were dictated by Hegel.

are its own productions, but in the shape of *subsistent* and *necessary* determinations. But the will has *purpose*, i.e., (1) its content consists in its own determinations; (2) the latter are defined as merely possible, as the *will's* determinations or as *subjective*, thus contradicting its absolute objectivity or the fact that the determinations do not also *exist*. The will's drive is to realize itself | in such a way that the will and the intelligence are identical.

10

§ 8

Right expresses in general a relationship constituted by the freedom of the will and its realization. One such relationship is *duty* [*Pflicht*], insofar as I regard it as essential and have to recognize this relationship, respect it, or bring it about. The merely formal character of right, as opposed to genuine right, derives from the fact that the realization of freedom has stages or that the spirit of freedom can be more abstract or more concrete.

In positive right, right is what is in the laws; in philosophical right, what is right *is* law and no law affords the criterion of right. The function of laws is to express the rational will and the way in which it enters into existence [*Existenz*]. Strictly speaking, right demands primarily only a negative comportment, although positive actions, arising for example through contracts, may also be required in it. Right is sacrosanct because it rests on the freedom of the will; and this also follows from the basic determination of the essence of God. What is free—pure spirit—is the basic concept of God.

Right has manifold stages; sometimes it is more abstract, sometimes more concrete; so it can be unjust, wrong [*unrecht*]. For instance, slavery may be lawful although it is absolutely wrong, and positive right may contain something unholy. The fact that something is a positive, long-established right does not make it right in and for itself. As circumstances change, the right that derives from them automatically ceases. The guarantee and confirmation of right, its formal character, is opposed to genuine right; this contradiction does indeed occur. The realization of freedom has necessary stages. And to study this process is the aim of our science.

Morality and right are often mutually opposed. There are, however, also moral points of view that limit abstract right; for example, if a debtor would be ruined by paying his debts, | the   11
right that strictly accrues to the creditors is limited by this point of view. The artisan must be allowed to keep his tools; and so right in the strict sense recognizes morality, and strictly, formally conceived right is not deemed sacrosanct. To this extent moral right is more concrete than abstract, strict right; still more concrete is the formation of an entire state, and this concrete spirit is possessed of a much higher right than abstract right, so that private right is limited by the right of the state. The spirit of the state and its realization is something higher than the spirit of the individual; and still higher than the spirit or the right of one people is the right of the universal state, the spirit of the world, which strikes down the inferior spirits when they oppose it or stand in its way. Then we see these great ethical collisions. For example, there was no greater right than that Rome should be a republic; but for the sake of the spirit of the world, whose tool he was, Caesar had the right to overturn the republic, yet Brutus meted out justice, his right deserts, to Caesar as an individual. The single individual who sets himself up as the embodiment of the will of the world ends by being destroyed. In order that right should not be merely formal in character, there are more concrete spirits that surpass the more abstract ones.

What is therefore essential in right is philosophical insight into the different standpoints. But the general feeling of right one has from a lower standpoint can make one believe one is suffering wrong. In this matter insight is one thing, general opinion another.

§ 9

As the *concept* [*Begriff*] of the freedom that is for itself and so has no particular content and purpose, the will is, to begin with, *merely formal* [*formell*], insofar as, in the process of distinguishing itself from itself, it is nonetheless not yet distinct, and so has not yet any *determinate existence* [*Dasein*]. But since freedom is essentially only absolute identity through its absolute negativity,

12   its determining must essentially | acquire the element of being other and of being in general, but in such a way that this being occurs in it only as a *seeming* [*Scheinen*], as something immediately sublated or merely ideal [*ideell*], while freedom itself remains within itself.

The will as concept is merely formal because the free will is its own purpose, and we have here the unity of subjective and objective; no differentiation has yet taken place between them, and the free will is wholly abstract form. It can likewise be said that the free will is devoid of form because form is not yet posited in a distinction. The content is what is identical with itself, with the quality of being indifferent vis-à-vis the form as distinct. Thus God is the absolute content, and the idea is the unity of subjective and objective (which are something distinct). Freedom is absolute negativity since it is living, and it must include the moment of being, of abstract identity. Seeming [*Scheinen*] is the unification of positive being and nonbeing. The will must will something, it must have a content, but this content is not an other. If we have formed a concept of something, it is no longer something alien for us because it is permeated by us. In love another is object, each is an ego, an unyielding atom on its own account, and in this absolute independence the object of my love is my other self, and one self is the other self. The necessity is that the concept, freedom, realizes itself; the will is absolute idealism, and what is for the will is distinct from what wills, but insofar as it is the object of my will, it is only ideal, and has no independence.

§ 10

The free will is initially abstract and immediate, as is its determinate existence or realization; this constitutes the sphere of *abstract right* [*abstraktes Recht*] [Part I]. The second [sphere] is where these two moments, the will in its concept and its determinate existence, break apart into independent extremes, the will in its concept becoming the particular inner will of a subject and its existence becoming the subject's well-being; and [where] the unity of these moments, the good as idea, on the one hand *is* their abso-

13   lute | content and determination but on the other hand is at the

same time contingent in relation to them: this is the sphere of *morality* [*Moralität*] [Part II]. The third sphere is the unity of both these moments, in which the idea of the good is realized in subjective freedom and [in] determinate existence, in such a way that freedom exists equally as necessity and actuality. The universal will comes about: *ethical life* [*Sittlichkeit*] and the state [Part III].

That these three stages exist derives from the idea: first we always have what is abstract, the free will in its concept, abstract right, the realization of which is only abstract realization. To this pertains personality, i.e., abstract freedom. The second sphere is the sphere of morality in general, although we here leave aside the doctrine of virtue. It is here that the concept of the action of *dolus* [fraud] and *culpa* [fault] comes into play, as do human attitudes and human well-being—all questions that do not arise with abstract right. This is the sphere of reflection, of difference, of distinction, of mutual exclusion. Abstract right becomes external to itself, and in this second sphere the first two moments are independent and mutually exclusive; the differentiation must be accentuated to the utmost. We take the subject in its will over against the object, the subject that in its arbitrariness posits itself utterly for itself; the externality of the subject becomes human well-being and happiness. (Above the two moments stands their identity, their absolute unity, the good as idea as distinct from reality.) Good is supposedly accomplished by the conscience, while well-being is regarded as subordinate to good; at the same time, good ought to be actualized. The conscience may be good or evil, individuals may enjoy happiness or they may not. In the third place we have the resolution of this contradiction, ethical life or the state; here it is not only abstract right that is realized, but the idea of the good. Here the idea of the good, whose soul is the concept of freedom, is actualized. Here the free will no longer stands over against necessity, but the absolute and the necessary are equated, and the universal will is the good.

I. ABSTRACT RIGHT

§ 11

The free will, at the stage when its concept is still abstract, occurs as an immediate existence [*unmittelbares Dasein*]; for while the concept is found utterly and solely as idea, its immediate reality is abstract being, and as the reality of absolute negativity its reality is here the *being of the individual* [*das Sein des Einzelnen*].

The pure free will is divinity, while the individual free will is that of a human being. It is plain to us that the human being is a free being [*ein freies Wesen*]. The free will has being, and this being is determined as the being of the individual. Now because the free will is absolute negativity, absolute being-for-self, the starting point must be the being of the individual free will. Absolute spirit appears within itself, is a distinction that in itself is not a distinction. Absolute being [*Wesen*] is the intuition, or differentiation of itself. The concept of the absolute free will is the finite free being. We begin with the individual free being, and then consider how it frees itself from this finitude.

§ 12

The free individual is the *person*. *Personality* implies that— determined as I am on all sides in this absolute finitude, this pure and utter self-relation—I am within myself infinite and universal.

The individual has immediate being. I am this particular

being, [one] determined on all sides, something completely finite: this is my status, my character. This complete finitude constitutes the immediate being of the individual, but in this finitude I am myself, I am utterly self-contained, I am pure self-relation, I can reject all these other elements that | impinge on me. I am dependent on all sides, yet I am also my own, I am therefore infinite and universal in that I comprehend myself as "I." This is the concept of personality: I am the force that can hold these contradictory elements apart; I am this absolute bond. All human value consists in knowing oneself as person. Contained within myself, I am absolute negativity, the absolute activity of my self-relating; what the immediacy of being corresponds to is that my being becomes freedom, that my reality is freedom itself.

16

§ 13

The general imperative of right is therefore to *respect human beings* (yourself and others) *as persons.* But because the principle of abstract right is only pure personality and the individual's own will, imperatives of right and duties, as well as actions in the sphere of right, are ultimately and properly speaking only *negative*; in other words [it is] merely *forbidden* to impair the freedom of others. Since abstract freedom does not contain any *particular* content, actions with such a content are, in regard to abstract right, only *possible* actions (as neither contrary to abstract right nor necessary actions); in other words they are *permitted.*

"Respect human beings as persons" is the imperative of abstract right; thus all imperatives of right (other than the command, "Be a person") are merely prohibitions. Right does not yet contain duties; actions in the sphere of right are always merely negative. For example, "Abide by contracts" embraces positive actions, but the ultimate purpose is only negative: I place others in possession of something that they already own; the aim is that what they own, their freedom, their personality, should not be impaired. An action affects something outside itself; but I cannot affect the personality, which has no external aspect. For something to be "permitted" means what is possible from the standpoint of right, since in right there are only prohibitions; thus | positive action is only permitted. Right still contains no particular purposes, as do morality and human attitudes. To the extent that something is necessary (as in the case of morality), we have [positive] commands. *What* is permitted is not determined by right; in right, particular purposes are only possible, not necessary. Permission refers to abstract right; in the case of immediate rights we have duties as well.

§ 14

The sphere of abstract right is concerned only with the immediate personality and its equally immediate realization, not yet with more concrete relationships. It contains three relationships: (1) that of immediate *possession* [*Besitz*], which is defined as *property* or *ownership* [*Eigentum*]; (2) that of a change of ownership as legal transference into the ownership of another, i.e., *contract* [*Vertrag*]; (3) the infringement of my ownership in general.

Here we are considering only abstract personality, not the right of persons. My relation to something external to myself is possession. A contract is a change that occurs by free will, not by nature. This change can have two forms: either my will remains in it, regardless of the change, which is merely external; or my ownership is changed by virtue of an infringement that restricts my freedom, and so injures me in what is my own.

1. Possession and Ownership

§ 15

In their immediate being, persons have a *natural* existence [*Existenz*]: partly [they have] in themselves an external mode of being [*Dasein*]; partly they stand in relation to things outside them. But they are, | in the first place, absolutely free in relation to these things; and in the second place these external *things* are not absolute ends in themselves and are consequently something unfree and impersonal. However real they may be for feeling [*Empfindung*], for need, and for consciousness, they are something merely ideal for the freedom of the person, something devoid of rights.

In their immediacy persons are individuals; the form of immediacy applying to them is the externality of nature. A person who exists at the level of immediacy is in fact natural; and at this level we first have the sphere of consciousness, for which external things have positive being. But philosophically speaking, this is no longer valid, it is subordinate. The natural human being is quite content with this, without recognizing that it is sublated. As free persons, persons have in the first place gone back into themselves out of externality; as free beings humans have knowledge of themselves, knowing that as egos their independence is not merely that of their bodies. In the second place, externality is, for the free person, something sublated, something merely ideal. What is free has freedom as its end, that is an absolute end. As a living being the external exists in individuality, is an organic whole, an end in itself, the concept itself as an individual. The species as such does not exist in nature, only the individual. A living being lives in its body, in its natural needs. The members of a living being are not parts but an organic whole.

For feeling, externality has reality, we can love it. Natural existence [*Existenz*] is a limited, relative existence since it has needs, and something other [than itself] is necessary for it. It is only when we reach the standpoint of consciousness that there is perception. For the standpoints of finitude external things have reality, but not for freedom. What is free knows itself as absolute end. What we call things are not persons, and regardless of the fact that they exist they are not ends for themselves. Things are devoid of rights; to be sure, they have the right to exist, but | right, properly speaking, is a relationship in which the will is free. By "thing" we understand what is not personal, what is subordinate.

§ 16

Persons can therefore imbue this impersonal externality with their free will, and they must thereby endow themselves with a sphere in which their freedom exists, namely *possession* [*Besitz*]. Through possession, on the one hand, *I become external*; and, on the other hand (which amounts to the same thing), an external thing becomes *mine* and has my will as its determination and substantial end. I possess my own body, like other things, only insofar as it is my will to do so.

Human beings can take possession of whatever is impersonal and claim that it is mine; things have within themselves no higher end, no more substantial end. Because they do not belong to themselves, I can imbue them with my will and by this means give my freedom an external sphere, a form of immediacy. I become external, and what is external becomes mine, it acquires inwardness, my will, an absolute determination that it does not have on its own account. I only possess my organic body insofar as I will to have it; an animal cannot separate itself wholly or in part from its body. Things have being in immediate fashion, and I in immediate fashion am an individual; the higher unification occurs in the state, in ethical life. Possession is the immediate relation of my will to a thing; I need no other mediation than that I will or want the thing. By this means the thing becomes mine, it cannot offer any resistance to me. Mediation occurs when two are independent in relation to each other, and a third sublates this independence. | 20

§ 17

Persons have their bodies by virtue of nature. As far as all other external things are concerned, as far as the earth is concerned, it is only in the abstract sense that human beings have an *equal right* to them. The essential externalization [*Äusserung*] of free will in possession involves from the outset the element of contingency, of empirical singularity, of mere need and arbitrariness. For this very reason the natural will of others can be limited; and through the accident of time the thing belongs to *the first* to take possession of it.

It is only in a universal sense that each individual has a right to what is external; but once individuals take possession of something, they enter the sphere of the external. Insofar as they are personal they have [a right] to external things in general, but nonetheless by taking possession of something they enter the sphere of singularity. Each person has a right to the whole earth because it is something devoid of rights, but the right must be externalized or uttered,[1] and as a result it has to do with individual things. When I take possession of something, contingency and need come into play, and I enter the sphere of singularity; and in so doing limit my will. *Res nullius cedit primo occupanti* [a thing belonging to no one is ceded to the first occupant][2] means that someone is the first, which is a matter of contingency. As soon as one takes possession of something, one imbues it with one's will and excludes others. Although it is a matter of contingency that one is the first, one has the absolute right to imbue something external with one's will. Each of us has, so we are told, equality of right, properly speaking, in regard to the whole earth; such a distribution is immensely difficult, and with each newborn child the division should really be undertaken again. Equality is an attribute which expresses an external relation. All have equal rights since each has equal abstract right in regard to the world; but abstract right must be realized, and in the process of realization right enters the sphere of contingency, e.g., of whim and need, and thus the sphere of inequality. |

21

§ 18

In order that a thing should become my possession, my inner will is not sufficient; it is also necessary that I *take possession* of it [*Besitzergreifung*]. By this means the determination of it as mine attains external existence [*Dasein*] and becomes recognizable for others. The negative condition [for my taking possession], namely that the thing should be *ownerless (res nullius)*, is here self-evident, or rather relates to the anticipated relationship to others.

1. [*Tr.*] The everyday sense of the German words *Äusserung* and *äussern* is "utterance" and "to utter," and in many cases Hegel seems to have this as well as the philosophical sense of "externalization"—and, from § 29 on, the legal sense of "alienation" (*Entäusserung, Veräusserung*)—in mind.
2. [*Tr.*] Throughout "Abstract Right" Hegel draws on many concepts from Roman law. His sources include Justinian, *Institutes*; Justinian, *Digest*; Gaius, *Institutes*; and among modern authors, J. G. Heineccius, *Elementa Iuris Civilis* (Amsterdam, 1726).

Possession is essentially the externality of the will: through the sphere of determinate existence [*Dasein*] I bring my personality into externality, so that what is inward may become external. Through the determinate existence, the external being of the will, there arises a being for others; in this way my will becomes recognizable for others (determinate being is being for another [*das Dasein ist das Sein für ein Anderes*]). The thing must be either *res nullius* or a *res abjecta*, relinquished by its owner with the thought that he ceases to own it. So the relation to others is here anticipated.

§ 19

Taking possession makes the *material* of the thing my property. I take possession either by directly *seizing* the thing *physically*, or by *imposing a form* [*Formierung*] on it (*specificatio*), or by merely *marking* [*Bezeichnung*] it.

Matter is devoid of rights, it does not belong to itself, so when I seize it, it is mine. (Fichte is of the view that matter belongs to God and that human beings only have a right of appropriation in regard to it, but this amounts to the same thing.)[3] Within God, matter is something merely ideal; if God causes matter to exist, God has himself surrendered it. For the philosophical consideration of spirit, matter possesses no independence, while its independence for consciousness is only subordinate. Marking is the merely objective representation of taking possession. To take possession is to appropriate through externality and the will. |

22

§ 20

It is, to be sure, in *seizing something physically* that my will most perfectly achieves determinate existence and becomes recognizable; but in scope this mode of taking possession is in the highest degree limited and temporary. It can, however, acquire a

---

3. [*Ed.*] Fichte, *Beitrag*, pp. 135–136. However, in Fichte's view this expression should be understood figuratively. See p. 136: "It can rightly be said, in figurative even if not in strictly philosophical fashion, that God is the owner of the raw material." Cf. Fichte, *Gesamtausgabe* 1:268–269.

further extension in scope in a mediated fashion as a result of the connection between a thing that is already in my possession and other things; property can also accrue to me as a result of such natural, chance connection. In addition, physical seizure is limited by the qualitative nature of the objects seized. By virtue of their quality of intrinsic externality, i.e., their inner dividedness [in respect] of their different aspects, things can be taken in possession by more than one [claimant]; this is where disputes arise, and the understanding [decides] how essential one or the other part or aspect is, and so [determines] the right to the thing itself.

Herein lies the imperfection of laws, because physical seizure is highly insignificant in terms of its scope (i.e., what I can grasp with my body), and I cannot go on holding things in detention, in bodily possession, indefinitely. If I have a stick in my hand, it is not only the part that I am grasping that is mine, but the whole stick, by virtue of the external connection, the external physical relation, to the part of which I have taken possession—from this [stems] the *accessio* [accession]. Under this head belongs hunting, in that wild animals are *res nullius*. I must kill them; in other words, taking possession of them, the means whereby I take them in my possession, is to kill them—an external action, one that is external to itself in that, like the external thing, it [has] on its own account a multiplicity of parts. But if, for example, the animal is wounded by several [huntsmen] and then falls, a legal dispute ensues; the dispute arises because of the animal's sensuous manifoldness, its various levels of life. In this way others can take possession, with me or after me, of part of the very thing of which I have possession of another part. And here philosophical right does not suffice, for | the thing becomes a multiple possession and is in itself a multiple thing, so that more than one person can each have a part.

Positive right must therefore seek to settle these conflicts and make application to different cases, and this is no longer a matter of reason [*Vernunft*] but of the understanding [*Verstand*]. Moreover, it is always better that a decision should be reached than that the case should be unresolved. In such conflicts each

23

has a right, but where there is no absolute determination, the question becomes one of degree. The concept involves only the decision that all parties have a right in regard to the matter in dispute.

What causes these conflicts is the nature of the things seized and the nature of the action whereby they are taken into possession. *Occupatio bellica* [military seizure] does not belong under this head, but to international law. A thing I have relinquished ceases to be mine insofar as I no longer have the *animus tenendi* [resolve to hold]. The situation in regard to jetsam is that the "right" to collect jetsam is obviously a denial of right. By *accessio* is meant that a thing is conjoined with what is mine; thus the fruit from my tree is mine. I must, however, give effect to the *animus*. *Accessio* is [defined] by what is mine. *Alluvio* [alluvial accession] is a chance conjunction with what is mine; it is another matter if this does not come about gradually but suddenly, in very marked manner, to the extent that the previous owner's mark, or the form he gave the thing, is still visible on or in it. Still more complex is *accessio* when another, by his action, has produced something on what belongs to me with the intention that his product should belong to him. Here it is a matter of good and bad faith, where for instance someone writes or paints on my paper, or cultivates my field. Where there is good faith, right must determine in such a way that no party incurs serious damage (the Sabinian and Proculian Schools[4]).

I can never take possession of something universal; it is mine only so long as I have it. So [it is] with breathing in the air. The sea is also a universal possession and is for the use of all because no one else is excluded from it by my using it. | Yet the   24
Danes levy a duty on the sea. It may be a different matter if this levy is imposed as an indirect levy, not as arising from something owned; the basic factor here is the power relationship. All nations lay claim to right over the sea to the furthest limit at

---

4. [Tr.] Two opposing schools of Roman jurisprudence, named after Sabinus and Proculus, jurists of the first century C.E.

which their guns can protect them. This is an important matter for fishing. Rivers, harbors, and the like can more readily be laid claim to by reason of possession of the banks or shores, despite the fact that rivers are something universal.

§ 21

To *impose a form* [*Formierung*] on a thing is the most essential mode of taking possession; by it possession is made durable, and taking possession becomes acquisition [*Erwerb*]. Under this head belongs tilling the fields, sowing and cultivating crops, and domesticating and feeding animals. The form given to something organic does not, it is true, remain precisely external in regard to it, but [is] assimilated by it. The mere use of land for hunting or pasture or of the seashore for fishing, etc., does not, properly speaking, impose a form on it, but it does involve the will to employ it for one's use, and genuine use involves the declaration of this will.

By imposing a form on a thing I predicate of it that it is mine. Others cannot take possession of it because the imposition of form, the predicate, is my will, and if another took the thing from me, he or she would be encroaching on my freedom. In the case of giving form to an inorganic body there is the ambiguity as to whether in so doing I had the *animus tenendi*. But usually I form things for my use, and by making them appropriate for my use I express my will that they should be mine. When I feed an animal, I enable it to live for as long as I do so, and in this way I come to own it. One does not acquire ownership over human beings by feeding them or even by educating them. A wild animal is something independent, and loses its independence by being tamed. But what education | gives rise to in the human being is the sense of freedom; and what principally matters for human beings is not just that they are kept alive by the food they eat.

To use something means, by and large, to ruin it because one uses it up, makes it a means. In land use too conflicts occur, in that the land is something concrete, can be used in many different ways: peoples who live by hunting use the land on which

25

they hunt, the nomad uses it for pasture, and the farmer makes even fuller use of it. Moreover, one farmer may have the right to do so and may cultivate the land, and then in autumn another has the right to pasture his cattle on the same land. Civilized peoples may [take] possession of land that is merely used for grazing or hunting [and] use it for agriculture, saying that the nomad and the huntsman do not wholly possess the land and that it is only the imposition of form, i.e., the cultivation of the soil, that yields possession properly speaking. However, the nomad does have the abstract right to make whatever use he wills of his ownership in the land. It is only *jus gentium* [law of nations] that makes the imposition of form the most complete mode of use and gives the most advanced, more civilized peoples, who use the land better, a right to it—a right that does not, however, derive from personality.

§ 22

The imposition of form also includes the human development of one's own body and spirit, the acquisition of capabilities and aptitudes. It is only through education or formation [*Bildung*] that I make the universal within me, my potentialities or capacities, something determinate and distinct from me; and it is by practice that I make the determinate mode of activity [I have learned] habitual. By this means I enter into possession of this mode of activity and gain mastery of it for the unhampered execution of my purposes. |

26

The acquisition of aptitudes also is one way of taking possession by the imposition of form. My inner capacities are potentialities, universal, but in developing them, I particularize them, I have to set the activity involved in imposing form apart from me as universal. I only have mastery of my habits to the extent that I distinguish them from myself, for if they are merely within me, they have mastery of me. The essence of spirit is not to *be*, but to posit itself by means of activity [*Tätigkeit*]. It is only by education or formation that I gain mastery over my activities and can perform them in a manner suited to the object I wish to work on. By imposing form I determine myself, I separate the determinate activities from me. These particularizations, these capabilities belong to me, and they only occur because I have no longer remained in identity [with myself].

§ 23

The act of *marking* [*Bezeichnung*] an object externally to show that it is purportedly mine is on the one hand not genuinely taking possession but only a representation thereof; on the other hand it is indeterminate in regard to its objective scope [and] thus its meaning.

A mark merely furnishes an indication of my will; it is only through imposing form that I make the thing my own. Another is at liberty to disregard the mark because it is not determinate, since the sign may be arbitrary or more or less natural. So marking is the most imperfect way of taking possession. For a genuine act of taking possession the will must be involved as well as the external aspect of seizing.

§ 24

Possession entails the external aspect of my relation to the thing. When at the same time the thing is essentially taken up into my will, possession becomes *ownership* [*Eigentum*]: ownership is the timeless, substantive relation of freedom. To the extent that possession and ownership are distinguished, | possession in general is defined solely in terms of my external appropriation and external relation to the thing.

Possession and ownership are essentially one; ownership is where the possessive relation is governed by right, and if the two are separated, possession covers only the aspect of the external relation. Ownership is the aspect governed by right, where there must be the will as well as external retention, while possession is mere retention. In the case of a contract, when I hire something out, I continue to own it; the other has possession of it. But the contract can only be temporary, for if the other is always in possession, his possession is no longer limited, and he is the owner. "For all time" is the universal, the concept, of time: eternity. The will introduces the nonsensible, timeless aspect. Human beings can hire themselves out, temporarily, for labor, possibly not even for specific types of labor; but it must be for a certain time, for if it were for all time, they would make those who hire their labor their owners. Possession can be separated from ownership, but not possession in general, only a specific possession or property; for rightful possession as such *is* ownership, which is the aspect of right.

<h2 style="text-align:center">§ 25</h2>

Possession is not an abstract externality of my will, for externality is of itself nothing abstract; on the contrary, possession is *concrete possession*, partly in that I actually have the thing in my grasp, partly in that I may employ, use, and enjoy it. If this concrete possession is mine—including also its matter—then I own it. But if it is only this concrete possession that is deemed to be mine, and ownership—as what is ideal, essential—is deemed to accrue to another, then this is an empty distinction, and the other has a merely abstract mastery, not over the things in question but over me, a mastery that can only consist in an indebtedness on my part to him as a condition of my ownership. If there is such indebtedness, it ought not to be insuperable, and my ownership should be capable of becoming *full ownership.* | 28

The lecturer here speaks of *dominium directum* [absolute ownership] and *dominium utile* [ownership based on use]. Possession is something external to itself, constituting something inwardly multiple, something concrete or manifold; it is accordingly also in manifold fashion that it appears in it. What is evinced in the thing possessed is not something at rest, but an activity; will shows itself as manifold. Depending on the quality of the objects and of my needs, concrete possession has different aspects, so a thing can be possessed in ownership by several persons, according to the different aspects of its possible use. One person may use a field for agriculture and another for grazing, and in this case agriculture is the principal use. The criterion here is whether a thing is universal or particular, for particular things are consumed by use, whereas universal things, such as the sea, air, etc., are not consumed. A field's operation is organic, and it is therefore not consumed provided I maintain and manure it. The use of pictures by looking at them is merely a theoretical kind of use, and the object is for me an organic, universal object. One mode of use may be more important than another, so that the *accessorium sequitur suum principale* [accessory use follows upon principal use]; and what has then to be established is what precisely in the individual case the *principale* is. But the *accessorium* may also require compensation. However, where I am in rightful concrete possession, I own the whole thing.

Dominium directum and *utile* give rise to ground rents, *laudemium*, fiefs. Here the *dominus* [possessor] has no use of the thing, but the person who uses it has an obligation to the *dominus directus* [absolute owner]. Whoever possesses an estate or receives rents for it, be it the ruler or the state, must therefore [be] regarded solely as private owner. Possession here rests invariably on a contract. Hereditary tenure is also something of this kind. This division into *dominium directum* and *utile* is an empty distinction inasmuch as | the *dominus directus* only has a right vis-à-vis the occupier but not the thing itself. A liability of this kind ought to be terminable, but as long as it subsists one must respect it, and one cannot approve of its simply being annulled as in France. The whole thing, in this case, is a contract of ownership in a form it ought not to have, for the *dominus directus* has only an empty right and must therefore also be held willing to abandon this empty right. With servitudes the *principale*, i.e., the more complete use, must take precedence over the *accessorium*, and the possessor of the former must be able to require the possessor of the latter to abandon his *accessorium*, against payment of compensation.

§ 26

The aspect of ownership as the rightful, i.e., universal ideal relation of will is the aspect of absolute personality; however, this equally includes the moment of *individuality* [*Einzelheit*]. This moment is therefore no less essential in real ownership. Ownership is thus to be complete and free, excluding any other [owner]; and *private ownership* as such should be the complete embodiment of the personality in possession, although this does not exclude servitudes, which are essential for the purpose of safeguarding and using what is privately owned by another, and which stem from the empirical nature of possession or property as such.

As person I am a free being; in the sphere of universality I am wholly an individual; in the thing [I own] I must be for myself in all my individuality, and so I must own it fully, freely; and [it follows] that there must be private ownership. It was Christianity that first made human beings free, but with the feudal constitution ownership became unfree, and this was one of the causes of the French Revolution. The principle that feudalism should be overcome was wholly good, but it had to be accompanied by compensation. It is therefore necessary | that every servitude should be terminable, and the price must be determined by law. From this it follows that there must be private ownership. With the rise of states no regard was had to the single individual. The field was owned by the family, and the individual had to take in fief from the head of the family what he wanted to cultivate. It was Christianity that first introduced the principle of personality, of private ownership. People who possess something they own freely, privately, have a quite different feeling from those who still have over them a master with *dominium*. Servitudes are *jura in re* [rights in a thing], but they must have a rational external determination. The many limitations on ownership in Roman law make it defective, and a history of how ownership became free would be a very important matter [for study].

30

§ 27

For there to be ownership another necessary factor is *time*, and in this manifestation [of the will], the will, as the universal, receives the characteristic of an utterance that has *duration in time*. Otherwise the thing becomes *res nullius*; I lose ownership by *prescription* [*Verjährung*] and can acquire [it] through *usucapion* [*Ersitzung*].

That I own a thing is something that happens in time, and my will—what is timeless—must become manifest; consequently it manifests itself as an utterance that has duration in time. The form of universality in time derives from my will. I must use what I own in order that my will may become manifest in that it wills; and it must manifest itself in a universal manner. Without this continuing utterance, without the reality of my will in regard to it, the thing becomes *res nullius*. In having the thing within the ambit of what I own and use, however, I express my will to have it. As this falls within time, prescription together with its determinations comes within positive right. But prescription and usucapion also rightly arise in the philosophical doctrine of right, for my will only exists as external.

31   It is true that prescription also has a political aspect | owing to the consequences we would have without it, namely the insecurity of ownership; but these are not necessary consequences, only contingent, for they do not develop of themselves, they do not pertain to the action itself, as is the case with necessary consequences. But as one inherent aspect of ownership is utterance [*Äusserung*], ownership lapses as soon as I stop giving utterance to it. Prescription is known [in Latin] as *praescriptio*, usucapion as *usucapio*. Usucapion was accordingly more general among the Romans than prescription.

Possession is an essential moment of ownership, and Savigny is therefore one-sided in his [view of] possession, for he regards it as merely a way of preventing prescription.[5] The more important aspect is undoubtedly the relationship of possession to ownership. The time needed for prescription, together with its determinations, belongs to positive right. Owing to the general constraints of the empirical world, the necessity of having fixed

---

5. [*Ed.*] The reference is to Friedrich Karl von Savigny, *Abhandlung der Lehre vom Besitz* (Giessen, 1803). The second edition also appeared under the title *Das Recht des Besitzes* (Giessen, 1806).

norms means that the period of prescription is too long for one case, too short for another.

§ 28

A thing placed completely beyond all further use as being owned by a non-actual person contradicts the element of ownership, namely that the will should be actualized in it and possession should be something actual.

Here belong, for example, *res sacrae* [consecrated things]. The purpose may be highly worthy of respect. But prescription may occur here if the purpose and the remembrance of it are no longer known, for instance if someone intends a grave merely for him- or herself. It runs counter to ownership that a non-actual person, who consequently has no will, as is necessary for the externality of possession, should withdraw things permanently from the use of which they are capable.

§ 29

I can *alienate* or *divest* [*entäussern*] what I own to the extent that the thing in question is a thing *external* [*äusserlich*] by nature. | Those goods that are not so much my possession as rather constitute my very own person—my personality as such, freedom of the will, ethical life, religion—are accordingly *inalienable* [*unveräusserlich*] and *imprescriptible* [*unverjährbar*].

Thus there are inalienable and imprescriptible things, things of which, to the extent that I possess them, I cannot divest myself and of which, even to the extent that they are possessed by another, I am not prevented thereby from regaining possession should I so will. To this category belong all goods that pertain to my personality, to the universal freedom of my will. Thus I cannot freely make myself a slave, for this possession vouchsafed by me to another ceases as soon as I so will. Even if I am born a slave and am fed and brought up by my master, and my parents and ancestors were all slaves, I am free the moment I so will it, the moment I come to the consciousness of my freedom. For my personality and the freedom of my will are essential

32

parts of myself, of my personality. All I am, I am only as in my personality. All these goods [constitutive] of my personality are equally imprescriptible and not subject to restriction; and the *justus titulus* [lawful title] and good faith of a slaveowner is of no avail to him. I can and should, however, divest myself of arbitrariness, and the aim must be to restrict it. The ability to own things belongs to the concept of freedom, for it is this that first gives freedom determinate existence [*Dasein*]. The capability of owning is part and parcel of personality. Rehberg sought to attack these basic concepts of natural right, and Fichte wrote against him in his "Spirit of the French Revolution."[6] Rehberg maintained that freedom as pure freedom could not be assailed by external actions, and that if I had someone beaten, this did not impair his freedom. But there is freedom only when it receives determinate existence, actuality, when it externalizes itself. Ethical life too is something inalienable, for I cannot hand over to others my conscience, which is after all the judge of the ethical life. No less inalienable is religion; the laity cannot therefore renounce religion and leave it to the priests, as | it were on trust, in order that the priests should say what religion involves and what someone must do in order to be religious. But even if the people did hand their religious rights over to the priests, they could at any time take them back.

Admittedly the stipulation that all rights which rest on personality should be inalienable and imprescriptible is a demanding one, yet freedom is only freedom [when it is known]. In other words all these rights enter on the scene only with the

33

6. [*Ed.*] Hegel is referring to the criticism which Fichte directed in his *Beitrag*, pp. 132 ff., against August Wilhelm Rehberg's *Untersuchungen über die Französische Revolution*, part 1 (Hannover and Osnabrück, 1793). Cf. Fichte, *Gesamtausgabe* 1:267 ff. According to Fichte, Rehberg argues that on the basis of natural right human beings can prove no rightful claim to the material to which in the course of production they impart their form. Since according to this no one, for example, can be the owner of land or landed estates, one must derive this right from the state. Against this Fichte argues "that it is not the state but rational human nature that is in itself the source of ownership." However, Rehberg did not maintain that an attack on my body leaves my freedom unimpaired, nor did Fichte impute this view to him.

consciousness of them, and as soon as the people gain this consciousness of their rights, they necessarily accrue to them.

§ 30

I can hand over to another for a limited time the use of my particular physical and mental powers and aptitudes because, as determinate, they have the aspect of an external relationship to my personality. This relationship is characterized and exists as external, however, only insofar as the handing over or alienation [*Veräusserung*] is restricted to single products or to a definite time. If the handing over were to be for an unrestricted period, my powers would be alienated [*entäussert*] as a totality, and this totality is the manifestation of my universal being. In the same way too I can only hand over what I own in general, and what I produce, as individual [goods and services].

My aptitudes and powers are grounded in my intelligence, my reason; they are my own and something inward. But they have the relationship of something external to the extent that they have a distinctive content and belong to the particular, not the universal side. And to the extent that they are something external I can hand them over; I can bind myself to do something for another or can enter the service of another, but even if I undertake to perform all kinds of service for someone, there is the limitation that I retain my personality, as indicated in the previous section. However, I can only hand over my services for a definite time, and I cannot assign to another rights over all my labors. This | restriction in time and restriction in terms of number and degree constitute the aspect of externality. But if I were to hand over to someone the generality of my services, my ability to produce something that is a universal or contains all particularizations, everything external, I would in so doing divest myself of what is universal, what lies within. In the totality of my production for an unrestricted period, a universal [element] is present. So I cannot give away this externalization of my capability in its entirety. I cannot hand over my inner [element] to anyone, but only my services as limited in time and confined

34

79

to particular functions. Similarly I cannot hand over to anyone, along with what I own, my capability of ownership. A criminal who is imprisoned can only lose his freedom for a definite time, a limited time. In this way it does become possible for me to hand over or alienate my inner [element] to another, and this alienation [*Veräusserung*] has the shape of externality [*Äusserlichkeit*].

§ 31

Through the sphere of my freedom that I have in ownership I come into relationship with other persons. The immediate unit of personality is a repulsion into infinitely many units. The *essential being* [*wesentliche Dasein*] of ownership is the *determinate existence* [*Dasein*] of its right-governed absolute aspect, namely that in ownership persons *recognize* [*anerkennen*] one another as persons. This means that in the consciousness of their self-identity they know themselves to be identical with others through the mediation of external existence, and they accept one another as mutually free and independent.

By virtue of the fact that I give reality to my will through ownership, there arise relationships between me and others, between what I own and what others own. The unit is the relation of the negative to itself, repulsion from itself. But the concept of the unit is being-for-self, i.e., the negativity of positedness by something else. The existence of many persons is what constitutes necessity as such, but this is no immediate plurality but a necessary plurality. | My existing determinately [*Dasein*] in my ownership is a relationship to other persons, and from this stems reciprocal recognition: the free is for the free. Since I know myself to be free, I know myself to be universal and know others to be free; and since I know others to be free, I know myself to be free. The principle of right accordingly [runs]: Respect yourself and others in their ownership as persons.

§ 32

Ownership involves the free will as such, with no distinction as yet between universal and particular will. In the mutual relationship between persons, however, each person's own will becomes determinate since it appears as other in relation to another, as *particular will* [*besonderer Wille*] or as *arbitrary will* [*Willkür*].[7] But since the free will is in and for itself universal will, arbitrary will must sublate its particularity and posit itself as a universal will, a will identical with another; this constitutes the inner necessity and essence of *contract.*

It is an optional matter whether to conclude a contract with another, but although it depends on me whether to conclude this or that contract, necessity is the [essential] aspect of contract. As indicated in the preceding paragraph, ownership gives rise to a mutual relationship between persons; as others for one another, each person has a particular will, an arbitrary will. But the will is free and something universal, and the freedom of the will is not annulled through particularization. The single individual must, however, sublate his particular will and acknowledge, give reality to, a common will shared with another; and this is what gives rise to contracts.

2. Contract

§ 33

Contract [*Vertrag*] is the acquisition of a thing that is no longer devoid of rights and independence over against me, but involves the will of another and is consequently impenetrable for me. This | 36 acquisition is accordingly mediated, mediated by the fact that the will inherent in it withdraws from it with the specification that the thing should pass over into my ownership and that I should be willing to accept it. This mutual agreement constitutes the *manifestation* [*Erscheinung*] of the common, universal will; for the

7. [*Tr.*] *Willkür* is one of the most fluid of Hegel's concepts. It refers to a will that chooses in an arbitrary, capricious, or spontaneous fashion, as opposed to a will whose decisions are based on necessary and universal principles. It is free in the sense of being unconstrained, but not in the sense of the *idea* of freedom, namely self-relatedness (presence to self) achieved in and through relatedness to others. Authentic free will is communal, while *Willkür* is individual and particular. We translate *Willkür* variously as "arbitrariness," "caprice," "arbitrary will," "free will," "choice," or "free choice," depending on context.

latter *is posited* by the positive choice [*Willkür*] from which the contract stems and the negative choice involved in sublating the particularity of my possession, and it concerns a *particular object*.

With contracts we are no longer concerned, as in the case of possession, with abstract things but with things whose matter involves the will of another. Here I cannot acquire something by merely laying hold of it but only through mediation, in that the will of the other withdraws from it. What the mediation involves is that the other side too has a part to play, not solely my external action: the will inherent in the thing must withdraw from it. But the thing's surrender also implies that the relationship to me is determined positively, i.e., the thing passes into my ownership, and I am willing to accept it. On the one side there must be surrender, and on the other acceptance; such a contract is *gift*. If, however, there is surrender and acceptance on both sides, then we have *exchange*. The surrender and acceptance willed on each side gives rise to a common, universal will because the particular will was surrendered; but the manifestation of the universal will is due solely to the fact that it is a posited will and that the conclusion of a contract depends on the decision of the contracting parties.

By contract we move from individuality to universality, although this universality is still only a seeming universality. For a contract proceeds from my desire, my need. The object in regard to which I conclude a contract is likewise a particular [thing]. It is often said that the state rests on a contract of all with one and one with all. Here the starting point is individual persons, and the contract becomes one with the government or the sovereign. If one party does not keep the contract, so it is said, then the other too, if one believes this, is no longer bound to the contract. However, this view | stems from the fact that constitutional law is derived from private law, as has occurred with us too. The view that the constitutional relationship as such is contractual is mistaken in that it takes for its starting point individual persons and the possible way in which one or another state may have been formed. But the state does not start,

37

is not founded, on individual persons but their universal will, the substance of their being; it is founded on no arbitrary object but the power within them and over them. A contract, on the other hand, can derive only from choice [*Willkür*].

So it is not the choice of the individual person whether he or she wishes to have a government or not, nor the choice of the government whether it wants to have citizens or not. But might there not be a contract between the people and its government against a sovereign dynasty? But with every monarchy it is a necessity that the highest point, the ruler, should not depend on the choice of the people. In the state everything must be necessary, so no choice, no contract of the individual citizens with the sovereign [*Fürst*], is acceptable. The former German principalities had over them emperor and empire, and it was a feudal relationship in which the princes [*Fürsten*] held private status within the universal state. This was wholly contrary to reason [because] the rights of the states were determined by contract. The view that the state is a social contract between individual persons also had a great influence on the French Revolution, the idea being that the decision to constitute a people depended on the whim of the individual citizens.

§ 34

Since in contract what is intellectual enters into relation with what is intellectual, and the will of the two parties becomes identical, this intellectual identification, which is an explicit feature of contract as such as opposed to possessions and the transfer of possessions, must give itself determinate existence [*Dasein*] in a real [*reellen*]⁸ element, as a *declaration*, | either through signs and ges- 38 tures or, most commonly, through speech, as the *stipulation* of the contract.

Of itself contract is the positing of a universal will, but the will in the form of the particular decision [*Willkür*] that I own this is sublated. Possession is in fact universal existence, while

8. *Ms. reads:* ideal [*ideellen*]

of itself contract exists as what is intellectual, which is a merely ideal mode of existence [*ein ideelles Dasein*]. The body is a representation of the mind [*Geist*], expresses the will of the mind, and in this way the universal will becomes theoretically existent, while the practical existence of contract derives from performance or execution. The mind expresses itself through speech, through sound, which is merely a vibration, and it is in this way that the theoretical will expresses itself in contract. The mode of expression conveyed in a handshake is a sign of agreement. The stipulation of the contract is expressed in more determinate fashion through speech. With many things the stipulation and the execution of the contract are simultaneous (e.g., in the case of buns for sale in a shop).

§ 35

The stipulation of the contract is also distinct from the real passing of ownership from one to the other, distinct, that is, from *performance* or *execution* [*Leistung*]. The contract itself binds me immediately to performance as a pure matter of right, for it has made what previously belonged to me already something owned by another. In the agreement as [the expression of a] universal will I have sublated my arbitrary will. This agreement contains what is essential in the determination of ownership; and, in the mutual recognition [of the contract], it also involves essential, authentic existence, whereas continued possession is only something inessential. If I did not perform what is stipulated, I would therefore be injuring what the other owns.

That I should keep my promise is a matter of morality, but in contract I pledge myself. The things governed by contract are also called real personal rights because I only come by them through another person. The contention that, as Fichte says,[9]

9. [*Ed.*] The transcript does not accurately reproduce the statement by Fichte to which it refers. See Fichte, *Beitrag*, pp. 123–125 (cf. Fichte, *Gesamtausgabe* 1:263–264): "So even by performance on my part I acquire no right to the performance of the other, unless his free will, whose direction I do not know, has given me this right, and continues to give it." This statement by Fichte occurs in the context of his theory of the distinction between morality and legality. Only the

each is bound | to perform [a contract] only when and to the   39
extent that the other party has performed [it], is not valid, for
then no one could begin; the contract binds me to performance
as a pure matter of right, and the contract is concluded by virtue of the stipulation itself. With a contract and its performance
moral aspects do not yet arise. Performance is necessary for
the simple reason that [otherwise] what the other owns would
incur injury, since as a result of the stipulation the thing has
passed completely into the other's ownership. In the [mutual]
recognition I am confronted by another will, and the other is
confronted by my will, and through recognition the common
will has existence. For I have sublated my arbitrary will to possess the thing, and the performance is the external reality of the
universal will, i.e., something inessential. Performance is therefore not a moral consequence; nor is it a consequence dependent on an external manifestation, but a consequence as a pure
matter of right, that I should not injure what I have recognized
as owned by the other. The classification of contracts is an affair of the understanding.

§ 36

The *classification* of contracts must be based on the main distinction deriving from the subject matter, namely ownership: this
may be either full ownership or merely possession. However, possession differs from ownership only insofar as it is in general something temporary and, in contrast with ownership, something restricted. Furthermore, contracts may involve only a willingness of
one side to hand the thing over to the other side and the agreement of the other side to accept it; or they may involve both kinds
of willingness on both sides. On this basis they are either contracts
of gift or contracts of exchange.

Supreme Judge of morality knows the other's true intentions; I cannot have such
insight. It is only when the other's intentions become manifest in the world of phenomena that they become knowable for everyone. If the other withholds his performance, my performance does not become mine again, but remains unaffected, since
the contract as such has not come into being. Only by his performance can the other
make my performance part of what he owns.

Substance does not occur in isolation from its accidents; since they are a totality, they have returned into their inner being. But possession cannot contain the totality of the accidents, for otherwise ownership passes over along with it. So if I am not to lose ownership itself, it is only individual accidents of my ownership that can pass over. |

40

§ 37

Contracts are therefore:

I. Contracts of gift [*Schenkung*], comprising:

(1) Gift of a thing as such;

(2) The performance of a service [*Dienst*], e.g., the safekeeping of something deposited;

(3) The loan [*Verleihen*] of a thing, i.e., the bestowal of a portion of it or in general of a restricted use or enjoyment of it.

The thing deposited or *depositum* is, properly speaking, given away. In point of form it also seems a *depositum* if I deposit money in a bank, but in return the bank gives me a voucher, which is my property, so the contract is a contract of exchange. The bank has the use of my money, and I have the use of the bank's voucher. If I lend something to anyone, I give them the employment or use of it (*commodatum*).

(4) The capacity to make a *will* or *testament* [*Testament*] rests on the fact that I have in general the right to dispose of what I own in favor of another and also to determine the point of time at which that other person is to enter into enjoyment of it. But as in this case this point of time is the time of death, there is a contradiction in the fact that I give for an eventuality when I am in any case no longer owner or possessor. Testamentary capacity can therefore derive only from social right in general, that is, only from reciprocal recognition.

The contradictory element in wills or testaments is that testators give away something at a time when they no longer own it. Inheritance *ab intestato* [without a will] falls within the law governing family relationships. Testamentary dispositions are therefore valid and governed by right only to the extent that they are deemed rightfully possible in the state in question and to the extent that the others are prepared to honor and acknowledge the will of the deceased; for otherwise, following the possessor's death, the property becomes *res nullius* [a thing belonging to no one]. According to their own will expressed in the testament, testators retain full ownership until they | are   41 dead. The Romans accordingly regarded testation as part of *jus publicum* [public law], and testaments had to be executed before the people *in comitiis* [in assemblies], thus indicating the people's assent to the testament.

II. Contracts of exchange [*Tausch*]. Since these are not contracts of gift, they imply that, whatever their qualitative diversity, the things exchanged ought to be *equal*. This abstract or universal way of regarding them, which makes it impossible to measure them against one another and set them as equal or unequal in a solely *quantitative* determination, is their value.

    With contracts of exchange one has to envisage comparing things in their diversity; they may be dissimilar, but what makes them similar, their value, is an abstraction. I merely posit an identity between the two things according to their externality. It is I who, in comparing them, bring them into relation. This likeness between them is their value, an abstract way of viewing them, according to which they can be assimilated to one another despite being qualitatively diverse. Now the value depends on the labor needed to produce the thing, value being determined by the art and effort involved, the rarity of the object, etc. The comparison is made on the basis of this value, which is a quantitative determination, a measure. Price is the value in an empirical case. Value may also reside in a subjective, particular opinion.

    (1) *Exchange* of a thing as such, of a commodity, i.e., of one specific thing for another, which is likewise of a specific nature.

    A commodity is in fact a thing with determinate qualities.

    (2) *Purchase* [*Kauf*] and *sale* [*Verkauf*] (*emptio, venditio*). Exchange of a commodity for *money* [*Geld*], i.e., a thing that is not

specific but universal, or a commodity that only has value, with no other specific determination as to use.

The definition of money is only that it is mere value; but money also becomes a commodity in relationship to a bank voucher. Money is a commodity existing according to the abstraction that it is used for no other use than as value. The monetary standard makes money | reciprocally a commodity by virtue of the fact that our coins are of different metals. To the extent that money is regarded as money, all that matters is that the value should be present. But since money abstracts from the [specific] commodity to pure value, a primitive people does not yet have money, and makes do with inconvenient barter—inconvenient because I have to look a long time before I find someone whose need is precisely the converse of mine.

(3) *Rental* [*Vermietung*] of what is mine—house, garden, etc.—to another (*locatio, conductio* [rental, lease]) is handing over its temporary use in return for rent, while I remain the owner. That my specific property passes into the possession of another to use and I at the same time as actual owner remain in possession can be mediated by the fact that I remain in possession of the *value*; this comes about through *pledge* or *surety*. Pledge and surety may also be found in the case of contracts of gift (numbers 2 and 3) as well as in the case of the other contracts of exchange when it is possible to separate in time the delivery [*Tradition*] or performance of the contract by the one party from its performance by the other party, or in general to separate the performance from the stipulation.

The use must be temporary since otherwise I hand over what belongs to me to the other and there would then be no reason for the other, as owner, to pay me, the former owner, rent for the use of his property. After use I reenter into possession. The pledge relationship arises by virtue of the fact that, in entrusting another with what belongs to me, I wish to be safeguarded for so doing since I cannot then momentarily remain in possession with the other. He gives me in return part of what belongs to him as a pledge in substitution, and so I remain in possession

42

of the value of my property, but have too a particular thing in my hand. A pledge differs from ownership and purchase in that each remains in possession of what he owns and the specific thing is not handed over. Pledging may also figure in the other kinds of exchange contract, in that the two parties may perform the contract at different times, and I remain in specific | 43 ownership as long as I have not received performance from the other. It is the same with surety in that there a third party, by whom I set greater credit, intervenes on behalf of the second party.

(4) *Lending on interest* [*Anleihen*] (*mutuum*) is the same as renting, except that lenders remain owners solely of the value but have divested themselves of the specific thing.

The difference between lending on interest and renting is that lenders remain solely owners of the value and hand over the specific thing to the other. The value remains in the ownership of the lender, so lending is not divestment or alienation. If lenders are given a pledge, they keep the value of the capital in their hands.

(5) In a *wages contract* [*Lohnvertrag*] (*locatio operarum*) I divest myself of or alienate to another [*veräussern*] my productive capacity or what it produces, to the extent that it is alienable and for a definite time. Related to this is the *mandatum* [a counsel's acceptance of a brief] and other service contracts, which rest on trust, good will, particular talent and aptitude, and to that extent possess an infinite value.

The object of the contract must here be a [form of] labor that is *honesta* [honorable], and so is alienable, provided moreover it is only a part of the manifestation of my capability, for the entire manifestation is inalienable. Acceptance of a brief [*Mandat*] and the ensuing contracts are unassessable, for here the good will, aptitude, genius, and trust belong to the infinite personality and are consequently incommensurable, however limited the products may be. This category also includes state offices, which are neither wage contracts nor contracts at all, although I enter into an agreement with the state by serving it for my remuneration. For every citizen is in general under an obligation to serve the state. The citizen who is a soldier is under an obligation to be a soldier because of his duty, as citizen, to defend the state, not because of the pay he receives. State offices involve this aspect of the duty of service to the state, and this prevents them from becoming wholly contracts, for duty to the state comes first. For this reason it was previously the case, especially in republics, and still [is] so [today], that | officials receive no salaries but only emoluments to defray their expenses. For this reason too everyone is equally under an obligation to serve the state, [one] no more than another. But because I wish to be appointed, I insist that I can do more; I wish to do more, according to my particular aptitude. The relationship of particularity here comes into play, and the state can use me as it wills, for it is not bounden to me but can choose among several; I on the other hand am bounden to the state. So a civil servant who seeks to be appointed according to his particular aptitude can also demand payment for this particular aptitude, and in this way the aspect of contract comes into play. But to the extent that my services are mental rather than physical, approximating to the acceptance of a brief and similar contracts, to that extent the relationship differs from what constitutes a wage contract, properly speaking.

The main distinction in regard to contracts may be said to be that in some cases what is owned is handed over in its entirety, in other cases only a use of what is owned.

3. Wrong

§ 38

Contract is in principle a finite agreement and leaves the remaining, wholly universal particularity of individuals still in mutual opposition, including all of their contingency and arbitrariness [*Willkür*]. Ownership is the subsumption of a particular thing under my personal will; in this respect the subsumption is in itself infinite and universal, but by virtue of its particularity it contains contingency and arbitrariness. It is therefore a matter of chance whether others do not regard it as wrong [*unrecht*], in that they may recognize in it the universal, namely my personality and capacity for rights, but not the particular.

In right my ownership is posited in differentiated fashion, as a relationship that has to be recognized by the other. In contract the arbitrary will [*Willkür*] of individuals, the particular will, has, to be sure, been sublated into the universal will, but this universal will is only posited, because the contract is only posited by the | independent choice [*Willkür*] of the individuals; one of them cannot sublate it, but both can by mutual agreement. The rest of the arbitrary will is not sublated by such agreement, and contract is only an exception to personal, natural free choice, to contingency in general. My ownership of a thing implies that the infinite [element] of my will in and for itself, which is involved in it, is recognized, but the arbitrary will may oppose this. Insofar as ownership as personal will is abstract and universal, however, it must particularize itself, it must embody its universality in something external. In taking possession I subsume a particular thing under the universal [element] of my will. In the same way others may subsume it under their will and believe that they have already acquired it and that my claim to it is wrong. Collisions of this kind are unavoidable where particularity stands opposed to particularity, and these clashes concern only the particularity [of ownership], not universality. Each recognizes the personality and the capacity for rights of the other, but the thing in question is not, so each believes, owned by the other. This is where civil lawsuits arise.

45

§ 39

In this case there arises what pertains to the sphere of *civil lawsuits*: a straightforwardly negative judgment—that is, [the negating] of only the particular, not the universal, element in the predicate "mine" that I bestow on something; this happens in such a way that the thing in dispute is laid claim to solely on grounds of right, and it is conceded that it should belong to the party who has the right to it.

When I say "This is not yours," only the particular aspect is here negated, not the other's capacity for rights or his personality. A negative judgment still involves a relation to the universal. In a civil lawsuit each party should be accorded its rights, but only one party can have right on its side; however, the other party is not denied what pertains to its capacity for rights, but only what pertains to possession, to subsumption. | It is on the contrary affirmed that if that party were rightly entitled to the thing in question, then it ought to have it.

46

§ 40

Since in both parties the recognized status [*Anerkanntsein*] of the universal will or of right is bound up with the particular interest and the particular viewpoint in regard to subsumption of the thing in question, it is necessary to have, for the universal will of right, another actuality than that of the parties, namely a *judge* [*Richter*] who, as a particular will, has only the universal [will], and who has the power [to ensure] that the parties will waive their viewpoint over against his and acknowledge it.

Each party has the natural will to possess the thing, but they demand to possess it on the ground that it is right; they recognize the universal will. But each has a viewpoint that is subjective since it is opposed to the viewpoint of the other; the one that is in the wrong also wills right. The particular will must here come on the scene as universal will, and the subjectivity of this will must be solely a universal will; it must have the viewpoint of the universal will. This judge must have insight in regard to the universal will, must have familiarity with it; and he must be impartial. In addition the judge must be recognized; he must be recognized as willing (and being familiar with) the universal will, and he must have the power to decide. Here the moral aspect comes into play, since the subjective arbitrariness of the individual must accept the universal will, and this is a higher aspect. What is required here is the universal will in and for itself, free from all arbitrariness and bound up with power (i.e., a power that has necessary force). Thus it is only in the state that there can be a judge, for if the parties do not like the decision of an arbitrator, they can mutually disregard his decision; whereas the judge, who has power, renders a firm decision, which must be put into effect. |

§ 41

In addition, the arbitrary will is no less contingent in regard to recognition in general. Initially recognition has only determinate existence, for in order for the universal [will], [the will] that has being in and for itself, to achieve actuality, the subjective will would have to sublate itself over against the universal will, and it has not yet done so. The will *does now* contain an objective element, and the arbitrary will can therefore turn against it. As my will is positively related to a thing, the thing can in general [be] seized by the external force of another and placed under necessity. I can be prevented from using what belongs to me, from exercising my right; the exercise of my right can be made conditional on my doing or giving up something: *coercion* [*Zwang*].

At our [present] standpoint not only the subjective but the universal will is injured. The recognized status of the personality is only immediate; for it to be actual, mediation must be accomplished, the arbitrary will must have sublated itself, there must be present the particular objective will of each individual, and the subjective will in its particularity must be sublated. This mediation first occurs in the moral standpoint. Since I own something—an external thing, or even my body, which also belongs to what I own—and my will has externality, it is capable of being treated in an external manner. The violent external action of another is possible, and my will, which inheres in the thing, can in this way be laid hold of, in that it is present in autonomous manner, as substance in the accident. Substance or will can therefore be laid hold of in what is owned, and can be placed under necessity. Of itself my will is autonomous, but since it has determinate existence in a thing, it inheres in it; at the same time, however, something else inheres in it, since the thing is something external. So I can be prevented from using what belongs to me, from exercising my rights; and if I want to recover them, I can be compelled to do or to abandon something else: "If you want to keep this, you must do something else." By reason of my will's having determinate, external existence, coercion can therefore enter into play and affect it. |

§ 42

Because, however, the will is free and can withdraw from every [form of] externality, human beings can be coerced, i.e., their physical side can be brought under the power of another; but the will cannot be *coerced* in and for itself, and whoever is coerced is to that extent coerced in accordance with his own will.

The will can therefore be coerced in regard to its various external aspects, because its physical existence can be opposed by a greater, stronger physical existence. Here power lies with the greater, the more intensive element. In and for themselves human beings cannot be coerced, for there is no superior power to which a free will would have to yield. In the same way a people may be conquered, compelled [to submit], but it cannot be coerced, for it can sacrifice itself in order not to be coerced. [Even] when the will deems itself compelled [to submit], one still seeks to keep something external for oneself; and [a people] loses its autonomy or independence if it does not regard this as something infinite and inalienable. Accordingly no conquered people can rightly complain, since its will was always involved in the conquest.

§ 43

Since, however, the will ought not only to be free in and for itself or in its concept but also to have determinate existence, and to be free in its existence, it ought not in principle to be coerced at all. Coercion is, generally speaking, wrongful. It is [also] self-destructive in its concept; and the way this is portrayed is that coercion is annulled by coercion, or it is *conditionally rightful* to the extent that it is an annulment of [previous] coercion.

The person who is coerced gives up one mode of existence, preferring to it a mode of existence he is still vouchsafed. What has to be examined here is whether the existence that is preferred to what is given up is worth the sacrifice, and what existence has to be given up. Cato, for example, preferred freedom to a servile life in a nonrepublican state; he was | unwilling   49 to see his great individuality brought into subjection. In this respect much depends on the particularity of the individual, whether to yield to necessity or not. In Greek dramas the chorus is usually in favor of yielding to necessity, but the heroes make their individual viewpoint prevail. The one who coerces always does wrong, even if the one who is coerced [also] does wrong in allowing himself to be coerced. As free will the will ought to be respected in its existence by the other, insofar as it exists for the other. In the state there must be recourse to coercion, and this coercion is here rightful, since by it [another] coercion is annulled. But the coercion imposed by nature cannot be regarded as coercion, for I can liberate myself from the coercion of nature. I can only will to be free for something free, so it is only from something free that coercion too can stem. In its concept the will cannot be coerced. Only something that is free can coerce, but in coercing it annuls freedom. This is a contradiction, and it is consequently possible in society for coercion to be annulled by coercion; only to this extent is coercion rightful. We shall see here to what extent a people that is not yet at the level of the state, a people in the state of nature, a condition of [subjection to] the coercion of nature, can be obliged to enter into the state and give itself a constitution, since this latter [form of] coercion annuls the former coercion, that of nature.

§ 44

Strict right is called *coercive right* insofar as it concerns the will in its immediate identity with a thing or according to its *abstract being*. This right therefore *is* and *must be*. In other words the reason why coercion is *permissible* here as a counter to coercion is that it *can* take place according to the concept, and this is because the will—which as subjective stands in infinite relation to itself as the inner certainty of its freedom—is not yet object.

In natural right strict right is usually called coercive right, and it is permissible here in that it occurs here in its concept, but only as a counter to coercion. The possibility of coercing | makes coercion possible. The moral will is the will in infinite relation to itself, the will that not only is but also has inward knowledge of itself. The existence that the free will has in itself has no externality; its self-knowledge is the existence of the free will. This existence is a purely intellectual existence, and according to the concept there can be no coercion here. So there ought also to be no coercion here, even if empirically it can occur, since arbitrariness here comes into play. The moral will is the mediated will, which is for itself as a result of the negation of its arbitrariness. Right is and must be (as abstract right), for it is the being of the will; and what *is*, and is in conformity with its concept, *must* be. In this sphere coercion is possible, but it is only rightful insofar as it destroys coercion; for coercion must be annulled by coercion, not by morality, since whether one wishes to be moral or not is a matter for one's own free choice, whereas right must *be*, and the being of right must here be present.

§ 45

Crime [*Verbrechen*] is any form of coercion whereby the principle of the will is attacked and right is infringed as right. The sphere of *criminal law* [*peinliches Recht*], the infringement of personal freedom in an individual case or in general, [the practice of] slavery, injury to life and limb and what belongs to me generally— [all this is] an infinite judgment through which is negated not only the particularity but also the universality inherent in the predicate "mine." Since it is only the *existent* will that can be injured, this gives rise to a distinction based on the objective aspect of crimes; this aspect involves consideration not only of the abstract injury done to the infinite [element] but just as importantly of the qualitative and quantitative manner of its existence.

Crime is the infinite judgment whereby right is infringed as right and what is mine is assailed, negated in such a way that if

I were to allow it to happen, I should lose not only what belongs to me but in general the capacity for ownership, the universal [element] of my being, | which in such a case is not recognized. Here right as right is infringed, the universal [element] of the free will. The one who commits a crime against me simply does not admit, or denies, that I have a right. To make and keep a human being as slave is the absolute crime, since the personality of the slave is negated in all its expressions. Murder does not, properly speaking, affect freedom in all its expressions; instead it is the infinitude of the personality that is annulled, and what is negated is only the possibility of all expressions of my personality, not, as by slavery, their actuality. Since I possess my body, since my will is in it, the one who causes injury to my body infringes my right as right. This extends also to the honor of the injured party, which is another mode of external existence consisting in the ways [other] individuals and I view myself; and the injury to me occurs because I am the content of these views.

In crimes right is infringed as right, and to this extent all crimes are equal. What is absolutely qualitative, the freedom of the will, is infringed. Consequently the Stoics maintained that there is only one virtue and one crime in the sense that crime infringes the law, infringes right.[10] It is the same with honor, because I can attach this feeling to everything. Yet one can also receive infinite injury in this fashion through a purely civil dispute, because the inward element, honor, is thereby infringed, and because one accuses the other of wrongdoing.

10. [Ed.] See Plutarch, De stoicorum repugnantiis, in Plutarchi Chaeronensis omnium, quae exstant, operum Tomus Secundus continens Moralia Gulielmo Xylandro interprete (Frankfurt, 1599), p. 1034 (Plutarch's Moralia, vol. 13, part 2, with an English translation by Harold Cherniss [Cambridge, Mass., and London, 1976], p. 425); Johannes Stobaios, Eclogae ethicae, book 2, chap. 7, in Johannes Stobaios, Eclogarum physicarum et ethicarum libri duo, ed. A. H. L. Heeren (Göttingen, 1792–1801), 2:36, 110; Diogenes Laertius, De vitis, dogmatibus et apophthegmatibus clarorum philosophorum libri decem (Leipzig, 1759), book 7, chap. 1 (§ 125), pp. 472–473. For a modern conspectus see Stoicorum Veterum Fragmenta, ed. J. von Arnim, 3 vols. (Leipzig, 1903–5), 1:49–50 (frags. 199–204), 85–86 (frags. 373–375); 3:48–51, 62 (frags. 258–259).

Only the will that has determinate existence can be infringed or coerced because only in this way is it for others, only in this way is it qualitative—but not the will in [its] concept. In being infringed, the will is thus infringed as a determinate will, not in its infinitude. This is to posit qualitative and quantitative relationships; for instance, murder is qualitatively distinct from theft, and theft, according to its scale, quantitatively distinct from greater or lesser theft. In the absolute crime too, when someone is made a slave, a temporal distinction comes into play: the slave can secure release today, tomorrow, or sometime during his life. In determining the qualitative and quantitative distinction (an affair of the understanding, for here we are not speaking of the concept of crime), a positive aspect comes into play, | and the judge's decision has to embrace a great deal in this respect, not solely the law.

52

§ 46

Not only must the coercion that [has] been posited by such an action be annulled as product, to the extent that this can happen, but the *inner nullity* [*innere Nichtigkeit*] of the action must be brought out in and for itself or in its *totality*. Since criminals are rational agents, it is implicit that their actions are something universal and establish a *law* that they have recognized in them [as valid] for themselves. They *may* therefore be subsumed under the mode of action they have established, indeed they *must* [be] subsumed under it; and the action, which resides not merely in the product but—as particular action opposed to the universal will—essentially in the subject, and which has positive existence in the subject too, [must] be annulled. The way in which this comes about is for the law established by criminals, whose content is a transgression, to be applied to them. In this way both the positive validity of their action and its negative validity, the injury they have also done to themselves in causing injury to others (all others), are done away with and wrong is turned into right.

Since our theory is based on the concept, the crux of the matter, crime, is an action that is essentially a nullity. This nullity must come into existence, and this must be the basis of punishment—the realization of an action that is in and for itself null. Crime is in and for itself a null form of action, an infringement of right as right, of the free will as free will; but the free will cannot be infringed in its concept; so crime contradicts the concept of the free will, and this is the nullity of crime. The will must have its determinate being [*Dasein*] in its concrete existence [*Existenz*], and this existence [*Existenz*] is infringed. The action of criminals is universal because they are rational beings; so they have established something universal, a law proclaiming that it is right to infringe freedom; and by their action they have recognized this law. Beccaria[11] repudiated capital punishment because, following Rousseau,[12] he regarded the state as a contract between individuals, | and he then assumed that no one could allow one's fellow citizens to put one to death in certain circumstances because this was contrary to human nature.

However, crime is in and for itself (without regard to the state) a law that criminals establish through their action. In killing, they establish as universal that it is permissible to kill—they have acknowledged as much. Since it is a negative action, criminals have injured individual [victims], all [others] and themselves; they have infringed the universal, negatively that is, while positively they have acknowledged it because theirs is the action of rational beings. They may therefore be subsumed under the same way [of viewing things]; they have granted the right for evil to strike themselves. Crime is an action, i.e., a change in an external mode of existence; crime brings something forth. There are actions or crimes for which one can make restitution, such as robbery and theft, but life cannot be restored. A person who has been killed is no more, and consequently has also lost nothing, for whoever is dead no longer has anything.

53

11. [*Ed.*] Cesare Beccaria, *Dei delitti e delle pene* (Leghorn, 1764), chap. 16: "Chi è mai colui che abbia voluto lasciare ad altri uomini l'arbitrio di ucciderlo?"

12. [*Ed.*] Rousseau, *Principes du droit politique* (Amsterdam, 1762), esp. book 1, chap. 6, pp. 26 ff. Cf. Rousseau, *Du contrat social; ou, Principes du droit politique*, in Rousseau, *Œuvres complètes*, vol. 3 (Paris, 1964), pp. 360 ff.

But the dead person's friends have lost, and they can demand reparation.

This means that the mere outcome of crime is annulled, and this annulling is civil punishment. However, criminal punishment also has a role to play, for the *action* is not yet annulled. The crime has gone scot-free, is not yet annulled, and this is the intellectual aspect of the action, for the crime has still a positive validity, which lies in the subject. Crime is, however, a particular will, the infringement of the universal, of right in itself; this is an affair of the particular will, and crime remains something subjective. (A good action, a beautiful work of art, is something objective, and they do not involve subjectivity, for what is good or beautiful is a universal work. What is peculiar to the doer of an evil[13] action, what is his or hers, is something subjective, basely motivated.) The reason why crime is a bad action is that it is something particular, opposed to the universal will. As long as the negativity has not yet been made actual in regard to criminals themselves, the crime still goes scot-free, it is still | something subjective. The law that criminals have established through the crime must therefore be accomplished in regard to them; it must recoil on them. The action of criminals is against others but also against themselves. The law established by criminals is a universal law, but only they have recognized it. By means of punishment their action, in its positive validity, is brought to naught; but the negative side too, the injury, the coercion they have brought about, is annulled by the coercion [exerted by punishment]. Since crime is a positive, inwardly null mode of action, a mode of action having an existence it ought not to have, the second negation must come into play; the universal injury is annulled by the punishment criminals undergo. Restoration is the negation of negation. The evil conscience of criminals, their unrest in their self-consciousness, must be annulled by means of punishment; for nullity is brought to naught in them by punishment, and so wrong is turned into right.

Coercion *in abstracto* is wrong, but to the extent that it is

13. *Ms. reads:* good

coercion exercised against coercion, it is right; the negation of negation is affirmation. Punishment follows crime as absolute law; law and punishment directed against the transgressor of the law are the opposing sides, which are absolutely necessary. All other theories of penal law are only a particular aspect in regard to crime and punishment, a further and more concrete aspect, but not the concept, the abstract element. For the state may do nothing that is not right in and for itself, so the deterrence theory is of no avail, unless the will is here assumed to be necessarily weak, which is after all only a matter of contingency. It is therefore false to assume that human free will is essentially determinable—and this is after all only a second aspect. In deterrence the criminal is regarded as a means for others. The fact of deterring is a matter of chance; it all depends whether the others will allow themselves to be deterred or not. Where punishment is most severe, dispositions become savage, and the effect of the deterrence theory is to make crimes more numerous. According to Feuerbach deterrence is achieved by threat, and punishment ensues because [criminals] | have not let them-   55
selves be deterred by the threat.[14] The psychology of spirit of those who rely on deterrence is flawed in that they regard spirit as dependent. Feuerbach's way around the difficulty is a vain contrivance, even though it found such wide acceptance. Where there is no state, there is revenge, and revenge may be just; punishment and revenge differ only in form. Moreover the state can only threaten with what is right. Threatening involves an effeminate element such as deterring, because this runs counter to the elasticity of freedom; for the will there is no cause, it is absolute inner self-determination. With threat, criminals are supposed to be deterred by the specter of punishment. The state may not threaten with anything that is not right in and for itself; moreover, threats are in principle unsuited to the state.

The reform of criminals has also been made the principle of

14. [Ed.] Paul Johann Anselm Ritter von Feuerbach's theory of general prevention was presented in his *Revision der Grundsätze und Grundbegriffe des positiven peinlichen Rechts*, part 1 (Erfurt, 1800), esp. pp. xix–xxx, 49–108.

punishment; but this is an intention that relates to the criminal as subject. Reform is indeed a positive mode of existence [*Existenz*], but only for the inward core of the crime, not for what is external; and since there is no possibility of knowing whether criminals can be reformed or not, nor whether they are reformed or not, reform is nothing external, whereas an external punishment must impinge on the external crime. The right of pardon makes what has happened as if it had not; the deed is made individual, it is made naught. Reform is at all events an essential moment; if therefore criminals make good their crime, they have annulled the product or outcome of the crime and recognized the rights of others. So in most cases private citizens will be content with restitution; that [criminals] mend their ways from a pure impulse is, however, a matter of contingency, for it may also be the result of fear of punishment, so reform is something ambiguous. But a judge will always have regard to the fact that a criminal *sought* to make good his crime. Yet the truth is that crime is only genuinely brought to naught through punishment, both for others and for criminals themselves, for whom punishment makes the crime as though it had not happened. Crime is something in and for itself null, and this nullity must be itself annulled, sublated into actuality: such is the idea on which punishment rests. |

56

§ 47

The annulment of crime is in principle *retribution* [*Wiedervergeltung*]—the bringing to naught of the nullity brought about by the crime insofar as the crime, as existent, has a definite qualitative and quantitative scope, so that its negation is itself conditioned and determinate. Because of this external side, however, the annulment of crime is not tied to specific equality but to equality of *value* [*Wert*], which also can depend on manifold circumstances, irrespective of the moral side, namely the subjectivity of the will.

The moral point of view extends no higher than that right should be done. The annulment of crime is retribution, because retribution is the negation of the negative, of the crime. As actual crime, crime enters the sphere where qualitative and quantitative differences arise; e.g., murder ranks higher than theft, or petty theft is of less account than major theft. Crime is something determinate, and the negation of crime is the negation of just this crime, not of crime in general. So the negation is determined by quality and quantity, no more ought to happen and no less. But the retribution ought not to be a *talio*.[15] On the contrary, here in actuality, many qualitative and quantitative determinations come together comparatively; they are only equal to one another on the universal plane, according to their abstract, universal being, wherein they are equal in terms of value. It is therefore a false view to think, in matters of retribution, of the *talio*; on the contrary, retribution must rest on the equality of value.

Difficulties do indeed arise in ascertaining this value, and here, as with exchange, the empirical enters in. But if this difficulty were to be adduced against retribution, then it would have to be said too that all exchange and all compensation for damages are quite impossible. If for example imprisonment is decreed for theft, | [it] is difficult to define imprisonment in terms   57
of its length. But the two things have this in common, that they both involve an infringement, and so they are equal to one another in concept. As regards the quantitative aspect, with how long a prison term theft should be punished, it is very difficult [to determine], but this difficulty resides on the level of determinate existence as such because such existence constitutes an external level, the level of otherness for the concept; and this lies in the nature of the case. Now this quantitative determination depends on many circumstances: crimes must be compared with one another and the punishment accordingly increased or reduced. But this comparison is once again an external aspect, which does not, properly speaking, impinge on the individual crime. The determining factor here is ethical concepts, the state

15. [*Ed.*] The reference is to the *lex talionis*, the law of retaliation.

of the nation. But this pertains to the positive treatment of criminal law.

§ 48

The annulment of crime is in the first place *revenge* [*Rache*], and *just* revenge insofar as it is retributive. But as revenge this annulment is carried out by the injured individual or relatives or by other individuals, and it is the action not of the universal but of a subjective will, and hence a new transgression. Thus the revenge falls immediately into infinite progression because it is a contradiction that the universal will should have actuality through an immediately particular [will]. What is then required is a will that has being for itself, a universal will, a judge.

With the ancients revenge and punishment are not yet distinguished: Dike is revenge and punishment, the Eumenides are goddesses of revenge and of punishment. Punishment is the annulling of crime insofar as it occurs through a court, in the state, through a will that is only the will of the universal, not the subjective will of the injured individual or of the family, of the injured parties themselves. In point of form, therefore, revenge and punishment are distinct. In revenge | justice is mingled with contingent subjective feelings; contingency of insight, of will, and of feeling is here mingled with the universal will. Revenge is in the first place the implementation of right, insofar as right is the annulment of crime, but a subjective implementation. In several countries a number of crimes are punished only if they are brought before the courts by the injured party and form the subject of an accusation made to the judge; and no one, not even the judge himself, can do anything in the absence of such a denunciation. So here revenge is viewed as something governed by right, as for example in England, where, if the evidence against a criminal is insufficient, he can be invited to engage in a duel and forced to do so. [It is] the same in other countries with theft, where only the person who has been robbed can be the accuser.

To the extent that revenge derives from a subjective will, it is

58

104

only a subjective, and not a pure, annulment of the transgression, and is therefore in turn a new transgression; and so revenge falls into an infinite progression, as in Arabia and North America it passes down from generation to generation. For here the contradiction remains present, and they (the two revenge-seeking parties) stand over against each other in reciprocal negation. The contradiction is that the crime is to be annulled whereas the will occurs only as particular will. The judge has only the universal will, for he is not injured, and in his being-for-self he wills only the universal will. Among uncivilized peoples anyone not satisfied with the judge's decision would challenge the judge to a duel. Only in a civilized people is a judge of the kind portrayed conceivable and possible.

§ 49

What constitutes right in the first, immediate relationship of persons to persons is the fact of being recognized [*Anerkanntsein*], the fact that the free will *exists for the intellect* [*das intellektuelle Dasein*], that the particular will of *the individual* knows itself to be identical with the other [wills] in *immediate* fashion and accepts their validity on a reciprocal basis. | For right to exist in this way is accordingly a matter of *contingency*, but at the same time right attains actuality only through the subjective will. Likewise the *external existence* [*äusserliche Dasein*] of a thing, its subsumption under a subjective will (in accordance with a felt need, etc.) is contingent and at the same time an essential moment in the existence [*Existenz*] of right. As the substantive [element], however, the universal will is still distinct in this relationship from its essential moments; it is an *ought* whereby their contingency is to be sublated and they [the will and its moments] are made identical. The sphere of this *mediation* is *morality*.

The aspect that concerns right as right is that individuals are identical in immediate fashion, that they know themselves immediately as identical, recognize each other as persons. This recognized status of personality is what raises the intellectual level to determinate existence in the sphere of right. Persons are *for* persons, and they have immediate actuality, a contingent, not a necessary actuality, for the necessary is the sublating of immediacy.[16] The effect is mediated by the cause, but it is only in the effect that the cause is cause, and the product or outcome is pure mediation. Mediation is an utterly necessary moment. This first recognized status of personality is contingent, for the subjective will has not yet posited itself as identical with the universal will and does not yet recognize the particular will as a differentiated will. Only through the subjective will does right attain actuality, and in this way right is contingent. The essential moment is the contradiction; the subjective will is essential in the universal will, yet it occurs here as a contingent will. The subjective will subsumes things in contingent manner, according to felt need, caprice, etc. The sphere of mediation, the sublating of this contradiction, is the standpoint of morality, of what "ought" to be. But as long as the accidents are not identical with the universal will, it is *merely* an "ought" and still something subjective. As expressing what ought to be, the universal will is only the infinite concept, but the universal will must realize itself in the subjective will. The universal will has as its material the subjective will, in which it must bring itself forth.

16. *Ms. reads:* mediation

II. MORALITY

§ 50

Morality does not concern the *person* as such, the will as immediate singularity [*Einzelheit*], but as individual [*individuelles*] subject, the will that is for itself and whose singularity is determined in such a way as to become *particularity*, i.e., the relation of the will that is for itself to the will that is *in and for itself*.

Morality no longer concerns immediate singularity but what we call the subject. The universal will is the will that is in and for itself, free from determinacy. This relation of the universal will to the singular will is the particular will. The will exists as recognized will to the extent that it has validity in another will. The particular is not the singular but has universality within itself in immediate fashion; the particular color "red" always includes the universal characteristic of being a color.

§ 51

From a general standpoint morality involves three aspects:
(1) Formal action [*formelle Handlung*] and disposition [*Gesinnung*].
(2) Subjective purposes, [my] welfare [*Wohl*] and intention [*Absicht*].
(3) Good [*Gute*] and conscience [*Gewissen*].

The first aspect [to be considered] is action, the particular way in which the subject realizes [itself], the fact that it gives itself determinate existence—disposition is the universal. Secondly there is intention, the particular purpose accompanying something; it is here that contradiction arises between subjective welfare and the right constituted by objective welfare. And thirdly there is the standpoint where the objective purpose is made one with the subjective purpose; this is the standpoint of ethical life. |

61

1. Actions and Dispositions

§ 52

In the will that is for itself, the particular [mode of] self-determination has, *in terms of form*, the determinateness of subjectivity; it is lacking something by comparison with the will that is in and for itself, and is contradictory to it. Thus it is the sublating of this negation, the transposition of the will that is only for itself into determinate existence, that is, an objective universal such as the will gives to itself *as will*, namely as *relating to the will* of other subjects: an *action* [*Handlung*].

The will that is for itself is[1] for itself and within itself, or self-contained, but the will is the totality, the subjective will, and as subjective will it is the will that is [only] in and for itself; this concerns the form of the action. The will is not yet determined here in its content, but only in terms of form. In its being-for-self, however, in its singularity, it is infinite. Freedom consists in having a limitation but transcending it. The infinitude of self-consciousness consists in the fact that its barrier is something negative for it and that, in this negation, it nevertheless *is*. As what is free, the ego can endure the contradiction and is itself its positive resolution; but finite nature is only negative. For itself the subject is something subjective, and for the subject itself this subjectivity is a lack; but the subject is itself the sublating of this contradiction. This sublating is *action*. Action consists in the subject's sublating its subjectivity and making its inner element external. Action is a transposing or translating of the will, [a mode of being] that the will gives to itself

1. *Ms. adds:* (1)

108

as existent being [*Dasein*]. Taking possession is only an action insofar as it relates to the will of other subjects, to the fact of being recognized. Contract is an action because in it I give myself a determinate existence for the will of another. Action derives from the subject, and realizes itself in immediate fashion in the case of contract, and still more in the case of wrong and crime, but we have not yet considered this subjective aspect. | 62

§ 53

Particular self-determination, as the inward self-determination of the will that is for itself, and as a mode of self-determination that is intended to be realized, is known by the subject and is its *purpose* [*Zweck*]; [it is] a judgment that in its determinacy comprises universal thought. The *disposition* [*Gesinnung*] is this universality as belonging to the subject; and, as singled out and set apart on its own account, it is the *maxim* of the subjective will. Once right is enacted, the disposition is of no essential significance for it.

Action is the transposing or translating of inwardness into externality, but externality is the form in which the will posits itself. The subject wills something; this is its purpose, but purpose is still something inward. Purpose is self-determination of the will in a way that is not intended to remain subjective, to keep this defect of non-externality. The subject has knowledge of the purpose insofar as it is still in the subject's inner being. In the purpose a universal thought is present, [for] the will consists in being in and for itself universal as well as in and for itself determinate. What I posit inwardly is mine; my purpose is a universal, which is, however, also determinate. In the will I do not remain at the stage of universality, but determine my will. The purpose is my image, but it is as yet only subjective and has to become objective.

The purpose is the concept. In what is living the concept (purpose) has immediate being in external existence [*Existenz*]; only in spirit does the concept have being as something inward. The will has the concept that is in the element of thinking; it

109

has knowledge of it. To the extent that it belongs to the subject, this universal is the disposition; but if we express the disposition in abstract terms, we say it is the maxim of a will.

If maxims are considered wholly [on their own account], then they are principles; if the principle belongs to a subjective will, it is "my" maxim. Principles have to be made into maxims. It is the endeavor of moral education that these principles should always be present to the imagination, but they must be appropriated, | awakened within the subject itself, not merely represented to pupils as external, for in that case what impinges on the pupils is always in the form of something external. Pupils must view the good as their own will. The principle must become the subject's own. Once right comes about, the disposition is immaterial, for right is a genuine mode of acting, an inwardly substantive mode of existence [*Dasein*] that has been brought forth. Here the subjectivity of the will does not enter into consideration; all that is required of the subject is to do the right on the basis of moral principles.

§ 54

The subjective will is more precisely a finite will insofar as its standpoint is that of consciousness. It has a presupposed object for its action, and also has in its purpose the representation of this object and the application of its maxims to the conditioning circumstances. The *deed* [*Tat*] is the alteration brought about in the existent situation, and the will *is responsible* for such alteration and its consequences.

Here we consider a further aspect of action. The will is subjective, not objective; it is at the standpoint of consciousness, of the finitude of consciousness, [which means] that spirit is not in and for self, but its reality subsists for it as an object on which it acts. External circumstances are the conditions within which it acts, and its purpose involves representing these external circumstances in general and subsuming the determining circumstances under the purpose. Action bears on the concrete situation; as activity, the will effects the alteration and is responsible (not "chargeable")[2] for the alteration and its consequences. This is the concept of "being responsible" as such. "Being chargeable" or imputation is something else. A deed is as such a transformation into objective existence. That a human being is responsible | for something expresses immediacy, the emerging from the subjective into objectivity, and the deed is the wholly immediate mediation. The consequences are at least dependent on the deed. Liability in the civil sense [means that] if I owe someone something, I am the possessor under civil law and the other is the owner.

64

§ 55

But since this will, as consciousness, is finite, the world of objects as it appears [*die gegenständliche Erscheinung*] is contingent for it and may of itself be something quite different from what it is in the will's representation. In the same way the deed, as the purpose transposed into externality, is the prey of external forces, can attach to externality in quite different fashion, and can give rise to a chain of remote consequences alien [to the purpose]. In its *deed*, however, the will recognizes as its action and *is chargeable* for only those elements of the deed of which it has knowledge in its purpose, and it repudiates the imputation to it of anything else.

An animal does not, properly speaking, *do* anything, but still less can it *act*. Prior to actualization the will has its purpose within itself, and it is a matter of contingency how the world of objects as it appears exists for it as consciousness. However, the representation of consciousness may be very different from actuality. Human beings, who do act, operate on the circumstances as they conceive them. If someone out hunting shoots someone, in the belief he is killing a wild animal, he is not chargeable for this and will not let it be imputed to him. An action is mine only insofar as my purpose includes the circumstances. Something quite different may also attach to the

2. [*Tr.*] The text distinguishes between *schuld sein* and *schuld haben*, rendered here by "to be responsible" and "to be chargeable" respectively.

externality; consequences may ensue that were not inherent in the deed, and persons will not let such consequences be imputed to them either. For only what inheres in the purpose of the action can in fact be imputed. The heroic consciousness saw itself as infinite intelligence and regarded its deeds as in all circumstances its own. Oedipus slew a man | who met him on the way, but it was part of the action that this man was his father. However, the ensuing anguish he experienced was as great as if this circumstance too had been in his awareness. Human beings here credit themselves with knowing everything; they impute to themselves that they *should* know everything, and experience the anguish as of one who has *acted*.

§ 56

Because crimes are actions that are in and for themselves null, the subjective knowing and willing of such an action forms the disposition in regard to the universal implicit in it. Apart from awareness with regard to the objective circumstances, [this means] that as action it formed part of the purpose, i.e., that it was *premeditated*; this constitutes an essential moment in the imputation and punishment of crime.

For a crime to be judged as such depends on the disposition. Crime is properly speaking an empty phenomenon, for it is an action that is in and for itself null, whose positive aspect continues to belong to the subject; to this extent revenge or punishment must be directed toward the subject.

Whether an action is a crime depends on whether (1) the circumstances were present in [the subject's] consciousness, and (2) the universal element in the action, the maxim, formed part of the subject's purpose, or both together; the action must have been premeditated. The subject must have known that the crime or action is something contrary to right; this brings in the positive, empirical aspect. (In Germany children cannot be summoned to appear at court and convicted, but there are frequent conflicts on this point in England, in London; children are frequently given penal sentences, admittedly to a lesser extent [than adults].) The child's actions are still imbued with singularity; the child cannot yet have the aspect of universality, of rationality. Here the law must determine in firm manner, so as not to leave too much to the judge's arbitrary decision. For different kinds of personal right may be pronounced in the space of a day. | Other conditions such as anger, drunkenness, or madness are conditions that weaken a human being's awareness.[3] It has been said that every crime is insanity, but even the insane have to be penalized on account of evil actions, though without severity. Madmen who commit crimes in a moment of pure rage are to be regarded as animals, and like animals they can be deterred; we can try to protect ourselves from them, we can make them harmless. But we must always assume, we must pay humans the honor of assuming, that they were aware of the universal aspect of their crime. The punishment may be mitigated on the ground that the criminal was not aware of the true value of the action. But the whole gamut of mitigating circumstances should not lie within the competence of the courts; the main responsibility in this regard must belong to a higher power, the ruler. Milder customs also result in milder penalties.

An action comprises two aspects, [the deed and] the universal aspect, the maxim, which essentially concerns the disposition. It is assumed of the criminal that he knows the law. However, lack of mental development can justify lesser degrees of punishment, but only if the criminal is a child or insane. Otherwise human beings are always paid the honor of assuming that

3. [Ed.] Cf. Paul Johann Anselm Ritter von Feuerbach, *Lehrbuch des gemeinen in Deutschland geltenden Peinlichen Rechts* (Giessen, 1801), pp. 75–76: "§ 96: The individual states that preclude imputability include . . . I: any nonaccountable state of mind such as makes impossible any awareness of the punishable nature of the deed. . . . Immunity from punishment is also conferred by (1) the natural state of childhood; (2) the unnatural state of childhood (usually) in deaf-mutes from birth and wholly childlike old people; (3) mental illness, specifically mania and delusion . . . ; (4) extreme drunkenness incurred through no fault of the person concerned; (5) uncontrolled righteous emotion; (6) innocent sleep; (7) error or ignorance for which one cannot be held accountable in regard to the existence of the penal law as such or in regard to whether the deed in question is subsumed under it."

they have this universal rationality within them. So to the extent that their actions are contrary to universal human rationality, they are punishable. But the state prescribes very severe and heavy punishments for wholly positive crimes, whose only universal aspect is that the state proclaimed them but which in other respects do not accord with what is rational. However, the subject [of the state] must make it his concern to familiarize himself with these laws. Thus stealing in general is prohibited, but awareness that a particular theft is regarded as so serious is something contingent; the criminal could be wholly unaware of this particular aspect or be aware of it to a greater or lesser degree. However, these penalties are subject to mitigation and pardon.

67   Where the universal | aspect of crime is present, there is *dolus* [evil intent], but [only] to the extent that the single individual in question was aware of this universal aspect. Milder customs result in less serious crimes. In this respect a sharper distinction is drawn in regard to the determinations of [the criminal's] awareness; abstractions figure in it to a greater extent on their own account, and the crime becomes greater. On the other hand, the good too is more certain. An uncultured people undergoes total injury in everything, feels infinitely injured in each and every external injury. People at a higher cultural level feel themselves to be less injured when an external object they have imbued with their will suffers injury [than in the event of an injury suffered] in their inner feelings, in the feeling of inner freedom; their anger and desire for revenge are not so great. In a highly cultivated state each citizen enjoys better protection against crimes, and the milder practice of the courts of justice is warranted by the fact that very severe, deterrent punishments are seen to be no longer so necessary. People at a high cultural level, who set their honor within themselves, are not so deeply injured in regard to something external, because their inner independence abstracts to a greater extent from its external presentation.

Such are the chief points that arise in regard to the form of action.

2. Particular Purposes; Welfare and Intention

§ 57

The subjective will is not only formally determined and finite vis-à-vis reality in general; since its determinacy is at the same time infinite inward self-determination of the subjective individual, its determinacy is indifferent to the difference of form and turns [into] the content which, as the reflection of the particular subject into itself, is initially a *particular* content; and in its whole extension is the subject's *welfare.*

The content is the form reflected into self, the inwardly determined form. This relation to self is a determinate reference; its distinction has become simple. The content is determined in opposition to the | form, yet it is indifferent to it. What we have   68
to consider here is that it is the form itself that turns into the content. As subject, the subject is the ego, absolute infinitude reflected within itself, and this reflection within self—self as this difference—constitutes its content. This content is infinite reflection within self, determined over against form, but by virtue of the fact that the content is opposed to form, it is a determinate, finite, particular content. This particular content constitutes the distinctive purposes of the individual, the individual's welfare.

§ 58

Welfare includes the individual's natural requirement. In the first place this comprises what pertains to *particularity* in taking possession of and acquiring property, but also what pertains to spiritual requirements—to educate oneself and in general to bring one's *own sense* of one's particular actuality into conformity with the *universal concept* of one's life and its diverse aspects and with the *idea* of one's intellectual and volitional being.

Here the subject gives itself a particular sphere of its existence; here there arises the conflict between the individual's welfare and purposes and *right,* the clash of particularity and the universal. Properly speaking, all one acquires is acquired in arbitrary fashion, according to a particular requirement; in other words, one wills this particular [thing or event]. Human life is organic, and this organic life wills to subject inorganic life to itself. Immediate concordance [between the organic and the inorganic] consists in having a feeling of oneself, of one's welfare, one's enjoyment; it consists in the individual's returning into self. Spiritual requirements include whatever pertains to the development of spirit. The various requirements of spirit constitute the spirit's self-realization. The forces of spirit are drives or requirements to the extent that human beings are implicitly spirit in their concept, but are not something explicitly existent for the spirit; and this | contradiction actuates the impulses, so that the forces may be existent for the spirit, so that it may encounter no impediment in them but have completely permeated them. This is in general what pertains to welfare.

§ 59

Welfare has, to be sure, as its principle the particularity of the subject, but it is an essential moment for acting and for realizing the universal will because the activity of acting in general is the *negative relation of the will to itself*, and so lies in the sphere of individuality. Welfare is consequently an essential purpose of the will or a [form of] right; and, insofar as it must be brought about by positive action, it is *duty*. In general terms, what duty involves is that all action must comprise an *interest*, because in such interest the subject has self-awareness; and in its deed, whatever else it may contain, it must recognize itself as this single individual.

Welfare is an essential moment of the will; it is a [form of] right, and a duty insofar as it must be brought about through positive action. What constitutes the limited character of the will is naturalness. This primary division into universal will and particular will is a necessary moment. Welfare has, to be sure, as its principle the particularity of the subject, but acting contains the mediation between subjectivity and objectivity. It is only through action that the absolute final purpose of the world is brought about. But only the subject is active, acts, for activity is the negative relation of the will to itself. But the self-mediating will is individuality; a will inwardly mediated with itself has being-for-self. In the East the moment of particularity does not occur; it is not posited on its own account as an essential moment. It was only through Christianity that there arose individuality, having existence as singular, as particular. Welfare is a [form of] right, and it is a duty, for it must be brought about. The subject that acts recognizes itself in its action; this is its interest [in acting]. In its complete universality the interest is not yet distinct from the purpose of the action itself. All that is involved in interest is that it arises through the individual, which | in its action enjoys itself. In what human beings do they 70 have awareness of their deeds, and this is nothing evil.

§ 60

For the natural will as such, welfare is only purpose as [the welfare] of this individual subject. With the person, however, we already have, to be sure, the single individual, but free from mere naturalness of will. And happiness enters the moral sphere as duty to the extent that the particularity of the subject does not exist abstractly on its own account, but is determined by, and subsumed under, the will that has being in and for itself. Moreover, it is in consequence determined as universal in such a way that the purpose extends to the welfare of others and, in so doing, is equally moral purpose and duty.

Happiness is enjoyment, the satisfaction of impulses, presented in the reflection of universality, but it is not yet universality in and for itself. Happiness does enter the moral sphere, however, not as particular purpose but as subsumed under the universal will. The will of the individual is an essential moment, but only insofar as it is subsumed under the universal will. The purposes of morality are essential purposes, but not in accordance with their particularity. There is always an antithesis between form or universality and content or particularity. Of itself, duty is what is universal, absolute, but it must have a content, and so it enters the sphere of particularity. The particularity of the will must be subsumed under the universal will; and to this extent it is also a duty to make one's purpose the

117

welfare of others—the welfare of one's neighbor but not the welfare of all, for it is not possible for individuals, as particular, to relate to all; their sphere of effective action is confined to those with whom they come in contact.

§ 61

Since their content is particular, these moral purposes are in principle contingent in relation to right, and may therefore be in 71 concordance with it, | but they also may not be. So in the action too its particular aspect may [be] the essential purpose or end for the subject, the objective action may be reduced to being a *means* to the end, and this particular aspect [may] be the *intention [Absicht]*.

This paragraph touches on the collision between moral duties and right. Moral purposes or ends concern the particularity of the subject, whereas right is the determinate existence of the free will in general. The universal and the particular may be congruent with each other, but they may also not be in concordance. In a [given] action, which, as action, includes the universal and the particular aspect, the particularity may therefore constitute the purpose—the moral purpose consisting in the welfare of others. This particular aspect of welfare as such may be the subject's intention in its action, in which case the objective action, the rightfulness of this action, the universal element, is only a means to the particular intention. The particular that is the consequence of the action may be the intention of the action, and this intention may in turn be intention for another intention, and so on. As particular, the intention may always be mediated in this way ad infinitum.

The disposition refers to the moral element, to welfare, but the content is always a particular content. Intention is often equated with premeditation. In the case of a crime the differences between intention and premeditation or disposition relate to *dolus* [evil intention]. An action that is of itself a crime may be a means to another intention, which may be a moral one. For the presumption of *dolus* the following distinction must be made: if agents are merely responsible for the crime, it is not a crime for them; but insofar as, for example, the death of another formed part of their intention, so that they are chargeable, it is a crime, and there can be no question here but that the *dolus* resulted from evil premeditation. With *dolus indirectus* [indirect evil intention] what is meant is that if, for example, someone starts a conflagration, the intention is to burn [whatever it may be], but the people who perish in the flames are an indirect[4] consequence of the action; the action is a crime, but the consequence did not directly form part of one's intention. If people are injured, it depends on their constitution, | on   72 the skill of the doctors, etc., whether the injury will result in death. If someone poisons a well in order to kill his neighbor's cattle, it is an indirect consequence that people who drink from it die [too]. But the action here entails involvement with an element over which one subsequently no longer has mastery, so there is no question here of *dolus indirectus*; instead it inheres in the action itself that it may extend to immeasurable consequences. If by chance the arson causes little damage, so much the better for the agent. By such actions, agents deliver themselves up to external circumstances, and the ill that ensues from them serves them ill too.

If an action is a crime, *dolus* is automatically proven, and the judge no longer needs proof of *dolus*.

§ 62

Moral purposes differ in kind, and which is higher in comparison with others belongs to the discussion of morals. With regard to right, however, I can admittedly renounce my right for the sake of a moral intention, but the moral intention does not justify a wrong action; still less does it make it a duty. In merely moral intentions only a subjective particularity should be recognized, but the wrongful action would infringe the universal principle, the freedom of the will. The genuine moral disposition consists rather

4. *Ms. reads:* direct

in doing first what is right; it is moral to the extent that right exists as the subject's own self-determination. An evil disposition in the merely moral sense is one directed against the welfare of others.

If I fulfill one duty, this may exclude other duties; which duty is the higher is for morality to decide. Moral duty involves the incongruity that duty is a universal, yet belongs to a particular. | The conflict of duties must be decided in the last resort by conscience, but its decision lacks a rational basis. The duty that involves more universality is the higher. While I can renounce my particular right for the sake of a moral intention, I cannot for that reason infringe the rights of others. I also cannot renounce my capacity for rights from a moral intention, for I cannot renounce my freedom. People would rather be governed by morality than by right; but the content of right is universality, whereas the content of moral intention is particularity.

Right can therefore never be infringed for a moral purpose, whatever it may be. For a wrongful action infringes freedom. The prime moral duty is rather, in the first place, to be rightful, governed by right; only then can moral purposes enter in. Rightful action as such, the truth of rightful action, is where right is done for its own sake. The moral disposition contains the danger that, since my maxim is to do right but I at the same time have this maxim and know that I have this disposition, moral self-conceit arises. In determining itself to right, the subject also reflects on the fact that it itself so determines itself. The truth is that one does the right because it is right, not the reflection that the maxim is one's own maxim. Certainly those who wish to be moral must make the moral maxims their own, but what they must be concerned about is that the maxim has come into being, not that they have enacted it. What is morally evil is the disposition that is opposed to the welfare of others. So someone who is very much governed by right may nonetheless be evil; in the state, however, people must set less store by their welfare and the welfare of others than by rightful duties, the welfare of the state. Here we can see the meaning of the expression, "He

73

is a good man who sets less store by universal right than by the welfare of others." Evil in the disposition is when someone executes his egoistical plans at the expense of the welfare of others. The civil servant as such must set less store by the welfare of single individuals than by right. |

§ 63

The particular determinations that initially constitute the content of moral purposes, taken in their entirety as a single whole, are themselves a universal and, to that extent, infinite. In *life* there inheres at the same time the possibility of the determinate existence of freedom as such, of right; and if life is in extreme danger, it may appeal to a right of distress, since in relation to the infinite infringement of this possibility, or in relation to the [complete] absence of right, the right of another or the property of another acquires the status of a merely *particular* existence of freedom. In other words, if one life that is at risk is set against another life, both are reduced to this latter abstraction.

All particularity taken together is a whole, something infinite, the particular returned from its particularity. This whole particularity is life, the possibility not only of particular purposes but also of right; life forms an essential sphere of right. So where life is endangered, it claims a right of distress. The danger of infinite injury is the danger of complete loss of right. In the face of this loss of right, right as such disappears—the welfare of others, their particular moral purposes and their right—because my determinate existence, which is my freedom, is in danger. Equality in this case means that the other should not take precedence over it [i.e., my existence], and the other's right disappears in face of it. The wish that no one should have a prior claim to anything in the sphere of the particular, of inequality, is envy. Equality of external goods is something false because this belongs to the sphere of the particular, the contingent, the unequal. But in relation to the absolute claim to freedom of each human being, of life itself, the particularity of the other's rights disappears. If both are in mortal danger and there is only room for one on the plank, we have here the condition in which right is absent, and the decision is left to subjective feeling; it is no longer a question here of right and wrong, but only of nobility of mind.

75   Because all human existence in its externality | is a matter of contingency, such a case can arise. For instance, a woman who was traveling with her husband and children, when surrounded by a large pack of wolves and in danger of their all being lost, threw one child to the wolves and so saved herself and her husband and her other children. It cannot be said that she did wrong, but her peace of mind never returned. The state, however, has laws governing the right of distress. If an artisan owes all he possesses, the creditors not only cannot oblige him to work for them till the end of his days, but may not even take from him the tools he needs for his work, so that this extremity of need may be averted from him.

§ 64

Need exhibits not only the nullity of welfare as such, as the realization of particular subjectivity, but also the nullity of the existence of freedom, namely right; and the particularity of purposes, regarded on its own account, dissolves in the universality of thought so far as its content is concerned. In the ideality of this particular content and of external existence, the universality of the will—pure right and abstract duty—has returned within itself. In this way, as ideal, particularity, which from the moral standpoint is supposedly determined by the *universal will*, is equivalent to and identical with the latter; and, in this universal ideality of the particular, *subjectivity* has an ideal mode of existence and is therein likewise returned within itself—as the *good* and as *conscience*.

Here we have the transition to the good and to conscience. The good is what is utterly universal, the universal final purpose of the world; conscience is singularity as such. In need the particularity of the subject exhibits itself in immediate fashion as null. The particularity of the subject also includes the existence of freedom and right, and need exhibits the limitedness of this aspect in general. But it is not only this immediate need that exhibits this nullity; for universal thought there are no absolute duties. Such duties arise only in the ethical state. Every absolute duty is a limitation. The free will, as conscious of itself, the pure will, comprises no aspect in which it still has to realize itself. | The freedom of the will that is for itself now exists solely in self-consciousness, the universal will has only itself as its object and purpose, and the subject exists solely in its pure ideality. This freedom is therefore the negative of the particular, and this negativity indicates need. Heart and mind cut themselves off completely from the external world and shut themselves within themselves; all particularity is here evaporated. Here all reality has disappeared, and self-consciousness resides in the pure certainty of itself. This is the transition to the state. 76

The transition to conscience and to the good is a dialectic. Need sets a dialectical moment in motion. The universal will, the will that is in and for itself, the will defined as all that is encompassed by welfare, and the will that is in and for itself, having passed through the mediation of subjectivity and possessing an unlimited [mode of] existence, [is] an existence [*Dasein*] that is in and for itself universal; it is the will that has being in and for itself in its existence [*Existenz*].

[3.] The Good and Conscience

§ 65

The good [*das Gute*] is the universal will as absolute final purpose and object. It is the idea wherein [are] sublated for spirit the particular purposes involved in its welfare as well as the determinate existence of right as something self-sufficient, and the absolute final purpose of the world is in consequence accomplished.

The universal will is the absolute final purpose and object, what is and ought to be. In contrast with freedom, nature is something lacking self-sufficiency. From the moral standpoint, there is as a result of the dialectic no longer anything self-sufficient over against the universal will. The concept has passed through its mediation by its antithesis and has the antithesis within itself. The good is not only the free universal, but the free universal in its determinate existence, which is equal to the universal. This is the idea of the good or of the final purpose of the world. It was this idea to which | Kantian philosophy attained, but got no further. But [here] the good is eternal rest, it has no activity, it is not yet determined as substance, [whereas] it must be actual, must realize itself; as the idea of the good it is still without movement. This good is accordingly given in Kantian philosophy as an "ought to be," but "ought" as such implies something incomplete—the good is not yet portrayed as idea. Happiness ought to be present, the subject ought to be inwardly in accordance with this good; but the subject makes it a matter of contingency that it is so. Kant based the immortality of the soul on the fact that the good ought more and more to resemble the universal good; this postulate is the infinite progression.[5] But since both moments are posited—the subject in its particularity and the universal substance—both cannot be self-sufficient; subjective particularity must sublate itself. In its concept the good contains the particular, the negative, and this is the aspect of activity, where the subject is in an infinite relation to itself.

77

§ 66

Self-determination within this abstract idea and its actualization constitute pure subjectivity, simple certainty of oneself, in which all determinacy of right, duty, and existence evaporates: *conscience* [*Gewissen*]. [Conscience is] this absolute power of the free will, which grasps itself as absolute self-determinacy and as utterly free being-for-self, and in which alone lies the determination of *what is good*.

Here the moment of subjectivity is no longer regarded from the viewpoint of subjectivity. Within the universal everything particular is contained, but the particular is negated; so the

5. [*Ed.*] Hegel is referring to the doctrine of postulates in Kant's *Critique of Practical Reason*. See Kant, *Schriften* 5:107 ff.

moment of pure self-consciousness is contained in the good—
this pure | inner certainty of oneself, this complete inner clarity.   78
(Actualization is the determining of the particular purpose.) For
conscience nothing counts but right and duty; determinate existence is altogether of no account. It is conscience that determines what good is. But it is the very same conscience that
knows itself as law; it is the absolute power of substance, of the
good. In this inner certainty the subject is completely present
to itself in its purity. The genuine idea is only the unity of the
good and conscience. The concrete conscience acknowledges objective duties, and to the extent that it is concrete and decides
in regard to conflicting duties, [it must choose], and the higher
duty for which it decides is an objective duty: it is acknowledged as the higher in all consciences. If I have genuinely acted
in accord with my conscience, this is nothing subjective, but is
a universal, objective duty. Conscience is this pure subjectivity;
my genuine conscience is universal conscience.

§ 67

Where self-consciousness, in this vanity of all determinations and
in pure inwardness of the will, still clings to its own particularity
and imbues this with the idea of the good and of its absolute self-
determination—there we have *hypocrisy* and *absolute evil*.

When the subject has attained this level and yet holds fast to
the particular, it has transcended all specific duties. But where it
still, after disposing of everything, makes itself, in its particularity, the purpose, then it is absolute evil, hypocrisy. Conscience is
the pure certainty of oneself, the pure relation to itself of absolute freedom; it is the absolute majesty that proclaims itself free
from everything and itself determines the good. But if it makes
its particularity the principle of its determining, this is the highest pitch of hypocrisy, directly identical with evil. A subject that
has conceived itself in this way determines *from itself* what is
good and evil. But these are its particular purposes; its action
[is] accordingly not in conformity with conscience, but [is] hy-
pocrisy. The subject then gives its action the status of | duty and   79

something governed by right, and so justifies it for its particular view. This can be termed the absolute hypochondria of spirit, seeing only itself and annulling all ties and friendly relationships and duty because it is afraid of losing itself in them. What is good depends on how the subject defines it; the subject deceives its conscience itself when it regards everything it does [as] in accord with conscience, whether it is actually so or not.

It is said in praise of human nature that human beings will nothing evil for the sake of evil. Evil is what is null, infringement, the positing of a negative; but as action it is also always something positive, even if it were only revenge, which can even claim life. If, for example, no one seeks an advantage from the action, then we may well have here something negative as regards the advantage, but it is a positive action because the subject carries out its revenge. It restores to itself consciousness of its impaired validity, the reestablishment of which is something positive. It is not because it is something negative, nor because the agent derives no positive advantage from it, that the evil is regarded as having occurred for evil's sake; rather it is positive evil because the agent's purpose is envy and revenge. A man who flees from the field of battle may appease his conscience, for he has preserved his life; and this is an essential moment, which should, however, have been subordinated to duty. Evil consists in infringing a duty; it is hypocrisy to raise evil above duty and so deprive duty of the essential aspect. What is congruent with the conscience is what can be acknowledged by all as in congruity with conscience.

§ 68

The inner certainty of oneself in which particularity is purified to abstract subjectivity is, however, only abstract activity, devoid of deed and action, because it is the immediate taking back of all determination within itself, and because its determination is only the universal good. This undifferentiated fading away into itself is a reduction | to *simple immediacy*, which, however, has as its essence the absolute unity of freedom with itself. The good and absolute subjectivity are in themselves identical, and one is only the

80

126

determinate existence of the other. In the good, subjectivity accordingly has the element that subsists in and for itself, in which its differentiation attains the level of subsistence and becomes objective, in the same way as this its particularization is merely ideal and exists only in the unity over against which it preserves nothing peculiarly its own: free *substantiality* or *ethical life*.

The point we are now at is pure inner certainty. It is the concept of freedom in its negative relation to self, it is abstract activity, in which no action ensues. The universal element in subjectivity is the good. The Fichtean philosophy,[6] which makes the ego the absolute principle, has in subjective form remained on one side; the objective side has always been given the side of negativity, but the identity [between the two sides] remained incomplete. Objectivity ought to be congruent with pure certainty of oneself, but has remained [self-]perpetuating. The highest standpoint of Fichte's philosophy is *striving, yearning*; the inner good has remained merely what ought to be, and what this philosophy amounts to is merely a yearning for what is supposedly good. Beautiful souls, who have within themselves this infinite self-consciousness, this clarity, have held fast to this standpoint. If, however, they go over to action, they enter the sphere of limitedness. They foresee this and therefore fear every contact, remain enclosed within themselves, and revere their inner infinitude, all of which led them to make themselves, their ego, God; they are only inwardly subjective, inwardly intuitive. They regard the good only as what ought to be, not as actual. In this way they border on hypocrisy; their essence is inner vanity. In their relation to others they acknowledge only their subjective concepts but not duty toward others. This is true for instance of Novalis and Spinoza, who died of consumption because they regarded pure objectivity only as something vanishing or consuming away,[7] as an "ought," not as something actual. They

6. [*Ed.*] See Johann Gottlieb Fichte, *Grundlage der gesammten Wissenschaftslehre* (Leipzig, 1794). Cf. Fichte, *Gesamtausgabe* 2:173 ff.

7. [*Tr.*] In German "consumption" is *Schwindsucht* and "vanishing" is *Verschwinden*. Hegel is thus making a play on words that can be only partially rendered into English.

81   lack the confidence to posit themselves objectively, | to let themselves go, i.e., in such a way as to remain completely sure of themselves. With them the concept is not differentiated; it remains pure intuition. The concept must break in two and posit itself as universality, in which all differences cease, because its elements form an inseparable totality.

As the will that is in and for itself universal, into which subjectivity has passed over, good is the substantive unity that determines itself inwardly. For example the classes or estates [*Stände*] making up a people are single organs that have their own life, that subsist on their own account, but that do not have their life in isolation from the body politic as a whole, but only as organic components. Being, in relation to what is free, means that its distinct phases achieve being.

III. ETHICAL LIFE

§ 69

Ethical life [*Sittlichkeit*] comprises as its merely ideal [*ideellen*] moments right as the unmediated existence [*Dasein*] of freedom and morality [*Moralität*] as the reflection of the free subject into itself. It is itself its truth, the idea as the free will purified to universality, which has its actuality in the disposition of the subjective will, in the same way that the subjective will has its foundation and substance—freedom become nature—in the will that has been purified to universality. We are thus faced with *two kinds of right*, the absolute right of substance and the right of individuals—the latter as both substantial right (as opposed to individuality or subjectivity as such) and the right of individuals for themselves (this being, however, essentially subordinate to substantial right).

A distinction is made here between morality and ethical life. Morality is what is reflected, whereas ethical life is the interpenetration of the subjective and the objective. (Desirable though it is that we should be able to denote everything in our own language, in philosophy the situation has arisen that we use a foreign term for what is more remote, for what is reflected, e.g., "being" [*Sein*] and "existence" [*Existenz*].[1]) Right and morality

1. [*Tr.*] The "foreign terms," i.e., the terms foreign to German, are in this instance *Moralität* (morality) and *Existenz* (existence), while the indigenous terms

129

are only ideal [*nur ideelle*] moments; it is only in ethical life that they come to existence [*Existenz*]. Actual morality is only the morality of the whole, in ethical life. So what must first be shown here is that the two earlier moments—right and morality—are only ideal. What comes first is the ethical substance, the substantive life of a people, of a family; and it is only later, when custom is no longer good, that the subject returns within itself and seeks its point of support in morality; it seeks in itself what is good, no longer in custom, in actuality. Once spirit no longer recognized itself among us in its old mode of life, there occurred the periods during which | right and morality were developed. The subject no longer knows itself as infinite, as perfect; it knows what is good, and knows that the good is found in its self-consciousness yet also transcends it and [that] in this way hypocrisy comes about. But historically the substantive is what comes first.

Ethical life is not only the absolutely good but also the absolutely true. It is the truth because actuality is here identical with the concept. Truth is where the subject takes up what is objective in its purity, not allowing free play to its particular reflections within itself. The good is the determination of the subject's self-consciousness, and activity is where the subject realizes what is objective and brings it forth from itself; it is at the standpoint of truth that the subject realizes what is objective within itself. The concept that is immediately realized and realizes itself is the truth. What is living reproduces itself; it is only a game with itself, it brings forth only what already is. The rational as such, law, can be called the concept, but it has its determinate existence [*Dasein*] in the individual subject, in its intelligence. The subject is the free concept, the concept that exists [*existiert*] as concept; the ego is the subjective concept. If I have an aim, I

are *Sittlichkeit* (ethical life) and *Sein* (being). Another indigenous-foreign contrast is found in Hegel's use of the terms *Dasein* and *Existenz*—the former indicating a mediation of the subjective and objective, and the latter a reflection into subjectivity; it does not appear, however, that Hegel maintains a systematic distinction between these terms in this work (see Introduction, n. 1).

know it immediately as mine. But reality, the ethical life of a people or family, is no longer this subjective concept; instead the subject's relationship to them is as to what is objective. Because ethical life is the standpoint of truth, it must have existence [*Existenz*], must be actualized; the good must be actualized by the ethical subject. What we have then is a movement of spirit in its reality. The standpoint is not that the good is not present; on the contrary, substance is eternally present. All that happens is that what is already present is brought forth. The spirit must be immune to the one-sidedness of subjectivity. It is the free will that is purified to universality. Right and disposition have completely permeated each other, [in such a way that] what happens should be the universal will; this its being is the essential disposition of the subject. The substance occurs as the universal actuality, and dissolves into many individuals, but in their disposition these individuals have returned to the universal.

We are confronted here with two forms of right, the substance and its determinate existence [*Dasein*], the universal volition | of all—the substantive right—and the right of individuals. Substance must *be*, and the individual must *be*; and since their roots intertwine, the individual subjects must be *within* the substance. The right of the individual subjects is the substantive right itself, in which they participate. Family right as [the right] of individuals to lead their natural life is a necessary moment, but only to the extent that it lies within the substance. Substantiality, what is purely ethical, is the foundation. We do not have to regard peoples as an aggregate of individuals; on the contrary [it is] only the whole, the [sphere of] determinate existence, that has to be recognized, wherein individuals have their existence insofar as they are the actuality of the universal substance itself.

§ 70

An ethical disposition on the part of the subject involves setting aside reflection, which is always ready to pass over from universal substance to the particular. It involves knowing and recognizing the universal element of substance, the laws, as an eternal mode of being subsisting in and for itself and as the distinctive essence of self-consciousness; and it involves acting in, and being simply oriented toward, its substantive vocation, which for the individual is both a particular sphere and the sphere of universal substance. In the same way the ethical disposition in relation to natural and contingent circumstances consists in being oriented toward the situation in question as to a *mode of being* from which, to the extent that such being involves injury to the subject, the latter abstracts the infinitude of its will. In this way of looking at it, as positive relation to what is necessary, the subject salvages its free relation to the situation and to itself; and, while it may well experience natural pain, it does not regard itself as suffering wrong.

Substantiality is essentially disposition. Insofar as this disposition pertains essentially to the subject, it consists in recognizing the laws; and insofar as this cognition of the laws is subjective knowledge, a universal element is already posited as inherent in it. It is essential for the ethical disposition that the subject be educated in this way; what one has to do, one must do straight away without further hesitation. What is, what | must be, must be grasped immediately and done without more ado. This is where moral conceit intrudes. In the same way that it is one aspect of love, self-forgetfulness is also an essential aspect of ethical life. This constituted the character of Roman and Greek virtue, namely that all did straight away what was their duty, without moral hesitation and without the presumption of knowing better—the simple consciousness that the laws exist. This simple, undeviating, fixed orientation is a feature of the ethical disposition. Now individuals are assigned to a particular sphere in the whole substance, they have their particular sphere. In their ethical attitude they will the universal, but the particularity attaching to their activity—which has the universal as its end—means that each at his standpoint must do only what that standpoint requires. The whole is an organic life, in which the universal element is maintained only by each organ being active in its particular function—equipping oneself for one's particular sphere and, by being thus equipped, promoting the universal.

The subject also has a [detached[2]] attitude to contingent circumstances, insofar as it is itself external. Its life in the whole and its life in its particular sphere are spiritually identical. But for human beings destiny consists in becoming entangled with necessity. The ethical character here consists in having a straight and simple orientation toward circumstances, being rigidly oriented toward one's situation in which the subject's freedom is infringed. The subject must see and judge: such are the circumstances, and in face of them this is what I have to do. But where the ethical disposition enters in is that the subject withdraws its will from that part of itself which is injured and makes it something external in relation to itself. All that belongs to human unhappiness is grounded in dependence on contingent circumstances. The extent to which human beings will feel the ensuing pain depends on the extent to which the injury involved higher interests for them, but they are aware that as far as their own inner being is concerned, these interests have the nature of contingency, that it is not for them to invest their ego | in the contingent injury. The loss results in pain, for there is a lack of concordance with their needs.

The truth is that the freedom of spirit does not reside in these things and that human beings do not believe they are being unjustly treated by destiny since they withdraw their will from these things; what they have to do is sacrifice those aspects that have sustained injury. But the individual can also endure wrong by demoting it to the level of mere being, [by taking the view that] wrong simply *is*. To linger in the feeling of being wronged gives rise to inaction because this feeling is confined to the negative attitude. If I am not "in" the injury with my free being, then the injury too becomes only a particular thing, and the universal is salvaged. Pity is also something inessential here. The intuition that "this is so" is one kind of intuition, a positive relation to negative circumstances. Those who merely

2. [*Tr.*] The German editors, in an attempt to make the sentence meaningful, have inserted the preposition *hin*, which usually suggests something further off or remote. The insertion of "detached" is our attempt to render this in English.

suffer have merely the feeling of the negative, but this fixed orientation results in the subject's still having its positivity in this negativity. Antigone laments her destiny, and feels the injury deeply; but in this inconstancy of the external state she still has knowledge of herself.[3] The positive resides in the act of intuiting that "it is." If one does not advance beyond saying "it shall not be," the individual remains at the stage of negativity that consists in saying "because it must be, I so will it," and force is denied the coercion it seeks to apply. Subjective willing, the subjective disposition is the right disposition to the extent that the will and disposition are the universal. Now this substantiality has a religious aspect.

§ 71

The ethical substance is absolute foundation. The spirit that is free from the particularity of subjectivity but that through subjectivity has become actual as the disposition and activity of spirit, set apart in this way for itself and known by the subject as its substance, is the object of religious feeling, of religious intuition and contemplation. But the religious element [das Religiöse] remains partly in [the sphere of] feeling and in [a state of] indeterminacy with regard to the organic | particularization and actuality of the substance, and contains only contingent thoughts. In part the substance itself is limited at its various stages, and to this extent religion [is] negative toward these its aspects, or else [it] grasps their universal element only in its entirety. While religion can accordingly be called a *form of the ground* of ethical life, it is no more than the feeling and intuition of this ground.

In recent times several things have been made merely civil matters. For instance marriage has been made to depend on the mere arbitrariness of contract, and the root of family ties has been located in something arbitrary. In the same way the state has been regarded as stemming from the individuality of the

87

3. [Ed.] Hegel is probably referring here to Sophocles' *Antigone* 450–470. In another connection he refers in his *Phenomenology of Spirit* (trans. A. V. Miller, Oxford, 1977) to the same passage (p. 261). Cf. *Gesammelte Werke* 9:236, 509.

subjects. Once the freedom of individuals was made the sole ground of the state, the aim of the state became their mutual limitation. And since the individuality of the person was thus made the basis, the state became a state based on need [*Notstaat*], on coercion; for the individual subjects it became a third party. In opposition to this relationship of a merely civil contract in the family, and in opposition to the state based on need, the contrary view has been advanced that it is universal spirit, the unity of spirit, that must constitute the [ethical] substance, not spirit as individual volition.

The ethical substance is free from this particularity; individuality is sublated. Spirit that is actual is the substantive spirit, and it is in its disposition as universal attitude that it has its essence, to the extent that it is set apart for itself. In relation to public life the substantive spirit is the peculiar spirit of the people, the spirit that is within all, yet remains in undisturbed unity. In family life it is the basis of the *lares* [protecting deities]. Now religion is nothing other than the consciousness of spirit as universal, absolute spirit. Heathen religion differs from the Christian religion in that the spirits are limited spirits [by reason of] the transition to universal spirit. The spirit that a people worships as essential being ought not to be merely the spirit of the particular people in question, as with the Greeks and Romans, but to coalesce with the universal spirit. God is not to be represented as something otherworldly, as an ideal to be striven toward; in the ethical | substance God is omnipresent, is something living. This relationship characterizing religion lies in the [sphere of] feeling, and extends no further: it is a knowing of the substance, an immediate knowing, a believing, i.e., an immediate knowing that the subject has its essential being in this substance, the feeling of the nullity of the external side of the subject. Religion may be a relationship of fear, in which[4] the individual remains confined to the negative side, but the [cause of] trepidation resides in the fact that particular subjectivity for its part is the negativity of the substance in the consciousness of

88

4. *Ms. may also be read:* in that

nullity. Without fear there is no genuine love, for love is to feel the particular as of no account and to submerge it in universal consciousness. As actualized spirit the ethical substance particularizes itself and thus becomes actual. But since religion remains fixed on the deity as such, particularization remains extraneous to the deity, and the religious side contains thoughts, reverence, but only thought directed to something remote.[5] Religion is essentially a mode of thinking; the element of religion is at all events thought, but it is only an immediate thinking, an intuiting.

The extension of thought, in such a way that the concept differentiates itself as something concrete, no longer belongs to the aspect of religion. The [ethical] substance is a particular substance; it has different stages, e.g., family and state, and these in turn particularize themselves inwardly. The attitude of religion to such particularization is negative. What the religious sphere comprises is the fact of rising above particularization. If it remains solely a religious sphere, it eschews all particularization; and if particularization is carried over into life, is made existent [existent], it gives rise to religious fanaticism. With this form all distinction of particularization disappears. Freedom and equality ought to be actual, and all ordering had the form of the negative; such was religious fury. If the religious sphere seeks to be the only form, without fanaticism, then we have the piety of inactivity, content merely for human beings to love each other as Christians. This piety spells the disappearance of public life. So 89 [it is] with the Quakers. | Nevertheless they have no choice but to renege on their principle of living as purely private persons and live in the state and engage in business.

Religion can be called the form of the ground of ethical life, but this ground must pass over into existence [Existenz]. God would not be God if he did not become finite and know himself in this finite condition. Authentic actuality is to know oneself in one's reality. In religion it must come to consciousness that the true constitutes the ground [of actuality]. Religion does involve

5. [Tr.] The German plays on three forms of the word Denken, "thinking." Gedanken means "thoughts"; Andacht, "reverence" or "devotion," suggests "thinking of"; and Hindenken is a thinking directed to something far off (hin).

the relation of the particular to the universal, e.g., that supreme authority rests with God or that the individual laws derive from God. Now the aspect that one has in mind here is that these things have within them something divine, but as it occurs in the positive religions it is something false.

§ 72

The ethical substance is:

(1) the immediate or natural ethical substance, the *family* [*Familie*], which passes over into

(2) *civil society* [*bürgerliche Gesellschaft*], which has initially as its aim the relationships and protection of individuals in their particular interests, but essentially it draws itself together into

(3) a *constitution of the state* [*Staatsverfassung*], a public life and activity in and for the universal.

In its immediate, natural mode the ethical substance is family, which is based on unity of sentiment, on love. The family cannot remain in this immediate state; through its activity it comes in contact with others, who are also members of a family. In this way there comes into being *civil society*, in which each family exists as individual. The purpose of this association is to protect individuals in their relationships, in their particular interests. The basis here is an external civil relationship; families confront each other in business and occupational affairs. Concern for individuals is also useful and is thus the concern of all. Here the burgher [*Bürger*] is a bourgeois.[6] The relationship [between families or individuals] is here one of civil trade, and this concerns the state economy and the right of jurisdiction and authority exercised by the police. The third stage is public life, | where life in and for the universal is the aim, where substantive life has determinate existence, and where the individual exists for universal life as a public person, in other words is a

90

6. [*Tr.*] The German word for "citizen" (*Bürger*) is similar to the French *bourgeois*, which conveys the idea of an inhabitant of a market town (*bourg*) and hence refers to an economic as opposed to a political or public function; the latter is designated in French by the term *citoyen*. Hegel alludes to this distinction here and in § 89.

citizen [*Citoyen*]. Here it is the state that is taken as individual for itself, one state as over against others.

1. The Family

§ 73

The family has as its foundation the immediate substantiality of spirit, in other words self-*sensing* unity or *love*, the disposition of individual persons whereby they have their essential self-consciousness in this unity.

That the free will of the person occurs as an individual will is a subordinate standpoint. The rights that are founded on the family are different from the rights we dealt with in the case of property; their foundation is quite distinct and of another kind. Here we are dealing with substantive freedom and the foundation is a universal will, whereas the will on which property rests is of a kind remote from substantive freedom. Personality, which is at the basis of ownership or property, is here rather dissolved. The family is here founded on an identity of will. This is the truth of the will, namely that according to its concept it is a universal will. The disposition is here an essential moment, the moral moment, in which, however, the good itself constitutes the actual identity. This consciousness, or ethical life, has the shape of love, of the self-consciousness that one has not in oneself but in another, in whom one has one's own self-consciousness in such a way that this knowledge of the identity [of self and other] is the essential matter. Self-consciousness knows itself to be conscious of itself in the other, and is the intuiting, the feeling of this unity. | The consequences of this family relationship will emerge as we consider the aspects of family life in more detail.

91

§ 74

There are three aspects of the family to be considered:

(1) The family relationship itself in its immediacy.

(2) In terms of the external existence in which it invests itself: family property [*Eigentum*] and capital [*Gut*].

(3) The education of children and the dissolution of the family.

The second aspect involves the process whereby the will of the family invests itself with external existence. This is where the relationship of right as such enters into play, but in a manner subordinate to universal substantiality. The third aspect comprises the transition upon which the family enters, the departure of children to found new families of their own.

A. The Family as Relationship in Its Concept

§ 75

Because this substantiality is immediate, it implies the aspect of *naturalness* [*Natürlichkeit*], of organic vitality. To this extent the idea is the universal in the form of species, the latter being differentiated into natural sexes, whose *particularity*, however, is at variance with their immanent universality, the universality of the species, and is accordingly the drive toward self-sublation. In the natural state the identity of the sexes is distinct from themselves as natural beings, particularly as beings existing for themselves; [it is] a third factor that is *produced*, in which both sexes intuit their identity as a natural actuality and which itself both has the feeling of this unity and also, by its nature, needs help because it does not yet exist for itself.

The universal exists in nature in such a way that existence [*Existenz*] is always individuality; and only the species, the inner being, is the universal. Particularization is male and female, [the second stage] is the union of the sexes, and the third is what is produced, the product. In its immediacy the [ethical] substance is | what is living, the totality of the natural order in general. The moment of immediacy involves setting oneself up in opposition. The transition from the general concept of the ethical to what is living has been made in such a way that the first stage, the natural order, exists. All we have here as yet is the immediate substance; subsequently this immediacy passes over and is sublated. At the higher standpoint we no longer have, as here, something merely posited. Absolute totality in fact consists in this process of self-diremption. And to this extent natural, organic life is something posited. Life is the highest level

92

that nature can attain. What has being in and for itself only becomes for itself by opposing something to itself, and for it to do so being must first be posited. The universal does not yet exist in nature as universal, but only in thought; in spirit the species has being for itself.

The immediate mode of the universal's existence [*Existenz*] is the difference between the sexes; this constitutes particularization, the aspect of determinacy, of determinate existence [*Dasein*]. So we have the contradiction that this particularity is at variance with the species, and this contradiction is a deficiency for the universal; this feeling of an inner negative constitutes the drive [for self-sublation]. The inorganic cannot be its own and its other, or else it is neutralized; but what is living feels this deficiency, and this feeling of deficiency constitutes the drive to make itself the species. In its determinate existence the substantive will is totality; the universal concept is the inner being, the species; particularization is the difference between the sexes. The organic is in the first place inner process. This does not belong here; here we are dealing only with the species. The one particular entity has the feeling of its identity in the other particular entity. In them is the drive to posit the species; there is the contradiction that in their determinate existence they are only particular beings yet have the species within them. They are restricted and have their restriction within themselves, in their power.

This is the necessary contradiction that belongs to the complement of the concept; since the deficiency is made good by union with the opposite, the drive, one's own | feeling, is satisfied. Human beings feel themselves in otherness; only in otherness are they conscious of their own preservation. In the natural order the unity is an existing, self-posited unity, whereas in the spirit this is not the case. At the standpoint of consciousness the concept is my concept, not distinct from me: both are identical. Actualized identity is reproduction, the result, the product. Those who reproduce intuit their identity in their offspring, and their offspring have the feeling of unity; [the child has] its roots in the family from which it [has] sprung. In it, in the child, the species has attained determinate existence. The germ of a plant contains the whole determination, the whole nature of the plant, the leaves, flowers, and fruit according to their particular properties. This is ideally present in the germ, as thought. With this offspring the species begins; and the offspring is in need of help, for it has not yet posited itself in opposition to the external world or in the opposition between the sexes. For human beings to become what they ought to be, a major process of development is required.

§ 76

The way in which this merely natural relationship is raised and transformed to the *ethical* is that the species is rationality, i.e., the *inner* unity and universality of the purely natural sexes in self-consciousness, occurring here as the disposition of substantive unity; and that this love, along with the knowing and actuality inherent in it, is the essential element and goal. The drive and passion vanishes in its satisfaction, turning into this relationship itself; and the rational, purified through this sublation of the natural, subjective side, emerges as conjugal love.

The merely natural relationship becomes immediately an ethical one; this is in principle the transition from the animal to the ethical. The animal is species, but not species for itself; in nature existence [*Existenz*] takes the form of species. The species becomes *for* the species through the death of the individual; but the power of the species—a power it demonstrates in the successive generations[7]—is such that of its own doing it emerges again as individual. The species, the inner universality, becomes intelligence, will, the universal knowing itself, and this is what | 94 being-for-self is. In self-consciousness the species is rationality knowing itself as universal; the sexes know universality, and this immediate knowing, this feeling, is love. This makes family life something rational and ethical. Now the aim of sexual union is that this love, this rationality, should take on determinate existence in the partners' life. The drive and passion vanishes, etc.

7. [*Tr.*] The German word *Geschlecht* can mean either "sex" or "generation."

141

Love is a universal term: sometimes it means the unsatisfied feeling of the sexes for one another. Where this unity is not yet actualized, we have unsatisfied love, love as drive, as passion. Passion means that the subject feels the disappearance of its particular subjectivity and is gripped by a feeling of universal self-consciousness. To love is therefore to feel the potency of negative unity and to suffer in the feeling that what ought to be—the feeling of extinction as a wholly separate subject and rebirth in the other—does not yet exist. Passion has only one object, in which the universal self-consciousness is bound up; being in love means that one is of the opinion that only through this specific object can [one] pass over into universality. This moment of particularity is based on the view that one's own particular qualities must be one's starting point. It used to be otherwise, when parents chose spouses for their children according to their insight and sense of duty, the basis being that the parents have the thought of duty and the insight that children must be married. The girl then loved the husband determined for her because he was to be her husband, and vice versa. Here love does not begin in chance inclination, in the free choice [Willkür] of the subject, but in the thought of determination; it can be said that this way of doing things is the more ethical. But with us, the particular inclination contains the thought that there can be only this one subject with whom one can enter into matrimony. Infinite and lofty as this feeling may be, nonetheless | only the particular interest of these two lovers is involved, and it arises only out of a sympathy for others. Antigone is destined for the son of Creon, yet it is not the interest of love that leads Creon to choose her, but the interest of the state.[8] And this love, or being in love, is for the most part the object of our comedies and tragedies.

But this being in love vanishes through satisfaction, and this subjectivity disappears as soon as marriage comes on the scene; the heroes of novels become like everyone else. Animals and weaker [forms of] nature do not survive mating; for example

8. [Ed.] Hegel is probably referring here to the conversation between Creon and Haemon in Sophocles' Antigone 726 ff.

the plant or its blossom dies off with pollination, and weaker animals too die in the satisfaction of passion. This negativity issues in ethicality; through the sacrifice of passion there arises platonic love. Since it is the particular personality that sacrifices itself in this relationship, it is it too that opposes the difficulties of entering into this relationship. The subject demands that its particular inclination, its particular free choice be satisfied, and it hesitates to place itself in a universal relationship. Love has many particular modifications, depending on its different relationships in actuality and on the immediate personality. Platonic love is the intuition of the beauty of soul, and it views the moment of transition to the sensual relationship as a debasement of this lofty conception. By its nature, everything negative has also a positive side, and it is the negative side that results in the ethical relationship. The drive and passion vanish in satisfaction, and so it is from the natural drive itself that the spiritual, substantive relationship arises. It is precisely through the satisfaction of the drive that platonic love attains its truth. For example in all of Wieland's novels there is first of all platonic love, which is then made ridiculous as a result of being actualized.[9] We are told in the Bible that Adam knew his wife Eve [Gen. 4:1]; the relationship of passion was past, and there emerged the relationship of conjugal love devoid of passion. | 96

§ 77

It is also through their rationality that the two natural sexes acquire their intellectual and ethical significance. Their differences are the moments of the concept, and each has in the other the intuition of its reality. Thus the one moment is the knowledge of its free universality, the self-consciousness of thought, and the willing of the universal, objective final end, while the other is the knowing

9. [Ed.] Despite the general terms in which the reference is couched, the following works by Christoph Martin Wieland are in all probability chiefly relevant in this regard: Der Sieg der Natur über die Schwärmerey, oder, Die Abenteuer des Don Silvio von Rosalva (Ulm, 1764); Geschichte des Agathon (Frankfurt am Main and Leipzig, 1766–1767); and Geheime Geschichte des philosophischen Peregrinus Proteus (Weimar, 1788–1789).

and willing of subjective individuality. In the natural relationship the former is therefore the powerful, actuating element in relation to the latter, which, as confining itself within subjectivity, is the receptive, submissive, abstractly universal element, like matter. The substantive life of the man is accordingly in the state; what pertains to natural needs, sensibility, and the particularity of life he finds in the family, in which the woman has her substantive life and in which her vocation lies.

The sexes are naturally different, but this difference is reconstructed within them by virtue of their rationality. Each sex contains both moments, but developed in different directions. In their relationship to each other, in being opposed in this way, both together constitute the whole; each has in the other the intuition of its reality. In general the man is the knowledge of free universality; his character is such that it is his element, his vocation, to bring forth what is rational. To the woman belongs the moment of the individuality of immediate life. At one time it was doubted whether the female sex formed part of the human race. Woman is a free being for herself, but the distinction between woman and man is presented by experience.

Man is made for the universal interest, disregarding subjectivity; to him belongs living and acting in the state, the realm of science and art. In nature a chance event may occur, a chance deviation from the essential vocation [of the sexes]. There have been women who applied themselves to the sciences, but they never penetrated deeply or made any discoveries; they can produce what is pleasing in art, but its ideal, plastic element is beyond the scope of their action. If women play a major role in a state, this is a | sign that the state is in its decline, for they introduce the subjectivity of interests. Women are oriented toward subjective individuality; their principal sphere of action is the family, the *lares* [protecting deities] and *hestia* [goddess of the hearth] are their concern. The man has within himself the absolutely substantive, the force, might, and form of activity. As the abstractly universal, whose basis is the interest of particularity, the woman does not have substantive but only abstract univer-

97

sality; she is the matter, the receptive material. The man must live in the state and seek to promote universal ends. The woman is responsible for the [other] side of substantive life, namely the family; the man only turns to the family to meet his substantive needs. The woman must supply the man with his needs, and the man must find mental refreshment [*Gemüt*] from his wife within the family so that, reinvigorated, he may rejoin the quest to further the universal. Only the imagination [*Einbildung*], the direct result of which, however, is to give a false image [*Verbildung*] of the two sexes, can tear them away from their [proper] vocation.

§ 78

Marriage is the formal union of two persons of differing sex, brought to public recognition and so acquiring the status of a legal relationship vis-à-vis others. It is a union by virtue of which they bind themselves to make *one* person in love and mutual trust and to recognize this substantive unity as their essential vocation and duty. While it is true that such unity rests essentially on their disposition, it is at the same time, as a rational, universal unity, a bond raised above the contingency of passion and of particular predilection, and it encompasses the different aspects of a particular determinate existence.

By means of marriage the union of the sexes becomes a legal relationship, entered into publicly, and this can be done in the state before either a religious or a secular authority. It is of the nature of the legal relationship that it must be protected against others in this relationship. But insofar as this relationship rests on the inner | disposition, the authorities can give [it] legal protection only to the extent that it possesses external moments. Trust is the awareness that my interest is the other party's own interest and duty. When two people marry, it is their common will to make one person; the wife loses her name and no longer belongs to her family. A disposition in the sense of a particular and passionate predilection is excluded here, because the union is a universal union, a union for the duration of life. To the

98

extent that an estrangement is only partial, only momentary, this does not affect the relationship as a whole, does not annul the universality of the relationship. It is only when the estrangement affects the general disposition that the whole relationship is annulled or can be annulled by the authorities. The underlying substantive unity is a divine, essentially substantive relationship, which in its determinate existence has various aspects. A particular aspect, such as the procreation of children, does not constitute its end, as in the case of animals, where perpetuation of the species is the highest end. In concubinage, the memory of the sexual relationship is predominant, whereas in marriage the principal element is unity. In the same way the *mutuum adjutorium* [reciprocity of assistance] is only a particular end. So it is possible for people to marry even if one of them can no longer have children. The marriage union unites the different aspects of a particular determinate existence, and no single aspect is an absolute end on its own account.

§ 79

Marriage is indeed based on the particular consent of the two parties, but this does not make it a contract *properly* speaking, a *civil contract*, because the parties do not give up only their particular right to individual objects. On the contrary, the whole immediate personality is mutually sublated and enters into union, which for this very reason comprises the essential moment of the [marital] disposition.

Marriage is not a contract properly speaking, not a civil contract. It has been regarded as an improvement that marriage is currently | viewed as a civil contract and [has been] wrested away from the church. Marriage can be an ecclesiastical contract to the extent that it is an ethical relationship in which the individual partners give up their arbitrary will and make unity, which is an ethical and thus religious quality, their end. Contracts regarding the actual property of the spouses do not affect the marriage itself. The authority whose guarantee is needed for the marriage may indeed be the ecclesiastical authority, though this is not necessarily so; it may also be the authority of the state qua ethical state. For example in France a family court constituting an ethical authority was ordained as court in marital cases.

Kant presents marriage in a shameful, ugly manner; he says that marriage is a contract whereby each of the spouses gives his or her sexual parts to the other to use.[10] In this contract human beings make themselves a thing, though Kant believes that personality is restored to both by virtue of the fact that making oneself a thing is reciprocal. He goes on to say that to acquire a limb or member of a human being is to acquire the whole person.[11] If one spouse leaves the other, the fact that the marriage is publicly recognized means that the external authority can decide in regard to this external action, for this does not extend to the disposition. Moreover, the relationship is on a higher plane than mere predilection, and the fact of leaving one's spouse in no way implies the total alienation of the spouse's disposition. But Kant is wrong in saying that the other spouse has the right to lay claim to the absconding spouse as a *thing*.[12] It is the same with abandoning some piece of mental or physical labor for the other spouse. [This] always involves the particularity of work and limitation of time; what I surrender is only a particular right, the subsumption of a particular thing under my will. But what enters into the marriage relationship is the whole personality; the parties mutually surrender themselves as

10. [*Ed.*] Hegel is here referring to Kant's *Rechtslehre*, p. 107 (§ 24). Cf. Kant, *Schriften* 6:277–278.

11. [*Ed.*] Hegel is here referring, in part almost verbatim, to Kant's *Rechtslehre*, pp. 108–109 (§ 25): "[The] natural use that one sex makes of the sexual organs of the other is an enjoyment for which one party surrenders itself to the other. In this act persons make themselves into things, which conflicts with their human rights in regard to their own person. The sole condition under which this is possible is that, in one person's being acquired by the other (as it were as a thing), the latter in reciprocal fashion acquires the former; for in this way each regains himself and reestablishes his personality. But to acquire one of the limbs of a person is to acquire his entire person. . . ." Cf. Kant, *Schriften* 6:278.

12. [*Ed.*] Kant, *Rechtslehre*, p. 108 (§ 25). Cf. Kant, *Schriften* 6:278.

a whole. The man retains for himself the universal side, what pertains to activity for the rational universal.

In the field of right the disposition | is superfluous; it makes no difference what my disposition is when I act, whereas in marriage the disposition itself is an absolute moment. The question of what authority is the guarantor of the marriage has been discussed, but it is a matter for the constitution of the state whether the guarantee is the responsibility of the ethical state, acting through its official agencies, or of the church.

§ 80

In essence marriage is *monogamous* because it is only between *two* persons of different sex that this specific relationship of inwardness can occur. Any other number distorts it, because it is inherent in the very concept of this union that one enters it as an immediate person, in exclusive individuality. Moreover because the disposition is an essential moment—the foundation of marriage—there can be as little compulsion to enter into marriage as there can be of any other positive bond capable of holding it together when there is *total* revulsion and hostility of disposition. A third, ethical authority is necessary, however, partly to counter mere opinion about such a disposition and the detailed circumstances comprising it, partly to distinguish such circumstances from total estrangement, and [finally] to take official notice of total estrangement where it has occurred in order to pronounce a *divorce*.

The third point, that of a ban on marriage on the count of consanguinity, belongs to the third moment, that of the dissolution of marriage. It has been held that monogamy, like marriage itself, could not be justified on the basis of the natural right that obtains at the natural standpoint.[13] It is only what pertains to freedom that provides the basis for marriage. There is in principle no distinction between bigamy and polygamy, in that plu-

---

13. [*Ed.*] Hegel is possibly referring here to Kant's *Rechtslehre*, pp. 109–110 (§ 26). Cf. Kant, *Schriften* 6:278–279. He is possibly also thinking of Montesquieu's *De l'esprit des lois*, book 16, chap. 4, pp. 352–353. Cf. Montesquieu, *Œuvres complètes*, p. 511.

rality knows no limit. The natural ratio of male to female births has [also] been taken as a basis; but these natural data do not affect rationality—this is one of the chance circumstances that manifest themselves in the state. (It was in fact found that there were more marriageable persons of female gender.) | Because in marriage the immediate personality is given up and unity enters on the scene, this unity is not possible in polygamy, particularly [since] the two or more husbands or wives of a marriage partner cannot enter into unity with one another, or be married to one another. If the husband has several wives, the wife does not attain to her rights, and the marriage does not become a genuinely ethical relationship, but remains at the natural standpoint. In India women are capable of having children only from twelve to twenty years of age.

101

But this very disparity of the two sexes in creating and procreating is a proof that the procreation of children cannot be the essential, sole end of marriage. Disposition is an essential feature of marriage, which rests on the voluntary consent of both parties so that, even if the parents are opposed, the laws recognize the will of the parties as sufficient. The opposition of the parents cannot be an absolute obstacle. The more cultivated a people is, the wider the sphere assigned to the purely private disposition, etc. There may be estrangement in the marriage; the spouses may not have known each other sufficiently. Marriage ought in principle to be indissoluble, for it ought not to rest on the passion of an instant from which estrangement could arise. In any event a third authority, an ethical authority, is needed to act in the case of disputes between spouses. It is often the case that relatives themselves seek to settle such disputes. The authority may be an ecclesiastical or secular court. But since it is customs that constitute the essential moment of marriage, it is principally customs that such courts must bear in mind. There would be nothing more desirable than that marriage should be declared inviolable and that the spouses should live for each other in mutual relationship. When the question was under discussion in France the view was expressed that it was ridiculous for a husband to complain of his wife's infidelity, particularly since it was shameful for him not to have managed to prevent it. Customs make laws and laws make customs. |

B. Family Property and Capital

§ 81

As family property, property acquires the character of a possession that is independent of contingencies and is secure and enduring, namely, *capital* [*Gut*].[14] It is only with the family that continuous income becomes requisite and that the self-interestedness of desires becomes a communally beneficial concern for something held in common, becomes a duty.

Family possessions are something universal, to be used to care for the whole. They are independent of contingencies and time. For the family is something enduring, something lasting, so its possessions also do not depend on individual circumstances. Property relates to the legal aspect of possession; the family requires to have capital, lasting possessions and income. What individuals do they do not do for themselves, so it is not a matter of self-interestedness, directed to satisfying individual needs, but rather each is concerned for something universal.

§ 82

The husband is the head of the family and has to represent it externally to the extent that it exists as a legal person in relation to others. It is also for him to control and administer the family capital; but this capital is common property, and no member of the immediate family has particular property.

To the extent that the family has property, it enters into a re-

---

14. [*Tr.*] *Gut* here means the goods, possessions, wealth, resources, estate owned by a family. As used by Hegel, it is a term related to but distinct from *Eigentum* ("property") and *Besitz* ("possession"), and functions as a synonym for *Vermögen* ("resources," "estate"). In the published edition of the *Philosophy of Right* (1821), *Vermögen* is used in the corresponding paragraph (§ 170). In the Heidelberg lectures, Hegel uses several terms meaning "capital": *Gut, Fond, Kapital* (cf. § 118).

lationship to other persons, a legal relationship. In this relationship the husband's role is to represent the family, while the wife's essential activity is inside the home.

§ 83

With the husband's authority over the family property, an authority that includes only the ethical duty to conserve it and to care for the family's subsistence, the communal nature of property | and the right that all members have to it come into conflict. This 103 is the reason for marriage settlements between spouses that would otherwise be invalid, and for arrangements to secure, or attempt to secure, the family property in some other way inconsistent with the free ownership of property (which by nature is a thing, not an item of capital) and with the changing character of external existence in general. Something universal is therefore required in which the conflict is resolved in both its legal and its economic aspects, as well as detailed provisions governing among other things the family's capacity to inherit property in light of civic interests and dependent on recognition by the state.

The conflict that arises here is as follows. Family property is supposed to be something solid, lasting, universal, for here we are considering an ethical aspect where whim no longer has any place, since [it] is the property of the family, of an ethical, essential, inner whole. As head of the family the husband is necessarily responsible for the control and administration of the estate [*Vermögen*]—and the conflict lies in the fact that he has the ethical duty to preserve and increase the family property, but also has the right of control over it, whereas all other members of the family should not have any rights over against him, who is its head.

Many institutions in the different nations are concerned with the enduring character of family capital. But the true relationship is one of common ownership: the spouses may not own particular property as particular individuals. In marriage settlements the husband secures to the wife certain property which remains hers even after his death, and in this way the wife's property is preserved for the family and is safeguarded against all contingencies and the dangers to which the husband is exposed by the requirement to earn a living for the family and by his freedom to act as he chooses. These contracts have often, however, had the peculiarity that the wife continued to be regarded as still remaining in her [former] family, and if she died without children her estate reverted to her family. But this is wrong, for the new bond of marriage is not seen as what is alone essential. When the Israelites conquered Canaan, each family received its own plot of land, and even if it sold | or mortgaged it, etc., after forty-nine years, in the so-called jubilee year, it got it back free.[15] These measures to confer an enduring character on family property are in conflict with the free ownership of property in general, as an essential corollary of the concept of full ownership. From the point of view of political economy, however, it was found that landed property in the hands of private owners was better cultivated than property that the person concerned tends only for a community and in which he has not the same interest as in what he owns freehold. A further factor is that the members of families are *glebae adscripti* [assigned to a plot of land], and usually the only reason why communal ownership holds them together is that this is inherent in the nature of this relationship.

In general terms family capital constitutes an indestructible stem, but it is contrary to the nature of the case to form so solid a relationship from something external. Civil society as such, however, is the essential, ethically abiding soil in regard to which each can gain a portion for himself; and here there comes into play the system wherein all labor for the benefit of all, each participating as his own capability and aptitudes permit. This conflict, i.e., its ethical aspect, is thus resolved by the state. The state must see to it that the family is given the right that the husband should use his aptitudes for the benefit of the family, so the state is fully entitled to take charge of the family estate if

15. [*Ed.*] For the "jubilee year" and its associated customs see Leviticus 25: 8–34.

the husband is a spendthrift. If the family property is ruined by chance or misfortune, the state, as universal entity, also has the duty to maintain the particular individual members of the family. On the political plane many different nations have ensured [the permanence of] family property by providing that spouses who have children could not make testamentary dispositions such as would prove ruinous to the family property. The right of primogeniture can also be introduced in the interests of the constitution where it is the intention of the constitution to have an aristocracy. The conflict consists in the fact that no single member of the family has an exclusive particular right to family property, while the husband as head of the family must have the right of control. |

105

§ 84

The common ownership of family property forms the basis for the *right of inheritance*, which is not an acquisition of alien property or property that no longer has any owner, but the coming into one's right of control or distinctive possession of capital that is essentially owned in common—a process that becomes more and more indeterminate as the degree of kinship becomes more remote.

The doctrine of inheritance cannot therefore be dealt with under the acquisition of property. By virtue of the supposition that the members of the family were closest to the deceased, it might be said that, in order to obviate the inconveniences of the seizure of an estate that as a result of death had become *res nullius* [owned by no one], it can be assumed that the family members would normally seize [it]; and it was consequently handed over to them. This is Fichte's conclusion.[16] But according to the principles we have laid down, the situation is different. In dividing the inheritance regard must be had to degrees of kinship. In the case of more distant relatives there can be the right to

16. [*Ed.*] Fichte, *Beitrag*, pp. 147 ff. Cf. Fichte, *Gesamtausgabe* 1:274–275. See also Johann Gottlieb Fichte, *Grundlage des Naturrechts nach Principien der Wissenschaftslehre, Zweiter Theil, oder Angewandtes Naturrecht* (Jena and Leipzig, 1797), pp. 92 ff. Cf. Fichte, *Gesamtausgabe* 4:57.

bequeath property by will, whereas children must receive their obligatory share. In many states the state inherited if there were no close relatives. One aspect of this is the taxes that can be imposed on an entailed estate. It is also the case that the more distant the relationship, the less do these distant relatives have this definite right to common ownership of the family estate. When the heirs are children, however, they are exempt from this estate duty. Equality of inheritance for relatives of like degree is the immediate relationship on which the division of the inheritance must rest.

But there are also other ends that states have pursued in regard to the transfer of property. For instance with more primitive peoples the possession of property was what ensured the preservation of the family. Under ancient Roman law the goods of one family could not pass to another family: the *sui heredes* [one's own heirs] and agnates inherited before the cognates, and the wife's estate reverted to her former family and did not pass to her children; | nor did the mother inherit the estate of the children. Children had no property of their own. If there were no agnates, the estate passed to members of the same *gens* [clan], though later the praetor called on cognates and agnates together. But with the Romans the right to bequeath property by will was carried too far; they could disinherit their children. This is also the basis for the legacy-hunting that Juvenal and others took as the subject matter for their satires.[17] The right to bequeath property itself also explains the existence of a distasteful relationship between the testator and those who have hopes of the inheritance and seek to obtain it by servility. This is the origin of the Lex Voconia, which debars women from being made heirs so that too large an estate should not remain in their hands. Family ties, which were the foundation of the Roman law of inheritance, became looser and looser. The equal distribution of property led to the rule that daughters could not inherit, in or-

106

17. [*Ed.*] See in this regard Juvenal's *Satires* 1.1.37–41, 1.4.18–19, 4.12.94 ff., 5.16.54–56. Also in his lectures on aesthetics Hegel deals with Juvenal and Persius only in the form of general references. Cf. *Werke* 10/2:118.

der that they should not adjoin a large estate of their own to that of their husbands. From this [consideration originate] several laws of the Greeks, who took steps to prevent the unequal distribution of property as a prime reason for the decline of a republic. In Athens there were hard and fast provisions governing dowries, and in Sparta the fact that most landed estates were in the possession of women brought ruin to the state.

But the equal distribution of an estate can remain no more than a desideratum since the size of an estate is the affair of chance. This is why modern states allow wealth to accumulate without restraint and have institutions to care for the lower classes.

C. The Education of Children
and the Dissolution of the Family

§ 85

Children have the right to be maintained and educated out of the communal family property. The parents' right to their children's services is based upon and restricted to the common task of looking after the family and education generally. Similarly the parents' right | over their children in regard to their freedom and life is re- 107 stricted to the end in view, namely to discipline and educate them. In accord with the basic [family] relationship, the purpose of punishment is here essentially moral in nature, not a matter of justice but of the improvement and deterrence of a freedom that is still in the toils of nature.

Children are an element in the family, but their aim is to leave it. Children belong to the family as a whole, so have the right to call on the family estate for their needs and their education [*Erziehung*]. And should the parents refuse to do this for their children, the state must intervene in order to maintain and enforce this right. It must not be the parents' aim merely to derive benefit from their children's labors; the state has in consequence a duty to protect children. For example in England six-year-old children are obliged to sweep narrow chimneys, and it is the same in manufacturing towns in England where young children have to go out to work and only on Sundays is anything done for their education. Here the state has an absolute duty to ensure that children are educated.

The services children render within the family also must not conflict with their education. Children must be accustomed to obey and must be compelled to renounce at an early stage in their conduct subjective capriciousness and whim. Children must be trained [*gebildet*] and educated; this is the rational basis underlying the relationship. According to Kant, children form part of the home, so when they run away their parents have the right to seize them as things.[18] Among the Romans the fathers' power over their children extended to their life and liberty; they could punish their children as judges. But the judge is, as such, a universal person and must prosecute the right without regard to the individual's welfare; by contrast the father must be concerned with the welfare of his children, and this is a moral aspect. Parents may tend on the contrary to be harder on their children than the judge in that they may be under much greater provocation; | for they see themselves in their children, and there is often a sense of personal injury, whereas with the judge there is no question of any sense of injury being involved. For this reason parents are very often less effective at instructing their children than teachers from outside the family.

108

Children do not yet have actual free will, they are not yet persons; they are consequently ruled by their parents and made persons, educated. The relationship between parents and children is the bond of love, so a father cannot make his child a slave or kill it as happened with the ancient Romans. Otherwise the relationship is merely a heartless, external bond, not an ethical bond assuming a religious form; it is no more than a superstition, and spirit is no longer immanent within it. The parents' authority is restricted to the aim of having a disciplined home and educating the children; the sole purpose of punishments is the moral one of improvement. Deterrence can have an effect

18. [*Ed.*] Kant, *Rechtslehre*, p. 115 (§ 29). Cf. Kant, *Schriften* 6:282.

on the natural side because children are still, with their freedom, in the toils of nature. So deterrence plays an essential role here. For the educator, the child exists as a concrete object on whose disposition the educator has to work.

§ 86

In regard to the family relationship, the aim of education is in general to raise children out of natural immediacy, in which they find themselves originally, to independence and free personality, and so enable them to leave the family, the substantive natural unity of which is thus dissolved.

The aim of education is to subjugate the natural, immediate aspect and bring into prominence the aspect of self-determination or freedom. Spirit consists only in making itself what it is through its immediate activity. Human beings can only become free through the negativity involved in sublating natural life. Discipline | must begin with obedience, for one who has not learned 109 to serve cannot rule; the entire capriciousness of children must be sublated. Spirit must come to the consciousness of its negativity. The child must come to view the free personality of the older members of the family as its own and submit to their will. The child has the proper feeling of its dependence and obeys the rational personality of its parents, to whom it is bound by love. What sets children on the upward path is their impulse to grow or mature, dissatisfaction with their present self.

According to Montesquieu there are, unhappily, three kinds of education human beings undergo, from one's parents, [from one's] teachers and instructors, and from the world; and the education one receives from the world, fitting one as a citizen, stands in contrast to the other two kinds.[19] The first kind, education by one's parents, is characterized by love, trust, and obedience; parents must concern themselves with their children, whether they are good or bad. This kind of education does not depend on the moral worth of the child, whose status is still

---

19. [Ed.] Montesquieu, De l'esprit des lois, book 4, chap. 4, p. 45. Cf. Montesquieu, Œuvres complètes, p. 266.

that of a child only. At school the child is judged according to what it is, according to its deserts; here the aspect of merit does come partly into play. In the world, however, justice comes into play; human beings are of value not merely because they *are*, but through their merits. But the commonwealth also has the right to pay heed to the education of children.

The character of the parents and the character of the world both play a principal role. A distinction has often been drawn between cultivation [*Bildung*] of the heart and cultivation of the intellect, but to the extent that both constitute true education (not formal education), they are interconnected. Of necessity children exist at first essentially in the sphere of love, of the family; it is dangerous to remove children even from parents who have a bad influence on them, for even bad parents love their children, and in this feeling the children must necessarily grow stronger. The initial education of children comes essentially from the character of the parents; it is this that draws them into the actual world. But this does not mean that children acquire precisely | the character of their parents: for instance, a very industrious mother may bring up lazy daughters, or a violent father may by his violence bring up timid sons. Morally religious parents can make their children sick of the moral commandments because the children get the feeling of not acting from themselves. The character of the world colors the child's every representation of the positive or negative value of things. All of us are children of our time; it is only those who follow wholly the spirit of their age that attain greatness in their time. It is true that high-minded teachers can achieve a great deal with children, but it is a mistake to do as Pestalozzi and others have done and withdraw children from the world and educate them in such a way as to give them [only] their own interests.[20] This kind of education makes good private persons but not good citizens. It is by sensing higher aims in their parents that children become inwardly dissatisfied [with their present level]. For ex-

110

20. [*Ed.*] In this very generally worded reference criticizing and apparently reinterpreting the Swiss educator Johann Heinrich Pestalozzi, Hegel is probably

ample they are taught to make cardboard boxes, and since those teaching them pay a great deal of regard to the good workmanship of the boxes, the children believe they are thereby attaining a higher level of interests since they see their teachers very interested in their work. Once children leave the parental home for school, the principle that comes into play is no longer that of immediate validity but of merit. Now the aim of education is for children to become independent persons and pass over from the sphere of love and obedience into that of free personality. For the members of the family form only one whole. This is the basis for the transition from the family to civil society.

But we still have to consider the further aspect that the founding of new families, which enters on the scene with the emergence of free personality, does not take place within blood relationships. The aim of education is negative in relation to the immersion of freedom in nature. The dissolution of the family has two aspects: (1) that those who have left the family themselves reenter the family, and (2) so form other families for themselves. |

111

§ 87

One specific feature of the dissolution of the family is that the natural unity, the blood relationship, endures merely as ethical love, and that those [who] are so related by nature for that very reason introduce mutual separation, avoid entering into a marital relationship with each other, and when entering upon marriage take as their point of departure natural nonrelatedness.

It has been maintained that marriage between blood relatives is not forbidden by nature; however, most peoples find it repugnant. The rational basis of this feeling has been indicated in the above paragraph. For one thing, it is in accord with nature, since otherwise the race degenerates. But it is already inherent in rationality itself that the previous unity within the family

referring to his *Lienhard und Gertrud* (4 vols., Basel, 1781–1789), and specifically the volume *Wie Gertrud ihre Kinder lehrt* (Bern and Zurich, 1801). But possibly he is also referring to Pestalozzi's practical activity in the children's homes and educational institutions he founded, especially the one in Yverdon.

should be sublated and that poles of the same name repel each other—those things that are already identical repel each other—and only those who are not of the same name attract each other. All strength, all energy rests on the opposition from which unity arises. Montesquieu adduces the fact of having previously lived together as the ground for keeping a sense of shame among members of a family;[21] but marriage has after all an ethical significance, while the sense of shame is in fact based on this mutual avoidance which is incumbent on blood relatives. Love between brothers and sisters must remain as an ethical feeling. A sister cherishes in more inward fashion love for her brother, whose action reaches out into the world. Antigone indicates the reason why, in order to pay the last honors to her brother, she risked her life for love of him: she would not have exposed herself to death for her children's or her husband's sake because she could get another husband and other children, but never another brother.[22] What makes *our* tragedies so lifeless is the chance nature of the object that is loved. But with Antigone what happens is necessary: she is so firmly attached to this original bond of her family. |

112

§ 88

The family disintegrates in natural fashion into a plurality of families whose reciprocal conduct is governed by their freedom as independent persons. Based on the substantive unity of the family, their individuality remains at the same time contained within the principle of universality—even if initially, by virtue of its separation from that of individuality, this principle is one of formal universality. This reflexive relationship of the two principles constitutes *civil society [bürgerliche Gesellschaft]*.

In the case of the family, the universality is absorbed by one member. The principle of universality [of the one member] and the principle of universality [of the family] confront each other

21. [*Ed.*] Montesquieu, *De l'esprit des lois*, book 26, chap. 14, pp. 142 ff. Cf. Montesquieu, *Œuvres complètes*, pp. 763 ff.
22. [*Ed.*] See Sophocles, *Antigone* 905–911.

[as independent principles]. The fact that it is independent means that the universality is not an essential universality. One family grows into many families, and once the many families form a people [*Volk*], the patriarchal aspect of the families [in originating] from one family disappears. The Jewish people originated from one family. It also happens, however, that many scattered families may be brought together to form one people, for instance by a conqueror.

2. Civil Society

§ 89

The more precise concrete characteristic of universality in civil society is that the subsistence and welfare of individuals is conditioned by and interwoven with the subsistence and welfare of all other individuals. This communal system provides individuals with the framework of their existence [*Existenz*] and with security both externally and in regard to right. So civil society is in the first place the *external state* or the *state as the understanding envisages it* [*Verstandesstaat*], since universality does not as such take the form of purpose in and for itself, but of means for the existence [*Existenz*] and preservation of single individuals—the *state based on need* [*Notstaat*]—because the main purpose is to secure the needs [*Bedürfnisse*]²³ [of individuals].

Here the burghers are *bourgeois*, not *citoyens*.²⁴ | Individuals ¹¹³ have their own welfare as their purpose, they are persons governed by right, and the moment of right emerges in a universal form. But the individual's welfare and subsistence are conditioned by the welfare and preservation of all. Individuals care only for themselves, have only themselves as purpose, but they cannot care for themselves without caring for all and without all caring for them. With their own selfish purposes they also

---

23. [*Tr.*] In this and the following paragraphs, Hegel uses two closely related terms: *Bedürfnis(se)*, which we translate as "need" or "needs," and *Not*, translated as "need" or "necessity."
24. [*Tr.*] See above, § 72, n. 6.

labor at the same time for others. Here everything, including all acquisition of property, rests on contract. Every product is a product of many others; every individual product that satisfies my needs presupposes this chain of production. All work in confidence that their work will be used. Here is the sphere of the mediation involved in the fact that the individual's purpose also has universality as one of its aspects. But here we do not yet have life within the universal *for* the universal. Here the purpose is the subsistence and right of the individual. The universality that is in question here is only abstract universality, a universality that is only means, so that this is the state as the understanding envisages it.

The purpose of acquiring rights is to satisfy one's needs; the protection and safeguarding of property in particular is the purpose of the state based on need. The unity of the family has fragmented, the ethical relationship of the family has dissolved, and the state based on need is not an ethical state. The family is something substantive and must raise itself to the being in and for self of ethical life by transcending the antithesis. The antithetical stage of the family is the state based on need, or abstract universality. Here individuals as independent agents have to see to their needs in one-sided fashion; these needs constitute necessity, and this necessity finds satisfaction only in the universal context.

§ 90

This sphere, in which human beings come on the scene as the concrete totality of their particularity and needs and have their particularity as their purpose, is the necessary moment of difference—the moment in which particular subjectivity, freedom of choice, arbitrary activity, and all the contingency attaching to nature | and happiness have their full play. The needs in question are not solely the immediate natural needs of animal life; nor are they the needs of the intelligence as it occurs in ethical life and scientific knowledge, the intelligence that has being in and for itself and has returned to itself from the sphere of difference and mediation. They are instead the former needs raising themselves to universality, and

114

the needs of the ethico-scientific intelligence shining through into the particular. In this sphere spirit is accordingly, in its formal universality and honesty, implicated in necessity and inconsistency with itself.

By "human being" [*Mensch*] we mean the concrete totality of our many energies. Issued from the substantive universality, human beings *are* this universality, but they have here for their purpose particularity. This is the moment of fragmentation, out of which ethical life comes to itself. It is by differentiating itself inwardly and then completing itself, making itself whole, for itself, that the idea is strengthened. And the absolute force of the idea consists in maintaining itself in the sphere of difference and returning to itself from the absolute loss of its essence; in their antithesis [by contrast] natural things perish. At the stage we are here dealing with, all the contingency attaching to nature and happiness has full play. In terms of existence [*Existenz*] the sphere of the state based on need is subsequent to the sphere of ethical life. The formal aspects of ethical life emerge later than the ethical totality itself.

Insofar as we are concerned with conceiving what is true, namely the ethical idea, the concept is what is concrete. What is primary and immediate is not yet in its truth. At the stage we have here, particular subjectivity is the purpose. The Christian principle is that each individual, as individual, is an infinite end. With the Oriental principle the individual disappears and is only an accident of the monarch or the priests. No state can subsist without the ends of universality, whereas in our modern states it is the viewpoint of subjectivity that is predominant, and much attention is paid to the welfare of the individual. Whenever this principle comes into play, the opposing aspect also manifests itself: in Athens, for instance, Diogenes and the Cynics arose to berate the proliferation of needs and pleasures and the resulting degeneration, | and to call people back to natural life, to the state of nature;[25] it was the same in Rome with Persius and Juvenal.[26]   115

---

25. [*Ed.*] See Hegel's treatment of Diogenes of Sinope and the later Cynics in his *Lectures on the History of Philosophy*, trans. E. S. Haldane and H. S. Simson,

Christ called on his followers to renounce riches, and so did Diogenes of Sinope. Tacitus and Rousseau call for both outer and inner simplicity.[27] But a people can no more be made up of Cynics than of Quakers. This simplicity they visualized is merely a turning one's back on the prevailing level of culture, and the distribution of one's goods to the poor is a limited matter, for if this is done there are no longer any poor. It is necessary not [only] to remain in this sphere but also to accept the need for transition into it. It is necessary that a people should pass over from the simple state of nature into the proliferation of needs; but it is incumbent on human beings to raise themselves above this state of nature. Tacitus sees it as an expedient that Agricola sought to ruin the Germanic tribes by civilizing them, but this is not so.[28] Human beings share with the animals drives pertaining to immediate natural needs, and if they do not rise above them they remain at the level of the beasts.

The moment of necessity that we are considering here also does not involve the sphere of ethical life and scientific knowledge; it does not yet include the aim of the intelligence that grasps, knows, and enjoys itself on its own account. Ethical life and scientific knowledge consist in being raised above mere needs. What introduces an ethical dimension into this sphere is honesty. The need here is to issue forth into universality; ethical

---

3 vols. (London, 1892), 1:484–487 (*Werke* 14:164–169). See also Diogenes Laertius, *De vitis* 6.1–7. For Antisthenes see Wilhelm Gottlieb Tennemann, *Geschichte der Philosophie*, 11 vols. (Leipzig, 1798 ff.), 2:87 ff.

26. [*Ed.*] See for example the second satire of Juvenal and the fourth satire of Persius.

27. [*Ed.*] The allusions here are to Tacitus's portrayal of the northern peoples in his *De Germania* and *De vita et moribus Iulii Agricolae*; see *Cornelii Taciti Libri Qui Supersunt*, vol. 2, fasc. 2 (Leipzig, 1907), pp. 220 ff., 245 ff.; and, possibly, to Rousseau's *Lettres écrites de la montagne* (Amsterdam, 1764). The latter led to a controversy with Voltaire, who responded with his anonymous article *Sentiment des citoyens* (n.p., n.d.). Hegel refers in comparable fashion to the controversy between Rousseau and Voltaire in his *Phenomenology of Spirit*, p. 319 (*Gesammelte Werke* 9:285, 511).

28. [*Ed.*] Although he mentions the "Germans" here, Hegel is obviously thinking of Tacitus's portrayal of the way in which his father-in-law operated in Roman Britain. See *De vita et moribus Iulii Agricolae*, § 21.

life, scientific knowledge, and religion are not to be found in this sphere as essential, but merely shine through into it. Spirit exists in inconsistency with itself and seeks to pass beyond the [level of] need.

§ 91

The citizens [*Bürger*] of this state are *private persons*, linked to the universal by their needs. Their essential activity consists in | 116 imparting the form of universality to, and thereby conferring validity upon, arbitrary desires as well as needs and their satisfaction (since this satisfaction has a wholly particular purpose). This formative process constitutes education or cultivation [*Bildung*] in general.

Our sphere is in the first place that of education or cultivation in general. Education is concerned with form, and the content can be of widely differing nature. The form of universality imparted here to the particular *is* education. The two extremes of particularity and universality are here [present]. Particular needs are linked with the universal, and it is a question of raising their form to universality. But again it is this form of universality itself that is the means whereby individuals obtain their needs. The satisfaction of needs comes about through universality; by means of it human beings can subsist. The particular raises up the universal and again lowers it to particularity. Needs must obtain the form of universality and lose the singularity they have in the state of nature. Collaborative effort and the needs of others bring means into play. Labor is an abstract, not a particular activity. This is education in relation to needs. In the same way education of the mind means that my thoughts are not my thoughts but universal thoughts, something objective. It pertains to education that in their relation to self all individuals in their vanity give due scope to the ends, needs, and vanity of others. The highest form of education is also a form of simplicity. There are two kinds of educational deficiency: lack of cultivation and the kind of education whose practice is always surrounded and restricted by a host of specific considerations. True education knows only one consideration, the sole

means that is appropriate to the case in question, and has thus
117   returned to the simplicity of nature. |

§ 92

Civil society contains three elements:

(1) The mediation of needs and their satisfaction in a system
involving the needs of all: *political economy* [*Staatsökonomie*].

(2) The protection of property through the *legal system* [*Rechts-*
verfassung].

(3) General provision for the welfare of individuals both individually and to ensure the existence of right: the *police* or *public*
authority [*Polizei*].

The first sphere is a system involving the needs of all. Universality is here internal to the need—the mutual mediation of
the needs of citizens. But we are not speaking here of the sort of
political economy [*Staatswirtschaft*] where the universal subsists for the universal. The science we are considering here deals
simply with the contingency of the needs of individuals. So the
foundation is utter contingency. But this interweaving itself produces a universality, although conversely it is this very universality that actuates and fosters the needs and satisfies the particular needs. However, this contingency always raises itself to a
necessity. We are considering only the basic elements of this system. Here the universality is internal to the [system of] needs.

The second point is the legal system. Here the purpose of
formal freedom is to protect individual ownership, both for the
sake of possession, which is a need, and for the sake of right itself. In civil society the legal system has its essential standpoint;
in the ethical sphere it is a subordinate purpose.

The third sphere is where the universal as such emerges, although its purpose is still only the welfare of the individual. Provision is made for the right and welfare of individuals through
external arrangements of universal scope. The role of the legal
system is to annul infringements of right; that of the police is to
prevent them. The *Politeia*[29] teaches the form of government of

29. [*Ed.*] Plato's *Republic*.

the people. With us "the police"[30] may also mean something universal over against the particular citizen, but this universal has as its end the welfare of individuals as individuals, not, as | in   118 the *Politeia*, as a universality. In regard to needs and their satisfaction, the system of social classes [*Stände*] here comes into play.

A. The System of Needs: Political Economy

§ 93

An animal has a definite range of needs. In this sphere of dependence, too, human beings prove their transcendence over animals and their universality. Immediate *universality* in the singularity of concrete needs consists in the *proliferation* [*Verfielfältigung*] of needs; more precisely, it consists in their division and differentiation into single parts and aspects, which in this way become different needs, more particularized and at the same time less concrete, *more abstract.*

What we have to consider here are needs [and] the means of satisfying them. One human being's needs are mediated by others. The means of satisfying needs, i.e., work, is work for others in order to work for oneself; one procures one's needs through others. As universality, human beings should rise above their immediate single needs; this transcendence is initially only proliferation, or particularity. Allness is complete universality. Formally, the proliferation of needs comprises the character of rationality. A natural need, for instance to clothe oneself, is something concrete. Animals are cared for by nature. Humanity rises above the soil [from which it is sprung] and can live anywhere in the world. Hercules was attired in a lion skin, and this is a simple way of satisfying [the need for clothing]. Reflection fragments this simple need and divides it into many parts; according to its particular nature, each individual part of the

30. [Tr.] Hegel is here playing on the root sense of *Polizei* and its derivation from Latin *politia* and Greek *politeia*, meaning "political authority," "political administration," "government," or "commonwealth." See § 117, n. 46.

body—head, neck, feet—is given particular clothing, and so one concrete need is divided into many needs and these in turn into many others. Comfort consists in hitting on just the suitable means | of satisfaction. Division of the need makes it more universal, more abstract. The quest to discover means of satisfying [needs] is stimulated anew by each new means. This proliferation of means promotes comfort, but discomfort is introduced by the fact that so very many means are required.

§ 94

This proliferation of means is mediated, for the specific sphere of need is immediate need, the requirements of nature; what constitutes the mediation is that a self-consciousness relates to itself through identity with another self-consciousness. This universality has

(1) a *restricted, finite* content because the individuals stand in relation to one another as independent, particular beings; so it is not inherent in their substance that they are identical but only in a content that, although it belongs to them, is distinct from them as a totality. Consequently this unity is

(2) only a *represented* [*vorgestellte*] unity and exists only in *opinion* [*Meinung*]. For representation is subjective knowledge, whose content has the shape of something other or alien, and this represented unity is only *equality* [*Gleichheit*].

In regard to their needs, too, human beings evince the character of universality. As self-sufficient consciousness they are essentially relation, and the consciousness of identity is only a fragmented,[31] restricted consciousness because they are separate from one another, essentially distinct. All individuals have their own peculiarities. In consequence consciousness enters the sphere of opinion and representation; representation is the knowledge of a restricted content. The identity of knowledge in representation is not posited by me. There is merely unity of representation, not of knowledge. The consciousness of identity | relates to single representations, to single needs, and is thus merely an

31. *Ms. could also be read:* fragmenting

opinion. Unity is here no more than an equality; the equality between one thing and another is an external relation.

§ 95

This mediation has its starting point as such in the contingency and inequality that are to be found among different individuals in regard to modifications and needs, in particular to the way they are satisfied or to kinds of enjoyment. This perception involves the contradiction implied by inequality with the other in the consciousness of equality, and justifies the drive to bring about and represent to oneself one's equality with others, the imitative drive, which affords the stimulus to obtain the same unknown enjoyment for oneself or in general to acquire what the other has. By dint of repetition the enjoyment becomes something subjectively universal, a habit and need. It is then no less necessary to give this equality determinate existence for the other, and to make oneself aware of being regarded and *recognized* [*anerkannt*] by the other as his equal.

This is the well-known drive to be recognized by the other as equal. The drive and the energy [directed to it] must be regarded as grounded in rationality. The way universality appears in this sphere is that one perceives that others have this particular enjoyment, and there appears to be a particular need. Since needs exist in the realm of natural life and contingency, a diversity of needs arises. All drives are based on contradiction. One is faced with the consciousness of one's identity with the other and at the same time the consciousness of inequality. The imitative drive comes into play, coupled with confidence that what the other has must be pleasing to oneself too. The upbringing of children rests on this drive: grown-ups do it, and we want | to do it too. It is the drive to imitate and to give oneself the notion that the other has nothing we do not have. Fashion is one aspect of this, and to dress according to fashion is the most rational course, whereas we can leave it to others to bother about new fashions: one should not take the lead oneself, but one should also avoid idiosyncrasy. By dint of repetition, an enjoyment becomes habit and a self-imposed need (e.g., smoking). One asserts oneself in order to be equal with others.

121

169

§ 96

The other aspect that is likewise linked to this is the opposing one, namely that of annulling this equality, giving oneself value as something *particular*, the competitive desire to distinguish oneself, but to do so at the same time in a generally valid way, provided only it is a pleasant way.

Once one is on an equal footing with the other, there is also a drive to give oneself value as something particular; but this quest for particularity leads to the greatest lapses in taste, for what is stupid is always something particular. However, everything particular must have something pleasant to it. This drive to present oneself as particular also [occurs] in excess, and one aspect of education is that particularity annuls itself in particularity. The sacrifice of vanity is at the same time a gratification of vanity, for instance in the case of compliments and the refined conversation of society. This urbanity consists in making oneself interesting through the views one advances and by respecting the validity of the thoughts of others. In courtesy, vanity is gratified in being sacrificed. Universality must still shine through even in particularization.

§ 97

The *means* of satisfying needs are specific external things, the *utility* of nature. To the extent that the need is already present, one has a great choice among them. Conversely, their | particularity also gives rise to the specific nature of enjoyments and needs, in the same way that the drive to imitate and to excel leads in turn from the means to the proliferation of needs.

Means are natural things, and with each thing the particular qualities in nature are essential. Natural things are useful insofar as human beings posit themselves as ends and the natural things serve them as means. Inorganic nature is nonliving nature by reason of the fact that the concept is only something inward. In what is actually living, each member is necessary for self-subsistence. It is the essence of natural things to perish, and it is for human beings to make this finitude of things manifest;

they need not therefore scruple about using natural things. Humans comb the whole earth to find the most suitable means for their needs, even for the most humble end. The specificity of natural things is again primary, and enjoyment in turn is determined accordingly. Again it is a matter of chance that one human being is familiar with the particular use another makes of natural things (philosophy on the properties of coffee). This is where imitation and the drive toward a particular use arises. Our purpose here is not to portray the satisfaction of needs but the means people use to satisfy them.

§ 98

There is no limit to this proliferation of needs, in the same way that there is no means of delimiting what is *natural* need and what is a need based on representation, an *imagined* need. *Luxury*, which arises when social conditions tend to multiply needs, enjoyments, and means indefinitely, and make them more specific, gives rise to a no less infinite proliferation of need. And this need is confronted by an impenetrable, infinitely resistant material—namely nature as a means, the sort of nature that is possessed by free | will. But since this need with its satisfaction has a mediation of this kind, it is entirely removed from the immediate necessity of nature; it is raised to the realm of representations and governed by inner freedom of choice [*Willkür*] instead of external necessity and contingency. It becomes a system of universal and abiding *resources* [*Vermögen*] in which all have the right and possibility—or capability—to participate by virtue of their subjective aptitude and education, by virtue of what they make of themselves.

123

We are here concerned with the distinctive shape of need in this sphere. Needs and means are something external, natural, so that what has been subdivided assumes once again the nature of externality and thus can be subdivided anew. To drink wine is a simple need, but people in wine-growing regions are exceptionally well informed about wine. The imagined need originates in the natural need, but the need of spirit is to transcend nature. This tendency toward an infinity of needs is luxury. This proliferation of needs is made the subject of scorn by the Roman satirists,[32] who tell us how hundreds sometimes have to busy themselves to satisfy a momentary need and that just by so doing they in turn satisfy their needs. The entire system of the subsistence of the whole is founded on this superfluity of means and enjoyment. Where there is less luxury, there are fewer forms of universality and refinement, and less possibility of subsistence for many.

It does not depend solely on the free choice of the individual to remove from need the character of a necessity; one is confronted by a material that is owned by another. But even so the necessity ceases to be an immediately compelling one and is a necessity founded in representations, on free choice. In the representational realm [and] in language the name is thus taken for the thing; only the names of things continue to be used, as with the means for [satisfying] needs, which in the system of means belong to the realm of free choice. So human beings are confronted here with the freedom of choice of their fellows. In this way the natural character | of the means is annulled and nature becomes enduring.

124

What we have here is a universal resource [*Vermögen*], not changeable nature but an ever-enduring wealth of society, made independent of nature. Participation in this wealth does not, however, depend merely on taking control of it, as in nature; instead it depends on one's education, i.e., on one's capability to satisfy one's needs by aptitude. Human beings are therefore thrown back on themselves in order to train themselves and give themselves aptitude. But the possibility of educating oneself in this way again calls for a capital resource [*ein Kapital*]; and the possession of this is again something contingent, a contingency that must, however, be sublated by the state.

§ 99

On the immediate level the proliferation of need leads to a like proliferation in stimulating infinitely manifold and ever more

32. [*Ed.*] The reference is to Juvenal and Persius; cf. Hegel, *Werke* 10/2:118.

strenuous activity. On the theoretical plane this involves a rapid succession of representations, the ability to grasp complex and universal relations, and refinement of the understanding and of language; but it also involves a need for occupation [*Beschäftigung*]— occupation in the form of work that must be appropriate to the needs of others and is refined or general in form.

All activity is founded on some need. Activity contradicts a demand in regard to the determinate existence of spirit, and this contradiction is the feeling of need. Educated persons can be recognized by the fact that they have an unending succession of representations in a short space of time and pass over rapidly from one representation to the other; so with educated people the representations are more general whereas uneducated persons do not get beyond single representations. A businessman or [government] minister must be able to pass over instantaneously from the weightiest subject to the most petty. There is a vast contrast between the rapidity with which a minister and a shepherd pass over to another thought. The act of passing over from one to the other reduces the single thought to just one moment, and the universal aspect of the case comes to light. People of mature years, who are already | familiar with objects, per- 125 ceive the universal aspect and hold fast to it, forgetting the individual aspects of sense phenomena, which no longer have any particular interest for them. Children by contrast find the single phenomenon more striking and remember it better.

The word "example" [*Beispiel*] implies that the universal is the essential while the single action [is] merely incidental.[33] Humans live in the realm of representations: the sound of speech is important for what it denotes, and not [merely] as sound. Words have determinate existence, but only through and for the act of representing. Speech in general is the system according to which things subsist in the representational realm, and it gains in universality to the extent that it becomes less concerned with expressing objects of sense. The true richness of a language is not

---

33. [*Tr.*] The prefix *bei-* often suggests something standing alongside, extra, or accessory (e.g., *die Beistehenden*, "bystanders").

its richness for sense phenomena in their particularity, but for universal relationships and definitions of relationships.

Need gives rise to the necessity of occupation. Activity is diversified, and the restless urge always to have something to do becomes itself a need. A savage on the contrary is always lounging about and only engages in activity when he is compelled to. Restlessness is a constant process of passing over [from one thing to another]. In the state this activity is a form of work that relates to the needs of others; one's own indeterminateness, imagination, and opinion must be given up, and one must direct one's work to a determinate end, for the sake of a need. This is why it is so good a training for people to work toward determinate ends since in doing so they are obliged to give up their subjectivity.

§ 100

The contingent circumstance that one person has a surplus of one means [of satisfaction] leads of itself to *exchange* [*Tausch*] against means that the other has in surplus. But the multiplication of needs demands the preparation of specific means for their satisfaction; and the rationality involved in this is expressed by the fact that the use of natural things no longer consists in immediate appropriation and enjoyment of them but is on the one hand *prepared for in advance* by *labor* or *work* [*Arbeit*], while on the other hand labor itself is mediated by the use of *tools* [*Werkzeuge*], by means of which | individuals make their activity specific and at the same time protect themselves against the mechanical relationship of wear and tear [*Abnutzung*].

Need generally speaking produces activity. To be sure, exchange rests on the contingent circumstance that one person has a surplus of something; but to produce such a surplus here becomes an end, and the preparation of specific means to this end is called for. In our mode of life there are very few means that are used just as they are taken from nature. Most [means], even those to meet natural needs that animals have [in common] with us, such as food, are rarely used by humans without being pre-

126

formed; we have already imparted our form to them, taken their strangeness from them by mixing them with other natural products that are opposed to them. For example, in preparing dishes for enjoyment, fat is removed from the animal tissue; at the same time the compounded dishes must be homogeneous. In this way we make nature homogeneous with ourselves, we assimilate it to ourselves; and the fact that we diminish the animal function, e.g., of digestion, cannot be called a loss of vigor.

The character of rationality in human beings shows itself in the means, the tools that they use. Through these tools activity is made more specific. By using a tool people insert a means between themselves and nature, and prevent the attrition of their energies by allowing the means to suffer the wear and tear and so preserving themselves. What is rational is in general what preserves itself, what exempts itself from change. This mediating use of tools is the invention of reason, and self-preservation makes this a duty for humanity.

§ 101

Furthermore, the preparation of specific means calls for a particular aptitude and familiarity, and individuals must confine themselves to only one of these. This gives rise to the *division of labor*, [a multiplicity of labors,][34] | as a result of which labor or work becomes less concrete in character, becomes abstract, homogeneous, and easier, so that a far greater quantity of products can be prepared in the same time. In the final stage of abstractness, the homogeneity of labor makes it mechanical, and it becomes possible to install machines in place of people, replacing human motion by a principle of natural motion that is harnessed to secure uniformity and to promote human ends.

This is the basis for all factory and manufacturing labor. Each single operation is assigned to a single individual. In a smallish factory employing ten persons the daily output [per person] is

127

34. [*Tr.*] The text reads, *die Teilung der Arbeit*, to which the German editors have added in brackets, *eine Vielfalt von Arbeiten*.

4,800 pins, whereas an individual working wholly on his own can make 20 pins at most.[35] The subjective change of representations[36] and [the change] in the work being done—this change-over requires a certain time, more time than when the individual subject constantly repeats the operation in question. So [in a factory] the work becomes abstract, uniform, and thus easier, since there is only one skill the individual subject learns, only one routine he practices, and so he can acquire more readiness at this single operation. [By contrast] the work done by any artisan is more concrete: frequent changeovers are a necessity for him, and his practical knowledge must be manifold and extend to many different kinds of objects. This is why factory workers

35. [Ed.] By way of explanation see Adam Smith, An Inquiry into the Nature and Causes of the Wealth of Nations, vol. 1 (Basel, 1791), pp. 7–9: "To take an example, therefore, from a very trifling manufacture; but one in which the division of labor has been very often taken notice of, the trade of the pinmaker; a workman not educated to this business, which the division of labor has rendered a distinct trade, nor acquainted with the use of the machinery employed in it, to the invention of which the same division of labor has probably given occasion, could scarce, perhaps, with his utmost industry, make one pin in a day, and certainly could not make twenty. But in the way in which this business is now carried on, not only the whole work is a peculiar trade, but it is divided into a number of branches, of which the greater part are likewise peculiar trades . . . and the important business of making a pin is, in this manner, divided into about eighteen distinct operations, which, in some manufactories, are all performed by distinct hands, though in others the same man will sometimes perform two or three of them. I have seen a small manufactory of this kind where ten men only were employed, and where some of them consequently performed two or three distinct operations. But though they were very poor, and therefore but indifferently accommodated with the necessary machinery, they could, when they exerted themselves, make among them about twelve pounds of pins in a day. There are in a pound upwards of four thousand pins of a middling size. Those ten persons, therefore, could make among them upwards of forty-eight thousand pins in a day. Each person, therefore, making a tenth part of forty-eight thousand pins, might be considered as making four thousand eight hundred pins in a day. But if they had all wrought separately and independently, and without any of them having been educated to this particular business, they certainly could not each of them have made twenty, perhaps not one pin in a day; that is, certainly, not the two hundred and fortieth, perhaps not the four thousand eight hundredth part of what they are at present capable of performing, in consequence of a proper division and combination of their different operations."

36. [Tr.] That is, the mental activity required in switching from one operation to another when an individual is working alone.

become deadened [*stumpf*] and tied to their factory and dependent on it, since with this single aptitude they cannot earn a living anywhere else.

A factory presents a sad picture of the deadening [*Abstumpfung*]³⁷ of human beings, which is also why on Sundays factory workers lose no time in spending and squandering their entire weekly wages. But once factory work has reached a certain degree of perfection, of simplification, mechanical human labor can be replaced by the work of machines, and this is what usually comes about in factories. In this way, through the consummation of this mechanical progress, human freedom is restored. A factory can thrive in a country where there is great poverty and people have to make do with little; but in England | the cost   128
of labor is exceedingly high, and yet the factories prosper because machinery does away with the need for human labor, so the English can supply cheaper goods than other nations in which workers cost much less.

The mechanical tools people use are also machines, since they are not wholly dependent on human activity and instead human strength is largely replaced by mechanical means. But with all mechanical motion the uniformity achieved is not lasting: the tension on a watch spring is always greater at the beginning than later, and it is we who have to introduce the uniformity of movement. Human beings are accordingly first sacrificed, after which they emerge through the more highly mechanized condition as free once more.

§ 102

With the transformation of contingency from that of external nature into the form of free choice [*Willkür*], the scope of contingency is made infinitely more extensive as a result of the inequality of natural bodily and mental talents and the infinitely diverse and complex circumstances underlying in general the indeterminate *inequality of resources*. However, the essential inequality based on

37. [*Tr.*] See below, § 118, n. 48.

this system of needs and means constitutes the *difference of classes or estates* [*Stände*]³⁸—the difference of the particular subsystems contained in the universal system of needs, the different kinds of means they have and work they do.

Instead of the dependence of humanity on external nature, we are now in the presence of subjective contingency. The whole is raised above immediate dependence on nature, but subjective contingency, human free choice, comes into play in regard to people's mental and bodily talents, and this contingency is infinitely greater than that of nature. The individual's participation in and contribution to the collective estate depends on that individual's talents. In this respect the class or estate individuals attain to is in each case a matter of particular destiny, which depends partly on their talents, partly on inclination and chance occurrences. People have little choice as to what they determine themselves to become. The | opportunities to acquire aptitudes are also few and far between, and there is in addition little in the way of particular incentives to enter certain vocations [in preference to others]; all the greater is the part played by contingency. And this is the reason for the subjective *inequality of resources*, the antithesis of which is an insubstantial chimera; for the whole system rests on the subjective character of talents and the variously contingent character that in turn attaches to these subjective talents. In more determinate terms, the differentiation constitutes the *division of classes or estates*. The state must respect the aspect of inequality because it is one aspect of the free choice present in the contingency and freedom of the individual. Admittedly something universal must endeavor to avert the consequences that might ensue from this if they are

129

---

38. [*Tr.*] The word *Stand* means "(social) class," "status," "standing," or "estate," while the plural *Stände* can also refer to the groups (the "estates") comprising a parliament, or to the parliamentary institution itself (the "estates assembly," see § 148). The traditional estates were the clergy, the nobility, and the commoners (bourgeoisie). For Hegel the social classes are identified not so much by degrees of wealth (upper, middle, lower, etc.) as by function (agricultural, commercial, manufacturing, civil, religious, etc.).

harmful. The whole must articulate itself, and this articulation in regard to the manifold character of needs and work is the necessity of classes, whose higher necessity is founded in reason since each living thing must become inwardly unequal. To feel pity that one human being must suffer more because of his needs than another is an unjustified sentiment.

§ 103

These classes are specified conceptually as the substantive [*substantielle*] class, the formal [*formelle*] class, and the universal [*allgemeine*] class.

(1) The immediate [i.e., substantive] class satisfies its needs from resources in the form of *property* [*Gut*]: the agricultural class. By agriculture the nomadic life of savages, who seek their livelihood from place to place, is tied in tranquillity to the soil, and the contingency of external change is likewise restricted to the regular processes of elemental nature. The procurement of means too is confined by agriculture to a definite single season, which in consequence gives rise to a concern to make these temporarily available means permanent and creates the need for recognized ownership of possessions. The resulting form of work determines the living productive activity of nature; on the other hand it has no value on its own account but is only a means, and | the main purpose of the 130 natural products amassed is to provide subsistence that is not further mediated.

The sphere we considered under family is an integral feature of the agricultural class. The era during which agriculture comes into being is one of the principal eras in the history and religion of all peoples; this is how the mysteries of Ceres came about. The savage ceases to direct his reflection to the whole gamut of contingency and directs it instead to what lies before him, to the soil. Hunting involves a nomadic existence in which the means to satisfy need depend on the chance character of obtaining or finding something, and it is the same with fishing.

Agriculture spells the end of nomadism, with its alternating extremes of dire need and momentary surplus that cannot be stored for the future. To be sure, agriculture also involves the elemental aspect of nature, but no longer nature in its contingency, but nature that changes in necessary fashion and must always return. On the temporal plane too, there is only one season in which one can procure for oneself the means of subsistence, which gives rise to concern for the other seasons, so farmers acquire a sense of present and future. The need for ownership arises. For ownership comprises the aspect of freedom and that of the universal, i.e., of something that has to be respected by all. The ideal form of taking possession, the cultivation of the land, denotes my possession, and this form must be respected. Ceres and Triptolemus did not merely found agriculture but also laid the bases of lawful ownership. One's land is a lasting, permanent possession, especially insofar as the inner universality must have a determinate existence; right must be known and respected.

The farmer is not mainly concerned with the form, namely that the land must be cultivated or the animals fed; this happens only in order to increase and facilitate the life of nature itself. It is gifts of nature that ensure the farmer's existence [*Existenz*]; the relationship here is between what is living and what is living, | not between human beings and their own invention. They do not have themselves to thank for everything, but intuit organic life in general. So what we have here is rather the class of innocence [*Unschuld*], of faith; heart and mind do not yet have the consciousness of obligation [*Schuld*], the awareness that what one has is one's own. Nor does any major mediation enter into the system of satisfaction of needs. The family itself prepares manual tools, clothing, etc. Subsistence does not depend on the work and needs of everyone else.

§ 104

[(2)] With *business* or *trade* [*Gewerbe*], the reflective [i.e., formal] class, the chief aspect is the form and an abstract profit, one that does not serve directly for gratification. A man belonging to this class processes raw material, and the form he gives it is what makes the thing of value. He is therefore impelled in the direction of mediation with others in a variety of ways, in his reflection and in regard to his need to exchange the products of his work, and also in regard to his tools. As more abstract in character, the *manufacturing class* [*Klasse der Fabrikant*] has to deal both with a lifeless material and with a mechanical form; and the more perfect, i.e., the more limited, the aptitude required, the more dependent is the value of its output on a contingent factor, that of the further perfecting of the aptitude of others, and other external circumstances. For the purposes of universal exchange, money—the abstract value of the commodity—becomes a need and by its circulation multiplies the amount of property indefinitely. The *commercial class* [*Handelsstand*], whose business is to act as a universal intermediary in the reciprocal exchange of manufactured articles, accumulates wealth, which is subject to no inherent qualitative limit, so that the pursuit of wealth extends indefinitely and for its part in turn gives rise to the proliferation of needs and means.

In the manufacturing class work is abstract in character, whereas the third class again involves universality; it is here [in the manufacturing class] that wealth originates. The main thing in business is the form, one's own | aptitude, but this form is not due to nature but to oneself. The articles produced by the business class are not those that serve the needs of the producer; his aim is rather to make a general profit, out of which he can supply his needs. With us, the agricultural class has also joined the business class, and the main thing is no longer to preserve the farmer's [means of] satisfaction. Instead the farmer has an eye to what is most profitable in order to exchange it for other people's products—[an eye,] in other words, [to] the kinds of produce for which human labor is least needed since he no longer regards the people in his service as belonging to his family.

In the business class the principal concern is not the raw material but the form produced by the worker's activity; he therefore has himself and his own activity to thank for everything. This is the reflective class, where one becomes aware of oneself

132

and one's activity. One only produces means in order to obtain the means for the satisfaction of one's needs. The business class, the individual member of it, has the self-awareness that it is through his own activity that he subsists. Its main aspect is not to be dependent on external nature; yet the members of this class are partly dependent, since they must obtain from others their raw materials and their tools, which others manufacture for them. The needs of others also make possible the sale of their products, and they are dependent to this extent. But exchange occurs only when the one has a superfluity of one thing and the other of another thing, and is possible only when people live side by side; hence business is essentially an urban growth. While it costs more to satisfy needs in a large town, some non-immediate, derivative needs such as tools can be had more cheaply.

The artisans of this class see, it is true, to their individual needs, but there is not the same degree of abstractness present in their workshops as with the *manufacturer*, for whom the mechanical plays a greater part, the essential purpose being to simplify work. The more mechanical factory work becomes, 133 the more dependent people are on the factory, and in order | to ensure their livelihood the public authority [*Polizei*] intervenes, according privileges and restricting the number of workers; guilds [*Zünfte*] come into being, so that excessive competition is prevented. If there are too many craftsmen in a town, the individual craftsmen automatically suffer, and the influx of further craftsmen cancels itself out. With factories it is otherwise: since their work is abstract and they need a larger market for their large quantity of products, manufacturers have to seek a wider circle in which to sell their products. The artisan producer, on the other hand, works only for a specific circle. The manufacturer is confronted by a greater degree of contingency—the fact that other factories open, which invent better machines or have cheaper workers or an easier supply of materials; and in this way factories are ruined if other factories open in the area where they sell their products. For example most of the Dutch factories have been ruined by the English. And as factory workers, who always have a single abstract type of work, have great difficulty in switching to another kind of work, and factories are easily ruined by [changing] fashions and all the contingent factors mentioned above, poverty easily arises.

Commerce [*Handel*] comes into play as means, while money is needed as the universal means of exchange of needs (the agricultural class affords more scope for exchanging needs [directly] against needs, and here [monetary] exchange plays a minor role). That one country should have much money is not by itself the criterion of its wealth, for in this country money is cheap, i.e., the goods are dear; but where money is in short supply, it is dear and the goods are cheap. An essential factor in the case of money is circulation. In a country where there is little money, exchange is inhibited. Where the circulation of money is greatest, there wealth is greatest. The more money circulates, the faster does the same sum of money become a means for everyone through whose hands it passes, and each of these has the possibility of profiting through the sum of money in question. If there is insufficient coinage to serve as means of exchange, its place is taken by paper money; | the relative position of goods   134 is fixed in relation to paper money, but circulation is facilitated. The wealth of the nation is not increased by increasing the amount of money; it is only the circulation that is increased. For example, in times gone by, France experienced a great increase in wealth through paper money. It is admittedly better if coinage is in use, but even paper money is not to be regarded as a national misfortune insofar as it conduces to increased circulation.

Within the business class the *commercial class* constitutes the universal class; its business is to trade the means produced for other means, to exchange the surplus of the one, be it in artificial or natural products, for the surplus of the other. The main thing is profit. The commercial class has to do with means as universal means; it has to do with *the* universal means, money, and to this extent its efficacy extends to the universal. And the great man of commerce, who has to do with what is universal in the needs of nations, who has the map lying before him, has a great status. Wealth and profit become an indeterminate quest, not merely to the extent necessary to satisfy his needs, and the relation to individual need is more or less general.

In republics an inordinate increase in wealth is dangerous, so legislators have sought to counteract it. For example the richest citizen in a *demos* [populace] had to pay for the plays; in this way wealth was honored, but he was obliged to reduce his estate, or limits were placed on accumulation. The inheritance laws were also directed against excessive enrichment. However, commerce seeks to awaken new needs among the nations; for this reason the English, for example, make the Chinese such great presents of woolen material, in order to give them the need for it and so gain a new market for selling their goods.

§ 105

(3) The *universal class* [the class of civil servants] in general has as the aim of its work the universal element in the social condition itself; and for this reason | the universal element itself must make provision for the needs of this class, and it must be raised altogether above want and [the necessity of] working directly to relieve want.

135

The universal class pertains to the essential organization of the state, and has its actual existence in the constitution of the people. It has as its aim the universal as such, namely that right should come about and that there should be security. In all other classes the aim of each is to look after himself; but this class must be removed from want and must be looked after by the universal. The task of providing for its needs must be assumed by the state. The individuals [of this class] may each also have particular aims in the form of remuneration, etc.; this is not an essential aim, however, but must be regarded as a means to attaining the universal aim. In order that this may be the pure aim of their work, they must not have to work in order to relieve need; by virtue of their office they must be independent as far as needs are concerned. The relationship must be so determined that in performing their official duties they are not bound in regard to their needs. This must be taken care of through taxes or independent possession of property, as used to happen in earlier states where various state employees were given property so that independence enabled them to devote themselves to effective action for the general interest. The universal class also includes teachers, who apply themselves to the various fields of knowledge for the greatest good of the community. It is honorable for a state if, in order to support the universal class and in particular develop knowledge, it confers on individuals who devote their whole lives exclusively to this purpose certain privileges or independence of means. Instead of this it was the custom in Germany to give privileges to the nobility, who abandoned themselves to the most shameful passions at the expense of their few vassals.

§ 106

This differentiation of classes, which lies in the concept of the matter under consideration, must also be only a differentiation posited [as] such by the different determinations of the concept. | So regardless of all accidents of birth and nature governing the class to which individuals first belong, it must be left to their own activity to determine to what class they themselves wish to belong. Only in this way will more honor and power be ascribed to subjective contingency, free choice, and self-determining consciousness than to natural contingency.

136

It must be a matter of chance for individuals to what class they belong, in which they are born; but our entire environment at birth consists in relationships whereby we must belong immediately to the class in which we are born. However, this conceptually necessary differentiation of classes was regarded for instance by Egyptians and Hindus as naturally necessary, and so made permanent, and this gave rise to castes. The result is to deprive human beings of the freedom to rise above these natural circumstances. No personal advantages can raise the barrier of the castes, and subjective contingency and the consciousness of freedom cannot take effect. In the Roman state too we see the abrupt distinctions between patricians and plebeians, resulting in constant inner strife. For privileges accorded to one class in regard to communal tasks are very oppressive. For instance the Prussian nobility used to have the sole right to be commissioned officers. This class distinction based on privilege, where one class participates to a greater extent in communal tasks, is one of the most repugnant forms of distinction. In England and France large property owners are regarded as a true nerve of the state because they can be independent of the sovereign's favor and all [thought of] profit, and this is an essential relationship.

§ 107

It is in the class system that human *particularity* in fact receives its rights. The ethical disposition here is *rectitude* [*Rechtschaffen-heit*] and *esprit de corps* [*Standesehre*], i.e., the disposition | to make oneself a member of one of these necessary elements of civil society through one's own activity, industry, skill, and conformity to right; and, through this process of mediating with the universal, to *be* something and to be *recognized* both in one's own eyes and in the eyes of others. Moreover, morality has its proper place in this sphere characterized by reflection on one's own doings, and where the contingent nature of individual need makes a single, contingent act of assistance a duty.

As concrete individuals we each exist in particular external circumstances. But apart from their particularity human beings must also have as their aim universality. The other aspect, however, is the ethical disposition, which consists in the fact that all human beings must have a class status and educate themselves for it; but the class they educate themselves for depends in part on chance circumstances. It depends upon the opinion the individual has of a particular class, and the material circumstances and other properties that constitute it. In Plato's state the rulers allocate children as they judge fit to the class for which they

137

186

seem suited, and educate them for it.[39] But here subjective free choice, or self-determination, is suppressed. Freedom in particularity *is* free choice. To maintain oneself in the chosen status and carry out the corresponding duties is rectitude. Now each class is something universal, and rectitude is ethical life in the sphere in question. It is not yet ethical life [as such], because human beings must have still higher aims. Thus rectitude cannot be regarded as the aim, for there must be other ends that transcend this sphere.

Esprit de corps [*Standesehre*] is the consciousness of rectitude, of being regarded as upright by one's class and having the appropriate standing within it. Human beings must resolve to be something particular in the class relationship, they must assign to themselves a class status. In maintaining themselves within the | restricting confines [of class status], they confer on   138
themselves the essential moment of actuality, a moment that is necessary in order for them to attain their freedom. Rectitude consists in giving oneself a status and being rightly what people *are* in the status one has assumed, and in this rightfulness one rises *in* one's sphere *above* it. By esprit de corps we mean that the individual is a useful moment for the universal. "Serviceable" or "useful" is said of something that is a means for something else. As we ourselves are our own end, we cannot be means, cannot be serviceable or useful. But though we may be ends in ourselves in our activity, our activity here becomes entangled with the end pursued by all others. By their particularity human beings are restricted to the determinate existence of all others, but they must raise themselves from this particularity [while still] in it. In this sense people ask what someone is, i.e., what status a person has, and someone with no status is nothing. However, by virtue of their determinate existence, humans have to make themselves actual and to maintain themselves in this particularity. This is the ethical aspect of this class [system].

39. [*Ed.*] Hegel is referring to Plato's *Republic* 460b–d.

The determinate existence of morality constitutes this sphere, properly speaking; as moral beings, humans must here do their duty for duty's sake, but morality does not indicate where duty lies, and does not comprise duties in their determinateness. The stage of morality comes into play once one seeks to return wholly within oneself; it is one's class status that constitutes the real content for duty, that imposes determinate duties that can be known to everyone.

One feature of virtue is that individuality, by self-determination, endows itself with a specific character; the essential feature of virtue is that one has endowed oneself with a virtuous end or purpose. Now insofar as it is one's class status that occasions virtue, virtue is no longer contingent, conferred by individuality; for one's freedom lies solely in the fact that one confers status on oneself. However, it is this status, and not individuality as such, that prescribes duties for all persons of the class in question. A benevolent person has the intention of helping others, and this depends on his free choice. But in this system of mediation those who care for themselves are also caring for others; they are acting for themselves and [at the same time] looking after others. | The very actions that are in other spheres a matter of free choice become necessary actions in the sphere of mediation, and little of the merit for this accrues to the individual. If we spend our money on our needs we are giving our money to others, though on condition that they do their duty and are industrious; in so doing we give them a juster feeling of themselves than if we give our money away to the poor, for the poor, when given alms, have no feeling of independence.

139

This is the necessary connection underlying this [system of] mediation: that those who look after themselves are also looking after others. Nevertheless an element of contingency can enter in here, namely that provision is not made for others: want or need. On the general plane it is for the state to prevent universal need by taking appropriate measures, but there can also be subjective want or need, where people have to be helped in their frame of mind by word and deed; but even in the case of individual need it is better for provision to be made by the state.

It is true that people usually prefer to retain their freedom of choice in helping others in need rather than leave the state to help by means of general provisions. And the free will is after all involved here too if the individual regards this concern on the part of the state as something rational; in this way individuals *can* act in benevolent fashion using the machinery provided by the state. Subjective assistance must be reduced to the minimum because it can harm instead of helping.

§ 108

By means of education [*Bildung*], through whose universality individuals work off their immediate subjectivity, and through the mediation of the universal interchange of work and means [of satisfaction], individuals *become* and *emerge* for themselves as free will [*freie Willkür*] or subjectivity of will, a subjectivity that is, however, inwardly universal. *Formal right* makes its appearance, and, however intimately it is implicated and has its essential content in the aim of [satisfying] needs, it must also, as the substantive element underlying this aim, be embodied in something independent of it, namely the *administration of justice*. | 140

This negativity of singularity involves the emergence of universality, and as free will in general, this universality is an essential element of myself. All people are, have, work, enjoy, etc., to the extent that everything they do, have, and enjoy is mediated by others; yet in this mediation they return to themselves, exist for themselves. This being-for-self is the moment of right. The whole sphere exists only because there is such a thing as right; we all view ourselves as persons governed by right, and the fact that we are recognized [as such] is the subjective element.

B. The Administration of Justice

§ 109

Both the administration of justice [*Rechtspflege*] and actual legal relationships *presuppose laws founded on right* [*Rechtsgesetze*] as something valid in and for itself; and such laws must be regarded essentially in this light. Legislation itself belongs to another sphere than this; it is at the same time the practice of the courts and the distinctions that arise out of the indeterminately differing cases that come before them which give rise to the need for further determinations and the indeterminate further development of the legal understanding as opposed to the no less necessary simplicity of the laws.

We are here considering the universal determinations of the administration of justice, namely laws founded on right. The administration of justice is not concerned with legislation, where the laws are handed down by a higher authority; the laws are assumed to be already there. The fact that the legislative and judicial functions cannot be combined in one person is clear from the consideration that, if they were, the judicial authority would itself make the law for the case that was to be judged, and there would then be no subsumption.

The development of law founded on right and the differentiation of cases is an affair of the understanding. In his *Republic* Plato finds it unworthy of himself, and of honest men, | to pronounce on individual laws and how they are to be subsumed and further developed, a process that extends and continues infinitely.[40] What constitutes the formal character of law is that its concept is this infinite to which it tends, but that this is to be applied to the finite. A perfect, fully complete code of laws is an unattainable ideal; rather it must be continually improved. There should be a code, but it is continually being added to, is continually in the making. In this field of infinitude the material is empirical; the definitions established by the understanding are constantly subject to fission. This is the field of arguments and counterarguments, where there is no stopping.

It is from this actual adjudication or practice of the courts that all laws originate. The actual pronouncement of judgment gives decisions that, even though tailored to single cases, become universal laws; in this way a law takes shape on the basis of *similiter judicata* [similar judgments]. The courts cannot be

140

40. [*Ed.*] The allusion is to Plato's *Republic* 425c–e.

dead organs of the laws; the judge's own understanding, own insight, always has a part to play. The Roman practice of having each year a new praetor, who set limits to his caprice by rules of his own which he prescribed for himself before taking up office, was a very erroneous one owing to the fact that the judges changed too often. It was the Romans above all who developed the legal understanding; since public life was suppressed under despotism, the understanding directed all its lively attention to the development of law. Now on the one hand we have the requirement that the laws should in themselves be simple principles, in the same way that the principle of right is a simple principle and because this simplicity is necessary for the individual's insight into and familiarity with the laws; on the other hand the specific determinations of law must be able to keep on developing freely. |

142

§ 110

In being brought before the courts, right enters the essential relationship that it has to be *known* or *recognized* [*erkannt*]. This gives rise to the requirement that in order to be legally binding, actions should of themselves be invested with this form from start to finish. The legally binding character of contracts and other actions that call for implementation does not, according to this distinction, rest merely upon these transactions themselves but just as essentially on their formal character congruent with the laws. In other actions *recognizability* [*Erkennbarkeit*] resides partly in external circumstances, the way they are heeded, assessed, and combined, partly in the testimony of others; this testimony has the form of subjective assurances, to which taking the *oath* is designed to impart maximum objectivity.

Here we are dealing with the determinate existence of right, with its recognizability. Now what constitutes the existence of right, what is its recognizability? We have here the antithesis that persons may have right [on their side] but their right must be recognized. This gives rise to the requirement that actions that are to be recognizable should be brought to court

191

and recognized by the courts; these are the requisite legal formalities. Uneducated people may regard it as repugnant in the extreme that their right or its recognition should depend on something external, but it is its formality that constitutes the determinate existence of right. The laws have to determine what is necessary for the action to be sufficiently recognizable; but this is an affair of the understanding, subject to contingency and arbitrariness, and consideration must be given to what extent one circumstance is sufficient [for the purpose]. An action itself subdivides into many acts, and each act may be separate, [i.e.,] separate from the principal act, e.g., a contract and its performance. Consideration must also be given to what extent an *actus* is important or necessary for the subsistence of the contract. In order that there may be no more excuses, all necessary circumstances have to be taken into account.

The formalities and their validity rest then on their externality. In the case of other actions, especially such as are not directly | destined to be executed in court, there must be a combination of external circumstances; regard must be had to what is objective, circumstances that are present as effects or conditions from which it is possible to infer the cause. Account often has to be taken here of contingent circumstances, and the necessity of combining so many circumstances brings into play subjectivity, the moment of contingency, in connection with the subjective education and perceptiveness of the judge; the judge's zeal and diligence also necessarily play a part.

Of itself testimony is something subjective, circumstantial, to the extent that it is retained in the individual consciousness of something that is past. What it depends on is the chance presence of the subject. We have here an assurance or affirmation by the subject, and as affirmation this is something wholly subjective; but an attempt is made to impart objectivity to this subjectivity by means of taking the oath. (The aspect of the administration of justice we are considering here is that right must be recognized, must be recognizable for the courts, and this is the reason for legal formalities.) Witnesses should testify according

143

to their knowledge. In the oath I declare myself to be objective, I express my being [*Wesen*], and I link to this essentiality [*Wesenheit*] the specific affirmation I make. The oath is therefore something religious. In calling on the supreme being [*das höchste Wesen*] I transcend all particularity and leave aside all subjective aims. My deposition shall have the same certainty as my being has for me; I am trusted to leave aside all subjectivity. For this recognizability on the part of the court, it is necessary to go back to what is most objective in humankind, to religion, to morality. Since perjury is possible, taking the oath must be carried out as a religious *actus*, to be performed with a certain solemnity. Among the English it is also a dangerous custom that the cold formality of taking the oath, if it is sworn by two people, makes the issue wholly certain; and the mercantile spirit is such that perjury is easily committed, with the result that other citizens may innocently fall into extreme misfortune. Nor should witnesses have to take the oath in regard to wholly petty matters. | 144

Under German law, in addition to all other evidence, criminals cannot be condemned until they have confessed. This is a very humane provision, for the judge's cognition may be falsified by a strange concatenation of circumstances. Another reason why this acknowledgment by criminals is a very good idea is that the criminals themselves as judges must pronounce sentence against themselves, so this also does honor to rationality. Confession alone is not sufficient, for persons may be so tired of life as to accuse themselves falsely. In England the judge himself warns criminals not to harm themselves, not to confess anything. But this is to take the attitude that they must regard the court as if it were their enemy. Instead, the true attitude is that the court has to bring crimes to the light of day, and criminals are at the same time seen as human beings in general, who are expected to indicate what they know of the circumstances. The truth is that it is not contrary to [their] humanity but rather that the accused become universal persons (intelligence, reason, a being governed by right) when they contribute to revealing the truth and uncovering the crime.

Tortures were commonest when people believed in ghosts, in times of superstition. For example the Egyptians put to death whoever wittingly or unwittingly killed an ibis or a cat; this is certainly very degrading, but however bad it is, it is not as bad as the use of torture. For if someone did not confess under torture, it was supposed that he was being aided by the devil. The cramps and convulsions were attributed to the devil who was aiding the poor wretch, and instead of arousing pity these symptoms were themselves taken as evidence against him.

In these times we see the most fearful evil raging unchecked. Apart from the recognizability of crime there is a second aspect of crimes to be considered, which also belongs to this sphere. |

145

§ 111

In addition to being recognized as deed and action, crimes also involve the negative aspect whereby their nullity has to be given determinate existence. It is only through civil society that the concept of right receives the form of something that has being in and for itself, opposed to the particularity of self-related need and interest, and constituting, in the form of *law*, the ultimate, self-reflected ground. In this *universal* the subjective element, which involves the immediate annulling of crime in the form of *retribution* [*Wiedervergeltung*], falls away. This is because what is injured in crime is right as right; hence the party injured from the standpoint of right withdraws from the proceedings, and universal right, which now exists for itself, takes over the prosecution and punishment of crime.

In addition to the fact that the [criminal] action, as a positive action, must acquire determinate existence for the court, crime also involves a negative aspect, which must also be brought into existence, by means of which the nullity of the crime—which *is* null within itself—is sublated, is itself annulled. This came about through retribution in the form of revenge, but here we have the concept of right as law, as a universal or ground, as what is substantive or essential. As the ground or reason for which something is punished, we point to the law. Now that the concept of law has acquired universality, it constitutes the ground, but law expresses only the simple form of this logical connection. Now that right is the ground, it is not the injured party who has to be given satisfaction but the law. The injured party is a concrete person, and since this concrete person exercises right, particular interest, the infinitude[41] of personality, comes into play. In the state this subjective side falls away, and it is not so much that retribution is exacted from the wrongdoer as that he is requited for his action. The "re-" does not have here the meaning of abstract equality; what is requited is the value in general. Right exists in the law as something universal, and the courts are a form of activity devoid of particular interest. In crime right is infringed as right, the universal as | universal, and here it is not a matter of subsumption. The universal has been negated, so it is a universal instance, a public person, [e.g.,] a fiscal *accusateur public* [public arraigner], on whom the task of prosecuting falls. Nor can there be any role here for generosity or pity on the part of the injured party; instead it is the universal that enters into play as what has suffered injury.

146

§ 112

The exercise of right by the universal is no longer directed against criminals as something contingent and an external power. Right also belongs to criminals: it protects them and is accomplished in them as their own power and essence. This exercise of right thus becomes a *reconciliation* [*Versöhnung*] brought about by justice, both objectively and subjectively as far as the disposition is concerned; and revenge is transformed into *punishment* [*Strafe*].

The transition from revenge to punishment is as follows. The wrongdoer's relationship is not with the injured party but with injured right in itself, with the administration of justice. For in the case of revenge [the compensation exacted] does not

41. [*Tr.*] See below, § 114, exposition.

impinge on criminals as their right but as the rights of others, of the injured parties. Right in the form of law impinges on criminals as something majestic, something universal, free from subjectivity. Human beings are honored by the justice that punishment is, because it is their own will that is related to them in the form of essence. With retribution as revenge, where a subjective will comes into play, the progression of revenge extends ad infinitum, but [here] compensation takes the form of contradiction resolved. In punishment wrongdoers find themselves, are present to themselves, with the result that punishment is something self-enclosed; it disposes of the matter.

§ 113

In right, which exists in the form of universality that has being for itself, punishment too acquires a universal meaning according to its content. As annulment of the crime, the injury [done to the criminal] is, to be sure, necessarily proportionate to it, but in the presence of universal right this proportionality is found not in the individuality of existence [*Existenz*] but in accord with the essence of right. | This allows greater freedom to the manner in which the crime is atoned for, with the exception of [forfeiture of] life, the qualitative nature of which is infinitely varied. Since the determinate existence [*Dasein*] of the individual consists, in civil society, in being recognized, this stage also includes disgrace as a moment of punishment or as punishment itself. If disgrace is not mere shaming but destroys the reputation, it is something lasting whereby the offender loses his status.

147

What is expressed here is (1) that in retribution, in the principle of punishment, the equality involved should not extend to empirical qualitative equality; what is involved here is value. The qualitative character of crime is raised to universality, and punishment acquires the form of value, value viewed from its universal, essential side. In our sphere, the sphere of thought, of reflection, it is in general always the case that everything passes over into universality. This is characteristic of thinking beings, who raise themselves above existence [*Existenz*]. Outside the sphere of civil society, the commutation of punishment is an affair of caprice and whim, for it stands over against the offender as something immediate, and this arbitrary element is unrightful. Free rein is here given to the qualitative manner in which crime is punished, and the invidious equality which is not appropriate to a universal being that rises above immediate existence [*Existenz*] and appearance falls away. This universality introduces a liberality into the requiting of crime, even though the moment of equality is demanded by justice. As an inestimable possession life is something qualitative, and here no exchange is possible; and the punishment for murder must be capital punishment because life is beyond valuation.

(2) Another aspect here is injury to the determinate existence that is recognized, to honor. Punishments that involve no more than a momentary shaming in the eyes of others, to the devising and invention of which much ingenuity used to be devoted, have now largely been done away with. Here the whole punishment consisted in shaming. These punishments [where] one was content with this *actus* are no longer appropriate according to our customs, and more prominence is given to retaining | and main- 148 taining the thought of them. A punishment seen as a merely momentary shaming would be converted in our eyes—we being no longer so naive as our forebears—into a lasting loss of reputation, seeing that with us reflection has become preponderant and forgiveness no longer follows immediately after repentance. In ecclesiastical penitence too, transgressions are no longer annulled by repentance. Moreover these punishments were only for the lower classes.

Associated with the disgrace that is retained and is therefore permanent are branding and flogging, which was followed by banishment; this meant that disgraced subjects were no longer capable of earning their livelihood in their own locality but could again do so in foreign lands, where they were unknown. So it was customary to look at once at an offender's back to see if he had already been branded. A disgraced person can be reintegrated by society. With the substantive [agricultural] class, where there is more spontaneity and reflection is not so developed or adhered to, disgrace does not strike as hard as with the higher classes, so disgrace has not the same importance and value for all classes. It was also the custom for the common people and court bailiffs to seek to make their abomination of crime known through their own activity, but this is wrong. Hanging is also regarded as demeaning because the noble possession that is life is taken away by a mechanical implement that costs so little. Beheading is now more accepted, and the guillotine has been deemed an important invention because the chance character of the executioner's skill does not here enter into play. However, this form of punishment is more of an indignity than to be killed by the free action of a human being. It is repugnant to see this action brought about by lifeless machinery.

Now that crime assumes a universal form, it becomes possible to take into account the moral aspect, the moral improvement [of the criminal], which | does not influence the justice of the punishment.

149

§ 114

The universal that is infringed through wrongdoing is not merely the concept of right but is present as civil society, which has as its basis and the ground of its subsisting the task of securing the life and property of individuals; consequently it avenges, in the injury done to the individual, the injury done also to itself as universal, and it modifies the penal provisions accordingly.

In crime injury is done to civil society, to a universal. Individuals are injured in their personality, and it is open to them to regard this as something infinite; but as has been said,[42] the qualitative and quantitative must be defined in terms of their external being. Since civil society, [which] has its essential being in what constitutes life and possession of property, is injured as a universal, an offense may become more important, by reason of the threat it presents to the basis, the substance of civil society, than it would be if all it amounted to was injury to the individual—e.g., theft and robbery. In civil society the role of right

42. [Ed.] See above, § 47.

is to be the unity of the universal and the particular wills. Out-side civil society it is a matter of contingency whether I leave the other unimpaired or vice versa since we have not yet rec-ognized our rights reciprocally, and I know that I am related to the other in contingent fashion and have to guard against being injured by him, have to arm myself so as to defend my-self against him. In civil society right has validity as law, i.e., it is recognized, and an injury that occurs here is a wrong in a wider sense than where there is not yet a state. The criminal acts (1) wrongly in general, and (2) against his own recognition of the law. So in civil society offenses can be punished more severely | than they can be in the abstract, in and for them-selves. And it depends on the view taken by civil society what importance it attaches to an offense and how severely it accord-ingly punishes it.   150

An offense is intrinsically dangerous in proportion to the other offenses it makes possible. Yet it should be taken at its own inner value, according to its universality. A totality is the illumination of the singular by reflection. An offense is inwardly more important [by virtue of] this inner universality: if the uni-versality is regarded as a totality the offense is punished by ref-erence to other single actions; but an offense must be punished according to its own inner importance. And since security of life and security of property are the basis of civil society, an of-fense against this basis is an offense against the universality and is punished more severely as harming the universality. It seems quite disproportionate for theft to be punished by death. The loss another incurs through theft may be minimal; but since the security of civil society is thereby impaired, it can impose more severe penalties. However, civil society can only modify the pun-ishment in light of the injury done to the universality; overall it must take into account equality of value, and the injury done to the universality is only one aspect to be considered. To be sure, the offense must be elevated to the [plane of] universality, but not indeterminate, abstract universality.

There are also other considerations that may render punish-ment more severe, e.g., if there was a conspiracy or if it is not the offender's first offense. An essential aspect of the action is the will, and the will that acts is subject to quantitative differences and gradations. Anyone who conspires has overcome aversion to crime, and has strengthened his will by using people who serve him rather as means; and the action is that of a more intensive will. It is the same when the will has passed through several stages. Repetition of the offense shows, for instance, that 151 | crime or evil has become the general, continuing element, has become a habit. And in imposing punishment all this must be taken into account. But the degree of danger is only one aspect, and a misleading one at that, for the implied idea is that what is punished in the offense is the possibility of something extraneous to it.

§ 115

Right as it exists in and for itself in a given case, and [right] as it has determinate existence according to legally determined norms (in other words, as recognizable and subject to proof in court), are in one respect extraneous to each other and also contingent insofar as the latter, existence for its own sake, is the external side, whereas right should come about in and for itself. Moreover, the more highly developed the laws are, the more manifold do they become for the concrete case and the more therefore do the judgment and application of the laws depend on the subjectivity of the judge. As a consequence it is necessary to have not only a *judicial system based on legal forms* [*Rechtspflege der Förmlichkeit*] but also one based on *equity* [*Billigkeit*]—not merely to the extent that in the event of loss, regard is had to equitable assessment of the thing in question and the condition and well-being of the parties, but also to the extent that in regard to form, judgment is pronounced in such a way as to be subjectively and adequately recognizable. The demand for a simple legal process as opposed to the long course of a more formal process also becomes important with regard to the difference between the classes—the simple, substantive mode of thought of the one and the more refined, formal, obdurate reflective thought of the other.

One knows one is in the right, but one cannot enforce one's

right, cannot make it recognizable because its determinate existence lacks the recognizable norms, and this is a terrible feeling for us. Both are necessary, that one should be in the right and that one's right should be recognizable. In the event of conflict actual right must take precedence over the formalities. For example in a testament or will, if certain seemingly quite inessential formalities are lacking, the whole will is | invalidated. Certainly the judge can argue that if these formalities are neglected false wills can easily be made; but in so arguing he is taking the part of the law and seeking to give a possibility, the possibility of something extraneous, precedence over right properly speaking.

152

To an unsophisticated person it must seem terrible that lack of a formality, the mere possibility of falsification of a deed, causes judgment to be rendered against the true right. The judicial system is nearly as important as the law itself, and among civilized peoples should be as fully developed as possible. But in England the most erudite jurist is incapable of knowing all the laws and how they qualify each other; so the laws are in the utmost confusion, but the judicial system makes the deficiencies imperceptible or almost so, and for the freedom and right of the citizens a good judicial system is more necessary than a new legal code.

For rights to be recognizable the judicial system must pay due regard to formalities; but these formalities should not impede right, and in the conflict between right and formalities, formalities are to take second place. It is not only the formalities that proliferate as the cultural level rises, but also the laws themselves. It is not the judge's role to be a mere organ of justice; there are a great many calls on his reflective thought.

Moreover, there must be courts of equity, over against the courts of law, in order that regard may be had not merely to right as right but also to the welfare of the parties; it is these questions of welfare, sympathy, etc., that have to be taken into account in equity proceedings. When the damage caused to one party by nonfulfillment by the other party of a contract entered into between them cannot be wholly demonstrated and has to be evaluated approximately, we have a proceeding in equity, where the [mode of] existence [*Existenz*] of both parties is also taken into account. Right ought to come about as right, but the courts have to decide according to their formulae and cannot deviate from the formal law. But a court of equity | could obviate the resulting wrong, and the evidence here must consist in individual circumstances. In England, for example, one can choose freely whether to leave the decision to the rigor of the law or to equity. Such decisions in equity make people conscious that they are getting their rights, and this is worth a great deal. Thus the Lord Chancellor attaches more weight to a draft will, a rough copy often without a trace of formality, than to an earlier will concluded in due and proper form.

153

The difference between the classes must also essentially result in differing forms in law. Thus the substantive class is concerned with its own distinctive right; not every single detail is essential to it, all it wants is right in general, its attitude is the substantive attitude; and it is only in the reflective class that each individual circumstance has to be explored.

§ 116

Proliferation of the laws makes comprehensive knowledge of them a distinct profession to which individuals must devote themselves completely, and [knowledge of the laws] becomes all the more alien to the mass of the people, although they form the basis and embodiment of its right. So it is not so much by virtue of their own insight that the parties are subjectively convinced of their right as by *trust* [*Zutrauen*]. They gain this conviction partly through jury courts made up of their peers, partly through the publicity of the proceedings; together these two form the main guarantees of the impartial administration of justice. Further requirements in regard to the formal constitution of the courts concern their collegiate form, the plurality of instances, and especially the independence of the judges both in their functions and in the terms on which they hold their office.

Since individuals must devote their entire course of study to knowledge of the law, this knowledge, and the means whereby one comes by one's right, become a closed, incomprehensible book for the great mass of the people. For the individual the administration and course of justice become no more than a matter of fate, a wholly alien power. | Right—the very thing in which   154 human beings ought to have their consciousness of freedom— and the process of right become for them an alien power: the costs levied by lawyers and the state result in litigants seeing a higher conspiracy directed against them, a conspiracy of the higher classes, whereby a gulf opens up between them and their right; all they get to know of the law are the legal costs. What is wholly lacking is precisely the subjective aspect, that individuals know how right comes about for them. For this alienation of right from subjective consciousness we have to thank our German youth who went, some ten thousand strong, to Bologna to study Roman law.

One of the most important things would be—since one's own insight is not possible owing to the proliferation of the laws— for trust to develop between lawyers and those who seek right. And trial by jury and the publicity of legal proceedings are the main means of maintaining trust and leaving it to the subjects to choose between arbitration and the formal process of law. Courts of first instance should also first seek to bring about an amicable settlement; but there is an ambivalence here, in that the office of arbitrator is simultaneously held by the judge, to whom it is accordingly all the same how he puts an end to the dispute, whether by legal process or by mediation. In fact there should be a separate authority for each function, having just the single purpose and concerned to realize it. Another factor that comes into play if the two are combined is the judge's subjective financial interests, partly for himself, partly for his friends the advocates. With jury courts composed of peers there are two aspects, the facts of the case being established by the jury and the president of the court confining himself to pronouncing the law in regard to the facts as established, subsuming them under the law.

But there must also be the subjective conviction that right is being implemented; care must be taken to foster a trust and awareness that one is receiving one's right. | The chief necessity for this, however, in the case of a fully developed legal system is that all should know themselves to be involved in the process; and this is ensured by the jury courts, which must be chosen by the people, not as in France solely by the prefect. Nor may they be chosen judicially but only according to the trust the electors have in particular in the candidate's morality. The members of the jury must be independent men in relation to their superiors, and it is very important that they should not have to keep looking over their shoulders; they must also be of independent character. A citizen who has lost interest in the state and is accustomed to doze his life away in mental dullness and political inactivity may be very disinclined to occupy a public office of this kind without remuneration, and in despotic states this state of affairs is quite acceptable to the common people. The upper classes, on the other hand, find it more oppressive, since they stand nearer to the despot. The fact that people have lost the habit of public service in this way may be one reason why jury courts have not become as firmly established in France as one must wish. The jury members must be of equal birth with the accused, and he must be confident that they have the same interests and the same circumstances as he has.

It is for the jury to determine the nature of the crime, who committed it, and in general to investigate the facts of the case, and this is within the ken of every educated citizen. The assistant magistrates of our forebears were citizens of the municipality; they were not lawyers and they were unpaid. But these courts had the shortcoming that they consisted of permanent members and they filled any vacancies that arose themselves. This ability to appoint new members themselves is a very common feature of our municipal administrations, despite its fallibility; and the administrators are not even properly accountable. It is true that no supervision is possible with regard to the courts, but the fact that they are permanent and self-renewing

in this way makes them alien to their fellow citizens and independent of them. This may also be the reason why these assistant magistrates have sunk to a very low status and [are] for the
most part inactive members | of the court.

156

Another *actus* is the application of the legal penalty to the
crime once it has been established, and this is for the judge as a
legal expert. But he must first once again put specific questions
to the jury concerning the facts of the case. If he can put particular questions to them concerning each single circumstance and
so more or less question them at his discretion, he can draw his
conclusion from the mass of answers, and yet still decide according to his will; and the jury ceases to be of any effect. In England there must be a unanimous decision by the jury because
the decision must be homogeneous, and this unanimity is to be
preferred to the French system, under which a two-thirds majority is sufficient and the judge's vote is decisive. The offender's
confidence in regard to his sentence is also necessarily greater
if unanimity is required. [For the jury] to pronounce sentence
would be contrary to the relationship between one citizen and
another, and the task of pronouncing [sentence on the basis of]
the laws belongs to a distinct court composed of judges designated [for the purpose]. It is not for them [i.e., the jury] to
pronounce on what is objective or abstract. What is essentially
distinct activity according to the concept must also involve a
particular, separate mode of acting, and so the jury's role is to
pronounce only on what is subjective. The police adopt a hostile attitude to the offender and seek to make him liable to punishment; the judge on the other hand, since he is pure justice, also
takes the part of the offender, so judge and police must also be
separate authorities.

Another essential feature, originating in Germany and still
quite widespread, is that legal proceedings should be public. All
citizens must themselves be able to hear why their fellow citizens are condemned, for it is not merely the accused's right that
is the object of judgment but the universal right of all. This also
eliminates divergence between the popular view of the offense

and the judgment of the court. The accused too, if his judgment is pronounced before his fellow citizens, is honored by the fact that the people are participating in the investigation. Action that has to be conducted in public has, however, a quite different significance in general terms. |

157

Another essential requirement is the collegiate form of the courts. This originates from Germany. The collegiate form of the courts does admittedly cause delay in reaching decisions, but without it there is all the more scope for arbitrariness and particular interests. But since each college must have an assessor, what happens is that since anyone can become an assessor each assents to the other's proposal since he hopes to be similarly treated himself; and because the responsibility rests on the whole college, the individual's responsibility becomes less. However, the assessor must so order his work that his proposal has universal validity within itself, and as far as answerability is concerned the assessor's is greater. Moreover, as a communal whole the college is in a stronger position to stand up to despotism, since the individual's freedom of action cannot here be so influenced as to sway matters unduly one way or the other. Each member of the college enters into an established whole, and there are not so many fluctuations in attitude and procedure. Plurality of instances is also very necessary, since anyone who believes himself wronged can still appeal to higher instances; the court of third instance is usually only a court of cassation, which merely examines whether the due forms[43] have been properly observed by the lower courts. This succession of instances does also hold up the rapidity of proceedings, and to this extent it has an inconvenient side. In times gone by, things in Germany had reached the point where a prince's subjects regarded it as fortunate if they were exempted from the court of third instance, the imperial court, where cases often got stuck for a century or more.

In monarchies it is an essential principle that the monarch should not act as a judge himself, in order that it should not be

43. *Ms. could also be read:* the formulae

his personal caprice that pronounces the verdict, and also because he has so much other power already. And the one who judges should have no other power over the parties than to judge them. Hence in recent times the prince only has the right to appoint the judge, who is independent in his | functions. The   158
prince has also the right of pardon, but not the right to make the penalty more severe. Regarding Frederick II's action in relation to the miller, when he dismissed several judges because they denied the miller his right in favor of the nobleman, the king's action was justifiable insofar as he believed the miller had been wronged.[44] But no member of the court can be deprived of his livelihood arbitrarily. It is also natural that accused persons should have defending counsel because they must be given someone in whom they have trust—this was the first point we dealt with.[45]

C. The Police or Public Authority[46]

§ 117

In the system of needs there are general resources [*Vermögen*] available for the needs of all. In the administration of justice the abstract right of individuals is maintained, but in the system of needs their welfare is an end only for themselves; nor is their end the universal connection between needs and the means of satisfying them, despite the fact that their subsistence depends on this.

44. [*Ed.*] Hegel is here referring to the case of Arnold the miller. Arnold's mill had been put up for auction by his feudal lord owing to his failure to pay his ground rent, and his counterplea was rejected on more than one occasion. His argument was that a carp pond had been constructed upstream from his mill, and this had deprived him of the water. Finally he appealed to the king, who eventually decided in his favor and sent the responsible magistrates to prison. See *Gespräche Friedrichs des Grossen*, ed. F. v. Oppeln-Bronikowski and G. B. Volz (Berlin, 1924), pp. 190–193.
45. [*Ed.*] See the dictated paragraph at the beginning of this section.
46. [*Tr.*] Hegel uses the word *Polizei* (cf. Greek *politeia*, Late Latin *politia*, "state," "commonwealth," "political administration") to denote what we would call "the public authority" or government regulation of industry and commerce, and this is how we have translated it except where the reference is clearly to the police as agency of law enforcement and prevention of crime (e.g., in § 119).

The universal must therefore become active for itself as such, and must eliminate and sublate the immediacy and contingency inherent in the system of needs as well as the external contingency that is to be found in the exercise of administrative justice.

Here we consider the concept of public authority and its object. The state based on need has as its end the system of needs and formal right; the universal is limited to this sphere of need and of right. On the whole, people are not well disposed to the public authority, but however unpopular it is, it is all the more necessary. | The system of needs continues to be strongly marked by contingency, which must be counteracted by means of something universal; the sphere of right too is marked by this contingency, and to sublate this must be the aim of the public authority. All citizens make their own welfare their sole end and rely on the universal connection [between their needs and those of others]. But the universal must have itself for its purpose, must become really existent as a universal. But each posits his interest as the sole end and lets it stand opposed to the interest of another class; the public authority then has to act as a moderating factor and seek to maintain equilibrium between all. The subsistence of the whole is subject to contingency, and in this struggle individual parts would be destroyed. The sphere of right by which formal right is actualized is also conditional; the administration of justice is contingent on the offender being brought to court, while the purpose of penal justice is that no crime should exist. We can deal only with the main aspects of the public authority.

§ 118

The first contingency is that involved in the individual's participation in the general resources, since this participation presupposes health, skill, capital [*Kapital*], and so on, and also a major conjunction of factors far removed from the individual's own orbit. As born within civil society, individuals are [dependent] on these resources for the actualization of their right to live [and] have to accept them as the inorganic nature and external conditions

governing such right. The whole community [*das Allgemeine*][47]
must therefore make provision for the *poor*, in regard both to
what they lack and to the idle, malevolent disposition that may result from their situation and the feeling of the wrong they have
suffered.[48]

Individuals have to rely for their capital [*Fond*] on the general resources. Their skill or work is not the only condition for
them to be able to draw on these resources, for this requires
skill, | health, and a certain capital [*Kapital*]. Now that states   160
have recently entered the field of business and commerce, it has
been said that this is no affair of the state and, even if individuals are ruined, only raises the level of the whole. All people have
the right to live, and not only must this right be protected, not
only do they have this negative right, but they also have a positive right. The aim of civil society is the actualization of freedom. The fact that human beings have the right to live means
that they have the positive, fulfilled right: the reality of freedom
should be an essential consideration.

The life and subsistence of individuals are accordingly a universal concern. This universal should itself be its own conscious
end. Since everyone works for himself, it is for civil society to
have as its end what is [the universal concern]. For individuals
the general resources belonging to society constitute the aspect
of inorganic nature, which has to present itself to them in such
a way that they can take possession of it. For the whole earth is
occupied, and they have in consequence to rely on civil society.
The reason individuals have a right to the earth is that they have
the right to live. [Even] if it is only individual factors that make

47. [*Tr.*] In this section Hegel frequently uses *Allgemeine* and *Gemeinsame* as
virtual synonyms.
48. [*Tr.*] In both the Heidelberg lectures and the Berlin lectures of 1818–19
and 1819–20, Hegel's description of poverty is more detailed and passionate, and
his critique of existing social conditions more thorough, than in the published version of the *Philosophy of Right*. To this discussion of poverty should be added his
depiction above (§ 101) of the "deadening" of human beings under the conditions
of factory labor. See Shlomo Avineri, "The Discovery of Hegel's Early Lectures on
the Philosophy of Right," *The Owl of Minerva* 16 (1985): 199–208, esp. 204.

this difficult for human beings, these are particular factors over against their right to live; the sick or insane are cases in point.

The right to live is what is absolutely essential in humanity, and civil society must make provision for it. A poor person is one who possesses neither capital [*Kapital*] nor skill. In states where the poor are left to fend for themselves their situation may become miserable in the extreme. For instance they have no clothing and, since they cannot go to church, they are deprived of the comforts of religion. It is not possible for them to obtain their right through formal justice—merely appearing in court—owing to the costs involved in the formal process of justice. They are at a great disadvantage in religion and justice, and also in medicine | because it is only from the goodness of their hearts that physicians attend them, and the hospital authorities also take a great deal off their patients for their own profit. This contingency must be overcome by the whole community [*das Allgemeine*]. In the first place special provision must be made for the indigent in a fatherly fashion, with due regard for particular circumstances. In addition, efforts must also be made to combat the idleness and malevolence that poverty usually brings in its train; and it is in the very areas where the poor are in fact most supported on compassionate grounds that laziness and a disinclination for work are found. In southern lands, where the necessities of life are few, we find this immediacy, this insouciance, out of which people have to be torn, for they should be self-dependent by virtue of their work. Idleness easily becomes vice, and the feeling of having suffered wrong and of not being the equal of others leads to malevolence among the poor. Civil society must keep the poor working; in this way there awakens in them the feeling of standing on their own feet, which is the best counter to malevolence.

But whole classes, whole branches of industry can succumb to poverty when the means this sector of the population produces are no longer sold and their business stagnates. The conjunction of the different factors involved goes beyond what the individual can grasp, and here the state must provide. The complexity of civil society itself also leads to poverty, since the means of satisfying needs are too difficult [to obtain]. For very many people are invariably attracted by the possibility all have of earning their living among the numerous population of a wealthy country or town. For example, this far-reaching possibility draws many people into a capital city, but for the individual this possibility is a matter of chance, and the rabble [*Pöbel*] increases by leaps and bounds along with poverty. And because people know that their community has to support them, as in England, indolence increases. For this reason civil society also has the right to keep the poor occupied. |

162

§ 119

The contingency in regard to criminal law partly concerns the discovery and prosecution of the offenders. But above all, criminal jurisdiction is itself contingent and conditional insofar as it depends on the commission of crimes, which are contingent actions, for the prevention of which the police must be on their guard, with the admittedly ill-defined proviso that they do only what is necessary and that in other respects the freedom of action and movement of citizens should not be curtailed—above all, that they should not appear to be everywhere under supervision. Of themselves, actions governed by right and the private use of property also involve more general relations to others and to their use either of their own property or of property owned in common. To this extent it is the task of the public authority to supervise and regulate this general relation, which could give rise to damage and wrong to others.

Crime has to be punished, but all that pertains to identifying and apprehending criminals is the affair of the police. This cannot be the responsibility of the courts themselves because the role of the police here is to be as it were the enemy of criminals, and they seek in all possible ways, often by cunning, to uncover crimes—the courts must keep their dignity intact—and the detection of criminals is something subjective, not yet involving justice. Crimes are to be regarded as contingent actions; the fact that someone is evil must be seen as something contingent, and

211

the nullity that seeks to endow itself with positivity is crime. But the police should prevent crimes. Evil should not happen, and there should be an authority that prevents it. Here we are talking about what *should* be, and this is the standpoint pertaining to the organization of the state based on need. Fichte's state is centered on the police, to whom it seeks to accord particularly wide scope, | but his state is a state based on need. According to Fichte, no persons can go out without having their identity papers with them, and he deems this very important so as to prevent crimes.[49] But such a state becomes a world of galley slaves, where each is supposed to keep his fellow under constant supervision.

This police supervision must go no further than is necessary, though it is for the most part not possible to determine where necessity here begins. Thus it could be assumed that the police should not enter one's house without a special order, for what the family does within the home must be unobserved. In the same way it is repugnant to see policemen everywhere. In this respect secret police would be best, for people ought not to see that they are exercising supervision even though such supervision is necessary. But the purpose of what is hidden is [in this event] that public life should be free. The disposition of police officials to be false and do all they can to catch someone must be neither suppressed nor encouraged.

In London use is made of people who have no official role to go after criminals, but anyone who brings a criminal in is rewarded. These people, or police spies, hunt around, without being officials, out of subjective interest, and they seek themselves to make criminals or to impute crimes falsely. For example poor Irishmen were made counterfeiters without knowing what they were doing, and were then arrested.[50] This can give rise to an abyss of depravity.

49. [*Ed.*] Johann Gottlieb Fichte, *Grundlage des Naturrechts nach Principien der Wissenschaftslehre, Zweiter Theil, oder Angewandtes Naturrecht* (Jena and Leipzig, 1797), pp. 146 ff. Cf. Fichte, *Gesamtausgabe* 4:87 ff.

50. [*Ed.*] See *Allgemeine Zeitung*, 21 October 1816, p. 1177: "Great Britain (from a London paper, 9 Oct.). . . . The police officers Brook, Pelham, and Plower,

The police have necessarily to cause a good deal of inconvenience, e.g., by inspecting identity papers. But this is a necessary regulation, and the one who performs it is doing so from duty. His disposition does not come into the matter if he checks on someone, since people are after all supposed to be honorable; rather for the police official, I am a subjectively strange individual. The police also have to ensure that no one harms the communal property nor the rights of individuals through the use one makes of one's own property. With the rapid pace of life, and all the thrust and bustle of civil society, tasks of an ephemeral nature, which so many people perform, have to be made simple. What each single individual would have to do is taken over by the whole community. | The police enter on the scene and reckon how use of my private property could injure others. But there must be a certain liberality in this calculation, for otherwise the police can interfere ad infinitum in the use made of private property. Apart from this, no limit can be set within which this supervision must be confined. The police are hated because they [have to] proceed in such a petty fashion and have such petty things to do, and because in removing obstacles they act only negatively, not positively. It is only in countries where there is no police force at all or a very bad one that the value of good police is felt; for a good police force should not be noticed at all, and since it is not seen doing anything, it gains no praise either. 164

§ 120
What is absolutely necessary to promote the prosperity of all civil business is a rapid, clear system for the administration of justice, and civil and political freedom in general. But bearing in mind that satisfaction even of the most individual needs depends on the availability of means produced by others, these means, as

who suborned three ignorant Irish day laborers into taking part in counterfeiting in order to gain the blood money for denouncing them, were yesterday evening condemned to death for counterfeiting. As this crime is equated with treason, they will be dragged to the place of execution. The three Irishmen had already been pardoned by the Prince Regent."

something intended for general use, call for a system of supervision. Moreover, the mutually opposing interests of the different occupations and trades, coupled with the dependence of the major branches of industry and the individuals linked to them on the competition of others (including foreign concerns), call for a general system of care and oversight. Such care includes the means and institutions of general utility established for the use of all, and ultimately colonization, which becomes necessary with a people whose industry is continuing to progress.

Civil freedom in regard to the administration of justice and political freedom are necessary moments. For example our governments go to great pains to raise the level of the sciences. Their prime concern, however, in this respect should be to ease the burden under which [intellectual] property suffers. As long as it is permissible for scholars to be robbed in all due formality, it cannot be said that the sciences | are being given external protection. In the same way in all other lines of business, justice must be clear and expeditious. Thus the right of exchange must be executed promptly for the merchant. Provision is made for bondsmen and slaves: their needs are satisfied in exchange for their labor. Citizens also work for their needs, but there is a world of difference between the activity of free citizens and slaves because the former work in the feeling that their property is protected. Political freedom is likewise very important, and where it is lacking, where it is suppressed, the state declines. For example Poland, for all its great past, was brought low, initially in its industry, through the oppression of the nobility. The towns that once were so famous fell into decay, and now they are known only by name, and the whole country is partitioned. [It was] the same with the Italian cities, which used to be so famous but for want of political freedom and independence are now for the most part insignificant backwaters. For without the administration of justice and political freedom the desire to enjoy, own, and acquire property disappears. It is only when there is rapid and transparent administration of justice and freedom on the political scene that business activity becomes brisk.

165

Each one of us, however, is dependent on others in regard to even our most individual, trivial, and necessary requirements. We can say that we should examine this commodity or that article that we purchase to see whether it suits us, whether it is not too dear; but if we had to examine all such details it would require of us a great deal of time and trouble. So the community must relieve us of this trouble and effort. Now since all have this concern, the community too, as something universal, has the right to examine these articles; for otherwise it could be said that it is not the concern of anyone how buyers and sellers conclude contracts with one another. But the article, e.g., bread, is offered for sale as something universal, and the individuals who come to buy it do so in contingent fashion, as abstract individuals. Hence the community has to | supervise and inves-   166
tigate the general usability of the article; and the little effort it expends saves an infinite number of particular efforts of individuals, and those who work for others are relieved of this concern. The dividing line here is indeterminate. The concern of the public authority must be confined solely to general commodities; and more artificial articles, which satisfy only particular needs, ought to be none of its concern; but it is not possible to indicate how far this ought to be extended.

The whole community must also ensure that individual citizens can satisfy their needs, i.e., that the commodities are available in adequate quantity and at not too high a price; but it must also take care that prices do not fall so low as to make it impossible for the producer to subsist. The business class and the agricultural class come into opposition in this way; the farmer wants to sell his produce dear, and the artisan wants to have it cheap. This puts an end to the equilibrium between the different classes, and frequently for relatively long periods. In England this is often the subject of deliberations in Parliament, and some years ago the import of fruit was permitted only if its price reached a certain level on the internal market. The commercial class has an interest that its goods should not be too highly taxed in order that their consumption should not decrease, and since consumption rises disproportionately when prices are low, the exchequer draws in more when taxes are light than when they are heavier.

The commercial class also has an interest that, in order that the country's own factories may grow, the import of products that are to be manufactured by them should be made difficult or prohibited. The reason why the freedom of trade among all states gives rise to difficulty is that an international treaty of this kind is something contingent and each state's principal concern must be its own subjects. In England all enterprise is speculative in character, even the agricultural class tending in this direction. But the state must not be so closely tied to other nations' needs as to make it possible for one business class to be ruined if the link is destroyed. Commercial interests | and the interests of manufacturers are often in opposition here. And no interests of the one class may be exalted at the expense of those of another class. Thus annual fairs are organized where merchants from abroad can also sell their wares in order that the consumers are not delivered over unduly to the caprice of the manufacturers of their own district or state; and by imposing high factory-gate duties on outgoing materials a state may impel foreign manufacturers to come to it and use its nationals in their factories. If one class sells its goods in distant lands, the individual members of the class cannot clearly see how their affairs are going, and the state must see to it. [It is] the same with the introduction of new machinery, as a result of which manual workers lose their jobs. The community must facilitate the introduction of machines, but at the same time provide for those whose livelihood has disappeared. The state must look abroad, to obtain benefits for its subjects by trade negotiations. Roads and canals are particularly conducive to industry, but even more so the sea. It is also a distinctive feature of the sea that it imbues the commercial class with the dimension of courage: over against the principle of one's own utility, profit, and enjoyment, danger enters on the scene, and this gives rise to a courage, an indifference in regard to this end itself. For this reason the sat-

167

irists of old were unjustified in the strictures they passed on an adventurous spirit.

If the population increases too much, the result is *colonization*. Where property is indivisible, only one of the family becomes a freeholder and the others become servants, and here population remains stagnant. But where farm property can be divided up and there is freedom, there is a marked increase in population, and land becomes insufficient. People must then earn a necessitous living at factory work without free independence; or else the state must see to it that they are given some uncultivated land or land not fully used by its occupants on which to realize the demands they make on the state to earn their living, and where they | can live in the same way as in the 168 home country—and this is how colonies come into being. France and England have many colonies. Since these colonists forever remain citizens of their home country, they are very useful to it. But where a state faced with such land shortage makes no provision for its citizens, then the result, as with us here in Germany, is emigrations, caused by overpopulation and the demand to be able to lead a specific mode of life. Migrants from Germany, however, go out as individuals, and instead of being of use to the home country as colonists, they become assimilated to other peoples since their own country does not care for them. Initially colonies depend on the home country, but they gradually become independent and form states on their own.

§ 121

Lastly it is essential

(1) that each individual should be allocated to a specific class or estate [*Stand*] and should take steps to acquire any specific skill or property qualification required in order to enter it;

(2) that the classes in general, and also their various particular branches, should be formed into *corporations* [*Korporationen*] since they have the same vocation, [the same] concerns and interests, in order that what is implicitly alike should also become really existent in the shape of something communal [*Gemeinsame*]

217

and universal. [This is necessary in order to provide] for the communal interest and [to ensure] an esprit de corps and individual welfare, and also, since each individual in his particularity is rooted in a universal, [to ensure] the essential strength of the whole.

The natural diversity of the classes must not merely remain a natural diversity; it must also become really existent as a universal in order that it may be recognized as a universal. To have a real civil existence [*Existenz*] (qua bourgeois), everyone must belong to a specific class. However, it is first necessary to examine whether one has the appropriate skill and means to do so. These classes, which initially relate merely to need, must become firmly established corporations. The rational element in corporations is that the | universal represented by the communal interest must become actually existent in determinate form. The atomistic principle—that each individual fends merely for himself and does not bother about a communal [end], the principle of leaving it to each and every one whether one wishes to join a certain class, not examining a person's suitability from a political point of view since after all (as we are told by those who favor this principle) someone whose work fails to find any favor will shift to another line of business—such a principle abandons the individual to contingency.

The reflective standpoint of our time, this atomistic spirit, the spirit that consists in taking pride in one's individual interest and not in what is communal, is harmful and has brought about the decay of the corporations. Through this spirit Germany disintegrated into atoms and the empire went into decline. The onset of this period of disintegration, this spirit of barbarism, came at a time when every baron and petty municipality was crossing swords with the others, and so it came about that towns were formed through the conflict between burghers and nobles (the future patricians). The towns formed alliances, and so the Hanseatic and Swabian Leagues came into being, and in this way civil society was formed by means of corporations. In the towns all the trades were for their part also corporations, and we had the esprit de corps of the guilds. This was

169

the high tide of civil life; enjoyment lay in what was communal, and people did not amuse themselves for themselves but in the community.

Now this spirit is undermined, so that people are ashamed of their class, are unwilling to be seen as members of it, and take pride in themselves alone. The Greeks and Romans made the natural line of descent from a progenitor the basis of their divisions. The basis we use, resting on one's trade, on a common, enduring, and present interest one has freely chosen, is a superior one. To be sure, the citizens of a city can also be divided from the point of view of the public authority according to districts, but this is an external, purely spatial relationship—the basis here is the lifeless numerical one.

It is the same with the division of the civil militia into companies, this being done according to size, which is an external, unreal, and bad way of doing it as opposed to the way it was previously divided, according to corporations. But what also happened was that each corporation—not looking to the whole but | merely to itself, since the authority of the state was insufficient—amassed all the rights it could lay its hands on, disregarding the rights of other corporations. For the state to be able to subsist, it was therefore necessary for the corporations to be deprived of their power and prestige, and so they fell into decay. Corporations are useful in providing for the common interest, and the need to act in common is a constantly recurring feature. But everyone must also take pride essentially in belonging to a community, and the pride that consists in seeking to shine as an individual ought not to be. The whole, the state, only achieves inner stability when what is universal, what is implicit, is also recognized as universal. The sphere of needs involves particular ends, which are, however, ordered as something communal. The whole is divided into parts whose determinacy resides in the system of need. The essential interest of all particulars is to subsist, and this links them to the particular sphere. It rests on the particular vocation people elect for themselves; it is a real sphere, a concrete sphere pertaining to

170

activity. The particular ends of people are essential to them, but [together] they form something communal, and this is the most essential aspect of civil society.

3. The State

§ 122

The immediate substantiality of the family, substantiality at the level of feeling [*empfindende Substantialität*], or the ethical substance as individual, passes over, of itself, into civil society, whose particular aims and interests dissolve into a universal interest for one aim, the inner roots of which are the family, while its external reality, which must be brought back from unconscious necessity to universality, is civil society. Spirit in the natural state leads to an association of families, while particular needs lead to civil society; but as absolute duty, the universal that exists in and for itself leads to the *state* [*Staat*]. |

171

The state here differs from the state based on need that we encountered in the second sphere. The two principal moments are simple substantiality and its fragmentation into the sphere of difference. The former takes the form of feeling [*Empfindung*], love, trust, etc., while the latter takes the form of need to subsist for oneself, but in dependence, for something other than oneself.[51] This latter is the status of relationship—of independence, to be sure, but illuminated by something other than the self. It is the sphere of appearance[52] in general, in which freedom exists in formal fashion. The one is solid identity, the other its fragmentation; as the first [sphere] is marked by the tie of love, so here we have the tie of necessity, where people behave to one another as independent beings. The third is the unity of the two, which appears as consciousness of freedom. Freedom exists as necessity and necessity as freedom. In civil society freedom is not a product of separation but of the natural tie. Here in the state

51. *Ms. could also be read:* in dependence on something other than oneself
52. [*Tr.*] In the German there is a wordplay between *hereinscheint* ("illuminated") and *Erscheinung* ("appearance") that cannot be reproduced in English.

it is the product of separation and free, self-determined union. Absolute duty leads into the state. The ethical life of the state is that freedom should *be*, that what is rational, the universal will, should happen as a necessity and have external existence.[53] The inner roots of the state are the family. Family and state stand over against each other; the ruler is seen as the supreme head of a family, and the state continues to be based upon the family relationship as what is universal and all-embracing. The external reality of the one absolute end is civil society; however, this is the moment of negativity, where the form of universality emerges from need. This form of universality is a necessary moment of the state, but not for the purpose of particular needs; on the contrary, the essential end here is the free will. It is by reproducing themselves for the welfare of individuals that the ends or purposes constitute [themselves], but they dissolve in the welfare of the universal. The universal element in the state does not allow the particular purposes to ossify as such, but ensures that they keep on dissolving in the universal. | 172

§ 123

The state is the actuality of the ethical spirit as the manifest, self-transparent universal will, achieving knowledge and fulfillment in custom as it exists immediately in the individual self-consciousness. It is in the knowledge and activity of the individual self-consciousness that the state has its mediate actuality, just as

53. [Tr.] *dass Freiheit sei, dass das Vernünftige, der allgemeine Wille, als eine Notwendigkeit geschehe und äusserliches Dasein habe.* Cf. a similar formulation in the exposition to § 134: "what is rational must happen" (*was vernünftig ist, muss geschehen*). These formulations differ subtly but significantly from the famous dictum found in the Preface to the published version of the *Philosophy of Right*: "What is rational is actual; what is actual is rational." In the earlier lectures the emphasis is on a dynamic, unfinished process, and there is no legitimation of whatever exists as rational. (Such a legitimation is not intended in the later formulation either since what is "actual" differs from what is empirically "real.") See *Elements of the Philosophy of Right*, ed. Allen W. Wood, trans. H. B. Nisbet (Cambridge, 1991), p. 20 (incl. n. 22). See also Shlomo Avineri's discussion of this matter in "The Discovery of Hegel's Early Lectures on the Philosophy of Right," *The Owl of Minerva* 16 (1985): 202–204.

the individual self-consciousness, by virtue of its disposition to know the state as its substance and the end and product of its activity, has its freedom in the state.

In the state the universal will becomes actual; the universal has determinate existence as absolute end. Here there is no longing, nothing beyond our ken, no future; the purpose is actual and present. Identity is where what lies within is immediately external, so that inwardness occurs as externality and vice versa. The growth, etc., of a plant is something external, a determinate existence; but this concept constitutes its inner being, its nature. The essence of self-consciousness is what is rational; only in self-consciousness is the rational will present. Spirit is here what has been brought to the fore, what is clear to itself and universal; it does not occur as in the sphere of necessity and as in civil society, but occurs as freedom. What we have here is the universal that knows itself, the will whose form is that of universality.

In the same way that the universal is known here as law, which is revealed, so too it is actualized. Here the universal is the custom of a people, which *is* spirit and has the form of a universally natural event. A living organism is the first and the last because it has itself as the product of its activity. This activity constitutes the individuality of self-consciousness, which posits itself as negativity and is the free ego, infinite relation to itself. Spirit has its actuality in the individual self-consciousness. Reason is essentially concrete and thus spirit. Spiritual naturalness [*geistige Natürlichkeit*] gives rise to the family, need to civil society, and free will to the state. With the will as free will it is not only the good as an end that is required but the good in its actuality; however, the good is an idea, in the sense that it is not immediately actual. In the state the good is | actually present, not something beyond. Animal organisms continually produce themselves, but what they produce already exists—they only reproduce. [It is] the same with good in the state. The good is not a random disposition, not a disposition of the conscience; it is external, actual existence, and in order for it to be, the state can employ coercion.

§ 124

The right of the state consists in the idea of the state being recognized and actualized. Individuals have the right with their particular will to enter the state and form part of it. If they do not enter it of their own free will, they place themselves in the state of nature, where their right is not recognized, and this recognition must come about by natural means, through the struggle for recognition and use of force. In this relationship of force the divine right is on the side of the *founder of the state.*

The state is universal will, which is actual universal self-consciousness, the idea of God. For this reason the universal essence of the state has also been worshiped by the nations as a god. It is freedom in its universality and in its actuality; that this idea should *be,* is the supreme right. Freedom is pure activity, and this activity qua freedom is self-consciousness; thus the idea is realized in the individual self-consciousness. As in abstract right persons place their freedom in external, natural things, so the material form of substantial freedom is self-consciousness. Substantial freedom invests itself in the individual self-consciousness, which is devoid of rights over against it. If individuals oppose this idea, they are devoid of rights, wholly lacking in dignity. The absolute right of the state is to be actualized by means of the individual self-consciousness.

It is a matter of free choice for individuals, who have personal freedom, whether in principle they wish to enter the state. They ought to have their idea in the state, ought to become actually free through the negativity of their particularity. Self-consciousness is the essential moment in the idea of the state. [But] if it is the particular will of the individual not to be in the state, then that individual resolves to exist as an immediate entity | and enters the state of nature over against the state; the 174 consequence must be conflict between the state and the individual. What is free must have its knowledge in another self-consciousness: this is its higher mode of existence, existence at the representational level. It is only in the will of another that an individual can have this determinate existence through being recognized by the other's will. There is in consequence no longer a mutual indifference between persons; there must be mutual recognition, and there arises the struggle for recognition whereby one accepts the risk of giving up the natural mode of existence. In opposition to immediate being, freedom presents itself solely as negativity. Each of us incurs this risk in which we expose our natural being to being negated. Any who resolve on their own account to retain their freedom vis-à-vis the state thereby contend with the state for recognition; but divine right rests with the state, which therefore has the right of coercion in regard to those individuals who resolve to remain free in nature.

The founders of states must be regarded as heroes who are founders of the divine right [*göttliches Recht*] and who therefore have the right of coercion; they are regarded as heroes by the nations even if they have used force to bring their individual subjects together.

§ 125

Another feature of the founding of states is that in cases where corporations and associations of civil society, which rest in the first place on a common interest in a particular purpose, are in possession of a power that belongs conceptually to the state—possessing it not as an emanation from the state but as a purely private right of their own vis-à-vis the state—then the state as universal unity has the absolute right to annul such particular possession.

It is very often the case with us that states developed out of corporations, e.g., through feudalism; this explains the people's struggle against the magnates in our states. As third estate [*Stand*] the people | in turn formed corporations, by means of which they took advantage of the weakness of the state to secure privileges for themselves.

It has been these privileges against which the whole tendency of recent times has been directed. In other countries such as France and England the state established control over these particular rights. But in Italy for instance the opposite happened. The fact that private citizens reduced the state to ruins might give the semblance of being freedom. If single citizens, be they

175

individuals or corporations, possess rights belonging to the state, the state has divine right over against them, and can and must take these rights from them. Corporations claim their privileges as their private property, and they have form on their side. In Germany the supreme authority has sold or handed over one by one these rights belonging to the state. The constituent members of the state have arranged matters with the supreme authority in such a way that it handed over to them as purely private rights these rights belonging to the state, and in this way the rights of the state have become *jura singulorum* [private rights] in a manner absolutely contrary to right. No regard was had to where these rights came from or to the fact that they were state rights that cannot be possessed by individuals.

There is a work by Moser enumerating all these rights possessed by individuals, both state rights and their purely private rights.[54] Here belong the revolutions of recent times. There were classes [*Stände*] and individuals who possessed, as purely private rights, rights belonging to the state, especially in regard to taxes (e.g., freedom from taxation) and jurisdiction. And our day has seen a step taken toward the rational existence [*Existenz*] of the state that has not been taken for a thousand years past: the right of reason has been asserted over against the form of private right. Private circles protest loudly at this, and in France the *émigrés* still want to have their privileges back. In the same way the nobility in Germany invoke right in support of their former privileges. But only rarely can the state be bound by right to pay compensation. Thus no compensation can be demanded in regard to freedom from taxes, because the classes in question no longer have to render any services; if there were to be compensation, the state would take away with one hand what it gave with the other. There can be no question of demanding compensation for all such rights as that of jurisdiction or the exclusive right of appointment to the rank of officer and

54. [*Ed.*] Cf. Johann Jacob Moser, *Neues Teutsches Staatsrecht*, 23 vols. (Stuttgart, Frankfurt, Leipzig, 1766–1782).

176   other offices, | since it would rather be open to the state to present this class with a bill for its enjoyment of these rights. It is a different matter when there is vassalage, as in the case of *laudemium* [see § 25 exposition]; the form here becomes one of private property, and to the extent that the property is supposed to be, and to become, free of servitudes, those who gain thereby must pay compensation to the losers. The universal element constituted by the will that exists in and for itself is here confronted by nothing that could make itself particular.

§ 126

The life of the state is

(1) its organism in relation to itself in the form of *constitutional law* [*inneres Staatsrecht*];

(2) its self-sufficient individuality in relation to other states: *international law* [*äusseres Staatsrecht*];

(3) its universal idea as genus or generation [*Gattung*] and as absolute power vis-à-vis the individuality of single states: *history* [*Geschichte*].

For example an animal organism articulates itself in the first place from within. Secondly, organic nature is turned against a nature that is inorganic over against it. The third aspect is the process of generation [*Prozess der Gattung*]; as universal power, the genus pursues its development and presents itself as universal. In the same way the process of the state is, first, that it has its life within itself, then the need to exist over against other states as power and authority. This is the stage of irritability, of war and peace with other states, the state maintaining itself here as an independent, self-sufficient individual. Thirdly, universal spirit actualizes itself as world spirit [*Weltgeist*]; the genus manifests itself in solely negative fashion vis-à-vis individuality and relapses continually into singularity, while the universal becomes more manifest. The ensuing stage of history is always higher, and this is the perfectibility of spirit. It is not merely that the genera manifest themselves by means of the extinction of the individuals; in sublating its phenomenal form, the spirit of the age

177   [*Zeitgeist*] attains in the transition a higher stage. |

A. Constitutional Law

§ 127

The life-principle [*Lebendigkeit*] of the state as an ethical totality is actualized to such an extent that the universal free will brings itself forth with necessity; only to the extent that it does so is the state an organic whole. Its *constitution* or *system of government* [*Verfassung*]⁵⁵ is the rationality of a people and the organizing principle of its freedom.

For the will that is free in and for itself to be, it must be with necessity. Freedom must *be*, not in the sense of contingency but in that of necessity. Its actual being consists in its inner organization. A people is rational only to the extent that its constitution is rational. By "people" [*Volk*] we mean a unity in regard to customs, culture, etc., and this unity is existing substance [*die seiende Substanz*]. The people as pure and simple mass is still devoid of rationality, for rationality is only the whole system; thus the sun and the earth are not rational, but the solar system and its organization expressed in time and space is rationality. The mass is not what is rational: one cannot have respect for a people as mere people. A people that does not have a noble constitution is a bad people; only the universal can be genuinely respected. It is a different matter if one is comparing individuals with individuals in [the realm of] morality. The constitution means that the universal will must be brought forth.

§ 128

As an *external necessity* the state stands opposed to private individuals and to the system of needs and particularity in general, to the extent that this system's purpose and that of the state conflict. Since the former purpose becomes firmly fixed as an external purpose for itself, | the power of the state appears as coercive power and its right over against such purpose as a right of coercion.   178

Such external necessity is not the necessity of freedom. Such necessity occurs when purposes pertaining to the state based on

55. [*Tr.*] By "constitution" (*Verfassung*) Hegel means not merely a written document but the way in which a government is actually organized.

need clash with the state. The state must not allow the purposes of the state based on need to take root within it, but must constantly draw them back within its substance; its attitude to them is merely negative. If a corporation adopts an attitude counter to the universal purpose of the state, if what is private seeks to use the state merely for particular purposes, then the state appears as a coercive power. This struggle is on the one hand what gives life, on the other hand it is the state's inorganic nature, which it constantly has to bring back into universality. If something that has its particular purpose opposed to the purpose of the state becomes fixed on its own account, the state becomes an external over against this external. The state's right of coercion enters into play when the state departs in any respect from what is ideal [ideell].[56] We now have to consider the conditions of inner necessity.

§ 129

There are two aspects to be considered in regard to the constitution of the state:

(1) The concept of the state in terms of its inner organic determination.

(2) The allocation of individuals to its universal spheres of action and their participation in them.

But the concept of the state itself comprises two moments:

(a) to be universal, pure spirit, and

(b) to be actualized spirit, bringing itself forth through its own activity.

Actualized spirit involves the self-determination and individuality of the will, whereas universal, pure spirit is the substance, the end, and the self-consciousness of all. But where, as actuality and activity, this individual will of universal spirit behaves as an inwardly | inarticulated mass, it is caprice and contingency, and the whole is no more than an immediate actuality.

The concept of the state is in principle the universal as such.

179

56. Ms. could also be read: when the state contains anything not pertaining to the idea [ideal]

The first aspect is universal spirit viewed on its own account, while the second is how the individuals making up this material are allocated to universal spirit. There must be organic life within the state, and individuals must have a determinate share or participation in the universal sphere of action. The first aspect is the life of spirit on its own account, of which we say that it is active universal will, universal freedom determining itself inwardly. To this extent law plays no part, and it is thought [that is active]; however, where the will is concerned, law springs into action. The universal spirit is in the first place simply pure universal spirit, but it is also concrete universal spirit, which reproduces itself; together these two moments constitute spirit. An individual is the son of his people; all he knows is contained in the universal substance. The universal is the soil in which he has a mode of being, a position. So it is also the purpose of all individuals that this essence, this substance should be,[57] that it should be continually brought forth. Individuals are moments of this substance; their knowledge of themselves is as of particular beings, but all their knowing is mediated by substance, itself immediate. This substance is the real self-consciousness of all. As far as this self-consciousness is concerned, the universality of knowledge—the spirit inherent in the knowledge of all—is communal spirit. But if this spirit were to remain something whole, substantial, it would be something inwardly inarticulated, its will would be only whole, undifferentiated will, it would be caprice. Spirit is [here] immediately actual; it is what knows and what is known, and this knowledge is itself self-consciousness; the spirit has actuality. Individuals' certainty or certain assurance of themselves is the immediate actuality of spirit. But immediate actuality is contingent; it is a | possible actuality, one that either may be or may not be.   180

Substance, however, is immediate actuality, and as such has

57. [Tr.] *dass dieses Wesen diese Substanz sei.* Our translation construes the two nouns to stand in apposition (and thus adds a comma between them) rather than in a subject-predicate relation (which would translate as "that this essence should be this substance").

not yet genuine reality. It is to this that one is referring if one says there must be a corporate spirit in the state; this corporate spirit is then the universal foundation, but one must rise above it. A corporate spirit does not come about simply by encouraging or commanding people to display it; such encouragement is moral in character, since it is imputed to the subject. The corporate spirit is an attitude, but it must be an end in itself for each individual and cannot be left to the will of each individual as something moral. By command it is imputed externally as a duty. The corporate spirit exists; for it to do so, the life of the state must be actual. The English have a corporate spirit because they know all individuals receive their right, and the state, as universal will, is their will, the people's own will. In the state all nations find the essence of their freedom, find their substance. In Oriental despotism, however, there is no articulation, individuals disappear in the one will, and the unity is inwardly unarticulated. It is the same in a purely democratic state, to the extent that each individual has only to say his will and this will immediately comes to pass; and we are then not in the presence of necessity but of an undifferentiated mass, which can be as well one thing as another.

§ 130

It is in its organic inner *activity* [*Tätigkeit*], freedom as negative self-relation, that the spiritual substance brings itself forth in living fashion. Universal spirit is in consequence differentiated inwardly, and its universality is engendered from this differentiation, from the articulation and apportionment of its universal sphere of action and power into the different moments making up its concept as into distinct powers and spheres of action. The fact that the ultimate aim, which is a universal work and mode of being as well as a universal human attitude or disposition, is engendered from the determinate action of the different spheres of activity, constitutes the *inner necessity* [*innere Notwendigkeit*] of freedom.

Necessity involves the existence of two self-differentiating entities, two distinct self-determinants in which the concept | is divided; but the concept exists in both of them, and their move-

181

ment consists in dissolving into this identity. Absolute spirit determines itself and is nature, but is truly spirit in returning within itself. It is only through this differentiation that spirit is life. Animals that are less than perfect are those with a low degree of articulation, which exist as [mere] masses; with higher organisms reproduction involves the mediating action of movement. Animals that are all of one piece are those with a low degree of corporeal organization.

The essence of spirit as state is to differentiate itself inwardly, to divide itself; in this way it loses its contingent character. It is only as a result of this division that it is something living, organic. Enjoyment arises only in the form of coming back out of this differentiation. In religion the individual rises above the plane of work. Universal freedom is also no [mere] enjoyment, no rest, but something serious. Living actuality consists in the continual self-generation and self-determination of substance; this moment of negativity is the moment of freedom. The distinctions within the state must exist as members, each with its peculiar organization, which are inwardly independent and generate or reproduce the whole. Spirit exists as pure substantial unity, but in this self-differentiation it makes itself the cause [of the different powers and spheres of action]. To say that the best constitution is the one where the best people rule is to say something very trivial, since the question whether the constitution is to be good cannot be made dependent on contingency. Plato and Aristotle regard it as divine good fortune if government is in the hands of the best, and believe that necessity is to be found when they are at the helm.[58]

§ 131

The concept of the state comprises the following three moments: (1) The universal rational will, both as the constitution and constitutional laws and as laws properly speaking: *the constitution itself and the legislative power* [*gesetzgebende Gewalt*].

58. [*Ed.*] Hegel is referring to Plato, *Republic* 412c; and Aristotle, *Politics* 3.15.1286a38-b11.

(2) The particularization of the universal will by subsuming the particular under it as counsel and reflection, partly by raising it to 182 and equipping it for the form of universality, | partly by applying the universal to the individual: *the executive power* [*Regierungsgewalt*].

(3) The reflection of the whole into itself, the individual will as the ultimate power of decision and command: *the sovereign or princely power* [*fürstliche Gewalt*].

These three moments correspond to the moments of the concept itself, in the same way as in the organism we have sensibility, irritability, and reproduction as the unity of sensibility and irritability. The state is (1) a universal as universal; the universal as universal subsisting in and for itself is the constitution, and the universal in relation to the particular is law. Law is the universal element in the particular. The constitution is absolute power. In the state it is not given; the state has only the legislative power. (2) The executive power, whereby the universal is applied to the particular and the particular is raised to the universal: the application of the constitution and the laws. This includes equipping or preparing the particular for the laws, and also the power of enacting. Application of the universal to the particular is also one mode of enactment. (3) The subjectivity of the whole, whereby the whole becomes a subject: here we have the apex of the pyramid.

Kant declared that freedom is only ensured by the separation of powers, and he distinguished (1) the legislative, constituent power, (2) the judicial power, (3) the executive power.[59] The idea here is that each of the three powers retains the ultimate power of decision, and this makes them three powers; but since none of them is subordinate to the others, the whole is not an organic whole, and since each is separate from the others, they do not form moments of the concept. The legislative power gives laws, and the laws are only what is universal, and the universal as power of decision is something subjective; but the uni-

59. [*Ed.*] Kant, *Rechtslehre*, pp. 164–173 (§§ 45–49). Cf. Kant, *Schriften* 6:313–318.

versal must be transparent to itself. However, these different moments should be living, so each should include the other two
within itself. The legislative power is enacting, and | the execu-   183
tive power too has the power of decision. As living, the sovereign power is also, to be sure, what has the power of decision,
but it decides according to the universal and in the universal.

§ 132

This division is

(1) the absolute guarantee for freedom, because through it
alone freedom has actual *rights* within itself. Right is the *existence*
[*Dasein*] of freedom, but existence is to be found only in determination and differentiation. By virtue of the fact that in the constitution the particular spheres of action of the universal will are
present not only [as] duties but (as differentiated powers) also as
rights, the universal will is coupled to particularity, namely to the
sphere to which belong the peculiar activity and the interests of individuals—individuals who have to defend the rights of this sphere
as their own, in the same way that being assigned to such particular duties they are educated by means of this division of the universal labor and have their peculiar self-consciousness in sustain-
ing one essential moment of the universal will as a right that belongs
to them.

[We still have to describe] how the particular will of individuals as particular is and can be combined with the universal
will. For individuals to be active, for them to have an [active]
interest, they must possess something particularly their own.
Since they are living, actual subjects, it must be the case that in
working for the universal they attain their particular purposes.
If the state as individual has to maintain itself against another
individual, another state, the entire state and all its citizens are
involved. But things are different within the state itself. People take no share in the universal unless it is in their own self-
interest. But the universal must occur necessarily, and the moral
will can be disregarded here; instead, since the universal | must   184
occur, the individuality of each as such must reside in the universal. The universal must be accomplished and in such a way

that the individual, in accomplishing the universal, is working for himself. The particularity of the individual will must be
maintained in the universal will. Here we have universality and
particularity conjoined on the real plane. On the one hand this
is patriotism, while on the other it can be said that the individual is acting egoistically. The corporate spirit or patriotism does
not afford this guarantee; instead it is when the universal will
particularizes itself that it ceases to be a merely moral will and
becomes [a] necessary will.

Now the division consists in individuals being assigned a
sphere of action in which they have their existence [*Existenz*]
and in which their honor resides, a sphere that is of service to
the universal. Patriotism en masse has no inner necessity, and
involves no rights. Likewise there are no rights in despotism.
The well-known saying *divide et impera* [means] one must divide in order to have to deal with particulars as particulars and
not with everyone bound together; but it is just this principle of
"divide and rule" that also first gives rise to freedom since it
sublates the elementary level of volition and action. (The fact
that the state has rights vis-à-vis other states follows directly
from the fact that it is distinct from them, but we are speaking
initially of relationships within the state itself.)

For freedom to exist as right, it must endow itself with immediate externality. It is only through the process of differentiating and determining that this universal freedom attains existence [*Dasein*] within itself, attains being-for-other. Judgment
[*Urteil*][60] is the immediate existence of the concept; it is only as
judgment that the concept is made existent. Rights arise in that
the constitution is what makes freedom existent, i.e., particularizes the spheres of action of the universal will. As essential moments of the freedom of the whole these spheres exist in necessary fashion, and duties and rights come on the scene. By this

---

60. [*Tr.*] Hegel thought that this term, normally translated "judgment," contains within itself the idea of a primal division or differentiation (*ur-teilen*). However, *urteilen* derives from *erteilen* (to share out or distribute) and is not connected
etymologically with the idea of "primal division."

means the universal and the particular will are united. Individuals to whom such a sphere of action is assigned as they freely choose, and who devote themselves to it, have their aptitude in the specialized field in question and, as particulars, belong to it, | their own peculiar interests and activity being vested in it. 185 In patriotism the aim is that all should be alike, but here where we are dealing with education we have particularization. In a republic, where the educational stage has not yet been reached, we have this virtue of the ancients [patriotism]. But this moment of infinite value that individuals have within themselves as individuals, this principle of the Christian religion to the effect that each single individual should be deemed of value as such, [that there] should be no slavery, that all should know themselves equally in religion [as] objects of divine love—this requires that what is individual must give itself existence [*Existenz*], and its determinate existence [*Dasein*] is particularity. The subject is only what is singular; the particularity or determinate existence of the subject comes from the predicate or attribute, and particularity relates to universality. On the one hand the universal must particularize itself; [on the other hand] not only does the individual have its essence, its substance in particularity, but also it maintains itself in this particularity, and as this particular it knows itself as in the universal, it labors for the community [*Allgemeinheit*].

Only through its bringing forth does the individual subsist in its particularity, and this is its interest. Its pure interest is that this end should be brought about through it, that as the result of bringing forth it should posit itself, that it should have in the product the consciousness of itself; it must know the product as its own. The content is something particular, has determinate existence, and can therefore differ greatly: it may relate either solely to the subsistence and instincts of individuals (and this is self-interest) or to the universal. If in their patriotism the will of all is directed to doing what is universal, this particularization is overcome. After the Peloponnesian War, for instance, the Greeks became restless, each wanting to be involved in everything and do everything, and the whole then degenerates into powerlessness. It is by particular spheres of action being assigned to individuals that this division comes about. Labor becomes abstract and acquires the form of universality, and individuals must | educate or train themselves for their sphere of action. On the universal level, in the sphere of mass existence [*wo das Massenhafte existiert*], the universal becomes something contingent, since all believe that the only thing needed is their good will and no particular aptitude is necessary.

In regard to individuals, education or training is an absolute necessity. In recent times those who have acquired no aptitude for a particular class go into the universal sphere of the mass [*Massenhafte*], the military class, and there prove lacking (e.g., Colonel Massenbach, who as quartermaster-general failed to reconnoiter on the occasion of a number of engagements and so caused very serious damage to the Prussian army and showed himself completely incompetent, never knowing where he was; in recent times, being no longer of any significance for the military, he emerged as a patriot).

This education is something immediately necessary. If individuals vest their aptitude in a particular sphere of action, they must defend this status and view it as their own. A universal spirit of patriotism is formed by the fact that universal freedom comes about through particularization. There must be universal patriotism, but it must come about through esprit de corps.[61] Now if such corporations have many privileges, they can become dangerous to the whole; they must be given their purpose by the universal and for the universal. It is only through their actions, through their activity, that people proclaim what they are, but this activity must have its ground, its logical connection, in the universal. It must be a concern of the universal that they perform their functions not as single individuals through their contingent freedom of choice but as members of a corps. And in entering on a concern or sphere of action of the state, they make the state the center of their activity and attitude, and

186

61. [*Tr.*] Here the text uses the French phrase instead of *Standesehre*. And just below, the word *Korps* ("corps") is introduced.

the entire corps must defend its concern and becomes answerable for it. To be sure, individuals must stand at the apex, but the corporation causes them to operate through a corps of counselors. In the corps each defends his own honor and the honor of the corps as a whole. |

187

§ 133

Since this division makes the particular spheres of action self-subsistent bodies with their own peculiar rights, it cannot

(2) make the spheres mutually independent so that the unity of the whole should result from their self-subsistent action. But equally, as they are within themselves a totality, on the one hand they have their determination and their rights only in and through the general constitution [of the state], while on the other hand for the ultimate decision of will they must join together in an *actual* individual unity.

The different spheres of action and powers must essentially join together in a dual unity, in inner unity and in essentially individual unity. Each particular sphere of action subsists for itself and has within itself the whole concept, and to that extent a totality determined in such a way as to constitute a moment of the whole. Where individual classes or corporations cared for themselves (e.g., the Hanseatic League in Germany, which took to itself and invested itself with the state's duty and right to protect trade), this caring did not issue from the whole, and is a matter of their caprice. But the fact that all spheres of action or powers in the state must issue from what is universal is the inner unity and the external unity, the unity that exists in its own distinctive way.

It seems somewhat superfluous that a supreme power consisting in this subjective unity should unite all powers; when each single power is acting as it should, it seems that the universal thereby becomes existent *ipso facto*. All French constitutions had the defect that they lacked the subjective unity, the apex, which came necessarily into being in the form of imperial and then royal power. The interplay between juxtaposed powers none of which forms the apex of the pyramid inevitably results in one or another power rising above the others and standing over them. In France, where the king was only involved in negative fashion in the | universal power, being able to do no more than veto the proposals of the legislative body, the apex was too weak, and a state of tension became unavoidable the more the legislative body considered itself justified in its proposals that were rejected. In this mutual independence of the powers these two powers stood over against one another, and unity could only be decided by means of conflict. First the legislative power prevailed over the royal power, and the king was sentenced and executed by the legislative power. Then the Committee of Public Safety rose to the top, and the very top of the pinnacle was Robespierre. This point of unity centered in an individual, to whom the legislative power was slavishly subservient, performing deeds that attracted universal amazement. A wholly republican constitution was drafted, for the legislative body had collapsed. However, this democratic constitution could not take effect because of its inner nullity, and the Directory's constitution came into being. But the basic evil remained notwithstanding, in that the legislative power was quite independent of the Directory, which was surrounded by a great show of pomp and might. The inevitable struggle ensued, each side making it a point of duty to save the state; however, the power that was at the head of the army, the executive power, was the stronger. The apex of power was then reestablished by Bonaparte, first as consul, then as emperor; but because in so doing he did injury to the rational, the apex he established was overthrown despite the external power at its disposal.

This is why Fichte, in his constitution, set up two self-subsistent powers in opposition to each other, the executive and the ephorate. The ephorate's function was confined to supervising the laws, and its authority supposedly consisted in the fact that it first drew the executive's attention to any mistakes that occurred and, if they were not put right, it then imposed an interdict restraining the executive in all its branches and | overthrew it; and the entire might of the people was supposed to enforce

188

189

the interdict of the ephorate, in which its whole confidence rested.[62] However, the hollowness of this constitution is already apparent from the facts that two self-subsistent powers are opposed to each other and that the executive can easily send the whole ephorate into exile, as the French did. In Sparta, where the ephors were very strong, they gave rise to a terrible aristocracy, which Cleomenes and Agis—the noblest characters known to us in history—were unable to overthrow when they wanted to bring back the former constitution of Lycurgus. This simple subjectivity, this simple apex of power ([as] in the moral sphere the conscience) is necessary essentially in accord with the concept. In England the king is this ultimate apex too, but the constitution as a whole reduces him virtually to a cipher. Since 1692 there has never been a case of the king's vetoing a parliamentary decree, and the cabinet, which is responsible for everything, also becomes as nothing if it does not have the half of Parliament on its side. However, this inner unity of the concept must also be actualized.

§ 134

The first and most important question seems to be: By whom is the constitution of a people or nation [*Volk*] to be made? Yet the constitution should be regarded rather as the *foundation* of a people's life in the spheres of right and ethics, *existing in and for itself*, and essentially not as something *made* and *subjectively posited*. Its absolute cause is the principle of a national spirit [*Volksgeist*] as it develops in history. The causes of the individual factors determining this development may be very diverse in shape. This historical element in the development itself gives the constitution the shape of a higher authority.

In this section we pose the question: Who is to make the constitution—the people or someone else? And the answer | is: No   190

---

62. [*Ed.*] Johann Gottlieb Fichte, *Grundlage des Naturrechts nach Principien der Wissenschaftslehre* (Jena and Leipzig, 1796), pp. 192–193, 207–213 (§ 16). Cf. Fichte, *Gesamtausgabe* 3: 440, 448–452.

one, it makes itself. There is nothing easier than to formulate the general principles of a constitution, for in our day these concepts have become conventional abstractions. The past twenty-five years have seen a score or more of constitutions, all defective to a greater or lesser degree. The constitution is the foundation, the basis on which everything transpires. It must therefore be viewed as an eternal foundation, not as an artifact. All constitutions are also the inner developments of the national spirit, the foundation in which it expresses the stage of self-consciousness it has reached. In the constitution we have the people with its spirit, and this product of the national spirit can only be further determined in a specific individual way.

Above all, it is a wholly abstract, empty question to ask, Who is to make the constitution? Rousseau presented the constitution as a social contract of all with each and each with all;[63] but this implies the whim or freedom of individuals to choose whether to enter [into the contract] or not. The national spirit, however, is something necessary, and has merely to be known; and this knowledge cannot be the affair of the whole people, but only of the best educated, of the wise. It is false to leave the framing of the constitution to what is properly called the people [*Volk*], since the people do not have a mature inner awareness of the national spirit [*Volksgeist*]. Formerly legislation was regarded as something divine; Moses' constitution was given by God. In Athens civil strife made the constitution unworkable, so it was judged necessary to formulate what united all the citizens, and Solon was entrusted with the task of drawing up the constitution. Solon made use of the oracle as his authority. The heroic figure of Theseus united the people who were living dispersed. Louis XVIII gave his people an inviolable constitution; the king, as highest authority, gave the constitution, incorporating in it all the liberal ideas the national spirit had developed

63. [*Ed.*] Jean Jacques Rousseau, *Principes du droit politique* (Amsterdam, 1762), esp. book 1, chap. 6 (pp. 26 ff.). Cf. Rousseau, *Du contrat social; ou, Principes du droit politique*, in Rousseau, *Œuvres complètes*, vol. 3 (Paris, 1964), pp. 360 ff.

since the time of the Revolution. The people were dimly aware of what they had to have. Public opinion, this powerful lever | of today, includes an essential element of reason, but equally superficiality and falsities, and cannot be taken as an infallible guide. The authentic part of the [French] national spirit, what it produced, [the king] bestowed on the people in the Charter [of 1814]; and whether by calculation or free choice, he did not display the petty-mindedness of the *émigrés* and his own relatives. That he gave the people the constitution was only the act of authority, but the content was the national spirit refined. Now this charter is a beacon, and its basis is the form of permanence. The better is here the worse because it does not incorporate the form of permanence; and so, in order not to take away the form of permanence, which is essential, it is preferable to leave what is bad in the constitution. The constitution as a whole must be based absolutely on immutability. But the constitution itself, the national spirit, is something divine, which makes itself in history, through its own doing.

The princely authority in general was viewed as something divine, but the constitution must be so regarded. It is the spirit of the people that produces and develops the constitution; consequently it must be subjected to further individual determinations, but this can happen in many ways. Single provisions can be changed, but not the whole that is gradually evolving; and the nation cannot suddenly change the whole consciousness of its spirit, as would happen if the constitution were turned upside down. The vassals may engage in open conflict with the prince, or the prince may seek to exalt the crown, or the people its power, at the expense of the other. Educational processes bring about a peaceful change, a casting off of the old shell and a rejuvenation of the constitution. The executive, as middle estate, struggles with one of the other two sides, prince or people. If the prince subdues the vassals, a rational constitution can ensue, or at least one that constitutes a formal whole, and this is what happened in England and | France—the king subdued the vassals. The converse happened in Germany and Italy.

191

192

The national spirit is the substance; what is rational must happen.[64] Since in principle the constitution is a development, the individual moments acquire the form of something won by struggle, either by one side or the other, people or prince, by contractual means or by force. (The form of the state is not in fact essentially that of a contract.) The fact that the constitution appears as something won by the struggles of one's forebears confers a higher authority on the external shape; however, genuine rationality is the inner authority, being in harmony with the national spirit. The contractual form of constitutional development is not in fact the rational, but merely a formal property. But the rational must always find a way, for it possesses truth, and we must cease to fear that bad constitutions might be made.

§ 135

The general dividing line between constitutions is between those that are based on nature and those based on freedom of the will. In the case of those based on nature, people who are weaker in disposition, or in other ways, attach themselves to families of noble lineage or heroic dynasties and assume a stance of naturally divine dependence on them. According to this principle, however, private right and political right belong to the will of the individuals as such as their own property. The patriarchal and Oriental systems, then the aristocratic system, and finally the democratic system mark the transition from the natural principle, where dependence is envisaged in naturally divine fashion, to the principle of the will, the principle of the spiritually divine.

Whether the state coheres on the basis of nature or of the freedom of the will is what forms the dividing line between constitutions. | Every concept begins in immediacy, in nature, and strives toward rationality. Everything depends on the extent to which rationality has replaced nature.

Historically the nations see in the will of heroes something divine; this is the starting point in mythology, and this can be

193

64. [*Tr.*] *was vernünftig ist, muss geschehen.* See above, § 122, n. 53.

called the state based on nature. If it happens that someone sur-
rounds himself with satellites and brings cities under his sway,
this is only a passing moment of tyranny. Certainly there has
to be a concentration of physical and spiritual strength, but the
main factor is that the heroes are envisaged as divine beings.
The king is the priest, so the oldest form of monarchy is a
theocratic monarchy; with a few nations such as the Jews theoc-
racy predominated, whereas with the Greeks, Romans, and most
other nations the royal power predominated. Since human beings did not yet have a high degree of self-consciousness, they
did not make it the determinant for their actions but had recourse to oracles. The weaker obeys the stronger as having the
stronger will of freedom, but obeys him as something particular, as a superhuman being.

The main consideration is always the stronger disposition,
but also frequently physical strength, to give protection against
wild beasts. Thus we find originating among the Romans, Hindus, and Greeks a natural diversity of castes. The Hindus believe
the supreme being created four castes, and this system of caste
distinctions seems to have become permanent. In Rome it is
also very important which families founded the state; here the
plebeians seem to have come to the state without a master, as
a result of conquests, etc., and only later did they become conscious of the freedom that was their due.

The first principle to oppose this natural origin of states is the
contemplation of the divine will, while the second is the consciousness of freedom and the infinitude of self-consciousness.
It was necessary for the unity based on the king, founded as it
was on | the patriarchal constitution, to change into aristocracy   194
(as there is a transition from the unity of God to polytheism),
and only then did the democratic principle emerge, the principle in which each individual beholds his freedom. As opposed
to the naturally divine view this democratic principle could appear profane. Thus it is also said that God must be perceived in
nature, but in opposition to this first way of envisaging the divine the freedom of the individual was the profane element; yet
it was this that marked the transition to the spiritually divine.

The transition from envisaging the divine as an immediate property possessed by only a few to a democratic conception is a necessary transition. Democracy is the beginning of the freedom of the will; but democracy can no longer endure in the regulated state, for otherwise terrible conflicts arise. In other words, the principle of labor is the precondition for democracy. Aristotle's classification of constitutions as democracy, aristocracy, and monarchy is based on the old constitutions.[65] In this regard Montesquieu says of democracy that its principle is virtue, while the principle of monarchy is honor and the principle of despotism is terror.[66] Particularity of purposes does not enter into play in democracy, but the state as a whole; to the extent that customs in a democracy cease to be virtuous, freedom is lost. When virtue disappears, ambition and the quest for fame enter the hearts of those capable of it, and avarice into the hearts of all; for all persons seek to take from the state's resources as much for themselves as they possibly can. A republic is the rule of a few and the unrestrainedness of all. I would, says [Montesquieu],[67] have as scant regard for a young man who did not desire a republic as for an old man who did not execrate it. The principle of particularity is not contained in democracy, and if it comes on the scene, it has an annihilating effect on it. If it is not reconciled with the universal, the principle of particularity has a destructive effect, and this is what is lacking in democracy, namely that this principle, which must come into play, is not contained in it. It is only this reconciliation that makes the principle of particularity harmless.

195   Montesquieu goes on to say that the principle | of aristocracy

65. [Ed.] Aristotle, *Politics* 3.7.1279a–b. Aristotle describes how sovereign power in a state can lie with either the one or a few or the many. If rulers exercise their power to the maximum general good, the resulting forms of the state are monarchy, aristocracy, and polity; if they exercise it for their own advantage, the resulting forms are tyranny, oligarchy, and democracy.

66. [Ed.] Montesquieu, *De l'esprit des lois*, book 3, chap. 3 (pp. 26 ff.); chap. 6 (p. 33); chap. 9 (pp. 35–36). Cf. Montesquieu, *Œuvres complètes*, pp. 251 ff., 256–257, 258–259.

67. [Ed.] Montesquieu, *De l'esprit des lois*, book 3, chap. 3 (pp. 26 ff.). Cf. *Œuvres complètes*, p. 252.

is moderation;[68] for here we have a plurality of rulers, so as to moderate the aristocrats' envy of one another. The aristocrats have to moderate themselves vis-à-vis the burghers to whom they stand so close. In monarchy the place of all virtues is taken by the laws, although the motivation is honor.[69] Each contributes to the common welfare, believing that he is seeing to his own interest, and that by each making himself his own end the interweaving [of individual ends] gives rise to the whole, but not that everything should fall into ruin as in democracy.

Now if democratic virtue is opposed to monarchical egoism, monarchy seems something lower, but esprit de corps comes into play, and rectitude is virtue. In accord with these ends of particularity, civil society also passes over into concern for the universal, since the individual parts attach themselves to the whole. In monarchy the individual's disposition does not play an essential part, but as a result of the transition the universal qua universal becomes the end of political life. With honor the personality is the end in the eyes of others, but in reality, too, egoism must come into play.

In despotism the principle, according to Montesquieu, is fear. The grandees depend on the prince's caprice, and the head of the lowliest subject is under the protection of the laws.[70] For an attack on one individual among the people is an attack on the whole people, and the despot is lost; the grandees by contrast oppress the people and are too close to the despot. The reason why educational progress is impossible in Turkey among the better Turks is that if they or the despot deviate from [traditional] religion or customs and seek to distinguish themselves, the people fall upon them in droves. Fear of the grandees and of the people en masse holds the despot in check, and the more despotic and cruel he is toward the grandees—for it is only

68. [Ed.] Montesquieu, De l'esprit des lois, book 3, chap. 4 (pp. 29–30). Cf. Œuvres complètes, p. 254.

69. [Ed.] Montesquieu, De l'esprit des lois, book 4, chap. 6 (p. 33). Cf. Œuvres complètes, pp. 256–257.

70. [Ed.] Montesquieu, De l'esprit des lois, book 3, chap. 6 (pp. 35–36). Cf. Œuvres complètes, pp. 259–260.

toward them that he can be so—the easier the lot of the people usually is. In monarchy the powers that are available in despotism to the despot vis-à-vis the grandees (although not against the basic laws) must be divided; as a single individual the monarch cannot do everything, but must entrust the execution to others. | In a feudal monarchy the grandees have an inherited power, and the lesser burghers depend on them; Poland for instance was a monarchy but could be viewed as a republic. Both for his own safety and for the safety of the people, it is imperative for the monarch to divide the powers; if he combines them and gives them to his satraps, they need only to lift a little finger to be independent.

196

"Empire" [*Reich*] is to be distinguished from "monarchy"; for example, Germany was called the German Empire. "Empire" can here mean "anarchy," for the obligation of the princes to obey depended on their might, and the petty princes were the most loyal. In aristocracy the division of powers is less marked, for the council, made up of aristocrats, has the legislative and executive power, particularly since those nobles who are not in the council also draw to themselves the remaining branches of the executive power, so that in fact, even if not in law, the subjects are deprived of any share in the executive power. In democracy all powers merge together in immediate fashion, the people being the supreme lawgiver and the supreme judge. An individual, e.g., a general, is still needed for execution, but the power is not definitely transferred to him, and he does not know how far he can go. The people lack stability, and with them no laws are firm. In the same way as today one hears abuse of the rulers, so in Thucydides' day there were complaints about the people.

§ 136

More precisely, the nature of the constitution of a people or nation depends, leaving aside the question of what distinguishes it geographically, on the stage attained by its self-consciousness in regard to freedom, on its spiritual education in general. Of importance too is its external size, in terms of which the corporate interest becomes closer to or more remote from individuals, and their active participation in it more or less important, in the same way that a nation's self-consciousness of its | inner political independence is bound up with its relationships to other nations.   197

The spiritual education of a people or nation, which has the utmost influence on the constitution (as it does on what is animated by it), renders a constitution that is suitable for some other people unworkable for this one. What is rational must *be*,[71] but it has its existence [*Existenz*] only in the self-consciousness of a people. Thus there is nothing so irrational as for us to have recourse for our constitutions to those of the Greeks and Romans; much that was possible in these states is inapplicable in contemporary states. People are constantly complaining that so little use has been made of history; but individual cases are infinitely diverse, and laws too differ in the spiritual realm, for human consciousness, as perfectible, is constantly developing.

The geographical criterion makes a great difference in the constitutions of peoples who live in different climes, necessarily so, since climate plays so great a part. In the same way that, with birds, in the South everything is directed to the brilliantly colored outer plumage, while in the North it remains internal and their adornment consists in their beautiful song, so it is with human beings. Within the universal condition of being human, there is a very great diversity of views from one people to another.

The historical stage a people has reached also has a great influence on what constitution is suitable for it. The external size too makes for differences; thus despotisms can become immense, but democracies can occur only in small states. In Rome the empire's excessive extension over such heterogeneous peoples necessarily led to collapse; and it was the height of folly on the part of Brutus and Cicero, and so many other individually great

71. [*Tr.*] Das Vernünftige soll sein. See above, § 122, n. 53.

men, to imagine that Caesar's removal would restore the republic. In most cases the extension of the state introduces into the constitution elements | that can only be inimical to it. So inferences cannot properly be drawn from small states to large states, especially in regard to their external independence. Small states, which are independent only in name, are more in the condition of a merely civil society. The relationship to other [powers], the feeling of impotence, is such that both rulers and ruled do nothing to cause a disturbance. Large states, which have a lot to do with other nations, depend for their continued subsistence on the attitude they adopt toward them. The bigger the state, the more alien the corporate interest becomes for single individuals. There is not the same interest in unity in the consciousness of the farmer and of the merchant engaged in ocean trade. The larger the number of citizens, the less possibility is there for individuals to exert a significant influence on the whole, and they lose interest. What the single individual can do appears as of minimal importance.

The consciousness of the national honor of a small state is quite different from that of the citizens of a large state, and this makes for a different consciousness of the strength of rights in general. This is what is happening in regard to freedom of the press in the duchy of Weimar, where the duke, acting solely on his own, promulgates a decree against the freedom of the press granted by the constitution. The fact that England is separate from the Continent, and able to exert influence so widely through its mastery of the seas, makes for a distinctive spirit and a distinctive external constitution. It is the same with North America, where the excess population of other states has settled and agriculture, which is elsewhere the basis, is only now expanding. The remoteness from Europe makes a wholly distinctive constitution essential. It is only under such peculiar circumstances that Quakers, whose principles forbid them to be citizens, can yet be citizens of the state. So one cannot say that because this is possible in the North American republics, therefore [it must also be possible here in Germany]. |

§ 137

For a people that has developed to civil society, or in general to consciousness of the infinitude of the free ego in its determinate existence, in its needs, its freedom of choice, and its conscience, *constitutional monarchy* alone is possible. For particularity reflected into itself is on the one hand universal spirit articulating itself, as inwardly concrete individuality, into its particular moments: the constitution. On the other hand it is the moment of actualized individuality, of the individual subject: the monarch.

The highest form of a people is for all the individual moments to be developed and completely cultivated to form a self-contained system that, in its different moments, has constructed the whole. This national consciousness rests on the consciousness of the infinitude of the free ego. The being-for-itself of the individual, which appears as a vice in democracy, and the appearance of the arts and sciences, which was the main factor in the downfall of Athens (since the learned men and artists made themselves independent only for their art and science without regard for any political interest), were a sign of the height of cultivation attained in Greece, but at the same time of the ruin of the state, which did not include these elements in its constitution. To the extent that this principle comes into play, the mass character of democracy and despotism is eliminated, and fragmentation sets in. The intermediate moment between the two extremes is to have one's own choice in one's action, to be able to act freely according to one's conscience. Reflection exalts this particularity of the individual to universality; and the fact that particularity, in being for itself, is also for the universal, makes the constitution a whole in its tendency to separate out into totalities, which, as a result of this articulation, themselves constitute moments of a whole. This principle of particularization demands laws that guarantee its particularization and at the same time lead the particularizations | back to the universal. The particular raises itself to individuality or subjectivity and to universality. Now the constitution must contain particularity, while to bring universality into effect is to negate particularity; the other

200

249

extreme is the supreme apex [of power], which exists as individual subject, the monarch. These three moments are nothing other than the outward forms the concept itself assumes [in relation] to universal freedom. We now have to consider these three moments and how they pass over into the one whole.

a. The Power of the Sovereign[72]

§ 138

The power of the sovereign [*die fürstliche Gewalt*] itself contains three moments: that of the universality of the constitution and the laws, which provides its substantive basis; that of counsel [*Beratung*] in general; and that of ultimate decision. As the individual factor, this decision pertains to an actual individual as a numerical unity, to the *monarch*, who as the ultimate and immediate singularity of the abstract self of the will is destined for the role in immediate, i.e., *natural* fashion, in other words by *birth*. By this means the ultimate, actual unity of the state can be made the aim of arbitrary will [*Willkür*] and drawn down into the sphere of particularity as one particularity over against others. Interfactional strife around the throne itself and the enfeeblement of the power of the state for factional advantage are inhibited and sublated, and the contingent element in the personality of the monarch becomes a matter of less account thanks to the fact that the constitution and the executive power form an inwardly consistent whole.

Each of the three powers is [a] self-enclosed whole, but insofar as they are members of the whole, each of them in turn contains the three moments. The basis of the power of the sovereign is the constitution, and not everything covered by legislation is included in it. Constitution and laws make up the basis

---

72. [*Tr.*] Hegel's discussion of the power of the sovereign or prince (*Fürst*) in the Heidelberg lectures differs in certain respects from the treatment found in the published version of *The Philosophy of Right*. In the earlier lectures, the strictly limited powers of the monarch are more clearly articulated. See Shlomo Avineri, "The Discovery of Hegel's Early Lectures on the Philosophy of Right," *The Owl of Minerva* 16 (1985): 204–205.

of sovereign power, in accord with which the sovereign must rule. | In the second place, there is the moment of particulariza- 201 tion, of the application of the universal principles to the partic- ular laws: counsel. And third comes this final point, the individ- ual self, an actual individual, constituting the apex of the whole pyramid. The power of the sovereign is itself one moment of the constitution; and the rational element in accord with which the power of the sovereign has to regulate its decisions is the laws, which are already in existence for it. By counsel is meant that particular matters are subsumed under the universal, that consideration is given to what is practicable and most advan- tageous, at which point ingenuity intervenes in order further to derive the universal from the particular and give it the force of law; this is the moment of reflection. Counsel involves a council of ministers or cabinet [*Ministerium*]. Only what pertains to the ultimate formal decision is for the monarch as an individual. He has to say, "I so will it"; this is the final moment of individ- uality. This final certainty—mere deciding taken for itself—per- tains essentially to an immediate numerical unity. In the state this culminating element is something external; in morality it is internal, it is conscience, this focus of inwardness, which decides according to what it sees as best. This merely formal element pertains to the monarch as such.

The notion that the welfare of the peoples should depend on the contingent individuality of the monarch is in the main a modern view. For previously the sovereign was the focus wherein the nation's entire wealth, pomp, and splendor became visible. In modern times, however, this is no longer the case. The sub- stantial class alone still has this trusting belief in the monarch and believes it is only the officials who oppress them, all un- known to the good monarch and not at his behest. For the burgher class the monarch is a matter of indifference. They sub- scribe to the philistine philosophy that it is unjust that so much should depend on the monarch as one selected by the chance of fate, [asserting] how they would willingly rule themselves better and [complaining] how high the taxes | are. In a mature consti- 202 tution the individuality of the monarch becomes unimportant owing to the state's being organized in a rational, stable manner, and it is in this very insignificance of the person of the ruler that the strength and rationality of the constitution reside. At all events, however, more may depend on the ruler's personality in one constitution than in another.

The splendor that radiates from the monarch, and the money he consequently expends on his court, are in our day covered for the most part by the ruler's private estates and domains. It was formerly the case that the people saw in the monarch's splendor its own enjoyment. But if the monarch does not possess private property of his own, provision must be made for him by the community in such a way that he appears as the richest and also outshines all his subjects in pomp. The general view is that the former way of regarding things is even better, when the people laid store solely by the ruler's palaces, temples, and the like, not by his private property, and the whole realm was rich whereas the individual was poor, possessing his wealth in the common treasury.

Now because the immediate, ultimate decision pertains to the monarch, he must be monarch in immediate, natural fashion, as a result of birth. The ultimate abstraction of inner certainty is immediacy. With election one always has in mind what is objective, what is better, the pros and cons, whereas what is needed in the case of the monarch is the purely subjective, not the objective. We will be speaking more of this later in connection with the estates, the legislative power. This final decision is the principle of the monarch. In days gone by this final decision was to be seen in oracles, the flight of birds, etc. All things give rise to an endless series of pros and cons, and this final "I will" is needed to cut the matter short. In former days the priests used to live among the people without being involved in actuality and pronounced the final decision in instinctive fashion. As to deciding on the basis of the entrails of sacrificial animals, this is like allowing oneself to be guided by chance when one is of two minds within oneself. | But nowadays self-consciousness has reached the stage of internalizing this element of chance and no longer leaving it to external nature.

203

So this ultimate oracle, this contingent element represented by the final decision, resides in the monarch. In the same way that in ancient times this decision was removed from particularity [by oracles], so with us it is removed from particularity by birth; and monarchical succession becomes, by virtue of this birthright, a natural matter. An elective monarchy seems at first sight to be more rational if one says, "Let the best person rule." The whole assembly of free citizens meet together and to the plaudits of the whole people proclaim the candidate their ruler; but this can only occur with a relatively uncultivated people, where the ruler must be principally a commander. For in elective monarchy it depends on the opinion of the particular individuals who is to be monarch, so that arbitrary will [*Willkür*] is made the first power in the state. Particularity engenders factions. The particular interests of individuals enter into a compact with the ruler and, as a result of the privileges they annex to themselves, undermine the constitution. Those responsible for electing the ruler are concrete individuals, who are striving to attain particular aims. For it is [one] moment in the state that particular interests should exist, while election would be an act from which [particular] interests should be absent; and this would be a contradiction in the constitution. Much argument has been devoted to the fact that our rulers do almost nothing but sign their names, but the value of this formal element goes unperceived.

§ 139

The objective element in decision-making, the content, and also the legal and practical considerations, do not fall directly within the subjectivity of making decrees and are therefore the object of a counseling process [*Beratung*] distinct from the formal will of the monarch. The monarch is accordingly not answerable for all executive actions. He is the supreme representative of his people, but neither is he the highest functionary of the state, nor is he the paid agent of the people, nor again is he in | contractual relationship 204 with them. Such definitions imply a grounding through the will, incompatible with the immediate subjectivity that is the determining

253

characteristic of the concept of monarchy. The monarch is also responsible in particular for the final decision in the appointment of state functionaries and for the administration of justice in the pardoning of criminals.

The monarch acts solely as subjective agent, and it is only the objective element in an action that can be justified. So he is not answerable, for in his acts of government he is not responsible for this objective element but only for the wholly formal element of the will. In the same way that oracles, birds, and stars are not answerable for what they indicate, the monarch is not answerable either; and in this sense it is rightly said of him that he has no judge but himself and God above him. The divine nature of the monarch's authority is that he has within himself the moment of immediacy. What is rationally divine is the constitution, while the monarch is the naturally divine.

The monarch's freedom of choice [*Willkür*] is abstract freedom of choice. To be sure, negative unity is the most spiritual element, but at this highest level the element of subjectivity comes into play for the sake of reversion.[73] James II of England affirmed the divine authority of kings, but this implied that the objective element too—what right *is*—was a matter for the king's freedom of choice. For instance we are told God can do as God chooses, and that divinity is to be found not in nature but in miracles. James II retained his freedom of choice, but the objective element of willing was severed from the royal freedom of choice, and taken over by Parliament.

The monarch is the supreme representative of his people. He, and the state functionaries, are representatives of the people just as much as are those elected by them. In particular the monarch as the ultimate apex represents his people in relation to other states. He is not the highest functionary of the state, a paid agent of the people and in a contractual relationship with them. The monarch *is*; this supreme contingency *is*; the | externaliza-

205

---

73. [*Tr.*] Or: at this highest level reversion brings into play the element of subjectivity [*auf dieser letzten Spitze ist des Zurückgangs wegen das Moment der Subjektivität*].

tion of objective will *is*. What is introduced with the monarch is the element of ungrounded, groundless, formal decreeing. It is not a contract because then it would depend on the people's freedom of choice whether and how it wished to come to terms with this subject rather than another. In elective monarchy it is a blend of particular interests and objective considerations that determines the choice. But when a dynasty dies out, there is a break or vacillation in the natural order of things and another family has to be chosen.

We will discuss the appointment of state officials by the monarch later.[74] The sovereign power can only pardon on grounds presented to it. The act of pardoning is the responsibility of the one with whom right and wrong cease to exist (as they cease to exist with conscience). Courts of justice often recommend offenders to the ruler for pardon.

§ 140

The second moment in the power of the sovereign consists in a body of counselors [*eine beratende Stelle*], who bring before the monarch the universal aspect of the matter, its content and the considerations involved, its objective aspect in general. This may be a cabinet or council of ministers [*ein Ministerium*], which stands at the apex of the executive power for the purpose of deciding on particular matters; or it may be a council of state [*ein Staatsrat*] to prepare and advise on general matters as such and as laws. These counselors are answerable for the actions of the executive; their personal choice and dismissal alike rest with the free choice of the monarch, with whose particular person they have to deal. Since it is the ministers who are answerable for the power of the sovereign, there can be no action by the ruler determined in a merely personal manner (e.g., by the monarch's subjective environment, namely the court); his every decision must be signed by the competent minister.

74. [*Ed.*] See § 144.

It is the duty of the council of state and the council of ministers to lay before the monarch the objective side of the considerations involved; the minister has to sign the sovereign's decision and is answerable for it. Here we are considering the monarchical power to the extent that it relates to universality; 206 the moment of universality is the | second moment of monarchical power. It is the council of ministers that brings to the monarch the objective side of the question, the considerations involved, that in general informs him about it, and he can then decide one way or another on the basis of these considerations. The will can decide this way or that; but it is inherent in the way the state is organized that the rational must happen.[75] It is organized as an inwardly organic system, wherein particular caprice evaporates in the face of universal necessity. The power of the system is the rational, and it is in this that one must trust and not regard the power of the contingent as preponderant. The ultimate subjectivity is contingency; but how does it enter into the necessity of the whole without having a destructive effect? As the keystone of the edifice it is a necessary moment in the whole, and the whole and this necessary moment in the whole both subsist. A monarch at the head of a state that has no rational constitution extends his caprice over the whole and is capable of ruining everything. That what is necessary by virtue of the concept—that this *exists*, must inspire the people with confidence.

To make great demands of the sovereign implies in principle the notion of a despotic state, lacking a rational constitution. The monarch is surrounded by something mysterious, which the common man cannot and should not see through, so he attributes all power to the ruler, who shows himself in princely pomp and believes that everything depends on him. It is for the sovereign to decide according to the rationality of the matter, as demonstrated to him by the council of ministers. For this reason it used to be thought that the best course was to give sover-

75. [Tr.] *dass das Vernünftige geschehen muss.* See above, § 122, n. 53.

eigns a special training, since someone who was in himself well educated would certainly choose what was best. But the sovereign is first *by nature*, and so beyond all aims of particularity— beyond pride, conceit, envy, hatred, and the like. As immediately recognized by all as first, the sovereign cannot feel pride. This reverence is paid to him through the fact that he is recognized; with the sovereign all these passions of the intermediate estate fall away. Under the constitution that we are in the process of developing, the sovereign can only be avaricious for himself, but cannot so cause damage to the state, | for not he but the council of ministers has to administer the resources of the state, and his ample income must come from the household funds allocated to him. Debauchery [on the part of the monarch] can also have no effect on the whole for the further reason in particular that he can easily gratify all passions; and the position of the one extreme, the sovereign, is as simple as that of the other extreme, the man of the soil.

207

Since matters are brought to the sovereign by the ministries, his conceit no longer comes into play, for it is not he but the minister who has made the proposals, and it is no longer a question of his insisting on imposing something maintained by him. He views things in more indifferent fashion opposed to all spheres and aims of particularity, views them with a simply [*einfach*] educated understanding, and it is highly probable that he will choose what is rational. Since, however, the ministers have to deal with the person of the monarch, have to explain to him the whys and wherefores and persuade him, and accordingly have to adapt themselves to the personality of the monarch in order to bring their plans into effect, they must particularly avoid making him obstinate, and must flatter him by attributing all merit to the monarch, rather than to themselves who have done all the preliminary work. (For if anyone is desirous of imposing his particular will, naturally anyone who also has something to say on the matter comes treading on his heels.) This is why the course followed is often not the best, why it is that someone is very active on behalf of something, with a show of moral or empty vanity,[76] and evinces a self-relating interest; true zeal often accomplishes the least. All personal willing must remain hidden from sight. These are matters relating to the practical skill of ministries, for it is up to the ministries how they bring what they are answerable for to fruition. The person of the monarch may involve numerous chance attributes, so he must be a simple person, not answerable for anything [particular].

The ministers must be chosen by the sovereign; he also has to choose all other officials, | but it is only the ministers he is free to depose at will. Should it not be the case that ministers can be appointed and dismissed by the monarch, we would have a directory, and they would carry everything into effect, or else sovereign and ministry would be in hostile opposition to one another. A ruling council of this kind inevitably leads to the formation of factions, and the supreme power of the state would be drawn down into particularity, into faction. It must be for the monarch to choose his ministers, first because they have to deal with his personality, and also because otherwise one would get an aristocracy instead of a monarchy.

Because of his attitude, as a result of which any link to alien interests is foreign to him, the monarch will not choose his favorites because he will not wish to lay so great a burden on them and stand in this relationship to them. The impermanence of sovereign favor is an essential moment, because by flattery the sovereign can be brought to despise people and set no store by their personality. And precisely this attitude on the part of the monarch provides a guarantee that he will choose appropriate ministers. Moreover, given the extent of the business and the interests [he has to bear in mind], an incompetent minister will not remain in office for long. The mass of the nation repudiates the incompetence of ministers and stands firm against them. The main guarantee of the competence of ministers is

76. [Tr.] *Eitelkeit.* The text would make more sense if it read *Eiferkeit*, "zealousness." See the reference to "true zeal" immediately following.

their answerability to parliament, to which they have to indicate clearly what they intend. So a minister's position is the most dangerous in the state, for he has to defend himself against the monarch, against his colleagues, against public opinion, and against parliament. The French and English ministers are necessarily our examples here. Men who maintain their position as ministers, and show themselves good at the job, merit the highest respect.

The guarantee of parliament is specially effective in compelling the monarch to choose suitable subjects and to pay heed to talent, virtue, rectitude, and practical ability in the ministers he is to choose. The prince regent, who had his friends in the opposition party and his enemies in the cabinet, was not able, | 209 when he acceded to power, to make his friends ministers but had to keep on the former ministers. In the same way the present French cabinet is made up of enemies of the royal family, of ultraroyalists. These examples show that the choice of ministers in a monarchy with a good constitution is not merely a matter of the ruler's caprice.

The main function of the council of state is to advise on bills to be laid before the legislature, so it has no decisive power. The monarch cannot be answerable for all actions of the executive, but only the ministers. We can see from history how the previous coupling of the monarch's personality with the power of the ruler has given way to the ministerial system. A matter of particular complaint was the corruption of the courts, i.e., of the monarch's entourage, because so much depended on the personality of the monarch, and the basic interest of the court was to plunder the state and use it to its own advantage by mere favor, without regard to any ensuing harm to the state. There was at these courts an evident contradiction between [at one moment] making everything a point of honor and the next moment groveling abjectly. Thus under Louis XV one noble family had the important office of handing the king a towel when he retired to the privy, since this gave an opportunity to speak with the king; and a mother, in order that her son, who was still a minor, might retain this office, which otherwise was lost to the family, presented herself to the astonished monarch as he was in the privy. Here was to be seen maternal love and concern for her family contrasting with the most abject baseness. And among us too it is a matter of surprise if the king is not able to do something, e.g., make an appointment, as a matter of favor, without the consent of the competent ministers. |

210

b. The Executive Power

§ 141

The executive power [*die Regierungsgewalt*], here still seen only as directed within, concerns in general the preservation and well-being of the particular and the task of leading it back to the universal as well as providing public institutions for general purposes. Particular concerns as such are in the first place the particular property, aims, and interests of the individual local communities, guilds, estates, and corporations, and are administered by these bodies themselves as a matter of right. This self-administration also has the ethical aspect that individuals see their proximate, particular interest become a universal matter in which they find reflected the state as a whole—what binds them together, their activity and concern for the state, which imparts absolute subsistence to their sphere.

As the second moment the executive forms the mean, the particular, but only insofar as it is directed within, not yet without, vis-à-vis other states. Its object is to maintain the well-being of the particular spheres in their particularity: (1) that they subsist, and (2) to lead them back to the universal. For the particular continually seeks to grasp the universal to itself and to isolate itself at the expense of the universal. And the fact that the particular spheres are necessarily self-governed constitutes the democratic principle in a monarchy.

In considering the executive power two aspects have to be borne in mind, [first] the maintenance of the whole in the particular spheres of the executive, i.e., in such a way that the particular parts do not act in a manner contrary to the universal. Particular concerns are the estates or classes, guilds, corporations, provinces, cities, local communities—whatever has a determinate interest in common. What is communal must be present as actually so. A local community [*eine Gemeinde*] is constituted as a whole; in many respects it has a communal aspect [*ein Gemeinsames*]—the greater the community [*die Gemeinschaft*], the more respects in which it does so. The particular concerns must be preserved—must remain as they are. This must continue to be left to the estates themselves, | for it is   211 rightfully what belongs to them, their own concern, which they attend to on their own account.

The second moment is the universal, contrary to which they may not act. A local community must have property; as an independent corporation it is, moreover, in no way under age, and there is absolutely no reason why it should be unable to administer what belongs to it itself. This seems recently to have been quite forgotten, especially because the city magistrates, etc., administered very badly and, what is more, did not even defend the community's resources. This failure of the magistrates, as the proper authorities of the people, to discharge their functions made it necessary to take their administrative role from them. However, what should have been done was to organize this self-administration in another way, for the higher officials, in their thirst for power, took on the contrary almost all administration into their own hands.

This is the point of view of right, that individuals have the right to administer their resources, while the ethical aspect is that [citizens] find in their corporation a state in the government of which they share, and in which they carry their particularity over into the universal. Nowadays governments have relieved the citizens of all these cares for a universal. But this is the democratic principle, that the individual should share in the government of local communities, corporations, and guilds, which have within themselves the form of the universal.

In a thoroughgoing, complete democracy each individual

shares in all rights of government and administration; but as already demonstrated, a democratic constitution is not viable in a relatively large and civilized state. Corporations provide everyone with a state in which they can be active according to their concrete being. But it is only to the extent that they have rights through the corporations that individuals are duty-bound to cleave to them and make them their concern. This is particularly the case in England, and patriotism assumes the form that the preservation of the state is the concern of all, for all have their particular concern in their particular sphere, and it is only through the state that this particular sphere exists. Since they acquire this particular sphere in their class status, they are working for the universal, which only exists by virtue of this articulation. |

212

§ 142

Not only must the individual communities, districts, provinces, trades, and classes be bound together into a whole and as such have rights for promotion of the communal interest and their particular aims. First and foremost they must also be inwardly constituted and have advisory and decision-making authorities [*Behörden*] in the form of officers of their own—directors, managers, and the like. On the one hand these authorities have the power to make or endorse decisions, yet are at the same time subject to higher authority; on the other hand what they look after is what directly belongs to and concerns their circles. Hence the filling of posts for civil authorities must generally be a mixture of popular election by the commonalty [*Bürgerschaft*] (or class or those having the same class status) and a separate system of appointment by higher authority.

The fact of the individual classes being constituted must be recognized in the state; they must have rights, and they must look after their interests themselves, partly because they have a particular aptitude for so doing, but also partly and principally because they must have their activity in so doing, and have their interest in so doing. The members of the class must promote their concerns through the exercise of their will; and in this way the citizens become conscious that it is also open to them to be active in their corporation. It is only through this activity itself that a communal spirit (which is only contingently a moral spirit) is formed. This activity for a particular state must be carried out by particular officers, who deliberate in regard to it. It was a particular defect of earlier corporations that the officials themselves chose their successors; this gave rise to an aristocracy, which afforded an example of the particular interest that was taken into account in making the choice. But as members of a whole, corporations must in turn be subordinate to higher authorities. Since the officers [of the corporations] must themselves have authority, the corporations must, to be sure, have a voting procedure, but the directors or managers, whoever they may be, must have an authority over against those by whom they are chosen. There must also be a specific provision making them independent of the members of their local community, etc. | It 213 is necessary for guilds, etc., to elect their director, but he must then be confirmed in his office by the senior officials, so as to confer on him the seal of authority.

§ 143

Secondly, the executive power prevents the particular interests, classes, and officers from going outside the bounds of the universal. [If they do] they are brought back within it by the efforts of agents of the executive, the state officials and the higher authorities, who are constituted essentially on a departmental basis and form a pyramid at the apex of which stand the ministries. The essential point in regard to the organization of governmental authorities is that on the one hand civic life should be governed in concrete manner from below where it is concrete, but that on the other hand the business of the community should be divided into its abstract branches looked after by special authorities as different centers [of administration] but converging again in the supreme executive power to form a concrete [means of] supervision.

The point of view here is that the executive power brings

these spheres back within the universal and must take action against their infringements on one another and on the universal. Conflict arises in that the governmental authorities like to keep the civil authorities in their place, and their vanity and particularity come into play in this connection. Civic life is concrete, and where cases of civic matters come before the government, they too are concrete, and differences come into play which have to be allocated to particular authorities. The separate administration of the various branches is a necessity in government. They must converge in a unity both above and below themselves. The various branches are first divided and go their different ways, but then have to combine at a higher level from which the whole can be viewed.

214 Owing to the many affairs it has to deal with, a ministry must have several departments for | separate types of business, but at the same time too one department that takes account of the universal interest. This arrangement involves tremendous difficulties. Vertically, authorities must be organized on a departmental basis. A departmental system has the disadvantage of delay, but it has [in its favor] tradition and it upholds a cut-and-dried, definite mode of acting, since the personality of the individual involved makes no difference, has no influence on the course of the whole.

Another way in which authorities can be arranged is for a president to have officials working under him, but for him alone to be answerable and consequently [able] to annul or alter their work, as solely answerable for it. But this gives undue scope to caprice and personality, and there is undue delay until the new president has worked himself in; there can be no uniformity here. Only in the case of danger to the state may it be necessary to transfer more power to a single individual, but never in peacetime.

It seems to be the best thing for ministries if there is a central department, and the separate ministry departments for individual branches would have to include specialized technical advisers in addition to members of the central department; the minister must stand at the summit of the whole edifice. There must be one central point for particular types of business, namely the ministry; but this must in turn first particularize itself into ministerial departments, and the whole must be subordinate to the minister.

§ 144

The objective factor in the appointment of councils, authorities, and state officials is proof of ability—a proof that, as the sole condition, gives every citizen the possibility to seek, albeit at personal risk, to enter the universal class.[77] Individuals admitted to the universal class make it their concern to devote themselves to the service of the state in all that they are and do (both in the spiritual sphere and in regard to needs), and the authority they enter is a particular branch of the universal business, justified by the constitution. In view of their | particularity and their official duties alike, 215 it must be possible for them to be dismissed from the positions to which they have (as far as the subjective side of appointment is concerned) been called by the sovereign, not by arbitrary decision, but solely as the result of a formal judgment.

The objective aspect is that individuals who wish to enter the service of the state must first prove their ability. Herein lies the genesis of present-day higher education, that the possibility of participating in the service of the state is open to every citizen and is not confined exclusively to individual classes or conferred by birth. Not all can take part in the universal activity of government, but all must have the possibility of doing so, and must be given the right to do so by education directed to that end. Plato, who had not yet attained to the viewpoint of freedom, has everyone assigned to a particular class, without regard to their freedom of choice, by the supreme governmental authority according to its insight.[78] The [sole] condition for entry to the universal class is proof of ability. In addition the

77. [Tr.] The class of civil servants.
78. [Ed.] See Plato, *Republic*, esp. 412b–414b and 535a–536d.

state can fix the number of civil servants it needs, and in this way the intake declines. There must accordingly be a system of examinations in order to demonstrate ability. Large states are fortunate here in this regard because in them ability is all that needs to be taken into account, not, as in small states, subjective circumstances. For example in small provinces [*Lände*] where there are provincial universities, account is taken of the fact that an individual's uncle, father, and grandfather were learned men. But since all universities in Germany should form a whole, the compulsory university qualification should be eliminated and all teachers should be appointed solely on the basis of objective factors.

Appointment to a post is the responsibility of the sovereign, for which the individual subject is something contingent. But as civil servants the individuals appointed must have rights they can lose only as the result of a formal judgment. They have a right to their post; but this irremovability must affect not only the [officers attached to] courts but all officials. Individuals devote themselves to the service of the state and pin to it their spiritual existence [*Existenz*] and their existence [*Existenz*] as pertaining to their needs.

216 The state authorities | in which individuals work must be sanctioned, must be firmly defined, by the constitution. What the authority does must be based on right, and if a higher authority does not approve it, it can rescind it only by a formal process. By this means individuals have the opportunity to show their character and rectitude, but their rights and the rights of their entire authority, the corporation so to speak to which they belong, must be guaranteed. This constitutional justification of authorities is one of the main features in the constitution of a state.

The position of government officials is safeguarded in two ways. In the first place, they can be removed from their post only on the basis of a formal judgment; they have their rights and so are independent as far as their particularity is concerned. They have renounced [enrichment from] the communal resources of the state, profit, etc., and the state has accepted their attachment to the business and property of the state. And this sure protection necessarily restores their independence to them. Secondly, the authorities themselves are justified by the constitution, have certain firm rights by virtue of it. It is a major safeguard for servants of the state that they have rights, provided they are discharging their official duties.

§ 145

Civil servants are answerable in the first place to their superior authorities, whose essential concern it must be to maintain the authority of the government, represented as it is by civil servants, and whose members are drawn from within the same particular class. There must be a further safeguard outside this circle, partly at a further remove in the estates assembly,[79] but partly in the hierarchical organization of the civil service itself and the rights conferred on the particular spheres of civic life. By this means the power of government officials, which impinges directly on the citizens, | is in the first place limited primarily to supervising, advising, and taking formal decisions, and civil servants are obliged to become genuine officials of the state, i.e., officials of the citizenry as well as officials of the sovereign. This obviates one of the greatest ills that can befall states, namely that the class of officials—which makes up a major part of the middle class, and in which is to be found the intelligence and developed consciousness of right of the people—may become remote and alien, and, by its skill and education and use of official authority, may provide a channel for caprice and the oppression of citizens.

217

The principal ill to which our states are subject is that a middle class is forming in place of the old feudal nobility. And it is no longer birth but general education that is the distinctive feature of the middle class; this makes it necessary to the sovereign and peculiarly alien to the people. The privileged position this education confers on the middle class may enable it to impress the sovereign and oppress the citizens, although it is not something innate like nobility but something acquired. This undue

79. [Tr.] See below, § 148.

power of the middle class is commonly the essential ill affecting our states. It is usually now officials who pour abuse on sovereign and cabinet, aware of their rascally tricks and oppressive, discourteous behavior to citizens, and who assume the mantle of defenders of the people in order to distract their attention from themselves.

This form of oppression must be obviated but in such a way as not to impair the personal, essentially necessary authority of officials. The higher authorities must make it their concern to support the authority of the officials; and it is not enough to rely on the junior officials' being answerable to the senior officials as a safeguard against oppression, for the interests of junior and senior officials vis-à-vis the citizenry coincide. Recently an attempt has been made to keep a rein on the junior officials as far as possible through the superior authorities by getting them to submit reports on all their | official activities. But the fact that things got even worse after this is enough to show of how little use this is. Moreover, in itself the written word is lifeless and indefinite, and there are far too many special reports for the senior officials to be able to examine and appraise them, so there is precious little protection for the citizen who has to complain to officials about officials who are then judged in secret. A safeguard of this kind must therefore lie outside this circle itself, in the estates assembly. In order to obtain their rights, citizens must be able to turn, first, to the nearest responsible official, then to the senior official, and, if they get no satisfaction from that quarter, to the estates assembly.

218

One major safeguard must reside directly in the determination of the rights and duties of officials (it can easily be seen how much indeterminate freedom it is necessary and useful for the press to enjoy), and [in the fact] that all property belonging to corporations is administered by their own authorities, and the officials have only a formal power of decision. If the essential role falls to these officers of corporations, so that the officials cannot do exactly as they please but can only take the formal decision, then the officials become true officials of the state.

This ill of our times must be eliminated by organizing [the

civil service] from the bottom up, and all other plans are of no use or avail. If, in the mind of the official, his remuneration is the principal thing and he and his family exist for that alone, he easily comes to see his post as existing for his own sake, not that he is there for the sake of citizens, and he believes his only duties are to his superior, who can promote him. The educated middle class constitutes the people's consciousness of freedom and right; the developed consciousness of right is to be found in the middle class. But if this class does not have the interests of the citizens at heart, it is like a net thrown over the citizens in order to oppress them, particularly as the entire class forms a whole since its interests are one and the same. Alienated from the people, officials become, by reason of their skill, themselves the object of the people's | fear; even the way they talk strikes 219 the ears of citizens as gibberish, a kind of thieves' slang. They see only the consequences of their efforts to secure their rights, but not the course and manner of the proceedings. Officials must therefore accustom themselves to a popular approach, to popular language, and seek to overcome the difficulties this occasions them.

c. The Legislative Power

§ 146

The legislative power [*die gesetzgebende Gewalt*] is concerned with the state in its universality, partly as laws properly speaking, partly as internal concerns of government of a wholly universal nature, and partly [as it relates] to the basis in the constitution, which exists in and for itself but itself becomes more developed in the course of further elaboration of the laws and in the progressive character of the universal concerns of government. The development of spirit unaccompanied by a corresponding development of institutions, so that a contradiction arises between the two, is the source not only of discontent but also of revolutions.

As the omnipotence of the rational in general, the legislative power is not executive power [*exekutive Gewalt*], not the power of government [*Regierungsgewalt*]. As encompassing

269

individual cases, however, the concerns of government properly speaking are more universal in nature and, as such, the object of the legislative power. For instance, duties and taxes in a state are an essential, universal element, but their magnitude is a temporary consideration, as is the question what articles should be subject to taxes; so the system of taxes is a temporal system, subject to changes. But since taxes embrace all interests alike, they are an essential object of legislation. The finances of the state encompass only the resources required for administration, and here too the legislature has a part to play, though not a controlling part. The legislature is also responsible for the competence of particular authorities and the demarcation | of what should in principle be left to one type of officials for decision. The constitution must be presupposed, for the existence of a legislative power is itself a moment within the constitution, and the legislative power itself presupposes an ordered constitution, but the constitution as universal substance that takes on immediate existence in the legislature.

The constitution must provide an unassailable, sacrosanct basis, but the fact that it affects legislation and the executive implies that the spirit of the constitution develops, and the constitution is transformed; the substance alters under the influence of the legislative power. If the spirit [of the constitution] becomes of itself progressively more mature and institutions do not alter with it, there is genuine discontent, and if nothing is done to dispel this, we get disturbances of the peace owing to the fact that the self-conscious concept contains other institutions than actually exist; there is a revolution. Now revolutions derive either from the sovereign or from the people. For example Cardinal Richelieu suppressed the nobles and exalted the universal over them. This was despotism, but by suppressing the vassals' privileges he was doing what was true. In the case of the Germans, who were his enemies, he supported the vassals against the nation. He did not achieve recognition. His people, which he sought to raise, hated him, while the Germans saw in this ruination of Germany the palladium of German freedom; and this set the pattern for the Peace of Westphalia.

However, one must know how to recognize whether this is true discontent; for often the general grumbling of the people is not a call for what is better, so the government must scrutinize the people's wishes and should yield only when it is convinced. The executive must therefore wait until the thought that has been expressed has matured, and until the good thought has become the thought of the whole people. Sovereigns who have not waited long enough have done harm despite all their power and good | intentions. This insight into what is better must rise up from below, and must have permeated the lowest as well as the upper strata. This is why Joseph II's actions appeared despotic, because he did not wait for the proper moment to arrive— to do so is the mark of a very great spirit. For if it is planted in a still unready soil, the good on the contrary bears evil fruit. So the legislature must not be in the hands of those who, guided by their own interest, oppose such mature concepts of right, because this would prevent the constitution from ever developing to express the true concept of the self-consciousness of unity and right.

221

§ 147

The legislative power is an essential organ of state power, and one of the falsest ways of looking at it is to view it as essentially opposed to the executive. However, of necessity it cannot be entrusted to a council of state, to ministerial authorities and legislative commissions of the government. Its main feature is the *principle of classes or estates [das Ständische]*, in order that what is ordained as universal will and as the rational should be so not merely *contingently* and *implicitly*, but also *explicitly* and necessarily, involving active participation and the self-conscious trust of the general commonalty.

The legislative power is an essential moment of state power. This is inherent in the concept of the state itself. The classes or estates are a a major element in the legislative power. Contemporary discontent in this respect has resulted in peculiar attitudes and sentiments that have to be transcended, for instance the view that legislative power is solely the province of the estates assembly, or that the estates are all that is good and rational while the ministries represent the bad, so that the estates must oppose the ministries—the view that the excellent | and good comes solely from the people. These sentiments must be transcended. It is the highest interest of the estates themselves that the government should be strong and powerful and that the estates assembly should initially be subordinate to the government; it should not take the lead among the people in adopting a hostile attitude toward the executive power. Ultimately, a hostile attitude of this kind would result in revolution, whereby only those who hold the executive power in their hands would be changed, but what is conceptually necessary would nevertheless return.

The reason why legislation cannot be entrusted solely to a council of state or a ministry, despite the fact that they obviously understand it best, and why the estates also must have a role, [is as follows]: if it were merely a matter of ability to act for the universal interest, ministries would be sufficient for the purpose. In estates assemblies the most talented members are always those who have held high state office. But in regard to what has to be established as universal will, in the sphere of right, an essential feature is the self-consciousness of all, the interest that comes only with one's own activity. Only so is right present for itself, even if it may previously have been present in itself. For it is a matter of contingency if the government's actions bring about the universal, and the sole reason why there must be an organized state is that what is fitting may occur necessarily.

§ 148

The estates assembly [*Ständeversammlung*][80] contains in its concept on the one hand the moment of the universal will as what is

---

80. [*Tr.*] Cf. French *états généraux*, the legislative assembly in France prior to the Revolution of 1789, composed of representatives of the three estates (clergy, nobility, and commoners). The more normal English term is "parliament." The terms *Ständeversammlung* and *Parlament* occur synonymously in § 149 (see n. 81). Sometimes the abbreviated form *Stände* (estates) refers to the legislative body.

rational in and for itself. Here, where the executive is defined in opposition to it, the latter is the abstract individuality of sovereign power, [namely] contingency and arbitrary will. On the other hand the estates assembly gives visible expression to the people, in its abstract sense as a mass, distinct from its orderly government by the state; and to the extent that the mass of the people is viewed in its determinateness, | it is a mass of individuals and of particular 223 classes, whose interests are incumbent on the estates assembly, in contrast with which the executive characterizes itself as the universal element of the state. There has to be a twofold safeguard in the way the legislature is organized, ensuring that the assembly, as giving visible expression to the people en masse and upholding particular interests, does not become a power over against the state; and that the state itself, as executive, does not seize to itself the functions of legislation and become a merely sovereign power.

The estates assembly represents the people. It contains the moment of the universal will in the twofold sense: (1) [that it is] the will that is in and for itself rational; and (2) that it is not just in and for itself the universal will, but is also for itself since each individual has his self-consciousness in it. On the one hand the assembly represents the universal will; on the other, the people appear here as a mass—the individual and the individual classes with their particular interests. From the point of view of regarding the universal will as present in it, all that remains with respect to the government is that without the estates assembly it would represent the arbitrary and bad; this is the usual assertion of demagogues. It is to be hoped that God may grant that rationality should be a feature of the estates assemblies, but let us not accept the above assertion. After all, the people as they are found in the estates, in opposition to the government, are something coarse and elemental, a contingent mass. It is therefore very erroneous to oppose the people to the state; for without articulation, without the dimension of the state, the people lack rationality and are merely a mass.

With regard to the people as a mass, it is important to note that they never patently assume this form, for if they did they would appear as an untamed element. The people have to appear in the compartmentalized order of their civic life, as laid down in the constitution; only so are they recognizable by reason. To speak of "the people" is a completely empty phrase. If the people are viewed as a mass in its determinateness, then each head of a household, | each corporation retains its own particular interest. This individuality, this interest of the particular estates, has, in the estates assembly, to be set over against the rational universal.

The second aspect of the estates assembly is that the people, as separate entities, are present there in their corporations. It used to be the case in Germany that all estates—clergy, nobility, peasants—had their individual interests, which they sought to exalt to the exclusion of all else. But they were in any event debarred from participating in the overall whole (e.g., [decisions affecting] war and peace), and this universal was none of their concern, nor could they affect it indirectly. The constant quest was to extort something from the whole and take one's pride in particularity, and have as much in one's purse as possible.

From this second point of view the state's attitude is that it always has the interests of individuals [in mind], but always seeks to bring such interests back to the universal. In a well-organized state, however, neither of the two main viewpoints should dominate for its own sake. This must be ensured by the fact that (1) rationality does not rest solely with the citizens, (2) nor does it rest merely with the government—it is not particular interests that come to the fore, nor does the estates assembly exist solely for the interest of the individual classes. The one viewpoint is as erroneous as the other. It always used to be the spirit of the former provincial diets to look after their individual interests, the nobles for their own sake, the towns with an eye to their particular privileges, etc. To view the estates from the one side alone is false, and if one or the other side is present [and not the other], this undermines the constitution. Both points of view are one-sided; the estates assembly must be viewed in the light of neither the one [alone] nor the other, nor must the one feature or the other actually figure in the state [to the exclusion of the other].

§ 149

The above-mentioned safeguard derives from the universal, from the concept of the legislative power, the fact that for its actions [are needed]: |

225

(1) the monarchical principle as the universal individuality of state power, responsible for proposing laws in due form and confirming the resolutions of the other elements;

(2) cabinet [*Ministerium*] and council of state as advisory bodies, playing their part with knowledge and oversight of all branches of the state administration and its requirements;

(3) the estates assembly, [which] itself defends the viewpoint and interest of particularity and individuality, but in such a way that the members receive no instructions from their electors and are equally bound to foster the universal interest.

[(1)] As a result of this arrangement, the ministers, as answerable for their actions, have to propose what is good. It must always seem as if the action derives from the sovereign. Legislative proposals must therefore emanate from the sovereign, as far as form is concerned. The estates assembly cannot make any proposals on its own account; the initiative for laws rests essentially with the power of the sovereign. It must not seem as if, formally speaking, a law derives from the estates assembly; for the formal proposal the assembly must have recourse to the monarchical principle. For if the assembly formally proposes the laws itself, this implies its independence from the power of the sovereign. After all, laws also have to be enacted in regard to the executive sphere and administration, and if the assembly also had the power to propose legislation, it would be capable of embarrassing the state power through its demands. In England both the monarch and Parliament[81] can propose laws; but if it were to happen, as has not happened for a hundred years past, that a proposal by Parliament was not approved by the regent, this could easily endanger the state. In England the king must also have ministers in the lower house; however, they cannot be

81. [Tr.] The text here uses *Ständeversammlung*, but later in the sentence, *Parlament*.

made peers, since if they were, they could no longer sit in the lower house. The only reason why the celebrated Pitt was not a peer was so that he could carry weight in the lower house. Thus the [English] constitution itself is a grave danger to the good of the state, and only abuses—the ancient privileges—can preserve it. As a result of abuses, towns that have in some cases completely disappeared have the right of representation, and this makes it possible for the party in power | to be sustained, since something is always arranged by bribes. England is also not affected by the vulgar sense of being continually hostile to the cabinet and government, and many people who are concerned about the common good side with the party in power. If the cabinet no longer has the majority in important matters, there must be a change of cabinet, for in that case the party that does not in fact always declare itself in favor of the party in power, but only when it believes it owes it to the good of the state to do so, has come out against it, and the cabinet must fall. So the estates must only have the right to present to the cabinet their wishes in regard to a legislative proposal, in order that it may submit them as a proposal. In addition, the cabinet must endorse the assembly's resolutions.

(2) Cabinet and council of state must be given an essential role to play in the estates assembly. However, they must not have the right of vote but only to make proposals and examine and explain the issues involved. In addition, ministers and counselors of state must be present in order to elucidate the issues in regard to whatever the assembly wills. It is essential to have the concrete perception of the ministry that lives in the thick of the matters under discussion. This practical knowledge as to all the different effects a regulation will have is something that only the cabinet can have, overseeing as it does all departments; for regulations affect different parts of the state very differently. For if the ministries have no share in the assembly, the assembly as proposing and the government as not approving start libeling each other, which becomes unnecessary and avoidable by having the ministers speaking in the assembly. The opposition

too has a major and necessary part to play in enlivening the assembly's debates. Here ministers can be questioned on anything; here they can show their talent, skill, and presence of mind, since they are | under constant attack from the assembly, which   227
stands over against their ministry, and since the assembly's proceedings must always be public. And this is the most vexatious thing about being a minister, for here he often has to spend six to eight hours thinking and speaking about what are in part unexpected questions. This check on the executive is the best guarantee for having ministers who are competent and whose attitude is governed by right. It is an outstanding spectacle to see such matters examined by ministers and estates.

(3) The estates may not vote and act in the sense of a single city or class, but must vote and act in the sense of the whole. The parliamentary constitution is based on the interests of the particular estates, but for particular interests the members have no particular instructions for their corporation and from their corporation, but have [only] the communal interest. The state's impulse is to absorb all particular interests in the interest of the community. Its business is not to have regard to individuals as such, but to act according to universal rules, which may be very oppressive for particular spheres and individuals; and this is especially the task of the estates, to alleviate this inequality that results from these universal rules for particular classes or corporations. Members of the estates assembly are especially knowledgeable about the particular spheres, while the ministry has knowledge of the universal and has the task of regulating the particular will. The relationship between the estates provides an excellent basis on which to form a council of citizens to advise the government, but such joint advice is the product of the advice tendered by all three powers, those of the sovereign, the executive, and the estates.

§ 150

The guarantee that members of the estates assembly will have the necessary qualifications can be divided into, on the one hand, [the security that results] from their having wealth or resources independent of state resources and of executive favor as well as of 228 trade | (this being bound up with the interests of legality and the maintenance of civil order); and on the other hand their attributes of rectitude, skill, and familiarity with the interests and institutions of the state and civil life, gained through the actual transaction of business and governmental or other office and attested in fact. [It] also [resides] in a sense of governmental responsibility and the conception of the state formed and tested in the same manner.

Some people regard it as superfluous to say that certain qualifications should be possessed by members of the estates, and that the people themselves know who means well by them. But "meaning well" counts for very little, and is of no use; what is needed is general familiarity with the edifice of the state. Moreover, how are the people to know who means well by them?— by their opinion,[82] perchance? But this opinion is very much a matter of chance, and this empty possibility, this chance element, this opining must be excluded. For if it is merely a matter of opining, then it is those who for the most part hold the floor in taverns, who mean right ill by the government, and who know how to declaim, who are elected to estates assemblies. So it was in France, where actors, barristers, rough-mannered Capuchins, and the like [were elected] to the assembly. From an exaggerated sense of right, those members who had been in the first legislative body passed a law to the effect that those of their number who over a number of years had shown courage, resolve, and knowledge were [not] to be elected to the new legislative body. As a result these street-corner orators and Capuchins came to the helm, and it was they who caused the revolution to go off course.

The two necessary guarantees concerning members of es-

82. [Tr.] In the German there is a wordplay between the verb *meinen* (to mean) and the noun *Meinung* (opinion). In the next sentence, the verbal noun *Meinen* (opining) is used as well. And there is a play between *gut meinen* (to mean well) and (in the second sentence below) *recht feindlich meinen* (to mean right ill).

tates assemblies are as follows. In the first place, they must have wealth or resources independent of state resources, [so that] in order to support themselves and their families they do not need to enter the service of the state. In many states the opposite was the case, and posts for which no altogether exceptional aptitude seemed necessary were put up for sale. In | England all officers' 229 posts were sold, and the purchaser could sell them again as his own property; and yet the English armies acquitted themselves very creditably. This way of doing things is very pernicious, but where it is not introduced, there is scope for a system based on favor. Where the delegate has means independent of the resources of the state, there is no longer any room for favor. Above all the delegate's mode of acquisition [of his wealth] must not, like trade, be dependent on fortune, and his status must not unduly arouse avarice. The possession of independent means [ensures] the interests of legality, namely that the state should be preserved along with all particular interests and classes. Admittedly there may be individuals who sacrifice their own and their family's well-being for the well-being of the state. This is possible and desirable, but it is a matter of chance, and the state cannot expect a guarantee whereby it is necessary for individuals to sacrifice their own well-being and that of their family. In a well-organized state such tragic virtues should not be needed.

The second guarantee is the question of ability, but not solely of familiarity with where this or that state official is less than efficient, or familiarity with a multitude of well-appointed plans. The sole guarantee is that he [the member of the estates assembly] has attested his rectitude and aptitude by what he has done, through the actual transaction of business, by holding government office. To be familiar in the abstract is quite different from familiarity attested in practice. It could at all events be made a condition that only those who have proved their worth in government office should be elected to the estates assemblies, for the mere confidence of the citizens is something subjective. Moreover, a sense of governmental responsibility is tested by holding such offices, the majority of which—those for the particular spheres of civil life—must be held without remuneration. In these governmental posts one also gets to know the rabble and that it has to be ruled.[83] |

230

§ 151

These are the reasons for dividing the estates assembly into two chambers or houses [*Kammer*]:[84]

(1) By providing [houses of] the first and second instance—as with law courts and government authorities—one has a surer guarantee of ripeness of decision, specifically in regard to the most important matters, namely universal affairs of state; and one also removes the contingent character pertaining to the mood of the moment, which can attach to any decision by a numerical majority.

(2) But principally, there is less chance of the estates' being in direct opposition to the government in the event of diversity of views on important matters. Between the one [i.e., lower] house where the democratic principle must be predominant [and the government] there is a mediating element [the upper house], which if it takes the side of the democratic principle gives it all the more weight, and if it diverges from it prevents it from appearing in opposition to the supreme power of the state.

In the concrete circumstances of a state it is necessary for business to be divided, and it may become advisable to a greater or lesser degree to differentiate activities. In the same way as in the case of law courts there must be a higher court to which it is possible to appeal, so here too there must be a second house in the estates assembly. The government may have to suspend a single house and appeal to the people on important issues, but this can only occur in important cases, for the consequences are always harmful if the government comes into opposition with a

---

83. *The text continues, breaking off at the bottom of the page*: The sense of exercising right, in general the sense of the state, whereby the citizen differs from the rabble, whereby the sense that all particular spheres

84. [*Tr.*] The arguments for a bicameral legislature are much more explicit in the Heidelberg lectures than in the published version of the *Philosophy of Right* (see §§ 305–308).

single house in this way. To avoid this it is better for there to be two houses. Each house must have a veto; for something to be valid, it must have been accepted by both houses—a single house and the government are not sufficient. So neither house may be outvoted. In earlier times this was not the case in Germany; once the electors and colleges of princes had voted, the vote of the college of cities was not needed. [It was] the same in France, where there were previously three estates, one of which could be outvoted. | This at all events must not happen; all 231 estates must give their agreement and have the right of veto. Two houses are necessary, each must have a veto and a deciding vote. An assembly can be carried away by the mood of the moment. This does not happen so easily if there are two houses. Speedy and precipitate decisions are averted by this means as [well as] by having the necessary rules of procedure, namely that matters to be discussed should be the subject of prior examination by committees of the house, that proposals should be submitted and discussed more than once, that decisions should not be taken in haste, etc. In an emergency, it must be possible for the detailed rules to be set aside. The first decree acknowledges that there is an emergency, while the second sets out the text of the decision; so in this case it may be unnecessary for the proposal to be submitted three times over. Such exceptions may be called for frequently; but in this way a government that wants to have something approved can arbitrarily get it declared an emergency matter. The mood of the moment could be prejudicial in such cases if there were not two houses to counteract the contingency of the moment.

Often a small majority can decide the matter one way or the other. This appears as a matter of chance, since the equal votes for and against appear as negative votes, and the others, constituting the "majority,"[85] as deciding votes. Examples of this are

85. [Tr.] Here (and below) the text uses the loanword *Majorität*, whereas in the preceding sentence the normal German term *Mehrzahl* is employed. We have marked the difference by the use of quotation marks. Hegel's point is that in such cases the so-called "majority" consists in only the deciding votes.

to be found in the proceedings of the English Parliament. During the examination of the living allowance for a princess who was marrying a Prussian prince, the discussion bore on the question of increasing her income. An equal number of votes were cast for and against, and there was still one man to vote, a lord who had previously been infamously condemned, and he voted against the increase. So the decision depended on him. Now here we have the matter decided by chance, because it was only the "majority" that decided. This chance element must be avoided.

The decision must flow from repeated deliberations ensuring that the matter is abundantly ripe for decision, not from the contingent nature of a handful of subjects. If there is only one house, in the event | of its rejecting the government's proposal it would appear to it [i.e., the government] as an opponent, and hatred, tension, and friction would ensue. If there are two houses and they both vote against, the government has nothing more to say; the decision has double weight. If the houses differ in their opinions, the appearance of opposition is between the two of them. They do not in any way appear in opposition to the government, and there is no hatred or tension on the part of the government vis-à-vis the house that has voted against because the dispute is seen merely as one between the two houses. If there were not two houses, the only means available in the event of contradiction would be either to dismiss the government or to dissolve the house. The latter course would appear as an attack on the freedom of the people, while the former would endanger the existence [*Existenz*] of the state.

§ 152

The existence of two distinct houses is not merely a matter of numerical division but takes shape as the determinate difference that is inherent in the classes of civil society and in the qualifications of members of the estates that provide a guarantee [of their suitability]. These qualifications include in the first place the possession of permanent property that is independent of both state and trade, and that is free from the uncertainty of possession involved in such forms of ownership and from the quest for a profit to be gained from the want and needs of others—[that is,] *landed property* [*Grundvermögen*], which for this very reason is the property of a whole, of the family. Since it is important that there should be in the state a class of citizens or rather families who belong in this independent way to the universal class, and [that] these families should make up the natural substantive element in the state, this [class], and the first estate of civil society, that of *landowners* [*Güterbesitzer*], acquire in this way a political importance and vocation. This can be called a *hereditary nobility*, but one that enjoys no other privileges and feudal rights. On the contrary, by virtue of its | position it must do without the rights of   233 other citizens and families since its political preeminence must be limited to one member of the family, who has moreover to show himself in other respects suited to exercise his political quality, and who must be legally debarred from other forms of business and commerce, and even from rightfully disposing of a specific part of the family estate.

It used to be the case that if a noblewoman married into a bourgeois family, this was noted in the civil register. And the same thing happened if a bourgeois man married into a noble family, but in this case his name was marked with an inkblot in the register of nobility. There is no place here for these distinctions; members of the upper house must have more duties than privileges. Their means make them independent, and by reason of their fixed vocation for political life they are obliged to give themselves a higher political education. The various other estates in civil life are interested only in their particular classes, concerned only for them on an individual basis, and are thus cut off from the whole. But the higher, hereditary classes are tied to participation in the universal sphere by virtue of their situation. Their proximate aim may well be their particular [interest], but their essential aim is the universal. Members of the second house are chosen by the people, organized into corporations and estates.

The main characteristic of the first house is complete independence through having fixed means and a fixed vocation to pursue universal aims as a result of hereditary succession. There is no place here for the pursuit of abstract profit, for cunning or guile. The basic quality of this nobility is the possession of land [*Güterbesitz*], landed estate [*Grundvermögen*], not merely capital [*Kapital*] lent at interest, involving the pursuit of profit. Even large-scale traders, though they disregard petty gains and their business involves them in universal matters, are always after profits, albeit on a larger scale, and seek to accumulate indeterminate wealth. By the nature of the case landed property involves satisfaction of the family, making all pursuit of profits a matter of no account.

The first house contains the universal class, the landowning class. Members of the agricultural class who wish to enter the | estates assembly must not only belong to this immediate class but be wealthy landowners, having a universal quality through their education. They must be exempt from considerations of indeterminate profit, such as affect the mercantile class; their lands must be inalienable. It cannot be by accident that they possess property. For lands to be inalienable, there must be hereditary succession and, to that extent, a nobility. However, there is no longer any room for a nobility that lacks all recognized employment and is proud of the fact, nor must it take precedence over the middle classes in offices of state. A nobility of this kind must have no privileges, as in England; and the exercise of certain trades, and also the right to dispose of landed estate, must be forbidden to it. It has to accept the sacrifice of renouncing the general civil right of doing whatever does not adversely affect the rights of another. Patrimonial jurisdiction is not, properly speaking, of great importance; however, the state must not seek to derive profit from the administration of justice. There is still less cause for the president of the patrimonial court to pocket the legal fees; for if the state does profit from the administration of justice, at least this means that it needs to levy less in the way of other taxes from the population. Apart from the fact that someone is a landowner of this kind, he also has to prove his suitability, but such proof must not become a mere formality as in France.

234

§ 153

The *second house* comprises in general the second estate of civil society; and it does so in the form of *deputies* [*Deputierten*], who are elected without regard to property qualifications, unless it be their having held governmental or other office, and without salary. However, they are chosen not by an [agglomeration] dispersed into atomic units, but in the articulated system made up of their different associations [*Genossenschaften*] and thus by the vote of a commonalty [*Bürgerschaft*] from which no actual citizen [*Bürger*] is excluded, | regardless of means. The right to choose deputies and 235 the political action this represents is not, in consequence, a single, nonrecurrent action for the electors, nor is it handed over to single individuals as such but is essentially entrusted to local communities [*Gemeinden*] and other duly constituted associations. In this way these associations enter the state in a political context, and the election of deputies, and with it the existence [*Existenz*] of the estates assembly, rests on a duly constituted guarantee. Furthermore, there is such a close connection between the estates and the constitution of the whole that a free attitude on the part of the electors and also a free and constitutionally minded attitude on the part of the deputies is only possible if the *rights of individuals* are safeguarded by making the administration of justice and jury trials public, and if the *rights of the particular local communities and interests* are safeguarded by the free establishment of civic authorities and self-administering bodies.

For the first house, participation is based on the correlative attributes of landed estate and family. In the second house the family has been fragmented, and participation is based on the system of needs. No one in the state must be allowed not to be a member of an association. The system of needs comes into play in the form of deputies of the associations. Election must be by the commonalty in general, i.e., by the associates of one or another corporation [*Korporation*]. In regard both to electors and to deputies, there is no room here for the property qualification; it is superfluous. For since most of those elected will have held government posts, in electing them to such posts the electors will have already taken property or resources [*Vermögen*] into account. If these representatives of the people draw a salary or receive remuneration, their position alters completely; the office of deputy must not offer any financial advantage. Only in the case of small states may the state's external dependence so affect the spirit of the citizens that they are unwilling to take on the post of a deputy unless it offers advantages.

Electors do not participate in the election as single individuals but as an association. For the individual has no duties qua individual. One has duties | only to the extent that one exists and has to act for a universal. This is what makes corporations so strong. If it is for associations to send deputies, and all citizens must be members of an association, then every active citizen can also take part in the election. It goes without saying that day laborers, servants, etc., are not [allowed to vote, but] are excluded as not being members of an association. Voting rights must rest in commonalties, in corporations. Citizens must make their choice in ordered, recognized associations. Only in this way is the right to vote ensured; and the fact that an election is actually taking place [is ensured by the fact] that the right to vote rests with corporations, in that it is no longer left to the chance patriotism of individuals. Something must exist in the state that involves a commonality of right and duty. If the executive takes it into its head to carry out actions alone that ought only to be performed with the cooperation of the estates, there are specific authorities to remind the government of its duty. The public character of the courts, which must be jury courts, gives citizens the self-confident feeling that they are getting their rights and that the state's interest is being served. There must also be self-administration of the citizens' communal property. For if the citizens are harrassed by officials, there arises an indifference in regard to the universal, the view that the government is merely burdensome. All too frequently the character of authorities and officials is compounded of pride, sordidness, and dishonesty. There is a great call in recent times for estates, but if these estates were to lack a sense of the state,

236

286

they would bring with them hatred for officials, judges, and the government.

§ 154

A further point that can be noted in regard to an estates assembly is that its sessions must be held in public—partly as the means whereby its actions become universal property for the consciousness of individuals | (who thereby achieve correspondingly greater   237 power), partly in order that it and its members may gain from public opinion an oversight and weighty judgment of their work—but above all so that public opinion itself may attain both to an insight into the actual affairs and condition of the state and to a rational concept and correct judgment in regard to them, and also in regard to the personal element in ministries, government authorities, and members of the estates. Only in this way is an estates assembly both itself the antidote to self-conceit among its members and one of the most important means of education for the people.

The above desiderata were not to be found in the former German provincial assemblies or diets, and the citizens could not be blamed for shedding no tears at the loss of institutions that did more harm than good. [What was formerly regarded as] the good, if it [proves to be] bad, has by virtue of its authority all the more pernicious an effect. If the sessions of estates assemblies are held in public, this provides a means of keeping the people informed and enabling them to take part in the affairs of the community. The estates then have the opinion of the entire people behind them to support them. Where there is a revolution it is harmful for the proceedings of the estates to be public. This happened in France where the rabble followed what was going on and applauded or hissed, and if its opinion was unfavorable was only too ready to wreak revenge on whoever spoke against it. A member of the assembly who has aroused lively discussion in the chamber will moreover frequently continue the debate within his family, where everyone knows everything, and in this way his views too will be refined. And by this means the public gains familiarity with the administration of the state, and its judgment is formed. How vastly more advanced the English people are than the German. How false and silly is the judgment one usually hears [in Germany], even from those who shout the loudest, such as Colonel von Massenbach, by contrast with the judgment of the English. [It is] the same with the judgment in regard to the ministers and the sovereign, and the people's familiarity with affairs is confined to the purely private side, which is after all of subordinate importance in relation to the state. For great statesmen often pay very little heed to their private behavior, deeming it of small account by comparison with their office. It is only by holding sessions of the assembly in public that people get to know what is genuinely | important. The consequence is that no member of an assembly will get away with being only superficially or moderately well informed, and self-conceit is most severely punished and put in its place. Thus [it happened] with Count Waldeck in the Württemberg Diet when he accused the ministry of not having taken even one of ten apparently good measures to counter the previous year's scarcity; but the house had of necessity to reject all ten. The estates assembly, where the noblest and best of the people sit and where everything comes up for discussion, is the most important means of educating the public opinion of the people. In this way public opinion arrives at maxims that have immediate validity and at sound common sense. When a people obtains this education [Bildung], having regard to the self-consciousness of its freedom and its right, this provides the root of all public virtues [Volkstugenden].

238

§ 155

Directly bound up with the existence [Existenz] of an estates assembly and the public conduct of its business, as well as with a consistent constitution, is the possibility and efficacy of *freedom of the press* [Pressfreiheit] in regard to matters of state; [likewise the possibility] that other individuals from the general public should have their say publicly as they please; and the possibility for all to participate directly. For one thing, it is only if the assembly's proceedings are public that regular legal action can be taken against those who infringe freedom of the press; for another, people are in this way informed about affairs of state, public opinion is firmly based and oriented along the right lines; and for this very reason false judgments and public calumnies can be seen to be unimportant, and the government and public figures can therefore be indifferent to them.

Provincial assemblies and freedom of the press are two matters that engage attention more than any others. They can only exist within a consistent whole, but within the latter they are necessary links in the chain of the whole. In a large state freedom of the press is this complementary element. In such a state the local communities can only | be represented in the estates   239
assembly by deputies since not everyone can take part in it, the infinitely greater number being unable to do so owing to their occupation and education. This essential complementary element consists in gaining an immediate hearing for one's views.

But such freedom of the press is only possible where there is a good estates assembly whose proceedings are public, and where there are judicial proceedings involving jury courts, so that all know how and by whom they are being judged. If all people can write whatever they want, there is nothing to prevent all manner of libelous attacks on fellow citizens, officials, and rulers, and the revealing of all family secrets. But to enact laws as to where libel begins and ends is a difficult matter that causes endless trouble in France, Germany, and Holland, especially nowadays when the most libelous statements can be made using expressions that are not indictable. It is not possible to enact laws to cover this unless the libel is recognized. But this recognition must be by jury courts, for then the author of the libel and also the government, officials, and any private parties to the case are sure of getting their rights; and a decision can be taken by their peers, by judges they have chosen themselves, in regard to mere evidence of a libel. Someone accused of libel through the press is also not entitled to adduce as evidence the correctness of the facts; provided they are libelous, he is punishable. For example, someone who prints a parliamentary speech in which accusations are made may thereby be guilty of libel even though there was no libel on the part of the orator. A major point here—and this was introduced by Pitt in England—is that the jury does not judge solely on the facts of the case but primarily on whether there is libel or not.

Furthermore, if freedom of the press is to be introduced without doing harm, the people must already have attained a higher level of public education. Calumnies and false judgments concerning individuals and governmental affairs are of no consequence to the individuals and ministers concerned. They do 240 not need to worry about them, | they can pay no attention to them, since the people are fully informed as a result of the publicity [given to the assembly's proceedings], and in this way freedom of the press gives rise to indifference and insensitivity to the kind of respect one finds in other countries. It is open to one to lodge a complaint on this score, and one will certainly be accorded one's rights; but one deems it beneath one's notice, one rises above it. In England all the people read the abuse and censure directed at those who stand above them, whereby they see them dragged down, as it were, to their own level from posts they cannot themselves attain. Very many people spend whole days and nights thinking of caustic things to say about others. To judge from these articles, public opinion seems to be decisively opposed to the cabinet, but genuine public opinion shows itself in a very different light where it matters, in that in such a state the cabinet cannot remain in office if true public opinion is against it.

§ 156

An estates assembly cannot be regarded as having actually engaged in activity until it includes an opposition, i.e., until the universal interest becomes at the same time a particular interest within the assembly itself, and, on the basis of the constitution, the ministerial posts become an interest of ambition. Virtue in the state is not a moral abstraction from particularity of interest; it is rather that this particularity vests itself in a universal interest of the estate or of the state.

Here we are dealing with political virtue as opposed to moral and religious virtue. If the estates assembly is essentially of one mind in opposition to the government, then the government must either split or dissolve itself; and since this leads to the destruction of the state, the government as the repository of power must dismiss the assembly. If on the other hand the assembly were unanimously in favor of the government, it would not be fulfilling its vocation or attaining its goal. Of necessity there must be an opposition within the assembly itself; | the cabinet   241 must have the majority in an assembly, but the opposition must necessarily be there as well. The estates assembly is the main council of the state. The sovereign power, the cabinet must essentially have the majority, for this is implied in the concept of a cabinet; otherwise it is not the cabinet. If the cabinet is generally in a minority, it must be replaced by another cabinet, and this too can last only as long as it has, in general, the majority on its side. There must be three parties in the assembly, two that are directly opposed to each other, the party of the people and the party [that] is absolutely always on the side of the government, and then a sizable third party, which usually takes the side of the cabinet but on the whole is nonpartisan in its approach. This third party is an aristocratic party, based on noble families. It is usually thought that civil servants ought not to be members of an estates assembly on the ground that they are on the side of the government; but the government, as unity of the whole, is the foremost element that has to be preserved. As for civil servants, whose corporation must in itself have rights and who cannot simply be dismissed, they are not unduly dependent on the government. Yet they are for the most part the best educated, who were at universities, and bring with them into the assembly this mentality trained for office.

What is chiefly necessary in general is for the interests of particularity to merge into the interests of the universal. This is in fact one of the principal features in a large civilized state, that the interests of particularity should have been fully developed.

It is only in small states that there can be republican constitutions, where the main consideration is moral rectitude; in large states it is not possible to have regard to moral and religious motivations. Where ambition and status-seeking come into play, there is accordingly justification for an opposition as such. The ethical life which is present within the state specifically requires that the interest of particularity as such should exist, but should in turn be linked with the universal interest of the state or estate. The statesman's virtues are not solely moral virtues. What counts here is actuality, and the ethical consists solely | in this subjectivity's having its determinate existence in the universal. Ambition is this virtue within the state; particularity must make itself known along with the other virtues of the state. Miltiades' aim was the well-being of the state, but the virtue of such heroes was the element of nature. The prevailing moral standpoint of modern times has been apolitical in the sense that we seek to discredit someone's action (and believe that we do so) by saying he only acted in this way from ambition. We always consider the subjective side and through it become distrustful of proposals or actions. The necessary mistrust is that the others should not approve the matter in hand simply on trust; on the contrary, it is only when its real value has been ascertained that it becomes universal. But what we mean by virtue in the state is that what one person proposes partly from ambition others find to be concordant with the universal. Among the Romans [and other peoples] there were and are a multitude of philosophical and religious sects, such as Cynics, etc., or Quakers. But a state made up of such citizens could not subsist, and the latter subsist only to the extent that others take on the business of the community for them so that they are only parasitic plants, incapable of forming a state on their own. To be abstracted from particularity is to be severed from organic life.

242 (margin)

§ 157

Apart from collaborating on laws concerning the judicial and political sphere and determining the rights and mode of operation of the particular spheres of civic life, the estates are responsible, in regard to the executive power, for receiving and examining complaints by individuals concerning actions by officials and government authorities, for indicting ministers, and in particular for annually approving taxation, by which means they retain indirect control over governmental affairs in general without the government's actions themselves being subject to their decision. In regard to the sovereign power, they are responsible for supervising the succession to the throne, especially | in the event that the ruling dynasty dies out and a new one comes on the scene.   243

Here we are dealing with the responsibilities of the estates, initially their particular responsibilities. As the constitution is progressively developed, disharmony may ensue as a result of one branch's being more advanced than another, and in such a case the estates assembly must find a remedy. Laws differ from ordinances and from cabinet orders; in a well-ordered state there should be no place for cabinet orders since no one is responsible for them. It is not possible to indicate precisely the difference between laws and ordinances. Individual associations must have the right to present petitions to the estates assembly; this must be a sacred right, and the assembly must examine and check such petitions closely. In a well-regulated state there can be little necessity for formal indictments of ministers, especially as they have to render account of their actions; however, they must be under threat of such indictment in the event of their failure.

For the estates the approval of taxation is a way of controlling all government actions, since taxes are the means to all government actions and nowadays nothing can be done without money. Taxes must be regulated according to the revenue from crown lands, and to this extent account must also be rendered to the estates assembly concerning them. Formerly taxes had the form of a levy imposed on a particular piece of land, alongside which there might be a plot to all intents and purposes free from tax; and revenue was virtually the private property of the sovereign, out of which he had to meet expenditures. Customs duties had merely the form of taxes—it was not their purpose to facilitate trade. Only in modern times have taxes come into being, and the sovereign is given a civil list, for example in England. But all other levies imposed on landed estate as rights, ground rents, or tithes must be annulled before taxes can be imposed equally. In France all these levies were annulled by revolutionary decree.

Government actions themselves are not subject to the estates assembly, | but only the taxes that provide the means for them. Owing to the supervision exercised and the whole way the state is organized, the government cannot be extravagant; and the other extreme, the estates' stinginess with the necessary taxes, is also precluded by the political sense [actualized] in a constitution where everyone partakes in the universal—the sense of having one's pride and honor in the greatness of the state and the great deeds it performs. There is nothing that must not be given up for the sake of this whole, whereby one's particular interest is protected and furthered.

The monarch, as the ultimate pinnacle of the subjectivity of certainty, must be made permanent as a result of natural succession, and it is for the estates assembly to preserve this security of inheritance of the throne. If the dynasty dies out, the estates of the realm must see to it that a new dynasty ascends the throne without disturbances; and since nature ceases to determine the succession, it is for the estates themselves to make a choice.

§ 158

The wholly universal affairs of the state, however, concern both the public *training* [*Erziehung*] and *education* [*Bildung*] of individuals to serve the purposes of the state, and *art, religion,* and *science* in and for themselves—these being the intuition, feeling, representation, and knowledge[86] of the absolute essence of the state and of nature. The highest satisfaction of spirit, in which it recog-

---

86. [*Tr.*] Intuition (*Anschauung*) is the mode of cognition appropriate to art (*Kunst*); feeling (*Gefühl*) and representation (*Vorstellung*) are the modes appropriate to religion; and knowledge (*Wissen*) is the mode appropriate to science (*Wissenschaft*), meaning academic learning in general and philosophical knowledge in particular.

nizes the state, the lives and actions of individuals, and also history and nature as the absolute mirrored in actuality, [is] an intuition and occupation to which a people's express vocation, sphere, and status must be dedicated.

We are referring here in the first place to training and education on behalf of the state; training and education on their own account come later. The state has to see that this right of individuals to education and training is realized. Public educational establishments must in part afford opportunities for training, but in part they must be obligatory and necessary, and it must not be left to the free choice of individuals and parents whether to avail themselves of them. Children become children of the state. | Specific education by means of instruction is the objec-   245
tive element, and this is what the state must and can take notice of. Education in general takes place of itself, without the state's having to enforce it. The education of a succeeding generation is the direct consequence of the education given to the preceding one. The state is ethical spirit, spirit in and for itself, and constitutes the essence of all individuals; but the state appears as a state in time.

It is through religion, art, and science that the essence [Wesen] of the state, its freely emergent spirit, is intuited—this being an intuition [of] the intellectual element in actuality [das Intellektuelle der Wirklichkeit]. The state must regard this as an end in and for itself, an end such that it is justified by this very intuition. Spirit is actuality; hence the life of religion, science, and art must not exist for itself alone but must be the life of the state, and spirit must portray itself as actuality. The self-reflection of the ego must as such attain its freedom. The intuition of essence [die wesentliche Anschauung] is through art; religion involves still more, namely the intuition and consciousness of unity with the absolute object. The mystical element or inner core of religion is the self-consciousness of individuals in their absolute spirit; this is the supreme satisfaction of self-knowing reason. This world shows itself in history as a mirror image of the absolute. Science [Wissenschaft] is not merely believing in a general, abstract way but more precise cognition.

As the state is spirit in its actuality, these are essential elements in it. Knowledge of the absolute must also comprise actuality. There must accordingly be a church in the state, independent of the state but one with it. The understanding [*Verstand*] has recently arrogated so much to itself that the need [for a church] has emerged once more. The church must not portray itself as an earthly kingdom within the state, for otherwise the state must turn against it. Religion is a universal mode of representation [*Vorstellung*] and thought [*Denken*], but not yet conceptual thought [*Begreifen*]; this | higher level is science [i.e., philosophy]. The church has opposed science and has neglected to endow itself with this higher level, to raise the truth it contains to the sphere of science. Science and the church must not be mutually opposed, even though particular spheres are necessary for both.

246

We have spoken of the absolute concerns of a people: religion, art, and science. Knowing is the highest way in which reason is real, and this reality must come about in a people. There must be one class in the people that devotes itself to it. There used to be monasteries where people shut themselves off from the world but were of no benefit to the universal interest since they only looked after themselves. Contemporary states are still a far cry from establishing universal institutions for these spheres; the universities and academies of sciences have taken the place of the monasteries. It used to be the case that religion was attended to by fear of God, and the arts and sciences by the princes; but the needs of these spheres are not necessarily provided for in this way. However, people who devote themselves to them must not bury themselves so deeply in them as to lose themselves, as happened for instance in Egypt. The other extreme of our times is that the state is regarded as merely attending to the protection of its citizens. In its institutions the state must be a temple of reason. This is how philosophical cognition must comprehend the state; and even if individuals cannot know it in this way, at least they have the impression that the state is something rational.

B. International Law

§ 159

A people is a single entity, and it is only through determination and particularity that individuality has existence [*Dasein*] and actuality. Each people accordingly has its determinate anthropological principle, which | develops in its history, and to this extent is   247
a *nation* [*Nation*]. In this way at the same time it exists *for itself* over against other such individual entities, and as absolutely self-sufficient its relationship to them is that pertaining to a *state of nature* [*Naturzustand*]. *International law* [*äussere Staatsrecht*] is therefore a mixture of universal and positive right and of contingency and power.

What international law is concerned with is the being of a people for itself, but it involves only an "ought," that right should be. Here we are concerned only with the self-sufficient over against the self-sufficient. Existence [*Dasein*] means being something determinate in relation to something else. Each people has an immediate natural determinacy within itself, a particular character and particular geographical circumstances. It is not by chance that the spirit of each people differs from that of other peoples. The world-historical [principle] is a necessary principle; it is a particular principle that develops within the history of a people. World history is the portrayal of how these [national] characters constitute moments in the world spirit. We are all born, *natus*, in such a way as to belong to our *nation* and to a greater or lesser degree share our people's specific natural character. This "belonging to one's people by nature," [in contrast with] entering a specific state of one's own free will as an individual, gives rise to a conflict, which must be eliminated. According to the former principle none of us have the right to leave our people. In many states it was therefore made the rule for everyone to swear the oath of allegiance on reaching manhood. For instance the English government did not recognize emigration and recruited as a sailor every native-born Englishman it laid hold of on shipboard.

A further [cause for] conflict would be whether a nation has the absolute right to constitute a state. That is the natural thing, but a nation can also fragment into several states although it is enfeebled if it does so. If by contrast several nations constitute one state, the state retains a certain weakness, which is only eliminated after centuries of amalgamation. [It is] the same with the Jews. They have a religion of their own, which also contains a political ingredient in that they cleave to their religion and in conformity with it hold apart from all | other peoples and may not even eat or drink with a non-Jew. Now insofar as the Jews have in their religion principles that preclude all links with other citizens and impede the unity of the state, [their exclusion from the state seems to be necessary]. However, custom and the impulse imparted by universal rationality to abandon these disharmonies make such exclusion unnecessary. It is custom that prevails over principle; this is why governments are justified in not taking consistent measures against this unyielding opposition. Moreover, their constitutions are too firmly established for such opposition to be capable of causing any harm. At all events, international law contains something universal in the relationships [among the peoples]. Since the starting point is freedom of choice, these relationships rest on contracts, which however contain no guarantee.

§ 160

A people's highest honor is to maintain its independence or self-sufficiency [*Selbständigkeit*]; this is the being-for-self of its actual essence. This negative unity of the whole is the ideality of the particular spheres of civil life and of the subsisting-for-self of individuals. It is the domain in which the substance [of the state], as the power of actuality in relation to life and property and their rights, brings the nothingness of these things home to consciousness and makes sacrifice for the recognized status [*Anerkanntsein*] and independence of the whole a duty for all; whereas for the state of being recognized in regard to individual matters and external political relations in general, it specifies a particular part [of the people] as the *estate of courage* [*Stand der Tapferkeit*].

As negative vis-à-vis other peoples, a people therein exists for itself. Through the coherence of the whole all spheres converge together in the state, and all people attain their purposes in their sphere. It is in this ideality that the negativity, the power of the state, | comes into play. For those who live quietly in their 249 sphere, the nothingness of what they possess is brought to consciousness. Individuality involves the ascent to negative unity. All peoples strive to be a central point, and in Germany we find that every imperial city, every petty province regrets that it is no longer a central point. Nor is the people's wish in Germany directed to having just one central point, but to a federal union of the individual central points. The independence of the people is the element of all its negative unity, in which family life and all domestic happiness find their power. The particular must possess its right in the universal, and the universal must exist through the particular.

Wars may be condemned by morality, which can say that wars ought not to be; but the state is not merely an "ought." Rather wars must be regarded as necessary because independent peoples exist alongside one another. Individuals must feel the ethical substance, the spirit of the whole, in relation to which individuals are ephemeral. What is demanded is to sacrifice oneself to this substance willingly. Wars are like winds upon the sea; without them the water would become foul, and so it is with the state. This ethical aspect—the dimension the state acquires inwardly as a result of its external nature—is the highest viewpoint from which war can be regarded. In its manifestation, war is this orientation outward, which nevertheless operates inwardly and shows the nothingness of particularity.

This inner sacrifice is demanded not merely in disposition but in actuality. This element—to sacrifice life, property, and rights for the preservation of the whole—requires an independent people and a constitution that subsists within itself and preserves itself. In a small state that is not self-sufficient much can arise and endure that cannot endure in an independent state. Sometimes at the request of smaller states, sometimes on their own initiative, more powerful states may take upon themselves the task of preserving peace in smaller states.[87] The constitution cannot be guaranteed by a more powerful people, | for this would be the utmost disgrace. As a direct consequence, there is a duty incumbent upon all to sacrifice themselves for the preservation of the state. Individuals have their honor, their essential subsistence, in the state alone. Properly speaking, individuals can sacrifice themselves only for the state as a whole, for if a citizen were to go to war for his property, he would be staking his life for the sake of his property, although without his life his property would be of no use to him.

For the recognized status of specific individual matters, the state appoints a separate section of the people. For the only circumstance in which the whole people takes up arms is when the independence of the whole is jeopardized. It is just not possible for individual interests to be made an interest of this kind for the individual citizens. For these particular interests the state must have an army, representing the element of courage. This moment of negativity, of courageous sacrifice, demands an estate to which entry must be open to all. However, if there are not enough volunteers, the state can oblige certain citizens to enlist by law. A territorial militia, which must be held only in reserve, can only be used when the independence, the autonomy of the state is in danger. The dangerous feature about arming a whole people to ensure its independence is that one abandons a merely defensive system and acts offensively.

§ 161

Since the *right* of states vis-à-vis one another is based on their relationship as [that] of self-sufficient individuals, [which is] the relationship [that pertains to] a state of nature, it extends only to reciprocal recognition as independent entities—entities, that is, that attest themselves to be free by waging war and exercising power, with whom it is at the same time possible to live in a condition of peace.

87. *A sentence fragment follows*: But a state that is not independent

What states have to demand of one another is recognition— | 251
to be recognized [as] free, independent individual entities. What
is free as something naturally free only evinces itself by demon-
strating that its life is a matter of indifference to it; and this existence of what is free can be shown only in war. As a natural
mode of recognition, this recognition comprises an element of
contingency; and as natural attributes, strength, size, level of resources, talent all affect the outcome. The right of states on the
one hand is the demand that they reciprocally recognize one another; on the other hand it has to be proved that they in fact do
so. If a state has a constitution that threatens the independence
of other states or that is incompatible with a condition of peace,
the latter states can either refuse to recognize it or else call on it
to change its constitution in that respect. They cannot formulate this demand in the direct sense of requiring the state to deviate from its constitution, but the demand can be formulated
indirectly. For example the [other] states refused to recognize the
French Republic. The constitution is the inner life of the people,
and the people should have a constitution that enables other
states to live at peace with it. Insofar as uncivilized peoples
have virtually no constitution, and the civilized peoples who
live alongside them accordingly cannot rely on them and never
feel secure, they take it on themselves to compel these rough
peoples to accept a fixed constitution.

§ 162

The more specific obligations incumbent on states rest on *positive treaties*, and the fundamental principle of *international law* as
the universal right that ought to be valid in and for itself is that
treaties ought to be kept. But because of the principle of independence, the reciprocal rights of states are actualized only in their
particular wills and not in a constituted universal will. The proposition therefore does not go beyond an "ought." Numerous injuries
inevitably occur in the manifold relations between states and between their nationals. The question as to which of these are to be
regarded as assaults on the state as a whole and on | its honor, or   252

as a definite breach of treaties, or as a danger threatening from another state, is indeterminate. If states disagree over such questions, the matter can be settled only by war.

The universal obligation of states is that they recognize one another; if they wish to enter into other obligations toward one another, they conclude treaties. As with single individuals, the peoples or nations should have rights vis-à-vis each other. But since the rights they are willing to cede to each other are arbitrary, they have their determinate existence only in the particular will of the contracting parties. They achieve existence as a result of reciprocal free choice; by being actualized, their willing attains existence and ought to be recognized by others.

The universal element of will, i.e., the fact that they have defined their rights reciprocally, does not as such involve actuality; if this universal were actually present, their relation to one another would no longer be that of states confronting one another as particulars. All we have here is the proposition that treaties ought to be kept. This "ought" is a matter of contingency. A single individual of a state, or whole classes or corporations of its citizens, may be injured or adversely affected by another state, through its enactments. Now the aim of the state is the well-being of its subjects. It is a fact that states conclude numerous treaties with one another. In the absence of treaties, the state can regard the injury done to an individual as one done to itself or simply as an injury to the individual. If the states see it as a merely personal matter, they leave the individuals to themselves; and it depends on each state what it is prepared to tolerate from another state—it may regard its honor as at stake in minor injuries. The state does not have to wait for direct injury or attack; on the contrary, the mere danger of an attack or injury, or excessive growth in strength, may cause a state to resort to war. When Joseph II carried out domestic improvements | in Austria, he made other states jealous of him.

253

Such representations, views, and judgments determine whether the mutual relations between states will be peaceful or hostile, as also the strength of the injured state (which enjoys a kind of superabundance of health) and its power to provide all this [surplus] energy with an external outlet. After a lengthy period of peace, when the country's coffers are full and many of its young men are eager for war, a trivial insult readily becomes a cause for the outbreak of war. As we are here dealing merely with an "ought," it is just not possible to say anything against wars since states are opposed to one another as individuals living in nature [*Naturindividuen*]. Kant and others have spoken of perpetual peace,[88] and this is a well-meaning thought, which is also morally good; but the starting point has been that war is something that ought not to be. Yet without war peoples sink into merely private life—the security and weakness that make them an easy prey for other peoples. War is something ethically necessary. A league to preserve perpetual peace always necessarily involves the free decision of individual states whether to remain in the league or not; for without this freedom of decision they are no longer independent states.

It is also a well-meaning thought, advanced some thirty years ago, that the human race should form a single state.[89] What holds the individual states together in such a league of all states

88. [*Ed.*] Hegel is referring to Kant's *Zum ewigen Frieden: Ein philosophischer Entwurf* (Königsberg, 1795); cf. Kant, *Schriften* 8:341–386. In his article "Über den Gemeinspruch: Das mag in der Theorie richtig sein, taugt aber nicht für die Praxis," *Berlinische Monatsschrift* 22 (1793): 201–284, Kant himself refers to C. I. C. de St. Pierre's *Projet de paix universelle* (Utrecht, 1713) and also to Rousseau's treatment of the subject in his *Extrait du projet de paix perpetuelle de Monsieur l'Abbé de St. Pierre* (n.p., 1761) as precursors for the plan for universal international peace; cf. Kant, *Schriften* 8:312–313. In the *Metaphysics of Morals* Kant reverts to these problems in connection with his discussion of international law (§ 61). Cf. *Rechtslehre*, pp. 226 ff. (Kant, *Schriften* 6:350–351.)

89. [*Ed.*] Hegel may here be recalling Kant's article "Über den Gemeinspruch," in which he took issue with the "proposal for an international state" as envisaged by St. Pierre and Rousseau (see previous note). On the one hand Kant points to the impracticability of such a project; on the other hand he concludes that it is theoretically valid. In the short article "Idee zu einer allgemeinen Geschichte in weltbürgerlicher Absicht," which had first appeared in 1784 in the *Berlinische Monatsschrift* 4:385–411, Kant had discussed this idea—likewise with reference to St. Pierre and Rousseau—in the context of his scheme for a philosophy of history of humanity. In his "seventh proposition" Kant here sees as the historical goal of the human species the establishment of a "league of nations" such as would form the prerequisite for the introduction of a "perfect civil constitution." Cf. Kant, *Schriften* 8:24–26.

is merely an "ought," and the whole league is based on free choice [*Willkür*]. At all events the individual must desire the opposite of war; but war is a philosophically essential element of nature.

§ 163

War, being a condition devoid of right, a condition of violence and contingency, involves right—insofar as it is waged between peoples that recognize their independence on a reciprocal basis— only to the extent that it | preserves the possibility of peace and is not waged against purely private persons who are distinguished from the state. In other respects the way states behave to one another in general rests on a nation's *customs* [*Sitten*] as the inner universality of behavior that has being in and for itself and endures regardless of circumstances. A further point is that in war a people's independence is exposed to contingency. However, the higher right to which they are subject is contained in the universal world spirit.

Here the transition to a higher level is indicated. War draws all possible talents out into mutual antagonism; but even in the condition of universal absence of right [some] rights ought to be valid. In the first place, by virtue of the fact that war is waged by states that mutually recognize one another, the possibility of peace must remain, and envoys and members of parliament [may] not be harmed. Everything that does not belong to the actual state—civil life, religion, academic establishments, the law courts—ought to be spared insofar as it is only actual states as states that wage war upon one another. However, this too is by and large only an "ought," for, after all, these things belong to the state and provide it with means. Moreover, in the event of an emergency the state can seize [the] funds of particular spheres within it. For if the state is in danger of losing its freedom, the particular spheres have no rights in relation to it; and it must also sometimes deprive the state with which it is at war of these means or resources.

Custom is what most firmly regulates behavior in time of war. Where there is no longer any possibility of peace, where the independence of one of the peoples is threatened, it becomes a war whose sole aim is mutual destruction. If for example envoys were murdered, this would be a signal for a war of this kind. If a people in whom civil society has developed becomes embroiled with a people that has reached this level of civilization, they do not take it so much to heart if a | part or province is incorporated into another state, since those who pass over retain their rights, religion, etc. The Poles defended themselves honorably, but were too late in the attempt to equip themselves with a rational constitution. However, the [Polish] people were inwardly fragmented, torn by divisions. Among civilized peoples there are fewer and fewer such internecine wars because there is a more highly developed being-for-self of families and individuals. Thus unity is weaker and there is no danger for the totality of rights and institutions, for religion, education, etc. The Spartans made all Messenians who did not emigrate slaves. [It was] the same in the Orient [i.e., China], where in the capital all men, women, and children were murdered.

255

Since war dissolves international law, all that can remain is what exists as an inner element within peoples, namely ethical life. Our practice is to spare prisoners who are no longer dangerous; army chaplains and medical officers are not for the most part treated as prisoners. In the Polish War, Suvarov had every living thing in the suburbs of Prague massacred when he captured it. Since envoys represent their people, the murder of envoys is also a weighty occurrence. But as states are unwilling to stake their independence lightly, they view this latter insult as a single circumstance and disregard it. This [is what happened] with the French envoys who were murdered in Rastatt. The highest point a people can reach is to preserve their independence and sacrifice everything to it. But this independence is nothing absolute, and it can be destroyed. Something higher transcends it, world spirit, and where the latter emerges, the rights of the peoples disappear. |

256

C. World History

§ 164

The principles of the particular folk spirits [*Volksgeister*] are restricted. The unrestricted spirit is the universal spirit, which exercises its absolute right toward the folk spirits in *world history* as the *court of world judgment*[90]—a judgment, moreover, that is rendered not merely by its might and a blind destiny but by the necessary development of its self-consciousness, whereby a single nation or people is made responsible for implementing a single moment and stage, which it receives in the form of a principle. Such-and-such a people is dominant in world history during such-and-such an epoch; and in contrast with its absolute right of being the vehicle of this present highest stage in the development of world spirit [*Weltgeist*], the principles of other peoples are without rights.

Absolute spirit, existing in and for itself, is actual in self-consciousness. The state *is* this actuality. The state is inner life, but is something particular in relation to other peoples. All that is required of the universal constituted by the right of peoples is to *be*. But what is universal in and for itself is world spirit. Here spirit is striving to grasp itself in its highest form. And the highest moment is world history, the absolute process into which the independence of the peoples is transposed; in relation to this process the independence of the peoples is of no account.

Pragmatic history indicates the causes of the rise and decline of peoples. If one seeks to establish why a people fared as it did, the reasons are so closely interconnected that one continually encounters further causes. World history is this divine tragedy, where spirit rises up above pity, ethical life, and everything that in other spheres is sacred to it; it is where spirit brings itself forth. One is sad to see the decline of great peoples, the ruins of Palmyra and Persepolis, and how in Egypt everything has fallen into ruin. But what has been laid low, *has* been laid low and *had* to be laid low. World spirit is unsparing and pitiless. Even the finest, highest principle of a people is, | as the principle of a

257

90. [*Tr.*] See the next note.

306

particular people, a restricted principle, left behind by the advancing spirit of the age [*Zeitgeist*]. Nothing profounder can be said than Schiller's words, "World history is a court of world judgment [*die Weltgeschichte ist ein Weltgericht*]."[91] No people ever suffered wrong; what it suffered, it had merited. The court of world judgment is not to be viewed as the mere might of spirit; the genus has the might of the universal over individuals, which are accidents, but the genus in turn relapses into individuality. It is in these individuals that the genus in turn has its next determinate existence; this is a tedious process, where the same thing keeps on happening. World history, on the other hand, is always an advance to something higher. Moreover, it not merely "is"; "isness" [*das Ist*] is the ultimate, simple condition devoid of concept: something "is" because it "is."

The destinies of peoples do not involve merely being, which would be contingent in its manifestation, but a conceptualized being. To be sure, one must harden one's heart when contemplating the destinies of peoples, but they are not [what they are] merely because they are. Children do not yet comprehend themselves inwardly; it is only later that they make themselves free. In the same way epochs in world history are distinct stages in consciousness; each people has its development latent within itself, but in this great nexus of world history each people has a particular principle. Its history is only a development within itself, in an individual people.

Since one people is dominant in [a given epoch of] history, its principle is also introduced into the other peoples. A people whose principle coincides with the stage attained by the spirit of the age is the dominant people, and its deeds are the most excellent. The three hundred Spartans at Thermopylae form a moment of world history, even though several thousands have often fallen no less bravely. In contrast with such a people in whose deeds world spirit manifests itself, the rights of other

---

91. [*Ed.*] Friedrich Schiller, "Resignation: Eine Phantasie," line 95, in *Thalia* (1786). See Schiller, *Werke: Nationalausgabe*, vol. 1, *Gedichte, 1776–1799*, ed. Julius Petersen and Friedrich Beissner (Weimar, 1948), p. 168.

peoples are of no account; grievous though it may be to watch how it tramples them under foot, it fulfills its role. In the Roman people the injustice of continually interfering in everything was justified because it was the right of world spirit. Individuals who take the lead in such a people and at such a time, | even if they act in an immoral fashion by despising the rights of others, are nonetheless responsible for its being executed [i.e., the right of world spirit]. Here the absolute idea of spirit has absolute right against everything else.

258

§ 165

There have been four world-historical realms: (1) the Oriental, (2) the Greek, (3) the Roman, (4) the Germanic.[92]

World history was earlier dealt with in terms of the four monarchies, and this was based on the fact that the history of all other peoples is related to the world-historical peoples. It is in these four worldviews that spirit has attained knowledge of itself through these stages. There are peoples who lie on the periphery of this development and who are not world-historical. As folk spirit, determined by nature, spirit comprises many genera and species, since this natural side must also have its right; and the species in question are sometimes only dimly illuminated by world spirit in that they are to a greater or lesser degree closely related to the folk spirit of the leading people. In the Oriental realm we have despotism, in the Greek democracy, in the Roman aristocracy as opposed to democracy; while the absolute foundation in the Germanic realm is the principle of the inwardness of spirit.

§ 166

(1) The worldview of the Oriental realm is substantial, and it first arises as a natural whole, patriarchically governed, in which

92. [Tr.] The "Germanic" (germanisch as distinct from deutsch, "German") includes for Hegel virtually all of modern Europe and might be regarded as a synonym for "European" (a term Hegel rarely uses). Among the Europeans Hegel accords a special role to the so-called "Nordic principle" (§ 169) in developing the principle of inwardness.

individuals as sons have no personality, [no] right or property on their own account vis-à-vis the ruler, and in which distinctions of class, of civil | life are fixed by birth as separate castes. In it the sec-   259 ular government is at the same time theocratic, the ruler is also the high priest or a god, the constitution is religion, and religious and moral precepts and usages are at the same time laws of the state and laws of right.

This is the necessary first configuration, that of inward re- flection. Freedom is not yet present, and individuals know only the whole as their essence. As sons they have no right, no prop- erty of their own vis-à-vis the head of the family. World spirit passed beyond this immediacy to another people, but took the principles with it in order to develop them further—as in the Indian, Persian, Chinese, Babylonian, and Median empires. Of these the Chinese is the most highly developed. Here hierarchy and the patriarchal relationship extend down to the lowest mem- ber of society. Vis-à-vis the monarch no right, no property is valid. The viceroys are in their turn patriarchs of their province, and the father possesses all rights over his children, whom he can even have executed although he cannot kill them himself. If a son commits a crime against his father, this is the most hei- nous offense and plunges the whole province into confusion. And these original principles are further developed to encom- pass civil life.

We find the same basic view among the Persians; here the king was the reflection of the sun, and his princes represented the planets around him. In India the division into classes was more marked, and the prince is frequently distinct from the high priest. In their cosmogony they portray the caste system as of divine origin. The basis of the transmigration of souls is that al- though all human beings have emanated from God, their pres- ent status is a misfortune, and it is only through purification in the world that they can return once more into the godhead. This main dogma of the Hindus makes the sphere of finitude merely a contemplation of the beyond, merely a relation of ac- cidentality, to be taken up again into the infinite in merely un- conscious fashion, and not to grasp the infinite oneself in one's

260   consciousness. All constitutional laws | and laws of right are [for Muslims] contained in the Koran; in the same way even precepts governing etiquette, washing, eating, etc., are presented as religious laws. Muhammadanism is a purification of the Oriental worldview insofar as it does not accept the decline of spirit in humanity; this intellectual difference is the only essential one. In this worldview spirit is also seen as a natural element, as the sun.

§ 167

(2) The Greek realm has as its basis Oriental substantiality, which is, however, born out of spirit into spiritual individuality and transfigured into beauty. The one substance has dispersed into many peoples, in whom the essential element is unconstrained and serene ethical life. The principle of personal right emerges, but still compounded with and subordinate to the substantial, ideal unity— a self-determination whose resolutions come from within itself, although not yet ascribed to self-consciousness but to an external, superior [power]. The constitution is on the one hand democratic, but on the other hand this democracy still contains slavery.

The Greek realm can be regarded as the antithesis wherein Oriental substantiality is differentiated. The wild life of nature is here moderated, and what dominates is the individual spirit. The Greek realm is the world of ethical life, where the good resides in the communal spirit of one's people. The Greek gods represent spirits of the people, but the natural element is still present in them: Jupiter is the thunderer, Poseidon is still god of the sea, etc., but the ancient Titans, the natural elements, are banished to the fringes of the world. Art and industry can be recognized here.

Here we have a fragmentation into many peoples, but since they know themselves to be infinite they do not yet sever themselves from the universal. In the severe Doric character individuals are still more attached to the whole, whereas the Ionian
261   character displays this free | individuality. Here is the happy consciousness of being in ethical identity with one's whole. How-

ever, the laws are still directed wholly to the preservation of the state. In regard to inheritances the Athenians took steps to prevent the undue increase and accumulation of wealth. The wealthiest simply assumed, as the wealthiest, the cost of popular and also religious festivals. It was for the richest man in a demos to assume this, and if he was unwilling to do so anyone could offer to exchange his property with him. They laid store by the universal, but individuals were not here serfs for the construction of monumental works, as they were in the Oriental realm.

The final decision lay with the oracle, as self-consciousness did not yet have this subjective certainty. In Socrates we see the emergence of morality—the principle of being-for-self with its attendant dangers; this was also why Plato did not incorporate it in his Republic and made all property communal. It was, however, a necessary element that Socrates grasped; the Athenian people recognized its destructive effect and in punishing Socrates, who stood at the apex, punished themselves. With Socrates decision-making first becomes an inward process.

The principle informing democracy here was, as Montesquieu says, virtue, this unconstrained ethical life;[93] it is also possible to see here aristocratic principles. Personal freedom was not yet recognized as something absolutely universal; the free citizens were the aristocrats, and they were not yet conscious of the necessity of the freedom of all.

§ 168

(3) The Roman realm completed the tearing apart of ethical unity into the extremes of the being-for-self of self-consciousness and abstract universality. While the aristocracy was the starting point for the constitution, the aristocratic principle of substantial intuition did not come into play on its own account but in opposition to the opposing democratic principle, which was also present. | And as a result of this clash the former principle developed into   262

---

93. [Ed.] Montesquieu, De l'esprit des lois, book 3, chap. 3 (pp. 26 ff.); cf. Montesquieu, Œuvres complètes, p. 252.

superstition and power devoid of right, while the latter eventually led to the dissolution of the whole. In the ensuing general misfortune and death of ethical life, the particular individualities of the peoples died out, the formal right of personality was developed, individuals were degraded to the level of private persons, all equal with one another, and the only bond left to hold them together was an abstract arbitrary will whose growth assumed monstrous shapes.

The first realm is natural substantiality, the second spiritual substantiality, while the Roman realm introduced as the third element [formal right] and contains the opposition that is death. For the founders of the state were robbers, whom no ties could hold together. We can see the many forms fragmentation took: Numa was the first to introduce religion, while the Etruscans first brought aristocracy, which was opposed to the principle of personal freedom; and the whole history [of Rome] comprises this struggle between plebeians and patricians. During the aristocratic domination the principle of natural ethical life emerged only in opposition, and religion declined into superstition. The democratic principle also won rights for itself in the state, but this development of democracy brought down the whole. The appearance of the democratic principle brought about the dissolution of the whole. The shape this folk spirit assumed—this universal death of ethical life (all folk spirits were collected together in a pantheon)—was that of world spirit.

To this period belong the cessation of all public interest and the full development of formal right; [it is] as with a corpse, which in itself is dead, yet contains the life of the worms. The individual elements made up the whole without a central point; there was only one individual, bereft of universality, who was at the apex. Arbitrary will devoid of reason came on the scene. We see appearing these monstrous shapes, where individuals go so far as to view themselves as deity. This is the most monstrous thing that has been seen in regard to self-consciousness, that it is driven into Oriental forms; | yet these shapes were necessary. The character of the Roman realm was this tearing apart, this death.

263

§ 169

(4) In this unhappiness self-consciousness is pressed back upon itself. Yet from the infinite anguish, for whose embodiment world spirit had held in readiness the Jewish people, self-consciousness lays hold on the infinite positivity of its inner core; and the task of developing the world configuration [*Weltgestalt*] of this inwardness is entrusted to the Nordic principle, to the *Germanic peoples*. The beginning of national unity is not a religious or natural principle but the heartfelt comradeship and fidelity of free people, who attach themselves to a courageous leader and are rewarded by him with conquered land in return for which they owe him freely given loyal service. Once this had been formalized in a legal system which suppressed the other free subjects of the realm, it became the *feudal relationship*.

The Roman world is the world of difference, of disunity, out of which self-consciousness was pressed back upon itself. World spirit had prepared this infinite anguish for itself in the Jewish people. Earlier Jewish history pertains to the East. The Jewish God is not this substance that is actual in Oriental fashion, but a Beyond over against the plurality of nature and of spirit. This alienation, this anguish, this unhappiness was already present at an early stage in this people in order that, when it would become the anguish of the world, it should be set forth completely in the people of Israel. The Hindu principle still holds out the hope of the individual's being able to return again to divinity, but this was not the case for the Jews.

From these birth pangs there developed for humanity the consciousness of inwardness. This consciousness reached its full development among the Germanic peoples. For them the unity of the state was not a natural unity in the Oriental manner nor a religious unity, but a unity born of inwardness, from | the self. 264 Initially it rested on the free choice of a chief, to whom of its own free will and choice the people attach themselves with confidence. Here we have the principle of inwardness, out of which the feudal relationship arose. The apportionment and distribution of conquered land became the subject of obligation, where it is no longer a question of particular arbitrary will. So here we have particular choice along with obligation that is meant to be valid in and for itself; and this is a contradiction.

§ 170

In its immediacy this inwardness is a secular realm founded on congeniality [*Gemütlichkeit*], but because this principle is still abstract and undeveloped, it is also a realm of crude arbitrariness, of barbarous customs and a legalistic feudal constitution. As such it is opposed to the intellectual realm of truth derived from infinite inwardness. In the struggle between these two the realm of truth eventually lowered itself to the earthly level of actuality and representation while the secular realm raised itself to the principle of rational knowledge. In this way their inner reconciliation came about, a reconciliation in which the state as constitutional monarchy is both image and actuality of developed reason, and self-consciousness consequently has in the state its actual knowledge and volition. In the same way it has in religion the freedom and peculiar identity of its rational intuition and feeling, while in [philosophical] science the actual state, the [realm of] nature, and the ideal world are recognized as mutually complementary manifestations of one and the same reason.

This is the culmination of the entire presentation. The inwardness of self-consciousness in its infinitude, the principle of truth, initially came on the scene divided into a spiritual and a secular realm. The latter, founded on congeniality, was a realm of crude arbitrariness, of legalistic right, the realm of barbarism, [one] of whose main principles was that of congeniality. Barbarism properly speaking was present here— | congeniality passing over into vengefulness, into the most vehement self-will and passion. Particularity, the peculiar disposition of individual inclination, of arbitrariness, was not yet sublated in it. Opposite it stood the realm of the universal; but it only *stood* opposite it, and it was no easier for it than for the secular realm to develop. Beauty, where particularity is not yet subjugated by the universal, still involves this crude, untamed element. The intellectual realm also developed to the point where it formed a wholly

265

earthly realm; the life of the clergy displayed unbridled license along with self-mortification. The most temporal and common relationships were set alongside the eternal. The secular realm developed on the other hand toward the principle of the rational will. And as neither was any longer in advance of the other, there occurred this reconciliation, and the state became a constitutional monarchy, an image of developed reason, the articulation that becomes a whole.

Self-consciousness had also achieved its own volition and was no longer merely looking at something it did not understand. Freedom of self-consciousness in religion, constitutional monarchy, and cognition of the truth are the principles of our time. Rationality is to be found in the middle class, which is the intellectual estate. The people are a material extreme; to say that the people will what is good means that they do not want to be oppressed, and that they want to give as little as possible and get as much enjoyment as possible. It is through the middle class that the wishes of the people are laid before the sovereign.

Concluded on 14 March 1818
P. Wannenmann

APPENDIXES

INTRODUCTION

BERLIN, WINTER SEMESTER 1818–1819
Supplementary Notes[1]

To § 1

Natural right is the antithesis of positive right. The will is essentially freedom. The source of right is in spirit; it cannot be grounded in any external authority. God is adduced immediately as the source of the Mosaic laws; divine authority is also adduced as the source of royal power. This assertion has been interpreted erroneously as meaning that the actions of kings can be arbitrary and need only be grounded in the kings themselves. This has led to the utmost despotism, with God regarded as something otherworldly, alien to spirit and remote. This is not God; whatever is divine is rational, and vice versa. In regard to actual freedom, the will must be what is most rational; those at the head of the

---

1. [*Ed.*] Wannenmann's transcript of the 1818–19 Berlin lectures contains only the Introduction. This is also evident from the date given at the end of the transcript, "Berlin, 10 November 1818." But even the Introduction is not transmitted in full, as can be seen from comparison with C. G. Homeyer's transcription of these lectures: *Naturrecht und Staatswissenschaft nach der Vorlesungsnachschrift von C. G. Homeyer 1818–19* (in G. W. F. Hegel, *Vorlesungen über Rechtsphilosophie 1818–1831*, ed. K.-H. Ilting, vol. 1 [Stuttgart–Bad Canstatt, 1973], pp. 217–352). Wannenmann did not transcribe the text of the main paragraphs dictated by Hegel for §§ 1–6 but only Hegel's expositions. Only in the part headed "To § 7" did Wannenmann include both the dictated passages and the expositions. He probably only intended to record additional materials so as to supplement his transcript of the Heidelberg lectures. The headings given by him—"To § 1," etc.—also relate

state must have a wholly rational will. But this is no alien, other-worldly authority. The divine will is the will of reason; this reason is the universal element of the essence of the state. Natural right has no other determination than the realization of reason.

To remark (a).[2] Positive right is right to the extent that it possesses authority and is known publicly. There can be no constitution founded on right that contains provisions directly contrary to rational right; the distinction can only be one of form. Confidence and faith are the universal ingredients of the organization of the state. The individual's own consciousness ensures respect for positive right; where individuals depart from it, coercion is used, and fear keeps them on the right track. The universal must be in conformity with reason; authority and form constitute the positive element of the laws. There is a blending of this kind in all states; there are in fact no states where irrational determinations have not been preserved in positive right. Positive right is valid, whether or not it has been justified at the bar of reason, whether or not it has been recognized by individual subjects; so it may also contain arbitrary provisions that run counter to freedom. The constitution 270 of the state develops progressively; and all the institutions | it encompasses should develop concurrently and in equal measure. If one institution develops on its own account while others remain behind, a discrepancy arises, since they all ought to be in harmony, coherent and interacting. In Germany this has been neglected, and recently introduced institutions often do not fit in with those of longer standing. It is the same in England, where all disorders and

---

to the corresponding sections in the Heidelberg lectures, and for this reason his numbering of the sections does not coincide with Homeyer's. The dictated passages and expositions collected together under the heading "To § 7" correspond to §§ 7–10 of the Heidelberg lectures and to §§ 8–16 of Homeyer's transcript. Wannenmann separates only by dashes those materials assigned by Homeyer to distinct sections. In the dictated passages there is word-for-word agreement between the transcripts of Wannenmann and Homeyer. All the more astonishing is the divergence in their record of the expositions. The differences are so great it could be thought they are made up of materials from different lectures. In these cases it is for the present impossible to decide how the two texts relate to what Hegel said. Homeyer's text gives a stylized impression, almost as if it were the result of further reflection.

2. [*Tr.*] This corresponds to § 2 of the 1818–19 lectures.

discontents derive from the struggle that the rational constitution has to wage against the many privileges that impede it and conflict with it. On the one hand privileges are right; on the other hand they are wrong, because they infringe and curtail the rights of others; so they make a constitution founded on reason positive and arbitrary. In England there are villages of no importance, or villages have even been inundated by the sea and destroyed, that have the franchise, while large cities like Manchester that came into existence later do not.

To remark (b). Reason projects an ideal state, an ideal constitution, from which the shape of actuality is very different.

To § 2³

In nature the living being⁴ is directly identical with its concept; the inner core of natural beings is their concept. The freedom of human beings, however, consists precisely in transforming their nature, in making their nature for themselves. The principle of right, too, is not rooted in subjective human nature. The ground of natural right is not to be found in instincts and inclinations. Instincts or drives are forms that do not correspond to the essence of spirit; although the inner core, the content is objective, as inclination or instinct it exists in subjective form and may be intermingled with determinations of a private nature. However, rational organization of the system of right must contain nothing but the universal. The content of instincts is in any case the same as that of all determinations of the state, but the latter | must be grasped in their   271
objectivity.

By "nature" we understand on the one hand the concept or essence of something, but on the other hand it has a different meaning. The state of nature for humanity is not yet the condition of freedom but the condition of wrong. According to Hobbes, one must emerge from the state of nature.⁵ Human beings must pass

3. [Tr.] Wannenmann's §§ 2–6 correspond to §§ 3–7 of the 1818–19 lectures as transcribed by Homeyer.

4. Ms. reads: the concept

5. [Ed.] Hobbes, De Cive 1.13. Cf. Thomae Hobbes Malmesburiensis Opera Philosophica Quae Latine Scripsit, ed. G. Molesworth (London, 1839–1845), 2:166.

over to consciousness; they must be in a state not of innocence but of responsibility, i.e., what they do must be their work. Natural freedom, arbitrary will, and desire must surely be given up in the [political] state. As freedom has to express or realize itself, the concept has to enter the sphere of externality and to that extent enters into nature. The soil of nature is [not] the principle of natural right—neither immediate nature nor spiritual nature. In the child the will is still natural, it is not yet free; it is free will in potentiality, not yet in act.

It is said that human beings are instinctively drawn toward what is right, toward sociability. It is true that the content of this instinct comes from reason, but it is subjective and does not yet exist in a universal, objective free manner. We must take these determinations, such as sociability, objectively and consider them in their rational form. The basis of institutions governed by right is of necessity wholly objective, for what is subjective, feeling, assumes a different form from one person to another. People who appeal to their feelings or conscience are withdrawing from the universal; they all have the same right to have their own feelings, their own conscience. But the concept of freedom, the idea, must become existent, and this externality involves the element of mutual exclusion. However, this externality is only the sign of the concept; it is [not] permeated by the idea. Necessity consists in there being two self-subsistent and opposing entities that are essentially one within the concept. However, the natural must be in accord with the concept. Manifestation on its own account is a [form of] nature. Necessity is only appearance. Free will means to recognize nothing else as self-subsistent over against oneself. |

To § 3

Determinists believe that remorse and guilt are illusions. I find within myself that I determine myself. To be sure, this is a fact, but philosophy cannot rest here: it demands that freedom should be necessary, and the proof of this must be contained in the preceding parts of [philosophical] science. Dialectic is the soul of universal being [*Allesseiende*] itself. This soul passes over into consciousness; it is in spirit that the contradiction of consciousness is resolved. Truth resides in the free spirit, in freedom. In the other I am related only to myself, and subjective and objective are identical. The outcome of philosophy is at the same time also the substance. The pure indeterminacy of the ego, pure thinking, pure intuition, occurs in everyone; we all know that we can abstract from all sensations, even from the ultimate [one], that of life. The ego is perfect emptiness. The concept of the will can only be grasped as the unity of its two moments. The one is the consciousness that I can simply abstract from everything; the purity here is pure thinking, the pure ego, and its pure reflection within itself. I can negate everything, and this is one moment in my self-consciousness. And the Hindus confine themselves to this intuition: they cut themselves off from everything and know themselves in simple unity with self. In this sense the ego is utterly infinite, like space. [But] this is only what is universal in the will, the emptiness of abstraction. Freedom must externalize itself. Universality is in an absolute sense the basis.

To § 4

The second moment is the opposing one, the moment of determinacy, of restriction, of differentiation. If we consider what the first moment is, we see that the second is contained within it. The particular is itself contained in universality; the indeterminate | is 273 the negation of the determinate, and itself includes the determinate. The analysis of universality yields the moment of determinacy. That which has something opposed to it is only one of the two sides. The human being's first elevation above the finite is only an abstract infinite; both moments are merely ideal. The ego must pass over from the finite to the infinite; God must decide to pass over to the finite.[6] What is differentiated constitutes, as differentiated, the one side. Only by positing both am I totality. To posit something determinate in the will is to make a resolution; I invest myself in this determinacy, I *am* in the content of my purpose. A plant opens itself up; what is already contained in it emerges into

---

6. *Ms. reads*: The ego must pass over from the infinite to the finite; God must decide to pass over to the infinite.

determinate existence. Indeterminacy is expansion, while the second moment is contraction.

To § 5

The will is the concrete. The first two moments are merely moments of the understanding [*verständige Momente*] and of themselves possess no truth; it is only with the will that the rational [*das Vernünftige*] arises. Everything restricted is the dialectical within itself. The truth of the two moments is that the one is contained in the other. Actuality is the undivided unity of inner and outer. It is only through the will that the human being is, properly speaking, actual. So the will is genuine individuality, the totality of the two individual moments. Universality is equality with oneself. Universality is the return from something other to myself. What is dead is the universal, what is identical with itself, while it is only through negativity that what is living becomes identical with itself. The will arises only with affirmation as the negation of negation, of restriction. This unity is the genuine element in the will. It is only by the activity of sublating my restriction | that I am universality. I will something, I posit a barrier within me; but I posit this purpose as mine, I relate myself to myself. The only reason for positing a purpose is to posit myself identical with myself. The two moments are mere possibilities, but necessary moments of the will. Regardless of the fact that I posit for myself an actual purpose, I nonetheless know myself to be free in so doing; it is only a possibility for me, and I remain the controlling power. It is only when I have acted that it is no longer a possibility. In its concept, however, the will is not yet the will that has being for self, the will in the idea.

To § 6

The will consists in remaining, within its restriction, at home with itself [*bei sich*]. This is the concept of the will, but philosophy cannot stop at this point; the concept must be present in its determinate existence. As idea, the idea has no determinate existence in nature. The species does not appear in nature, it remains the hidden inward element; the power of the species is evident in the fact that individuals die, but this does not cause it to emerge. The free will by contrast is that for which this concept *is*. I must equal I, as Fichte says.[7] Self-consciousness [comes into being] in becoming the free will that has being in and for itself. The will determines itself, invests itself in an object, but this object is itself; in its object it is at home with itself. This is the absolutely real will. Children only possess freedom in its concept. The will has being for itself[8] when it has the concept as object. But what is free must, in its further development, have no other intuition but that of its freedom; this is the further goal of [philosophical] science. Humanity's vocation can only be absolute freedom. In nature God is identical with himself; nature is God's mirror wherein he recognizes himself. | 275

To § 7[9]

[§ 8] Insofar as it *is*, the abstract will has a [mode of] being, but only an abstract [mode of] being. Every desire consists in our wanting or willing something, but the content is still a natural content. What is mine is mine only because I will it. I am in this content, but it is not yet posited by freedom itself.

[§ 9] The natural will is the will in the sphere of instincts and inclinations, and it can be affected by the contingency of imagination and fancy. None of these determinations and no instinct is absolute with me as it is with an animal; I can choose, I am the universal over against them. Arbitrary will in general means that I, as the indeterminate, determine myself to something, I resolve; and this resolve constitutes my universality and my particularity. Since I have determined myself, I nonetheless remain at the same time

---

7. [*Ed.*] An allusion to Johann Gottlieb Fichte's *Grundlage der gesammten Wissenschaftslehre: Handschrift für seine Zuhörer* (Leipzig, 1794), pp. 1–17 (§ 1). Cf. Fichte, *Gesamtausgabe* 2:255–264.

8. *Ms. reads:* in itself

9. [*Tr.*] As indicated by the editors (above, n. 1), what Wannenmann designates as "To § 7" corresponds to §§ 7–10 of the Heidelberg lectures and to §§ 8–16 of the 1818–19 Berlin lectures as transcribed by Homeyer. Starting with § 10 of the latter, Wannenmann provides both Hegel's dictated paragraphs and the expositions recorded by auditors; and starting with § 11, he marks the transitions between dictation and exposition by dashes. We indicate in brackets the correlation of Wannenmann's text to the 1818–19 sections, and whether the material is from dictation (dict.) or exposition (exp.). This information is provided by a table in the appendix of the German edition.

something universal; I can give it [what I have determined myself to be] up. In my desires and instincts I can pass over from one purpose to the other, but in terms of its quality the other is also a natural purpose, so I do not by this means escape from finitude. The aim of this natural will is happiness, which is, however, only the semblance of an idea, as envisaged in reflection. To will nothing is likewise an abstract moment; if we were to hold fast to this abstraction, we would disappear within ourselves. The natural will or arbitrary will is the stage of reflection.

[§ 10 dict.] But the will that has being in and for itself has for its content its own infinite form. In this way it is *true* because it determines itself to be in its determinate existence or as standing over against itself what its concept is—the pure concept [that] has the intuition of itself as its reality. It is *free* because it relates itself to nothing other than itself; and it is *universal* because in it all limitation and individual particularization is sublated, the latter residing solely in the antithesis between the concept and its object or content.

[§ 10 exp.] Truth is the coincidence of concept and content; the will that has being in and for itself is the truth. In a good state freedom has actuality in the idea. An | untrue object is a bad object; it does not correspond to its concept. The standpoint of the will that has being in and for itself is the standpoint of truth. The will that has being in and for itself is universal, and individual particularization and all subjectivity of the will are dissolved in it. I am only evil to the extent that I will to act as an individual according to a particular principle. In the will that has being in and for itself, freedom wills itself. Universality is what is self-identical in what is differentiated; this is genuine universality. Presumably the universal will is also the will of all individual beings; but even if it is not, it nonetheless remains universal will. It is the criminal's own will in and for itself that he should be punished.

[§ 11 dict.] The *subjective* element in the will means, in the first place, that the will is the absolute unity of self-consciousness with itself; secondly, it means the particularity of the will as arbitrariness in the contingent content of its purposes; thirdly, it means a one-sidedness of form, insofar as the willed content, what-

276

ever its other properties may be, pertains only to thinking self-consciousness. —

[§ 11 exp.] If I am coerced, I do not possess myself in this activity: it is not subjective will. If people accomplish something as slaves, from superstition or faith, it is not theirs; the self is not in it. In action the self-consciousness ought to be identical with itself. In the second case the evil will is the subjective will, and it is opposed to the universal will; subjectivity consists in the particularity of the content. In the third case the subjective forms the antithesis to objectivity, to reality. The concept of the particular will is still confined within immediacy. —

[§ 12 dict.] To the extent that it has itself as its determination and is thus identical with itself, the will is the utterly *objective* will; but this identity and universality is at the same time form as opposed to the mode of determinacy of the will, which arises only in self-consciousness. Objectivity is thus the immediacy of determinate existence [*Dasein*] as external existence [*äusserliche Existenz*]. —

[§ 12 exp.] The objective has two meanings. In one sense it is no less one-sided than its antithesis, the subjective. In the other sense it is the will in the harmony of its concept. —

[§ 13 dict.] The will that has being in and for itself is | the idea, 277 and is in itself the unity of subjective and objective, in contrast with which the merely subjective determination of will is a contradiction. As opposed to the latter form, the unity of subjective and objective is what *ought to be*, the merely subjective determination losing its one-sidedness and becoming objective. This unity is to this extent a *purpose* of the will, and the will is the drive to realize itself and the activity involved in doing so. The absolute drive, and the determination of the free will, is for the universal will to come about, for freedom to be actual. —

[§ 13 exp.] The will is only alive as movement. All organic life consists in the fact that the universal posits a difference within itself, but continually sublates this difference. What ought to be suffers from a deficiency; it only ought to be, it still is not. Drive occurs where there is a contradiction; the rational is this drive to sublate the one-sidedness. Pain means that the negative exists as a deficiency for a living being, in regard to which the negative is purely a barrier. What is inorganic feels no pain. All drives are based on pain. This contradiction is the root of drive. What is one-sided about purpose is its form. Activity consists in sublating the negative and positing the subjective. Freedom, the inmost nature of the universal will, has also to become actual. And how it does so is the business of our science. Intelligence presupposes a pre-existent world; the case is different with the will, which must already be present for the intelligence. What comes last is objective spirit. The realizing of the will is the bringing forth of the reconciliation of intelligence and will. The idea must realize itself, and what we have to consider is the development, the realization of the idea. The will must be to itself the object, I = I. At the same time the will has to attain the form of being distinct from itself. The absolute idea must differentiate itself. The idea is concrete, it contains the moment of difference within itself. In the independence of the differentiated moments the idea must preserve its unity. The drive of the idea is to actualize itself, and in this way it gives its moments independence; but in this externality it must remain identical with itself. —

[§ 14 dict.] That a determinate existence is the existence of the will that has being in and for itself is what we mean by *right. Duty* is a relationship of this kind insofar as | it counts as essential for me, and insofar as I have to recognize it, respect it, or bring it about. —

[§ 14 exp.] That a concept or a determination is valid must first be deduced in philosophy. The will that has being in and for itself must exist determinately [*der an und für sich seiende Wille muss dasein*]. In everyday life we say that something is rightly made if it corresponds to a standard or a concept. I possess a right as a person, for this is the existence [*Existenz*] of spirit, it is freedom. Duty is the correlate of right. Freedom cannot be infringed; by infringing it I do something stupid. Determinate existence [*Dasein*] is a being for other [*Sein für Anderes*], so it has a side on which it can be grasped or infringed by others. The drive of the will that has being in and for itself is to realize itself; hence duty also [arises]. Duty means that I respect that wherein the free will is the univer-

278

sal will—and therefore my will too. So someone who has no rights has no duties, for he is not actual as free will. —

[§ 15 dict.] Right is something sacrosanct because it is the determinate existence of the absolute concept, of self-conscious freedom. However, the formalism of right and duty arises out of the difference in the development of the concept of freedom. As opposed to merely formal [*formelles*] (i.e., abstract and therefore limited) right, spirit, having brought the further moments contained within freedom to consciousness and actuality, has (as the more concrete and universal) a higher right. —

[§ 15 exp.] Self-conscious freedom is the highest thing on earth; the contemplation of this idea in its simple shape is the object of religion and philosophy. Right is everything wherein freedom *exists*. I have a right to live, whereas animals have no right to live. All the law has to tell us is what right contains; we cannot derive right from it. What is sacred as such must be utterly concrete; what is merely formal [*das Formelle*] is not sacred. According to its concept, right is the identity of freedom. In right in the strict sense it is only the abstract freedom of my will that has determinate existence, whereas in the state what is free is a universal, concrete spirit. The right of individuals is accordingly something subordinate, something merely formal as opposed to the right of the state. The determinate existence of individuals is also contained within the state, but their right | is present here as sublated. The moral element is formal [*formal*] only in relation to the concrete spirit. What I recognize as right ought to be in conformity with my conscience, but ethical spirit is on a higher plane than merely formal conscience. Right and morality are only moments in relation to ethical life, which stands above them as substance. A people that has a more developed spirit of freedom stands above another people that is less civilized, and the ethical life of the latter is merely formal in relation to the higher spirit, which as spirit has the right to impose itself. World spirit has the highest right because it is what is most concrete. Because it is idea it must invest itself with determinate existence, and its existence destroys what counted as valid with individual peoples. The merely formal element in right also arises in regard to one and the same relationship.

279

The family constitutes a whole, while a person as an individual person is something subordinate, wherein the rights of personality are absorbed. It is only when the ethical whole made up by the family is broken up, when marriage is dissolved, that the merely formal right of individuals, what belongs to them, reemerges. We always pass from the more abstract right to a higher, more concrete spirit. The free will as mere predisposition, as mere concept, must become identical with itself. In its beginning this idea is only the concept; it still has no immediate existence, it is merely abstract right. —

[§ 16 dict.] The idea of the will is (initially in abstract fashion and so in immediate existence) the sphere of *abstract right*. The second sphere is the reflection of the will into itself, entailing its division on the one hand into itself (as subjective will) and an external world, on the other hand into the idea of the good as the ultimate end possessing being in and for itself: the sphere of *morality*. The third sphere is the unity and truth of the first two, in which the thought idea of the good is realized in subjective freedom and existence [*Existenz*] in such a way that freedom exists just as much as necessity and actuality: *ethical life* and *the state*. —

[§ 16 exp.] In his *Republic* Plato attributes to Socrates the statement that justice is more evident in the state than in the individual.[10] Only in the state has right attained actuality. It is no coincidence that human beings have entered the state, in which alone the concept of freedom attains its independent determinate existence. In the beginning we see the idea in | its abstraction. The idea is still in immediate being; it is I, this particular individual, who am still the determinate existence of the idea. Right is here what the individual person does as a free person. If I, as an individual, call something mine, I have invested my freedom in it. The concept of freedom and its determinate existence are here still immediately identical. The second stage is the separation of the concept from its reality; the universal separates from the individual. It is only here that the idea of good as the ultimate end arises. The idea ought only to be realized. In the sphere of morality my freedom

280

10. [*Ed.*] Plato, *Republic* 368e–369a.

of choice ought to give itself the good as its object. My life is primarily that wherein freedom has its existence [*Existenz*]. My particular determinate existence [*Dasein*] ought likewise to receive satisfaction. The second sphere contains only the demand for such compensation; here we have only an "ought." In the third sphere freedom is also present with my knowledge and volition. It includes the element of morality. Ethical life [*Sittlichkeit*] must necessarily be the ethical life of everyone; it exists in necessity as custom [*Sitte*]. Determinate ethical existence [*das sittliche Dasein*] is the state in general.

End of the Introduction

Berlin, 10 November 1818

HEGEL'S PHILOSOPHY OF RIGHT

BIBLIOGRAPHICAL MATERIALS

Steinhauer, Kurt, comp. *Hegel Bibliography: Background Material on the International Reception of Hegel within the Context of the History of Philosophy = Hegel Bibliographie: Materialen zur Geschichte der internationalen Hegel-Rezeption und zur Philosophie-Geschichte*. Munich, New York, London, Paris, 1980.

Gründer, Karlfried. "Bibliographie zur politischen Theorie Hegels." In Joachim Ritter, *Hegel und die französische Revolution* (Cologne and Opladen, 1957), pp. 81–112.

EDITIONS AND OTHER PRIMARY MATERIALS

Hegel, Georg Wilhelm Friedrich. *Naturrecht und Staatswissenschaft im Grundrisse: Grundlinien der Philosophie des Rechts*. Berlin, 1821 (already published in 1820).

    Hegel's Philosophy of Right. Translated by T. M. Knox. Oxford, 1942.

    Elements of the Philosophy of Right. Edited by Allen W. Wood. Translated by H. B. Nisbet. Cambridge, 1991.

————. *Vorlesungen über Rechtsphilosophie 1818–1831*. Edited by Karl-Heinz Ilting. 4 vols. Stuttgart–Bad Cannstatt, 1973–1974.

————. *Philosophie des Rechts: Die Vorlesung von 1819/20 in einer Nachschrift*. Edited by Dieter Henrich. Frankfurt am Main, 1983.

————. *System der Sittlichkeit* (1802–3). Edited by Georg Lasson. 2d ed. Leipzig, 1923.

System of Ethical Life and First Philosophy of Spirit. Translated by H. S. Harris and T. M. Knox. Albany, 1979.
———. "Ueber die wissenschaftlichen Behandlungsarten des Naturrechts." *Kritisches Journal der Philosophie,* 1802–3. See *Gesammelte Werke* 4:415–485.
Natural Law. Translated by T. M. Knox. Philadelphia, 1975.
———. *Schriften zur Politik und Rechtsphilosophie.* Edited by Georg Lasson. 2d ed. Leipzig, 1923.
Hegel's Political Writings. Translated by T. M. Knox with an Introductory Essay by Z. A. Pelczynski. Oxford, 1964. Contains "The German Constitution" (1799–1803); "Proceedings of the Estates Assembly in the Kingdom of Württemberg, 1815–1816"; "The English Reform Bill" (1831).

SECONDARY LITERATURE:
NINETEENTH CENTURY

Gans, Eduard. *Naturrecht und Universalrechtsgeschichte* (1832–33). Edited by Manfred Riedel. Stuttgart, 1981.
Göschel, Carl Friedrich. *Zerstreute Blätter aus den Hand- und Hülfsacten eines Juristen.* 3 parts. Erfurt, 1832–1837.
Haym, Rudolf. *Hegel und seine Zeit: Vorlesungen über Enstehung und Entwicklung, Wesen und Wert der Hegelschen Philosophie.* Berlin and Leipzig, 1857. 2d ed. Edited by Hans Rosenberg. Leipzig, 1927.
Kahle, Carl Moritz. *Darstellung und Kritik der Hegelschen Rechtsphilosophie.* Berlin, 1845.
Köstlin, Karl. *Hegel in philosophisher, politischer und nationaler Beziehung für das deutsche Volk.* Tübingen, 1870.
Marx, Karl. *Aus der Kritik der Hegelschen Rechtsphilosophie.* See Karl Marx and Friedrich Engels, *Werke,* vol. 1 (Berlin, 1961), pp. 201–333. (Written in summer 1843; first published in 1927.)
Critique of Hegel's "Philosophy of Right." Translated by Annette Jolin and Joseph O'Malley. Cambridge, 1970.
———. "Zur Kritik der Hegel'schen Rechts-Philosophie." *Deutsch-Französische Jahrbücher,* 1844. See Marx-Engels, *Werke* 1:378–391. "Toward the Critique of Hegel's Philosophy of Law: Introduction." In *Writings of the Young Marx on Philosophy and Society,* translated and edited by Loyd D. Easton and Kurt H. Guddat, pp. 249–264. Garden City, N.Y., 1967.
Rosenkranz, Karl. *Hegel als deutscher Nationalphilosoph.* Leipzig, 1870. See pp. 148–163.
Schubart, Karl Ernst. *Über die Unvereinbarkeit der Hegelschen Staats-*

lehre mit dem obersten Lebens- und Entwicklungs-Princip des preussischen Staates. Breslau, 1839.

SECONDARY LITERATURE: TWENTIETH CENTURY

Ahrweiler, Georg. *Hegels Gesellschaftslehre.* Darmstadt and Neuwied, 1976.

Angehrn, Emil. *Freiheit und System bei Hegel.* Berlin and New York, 1977.

Avineri, Shlomo. "The Discovery of Hegel's Early Lectures on the Philosophy of Right." *The Owl of Minerva* 15 (1985): 199–208.

————. *Hegels Theorie des modernen Staates.* Frankfurt am Main, 1976.

Hegel's Theory of the Modern State. Cambridge, 1972.

Baum, Manfred. "Gemeinwohl und allgemeiner Wille in Hegels Rechtsphilosophie." *Archiv für Geschichte der Philosophie* 60 (1978): 175–198.

Baum, Manfred, and Kurt Rainer Meist. "Recht—Politik—Geschichte." In *Hegel: Einführung in seine Philosophie,* ed. Otto Pöggeler, pp. 106–126. Freiburg and Munich, 1977.

Beyer, Wilhelm Raimund. *Hegel—Der Triumph des neuen Rechts.* Hamburg, 1981.

Bodei, Remo; Roberto Racinaro; and Massimo Barale. *Hegel e l'economia politica.* Milan, 1975.

Böning, Peter. *Die Lehre vom Unrechtsbewusstsein in der Rechtsphilosophie Hegels.* Frankfurt am Main, 1978.

Bourgeois, Bernard. *La pensée politique de Hegel.* Paris, 1969.

Cullen, Bernard. *Hegel's Social and Political Thought: An Introduction.* Dublin, 1979.

Flechtheim, Ossip K. *Hegels Strafrechtstheorie.* Brünn, 1936. 2d ed., Berlin, 1975.

Fleischmann, Eugène. *La philosophie politique de Hegel sous forme d'un commentaire des fondements de la philosophie du droit.* Paris, 1964.

Fulda, Hans-Friedrich. *Das Recht der Philosophie in Hegels Philosophie des Rechts.* Frankfurt am Main, 1968.

Heller, Hermann. *Hegel und der nationale Machtstaatsgedanke in Deutschland: Ein Beitrag zur politischen Geistesgeschichte.* Leipzig and Berlin, 1921. Reprint, Aalen, 1963.

Henrich, Dieter, and Rolf-Peter Horstmann, eds. *Hegels Philosophie des Rechts: Die Theorie der Rechtsformen und ihre Logik.* Stuttgart, 1982.

Hochevar, Rolf Konrad. *Hegel und der preussische Staat: Ein Kommentar zur Rechtsphilosophie von 1821.* Munich, 1973.

_____. *Stände und Repräsentation beim jungen Hegel: Ein Beitrag zu seiner Staats- und Gesellschaftslehre sowie zur Theorie der Repräsentation.* Munich, 1968.

Hyppolite, Jean. *Introduction à la philosophie de l'histoire de Hegel.* Paris, 1948.

Jaeschke, Walter. "Staat aus christlichem Prinzip und christlicher Staat: Zur Ambivalenz der Berufung auf das Christentum in der Rechtsphilosophie Hegels und der Restauration." *Der Staat* 18 (1979): 349–374.

Kainz, Howard P. *Hegel's Philosophy of Right, with Marx's Commentary.* The Hague, 1974.

Kaufmann, Walter, ed. *Hegel's Political Philosophy.* New York, 1970.

Kelly, George Armstrong. *Hegel's Retreat from Eleusis: Studies in Political Thought.* Princeton, 1978.

Larenz, Karl. *Hegels Zurechnungslehre und der Begriff der objektiven Zurechnung: Ein Beitrag zur Rechtsphilosophie des kritischen Idealismus und zur Lehre der "juristischen Kausalität."* Leipzig, 1927.

Löwith, Karl. *Von Hegel zu Nietzsche: Der revolutionäre Bruch im Denken des neunzehnten Jahrhunderts, Marx und Kierkegaard.* Zürich, 1941. 2d ed., Stuttgart, 1950.

_____. *From Hegel to Nietzsche: The Revolution in Nineteenth-Century Thought.* Translated by David E. Green. New York, 1964.

Lucas, Hans-Christian, and Udo Rameil. "Furcht vor der Zensur? Zur Entstehungs- und Druckgeschichte von Hegels Grundlinien der Philosophie des Rechts." *Hegel-Studien* 15 (1980): 63–93.

Marcic, René. *Hegel und das Rechtsdenken im deutschen Sprachraum.* Salzburg, 1970.

Marcuse, Herbert. *Reason and Revolution: Hegel and the Rise of Social Theory.* London, 1941. 2d ed., New York, 1954.

von Martin, Alfred. *Macht as Problem: Hegel und seine politische Wirkung.* Wiesbaden, 1976.

Meinecke, Friedrich. "Hegel und die Anfänge des deutschen Machtstaatsgedankens im 19. Jahrhundert." *Zeitschrift für Politik* 13 (1924): 197–213.

_____. *Die Idee der Staatsräson in der neueren Geschichte.* Munich, 1924. 3d ed., 1963.

Meist, Kurt Rainer. "Altenstein und Gans: Eine frühe politische Option für Hegels Rechtsphilosophie." *Hegel-Studien* 14 (1979): 39–72.

Müller, Friedrich. *Korporation und Assoziation: Eine Problemgeschichte der Vereinigungsfreiheit im deutschen Vormärz.* Berlin, 1965.

Nicolin, Friedhelm. "Hegel über konstitutionelle Monarchie: Ein Splitter aus der ersten Rechtsphilosophie-Vorlesung." *Hegel-Studien* 10 (1975): 79–86.

Ottmann, Henning. "Hegels Rechtsphilosophie und das Problem der Akkommodation: Zu Iltings Hegelkritik und seiner Edition der Hegelschen Vorlesungen über Rechtsphilosophie." *Zeitschrift für philosophische Forschung* 33 (1979): 227–243.

Pelczynski, Z. A., ed. *Hegel's Political Philosophy: Problems and Perspectives*. Cambridge, 1971.

_____. Introduction to *Hegel's Political Writings*. Translated by T. M. Knox. Oxford, 1964. Pp. 3–137.

Peperzak, Adrian. *Philosophy and Politics: A Commentary on the Preface to Hegel's Philosophy of Right*. Dordrecht, 1987.

Piontkowski, Andrej Andreevich. *Hegels Lehre über Staat und Recht und seine Strafrechtstheorie*. Translated from Russian. Berlin, 1960.

Planty-Bonjour, Guy, ed. *Hegel et la philosophie du droit*. Paris, 1979.

Popper, Karl R. *The Open Society and Its Enemies*. Vol. 2, *The High Tide of Prophecy: Hegel, Marx, and the Aftermath*. 3d ed. London, 1957.

Rameil, Udo. "Sittliches Sein und Subjektivität: Zur Genese des Begriffs der Sittlichkeit in Hegels Rechtsphilosophie." *Hegel-Studien* 16 (1981): 123–162.

Reyburn, Hugh Adam. *The Ethical Theory of Hegel: A Study of the Philosophy of Right*. New York, 1968.

Riedel, Manfred. *Bürgerliche Gesellschaft und Staat: Grundproblem und Struktur der Hegelschen Rechtsphilosophie*. Neuwied and Berlin, 1970.

_____. *Studien zu Hegels Rechtsphilosophie*. Frankfurt am Main, 1969. New ed., Stuttgart, 1982.

_____, ed. *Materialien zu Hegels Rechtsphilosophie*. 2 vols. Frankfurt am Main, 1975.

Ritter, Joachim. *Hegel and the French Revolution: Essays on the Philosophy of Right*. Translated by Richard Dien Winfield. Cambridge, 1982.

_____. *Metaphysik und Politik: Studien zu Aristoteles und Hegel*. Frankfurt am Main, 1969.

Rosenzweig, Franz. *Hegel und der Staat*. 2 vols. Munich and Berlin, 1920. Reprint, Aalen, 1962.

Rothe, Klaus. *Selbstsein und bürgerliche Gesellschaft: Hegels Theorie der konkreten Freiheit*. Bonn, 1976.

Scheit, Herbert. *Geist und Gemeinde: Zum Verhältnis von Religion und Politik bei Hegel*. Munich and Salzburg, 1973.

Schild, Wolfgang. "Die Aktualität des Hegelschen Strafbegriffs." In *Philosophische Elemente der Tradition des politischen Denkens*, edited by Erich Heintel, pp. 199–233. Vienna and Munich, 1979.

Siep, Ludwig. *Anerkennung als Prinzip der praktischen Philosophie: Untersuchungen zu Hegels Jenaer Philosophie des Geistes*. Freiburg and Munich, 1979.

Steinberger, Peter J. *Logic and Politics: Hegel's Philosophy of Right.* New Haven, 1988.

Taylor, Charles. *Hegel and Modern Society.* Cambridge, 1979.

von Trott zu Solz, Adam. *Hegels Staatsphilosophie und das internationale Recht.* Göttingen, 1932. Reprint, Göttingen, 1967.

Verene, Donald Phillip, ed. *Hegel's Social and Political Thought: The Philosophy of Objective Spirit.* Atlantic Highlands, N.J., 1980.

Weil, Eric. *Hegel et l'état.* Paris, 1950.

GLOSSARY

The glossary contains a selection of frequently used and/or technical terms, especially those posing problems in translation. It has served as a guide, not an inflexible rule. When more than one English word is given, the generally preferred terms are listed first, while terms following a semicolon may be suitable in certain contexts. "Cf." indicates related but distinguished German terms, which generally are translated by different English equivalents. Adjectives are listed without endings. This glossary is indexed only on German terms; the index serves partially as an English-German glossary.

Absicht	intention
allgemein	universal, general; common
Allgemeine	the universal; whole community (cf. "Gemeinsame")
Allgemeinheit	universality
Anerkanntsein	(fact or state of) being recognized, recognized status
anerkennen	to recognize, acknowledge (cf. "erkennen")
Anerkennen, Anerkennung	recognition
Anschauung	intuition

an sich	in itself, implicit (cf. "in sich")
Arbeit	labor, work
aufheben	to sublate, annul
Aufhebung	sublation, annulment
äusseres Staatsrecht	international law
äusserlich	external
äussern	to utter, externalize (cf. "entäussern," "veräussern")
Äusserung	utterance, externalization (cf. "Entäusserung," "Veräusserung")
Beamte	official, civil servant
Bedeutung	significance, meaning
Bedürfnis(se)	need, needs (cf. "Not")
Begierde	desire
begreifen	to conceive
Begriff	concept
Behörde	(administrative) authority
bei sich	with self, present to self, at home
Benutzung	use, employment
Beratung	counsel
Berechtigung	justification, entitlement, authority
Besitz	possession(s)
besonder	particular (cf. "partikulär")
Besonderheit	particularity
bestehen	to subsist
Bestehen	subsisting
bestimmen	to determine, define
bestimmt	determinate, definite
Bestimmtheit	determinateness, determinacy
Bestimmung	determination, definition; destination, vocation
Bewusstsein	consciousness
Beziehung	relation, connection, reference (cf. "Verhältnis")

bildlich	imaginative, figurative
Bildung	education, culture; formation, cultivation
Boden	soil, ground, territory
Bürger	citizen, burgher
bürgerlich	civil, civic
Bürgerschaft	commonalty
Burschenschaft	(student) fraternity
darstellen	to present, portray
Darstellung	presentation, portrayal, exposition (cf. "Vorstellung")
Dasein	(determinate) existence (cf. "Existenz," "Sein")
Denken	thinking, thought
Ehre	honor, dignity (cf. "Würde")
Eigentum	ownership, property (cf. "Vermögen")
einfach	simple
Einzelheit	individuality, singularity (cf. "Individualität")
einzeln	single, individual
Einzelne	(single) individual
Element	element (cf. "Moment")
Empfindung	sensation, feeling (cf. "Gefühl")
entäussern	to alienate, divest, externalize (cf. "äussern," "veräussern")
Entäusserung	alienation, divestment, externalization
Entfremdung	estrangement
Entzweiung	cleavage, rupture, division
erkennen	to recognize, to know (cf. "anerkennen," "kennen")
Erkennen, Erkenntnis	cognition, recognition, knowledge (cf. "Wissen")
erscheinen	to appear (cf. "scheinen")
Erscheinung	appearance, phenomenon
Erziehung	education, upbringing
Existenz	existence (followed by "Existenz" in brackets; cf. "Dasein")

existieren	to exist; to become really existent (cf. "sein")
Forderung	requirement, demand
formell	(merely) formal
Freiheit	freedom
für sich	for (by, of) itself, on its own account, explicit
Fürsichsein	being-for-self
Fürst	sovereign, prince
Gattung	species, genus
gebildet	educated, cultivated, refined
Gebot	precept, commandment
Gefühl	feeling (cf. "Empfindung")
Gegensatz	antithesis, opposition, contrast
Gegenstand	object
Gegenstände (pl.)	objects, affairs, matters
gegenständlich	objective
Geist	spirit
Gemeinde	(local) community
gemeinsam	communal
Gemeinsame	the communal, community
Gemeinschaft	community (cf. "Gesellschaft")
Gemüt	emotion, disposition; soul, heart (cf. "Gesinnung")
Gemütlichkeit	congeniality
Genossenschaft	association (cf. "Korporation")
gerecht	just
Gerechtigkeit	justice (cf. "Recht")
Gericht	court (of law), law court, court of judgment
Geschäft	business, occupation
Gesellschaft	society (cf. "Gemeinschaft")
Gesetz	law (cf. "Recht")
Gesetzbuch	legal code
gesetzgebend	legislative

Gesetzgebung	legislation
gesetzlich	legal
Gesinnung	disposition (cf. "Gemüt")
Gestalt	shape, figure, form
Gestaltung	configuration, formation
Gewalt	force, power, violence (cf. "Kraft," "Macht")
Gewalttätigkeit	violence
Gewerbe	trade, business, industry
Gewissen	conscience
Gewohnheit	habit, practice, custom (cf. "Sitte")
Gliederung	articulation
Grund, Gründe	ground, reasons
Grundsatz	principle, maxim
Grundvermögen	landed estate or property
gültig	valid
Gültigkeit	validity
Gut	capital, goods, resources, property, wealth (cf. "Kapital," "Vermögen")
Gute	the good
Handel	commerce
handeln	to act
Handlung	action, act, transaction (cf. "Tätigkeit")
Ich	(the) I, ego
Ideal, Idealität	the ideal, ideality
Idee	idea
ideell	(merely) ideal
Individualität	individuality (cf. "Einzelheit")
inneres Staatsrecht	constitutional law
in sich	within itself, into self, inward, internal (cf. "an sich")
Insichsein	being-within-self
intellektuell	intellectual

Kammer	house, chamber (of parliament)
Kapital	capital
kennen	to know (cf. "erkennen," "wissen")
Korporation	corporation (cf. "Genossenschaft")
Kraft	force, strength (cf. "Gewalt," "Macht")
Lebendigkeit	vitality, life principle
Lehre	doctrine, teaching
Macht	power (cf. "Gewalt," "Kraft")
Mensch(en)	human being(s), humans
Menschheit	humanity
Ministerium	council of ministers, cabinet, ministry
Mittel	means, commodity
Mittelstand	middle class
Moment	moment, element (cf. "Element")
moral	moral (cf. "sittlich")
Moralität	morality (cf. "Sittlichkeit")
Nation	nation (cf. "Volk")
Naturrecht	natural right, natural law
Naturzustand	state (or condition) of nature
Nichtigkeit	nullity, nothingness
Not	need, necessity, want (cf. "Bedürfnis") .
Notstaat	state based on need
Obrigkeit	authority(ies)
partikulär	private, particular (cf. "besonder")
Pöbel	rabble
Polizei	police, public authority
Real	the real
Realität	reality (cf. "Wirklichkeit")
Recht	right, law, justice
rechtlich	rightful, legal
Rechtspflege	administration of justice
Rechtswissenschaft	science of right, jurisprudence

reell	(merely) real
Regierung	government, executive
Regierungsgewalt	executive power
Reich	empire, realm
Reichtum	wealth (cf. "Vermögen")
Richter	judge, magistrate
Sache	matter, subject matter; thing, fact, cause
Schein, Scheinen	semblance, show; seeming
scheinen	to seem (cf. "erscheinen")
schlecht	bad, wicked
schlechthinnig	utter, simple
Schlechtigkeit	wickedness
Schmerz	anguish, sorrow, pain
Schuld	responsibility, obligation, guilt
seiend (part., adj.)	having being, subsisting
sein (verb)	to be; to exist, to occur (cf. "existieren")
Sein (noun)	being (cf. "Wesen")
selbständig	self-sufficient, self-subsistent, independent
Selbständigkeit	independence, self-sufficiency
setzen	to posit
Sitte	custom, ethics
sittlich	ethical (cf. "moral")
Sittlichkeit	ethical life, ethics (cf. "Moralität")
Sollen	obligation, "ought"
Staat	state
Staatsrat	council of state
Staatswissenschaft	political science
Stand	(social) class, estate; status, standing
Stände (pl.)	estates (social group, parliamentary institution)
Standesehre	esprit de corps
Ständeversammlung	estates assembly (parliament)
Subjekt	subject

Tapferkeit	valor, bravery, courage
Tat	deed, act
Tätigkeit	activity (cf. "Handlung," "Wirksamkeit")
Teilung	division
Trennung	separation, division
Trieb	drive, instinct
überhaupt	generally, on the whole; altogether, after all, in fact, etc.
Ungerechtigkeit	injustice
Unrecht	wrong, wrongdoing, violation of right, injustice
unrechtmässig	unlawful
Untertan	subject (of a state or sovereign)
unveräusserlich	inalienable
Urteil	judgment
Veranstaltung	arrangement
Verantwortung	accountability, responsibility
veräussern	to alienate (goods or property) (cf. "entäussern")
Veräusserung	alienation (of goods or property)
Verbrechen	crime
Verfassung	constitution, system of government
Vergehen	misdemeanor, offense (cf. "Verletzung")
Verhalten	conduct, attitude
Verhältnis	relationship, relation
Verhältnisse (pl.)	conditions, circumstances
Verletzung	infringement, violation, offense (cf. "Vergehen")
vermitteln	to mediate
Vermittlung	mediation, means
Vermögen	resource(s), means, estate, wealth; ability, capacity (cf. "Gut," "Reichtum")
Vernunft	reason
vernünftig	rational
Verstand	understanding

Vertrag	contract
Verwaltung	administration, government
Volk	people, nation (cf. "Nation")
Völkerrecht	international law
Volksgeist	folk spirit, national spirit
Volkstugenden	public virtues
vorhanden	present, at hand, extant
vorhanden sein	to be present, to be at hand, to exist (cf. "sein")
vorstellen	to represent; to imagine, to envisage
Vorstellung	representation
wahr	true
wahrhaft(ig)	true, genuine, authentic
Wahrheit	truth
Weltgeist	world spirit
Weltgericht	(court of) world judgment
Wert	value, worth
Wesen	essence, essential being, being (cf. "Sein")
Wille	will
Willkür	arbitrariness, caprice, arbitrary will, free will, free choice
willkürlich	arbitrary, capricious
wirklich	actual
Wirklichkeit	actuality (cf. "Realität")
Wirksamkeit	activity, agency, efficacy (cf. "Tätigkeit")
wissen	to know (cf. "kennen")
Wissen	knowledge, knowing (cf. "Erkennen")
Wissenschaft	(philosophical) science, scientific knowledge
Wohl	welfare
Wollen	volition, willing
Würde	dignity (cf. "Ehre")
Zeitgeist	spirit of the age
Zufälligkeit	contingency, chance

Zusammenhang	connection, nexus, continuum, complex
Zustand	condition, state, situation
Zwang	coercion (cf. "Gewalt")
Zweck	purpose, end; goal, aim

INDEX

Only names of historical persons are indexed. Concepts and subjects are indexed on a selective basis when a brief or more sustained discussion of them occurs. When an entry is found in both text and footnote on a page, only the page number is referenced. The German for key concepts is given in parentheses.

Designer:	U.C. Press Staff
Compositor:	Prestige Typography
Text:	10/13 Sabon
Display:	Sabon
Printer and Binder:	BookCrafters

ONE WEEK LOAN

Sandhya Drew is a barrister at Tooks Chambers in London
specialising in equality, employment and human rights. She sits on
the Learning and Development Group of the UK Human Trafficking
Centre.

The purpose of Legal Action Group is to promote equal access to
justice for all members of society who are socially, economically or
otherwise disadvantaged. To this end, it seeks to improve law and
practice, the administration of justice and legal services.

Human Trafficking – Human Rights
Law and Practice

Sandhya Drew

Legal Action Group
2009

This edition published in Great Britain 2009
by LAG Education and Service Trust Limited
242 Pentonville Road, London N1 9UN
www.lag.org.uk

British Library Cataloguing in Publication Data
a CIP catalogue record for this book is available from the British Library.

This book has been produced using Forest Stewardship Council
(FSC) certified paper. The wood used to produce FSC certified
products with a 'Mixed Sources' label comes from FSC certified
well-managed forests, controlled sources and/or recycled
material.

ISBN 978 1 903307 65 6

Typeset by The Charlesworth Group, West Yorkshire
Printed in Great Britain by The Charlesworth Group, West Yorkshire

For my parents, with my love

Foreword

by Mrs Justice Laura Cox

As publicity surrounding the arrival in 2009 of a new US President rightly celebrates the abolition of slavery and the success of the civil rights movement that paved the way for his election, it is a sobering thought that the International Labour Organization currently estimates that there are still approximately 12.3 million people in slavery worldwide. Of these, some 2.45 million are in forced labour as a result of trafficking, an increasing number of them in the UK. In 2007 Anti-Slavery International estimated that at least 5000 people are being trafficked into the UK at any given time, for the purposes of domestic slavery or for sexual and labour exploitation. US data suggests that some 700,000 men, women and children are trafficked trans-nationally each year, the majority of whom are women and young girls trafficked for the purposes of sexual exploitation.

Much is being done at the regional and international level to tackle this problem, which is a long-standing and global phenomenon. Following the UN Convention and its Protocols in 2000, the Council of Europe adopted a convention on action against trafficking in May 2005. The International Labour Organization (ILO) has expressly prohibited all forms of slavery and slavery-like practices, including trafficking, in fundamental rights conventions (especially Conventions 29 and 182) addressing forced labour and the worst forms of child labour. They have done so on the basis that whilst these practices are crimes, they are also forms of economic exploitation. ILO activities in these areas proceed on the basis that the rare, criminal prosecutions of those perpetrators who are found will not begin to guarantee minimum standards of protection to trafficked persons; and that a collaborative, educational and promotional campaign is required, to run alongside the normal supervisory mechanisms for compliance by member states with international norms.

The problems are not just limited to developing or transition countries. Victims of trafficking are being transferred and exploited both within and between countries, in all the world's regions. Those involved in the trafficking of human beings for profit are no respecters of borders or boundaries, or of those laws at national or international level which attempt to address it.

States have positive obligations under international human rights instruments to protect the victims of trafficking and to punish the perpetrators. Yet there is still a general lack of knowledge and understanding of the nature and scale of this evil trade, and of the laws which seek to eradicate it. Trafficking is often confused with people smuggling, so that trafficked individuals who enter this country legally, though they are doing so as a result of coercion or deception, can be and often are overlooked. It is an essentially covert business, so that reliable information is hard to come by. Identifying the victims of trafficking poses a number of challenges, as does finding, arresting and sentencing those who traffic them. Employment laws do not penetrate the informal sector, where trafficked people labour without protection and usually without visibility, ruthlessly marketed by powerful, criminal organisations.

Those who are called upon to advise or act for people who are the victims of trafficking need, firstly, to recognise what they are dealing with and, secondly, to know how best to use the law or to offer practical help and support in an area where the law is new and developing, and is still largely contained in international instruments. Victims of trafficking may be reluctant to identify themselves as such, or are too distressed by their experience to talk about it to anyone, especially if there are other cultural barriers in play. Above and beyond the criminal law, the issues raised will encompass a wide range of employment, immigration, contract or public law issues, often informed by human rights principles. The unwary practitioner may suddenly find herself faced with a trafficking issue which calls for a multi-agency approach, and which may be outside her comfort zone.

How fortunate, then, that this book has now arrived on the scene. Published by the Legal Action Group, this timely, informative and highly practical contribution to a difficult subject will be welcomed by practitioners, advice workers, trade unionists, employers and students alike. In my view it will also deserve a place on judicial shelves. Judges too need to recognise and be aware of these issues if they arise in their courts, and to identify both the relevant legal principles and the context in which they can arise.

In easily accessible chapters, which include the national and international legal framework, the trafficking of women and children, practical measures of support for victims, securing compensation, labour inspection and useful resource and contact details, the author has succeeded in her aims of informing all those who may be called upon to advise upon or think about these issues, and enabling a better understanding of when and how they can arise and, most importantly, of what they can do about it. This text will be an essential reference for anyone who has to advise in this area or who wants to know more about the measures currently being taken at national and international level to combat a truly global problem.

Laura Cox
Royal Courts of Justice

Contents

Table of Cases

Table of statutes

References in the right-hand column are to paragraph numbers.

Table of statutory instruments

References in the right-hand column are to paragraph numbers.

Table of international legislation

References in the right-hand column are to paragraph numbers.

UN Conventions

Treaties

Other European Legislation

Decisions

Directives

Framework Decisions

International Statutes

Recommendations of the Committee of Ministers

Table of guidance

References in the right-hand column are to paragraph numbers.

International Guidance and Reports

Abbreviations

CEOP	Child Exploitation and Online Protection Centre
CETS 197	Council of Europe Convention on Human Trafficking 197
CICA	Criminal Injuries Compensation Authority
CPS	Crown Prosecution Service
EASI	Employment Agency Standards Inspectorate
ECHR	European Convention on Fundamental Freedoms and Human Rights
ECPAT	Coalition of charities to under umbrella heading End Child Prostitution, Child Pornography and the Trafficking of Children for Sexual Purposes
EEA	European Economic Area
EU	European Union
GLA	Gangmasters Licensing Authority
GMB	General Manufacturing and Boilermakers Union
HMRC	Her Majesty's Revenue and Customs
HRA	Human Rights Act 1998
HSE	Health and Safety Executive
ICC	International Criminal Court
ICJ	International Court of Justice
ICTY	International Criminal Tribunal for the Former Yugoslavia
ILO	International Labour Organisation
IOM	International Organization of Migration
LSCB	Local Safeguarding Children's Boards
LSC	Legal Services Commission
NMW	National Minimum Wage
OSCE	Organisation for Security and Cooperation in Europe
RMT	Rail and Maritime Workers Union
SOCA	Serious Organised Crime Agency
TUE	Treaty on European Union
TUC	Trades Union Congress
UKBA	United Kingdom Border Agency, Home Office
UKHTC	United Kingdom Human Trafficking Centre
UN	United Nations
UNCRC	United Nations Convention on the Rights of the Child

UNHCHR	United Nations High Commissioner for Human Rights
UNHCR	United National High Commissioner for Refugees
UNICEF	United Nations Children's Fund
UNODC	United Nations Office on Drugs and Crime

Introduction

An important understanding of this definition [of trafficking] is an understanding of trafficking as a process comprising a number of interrelated actions rather than a single act at a given point in time. Once initial control is secured, victims are generally moved to a place where there is a market for their services, often where they lack language skills and other basic knowledge that would enable them to seek help. While these actions can all take place within one country's borders, they can also take place across borders with the recruitment taking place in one country and the act of receiving the victim and the exploitation taking part in another. Whether or not an international border is crossed, the intention to exploit the individual concerned underpins the entire process.

> *UNHCR Guidelines on International Protection: The application of article 1A(2) of the 1951 Convention and/or 1967 Protocol relating to the Status of Refugees to victims of trafficking and persons at risk of being trafficked (7 April 2006)*
>
> www.unhcr.org.au/UNHCRguidelinesonInternationalProtection. shtml

Trafficking in human beings

1.1   Trafficking in human beings contains two elements: transfer and exploitation. Human beings are transferred in order to be subjected to very serious, criminal forms of exploitation. They can be exploited more easily once they have been transferred into an unfamiliar environment.

1.2   The process of securing control may be done by recruitment by way of complete coercion through abduction or kidnapping, sale of a child, deception by promises of legitimate employment and/or entry, deception about working conditions or abuse of vulnerability, or a combination of these.[1] Threats, abuse of vulnerability or debt bondage may be used to secure labour at the destination.

1.3   Interest in trafficking outstrips information as to its scale. Lack of information is in part due to the hidden nature of the business. The estimates are as fluid as the economics of supply and demand which leads to the problem. At the global level, four organisations have databases on trafficking in human beings: the US State Department, the International Labour Organization (ILO), the International Organization for Migration and the United Nations Office on Drugs

---

1   *Human trafficking: an overview*, United Nations, 2008 pp11–12 (www.ungift. org/docs/ungift/pdf/knowledge/ebook.pdf).

and Crime. The ILO has estimated[2] that the minimum number of human beings in forced labour (including sexual exploitation) as a result of trafficking, at any one time, is 2.5 million globally and 270,000 in industrialised countries. The US State Department has estimated that 800,000 people are trafficked across national borders annually.[3] The annual profits, according to the ILO, are estimated at $31.7 million globally and $15.5 million in industrialised economies.[4] The traffickers may be part of an efficient criminal organisation, or the chain of transfer may be carried out by individuals who are only loosely, or not at all, previously connected. Crucial to an understanding of the issue is the economics of trafficking, which, as regards trafficking within and into Europe, occurs at the intersection of global labour supply and demand. Thus, any nation that primarily receives trafficked human beings has to consider a strategy to address demand – for example, demand for cheap flexible labour in particular sectors such as care, construction, hospitality and agriculture, or the demand for cheap flexible sexual services. In each case, trafficking occurs in unregulated or inadequately regulated areas.

1.4   Representing clients who have been trafficked is a challenge for the practitioner. The law is novel and rapidly evolving, with significant aspects governed by international law. As a result, there is more history and theory and sometimes discussion on law reform in this book than is usual in Legal Action Group publications. However, this is neither a book for black letter lawyers nor a policy book. This is a practitioner's book which considers what can be done to assist clients now, using existing legal tools.

1.5   The adviser may be advising clients before as well as after they have been identified as victims of trafficking. The adviser therefore needs to be aware of what facts may point to the client having been trafficked and to be aware of what to do when they are alerted to the possibility that this may be the case. Indeed, the client may not initially self-identify as a victim of trafficking. Potential clients may have worked within a hidden economy[5] without regulation or

---

2   ILO, *A global alliance against forced labour*, Geneva, International Labour Office, 2005.

3   United States of America, Department of State, *Trafficking in persons report 2007* (www.state.gov/g/tip/ris/tiprpt/2007/).

4   Patrick Belser, *Forced labour and human trafficking: estimating the profits*, working paper, Geneva, International Labour Office, 2005, p17.

5   See the *Grabiner report on the informal economy*, HM Treasury March 2000, which touched briefly on unauthorised work by migrants (chapter 4).

protection. They may be traumatised. There may often be significant cultural and communication barriers, including, but not limited to, language barriers. Reaching the clients requires significant proactive outreach skills and linguistic accessibility.

A human rights approach

1.6   Anti-slavery agreements are often termed the first human rights agreements, concerned as they were with crimes against humans rather than against states per se. While a human rights model has existed for almost a century in ILO Conventions and other UN Conventions, only recently, with the coming into force of the UN Convention against Transnational Organized Crime, has that human rights model come fully into focus. However, even with a human rights model, the phenomenon of modern human trafficking does not sit easily within traditional human rights law which is orientated towards breaches by the state.[6] In contrast, human trafficking is a market activity often carried out by powerful private criminal organisations.

1.7   Human rights law has dealt with this so far through the imposition of positive obligations on the state. The nearest the UK has to a constitutional guarantee against the trafficking of human beings is Article 4 of the European Convention on Human Rights, set out in schedule 1 to the Human Rights Act 1998, prohibiting slavery, servitude and forced and compulsory labour. While both Article 4 and the ILO Conventions on forced labour were initially concerned with labour exacted by force by the state, it is now recognised that Article 4 entails obligations to take positive steps:

> The Court considers that limiting compliance with Article 4 of the Convention only to direct action by the State authorities would be inconsistent with the international instruments specifically concerned with this issue and would amount to rendering it ineffective.
>
> *Siliadin v France*, European Court of Human Rights, Application no 73316/01, 89.

1.8   Positive obligations involve the protection of victims and the taking of effective steps to prevent trafficking as well as prohibition

---

6   See generally 'The "not-a-cat" syndrome: can the international human rights regime accommodate non-state actors?' Philip Alston in *Non state actors and human rights*, ed Alston, OUP, 2005.

and punishment.[7] The creation and enforcement of specific criminal prohibitions represents a progression from the previous approach, focusing solely upon immigration control, which failed to distinguish between trafficker and trafficked.

1.9   However, criminal and immigration law are essentially reactive to a crisis. Preventive steps required to discharge the state's positive obligations will include addressing the causes of trafficking to prevent trafficking generally. They will also include putting in place a system of early warnings as specifically preventive steps. In a destination state such as the United Kingdom, this includes the inspection of relevant agencies and workplaces and the provision of civil law rights and remedies.

1.10   Finally, in furtherance of its positive obligations, the state has given itself considerable powers as against suspected individuals. These can be justified as measures necessary for the protection of the rights of others, but should be continually measured against the outcomes for that stated aim.

Multi-disciplinary law

1.11   The practitioner reaches for the existing law to provide a remedy for a wrong. There are now specific prohibitions in criminal law and a growing body of case-law. The civil law adviser has more diffuse sources of rights to consider. Issues raised by human trafficking cases may give rise to public law, immigration, employment, contract and tort as well as issues under the Human Rights Act 1998. There is a need for advice on immigration status, work, support and/or care and decisions on long-term future. Claims for compensation should be considered. Since there is at present no specific civil law framework for victims of trafficking, relevant pre-existing law has to be identified and used.

Partnership approach

1.12   A human rights lawyer interested in practising in this field will do well to set aside any automatically adversarial habits. This is an area

---

7   Sandhya Drew, *Human trafficking, a modern form of slavery?* [2002] EHRLR 481; Tom Obokata, *Trafficking of human beings from a human rights perspective*, Martinus Nijhoff, 2006; Sandra Fredman, *Human rights transformed: positive rights and positive duties*, OUP, 2008.

where a partnership approach is more effective.[8] A multi-agency approach by the state is combined with a partnership between the state, trade unions, employers and business, non-governmental organisations (NGOs) and civil society. In turn, advisers will be more effective and informed about the context in which their clients have been existing where they have adequate community links. Conversely, many community groups seek legal advice and this is likely to increase from 1 April 2009 with the system of support measures following identification as a victim.[9]

1.13   It will also sometimes be necessary to get information about conditions in other countries, where to get information about the sending state or information on why the client should not be returned.

1.14   This book will also focus on the circumstances in which advisers may be encountering victims of trafficking in the course of other work and applies the definitions of trafficking to a practical context. It is important to be aware that even the adviser who does not set out to specialise in this field may be faced with a request for advice. It is therefore important either to be able to provide initial advice or to be aware of where to refer the request.

Professional conduct, client care and practical issues

1.15   The usual professional conduct rules continue to apply to legal advisers.

Professional duty of confidentiality

1.16   A lawyer has a duty of confidentiality to his or her client or former client except where disclosure is required or permitted by law in advance or agreed by the client: Rule 4.01 of the Solicitors' Code of Conduct 2007 (Solicitors Regulation Authority);[10] para 702 of the Bar Code of Conduct, 8th edn.[11] There are very limited exceptions to that rule. The first is that notification duties arise where a lawyer who

---

8   The partnership approach was pioneered by the ILO.
9   See chapter 8.
10   Available at www.sra.org.uk/solicitors/code-of-conduct/214.article. The Code is dated 1 July 2007.
11   See www.barstandardsboard.org.uk/standardsandguidance/.

handles money has reason to believe that it may be connected to money laundering. The second exception is that it is necessary to breach confidentiality for the purposes of child protection. In practice, and subject to the exceptions, this means that where a client does not agree to disclosure, the adviser's role is limited to informing and advising the client. This does not prevent referral of the client for counselling.

Effective communication with the client

1.17   Many clients speak English and are happy to communicate in English. However, it is important that they be offered the choice of giving instructions in another language. Any interpreter used should be properly qualified, both linguistically and in dealing with traumatised clients.[12] If the client has been referred from a support network such as the POPPY Project, then it is likely that he or she would already have received counselling. If not, the adviser should consider directing the client to specialist counselling in tandem with legal advice given. Where the adviser is acting for a group of clients, it will be important to make contact with all claimants, but articularly all the test claimants.

1.18   Where the adviser suspects that trafficking may have taken place, it is important to explain to the client that the information is being asked for in order to provide full advice and support and to stress the duty of confidentiality. In assessing the facts, the diagnostic criteria may be considered, but should be no substitute for analysis of the full facts.

Registration with the Office of the Immigration Services Commission (OISC)?

1.19   An adviser who is not a lawyer or a legal executive needs to consider whether they are giving immigration advice or services and thus need to apply for registration or exemption with OISC (details at www.oisc.gov.uk).

Funding

1.20   CETS Convention 197 requires access to information on legal rights. Such advice should be independent. However, there has been no

---

12   See Resources.

visible attempt by the UK government to put such a system in place. Where the victim is currently a defendant, advice to them can be provided as part of the representation in the criminal proceedings.[13] This is not the case for advice on civil justice. In some cases, the support agencies working under contract will have the informal capacity to refer cases for legal advice. However, this is unlikely to satisfy the requirement for a properly structured system. As a matter of course, legal aid is not available for proceedings before the Criminal Injuries Compensation Authority (CICA), for personal injury claims, or for proceedings before the Immigration Tribunal or the Employment Tribunal. An adviser who is a registered provider of legal services may be able to make an application on the particular merits for funding to the Legal Services Commission.[14] Exceptionally, the Equality and Human Rights Commission may be able to fund a case.[15] A conditional fee agreement may be considered in multi-party actions.[16] Unions may also fund litigation.

Scope of this book

1.21   It is not within the scope of this book to consider the important long-term preventive actions which may be taken, such as the development of corporate social responsibility, the ILO Decent Work programme, or international bilateral work, whether between law enforcement or unions. One of the most effective steps to eliminate labour trafficking is corporations' proper monitoring of their supply chains to avoid exploitation, whether trafficked or in situ.

1.22   This book aims to set out the national legal framework on trafficking, broadly divided into the three areas of prohibition, protection and prevention. Chapters 2 and 3 set out the background at international and at regional level. Chapter 4 sets out basic principles of national law and practice. Chapters 5, 6 and 7 describe the relevant specific criminal offences. Chapter 8 sets out the law on immediate support which must be provided for a victim of trafficking. Chapter 9 sets out practical steps to support victims who find themselves in the criminal courts, whether as a victim or as a

---

13   See chapter 8.
14   See www.legalservices.gov.uk.
15   See legal strategy 2008/9 at www.equalityandhumanrights.com.
16   Such an agreement needs to comply with relevant professional guidance.

defendant. Chapter 10 describes how to recover compensation for trafficked people. Chapter 11 sets out how to secure long-term solutions on rehabilitation and resettlement. Chapter 12 considers the labour inspection regime in the UK and how victims may be protected under it. Chapter 13 considers issues arising in the representation of migrant workers. Chapter 14 considers the legal framework for asset recovery. Finally, there is an appendix with contacts details for available resources.

CHAPTER 2

Human trafficking in international law

Key points

- The prohibition on slavery forms part of jus cogens, peremptory norms of international law from which no derogation is permissible. The prohibition on slavery is regarded as the first declared human right.
- Since the almost universal elimination of slavery in the strict sense, the United Nations have identified and set norms on servitude and modern forms of slavery.
- International Labour Organization (ILO) conventions have had an important role in the development of prohibitions on forced labour.
- Unlike early 20th century forms of forced labour, effective action against human trafficking involves positive obligations protecting individuals against non-state actors.
- The ILO conventions and the United Nations Convention on Migrant Workers have been under-ratified by states in industrialised countries.
- The 2000 United Nations Convention against Transnational Organized Crime and its Protocols established human trafficking as a form of organised crime.

International law

2.1 Even purely national law practitioners need to be aware of the international legal framework on human trafficking. The definition of human trafficking derives from international law and international law developments continue to influence development at national level. In addition, human trafficking operates trans-nationally and therefore requires a response at global level. National law practitioners need to be aware of how to use bilateral agreements and to deal with transnational issues when they arise. International law comprises various sources, which in order of priority are: jus cogens or peremptory norms of international law; international conventions; international custom and practice; and general principles of law and judicial decisions.[1]

---

1 *Brownlie on International Law*, 2003.

Jus cogens

2.2 The prohibition on slavery forms part of jus cogens, together with the prohibition against race discrimination, including segregation;[2] the prohibition against genocide; and latterly against torture. Jus cogens are rules within customary international law which have a special status above treaty-based law or even other customary law. They are essential and intrangressible principles. No derogation can be permitted from them, and they can only be modified by a subsequent norm of general international law having the same character. Norms may evolve into forming part of jus cogens by being 'so widely and generally accepted, that it can hardly be supposed that any civilised State would repudiate it'.[3] These norms cannot be set aside by treaty or acquiescence, but only by the formation of a subsequent customary rule which has the contrary effect. These norms are seen as fundamental to the maintenance of an international legal order. They are thus obligations owed by each state towards the international community as a whole. A treaty is void insofar as it conflicts with a peremptory norm.[4]

International conventions

2.3 A treaty is an international agreement concluded between states[5] in written form and governed by international law, whether embodied in a single instrument or in two or more related instruments and whatever its particular designation.[6] It may be bilateral (concluded between two states) or multilateral (concluded between more than two).[7] Multilateral treaties may be regional or global. They may establish new rules to guide future conduct or they may be declaratory of existing law. The exact name for a treaty may vary and does not determine its position in any hierarchy.[8] However, the

---

2   *South West Africa Cases (Ethiopia v South Africa) (Liberia v South Africa) (Second Phase)* ICJ Reports 1996 p4 at 293.

3   *West Rand Central Gold Mining Company Limited v The King* [1905] 2 KB 391 (DC), 406–407 per Lord Alverstone CJ.

4   Article 53 of the Vienna Convention on the Law of Treaties ('The Vienna Convention').

5   Or some international organisations such as the United Nations or the European Community.

6   Article 2(1)(a) of the Vienna Convention.

7   Anthony Aust, *Modern treaty law and practice*, CUP, 2007.

8   Thus, the International *Covenant* on Civil and Political Rights has the same status as the Convention on the Rights of the Child.

United Nations Charter prevails over all other treaties. Human rights treaties differ in character from other treaties. They do not represent an exchange of interests and benefits between contracting states in the conventional sense, and in this respect may also be distinguished from the generality of multilateral treaties, many of which are concerned with the economic, security and other interests of the states. Human rights and humanitarian treaties represent, rather, a commitment of the particular states to certain norms and values recognised[9] by the international community. Or:

> In such a Convention the contracting states do not have any interests of their own; they merely have, one and all, a common interest, namely the accomplishment of those high purposes which are the *raison d'être* of the convention. Consequently, in a Convention of this type one cannot speak of individual advantages or disadvantages to states, or of the maintenance of a perfect contractual balance between rights and duties. The high ideals which inspired the Convention provide, by virtue of the common will of the parties, the foundation and measure of all its provisions.[10]

Initial agreements against slavery were bilateral and multilateral agreements between states, involving agreements between states on action to be taken. In the 1920s, this evolved and a more modern human rights approach emerged, granting rights to victims as well as imposing duties on states.[11]

Origins of the right to freedom from slavery

2.4   Even when slavery was recognised as a property right, human rights arguments were successfully raised against it. In the case of *Somerset v Stewart* 12 Geo 3 1772 KB. James Somerset had been sold on the African coast and worked as a slave on Charles Stewart's Virginia plantation. He escaped while in England, but was caught and detained in irons on a ship destined for slave markets in Jamaica. A writ of habeas corpus was lodged on his behalf. His lawyers identified the question as 'not whether slavery is lawful in the colonies ... but whether in England?'. They argued the inherent unlikelihood that a

---

9   *Case concerning application of the convention on the prevention and punishment of the crime of genocide (Bosnia and Herzegovina v Yugoslavia)* ICJ Reports 1996 p595, 115 ILR 1 at 57 per Judge Weeramantry.

10   *Reservations to the convention on the prevention and punishment of the crime of genocide* ICJ Reports 1951 p15, 18 ILR 364 at 370.

11   Sandhya Drew, *Human trafficking: a modern form of slavery?* [2002] EHRLR Issue 4, p481.

man would bind himself by contract to serve for life. They argued that any contract upon which the American relied was void as a matter of policy in England. They distinguished between 'the law of England' and 'the law of the Plantations'. They argued that any contract required power to give and to receive, and consideration. They argued that a man could not forfeit his and his descendants' rights: 'he cannot consent to part with them, without ceasing to be a man, for they immediately flow from, and are essential to, his condition as such. They cannot be taken from him for they are not his, as a citizen or a member of society merely, and are not to be resigned to a power inferior to that which gave them.' Freedom was asserted as a natural right and therefore unalienable and unrestrainable. They argued that Mr Stewart had to show his right by deed or contract. For the slaver, it was argued that there was no law against slavery, that it was common over the world. Lord Mansfield, in freeing the slave, held that the relatively narrow issue for him to decide was whether Charles Stewart had shown sufficient cause to answer the charge of habeas corpus. The court held he had not. The decision was thus relatively narrow:

> The state of slavery is of such a nature, that it is incapable of being introduced on any reasons, moral or political; but only positive law, which preserves its force long after the reasons, occasion and time itself from whence it was created, is erased from memory: It's so odious, that nothing can be suffered to support it, but positive law. Whatever inconveniences, therefore, may follow from such a decision, I cannot say this case is allowed or approved by the law of England; and therefore the black [sic] must be discharged.[12]

---

12 In *Bury the chains* (Macmillan, 2005), Adam Hochschild sets out the judge's view of the case (p49): 'The prospect of presiding over a case in which the right to property clashed with the right to liberty left him profoundly uneasy, and he did everything possible to avoid having the question be decided by trial. He urged Somerset, Stewart and their attorneys to negotiate.' This apparent speculation is in fact supported by judicial comments in *The Slave Grace* [1827] I 94, High Court of Admiralty. Hochschild astutely comments on the *Somerset* case (p50): 'this was a case in which what people *thought* was decided proved far more important than the actual wording.' The *Slave Grace* case, citing authority from 1749, attempted to limit the effect of *Somerset* to slaves in England, holding that the principle did not apply retrospectively to free a slave who had already left England and reached Antigua. In the later case, the court held that it was possible to be a slave in one country and to be free in another, stating (pp128–129): 'It has been said that the law of England discourages slavery, and so it does within the limits of these islands; but the law uses a very different language and exerts a very different force when it looks to her colonies; for to this trade in those colonies it gives an almost unbounded protection.'

In 1807, the British Parliament abolished the transatlantic slave trade (and its assistance by British ships). However, Britain agreed a series of bilateral treaties with other states permitting Britain to seize and confiscate ships carrying slaves (and later, ships preparing to carry slaves). Courts or Commissions made up of judges from different countries sat to hear the claims for seizure.[13] Slavery itself in the colonies was not abolished until 1834 through the 1833 Abolition of Slavery Act.

2.5   The 1815 General Treaty of the Congress of Vienna, forming the framework for European international politics until 1914, contained a declaration on the abolition of the slave trade. It was followed by the General Act of Berlin in 1885. Since then, slavery and its modern forms have been the concern of international law.[14]

Modern forms of slavery

2.6   In 1926, the League of Nations adopted the Slavery Convention.[15] This referred to the 1885 General Act of Berlin and to the Brussels conference of 1889–1890 and the ensuing Brussels Act of 1890. The convention defined slavery as 'the status or condition of a person over whom any or all of the powers attaching to the right of ownership are exercised'. The slave trade was defined as all acts 'involved in the capture, acquisition or disposal of a person with intent to reduce him to slavery; all acts involved in the acquisition of a slave with a view to selling or exchanging him; all acts of disposal by sale or exchange of a slave acquired with a view to being sold or exchanged, and, in general, any act of trade or transport in slaves'. Parties undertook to suppress the slave trade and to bring about the abolition of slavery in all its forms.

Relevant multilateral treaties

2.7   Once slavery in its narrow sense had been abolished almost worldwide, attention shifted to practices similar to slavery. On 7 September 1956, the Supplementary Convention on the Abolition

---

13   Jenny S Martinez, 'Antislavery courts and the dawn of international human rights law', Yale Law Journal 117:550 [2008] notes at p632 that the anti-slavery movement, compared to Nuremberg, 'places a much greater emphasis on non state actors – both the slave traders who were the human rights violators and the civil society leaders of the abolitionist movements in various countries'.

14   Consolidated Trealy Series Vol 63 No 473.

15   Entry into force: 9 March 1927.

of Slavery, the Slave Trade, and Institutions and Practices Similar to Slavery was agreed.[16] This convention widened the concerns to practices similar to slavery. It required states to act to bring about the abandonment of various practices, whether or not they fell within the definition of slavery contained in the Slavery Convention.[17] Broadly, the practices covered debt bondage, serfdom, slavery-like practices related to marriage and exploitation of a child.

Slavery-like practices

Debt bondage: The status or condition arising from a pledge by a debtor of his or her personal services or of those of a person under his or her control as security for a debt, if the value of those services as reasonably assessed is not applied towards the liquidation of the debt or the length of those services are not respectively limited and defined.

Serfdom: The condition or status of a tenant who is by law, custom or agreement bound to live and labour on land belonging to another person and to render some determinate service to such other person, whether for reward or not, and is not free to change his or her status.

Commodification of marriage: Any institution or practice whereby (i) a woman, without the right to refuse, is promised or given in marriage on payment of a consideration in money or in kind to her parents, guardian, family or any other person or group; (ii) the husband of a woman, his family or his clan, has the right to transfer her to another person for value received or otherwise; or (iii) a woman on the death of her husband is liable to be inherited by another person.

Exploitation of a child: Any institution or practice whereby a child or young person under the age of 18 years is delivered by either or both of the child's natural parents or by the child's guardian to another person, whether for reward or not, with a view to the exploitation of the child or young person or of his or her labour.

2.8   The convention requires states to prescribe minimum ages for marriage.[18] Section II of the convention deals with the slave trade:

---

16   Agreed by Economic and Social Council resolution on 7 September 1956. Entry into force: 30 April 1957.

17   Article 1.

18   Article 2.

it requires criminalisation of the trade and by article 4, specifically provides that 'Any slave who takes refuge on board the vessel of a State Party to this Convention shall ipso facto be free'. Section III requires the criminalisation of further acts, such as the branding of a slave, and of the act of enslavement itself. Section IV sets out definitions. In particular, the definition of 'slavery' from the 1926 convention is repeated. 'Slave trade' is also defined.[19] The convention also requires co-operation between states. Finally, the convention provides that no reservations shall be made to it.[20] It also provides that any disputes which cannot be settled by negotiation shall be referred to the International Court of Justice.[21]

Conventions on the trafficking of women and children

2.9   Meanwhile, a number of conventions were enacted in respect of traffic for the purposes of prostitution: in particular the 1910 Convention[22] for the suppression of the White Slave Traffic, the 1921 International Convention for the Suppression of the Traffic in Women and Children,[23] the 1933 Convention for the Suppression of the Traffic in Women of Full Age and the 1949 Convention for the Suppression of the Traffic in Persons and of the Exploitation of the Prostitution of others.[24]

Conventions of the International Labour Organization

2.10   The ILO was founded in 1919, immediately after the First World War. The ILO adopted a number of conventions[25] on forced labour which are very relevant to issues of human trafficking and have provided key definitions. The ILO has been particularly effective in its actions against human trafficking. It became the first specialised agency of the United Nations in 1946, immediately after the Second World War.

---

19   Article 7(c).
20   Article 9.
21   Article 10.
22   Adopted 4 May 1910.
23   Entry into force: 28 June 1922, ratified by the UK on 28 June 1922 as amended by the Protocol approved by the General Assembly of the United Nations on 20 October 1947.
24   Approved by General Assembly Resolution of 2 December 1949, entry into force: 25 July 1951.
25   Accessible at www.ilo.org/ilolex.

ILO conventions on forced and compulsory labour

2.11   Most relevant of all are the forced labour conventions. Although initially concerned with forced labour programmes enforced by the state, the definitions of forced labour remain very important to actions by non-state actors. Convention No 29 concerning forced labour[26] requires each ratifying member to undertake to suppress the use of forced or compulsory labour in all its forms within the shortest possible period. Article 2 of Convention No 29 defines forced or compulsory labour as 'all work or service which is exacted from any person under the menace of any penalty and for which the said person has not offered himself voluntarily'. However, exceptions were provided for:

(a) compulsory military service;

(b) normal civic obligations;

(c) any work or service exacted as a consequence of a conviction, provided the work is done for a public authority;

(d) any work or service exacted in cases of emergency, eg war or threatened calamity;

(e) minor communal services being performed by members of the community in the direct interest of the said community provided the members of the community have the right to be consulted about the need for such services.[27]

Restrictions were placed on who could be called upon in respect of exempted work. There was no provision for compensation where the principle was breached.

2.12   On 25 June 1957, the ILO also adopted Convention No 105 concerning the Abolition of Forced Labour.[28] By article 1, states members of the ILO undertook to suppress and not to make use of any form of forced or compulsory labour:

(a) as a means of political indoctrination;

(b) as a means of mobilising labour for economic development;

(c) as labour discipline;

---

26   Adopted on 28 June 1930 by the General Conference of the International Labour Organization, entry into force: 1 May 1932. Ratified by the UK on 3 June 1931.

27   This definition was adopted in article 4 of the European Convention on Human Rights.

28   Convention 105 was ratified by the UK on 30 December 1957 and entered into force on 17 January 1959.

(d) as a punishment for striking;

(e) as a means of racial, social, national or religious discrimination.[29]

At its 96th Session in 2007, the ILO Committee of Experts on the Application of Conventions and Recommendations issued a General Survey on ILO Conventions 29 and 105.[30]

ILO conventions on child labour

2.13　The ILO has also adopted conventions relating to child labour. On 26 June 1973, the ILO adopted Convention No 138: the Minimum Age Convention.[31] Convention 138 replaced various sector-specific conventions and was adopted with a view to achieving the total abolition of child labour. Article 1 required member states to undertake to pursue a national policy designed to ensure the effective abolition of child labour and to raise progressively the minimum age for admission to employment or work to a level consistent with the fullest physical and mental development of young persons. Article 2 required each member to specify a minimum age for admission to employment or work within its territory. Convention 138 came into force on 19 June 1976.

2.14　In 1998 the ILO issued a Declaration on Fundamental Principles and Rights at Work.[32] This identified four core labour standards by which all members of the ILO, regardless of whether they had ratified the relevant individual conventions, were bound. These were:

(a) freedom of association (Conventions 87 and 98);

(b) the elimination of forced and compulsory labour (Conventions 29 and 105);

(c) the elimination of child labour (Conventions 138 and 182); and

(d) the elimination of discrimination in employment (Conventions 100 and 111).[33]

29　Oddly, gender was not mentioned.

30　ILC 97 Report III (Part 1B). See http://www.ilo.org/global/What_we_do/InternationalLabourStandards/ApplyingandpromotingInternationalLabourStandards/CommitteeofExperts/lang--en/index.htm.

31　In force 19 June 1976. Not ratified by the UK until 7 June 2000.

32　Accessible at www.ilo.org/public/english/standards/decl/declaration/index.htm.

33　As seen above, these principles are in any event contained in the Universal Declaration of Human Rights (articles 5, 7, 20 and 23).

The result has been a targeted approach, focusing on immediate rather than incremental elimination of the worst breaches of labour rights. The ILO has an Infocus Programme promoting the declaration. The ILO has also instituted a special action programme to combat forced labour across the globe.[34]

2.15   Consistent with this targeted approach, in 1999 the ILO adopted Convention (No 182) on the Elimination of the Worst Forms of Child Labour.[35] This was a widely ratified convention which came into force on 19 November 2000. In recognition of the continuing use of child labour in developing countries, Convention 182 identified particular forms of child labour which needed to be eliminated as a matter of priority. These are set out at article 3:

(a) all forms of slavery or practices similar to slavery, such as the sale and trafficking of children, debt bondage and serfdom and forced or compulsory labour, including forced or compulsory recruitment of children for use in armed conflict;

(b) the use, procuring or offering of a child for illicit activities, in particular for the production of pornography or for pornographic performances;

(c) the use, procuring or offering of a child for illicit activities, in particular for the production and trafficking of drugs as defined in the relevant international treaties;

(d) work which, by its nature or the circumstances in which it is carried out, is likely to harm the health, safety or morals of children (this last to be determined at national level).

Article 6 requires each member to design and implement programmes of action to eliminate as a priority the worst forms of child labour. There is also a specialist project – ILO-IPEC – relating to the elimination of child labour.

ILO conventions on migrant labourers

2.16   The ILO and the UN also addressed migrant labour issues. Two ILO conventions addressed the issue: Convention 97, the Migration for Employment (Revised) Convention; and Convention 143 on Migrant Workers (Supplementary Provisions) (1975).[36] The Preamble of

---

34   ILO, *Human trafficking and forced labour exploitation*, Guidance for Legislation and Law Development (2005).

35   Ratified by the UK on 22 March 2000.

36   Adopted 24 June 1975. Entry into force: 9 December 1978.

Convention 143 specifically points out 'that evidence of the existence of illicit and clandestine trafficking in labour calls for further standards specifically aimed at eliminating these abuses'. Convention 143 drew a distinction, reflecting in the division of the convention into two parts, between migrant workers who were lawfully in the territory and those who were in an illegal or irregular situation. As regards those lawfully in the territory, the convention called for the promotion and guarantee of full equality of treatment, by methods appropriate to national conditions and practice, in respect of employment and occupation, social security, trade union and cultural rights and individual and collective freedoms for migrant workers and their families.[37] As regards those illegally in the country, the convention requires the state to undertake to respect the basic rights of *all* migrant workers.[38] Importantly, the convention called for information gathering exercises, in conjunction with employers and workers on the conditions of migrant workers. States were required to take measures against the organisers or employers of such migrant labour and to take part in information exchange with other states.[39] The stated purpose of such provisions was so that 'the authors of manpower trafficking can be prosecuted whatever the country from which they exercise their activities'.[40] Provision was made for the effective detection of illegal employment and for the application of administrative, civil and penal sanctions in respect of the illegal employment of migrants, in respect of the organisation of movements of migrants involving conditions prohibited in article 2, and in respect of knowing assistance to such movements, whether for profit or otherwise. A good faith defence was available to employers.[41] Article 8 prevented the loss of employment from depriving the worker of his or her legal status, *provided the worker had resided legally in the territory* and required the worker to enjoy equality of treatment with nationals in respect of guarantees of security of employment, the provision of alternative employment, relief work and retraining. Article 9 dealt with the position of a worker who was not lawfully in the territory. It required that the worker should enjoy equality of treatment for himself or herself and his or her family as regards rights for past pay, social security and other benefits. This

---

37   Article 10.
38   Article 1.
39   Articles 3 and 4.
40   Article 5.
41   Article 6.

was expressly stated to be without prejudice to 'measures designed to control movements of migrants for employment by ensuring that migrants enter national territory and are admitted to employment in conformity with the relevant laws and regulations'. Members were free to exclude either part from its acceptance of the convention. The UK did not ratify any part of either convention.

2.17   In 1990, the United Nations General Assembly adopted the new Convention on the Protection of the Rights of all Migrant Workers and Members of Their Families.[42] The convention has not been ratified by the UK. The preamble to the convention considers 'that recourse to the employment of migrant workers who are in an irregular situation will be discouraged if the fundamental human rights of all migrant workers are more widely recognised and, moreover, that granting certain additional rights to migrant workers and members of their families in a regular situation will encourage all migrants and employers to respect and comply with the laws and procedures established by the States concerned'. Like the two ILO conventions, the convention distinguishes between documented or regular migrant workers and those who are undocumented or irregular.[43] A worker is documented if he or she is authorised to enter, to stay and to engage in a remunerated activity in the state of employment pursuant to the law of that state and to international agreements to which that state is a party. Article 7 of the convention required non discrimination in respect of certain rights against all migrant workers. Those rights were: freedom to leave any state or enter their own (article 8), the right to life (article 9), freedom from torture or from cruel, inhuman or degrading treatment or punishment (article 10), freedom from slavery or servitude and from forced or compulsory labour[44] (article 11), freedom of religion (article 12), the right to hold opinions without interference and to freedom of expression (articles 12 and 13), the right to privacy (article 14) and to property (article 15), to liberty and security of person (article 16), and to equality with nationals before courts and tribunals (article 18). Article 20(2) provided that no migrant worker shall be deprived or his or her authorisation of residence or work permit or expelled merely because of failure to fulfil an obligation arising out of a work

---

42   In force 1 July 2003.

43   Article 5.

44   Except as allowed under international law, ie as a result of lawful order of a court, service exacted in an emergency threatening the life or well-being of the community or work carried out as part of normal civic obligations.

contract unless fulfilment of that obligation constitutes a condition for such authorisation or work permit. Part IV of the convention sets out economic and social rights for migrant workers and members of their families who are documented.

2.18   There was thus a substantial international legal framework on modern forms of slavery including debt bondage, trafficking in women and children, forced labour and the treatment of migrant workers. Most effective of the UN agencies was the ILO, unique in its tripartite model comprising governments, employers and workers to shape national policies and programmes. There was also cross-agency co-operation within the UN but despite this, wherever trafficking was addressed as a migration issue, states were reluctant, unless they had significant numbers of citizens who were emigrants, to agree to fundamental universal principles.

Human trafficking as organised crime

2.19   This changed when, on 15 November 2000, at its 62nd plenary meeting, the United Nations General Assembly adopted the United Nations Convention against Transnational Organized Crime and its Protocols on Smuggling and Trafficking.[45] The convention was opened for signature at Palermo between 12 and 15 December 2000. It was originally intended to have three protocols appended to it: the protocol to prevent, suppress and punish trafficking in persons, especially women and children; the protocol against the smuggling of migrants by land, sea and air; and the protocol against the illicit manufacturing of and trafficking in firearms, their parts, components and ammunition. The last of these protocols, on trafficking in firearms, was not in fact ready for adoption with the convention. That left the first two protocols.

2.20   The convention and its protocols were significant for three reasons: first, a clear distinction was drawn between smuggling (where the person being transported across the border is the *consumer*) and trafficking (where the person is the *commodity*). This was a distinction which had not up until then always been clearly drawn by states, and in particular by immigration authorities. Second, human trafficking was seen in the context of organised crime and therefore became a matter of concern, at national level, to criminal law enforcement agencies and not simply immigration authorities. Third, the protocol provided a definition of trafficking,

---

45   A/RES/55/25, annexes I, II and III.

drawn in part from ILO conventions, which has since been widely adopted. When considering the convention and its protocols, reference should be made to the respective travaux preparatoires and the interpretative notes contained in each of them.[46]

2.21 In the preamble to the convention, the General Assembly referred to the links between organised crime and terrorism and to the negative and social implications related to organised criminal activities and called for greater co-operation at the national, regional and international levels. The stated purpose of the convention is to promote co-operation to prevent and combat transnational organised crime more effectively. An organised crime group is defined as a structured group of three or more persons, existing for a period of time and acting in concert with the aim of committing one or more serious crimes or offences established in accordance with the convention, in order to obtain, directly or indirectly, a financial or other material benefit.[47] A serious crime is defined as conduct constituting an offence punishable by a maximum deprivation of liberty of at least four years or a more serious penalty.[48] By article 3 of the Organised Crime Convention, an offence is transnational if:

(a) it is committed in more than one state;

(b) it is committed in one state but a substantial part of its preparation, planning, direction and control takes place in another state;

(c) it is committed in one state but involves an organised criminal group that engages in criminal activities in more than one state; or

(d) it is committed in one state but has substantial effects in another state.

The convention preserves the principle of state sovereignty.[49] State parties are required to criminalise participation in an organised crime group and money laundering of the proceeds of crime and to co-operate in confiscation of profits.[50] They should also take preventive regulatory measures to combat money-laundering[51] and corruption.[52]

---

46 UNDOC, New York 2006 ISBN 92-1-133743-7.

47 Article 2(a) and (c).

48 Article 2(b). Earlier drafts contained a list of deemed serious offences, including traffic in persons.

49 Article 4.

50 Articles 5, 6, 8, 13 and 14.

51 Article 7.

52 Article 9.

Each State Party shall adopt, in accordance with fundamental principles of its domestic law, such legislative and other measures as may be necessary to establish as criminal offences, when committed intentionally:

(a)

   (i) The conversion or transfer of property, knowing that such property is the proceeds of crime, for the purpose of concealing or disguising the illicit origin of the property or of helping any person who is involved in the commission of the predicate offence to evade the legal consequences of his or her action;

   (ii) The concealment or disguise of the true nature, source, location, disposition, movement or ownership of or rights with respect to property, knowing that such property is the proceeds of crime;

(b) Subject to the basic concepts of its legal system:

   (i) The acquisition, possession or use of property, knowing, at the time of receipt, that such property is the proceeds of crime;

   (ii) Participation in, association with or conspiracy to commit, attempts to commit and aiding, abetting, facilitating and counselling the commission of any of the offences established in accordance with this article.

2.22   States parties are also required to adopt measures to criminalise corruption and to take measures against it.[53] States parties are required to adopt measures to establish the criminal, civil or administrative liability of legal persons for participation in serious crimes involving an organised criminal group and for the offences established in accordance with articles 5, 6, 8 and 23.[54] Sanctions should be effective, proportionate and dissuasive.[55] States parties are required to adopt measures necessary to enable confiscation of proceeds of crime, including identification, tracing, freezing or seizure.[56] This includes acting on requests from other states having jurisdiction over a relevant offence.[57]

---

53   Articles 8 and 9.

54   Article 10(1) and (2).

55   Article 10(4).

56   Article 12. This applies to both protocols. A proposal to include a text in the trafficking protocol calling for the proceeds from seizure and confiscation to be used to defray the costs of providing due assistance to the victim was rejected: see travaux preparatoires to the trafficking protocol at p444.

57   Article 13.

Jurisdiction, extradition and mutual legal assistance

2.23　Articles 15–22 deal with the transnational nature of much organised crime. States parties are required to establish jurisdiction over the offences of participation in an organised criminal group, laundering, corruption and obstruction of justice where the offence is committed on the territory of that state, including on board a vessel flying the state's flag and on an aircraft registered under the laws of that state.[58] Additionally, states parties may also establish jurisdiction over any such offences when the offence is committed against a national of that state or by a national or a resident of that state or the offence is one of participation in an organised criminal group or laundering outside the state's territory with a view to the commission of a serious crime within its territory.[59] Article 16 sets out measures relating to extradition, in particular article 16(3) requires that each of the offences covered by the convention shall be deemed to be included as an extraditable offence in any bilateral extradition treaty and records that states parties undertake to include such offences as extraditable offences in every extradition treaty to be concluded between them. The convention provides a legal treaty basis for extradition, where a state makes extradition conditional upon a treaty basis: article 16(4). Article 18 requires states parties to afford each other the widest measure of mutual legal assistance in investigations, prosecutions and judicial proceedings in relation to the offences covered by the convention. This may include:[60]

(a) taking evidence or statements from persons;
(b) effecting service of judicial documents;
(c) executing searches and seizures, and freezing;
(d) examining objects and sites;
(e) providing information, evidentiary items and expert evaluations;
(f) providing originals or certified copies of relevant documents and records, including government, bank, financial, corporate or business records;
(g) identifying or tracing proceeds of crime, property, instrumentalities or other things for evidentiary purposes;
(h) facilitating the voluntary appearance of persons in the requesting state party;

58　Article 15.
59　Article 15(2).
60　Article 18(3).

(i) any other type of assistance that is not contrary to the domestic law of the requested state party.

The provisions of the article do not affect the obligations under any other treaty, bilateral or multilateral, that governs or will govern, in whole or in part, mutual legal assistance.[61] Article 18(9)–(29) set out detailed guidelines and safeguards. These are displaced by a bilateral treaty of mutual legal assistance (whether preceding or postdating), unless the relevant states parties agree to apply article 18(9)–(29).[62]

Witness protection and assistance

2.24   Articles 24 and 25 require the state party to provide witness protection and victim protection and assistance. They are set out in full below.

Article 24
Protection of witnesses

1. Each State Party shall take appropriate measures within its means to provide effective protection from potential retaliation or intimidation for witnesses in criminal proceedings who give testimony concerning offences covered by this Convention[63] and, as appropriate, for their relatives and other persons close to them.

2. The measures envisaged in paragraph 1 of this article may include, inter alia, without prejudice to the rights of the defendant, including the right to due process:

   (a) Establishing procedures for the physical protection of such persons, such as, to the extent necessary and feasible, relocating them and permitting, where appropriate, non-disclosure or limitations on the disclosure of information concerning the identity and whereabouts of such persons;

   (b) Providing evidentiary rules to permit witness testimony to be given in a manner that ensures the safety of the witness, such a permitting testimony to be given through the use of communications technology such as video links or other adequate means.

---

61   Article 18(6).

62   Article 18(7). The interpretative notes point out that many of the costs arising in connection with requests under article 18(10), (11) and (18) would generally be extraordinary in nature and that developing countries should be provided with assistance to enable them to meet the requirements of this article.

63   An early draft referred to 'its' criminal proceedings. One delegation noted that the protection should extend to victims and witnesses involved in proceedings in other states. The final draft is wide enough to include that meaning.

3. States Parties shall consider entering into agreements or arrangements with other States for the relocation of persons referred to in paragraph 1 of this article.
4. The provisions of this article shall also apply to victims insofar as they are witnesses.

Article 25[64]
Assistance to and protection of victims

1. Each State Party shall take appropriate measures within its means to provide assistance and protection to victims of offences covered by this Convention, in particular in cases of threat of retaliation or intimidation.
2. Each State Party shall establish appropriate procedures to provide access to compensation and restitution for victims of offences covered by this Convention.
3. Each State Party shall, subject to its domestic law, enable views and concerns of victims to be presented and considered at appropriate stages of criminal proceedings against offenders in a manner not prejudicial to the rights of the defence.

2.25   The remaining substantive articles 26–31 are concerned with co-operation between law enforcement agencies on information, training and technical assistance, and prevention.

The Trafficking Protocol

2.26   The preamble to the protocol to prevent, suppress and punish trafficking in persons, especially women and children ('the Trafficking Protocol'), comments on the absence, hitherto, of a universal instrument that addresses all aspects of trafficking in persons. It comments on the need for a comprehensive international approach in the countries of origin, transit and destination, including protection, punishment and prevention. The protocol is intended to remedy that lack. It supplements the convention on transnational organised crime and is to be interpreted with it.[65] The provisions of the convention apply, mutatis mutandis, to it[66] and the offences

---

64   Interpretative note on article 25: while the purpose of this article is to concentrate on the physical protection of victims, the Ad Hoc Committee was cognisant of the need for protection of the rights of individuals as accorded under applicable international law. Article 25 was originally part of article 24.

65   Article 1(1). The protocol was signed by the UK on 14 December 2000 and ratified on 9 February 2006.

66   Article 1(2).

established in accordance with article 5 of the protocol are to be regarded as offences established in accordance with the convention.[67] This brings human trafficking squarely within the framework of organised crime. The protocol contains a purpose clause[68] which covers the prevention and combating of human trafficking, protection and assistance of victims and the promotion of inter-state co-operation.

Definition of human trafficking

2.27   Article 3 defines human trafficking by reference to three elements:

(1) *transfer:* defined as 'the recruitment, transportation, transfer, harbouring or receipt of persons';

(2) *force or fraud or some act negating consent:* 'the threat or use of force or other forms of coercion, of abduction or fraud, of deception, of the abuse of power or of a position of vulnerability[69] or of the giving or receiving of payments or benefits to achieve the consent of a person having control over another person';

(3) *intended exploitation* which 'shall include, at a minimum, the exploitation of the prostitution of others or other forms of sexual exploitation,[70] forced labour[71] or services, slavery or practices similar to slavery,[72] servitude or the removal of organs'.

---

67   Article 1(3).

68   Article 2.

69   Interpretative note (a): The reference to the abuse of a position of vulnerability is understood to refer to any situation in which the person involved has no real and acceptable alternative but to submit to the abuse involved.

70   Interpretative note (b): The protocol addresses the exploitation of the prostitution of others and other forms of sexual exploitation only in the context of trafficking in persons. The terms 'exploitation of the prostitution of others' or 'other forms of sexual exploitation' are not defined in the protocol, which is therefore without prejudice to how states parties address prostitution in their domestic laws.

71   The protocol does not expressly refer to the ILO conventions but they were discussed extensively during the negotiations.

72   Interpretative note (d): Where illegal adoption amounts to a practice similar to slavery as defined in article 1, paragraph (d), of the Supplementary Convention on the Abolition of Slavery, the Slave Trade, and Institutions and Practices Similar to Slavery, it will also fall within the scope of the protocol.

Articles 3(b) and 3(c) contain important riders to article 3(a). Article 3(b) provides:

(b) the consent of a victim of trafficking in persons to the intended exploitation set forth in subparagraph (a) ... shall be irrelevant where any of the means set forth in subparagraph (a) have been used.

Article 3(c) provides:

(c) the recruitment, transportation, transfer, harbouring or receipt of a child for the purpose of exploitation shall be considered 'trafficking in persons' even if this does not involve any of the means set forth in subparagraph (a).

The cumulative effect of these two provisions is that the consent of a child, either to the intended exploitation or to the transfer itself, is not a factor which a trafficker can rely on.

2.28   Having defined human trafficking, the protocol then requires states to act against trafficking as regards criminalisation, protection of victims and prevention and other co-operation. As regards criminalisation, the protocol requires[73] states parties to establish trafficking as a criminal offence in national law. Trafficking must be a criminal offence when committed intentionally,[74] when attempted,[75] when there has been participation as an accomplice in the offence[76] and when there has been organisation or direction of others to commit an offence.[77]

2.29   The second element of protection of victims of trafficking is dealt with by articles 6–8. These are less specific than the subsequent European legislation. Article 6(3) only provides that states shall *consider* implementing measures to provide for the physical, psychological and social recovery of victims of trafficking, in co-operation with non-governmental organisations (NGOs), other relevant organisations and other elements of civil society, and in particular the provision of appropriate housing, counselling and information, medical, psychological and material assistance and employment, educational and training opportunities.[78] The state

73   Article 5.
74   Article 5(1).
75   Article 5(2)(a).
76   Article 5(2)(b).
77   Article 5(2)(c).
78   Despite its optional nature, the relevant state under 6(3) is the state in whose territory the victim is. It applies to receiving states until the victim has returned to their state of origin, and to the state of origin thereafter: interpretative note.

party is required to take into account the age, gender and special needs of victims, in particular the special needs of children, including appropriate housing, education and care. The state party is required to ensure that its domestic legal system contains measures that offer victims the possibility of obtaining compensation for damage suffered. Article 7 requires states to consider adopting legislative or other measures to permit victims of trafficking to remain in its territory, temporarily or permanently, in appropriate cases and to give appropriate consideration to humanitarian and compassionate factors. As with article 6(3), this plainly leaves states considerable discretion. Article 8 requires states from which a victim had originated to facilitate their return. It also states that any such return shall be done with due regard for the victim's safety, any related legal proceedings and that the return shall preferably be voluntary. The article is without prejudice to any bilateral agreements between the relevant states.

2.30   Prevention is the third element of the response. The Trafficking Protocol sets out various ways in which states are required to do this including through public information campaigns, information exchange, border measures, security and control of documents.[79]

2.31   The protocol does not cover the status of refugees and is without prejudice to the existing rights, obligations or responsibilities of states parties under other international instruments.[80]

The Smuggling Protocol

2.32   The protocol against the smuggling of migrants by land, sea and air, supplementing the United Nations Convention against Transnational Organized Crime ('the Smuggling Protocol') is, like the Trafficking Protocol, to be interpreted with the convention. Its stated purpose is to prevent and combat the smuggling of migrants, as well as to promote co-operation among states parties to that end, while protecting the rights of smuggled migrants.[81] Smuggling is defined as 'the procurement, in order to obtain directly or indirectly, a

---

79   Articles 9–13.
80   Interpretative note to article 14.
81   Article 2.

financial or other material benefit,[82] of the illegal entry of a person into a State Party of which the person is not a national or a permanent resident'.[83] Article 5 provides that migrants shall not be liable to criminal prosecution under the protocol for the fact of having been the object of conduct criminalised through the protocol. Article 6 requires states parties to establish as criminal offences when committed intentionally and in order to obtain directly or indirectly a financial or other material benefit:

(a) the smuggling of migrants;
(b) when committed for the purpose of enabling the smuggling of migrants:

    (i) producing a fraudulent travel or identity document; or
    (ii) procuring, providing or possessing such a document;

(c) enabling a person who is not a national or a permanent resident to remain in the state concerned without complying with the necessary requirements for legally remaining in the state by the means mentioned. Attempting to commit the offence, or participating in the offence or organising or directing other persons to commit the offence. States are also required to establish as aggravating circumstances in the commission of an offence where:

    (i) the lives or safety of the migrants concerned are endangered;
    (ii) there is inhuman or degrading treatment, including for exploitation, of such migrants.

2.33   The protocol contains specific provisions on co-operation to prevent and suppress the smuggling of migrants by sea, in accordance

---

82 Interpretative note on (a): The reference to 'a financial or other material benefit' as an element of the definition in subparagraph (a) was included in order to emphasise that the intention was to include the activities of organised criminal groups acting for profit, but to exclude the activities of those who provided support to migrants for humanitarian reasons or on the basis of close family ties. It was not the intention of the protocol to criminalise the activities of family members or support groups such as religious or non-governmental organisations.

83 Article 3.

with the international law of the sea[84] and for the boarding and searching of vessels where there are reasonable grounds for suspecting that a vessel is engaged in smuggling of migrants, following authorisation by the flag state. The smuggling protocol also provides for measures of prevention and co-operation including border measures,[85] security and control of documents,[86] prompt verification of legitimacy and validity of documents upon a request[87] and for training and technical co-operation.[88] Article 18 provides for the return of smuggled migrants.

2.34   The UK signed the Trafficking Protocol on 14 December 2000 and ratified it on 9 February 2006. It did not enter any reservations or declarations. The convention entered into force on 29 September 2003 and the Trafficking Protocol entered into force on 25 December 2003.

2.35   The UN custodian of the convention and its protocols is the United Nations Office on Drugs and Crime (UNODC). UNODC has a global programme against Trafficking in Human Beings and offers technical help to states. In March 2007, UNODC, together with the ILO, the International Organization for Migration (IOM), UNICEF, UNHCR (the UN Refugee Agency) and the Organisation for Security and Cooperation in Europe (OSCE), launched the Global Initiative to Fight Human Trafficking (UN.GIFT).

UN Supervisory and monitoring bodies

2.36   The UN treaties each have supervisory or monitoring bodies. With the exception of the Human Rights Committee, which supervised the International Covenant on Civil and Political Rights, the monitoring bodies receive reports from the states on their compliance and sometimes hear from NGOs or social partners. In the case of

---

84   Articles 7–9. The provisions are derived from article 17 of the UN Convention against Illegal Traffic in Narcotic Drugs and Psychotropic Substances of 1988 ('the 1988 Convention') (United Nations, *Treaty Series*, Vol 1582, No 27627) and from the interim measures for combating unsafe practices associated with the trafficking or transport of migrants by sea (the interim measures), approved in December 1998 by the Maritime Safety Committee of the International Maritime Organisation (MSC/Circ.896, annex, and also reproduced in document A/Ac.254/CRP.3).

85   Articles 10–11.

86   Article 12.

87   Article 13.

88   Article 14.

ILO conventions, supervision is done by the Committee of Experts on the Application of Conventions and Recommendations and the Conference Committee on the Application of Standards. The ILO Committee also provides for inter-state complaints which are determined by a Commission of Inquiry appointed by the Governing Board. In addition, complaints by 'actors or individuals' about specific incidents may be made direct to the Special Rapporteur on trafficking in persons, especially women and children.[89] The 47-member Human Rights Council was established by the UN General Assembly in its Resolution 60/251 of 3 April 2006 to replace the Commission on Human Rights, hears confidential complaints and carries out a Universal Periodic Review,[90] designed to encompass all members of the United Nations regardless of reporting obligations.

International Court of Justice

2.37   The International Court of Justice[91] has a dual jurisdiction: it decides, in accordance with international law, disputes of a legal nature that are submitted to it by States (jurisdiction in contentious cases); and it gives advisory opinions on legal questions at the request of the organs of the United Nations or specialised agencies authorised[92] to make such a request (advisory jurisdiction). The advisory opinions are, unless agreed otherwise, not binding but carry obvious weight.[93] There are currently no cases in either jurisdiction directly concerning cases of human trafficking.

International Criminal Court and Tribunals

2.38   International criminal law is mainly concerned with breaches by state actors. However, that should not obscure the fact that actions by

---

89   See www2.ohchr.org/English/issues/trafficking/complaints.htm.

90   See Human Rights Council Resolution 5/1 (A/62/53. HRC res. A/HRC/5/21. Annex, para 15(a)) and the *General Guidelines for the preparation of information under the Universal Periodic Review* adopted by the Human Rights Council on 27 September 2007.

91   See www.icj-cij.org.

92   See list atwww.icj-cij.org/jurisdiction/index.php?p1=5&p2=2&p3=1.

93   See Rosalyn Higgins, *Problems and process: international law and how we use it*, 1994.

non-state actors may also fall within the competence of international concern and redress.[94]

2.39   International criminal law is primarily concerned with crimes against peace, war crimes, crimes against humanity and genocide. Enslavement is recognised as a crime against humanity under various statutes governing international criminal courts. Article 7 of the Rome Statute[95] prohibits enslavement, which by virtue of 7(2)(c) means: 'the exercise of any or all of the powers attaching to the right of ownership over a person and includes the exercise of such power in the course of trafficking in persons, in particular women and children'. Article 5(c) of the Statute of the International Criminal Tribunal for the Former Yugoslavia[96] prohibits enslavement but does not define it. In *Prosecutor v Kunarac, Kovac and Vukovic*[97] the Trial Chamber (on 22 February 2001) and the Appeals Chamber (on 12 June 2002) considered the issue of what acts would amount to enslavement as a crime against humanity. After a comprehensive survey (518–538) of the relevant international law, including ILO Conventions and the Nuremberg judgment, the Trial Chamber in *Kunarac* concluded that enslavement as a crime against humanity in customary international law consisted of the intentional[98] exercise of any or all of the powers attaching to the right of ownership over a person. They observed that this definition may be broader than the 'traditional and sometimes apparently distinct definitions of either slavery, the slave trade and servitude or forced or compulsory labour found in other areas of international law' and referred for support in this conclusion to the work of the International Law Commission.[99]

Definition of enslavement

542.   [I]ndications of enslavement include elements of control and ownership; the restriction or control of an individual's autonomy, freedom of choice or freedom of movement; and often, the accruing of some gain to the perpetrator. The consent or free

---

94 See 'The "not-a-cat" syndrome: can the international human rights regime accommodate non-state actors' Philip Alston in *Non state actors and human rights*, ed Alston, OUP, 2005.

95 In force from 1 July 2002.

96 See www.icty.org.

97 Case No IT-96-23_T and IT-96-23/1-T.

98 The relevant intention being simply the intention to commit the relevant act (cf genocide, which requires an underlying motive).

99 At 537.

will of the victim is absent.[100] It is often rendered impossible or irrelevant by, for example, the threat or use of force or other forms of coercion; the fear of violence, deception or false promises; the abuse of power; the victim's position of vulnerability; detention or captivity, psychological oppression or socioeconomic conditions. Further indications of enslavement include exploitation; the exaction of forced or compulsory labour or service, often without remuneration and often, though not necessarily, involving physical hardship; sex; prostitution; or human trafficking. With respect to forced or compulsory labour or service, international law, including some of the provisions of Geneva Convention IV and the Additional Protocols, make clear that not all labour or service by protected persons, including civilians, in armed conflicts, is prohibited – strict conditions are, however, set for such labour or service. The 'acquisition' or 'disposal' of someone for monetary or other compensation is not a requirement for enslavement. Doing so, however, is a prime example of the exercise of the rights of the rights of ownership over someone. The duration of the suspected exercise of powers attaching to the right of ownership is another factor that may be considered when determining whether someone was enslaved; however, its importance in any given case will depend on the existence of other indications of enslavement. Detaining or keeping someone in captivity, without more, would, depending on the circumstances of a case, usually not constitute enslavement.

543. The Trial Chamber is therefore in general agreement with the factors put forward by the Prosecutor, to be taken into consideration in determining whether enslavement was committed. These are the control of someone's movement, control of physical environment, psychological control, measures taken to prevent or deter escape, force, threat of force or coercion, duration, assertion of exclusivity, subjection to cruel treatment and abuse, control of sexuality and forced labour. The Prosecutor also submitted that the mere ability to buy sell, trade or inherit a person or his or her labours or services could be a relevant factor. The Trial Chamber considers that while the *mere ability* to do so is insufficient, such actions actually occurring could be a relevant factor.

Kunarac, Vukovic and Kovac, Judgment of Trial Chamber, 542–3

---

100 The Appeal Chamber held that the lack of consent was not an element of the crime of enslavement, although consent might be relevant from an evidential point of view as going to the question whether the prosecutor has established the element of the crime relating to the exercise by the accused of any or all of the powers attaching to the right of ownership.

2.40   Significantly, the tribunal regarded the transfer or trafficking of labour as an indicator of enslavement.[101] The tribunal also held (53) that for an act to constitute a crime against humanity:

(a) there must be an 'attack' by a state or organisation;
(b) the acts of the accused must be part of the attack;
(c) the attack must be directed against any civilian population;
(d) the attack must be widespread and systematic; and
(e) the principal offender must know of the wider context in which his or her acts occur and know that his or her acts are part of the attack.

The court went on to hold (54) that an attack can be defined as a course of conduct involving the commission of acts of violence. In practice, the attack could outlast, precede, or run parallel to the armed conflict, without necessarily being a part of it. At 55 they held that the acts of the accused need to be objectively part of the 'attack' against the civilian population, but need not be committed when that attack is at its height.

2.41   The Trial Chamber (15 March 2002) and Appeals Chamber (17 September 2002) further considered the issue of slavery[102] and forced labour and of enslavement as a crime against humanity in *Prosecutor v Krnojelac* Case No IT-97-25-T.

Trial Chamber

359.   It is clear from the Tribunal's jurisprudence that 'the exaction of forced or compulsory labour of service' is an 'indication of enslavement' and 'a factor to be taken into consideration in determining whether enslavement was committed'. In essence, the determination of whether protected persons laboured involuntarily is a factual question which has to be considered in light of all the relevant circumstances on a case by case basis. Such circumstances may include the following:

---

101 This will turn on how the transfer is carried out: hence the elements of coercion or deception in the UN protocol definition. See generally 'The "not-a-cat" syndrome: can the international human rights regime accommodate non state actors?' Philip Alston in *Non state actors and human rights*, ed Alston, OUP, 2005.

102 The Trial Chamber held that there was no difference between slavery and enslavement as regards the elements to be proved.

The consent or free will of the victim is absent. It is often rendered impossible or irrelevant by, for example, the threat or use of force or other forms of coercion; the fear of violence, deception or false promises; the abuse of power; the victim's position of vulnerability; detention or captivity; psychological oppression or socio-economic conditions.

What must be established is that the relevant persons had no real choice as to whether they would work.

2.42   On an appeal by the prosecution against acquittal, the Appeals Chamber held[103] that subjective belief by an individual that they had no choice but to work was not sufficient to establish forced labour. Personal conviction had to be proven with objective and not just subjective evidence.[104] Objective relevant evidence could (and in this case, did) include the substantially uncompensated nature of the work, the vulnerable position in which the detainees found themselves, alleged treatment of those who refused to work, claims of longer term consequences of the labour, the fact of detention and the inhumane conditions, which should have lead to a conclusion at first instance of coercive conditions.[105]

2.43   Finally, human rights deriving from international norms can be enforced in the regional and national sphere, which is the subject of the rest of this book.

103 See www.icty.org judgment of 17 September 2002.
104 At 195.
105 At 196.

CHAPTER 3

Legal framework at European level

Key points

- The European Community and the Council of Europe have separate legal frameworks addressing the issue of human trafficking.
- Article 4 of the European Convention on Human Rights and Fundamental Freedoms prohibits slavery, servitude, and forced and compulsory labour. The prohibition on slavery and servitude is non-derogable. It gives rise to positive obligations. Jurisprudence from the European Court of Human Rights, to whom claims of breaches of article 4 may be brought, will continue to be relevant when deciding cases under the Human Rights Act 1998 or in cases of a claim to the court itself.
- The Council of Europe Convention on Action against Trafficking in Human Beings (CETS 197) contains detailed provisions on the nature of states' obligations. It is intended to build upon and broaden the protection offered by the Trafficking Protocol to the UN Convention against Transnational Organised crime. It was signed by the UK on 23 March 2007, was ratified on 17 December 2008 with consequential amendments of UK law, and came into force in April 2009 in the UK.
- In matters of Community Law competence, Community Law remains supreme.
- The European Union has enacted EU Directives, Framework Decisions and Action Plans. These have generally been under the heading of justice and home affairs.

The two regional legal systems

3.1   There have been significant recent developments at European level against human trafficking, in particular the Council of Europe Convention on Action against Trafficking in Human Beings.[1] Other, European Union, initiatives continue to have relevance, as does the jurisprudence of the Strasbourg Court of Human Rights. It is important to bear in mind that there are of course two separate systems of regional law with different bases and different membership: the European Union and the Council of Europe. The

---

1   CETS 197.

European Union is a union with a legal and parliamentary system which has supremacy over national law. The founder members of the EU were Belgium, France, Germany, Italy, Luxembourg and the Netherlands. They were joined in 1973 by Denmark, Ireland and the United Kingdom, in 1981 by Greece, in 1986 by Portugal and Spain and in 1995 by Austria, Finland and Sweden. There was significant expansion to the east in 2004 when Cyprus, the Czech Republic, Estonia, Hungary, Latvia, Lithuania, Malta, Poland, Slovakia and Slovenia joined. In 2007 Bulgaria and Romania acceded to the Union. Membership thus stands at 27. Current candidate states are Croatia, the Former Yugoslav Republic of Macedonia, and Turkey.

3.2 European Community law has supremacy over national law and national laws must be set aside where they fail to implement Community law. The fundamental treaty is the Treaty on European Union (TEU), as signed in Maastricht on 7 February 1992[2] and as amended by the Treaty of Amsterdam. Title VI of the TEU for the first time provided for new forms of intergovernmental co-operation in the field of justice and home affairs. Action against human trafficking is dealt with under this title. Because the most significant recent developments have occurred in the Council of Europe and because it is the larger regional organisation, it will be considered first in this chapter.

Council of Europe

3.3 The membership of the Council of Europe is wider than that of the European Union, with significantly greater membership in Eastern Europe.[3] Unlike European Union law, the convention does not have internal effect in a national legal system. However, there is a presumption that a state will not act incompatibly with its international obligations. Further, the enactment of the Human

---

2 The TEU entered into force on 1 November 1993.

3 Current membership stands at 47: Albania, Andorra, Armenia, Austria, Azerbaijan, Belgium, Bosnia and Herzegovina, Bulgaria, Croatia, Cyprus, Czech Republic, Denmark, Estonia, Finland, France, Georgia, Germany, Greece, Hungary, Iceland, Ireland, Italy, Latvia, Liechtenstein, Lithuania, Luxembourg, Malta, Moldova, Monaco, Montenegro, Netherlands, Norway, Poland, Portugal, Romania, Russian Federation, San Marino, Serbia, Slovakia, Slovenia, Spain, Sweden, Switzerland, The former Yugoslav Republic of Macedonia, Turkey, Ukraine and the UK. Many of these states are sending states.

Rights Act 1998 has made the body of Council of Europe law very relevant. The two most significant Council of Europe conventions on the subject are the 1950 European Convention on Human Rights and Fundamental Freedoms[4] and the 2005 European Convention on Action against Trafficking in Human Beings.

1950 Convention on Human Rights and Fundamental Freedoms

3.4   The Convention for the Protection of Human Rights and Fundamental Freedoms, as amended by Protocol 11 ('the Convention on Human Rights') was agreed on 4 November 1950 in the aftermath of the Second World War. It entered into force on 3 September 1953. Compliance is supervised by the European Court of Human Rights which hears and determines applications[5] from any person, non-governmental organisation (NGO) or group of individuals claiming to have suffered a breach of a convention right. Nowhere does the convention refer to human trafficking. The Convention on Human Rights, and jurisprudence thereunder by the European Court of Human Rights, will, however, continue to be very relevant, because article 4 of the convention prohibits slavery, servitude and forced or compulsory labour.[6] The convention is a living instrument to be interpreted in the light of present-day conditions.[7] The criminal offence of trafficking is defined in national law in part by reference to article 4. In determining any question which arises in connection with article 4 (including whether or not a breach of article 4 has occurred), a court or tribunal must take into account any judgment, decision or declaration or advisory opinion of the European Court of Human Rights, opinion of the commission given in a report adopted under article 31 of the convention, decision of the commission in connection with article 26 or 27(2) of the convention or decision of the Committee of Ministers taken under article 46 of the convention, whenever made and insofar as it is relevant in the

---

4   European Treaty Series No 5.

5   Under article 34.

6   The false promise *Arbeit Macht Frei* being a recent memory. No derogation, even in times of emergency, is permitted in respect of the prohibition on slavery and servitude. Article 4(1) shares this non-derogable character as a substantive right with the right to life and the prohibition on torture: article 15. There are limited exceptions for forced and compulsory labour: see article 4(3).

7   *Soering v UK*, 7 July 1989 Series A, 161 para 90–91.

court's opinion.[8] In addition, the convention forms the basis of the rights set out in Schedule 1 to the Human Rights Act 1998, which gave further effect to (in essence, incorporated) the European Convention. Thus, a claim under the Human Rights Act 1998 or an argument regarding the duty of a public authority[9] may involve consideration of the jurisprudence of the Strasbourg Court. A claim by a person, NGO or group of individuals, that they have suffered a breach of their rights under article 4 must first be raised in national law and this will now usually be by express reference to the Human Rights Act 1998.[10] However, an application to the Strasbourg court remains available as a final resort.

Article 4: Strasbourg case-law

Definition of forced labour

3.5 The court considered the prohibition on forced labour in *Van der Mussele v Belgium*.[11] Mr Mussele, a Belgian trainee lawyer at the relevant time, contended that, in being required to carry out unremunerated representation of a client, he had been subjected to forced labour. His case failed on its facts, since he had voluntarily entered the legal profession, which involved a proportionate professional obligation to undertake some pro bono work.[12] However, the court set out some important principles. The court acknowledged the relevance of the International Labour Organization (ILO) conventions, in particular ILO Convention 29 concerning forced or compulsory labour.

---

8 Human Rights Act 1998 s2(1).

9 In private proceedings under Human Rights Act 1998 s7, or pursuant to the obligation of public authorities, under s6, not to act incompatibly with the convention rights, including article 4.

10 It is, however, not always necessary to exhaust all appellate avenues in national law. Expert advice should be sought on the particular circumstances of the case.

11 Application 8919/80.

12 Interestingly, the court declined to decide the matter as falling within the exception for 'normal civil obligations' set out in article 4(3), evincing perhaps a reluctance to call upon the exceptions set out in article 4(3) – or justifications as they called them at para 41. The court did, however, refer to article 4(3) in dismissing a claim brought under article 4 by a prisoner in respect of prison work: *Van Droogenbroeck v Belgium* App 7906/77 24 June 1982 at 57–60. A claim in respect of obligations on dentists was declared manifestly ill-founded: *Iversen v Norway* 1468/62 Yearbook of the Convention, Vol 6, pp327–329.

Article 4 (art. 4) does not define what is meant by 'forced or compulsory labour' and no guidance on this point is to be found in the various Council of Europe documents relating to the preparatory work of the European Convention ... it is evident that the authors of the European Convention – following the example of the authors of Article 8 of the draft International Covenant on Civil and Political Rights – based themselves, to a large extent, on an earlier treaty of the International Labour Organisation, namely Convention No 29 concerning Forced or Compulsory Labour.

...

There is in fact a striking similarity, which is not accidental, between paragraph 3 of Article 4 (art 4-3) of the European Convention and paragraph 2 of Article 2 of Convention No. 29. Paragraph 1 of the last-mentioned Article provides that 'for the purposes' of the latter Convention, the term 'forced or compulsory labour' shall mean 'all work or service which is exacted from any person under the menace of any penalty and for which the said person has not offered himself voluntarily.' This definition can provide a starting-point for interpretation of Article 4 (art. 4) of the European Convention.

3.6   ILO conventions and comments thereunder by the Committee of Experts will therefore be relevant to interpretation of article 4. The court concluded that article 4 covered all work, not simply work of a manual nature.[13] The court observed that the term 'forced' brought to mind the idea of physical or mental constraint. As to the term 'compulsory', the court held that the presence alone of sanctions in a freely negotiated contract would not suffice. They held, in line with the ILO definition in Convention 29, that what there has to be is work exacted under the menace of any penalty and also performed against the will of the person concerned – that is, work for which the person has not offered himself or herself voluntarily. Mr Van der Mussele had entered the ordre des avocats knowing that he would be required during pupillage to carry out some work free of charge. That notwithstanding, the court held that a considerable and unreasonable imbalance between the aim pursued (in that case to qualify as a lawyer), and the obligations undertaken in order to achieve that aim would alone be capable of warranting the conclusion that the services exacted were compulsory, despite the individual's consent.[14] The important principle set out is that in certain circumstances, a service cannot be deemed to have been consented

13   'Labour' was capable of covering all work and the French 'travail' certainly did: para 33. The court also referred to the very name of the ILO.

14   At 40.

to beforehand. This principle will have relevance to cases of debt bondage and where excessive charges have been made for travel and accommodation which are then deducted from wages.

3.7   The court also rejected a claim based on article 14 (non-discrimination in the enjoyment of the rights under the Convention on Human Rights in this case formulated as discrimination against lawyers) but in so doing, it observed that 'work or labour or labour that is in itself normal may in fact be rendered abnormal if the choice of groups or individuals bound to perform it is governed by discriminatory factors'.

Positive obligations

3.8   Governments have positive obligations[15] to adopt criminal law provisions which penalise the practices referred to in article 4 and to prevent, detect and punish breaches of such provisions: *Siliadin v France*.[16] Ms Siliadin was a Togolese national who had arrived in France aged under 16 on a three-month tourist visa. She agreed to carry out domestic work until her airfare (the cost of which had been lent to her by her employers) had been repaid and in exchange for regularisation of immigration status and attendance at school. In fact, she was never paid, apart from two ad hoc payments of 500 francs, did not attend school and her passport was confiscated. She was lent to and kept by another couple. After three years and one attempted escape into paid work, a complaint was filed by an NGO with the prosecutor's office on her behalf. The French Court of First Instance held that the applicant's vulnerability and dependence was established by the fact that she was unlawfully resident in France and was aware of that fact which was exploited by the couple she worked for. The offence, under 225-13 of the French Penal Code, of obtaining work with no or disproportionately little payment, through exploitation of vulnerability or a position of dependence, was made out. However, the Court of First Instance held that the offence of subjecting someone to working conditions incompatible with human dignity, contrary to 225-14, was not established. The court ordered the defendants to pay FFr 100,000 to Ms Siliadin. The defendants appealed to the Paris Court of Appeal. The Court of Appeal acquitted the defendants of all charges, and dismissed the

---

15   As with article 3.
16   Application No 73316/01.

associated compensation claim, holding that vulnerability could not be established simply on the basis that she was an alien and that she had been free to move about the city and had made phone calls to relatives. Her uncle, who had been a party to the arrangement, had given evidence that she had never complained to him. The applicant appealed against the judgment by the Court of Appeal but the public prosecutor's office did not, on the grounds that it was an assessment of elements of pure fact. The Court of Cassation quashed the judgment of the Court of Appeal as regards articles 225-13 and 225-14 on the grounds of inadequate reasoning. However, since there had been no appeal by the public prosecutor, the Court of Cassation only restored the claim of the civil party[17] for compensation. The Versailles Court of Appeal, to whom the case was remitted, restored the finding under 225-13 and dismissed the case under 225-14. The court ordered payment to compensate for psychological trauma. Ms Siliadin also received an award from the Paris industrial tribunal in respect of arrears of salary, notice period and holiday pay.

3.9   Ms Siliadin argued that the failure to convict amounted to a breach of article 4 and that civil compensation was not on its own sufficient. The European Court of Human Rights held that she had been subjected to forced labour and, having regard not only to the ILO Convention 29 on Forced Labour[18] but also to the UN Convention on the Rights of the Child, that she had been subjected to servitude. The court found that there are positive obligations under article 4, in the same way as for article 3, to adopt criminal law provisions which penalise slavery, slavery-like practices and forced labour. The court held that it was necessary for forced labour and servitude to be prohibited by the criminal law and that a civil remedy was not adequate to discharge that duty. In deciding that there had been a breach of the positive obligation, the court referred to the failure by the prosecutor's office to appeal the acquittal by the Court of Appeal. The court further held[19] that a criminal legal framework which was open to differing interpretations from one court to the next did not afford the applicant practical and effective protection against the actions of which she was a victim. Thus, Ms Siliadin had been the victim of a breach of article 4 by France.

---

17   Under French law, as with other civil law systems, the victim may become a party to the criminal proceedings and is referred to as the 'partie civile'.
18   See para 2.11.
19   At 147.

3.10   The extent of positive obligations will be further explored in *Rantsev v Cyprus and Russia*.[20] The case concerns the applicant's daughter, a Russian national who had left the cabaret in Cyprus where she had started working the week before. She was found by her employer, handed into the police and then released back to her employer, who took her to another employee's flat. Her body was found on the street below the flat the next morning. Questions have been put to the states parties,[21] in particular Cyprus has been asked to explain what measures were taken to ascertain whether Miss Rantsev had been the victim of human trafficking or sexual exploitation and to explain why she was handed back to her employer, whom she had sought to escape. Russia has been asked to explain what steps it took prior to Miss Rantsev's departure to ensure she was not a victim of trafficking.

Duties arising on expulsion

3.11   The Strasbourg court has appeared to accept that article 4 (like articles 2 and 3) may be relied upon to resist expulsion, where there would be a resultant risk of slavery or servitude. In *Ould Barar v Sweden*, Application No 42367/98 (1999) 28 EHRR CD 213, an admissibility decision, the applicant, the son of a slave, raised issues under articles 2, 3 and 4 based upon his fear that he would be enslaved on his return. The court did not appear to dispute (at 2) that article 4 would be engaged where there was a risk of slavery on return. The judgment is a very short one and the case essentially failed with the credibility of the applicant. There may be a distinction between the prohibition on slavery and servitude, under article 4(1), which, like articles 2 and 3, is non-derogable, and the prohibition on forced labour, which is derogable. The better view is that where there is a real risk of retrafficking amounting to slavery or servitude or (arguably) forced labour on return, article 4 will be engaged, in principle, and subject to the facts.[22] This principle will also apply where there has been trafficking in the past, provided the individual can establish a risk of re-trafficking in the future.[23]

---

20   Application No 25965/2004.
21   7 July 2008, www.coe.int.
22   See also *Regina (Ullah) v Special Adjudicator* [2004] 2 AC 323.
23   The standard level of proof may be considered in *M v the United Kingdom* Application 16081/2008 (www.bailii.org/eu/cases/ECHR/2008/522.html).

The Convention on Action against Human Trafficking

3.12   On 12 May 2005, at Warsaw, the Council of Europe Convention on Action against Trafficking in Human Beings CETS No 197 was opened for signature. The convention may be signed by member states, by non-member states which have participated in its elaboration and by the European Community. The convention entered into force on 1 February 2008, three months after it had been ratified by 10 states, of which eight were member states.[24] The UK Government signed the convention on 23 March 2007, ratified it on 17 December 2008 and the convention therefore[25] came into force on 1 April 2009.

3.13   The convention should be read together with the Explanatory Report attached to it, which sets out the background to the convention and explains the purpose of some of the provisions. The preamble of the convention refers to the Convention on Human Rights, the following Committee of Ministers Recommendations: No R (1991) on sexual exploitation, pornography and prostitution of, and trafficking in, children and young adults; R (1997) 13 concerning intimidation of witnesses and the rights of the defence; R (2000) 11 on action against trafficking in human beings for the purpose of sexual exploitation and R (2001) 16 on the protection of children against sexual exploitation and R (2002) 5 on the protection of women against violence.

3.14   The preamble also refers to recommendations of the Parliamentary Assembly of the Council of Europe: 1325 (1997) on traffic in women; 1450 (2000) on violence against women; 1545 (2002) on a campaign against trafficking in women; 1610 (2003) on migration in connection with trafficking in women and prostitution; 1611 (2003) on trafficking in organs; and 1663 (2004) on domestic slavery. The preamble

---

24   As of 12 October 2008, it had been ratified by Albania, Armenia, Austria, Bosnia and Herzegovina, Bulgaria, Croatia, Cyprus , Denmark, France, Georgia, Latvia, Malta, Moldova, Montenegro, Norway, Portugal, Romania and Slovakia. It had been signed, but not ratified, by Andorra, Belgium, Finland, Germany, Greece, Hungary, Iceland, Ireland, Italy, Lithuania, Luxembourg, the Netherlands, Poland, San Marino, Serbia, Slovenia, Spain, Sweden, Switzerland, the Former Yugoslav Republic of Macedonia, the Ukraine and the United Kingdom. Of the member States, it had not been signed by Azerbaijan, Czech Republic, Estonia, Liechtenstein, Monaco, Russia or Turkey. It had not been signed or acceded to by any of the non-Member States entitled to accede to it: Canada, Holy See, Japan, Mexico, the United States or the European Community. See http://conventions.coe.int/Treaty/Commun/ChercheSig.asp?NT=197.

25   Article 42.

also refers to the European Union Council Framework Decision of 19 July 2002, the Framework Decision of 15 March 2001 on the standing of victims in criminal proceedings and the European Union Council Directive of 29 April 2004 on the residence permit issued to third-country nationals who are victims of trafficking or who have been the subject of an action to facilitate illegal immigration, who co-operate with the relevant authorities. Lastly, the preamble refers to the UN Convention on organised crime and its protocols.

3.15   The convention merits close attention, given its recent ratification by the UK. It sets out in detail how the state is to implement its obligations, in a clear framework of prevention, prohibition and protection of the human rights of victims. The implementing steps came into force on 1 April 2009.[26]

Definition of trafficking

3.16   The definition of trafficking in article 4 of CETS 197 is taken from article 3 of the Trafficking Protocol to the UN Convention on organised crime. Article 4 provides:

> a 'Trafficking in human beings' shall mean the recruitment, transportation, transfer, harbouring or receipt of persons, by means of the threat or use of force or other forms of coercion, of abduction, of fraud, of deception, of the abuse of power or of a position of vulnerability or of the giving or receiving of payments or benefits to achieve the consent of a person having control over another person, for the purpose of exploitation. Exploitation shall include, at a minimum, the exploitation of the prostitution of others or other forms of sexual exploitation, forced labour or services, slavery or practices similar to slavery, servitude or the removal of organs;
>
> b The consent of a victim of 'trafficking in human beings' to the intended exploitation set forth in subparagraph (a) of this article shall be irrelevant where any means set forth in subparagraph (a) have been used;
>
> c The recruitment, transportation, transfer, harbouring or receipt of a child[27] for the purpose of exploitation shall be considered 'trafficking in human beings' even if this does not involve any of the means set forth in subparagraph (a) of this article ...

Importantly, the convention frees the definition from its moorings in transnational organised crime, since it applies to all forms of

---

26   See chapter 8.
27   Defined as any person under 18.

trafficking in human beings, whether national or transnational, whether or not connected with organised crime.[28] It also contains important guidance on the concept of vulnerability:

83. By abuse of a position of vulnerability is meant abuse of any situation in which the person involved has no real and acceptable alternative to submitting to the abuse. The vulnerability may be of any kind, whether physical, psychological, emotional, family-related, social or economic. The situation might, for example, involve insecurity or illegality of the victim's administrative status, economic dependence or fragile health. In short, the situation can be any state of hardship in which a human being is impelled to accept being exploited. Persons abusing such a situation flagrantly infringe human rights and violate human dignity and integrity, which no one can validly renounce.

84. A wide range of means therefore has to be contemplated: abduction of women for sexual exploitation, enticement of children for use in paedophile or prostitution rings, violence by pimps to keep prostitutes under their thumb, taking advantage of an adolescent's or adult's vulnerability, whether or not resulting from sexual assault, or abusing the economic insecurity or poverty of an adult hoping to better their own and their family's lot. However, these various cases reflect differences of degree rather than any difference in the nature of the phenomenon, which in each case can be classed as trafficking and is based on use of such methods.

...

87. Under the definition, it is not necessary that someone [has] been exploited for there to be trafficking in human beings. It is enough that they have been subjected to one of the actions referred to in the definition and by one of the means specified 'for the purpose of' exploitation. Trafficking in human beings is consequently present before the victim's actual exploitation.

...

97. Article 4(b) states: 'The consent of a victim of "trafficking in human beings" to the intended exploitation set forth in sub-paragraph (a) of this article shall be irrelevant where any of the means set forth in sub-paragraph (a) have been used'. The question of consent is not simple and it is not easy to determine where free will ends and constraint begins. In trafficking, some people do not know what is in store for them while others are perfectly aware that, for example, they will be engaging in prostitution. However, while someone may wish employment,

---

28   Article 2. The Explanatory Report makes it clear at #61 that it was intended to enhance the protection afforded by the UN Palermo Protocol.

and possibly be willing to engage in prostitution, that does not mean that they consent to be subjected to abuse of all kinds. For that reason, Article 4 (b) provides that there is trafficking in human beings whether or not the victim consents to be exploited.

Explanatory Report-Action against Trafficking in Human Beings,
16. V. 2005

3.17   The Explanatory Report also refers to jurisprudence of the Strasbourg Court, and to other Council of Europe legislative instruments, when considering the definition.[29]

Content of the convention

3.18   The convention is then divided into four further chapters relating to prevention, co-operation and other measures (Chapter II); measures to protect and promote the rights of victims, guaranteeing gender equality (Chapter III), substantive criminal law (Chapter IV); and investigation, prosecution and procedural law (Chapter V).

Measures of prevention and co-operation

3.19   Chapter II includes measures of national cooperation (5.1), effective awareness raising policies and programmes (5.2), the promotion of a human rights based approach (5.3), appropriate measures to enable migration to take place legally, in particular through the dissemination of accurate information by relevant offices, on the conditions enabling the legal entry into and stay on its territory (5.4), steps to reduce children's vulnerability by creating a protective environment[30] for them (5.5) with a requirement to involve non-governmental organisations committed to the prevention of trafficking in human beings (5.6). By article 6, the convention requires state parties to adopt or strengthen legislative, administrative, educational, social, cultural or other measures to discourage demand. Article 7 provides for border measures including the strengthening of border measures, and of cooperation between border agencies,

---

29   At 70–98.

30   106 of the Explanatory Report refers to the eight key components of a protective environment, as promoted by UNICEF: (1) protecting children's rights from adverse attitudes, practices, etc; (2) government commitment to realisation of rights; (3) open discussion of child protection issues; (4) enforced protective legislation; (5) the capacity of relevant individuals to protect children; (6) children's life skills, knowledge and participation; (7) a system for monitoring abuse cases; (8) programmes and services to enable child victims of trafficking to recover and reintegrate.

to tighten security and control of documents and article 9 provides for co-operation by the apparent issuing state where the validity of a document is in question.

Measures to protect and promote the rights of victims

3.20   Chapter III contains key provisions on protection of victims and promotion of their rights. Such steps are an essential element of a human rights approach. The chapter covers steps for initial identification of victims, in particular the training of state agencies in victim identification and assistance, including provisions for a stay on removal where there are reasonable grounds to believe that the person is a victim of trafficking in human beings and the correct approach in cases of children or where there is reason to believe that the victim is child (article 10), protection of private life (article 11), practical assistance to victims (article 12), the provision of a recovery and reflection period of at least 30 days (article 13), the provision of a renewable residence permit where the stay is necessary (a) owing to the persons personal situation or (b) for the purposes of their co-operation in investigation or criminal proceedings, or both (article 14), compensation and legal redress (article 15), co-operation in the repatriation and return of victims (article 16) and the promotion of gender equality (article 17).

3.21   The details of the victim protection and assistance provisions are worth setting out fully. Article 10 requires each state party to train competent authorities[31] in the identification of victims and to ensure that the relevant authorities co-operate with each other as well as with relevant support organisations. States parties are required to adopt legislative or other measures as may be necessary, in collaboration with other parties and with support organisations, to identify victims. States parties are required to ensure that if the competent authorities have reasonable grounds to believe that a person has been a victim of trafficking, that they will not be removed from its territory until the identification process has been completed by the competent authorities.[32] Where a victim's age is uncertain and

---

31   Paragraph 129 of the Explanatory Report states: 'By "competent authority" is meant the public authorities which may have contact with trafficking victims, such as the police, the labour inspectorates, customs, the immigration authorities and embassies or consulates. It is essential that these have people capable of identifying victims and channelling them towards the organisations and services who can assist them.'

32   Article 10.2.

where there are reasons to believe they are a child, they will be presumed to be a child and will be accorded special protection measures. Where the presumption is triggered, special protection measures are to be taken pending age verification.[33] As soon as an unaccompanied child is identified as a victim, the state party is required to provide for representation of the child by a legal guardian, organisation or authority which shall act in the best interests of the child; take the necessary steps to establish their identity and nationality. and make every effort to locate their family when this is in the best interests of the child.[34]

3.22   Each party is required to protect the private life and identity of the victim.[35] The specific requirements are that personal data is to be stored and used in conformity with the conditions provided for in the Council of Europe Convention for the protection of individuals with regard to automatic processing of personal data (CETS No 108). States parties are also required to adopt measures to ensure, in particular, that the identity, or details allowing the identification, of a child victim of trafficking are not made publicly known, through the media or by any other means, except in order to facilitate the tracing of family members or otherwise secure the well-being and protection of the child. States parties are also required to consider adopting, in accordance with article 10 of the Convention for the Protection of Human Rights and Fundamental Freedoms, measures aimed at encouraging the media to protect the private life and identity of victims through self-regulation or through regulatory or co-regulatory measures.

Assistance to victims

3.23   Article 12 requires each state party to adopt such legislative or other measures as may be necessary to assist victims in their physical, psychological and social recovery. It lists minimum assistance which must be provided to victims, which is:

(a) standards of living capable of ensuring their subsistence, through such measures as appropriate and secure accommodation, psychological and material assistance;
(b) access to emergency medical treatment;

---

33   Article 10.3.
34   Article 10.4.
35   Article 11.

(c) translation and interpretation services, when appropriate;

(d) counselling and information, in particular as regards their legal rights and the services available to them, in a language that they can understand;

(e) assistance to enable their rights and interests to be presented and considered at appropriate stages of criminal proceedings against offenders;

(f) access to education for children.

Article 12.3 also requires states parties to provide necessary medical and other assistance to victims lawfully resident within its territory who do not have adequate resources and need such help. Article 12.4 requires states parties to adopt the rules under which victims lawfully resident in its territory shall be authorised to have access to the labour market, to vocational training and education. Article 12.5 places emphasis on cooperation with NGOs, other relevant organisations and other elements of civil society engaged in assistance to victims. Importantly, article 12.6 requires states parties to adopt such legislative or other measures as may be necessary to ensure that assistance to a victim is not made conditional on his or her willingness to act as a witness. Finally, for the implementation of the provisions set out in the article, states parties must ensure that services are provided on a consensual and informed basis, taking due account of the special needs of persons in a vulnerable position and the rights of children in terms of accommodation, education and appropriate health care.[36] Article 13 requires state parties to provide a minimum recovery and reflection period. This must be of at least 30 days, when there are reasonable grounds to believe that the person concerned is a victim, although article 13.1 also refers to the need for the period to be sufficient for the person concerned to recover and escape the influence of traffickers and/or to take an informed decision on co-operating with the competent authorities. It is arguable, therefore, that if for some reason 30 days is not sufficient (for example, if recovery or access to advice takes longer), a greater period should be allowed for reflection. During the reflection period, whether it be 30 days or more, the convention provides that it shall not be possible to enforce any expulsion order against the person in question. That provision is without prejudice to the activities carried out by the competent authorities in all phases of the relevant national proceedings, and in particular when investigating and prosecuting

36   Article 12.7.

the offences concerned. During the reflection period, states parties are required to authorise persons concerned to stay in their territory. Article 13.3 provides that states parties are not required to observe the reflection period if grounds of public order prevent it or if it is found that victim status is being claimed improperly.

Renewable residence permit

3.24   A renewable residence permit is to be issued to victims if:

(a) the competent authority considers that the person's stay is necessary owing to their personal situation;

(b) the competent authority considers that their stay is necessary for the purpose of their cooperation with the competent authorities in investigation or criminal proceedings.

States are required to issue residence permits for children (where that is legally necessary) in accordance with the best interests of the child and, where appropriate, to renew it under the same conditions.[37] The non-renewal or withdrawal of a residence permit is subject to the conditions provided for in the internal law of the state party.[38] If a victim submits an application for another kind of residence permit, the state party concerned shall take into account that he or she holds, or has held, a residence permit in conformity with paragraph 1.[39] States parties, in accordance with their obligations under other international instruments including the 1951 Refugee Convention, are required to ensure that granting of a permit according to this provision shall be without prejudice to the right to seek and enjoy asylum.[40] Legal redress and compensation are provided for by article 15. The state party is required to ensure that victims have access, as from their first contact with the competent authorities, to information on relevant judicial and administrative proceedings in a language which they can understand.[41] The state party is required to provide, in its internal law, for the right to legal assistance and to free legal aid for victims under the conditions provided by its internal law.[42] The state party shall provide, in its

37   Article 14.2.
38   Article 14.3.
39   Article 14.4.
40   Article 14.5.
41   Article 15.1.
42   Article 15.2.

internal law, for the right of victims to compensation from the perpetrators.[43] The state party is required to adopt such legislative or other measures as may be necessary to guarantee compensation for victims in accordance with the conditions under its internal law,[44] for instance through the establishment of a fund for victim compensation or measures or programmes aimed at social assistance and social integration of victims, which could be funded by the assets resulting from the application of measures provided in article 23.[45]

Long-term solutions

3.25   Article 16 regulates the repatriation and return of victims. Any state party which is the sending state is required, with due regard to the victim's rights, safety and dignity, to facilitate and accept his or her return without undue or unreasonable delay.[46] When a party returns a victim to another state party, that return must be with due regard for the rights, safety and dignity of that person and for the status of any legal proceedings related to the fact that the person is a victim. Such return must preferably be voluntary.[47] A state party is required, at the request of a receiving party, to verify whether a person is its national or had the right of permanent residence in its territory at the time of entry into the territory of the receiving party.[48] In order to facilitate the return of a victim who is without proper documentation, the state party of which that person is a national or in which he or she had the right of permanent residence at the time of entry into the territory of the receiving party shall agree to issue, at the request of the receiving party, such travel documents or other authorisation as may be necessary to enable the person to travel to and re-enter

43   Article 15.3.
44   As against the traffickers, in civil law systems this is by way of a *partie civile*. However, the Explanatory Report makes it clear that the state is expected to guarantee compensation. It refers (#199) to the principles contained in the European Convention on the Compensation of Victims of Violent Crimes ETS, No 116, which is concerned with European-level harmonisation of the guiding principles on compensating victims of violent crime and with giving them binding force. European Union member states must also have regard to the Council Directive of 29 April 2004 on compensation of crime victims.
45   Article 15.4.
46   Article 16.1; cf article 8 of the Palermo Protocol.
47   Article 16.2.
48   Article 16.3.

its territory.[49] Each state party is required to adopt such legislative or other measures as may be necessary to establish repatriation and reintegration programmes, involving relevant national or international institutions and NGOs. The programmes should aim at avoiding re-victimisation.[50] Details of assistance available should also be provided.[51] Child victims must not be returned to a state if there is an indication, following a risk and security assessment, that such return would not be in the best interests of the child.[52] Article 17 refers to gender equality and requires the state party, in applying the measures in Chapter III, to aim to promote gender equality and use gender mainstreaming in the development, implementation and assessment of the measures. This is an important principle which runs through the convention, together with the necessity for a child-rights approach. This is in recognition of the over-representation of women among victims of trafficking. The convention commends a positive approach to gender equality, which is analogous to the positive duty to promote gender equality which arises in national law under the Sex Discrimination Act 1975.[53]

Substantive criminal law

3.26   Chapter IV is concerned with the substantive criminal law. Article 18 requires states parties to adopt such legislative and other measures as may be necessary to criminalise the conduct defined by the convention as trafficking. Article 19 requires the state party to consider adopting such legislative or other measures as may be necessary to criminalise the use of services which are the object of exploitation (article 4) with the knowledge that the person is a victim of trafficking in human beings. Article 20 requires states parties to adopt such legislative or other measures as may be necessary to establish as criminal offences the following conducts, when committed intentionally and for the purpose of enabling the trafficking in human beings:

(a) forging a travel or identity document;
(b) procuring or providing such a document;
(c) retaining, removing, concealing, damaging or destroying a travel or identity document of another person.

49   Article 16.4.
50   Article 16.5.
51   Article 16.6.
52   Article 16.7.
53   See 4.7–4.8.

Article 21 requires the state party to adopt such legislative or other measures as may be necessary to establish as criminal offences when committed intentionally, aiding or abetting the commission of any of the offences established in accordance with articles 18 and 20 of the convention as well as attempting to commit the offences in accordance with articles 18 and 20, paragraph a. Article 22 concerns corporate liability and requires the state party to adopt such legislative and other measures as may be necessary to ensure that a legal person can be held liable for a criminal offence established in accordance with this convention, when committed for its benefit by any natural person, acting either individually or as part of an organ of the legal person, who has a leading position within the legal person, based on:

(a) a power of representation of the legal person;
(b) an authority to take decisions on behalf of the legal person;
(c) an authority to exercise control within the legal person.

Thus, four conditions are required:

(1) an offence described in the convention must have been committed;
(2) the offence must have been committed for the entity's benefit;
(3) a person in a leading position – organisationally senior – must have committed the offence (including aiding and abetting); and
(4) the person must have acted on the basis of their powers.

3.27   In addition, the state party is required to take the measures necessary to ensure that a legal person can be held liable where the lack of supervision and control by a natural person referred to in paragraph 1 has made possible the criminal offence established in accordance with this convention for the benefit of that legal person by a natural person acting under its authority. Subject to the legal principles of the party, the liability of a legal person may be criminal, civil or administrative.[54] Such liability shall be without prejudice to the criminal liability of the natural persons who have committed the offence.[55] The offence of money laundering the proceeds of trafficking in human beings was considered but was dealt with separately through the Convention on Laundering, Search, Seizure and Confiscation of the Proceeds of Crime (ETS 141), a protocol which

54   Article 22.3.
55   Article 22.4.

requires that trafficking in human beings be treated as a relevant offence.[56]

3.28   Article 23 deals with sanctions and measures. It requires each state party to adopt such legislative and other measures as may be necessary to ensure that the criminal offences established in accordance with articles 18–21 are punishable by effective, proportionate and dissuasive sanctions. This means penalties involving deprivation of liberty which can give rise to extradition.[57] As to legal persons, the sanctions, whether criminal or non-criminal, must be effective, proportionate and dissuasive, and may be monetary sanctions.[58] The state party is required to adopt such legislative and other measures as may be necessary to enable it to confiscate or otherwise deprive the instrumentalities and proceeds of criminal offences (article 18/20 a) or property the value of which corresponds to such proceeds. The state party is required to adopt such legislative or other measure as may be necessary as may be necessary to enable the temporary or permanent closure of any establishment which was used to carry out trafficking in human beings, without prejudice to the rights of bona fide third parties or to deny the perpetrator, temporary or permanently, the exercise of the activity in the course of which this offence was committed.[59]

3.29   Aggravating circumstances are provided for by the convention and must be regarded as such in national law in the determination of penalty for the offences established in accordance with article 18.[60] They are where:

(a) the offence deliberately or by gross negligence endangered the life of the victim;

(b) the offence was committed against a child;

(c) the offence was committed by a public official in the performance of his or her duties;

(d) the offence was committed within the framework of a criminal organisation.[61]

The state party is required to adopt such legislative and other measures providing for the possibility to take into account final

---

56   Explanatory Report, 218–9.
57   Article 23.1.
58   Article 23.2.
59   Article 23.4.
60   Article 24.
61   Article 24.

sentences passed by another party in relation to offences established in accordance with this convention when determining the penalty.[62] In accordance with the basic principles of the national legal system, provision should be made for the possibility of not imposing penalties on victims for their involvement in unlawful activities, to the extent that they have been compelled to do so.

Investigation, prosecution and procedural law

3.30   Chapter V deals with investigation, prosecution and procedural law. The state party is required to ensure that investigations into or prosecution of relevant offences shall not be dependent on the report or accusation made by the victim, at least when the offence was committed in whole or in part on its territory.[63] The state party shall ensure that victims of an offence in the territory of a party other than the one where they reside may make a complaint before the competent authorities of their state of residence. The competent authority to which a complaint is made shall transmit it without delay to the competent authority of the territory in which the offence was committed. The complaint must be dealt with in accordance with the internal law of the state in which the offence was committed.[64] The state party must ensure, by legislative or other measures, in accordance with the conditions provided for by its internal law, to any group or foundation, association or NGO which aims at fighting trafficking in human beings or protection of human rights, the possibility to assist and/or support the victim with his or her consent during criminal proceedings concerning the offence established in accordance with article 18 of this convention.[65]

3.31   The state party is required to provide effective and appropriate protection from potential retaliation or intimidation in particular during and after investigation and prosecution of perpetrators, for:

(a) victims;

(b) as appropriate, those who report the relevant criminal offences[66] or who otherwise cooperate with the investigating or prosecuting authorities;

(c) witnesses who give testimony concerning relevant criminal offences;

---

62   Article 25.
63   Article 27.1.
64   Article 27.2.
65   Article 27.3.
66   Ie those defined in article 18.

(d) when necessary, members of the family of persons referred to in subparagraphs (a) and (c).[67]

The various kinds of protection may include physical protection, relocation, identity change and assistance in finding jobs.[68] A child victim must be afforded special protection measures taking into account the best interests of the child.[69] The state party is required to provide, where necessary, appropriate protection from potential retaliation or intimidation in particular during and after investigation and prosecution of perpetrators, for members of groups, foundation, associations or NGOs which carry out the activities set out in article 27, paragraph 3.[70] The state should also consider entering into bilateral or multilateral agreements with other states for the implementation of article 28.

3.32   Article 29 requires states to set up specialised persons or entities which shall be sufficiently independent to enable them to carry out their functions without undue pressure.[71] The state party is also required to adopt such coordinating measures as may be necessary, whether by the setting up of a coordinating body or otherwise.[72] The state party is required to provide or strengthen training by relevant officials in the prevention of and fight against trafficking in human beings, including human rights training. The training may be agency-specific and must, as appropriate, focus on: methods used in preventing such trafficking, prosecuting the traffickers and protecting the rights of the victims, including protecting the victims from the traffickers. Each state party is required to consider appointing a National Rapporteur or other monitoring mechanism.[73] As regards court proceedings, the convention refers to the European Convention and in particular article 6, and requires the state to adopt such legislative and other measures as may be necessary to ensure in the course of judicial proceedings: (a) the protection of victims' private life and, where appropriate, identity; (b) victims' safety and protection from intimidation in accordance with the conditions under its internal law and, in the case of child victims, by taking special care of children's needs and ensuring their right to special protection measures.

67   Article 28.1.
68   Article 28.2.
69   Article 28.3.
70   Article 28.4.
71   Article 29.1.
72   Article 29.2.
73   Article 29.4.

3.33   Article 31 deals with how jurisdiction is to be established. It is the only article in respect of which reservations may be made. The first and second bases of jurisdiction are territoriality and an extension of the principle to ships and aircraft. Thus, jurisdiction will be established when the offence is committed:

(a) in the state's territory; or
(b) on board a ship flying the flag of that state; or
(c) on board an aircraft registered under the laws of that state.

3.34   Article 31(1)(d) and (e) are the only parts of the convention in respect of which a declaration or reservation may be entered, at the time of signature or when depositing the instrument of ratification, acceptance, approval or accession, by a declaration addressed to the Secretary General of the Council of Europe.[74] They provide for jurisdiction to be established through the nationality principle, where the offence is committed:

(d) by one of the state's nationals or by a stateless person who has his or her habitual residence in its territory, if the offence is punishable under criminal law where it was committed or if the offence is committed outside the territorial jurisdiction of any state;
(e) against one of its nationals.

Reservations have been entered by some states to these provisions.[75]

3.35   The state party is required to adopt such measures as may be necessary to establish jurisdiction over the offences referred to in the convention, in cases where the alleged offender is present in its territory and it does not extradite him or her to another state party, solely on the basis of his or her nationality, after a request for extradition.[76] Where more than one state party claims jurisdiction over an alleged offence established in accordance with the convention, the parties involved shall, where appropriate, consult with a view to determining the most appropriate jurisdiction for prosecution.[77] The convention does not exclude any criminal jurisdiction exercised by a state party in accordance with internal law.[78]

---

74   Article 31.2.
75   http://conventions.coe.int/Treaty/Commun/ListeDeclarations.asp.
76   Article 31.3.
77   Article 31.4.
78   Article 31.5.

International co-operation and co-operation with civil society

3.36   Chapter VI sets out obligations to co-operate internationally and with civil society. Generally,[79] states parties are required to co-operate with each other through the convention, application of relevant international and regional instruments, agreed uniform or reciprocal arrangements and internal laws for the purpose of (a) prevention; (b) victim assistance and protection; (c) investigations or criminal proceedings.

3.37   As regards missing or endangered persons, where a state party has reason to believe that the life, the freedom or the physical integrity of a victim, witness or collaborator[80] is in immediate danger on the territory of another state, the state that has the information shall, in such a case of emergency, transmit it without delay to the latter so that protection measures can be taken.[81] The parties to the convention may consider reinforcing their cooperation in the search for missing people, in particular missing children, if the information leads them to believe that he or she is a victim of trafficking in human beings and may conclude bilateral or multilateral treaties to this end.[82] There are similar provisions requiring a state party to inform a requesting party of action taken or circumstances preventing action from being taken promptly or at all.[83] There are provisions allowing the impositions of conditions such as confidentiality.[84] Article 35 contains the important principle of cooperation with civil society, requiring each state party to encourage state authorities and public officials to cooperate with NGOs, other relevant organisations and members of civil society, in establishing strategic partnerships with the aim of achieving the purpose of the convention.

Monitoring mechanism

3.38   The group of experts on action against trafficking (GRETA) is named as the monitoring mechanism;[85] its members to be elected by the Committee of the States Parties. The Committee of the Parties[86]

---

79   Article 32.
80   Within the meaning of article 28.
81   Article 33.1.
82   Article 33.2.
83   Article 34.
84   Article 34.
85   Article 36.
86   Article 37.

shall be composed of the representatives of the Committee of Ministers of the Council of Europe of the member states parties to the Convention and representatives of the Parties to the Convention, which are not members of the Council of Europe. Article 38 provides for an evaluation procedure to be determined by GRETA. The convention does not affect the rights and obligations derived from the Protocol to the UN Convention against transnational organised crime[87] and other international instruments.[88] Proposals for amendments by a party must be communicated to the Secretary General of the Council of Europe and forwarded to members of the Council of Europe, signatories, states parties and any state which has signed or acceded to the convention. The opinion of GRETA will be given.[89]

Other provisions

3.39   Any state or the European Community may at the relevant time[90] specify the territory or territories to which the convention shall apply and may subsequently extend it.[91] Article 45 prohibits reservations to the convention apart from in respect of article 31.2. Any party may, however, denounce the convention by means of notification to the Secretary General of the Council of Europe.[92]

The European Union

3.40   The relationship between the Council of Europe Convention and the legal framework of the European Union is addressed within the Convention itself. Article 40(3) of the Convention CETS 197 provides that: 'Parties which are members of the European Union shall, in their mutual relations, apply Community and European Union rules in so far as there are Community or European Union rules governing the particular subject concerned and applicable to the specific case.'

3.41   Upon adoption of the convention, the European Community and the member states of the European Union made the following

---

87   Article 39.
88   Article 40.
89   Article 41.
90   See article 31.
91   Article 44.
92   Article 46.

declaration, explaining the disconnection clause in 40(3). The declaration, which forms part of the context to consider the clause, stated that the clause was necessary 'for those parts of the convention which fall within the competence of the Community/Union, in order to indicate that European Union Member States cannot invoke and apply the rights and obligations deriving from the Convention directly amongst themselves (or between themselves and the European Community/Union)'.

The European Community and the European Union

Relevant treaties

3.42   The consolidated version of the EC Treaty sets out the basis for and delineates the limits of European Union competence and involvement.[93] The treaty contains three sections, known as three pillars:

*   *Pillar I* – The 'Community' pillar concerns economic, social and environmental matters and is formed by Titles II (provisions on the European Community), III (provisions on the European Coal and Steel Community) and IV (provisions on the European Atomic Energy Community).

93   The main treaties constituting the consolidated version are: The Treaty establishing the European Coal and Steel Community, signed on 18 April 1951, in force 23 July 1952, expired 23 July 2002; The Treaty of Rome establishing the European Economic Community and the Treaty establishing the European Atomic Energy Community, both signed on 25 March 1957, in force 1 January 1958; The Merger Treaty, establishing a single Council and a single Commission, signed on 8 April 1965, in force 1 July 1967; The Treaty on European Union, signed at Maastricht on 7 February 1992, in force on 1 November 1993, creating a new – three-pillar – structure by adding intergovernmental co-operation on defence and on justice and home affairs to the existing 'Community' system. The Treaty of Amsterdam, signed on 2 October 1997, in force on 1 May 1999, was a Treaty amending and consolidating previous EU and EC Treaties. The Treaty of Nice, signed on 26 February 2001, in force 1 February 2003, reformed institutions in anticipation of enlargement of the Union. Treaties which have been signed but not ratified are the Treaty establishing a Constitution for Europe which was signed on 29 October 2004 but never ratified and the Treaty of Lisbon, which was signed on 13 December 2007 and will have to be ratified by all 27 member states before it can come into force.

This is supplemented by provisions on intergovernmental co-operation. These comprise:

- *Pillar II* – The 'Common Foreign and Security Policy' (CFSP) pillar (Title V); and
- *Pillar III* – The 'Police and Judicial Co-operation in Criminal Matters' (PJCC) pillar (originally called the 'Justice and Home Affairs' pillar) (Title VI).

Pillars II and III do not, unlike Pillar I, involve any transfer of sovereignty from national to community institutions, but remain matters of intergovernmental co-operation through co-operation by judicial and law enforcement bodies.

3.43   Measures to combat trafficking have so far been taken under Pillar III as measures of cooperation. However, they could arguably now be taken under Pillar I, given the transfer[94] of measures relating to visas and illegal immigration[95] and given the competence as regards the relevance of trafficking to labour rights and gender equality. The measures used to set out action against human trafficking have been joint actions, and latterly decisions[96] or framework decisions.[97] Joint actions are legal instruments of an intergovernmental nature adopted by the council. They are binding on member states. They are still used under Title V of the Treaty on European Union (Common Foreign and Security Policy – the second pillar). As regards Title VI (Police and Judicial Co-operation in Criminal Matters – the third pillar) joint actions have, since 1 May 1999 (when the Treaty of Amsterdam entered into force), been replaced by decisions and framework decisions. These are also legal instruments of an intergovernmental nature which are adopted by the council. A framework decision is binding on the member states as to the result to be achieved and leaves to the national authorities the choice of form and methods (like the directive in the community context, but without the direct effect). Decisions are used in the field of police and judicial cooperation in criminal matters for any purpose other than the approximation of the laws and regulations of the member state, which is the preserve of framework decisions. There is some debate as to the exact legal effect of framework decisions, which are an instrument introduced by the Amsterdam

---

94   Under the Treaty of Amsterdam.
95   See for example the proposed Directive COM(2007) 0249-C6-0143/2007-2007/0094(COD).
96   34(2)(c).
97   34(2)(b).

Treaty.[98] Framework decisions and decisions are binding on states as to the result to be achieved but leave to national authorities the choice of form and methods. They do not have direct effect, ie they cannot be relied on in national courts.[99] It has, however, been argued that implementing measures of those framework decisions do have direct effect.[100] Further, that framework decisions have indirect effect, ie that national measures taken in implementation must be interpreted in light of the obligations under the parent instrument. The uncertainty as to legal effect means that although framework decisions were intended as an instrument for the approximation of laws of the member states, in practice they have little success in achieving this aim since there is under-implementation as well as significant scope for variation.

3.44   The first significant call to action was in 1995, in the European Parliament's Resolution on Trafficking in Human Beings (A4-0326/95 OJ C 32/88). This was followed by the Joint Action 97/154/JHA of 24 February 1997 concerning action to combat trafficking in human beings and sexual exploitation of children (OJ L63 of 04.03.1997).[101] The Joint Action required member states to review national laws and practice and to make trafficking of human beings a criminal offence with dissuasive penalties. It also required effective enforcement including effective investigation, seizure of proceeds, judicial co-operation and the exchange of information on missing persons. It was amended and updated by the Framework Decision 2002/629/JHA, which followed the signing by the European Community, in December 2000, of the UN Convention against Transnational Organized Crime and the Protocols.[102]

The Council Framework Decision 2002/629/JHA of 19 July 2002 on combating trafficking in human beings[103]

3.45   The Council Framework Decision 2002/629/JHA contains three important elements: (1) a definition of trafficking; (2) provision for

98 First envisaged in the communication from the commission to the council and the European Parliament on Scoreboard to review progress on the creation of an area of 'Freedom, Security and Justice' in the European Union COM(2000) 167/final/2 (13/4/00).

99 Case 26/62 *Van Gend en Loos* [1983] ECR 1.

100 See article 34 and Craig and Barca – *EU law: text, cases and materials* OUP, 2003, p179.

101 See http://europa.eu/scadplus/leg/en/lvb/l33072.htm.

102 The framework decision was proposed by the European Commission on 22 January 2001.

103 Official Journal L 203 of 01.08.2002.

minimum penalties in certain circumstances; and (3) provisions on victim protection and assistance. In March 2009, the European Commission proposed a new council framework decision on preventing and combating human beings,[104] which will in due course repeal and replace the 2002 Framework Decision with an expanded version. Until then, the 2002 Framework Decision continues in force.

Definition of trafficking

3.46 The definition of trafficking is provided in article 1 of the framework decision. It is derived from the UN Protocol (see chapter 2) and defines trafficking as:

> the recruitment, transportation, transfer, harbouring, subsequent reception of a person, including exchange or transfer of control over that person, where:
>
> (a) use is made of coercion, force or threat, including abduction, or
> (b) use is made of deceit or fraud, or
> (c) there is an abuse of authority or of a position of vulnerability, which is such that the person has no real and acceptable alternative but to submit to the abuse involved, or
> (d) payments and benefits are given or received to achieve the consent of a person having control over another person
>
> for the purpose of exploitation of that person's labour or services, including at least forced or compulsory labour or services, slavery or practices similar to slavery or servitude, or
>
> for the purpose of the exploitation of prostitution of others or other forms of sexual exploitation, including in pornography.

Minimum penalties

3.47 Minimum penalties are dealt with in article 3(2)(b), which requires member states to set a minimum[105] of eight years' imprisonment when:

---

104 http://eur-lex.europa.eu/COMMonth.do?year=2009&month-03.

105 The prerequisite circumstances thus allow for a degree of discretion across member states as regards the imposition of the minimum penalty. In practice, the directive resulted in a range of penalties across member states ranging from six months to 20 years' imprisonment: 'EU action against trafficking of human beings: past, present and future', Obokata in *Immigration and criminal law in the European Union* (ed Guild and Minderhoud) Martinus Nijhoff, 2006 p397.

(a) the offence has deliberately or by gross negligence endangered the life of the victim;

(b) the offence has been committed against a victim who is particularly vulnerable. A victim shall be considered to have been particularly vulnerable at least when the victim was under the age of sexual majority under national law and the offence has been committed for the purpose of the exploitation of the prostitution of others, including pornography;

(c) the offence has been committed by use of serious violence or has caused particularly serious harm to the victims;

(d) the offence has been committed within the framework of a criminal organisation as defined in Joint Action 98/733/JHA,[106] apart from the personality level referred to therein.

Provisions on victim protection and assistance

3.48 The third element is victim protection and assistance. This is the most significant element. However, article 7(1) appears to envisage that the protection and assistance is conditional upon co-operation in the criminal process.

Lack of implementation

3.49 There has been uneven implementation of the framework decision, resulting in varying legal regimes across the EU on minimum penalties and on victim protection and assistance. Because of uncertainty as to its legal effect, it has not been possible to challenge defective or non-implementation in the courts. This is now mitigated through the European Convention CETS 197 (discussed earlier in this chapter).

Council Directive 2004/81/EC

3.50 The framework decision was followed by the Council Directive 2004/81/EC on the residence permit issued to third country nationals who are victims of trafficking in human beings or who have been the subject of an action to facilitate illegal immigration, who cooperate with the competent authorities 2004/81/EC of 29 April 2004.[107] The directive was adopted under article 63(3)(b) of the EC Treaty, which

---

106 Reference made to the Framework Decision 2001/220/JHA on standing of victims in criminal proceedings OJ L82/1 (22/3/2001).

107 OJ L 261 06/08/2004 P.0019-0023.

allows the council to adopt measures in relation to illegal immigration and residence. Like the framework decision, the directive flowed from the signing of the UN Convention and its protocols. The scope of the directive encompasses action against smuggling as well as trafficking. However, while member states are required to apply the directive in respect of victims of human trafficking, they are not so required in respect of those who have been the subject of an action to facilitate illegal immigration.[108] As to trafficking, the directive refers back to the 2002 framework decision.

3.51   In addition, two key features provide for victim protection by way of a reflection period and for short-term residence permits. The directive obliges member states to give a reflection period which would allow victims to decide whether or not they wish to cooperate with the authorities.[109] The directive leaves the duration and starting point of the reflection period to be determined according to national law, although the proposal mentioned a limit of 30 days. The reflection period operates as a stay on enforcement of any deportation order.[110] There is also an obligation on the member state to allow access to subsistence and to emergency medical treatment, and to attend to the special needs of the most vulnerable, and to provide translation and interpreting services and free legal aid, if established and under the conditions set by national law.[111] During or upon expiry of the reflection period, a renewable residence permit may be issued if certain minimum conditions are satisfied. These are that the stay will assist investigation or proceedings, that a clear intention to co-operate has been demonstrated and that links to the traffickers or smugglers have been severed.[112] The duration of the residence permit should be of at least six months and may be renewed if the minimum conditions continue to be satisfied.[113] It can be terminated if the conditions cease to apply or if relevant proceedings had terminated.[114] During the currency of the permit, victims may be granted employment, vocational training, education

108 Article 3(2).
109 Article 6.
110 Article 6, 7.
111 Article 7.
112 Article 8.
113 Article 8(3).
114 Articles 13 and 14.

and rehabilitation.[115] The directive allowed member states a considerable discretion as to the length of the reflection period and as to the grant of any short-term residence permits.

3.52 In addition, a protocol to the EC Treaty had provided for the UK[116] to be able to opt out of EU provisions on immigration, asylum and civil law and it did so in respect of this directive. Thus, the directive did not create any obligations as regards the UK. However, the two key obligations it contained to provide a reflection period and a short-term residence permit became the focus of campaigns on protection of victims, which then focused on the European Convention against Human Trafficking, adopted on 3 May 2005.

Other action

3.53 Much of the other action taken against trafficking has been by way of restrictive immigration control, eg visa requirements, carrier sanctions, fingerprinting, expulsion and action against illegal employment of third nationals. The risk of this approach is both of overreach and underreach: overreach in that it risks denying entry to those who may have grounds to stay under the Convention Relating to the Status of Refugees 1951; and underreach in that such an approach does not reach those victims of trafficking who enter the country legally. Instead restrictions on immigration promote the growth of an industry aimed at circumventing restrictive immigration policies. A more effective approach may be heralded by the draft directive providing for sanctions against employers of illegally staying nationals COM (2007) 249 final, proposed under Article

---

115 Articles 11 and 12. An early draft of the directive provided: 'Member States shall authorise the holders of a short-term residence permit to have access to the labour market, vocational training and education'. This draft was opposed, and the final wording of article 11 read: '1. Member States shall define the rules under which holders of the residence permit shall be authorised to have access to the labour market, vocational training and education. Such training shall be limited to the duration of the residence permit.' A similar position was taken in respect of the creation of social programmes for third party nationals, under article 12.

116 As well as Ireland and, in different terms, Denmark. The opt-outs are in Protocol of the EC Treaty, which took effect on 1 May 1999. The opt-out provides for the UK to decide whether to participate in discussion of legislation, which could go ahead without the participation of the UK. The UK could opt into legislation at a later stage, with the approval of the Commission.

63(3)(b) of the EC Treaty.[117] Another criticism of these provisions is that the protection and assistance of victims is seen not as an end in itself but as a means to the end of securing criminal convictions against traffickers, which ends once those convictions are secured. For example, the Framework Decision on Victims' Standing (applicable to victims of trafficking and referred to in the Framework Decision on Trafficking) sets out measures to protect and assist victims who assist the prosecution in criminal proceedings, such as the availability of legal aid, witness protection measures and compensation. However, there is no obligation on member states to provide any support at all once such proceedings are terminated.

Action plan, initiatives and technical assistance programmes

Tacis Programme

3.54   The Tacis programme (Technical Assistance Commonwealth of Independent States) was originally established under Council Regulation No 1279/96 of 25 June 1996 and renewed by Council Regulation No 99/2000 with an estimated budget of €3,138 million from 2000–06. While it covers a number of areas, such as economic development, environmental protection and rural economy, human trafficking has been identified as a priority.

EU Plan

3.55   The EU Plan[118] on best practices, standards and procedures for combating and preventing trafficking in human beings aimed at producing a co-ordinated policy approach across the European Union.[119] It has, however, not been recently updated.

STOP and Daphne programmes

3.56   The STOP programme ran from 1996–2000,[120] followed by STOP II which ran from 2001–2002. The aims of the programme were to develop a European policy and to encourage and fund information

---

117 See chapter 13.
118 Official Journal C311 of 9.12.2005.
119 See http://europa.eu/scadplus/eng/lvb/114168.htm.
120 Joint Action 96/700/JHA of 29 November 1996. See http://europa.eu/scadplus/leg/en/lvb/133015.htm.

sharing and development in the field of trafficking and child sexual exploitation. The Daphne initiative ran from 2000–2003, followed by Daphne II[121] and Daphne III.[122] The Daphne programme supports or funds the preventing and combatting of violence against children, young people (ie those aged 12–25 years) and women. The programme includes commercial sexual exploitation and human trafficking. Projects must cover at least two member states. Projects include identification of good practice, research, training, and treatment and support programmes.

---

121 2004–2008. Decision No 803/2004/EC. See http://europa.eu/scadplus/leg/en/ lvb/l33299.htm.

122 2007–2113. Decision No 779/2007/EC. See http://europa.eu/scadplus/leg/en/ lvb/l33600.htm.

National law and practice

Key points

- International law on human trafficking is not directly effective in the national sphere. However, this principle is not significant in practice since many international conventions may be relied upon through the Human Rights Act 1998 or in other ways.
- European Union law is directly effective in the national sphere.
- The Human Rights Act 1998 sets out a duty on all public authorities to act compatibly with the rights of the European Convention on Human Rights. This includes article 4. Courts have an interpretative duty.
- Public authorities must also adopt a gender equality approach in accordance with article 17 of CETS 197 and comply with their gender and race equality duties.
- Article 35 of CETS 197 requires an approach by the state which is not only multi-agency but involves partnership with non-governmental organisations (NGOs) and with civil society.
- The UK Human Trafficking Centre adopts this partnership approach as well as providing a specialist service.
- The UK launched an Action Plan on 23 March 2007. The Action Plan will be updated annually.
- A National Referral Mechanism provides a formal framework for the identification of victims.

4.1   This chapter is concerned with the law and practice on human trafficking within the UK national sphere. There are two aspects to national implementation of the UK's obligations to prohibit and prevent trafficking and to protect its victims. The first is how human trafficking is defined and prohibited: the legal framework. The most serious examples of human trafficking were already prohibited by the common law. However, specific prohibitions add clarity to the prohibition on human trafficking. The following three chapters describe the specific criminal offences as they relate to trafficking for sexual exploitation, trafficking of children and trafficking for labour exploitation. Victim rights in the courts and relevant rights and civil litigation are then considered in subsequent chapters. The second aspect is how the law is enforced in practice.

Law

4.2   In the absence of a constitutional framework or any developed national public or human rights law in this area, advocates for victims of trafficking may wish to rely on some of the international and regional law referred to in chapters 2 and 3 to delineate the scope of the obligations which the state has to victims to protect them against non-state actors.

4.3   With the exception of European Union law, these do not have automatic force in UK domestic law. However, this is unlikely to present a significant difficulty.[1] The Human Rights Act 1998,[2] in particular Article 4 in Schedule 1, provides the gateway for reliance on International Labour Organization (ILO) conventions.

Human Rights Act 1998

4.4   From 2 October 2000, the European Convention on Human Rights has been given further effect in the UK, through the Human Rights Act 1998. Most, but not all, of the convention rights are set out in Schedule 1 to the 1998 Act. The 1998 Act gives effect to the European convention rights in a number of ways:

(1) A court or tribunal which is determining a question which has arisen in connection with a convention right to take into account any judgment, decision, declaration or advisory opinion of the European Court of Human Rights; or decision of the Committee of Ministers under article 46: s2(1).

(2) There is an interpretative obligation on all courts and tribunals to read and give effect to primary and secondary legislation in a way which is compatible with the convention rights, so far as it is possible to do so: s3(1).

(3) Where primary legislation is incompatible with a convention right (and cannot be read compatibly), a court of record may make a declaration of incompatibility: s4(1) and (2). As a matter of law, this does not prevent the continuing validity of the legislation in question.

(4) Where secondary legislation is incompatible with a convention right (and cannot be read compatibly), it may be held to be invalid

---

1   For a general discussion, see Shaheed Fatima, *Using international law in domestic courts*, Hart Publishing, 2005.

2   See 4.6.

unless a provision of primary legislation prevents removal of the incompatibility: s4(3) and (4).

(5) It is unlawful for a public authority to act in a way which is incompatible with a convention right: s6(1). The 1998 Act does not define 'public authority'. Government departments, local authorities, the police and other public bodies are all public authorities. Section 6(3) of the 1998 Act includes 'any person certain of whose functions are functions of a public nature'.[3] This second category also falls within the 1998 as regards its public functions. Public functions should be generously interpreted: per Lord Nicholls in *Aston Cantlow and Wilmcote with Billesley Parochial Council v Walbank*.[4]

(6) A person who claims that a public authority has acted (or proposes to act) in a way which is made unlawful by s6(1) and of which he or she is or will be the victim may either bring freestanding proceedings in the appropriate court or may rely on the convention right or rights concerned in any legal proceedings.

(7) A claim may include a claim for damages if the court has power to award damages.[5] Such proceedings must be brought within a year of when the act took place, unless the relevant procedure (eg judicial review) has a shorter time limit.[6]

(8) The Act provides for the making of remedial orders by Ministerial Order following the making of a declaration of incompatibility: s10 and Schedule 2.

4.5   Where such reliance is not possible (for example, where the international obligation is not relevant to article 4), international obligations on human trafficking may still be relied on in national courts through the following arguments:

(1) There is a presumption that the state will act compatibly with its international obligations. *R v Secretary of State for the Home Department, ex p Venables*[7] per Lord Browne-Wilkinson: 'The [CRC] has not been incorporated into English law. But it is legitimate

---

3   This is intended to expand, not restrict, the categories of public authority: Home Secretary, *Hansard* HC 24 November 1997, Col 811.

4   [2004] 1 AC 546.

5   See further chapter 10. In practice, this means the County Court or the High Court.

6   There is a discretion to extend time if just and equitable: s7(5)(b).

7   [1998] AC 407 (HL), 499B–F.

in considering the nature of detention during Her Majesty's pleasure ... to assume that Parliament has not maintained on the statute book a power capable of being exercised in a manner inconsistent with the treaty obligations of this country.' This is particularly the case with an obligation relating to human trafficking which is a modern form of slavery, which itself is part of jus cogens.

(2) An international treaty may become part of national law in one of the following ways where national legislation which purports to give effect to it is enacted. This may be by express reference or by evidential nexus[8] or by the fact of the same subject matter.

(3) Ratification without more may not give rise to a legitimate expectation that the international obligations will be enforceable in the national sphere. The argument that a legitimate expectation arises on ratification seems to have run its course: *Tavita v Minister for Immigration;*[9] *Minister for Immigration and Ethnic Affairs and Teo* (1995); *R v Secretary of State for the Home Department, ex p Ahmed and Patel.*[10] The cases conclude that ratification of itself is not sufficient but statements by the government at the time of ratification may do so:[11] *R v Home Secretary ex p Launder.*[12]

(4) Relevant words may be construed by reference to international instruments containing the same words or concepts.

4.6   In UK law, unincorporated treaties provide evidence of (and in many cases, precision about) what the common law standard on fundamental rights is, or becomes.[13] Unincorporated treaties may be consulted in so far as they proclaim, reaffirm or elucidate the content of those human rights that are generally recognised throughout the European family of nations, in particular the nature or scope of those fundamental rights that are guaranteed by the European Convention, notwithstanding that they are not legally binding in domestic law and they are not sources of law in the strict sense.[14]

---

8   As with the Children Act 1989.

9   [1994] 2 NZLR 257.

10 [1999] Imm AR 22.

11 See, for instance, the clear intention to give domestic effect to CETS 197.

12 [1997] 1 WLR 839.

13 Per Lord Steyn in *R (Mullen) v Secretary of State for the Home Department* [2004] UKHL 18 [2005] 1 AC 1 at 26: 'Gradually a fundamental human right to compensation for miscarriages of justice evolved.'

14 *R (Howard League for Penal Reform) v Secretary of State for the Home Department* [2002] EWHC 2497 (Admin) [2003] 1 FLR 484 at 51.

Public authorities duties: gender and race equality

4.7   Article 17 of Convention CETS 197 requires the state, in applying its victim-protection measures, to promote gender equality and to use gender mainstreaming, in the development, implementation and assessment of the measures. At its minimum, this requires a gender sensitive approach – for example, through the use of female interviewers in cases of sexual exploitation. However, it goes beyond that to require positive promotion of gender equality.

> The main aim of Article 17 is to draw attention to the fact that women, according to existing data, are the main target group of trafficking in human beings and to the fact that women, who are susceptible to being victims, are often marginalised even more before becoming victims of trafficking and find themselves victims of poverty and unemployment more often than men. Therefore, measures to protect and promote the rights of women victims of trafficking must take into account this double marginalisation, as women and as victims. In short, these measures must take account of the social reality to which they apply, mainly that society is composed of women and men and that their needs are not always the same.
>
> *Explanatory Report to CETS 197* at 210

4.8   This is reflected in national law in the positive duty to promote gender equality in s76A and 76B of the Sex Discrimination Act 1975.[15] Similar duties exist in relation to race and equality.[16] Public authorities should now carry out equality impact assessments of any new policy, where the requirement of equality will have weight in proportion to its relevance to the policy. The impact of a proposed policy should be considered before it is adopted: *R (Elias) v Secretary of State for Defence* [2006] EWCA Civ 1293; [2006] WLR 321. In considering the impact, the authority must assess the risk and extent of any adverse impact and the ways in which such risk may be eliminated. Such an assessment should form part of the decision rather than an ex post facto exercise: *R (BAPI v another) v Secretary of State for the Home Department and the Secretary of State for Health.*[17] The duty to promote equality may require a targeted approach in order to act more effectively within ethnic minority communities

---

15   As inserted by ss84–85 of the Equality Act 2006.

16   Race Relations Act 1976 s71. Other more or less relevant equality strands are disability, gender identity, disability, religion or belief, sexual orientation and age.

17   [2007] EWCA Civ 1139 at 2–3.

where there is a particular problem: *The Queen (on the application of Kaur and Shah) v London Borough of Ealing*.[18] In addition to the general duty to promote equality which all public authorities have, there is also a more specific duty to promote equality which only specified public authorities have. The key question will often be whether in certain groups, a particular problem is higher, not what the overall number is as between different groups: *Kaur* 45. Thus, if trafficking occurs disproportionately highly amongst migrants, this justifies a targeted approach. If a change of policy is likely to impact adversely upon migrant domestic workers, almost all of whom are female, thought would have to be given as to whether the change can be justified in light of the gender equality duty. In practice, many equality impact assessments are not as careful as they should be.

Practice

4.9   The second aspect concerns how human trafficking is identified and the prohibition is enforced: the law in practice. This requires, in addition to prohibition, detection and punishment, focus on protection of victims and preventive steps. Effective state action depends upon good multi-agency working, including cross-agency communication and co-ordination. Getting this structure right is the most basic part of action against human trafficking. In its absence, genuine victims can be missed through belated or no action.

> **Operation Pentameter 2: An example of multi-agency working**
> Police led operation against trafficking for sexual exploitation with the participation of SOCA, UKHTC, HMRC, CPS, UK Border Agency, Home Office, Scottish Government and Crown Office, Northern Ireland Office and non governmental organisations including the POPPY Project and TARA in Scotland. Note that the figures relate to arrests, not charges or convictions.
> The operation focused on:
> - Rescuing and protecting victims;
> - Arresting, disrupting and bringing offenders to justice;
> - Pursuing the financial assets of traffickers;
> - Improving knowledge about the nature and scale of human trafficking in the UK; and
> - Maintaining and enhancing existing good work to tackle this area of criminality.

18   [2008] EWHC 2062.

99 people arrested for trafficking offences
13 people arrested for rape
179 people arrested for brothel offences
63 people arrested for money laundering offences
121 people arrested for immigration offences
34 people arrested for drugs related offences
Other offences charged include: kidnap (3); unlawful/false imprisonment (5); fraud/forgery (8); assault (3); perverting the course of justice (5); theft (1), obstructing the police (2)[19]
84 victims

The operation also involved research into the nature and extent of trafficking for labour exploitation. This involved a pilot set up through partnership working with the UK Border Agency, the Gangmaster Licensing Agency, the Department for Work and Pensions, Her Majesty's Revenue and Customs, the Ministry of Justice, the Department for Business, Enterprise and Regulatory Reform, the Department for Communities and Local Government, the Serious Organised Crime Agency, the Association of Chief Police Officers, and the Health and Safety Executive. Key non governmental organisations involved or consulted with include Kalayaan, the International Labour Organisation, Migrant Helpline, the POPPY Project, and Anti-Slavery International.

4.10   It is essential to have a mechanism whereby once it has been identified that someone *may* be a victim, that person is referred to a decision-making body and consequential decisions on victim protection are taken. Specialists are rarely the first point of contact with victims: in an early sex trafficking case, the victim ran onto Green Lanes in London and flagged down a police car. In a recent labour trafficking case, ex-employees called the police to complain about a GLA (Gangmaster Licensing Authority) licensed employer. This requires good awareness among, and communication from, those people who may come across, and thus be in a position to identify, victims. These may include NHS-employed doctors, nurses and other health workers, immigration officials, police officers and social workers and others. It will also include NGOs and individuals (including private practitioners such as lawyers and doctors). Effective detection and elimination requires co-operation between the state and non-state actors, including employers, unions, NGOs, medical and legal professionals and other members of civil society.

4.11   Identification involves a mechanism for referral to the relevant authority for victim protection by the state. This process is sometimes

19   Source: 2008 UK Action Plan.

referred to (eg in the OSCE Action Plan, though not in Convention CETS 197) as a National Referral Mechanism. The OSCE defines a National Referral Mechanism as a 'co-operative framework by which state actors fulfil their obligations to promote and protect the human rights of trafficked victims, coordinating their efforts in a strategic partnership with civil society'. This approach requires co-operation with people and communities as well as cross-agency co-operation and action. A similar approach of co-operation and strategic partnerships is required by article 35 of Convention CETS 197.[20]

4.12   This co-operative approach has been applied, though not entirely satisfactorily, in the UK.

UK Action Plan

4.13   Government policy, including specific action points, are set out in the Action Plan on Tackling Human Trafficking.[21] This is intended to be a living instrument which is updated annually. The first action plan was published on 23 March 2007. The second one, which updates and replaces the first, was published on 2 July 2008. The action plan refers to and sometimes draws on the Action Plan to Combat Trafficking in Human Beings adopted by the Organisation for Security and Co-operation in Europe (OSCE). It is issued jointly by the Home Office (for Scotland and Wales) and by the Scottish Government.[22] The action plan is divided into four chapters, which in turn address prevention, investigation, law enforcement and prosecution, protection and the specific aspects of child trafficking.[23] It is intended to reflect a multi-agency, co-operative approach. It sets out very specifically steps to be taken pursuant to the policy aims it describes.

---

20   Described in chapter 3.
21   Full text accessible at www.ukba.homeoffice.gov.uk. This follows the format of the EU Action Plan.
22   The plan is not co-written by the Northern Ireland Office. Some action points apply to Northern Ireland in any event. Northern Ireland agencies participated in Pentameter 2.
23   The lacunae in the action plan as regards child protection are identified and set out in *Rights here: rights now*, UNICEF and ECPAT (2007) chapter 3 pp16–20. These lacunae concern the appointment of a guardian, age determination, best interests and the principle of participation. This gap may be remedied with the withdrawal of the reservation to the CRC. These issues are dealt with in detail in chapter 6.

UK Human Trafficking Centre

4.14   A significant step towards a multi-agency approach is the UK Human Trafficking Centre (UKHTC), based in Sheffield and opened on 3 October 2006. The UKHTC co-ordinates and provides expertise to other agencies of the state. It has moved beyond its initial sole focus on co-ordination between police forces to co-ordination of other state agencies including prosecution and health and law enforcement, lawyers and judiciary. There is co-ordination not only through case contact but through thematic working groups.

The National Referral Mechanism

4.15   Convention CETS 197 requires victims of trafficking to be identified as such by trained, qualified staff within 'the competent authority' (ie one which has competence to make the decision in question). The convention does not require this to be one authority for all instances of identification and anticipates that the term covers a variety of public authorities. However, the UK Government has interpreted this as meaning one competent authority.

4.16   Under plans published in December 2008 (see flow charts on pp88 and 89) the UKBA and the UKHTC share responsibilities for determining whether there are reasonable grounds to believe that someone is a victim of trafficking in human beings, and thus able to access a range of support and protection.[24] The mechanism came into effect from 1 April 2009 and it is not yet clear how it works in practice. There has been criticism of what appears to be a model which is at once over-centralised (there is no reason why a first responder could make a decision on whether there are reasonable grounds which justify immediate short-term protection) and also leaves uncertainty on the respective roles of the UKHTC and the UKBA. How effectively this model will work will depend upon the willingness to seek expert recommendations (for example on identification of child victims) and to accept those recommendations. The UKHTC has pioneered a partnership approach, which should be followed through in the identification process. Guidance on a partnership approach is fully set out by the Organization for Security and Co-operation in Europe in its 2004 Handbook on National Referral Mechanisms.[25] The handbook defines a National Referral Mechanism

---

24   See chapter 8.
25   See www.osce.org.

(p15) as 'a co-operative framework through which state actors fulfil their obligations to protect and promote the human rights of trafficked persons, co-ordinating their efforts in a strategic partnership with civil society.' An over-reliance on the UKBA, including the UKBA within the UKHTC, in a decision on identification (which is distinct from a decision on the consequences of that identification) would not be consistent with the approach set out by the OSCE.

Public information campaigns

4.17   Public information campaigns are part of an effective strategy, as explained by the UKHTC:

> As part of the fight against human trafficking it is important that we are all aware of the scale and nature of the problem. Whether as employers, professionals in health and social services or simply as members of the public we all have a role to play in being vigilant and maintaining a high level of alertness to the possibility of trafficking crimes going on in our communities.

> It is important that if you have any suspicions you should contact the Crimestoppers Helpline on **0800 555 111**. What to look out for:

> 1. **On a farm or in a factory ...**
>   - **Non-UK** nationals doing farm or factory work
>   - Poor or non-existent safety equipment
>   - Workers do not have suitable clothing for the work they are doing
>   - Workers live in **overcrowded** private rented accommodation. They don't know the address of where they live or work
>   - Minibuses pick up non-UK nationals at **unusual hours** of the day and night
>   - Bins at the accommodation are full of fast food packaging
>   - Workers may seem **fearful** and poorly integrated into the wider community
>   - They have no days off or holiday time
>   - Employers or someone else is holding their **PASSPORT** and legal documents

> 2. **Domestic labour ...**
>   - A foreign national adult or child who lives with a family nearby, possibly as a domestic servant or nanny
>   - The person is rarely allowed out of the house, unless their employer or guardian is with them
>   - They are subject to **abuse**, insults, threats or violence

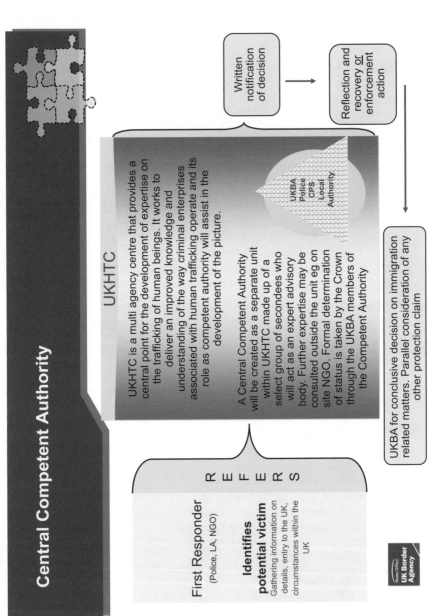

Central Competent Authority

UKHTC

UKHTC is a multi agency centre that provides a central point for the development of expertise on the trafficking of human beings. It works to deliver an improved knowledge and understanding of the way criminal enterprises associated with human trafficking operate and its role as competent authority will assist in the development of the picture.

A Central Competent Authority will be created as a separate unit within UKHTC made up of a select group of secondees who will act as an expert advisory body. Further expertise may be consulted outside the unit eg on site NGO. Formal determination of status is taken by the Crown through the UKBA members of the Competent Authority

UKBA
Police
CPS
Local
Authority

First Responder
(Police, LA, NGO)

Identifies potential victim
Gathering information on details, entry to the UK, circumstances within the UK

R
E
F
E
R
S

Written notification of decision

Reflection and recovery **or** enforcement action

UKBA for conclusive decision on immigration related matters. Parallel consideration of any other protection claim

UK Border Agency

Reproduced by kind permission of Bob Jones, UK Border Agency.

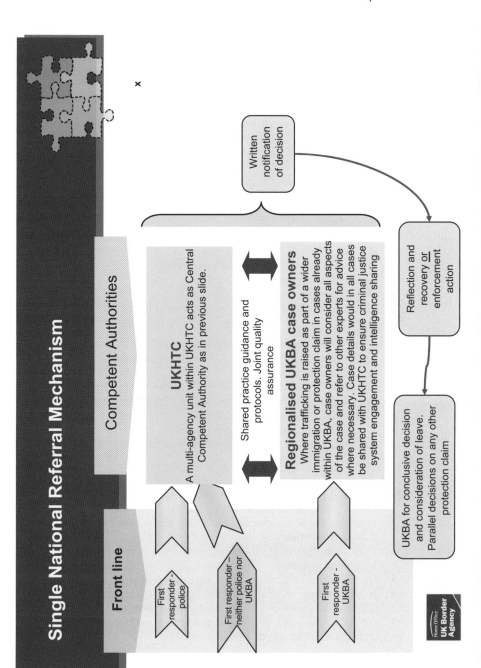

- They have no private space or a proper place to sleep i.e. on the floor or sofa
- They have a **poor diet** or are given the family's leftover food to eat
- If they are a child, they may have poor attendance at school, no access to education and no time to play
- The person does not **interact** much with the family

3. **In a sauna or massage parlour ...**
   - The women is a foreign national
   - She appears to be **unhappy and unwilling to perform sexual acts**
   - She is **frightened** or in physical **pain**
   - The women sees a large number of clients each day/night
   - She is able to keep little, or none, of the money she receives from clients
   - 'Special' services are offered including unprotected sex, often at a **low price**
   - She doesn't smile and is **reluctant** to cooperate
   - Food is paid for by another person
   - She has little or no time off
   - She may only know how to say sex-related words in English

1. **If you are traveling ...**
   - A non-UK national child is **travelling alone**
   - The child does not seem to have many possessions but does have a mobile phone
   - The child is not traveling to the UK to meet his or her parent or guardian
   - The child is **suspicious of adults**
   - They are very **afraid of being deported**
   - They may show signs of **inappropriate or sexualised behaviour** towards men

2. **On your high street ...**
   - A young, elderly or disabled foreign national who **begs in public places or on public transport**
   - They may show obvious signs of being **abused** such as **bruises, cuts or mutilation**
   - They seem fearful of adults (especially law enforcers) or their behaviour is jumpy
   - One adult is the guardian of a large group of children
   - A large group of adult or child beggars are **moved** daily to different locations but return to the same location every night
   - On public transport they **move as a group**, such as walking up and down the length or a train or bus

3. **Children in a home ...**
   - A **teenage girl** meets an older male who becomes her boyfriend. Initially he flatters her, buys her gifts such as a

mobile phone, and introduces her to alcohol or drugs. He makes her feel incredibly special

- The man **controls** her more and more. He claims she owes him for drugs and forces her to do sexual favours as a means of payment
- **She is taken** from her family home and returned after varying lengths of time; her relationship with her family or guardians gradually becomes severed
- Pictures or films of her engaging in sex activities are used to make her feel **guilty**, fearful her family will find out. Her 'boyfriend' uses this to control her, making her sleep with his friends
- He takes her to different flats (even in different towns or cities), getting her to sleep with different men
- She may not know he is taking **payment** from these men either in money or illegal drugs

Prevention: steps in sending states and steps to deal with demand

4.18   The UK is generally a destination state. The UK funds projects[26] in sending states (from where the supply of victims starts) focused on prevention of trafficking. There are also bilateral agreements with other states. It is not the intention of this book to examine such preventive projects in detail other than to signal their existence. Long-term preventive steps can also be taken in a destination state, through addressing the demand which creates the trafficking. Under Convention CETS 197,[27] the UK must consider making it a criminal offence to knowingly use the services of a victim of trafficking.

> 234. To be liable for punishment under Article 19, a person using the services of a trafficking victim must do so 'in the knowledge that the person is a victim of trafficking in human beings'. In other words the user must be aware that the person is a trafficking victim and cannot be penalised if unaware of it. Proving knowledge may be a difficult matter for the prosecution authorities. Similar difficulty arises with various other types of criminal law provision requiring evidence of some non-material ingredient of an offence. However, the difficulty of finding evidence is not necessarily a conclusive argument for not treating a given type of conduct as a criminal offence.

---

26   For example, the International Labour Organization (ILO) project in Myanmar: www.ilo.org.

27   Article 19.

235. The evidence problem is sometimes overcome – without injury to the principle of presumption of innocence – by inferring the perpetrator's intention from the factual circumstances. That approach has been expressly recommended in other international conventions. For instance, Article 6(2)(c) of the *Convention on Laundering, Search, Seizure and Confiscation of the Proceeds from Crime* [ETS No. 141] states that 'knowledge, intent or purpose required as an element of an offence set forth in that paragraph may be inferred from objective, factual circumstances.' Similarly, Article 6(2)(f), on criminalising the laundering of the proceeds of crime, of the *United Nations Convention against Transnational Organized Crime* states: 'Knowledge, intent or purpose required as an element of an offence set forth in paragraph 1 of this article may be inferred from objective, factual circumstances'.

Explanatory Report 234 and 235

4.19   Steps to address demand have proved the most controversial. Debate continues over whether regulation (or regularisation or licensing) is more effective than criminalisation, in the field of both labour and sex trafficking.

CHAPTER 5

The criminal offence of trafficking for sexual exploitation

Key points

- Sections 57–59 of the Sexual Offences Act 2003 specifically prohibit trafficking for sexual exploitation, defined as (1) intentionally arranging or facilitating transfer of a person into, within or out of the UK; and (2) intending to do anything which will amount to a 'relevant offence' or believing that someone else is likely to do so.
- Coercion or force in the transfer is not a necessary ingredient of the offence, unlike under the UN Trafficking Protocol.
- What is a 'relevant offence' is defined in the 2003 Act and consists of a range of sexual offences.
- Trafficking for sexual exploitation may also be prosecuted using common law and immigration offences.
- Sections 57–59 have significant extraterritorial effects. In particular, the UK courts have jurisdiction over arrangement or facilitation of transfer, whether committed inside or outside the UK. The destination offence may be intended to occur anywhere in the world, provided it would be an offence if committed in the UK.

Women are attractive as an entry-level commodity for criminals. They can cross borders legally and they do not attract the attention of sniffer dogs. The initial outlay is a fraction of the sum required to engage in car theft; overhead costs are minimal; and, as a service provider, the commodity (a trafficked woman) generates income again and again. Just one woman can make £3000–£6000 per month for her trafficker. These calculations do not take into account the frightful reality of multiple rape and unspeakable exploitation. But neither the supplier (the gangster) nor the consumer (rich western Europeans) understand this relationship in anything other than economic terms.[1]

5.1   On one analysis, most trafficking for exploitation is for labour exploitation. Prostitution is nothing other than sex work, voluntary or involuntary. It is true that, historically, action against prostitution was set out in different legal instruments and, as a supposedly moral issue, was treated differently to labour trafficking. This would not of itself be a reason to continue the distinction. However, the offence of trafficking for sexual exploitation, although most commonly applied

1   Misha Glenny *McMafia: Crime without frontiers,* The Bodley Head, 2008 p30.

to prostitution, also covers exploitation unrelated to work, such as sexual exploitation or abuse (of an adult or child) within a private context. The UN Trafficking Protocol has referred to the two categories of labour trafficking and sex trafficking. The two forms of trafficking do merit different approaches and are therefore dealt with in two separate chapters in this book. This chapter deals with trafficking for the purposes of sexual exploitation.

Prohibition at common law or use of other criminal offences

5.2   Until 2002, offences of labour or sex trafficking were prohibited and prosecuted at common law (kidnap, false imprisonment, murder, manslaughter, rape and incitement to rape and related inchoate offences) as immigration offences or as offences relating to prostitution.

5.3   The most commonly charged immigration offence was (and is) s25 of the Immigration Act 1971, which, as amended by s143 of the Nationality, Immigration and Asylum Act 2002, provides that a person commits an offence if he does an act which facilitates the commission of a breach of immigration law by an individual who is not a citizen of the European Union and knows or has reasonable cause for believing that (i) the act facilitates the commission of a breach of immigration law and (ii) that the individual is not a citizen of the European Union. Section 25(4) gives the section extra-territorial effect but only in respect of certain categories of British national. On indictment, the maximum sentence is 14 years' imprisonment. The defect in the offence, so far as trafficking is concerned, is that it did not, and does not, distinguish between smuggling and trafficking of illegal entrants. Further, aggravating features set out by Lord Bingham in *R v Van Binh Le and Rudi Heinrich Stark*,[2] a case concerning assisting illegal entry, did not include ill-treatment of the entrants. This was remedied in the first significant consideration of appropriate sentence in trafficking cases: *A-G's Reference (No 6 of 2004) (Plakici)*.[3] A British Citizen of Albanian national origin had been sentenced to 10 years' imprisonment for seven counts of facilitating illegal entry, three counts of living on the

2   [1999] 1 Cr App R (S) 422.
3   [2004] EWCA Crim 1275; [2005] 1 Cr App R (S) 19, p83.

earnings of prostitution, three counts of kidnapping and one count of incitement to rape.[4] The Attorney-General referred the sentence to the Court of Appeal on the grounds that the sentence was unduly lenient. The defendant was aged 26 and of previous good character. The victims were seven young women and girls from Moldova and Romania. The women and girls were brought into the country on false promises of lawful work and in some cases held against their will until they agreed to work as prostitutes. The crime was brought to light when one of the women escaped and flagged down a police car in Green Lanes, North London. The offender's premises were searched and condoms, lubricants and guides to massage parlours were found. Sums totalling £204,396 had been deposited in bank deposits controlled by the offender over the last three years. The Court of Appeal held that 'the offender occupied a principal position in a well-organised and international enterprise concerned in the illegal trafficking of women into the United Kingdom'. The court did not consider 'that 10 years' imprisonment in total in any way adequately reflects the criminality in this case or the need for a substantial and deterrent sentence' and increased the total sentence to 23 years.

Specific prohibition in criminal law

Nationality, Immigration and Asylum Act 2002

5.4   Section 145 of the Nationality, Immigration and Asylum Act 2002 made it a criminal offence to traffic in prostitution. This offence was committed where there was (a) arrangement or facilitation of arrival in, travel within or departure from, the UK by a passenger; (b) intention to exercise control or prostitution by the passenger, whether in the UK or elsewhere or belief that someone else was likely to do so. Control over prostitution was statutorily defined as the exercise of 'control, direction or influence over the prostitute's movements in a way which shows that he is aiding, abetting or compelling the prostitution'. The maximum term of imprisonment on indictment was 14 years. The offence had extraterritorial application, which was set out in s146. The offence was committed in respect of anything done in the UK but also, wherever committed,

---

4   The offences occurred between July 2000 and 29 October 2002.

by (a) a British citizen; (b) a British overseas territories citizen; (c) a British national (overseas); (d) a British overseas citizen; (e) a person who is a British subject under the British Nationality Act 1981; or (f) a British protected person within the meaning of the 1981 Act. The offence came into force on 10 February 2003.

Sexual Offences Act 2003

5.5 The prohibition contained in the 2002 Act was soon replaced by provisions in the Sexual Offences Act 2003 (SOA 2003), which came into force on 1 May 2004.[5] Part 1 of the Act extends only to England and Wales, with the exception of ss15–24, 46–54, 57–60 (the trafficking provisions), 66–72, 78 and 79 which extend to Northern Ireland. Part 2 (save for ss93 and 123–129) applies to the whole of the UK. The trafficking provisions apply to England, Wales and Northern Ireland. In Scotland, trafficking for the purposes of prostitution is prohibited by section 22 of the Criminal Justice (Scotland) Act 2003. Sexual offences against children, including transnational offences, are prohibited by the Protection of Children and Prevention of Sexual Offences (Scotland) Act 2005.

5.6 In the white paper which preceded the SOA 2003, the government described the provisions of the 2002 Act as a 'stop gap measure' which needed to be updated to take account of the changes to the law on sexual exploitation. It was explicitly intended to implement the commitment to introduce new offences of trafficking for sexual exploitation agreed in the UN Protocol and the EU Framework Decision on Trafficking.[6]

5.7 The 2003 Act reformed the Sex Offences Act 1956 which was not intended to, and did not, fit offences of trafficking. It also brought trafficking within the framework of sexual offences where before it was dealt with as an immigration offence and restricted to trafficking for the purposes of prostitution. A further consequence is that conviction of a relevant sexual offence requires inclusion on the sex offenders register held by the police under the Sex Offenders Act 1997 and associated notification duties.

5.8 The offence of sex trafficking is set out in ss57–60C of the SOA 2003. The offence comprises three elements:

---

5 Sexual Offences Act 2003 (Commencement Order) 2004/874.

6 *Protecting the public, strengthening protection against sex offenders and reforming the law on sexual offences* Cmd 5668 www.archive2.official-documents.co.uk/document/c,56/5668/5668pdf.

(1) *The trafficking element.* This consists of the intentional arranging or facilitating of arrival in,[7] entry into,[8] travel within[9] or departure from[10] the UK. The statute covers the arranging and facilitating of movement, whether or not it is in breach of immigration law.

(2) *The sexual exploitation element* is the identification of a relevant offence, which is to be found either in the 2003 Act itself or in other related legislation. The relevant offence may be committed or intended to be committed in the UK or in any part of the world. The statute also covers offences committed abroad which would be relevant offences if they were committed in the UK.[11] It may be an offence committed by the person arranging or facilitating the movement, or by someone else. The offence need not actually be committed ('which, *if done*, will involve the commission of a relevant offence'). Thus, the overall offence of trafficking may be committed before any exploitation has taken place. Equally, it may occur after exploitation but on further transfer.

(3) The *mental element* of intention to commit a relevant offence in the future or alternatively belief that another person is likely to commit a relevant offence in the future.

The relevant sections are set out below and their common structure can be seen (emphasis added).

57. Trafficking into the UK for sexual exploitation

(1) A person commits an offence if he **intentionally arranges or facilitates the arrival in the United Kingdom of another person (B)** and either–

    (a) **he intends to do anything to or in respect of B, after B's arrival but in any part of the world, which if done will involve the commission of a relevant offence,** or

    (b) **he believes that another person is likely to do something to or in respect of B**, after B's arrival but in any part of the world, which if done will involve the commission of a relevant offence.

---

7   Section 57.
8   As inserted, with effect from 31 January 2008, by s31(3) of the UK Borders Act 2007.
9   Section 58.
10 Section 59.
11 Section 60(3).

58. Trafficking within the UK for sexual exploitation

(1) A person commits an offence if he intentionally arranges or facilitates travel within the United Kingdom by another person (B) and either–

    (a) he intends to do anything to or in respect of B, during or after the journey and in any part of the world, which if done will involve the commission of a relevant offence, or

    (b) he believes that another person is likely to do something to or in respect of B, during or after the journey and in any part of the world, which if done will involve the commission of a relevant offence.

59. Trafficking out of the UK for sexual exploitation

(1) A person commits an offence if he intentionally arranges or facilitates the departure from the United Kingdom of another person (B) and either–

    (a) he intends to do anything to or in respect of B, after B's departure but in any part of the world, which if done will involve the commission of a relevant offence, or

    (b) he believes that another person is likely to do something to or in respect of B, after B's departure but in any part of the world, which if done will involve the commission of a relevant offence.

5.9   The section differs from the offence in the 2002 Act in that it mirrors more closely the definition in the UN Protocol. Unlike in the UN Protocol, however, there is no requirement in the legislation to prove coercion or force in the transfer, although that is very relevant in sentencing. Essentially, the offence requires proof of transfer and proof of intention to commit a relevant offence or belief that a relevant offence will be committed. Most significantly, the destination activity is no longer simply controlled prostitution, but a range of sexual offences, defined in s60. Section 60 also provides for extraterritorial effect in two important respects.

Extraterritorial reach of prohibition on arranging and facilitating

5.10   Section 60(2)[12] provides that ss57–59 apply to anything done whether inside or outside the UK. This means that arranging or facilitating, whether done inside or outside the UK, and whether or not an offence in the state in which committed, will be caught by ss57–59.

---

12   As substituted by s31 of the UK Borders Act 2007, with effect (SI 2008/99) from 31 January 2008. This replaced the original s60(2) and (3) which restricted the extra-territorial reach to offences by British citizens, British overseas territories citizens, British Nationals (Overseas), British Overseas citizens, British subjects under the British Nationality Act 1981; or British protected persons within the meaning given by s50(1) of that Act.

All relevant crimes along the trafficking chain can thus be prosecuted before courts in the UK.

Extraterritorial reach of relevant (destination) offences

5.11　The other extraterritorial element arises under the definition of what a 'relevant offence' (the destination activity) is. This is set out in s60(1) which provides that the 'relevant offence' may be:

(a) an offence under Part 1 of the SOA 2003;
(b) an offence under s1(1)(a) of the Protection of Children Act 1978 (c37);
(c) an offence listed in Schedule 1 to the Criminal Justice (Children) (Northern Ireland) Order 1998;[13]
(d) an offence under article 3(1)(a) of the Protection of Children (Northern Ireland) Order 1978.[14]

These offences are those set out in the SOA 2003 and the offence of making pseudo-photographs. A destination offence which is an offence at common law which does not fall within s60(1) would not suffice. The extraterritorial element arises by virtue of s60(1)(e) which provides that the relevant offence also includes anything done outside England and Wales and Northern Ireland which is not an offence within any of paras (a)–(d) but would be if done in England and Wales or Northern Ireland.

5.12　Thus, provided the destination activity would be unlawful under s60(1)(a)–(d) if done in England, Wales or Northern Ireland, it is caught by the trafficking provisions, whether the offence would as a matter of fact have taken place inside or outside the UK. This means that transfer of a person out of the UK with the intention of for example forcing her to have sex without consent in another country will be caught by ss57–59.

Relevant offences: Part 1 of the SOA 2003

5.13　As mentioned above, Part 1 contains the substantive offences in the SOA 2003. Part 1 of the 2003 Act creates over 50 offences and represents the most significant overhaul of the law governing sexual offences since at least the Victorian period. Section 140 repeals or revokes much of the previous legislation listed in Schedule 7 to the Act. The SOA 2003 is intended to cover offences across the genders

---

13　SI 1998/1504 (N.I. 9).
14　SI 1978/1047 (N.I. 17).

and sexual orientations and the terminology is therefore neutral.[15] The SOA 2003 also brought in reforms on critical principles such as consent (for example, where the victim had a learning disability to the extent that they did not have the capacity to consent or where they are a child) and sexual autonomy. There is significant overlap between different offences and prosecutorial discretion is therefore significant. The Crown Prosecution Service (CPS) has published guidelines on the exercise of such discretion: Sexual Offences Act 2003: Legal Guidance (July 2004).[16]

5.14   The offences cover:

- rape;[17]
- sexual penetration and assault;[18]
- causing a person to engage in sexual activity without consent;[19]
- rape and other sexual offences against children under 13;[20]
- child sex offences (applying to children under 16);[21]
- abuse of a position of trust (involving positions of responsibility in respect of children under 18);[22]
- familial child sex offences;[23]
- offences against persons with a mental disorder impeding choice;[24]
- inducements to person with a mental disorder;
- sexual offences committed by care workers for persons with a mental disorder;[25]
- indecent photographs of children;[26]
- abuse of children through prostitution and pornography;[27]

---

15   Apart from rape as a principal.
16   See www.cps.gov.uk.
17   Section 1.
18   Sections 2–3.
19   Section 4.
20   Sections 5–8.
21   Sections 9–15.
22   Sections 16–24.
23   Sections 25–29.
24   Sections 30–33.
25   Sections 34–44.
26   Sections 45–46. There is an exception to liability where photographs are made for the purposes of the prevention, detection or investigation of crime, or for the purposes of criminal proceedings, in any part of the world or when it is a necessary exercise by an individual of their security functions: s46. This protects those reproducing such photographs from prosecution.
27   Sections 46–51.

- exploitation of prostitution;[28] and
- sex with an adult relative.[29]

These offences will cover forms of sexual exploitation with no commercial element, and forced marriages in some cases.[30]

Exploitation of prostitution

5.15   As mentioned above, trafficking may be for the purposes of sexual exploitation which is not prostitution. Sections 52 and 53 concern the exploitation of prostitution. Both are governed by the interpretation provisions of ss51 and 54. Section 54 defines 'gain' as (a) any financial advantage, including the discharge of an obligation to pay, or the provision of goods and services (including sexual services) gratuitously or at a discount; or (b) the goodwill of any person which is or appears likely, in time, to bring financial advantage. Section 51(2) defines a 'prostitute' as 'a person (a) who, on at least one occasion and whether or not compelled to do so, offers or provides sexual services to another person in return for payment or a promise of payment to A or a third person'; and 'prostitution' is to be interpreted accordingly.

5.16   Both s52 and s53 are directed at so called 'pimping'. Section 52 provides that a person commits an offence if the person intentionally causes or incites another person to become a prostitute in any part of the world, and he does so for, or in the expectation of, gain for himself or a third person. An allegation of this offence is triable either way. If tried on indictment, it is a class 3 offence. The maximum penalty on conviction is seven years' imprisonment. If convicted after summary trial, the maximum penalty is six months or a fine not exceeding the statutory maximum, or both. Section 53 provides that a person commits an offence if the person intentionally controls any of the activities of another person relating to that

---

28   Sections 52–53.
29   Sections 64–65.
30   For an interesting examination of the arguments for and against criminalisation in Clark and Richards 'The prevention and prohibition of forced marriages – a comparative approach' ICLQ, Vol 57, July 2008, pp501–528. The offence is probably more effectively dealt with through family law in the first instance. See generally the Forced Marriages (Civil Protection) Act 2007 and the power under the Family Law Act to make a Forced Marriage Protection Order which can be made by an interested party on an ex parte basis.

person's prostitution in any part of the world, and the person does so for, or in the expectation of, gain for himself or a third person. The offence is triable either way. Tried on indictment it is a class 3 offence and conviction on indictment carries a maximum penalty of imprisonment of seven years, and on summary conviction a maximum penalty of six months' imprisonment or a fine not exceeding the statutory maximum, or both.

5.17   The acts must be committed in England and Wales to be punishable under the SOA 2003, since the extraterritorial provisions in s72 do not apply to ss52 and 53. However, the offence under s53 may relate to work by a prostitute anywhere in the world but the control must take place in the UK. In *R v Drew*[31] at Southwark Crown Court, December 2006, HHJ Rivlin held that 'control' was an ordinary term which ranged from compulsion to any form of influence over another person in connection with a particular activity. It could include ordering, directing and instructing. The fact that the prostituted person might consent to control might affect sentence but it did not affect guilt. Specific activities to be controlled might include days and hours of work, place of work, price to be charged, services to be offered, clothing and commission.

Sentencing guidelines for sex trafficking

5.18   The offence is triable either way. If the defendant is convicted in a magistrates' court, the offence is punishable by six months' imprisonment or by the maximum fine. On conviction on indictment, the maximum penalty is 14 years' imprisonment. The Sentencing Guidelines Council issued definitive guidelines in April 2007[32] which every sentencing court must have regard to.[33]

Factors to take into consideration

1. The sentences for public protection *must* be considered in all cases. They are designed to ensure that sexual offenders are not released into the community if they present a significant risk of serious harm.

---

31   No relation.
32   See www.sentencing-guidelines.gov.uk/docs/008_SexualOffencesAct1.pdf.
33   Criminal Justice Act 2003 s172.

2. The type of activity covered by the various trafficking offences in the SOA 2003 is broadly the same, the only difference being the geographical area within which the trafficked persons are moved. The harm being addressed is sexual exploitation, but here either children or adults may be involved as victims.

3. The offences are designed to cover anyone involved in any stage of the trafficking operation, whether or not there is evidence of gain. This is serious offending behaviour, which society as a whole finds repugnant, and a financial or community penalty would rarely be an appropriate disposal.

4. The degree of coercion used and the level of control over the trafficked person's liberty will be relevant to assessing the seriousness of the offender's behaviour. The nature of the sexual exploitation to which the victim is exposed will also be relevant, as will the victim's age and vulnerability.

5. In general terms the greater the level of involvement, the more serious the crime. Those at the top of an organised trafficking chain may have very little personal involvement with day-to-day operations and may have no knowledge at all of individual victims. However, being in control of a money-making operation that is based on the degradation, exploitation and abuse of vulnerable people may be equally, if not more, serious than the actions of an individual who is personally involved at an operational level.

6. The presence of any of the general aggravating factors identified in the council guideline on seriousness or any of the additional factors identified in the guidelines will indicate a sentence above the normal starting point.

7. Circumstances such as the fact that the offender is also a victim of trafficking and that their actions were governed by fear could be a mitigating factor if not accepted as a defence.

8. The starting point for sentencing of offences of trafficking for sexual exploitation should be a custodial sentence. Aggravating factors such as participation in a large-scale commercial enterprise involving a high degree of planning, organisation or sophistication, financial or other gain, and the coercion and vulnerability of victims should move sentences towards the maximum 14 years.

9. In cases where a number of children are involved, consecutive sentences may be appropriate, leading to cumulative sentences

significantly higher than the suggested starting point for individual offences.

10. Where an offender has profited from his or her involvement in the prostitution of others, the court should consider making a confiscation order approximately equivalent to the profits enjoyed.

11. The court may order the forfeiture of a vehicle used, or intended to be used, in connection with the offence.

Aggravating factors

1. Large-scale commercial operation
2. High degree of planning, organisation or sophistication
3. Large number of people trafficked
4. Substantial financial (in the region of £5,000 and upwards) or other gain
5. Fraud
6. Financial extortion of the victim
7. Deception
8. Use of force, threat of force or other forms of coercion
9. Threats against the victim or members of the victim's family
10. Proved or admitted abduction or detention (unless separately charged)
11. Restriction of the victim's liberty
12. Inhumane treatment
13. Confiscation of the victim's passport

Mitigating factors (apart from a guilty plea)

1. Coercion of the offender by a third party
2. No evidence of personal gain
3. Limited involvement

5.19   Despite the guidelines, earlier Court of Appeal decisions will still be relevant. In *R v Maka (Shaban)* [2005] EWCA 3365, a conviction under the SOA 2003, the Court of Appeal refused to intervene in a total sentence of 18 years (made up of consecutive sentences on different counts) reached by nine years each of two counts to run consecutively. In doing so, the court commented (para 10) that: 'The intention of the legislature in introducing the offence of trafficking for sexual exploitation, by the Sexual Offences Act 2003, was plainly to embrace a wide variety of different forms of conduct, identifiable as trafficking, for sexual exploitation. As [counsel] rightly recognises, the legislation contemplates that trafficking may be for the purposes of a whole range of sexual offences from rape downwards.' The court also confirmed that 'deterrence of those in Lithuania, or other Eastern European countries, or, indeed, in any other part of Europe, as well as of those, in this country, who take part in activities of this kind, is a highly material consideration'.

The Maka *case: Elena's story*

Elena was a 15-year-old living with her grandmother in Lithuania. Her friend was approached by a woman promising them work in England. A contract was signed, after advice from a local lawyer. The work promised was in a bar or restaurant. She arranged to meet her best friend in London. She was picked up from her home by an 18-year-old man named Kastas who drove her to the home of a middle-aged woman and her ten-year-old daughter. The next day they drove to Riga, from where flights to London are cheaper. On arrival at Heathrow on 12 July 2004, her passport was removed and she was taken to meet two men, Shaban Maka and Ilir Barjami. She was then taken to central London. The next day she was taken to a tube station and sold to a man named Bledi for £4,000. That night she was raped. The next day she was taken to a brothel in Birmingham. She escaped and contacted Maka. He picked her up with Bledi. Both then took her to a Coventry car park and there she was sold for £3,000 to Xhevashir Pisha who only took her out to buy fast food or to work in a Leicester sauna. She was sold again to three more men. She escaped and again contacted Maka. On about 6 September, she was sold back to Ilir Barjami for £1,500. She managed to escape on 11 September with the help of two English girls when she had been taken to a nightclub after the brothel had refused to take her. At the hearing in the Crown Court, Elena refused the offer of screens and gave her evidence in open court because she wanted to confront the defendants.

She has subsequently returned to school in Lithuania.

5.20   In *R v Roci and another* [2006] 2 Cr App R (S) 15, a sentence of 11 years was reduced to nine years on appeal in a case involving the importation, from Lithuania, of prostitutes who were aware that they would work as prostitutes and therefore could not be said to have been corrupted within the meaning of sentencing guidelines but who were then coerced to working in unpleasant circumstances and in ways contrary to their wishes (eg when they were menstruating and when clients were drunk) and who were required to pay over most of their earnings. The court said:

> It is to be noted in this case, in contrast to the case of *Maka* in which this constitution gave judgment earlier today, that the victims of these offences were not only adult prostitutes, but they came to this country for the purpose of carrying on a trade as prostitutes. The coercion to which they were subjected was extremely minor compared with the coercion and corruption to which the victim in *Maka* was subjected. That said, these activities were carried out by these two appellants for commercial gain, over a substantial period of time.

Further guidance on sentencing was given[34] when appeals by both prosecution and defence were heard in *Attorney-General's Reference Nos 129 and 132 of 2006 under section 36 of the Criminal Justice Act 1988; R v Delgado-Fernandez; R v Thanh Hue Thi*.[35] In *Delgado-Fernandez*, the defendants were convicted of conspiracy to traffic into the UK for sexual exploitation, conspiracy to control prostitution for gain and conspiracy to facilitate a breach of immigration law. Mr Zammit, who controlled a prostitution racket involving entry through Ireland, had sentences totalling seven years reduced to five because the case lacked features of deception or coercion. His co-conspirator, Miss Delgado-Fernandez, who was previously a prostitute, had her sentence reduced to four years in total, because she was very much under the control of Zammit and only received a modest share of the profits of the enterprise.[36] The court refused to increase a sentence of a total of five years in respect of Mr Thanh Hue Thi, despite evidence of coercion, and large (£2 million) personal profits. In *R v Ramaj*,[37] the defendant had been convicted of trafficking but acquitted of rape, false imprisonment and controlling prostitution for gain. An appeal against conviction failed.[38] A sentence for the trafficking of an 18-year-old Lithuania girl by the 20-year-old defendant was reduced from 10 years in a young offenders' institution to five. On the other hand, in *Kizlaite*,[39] the Court of

---

34 The sentencing guidelines were still in draft.
35 [2007] EWCA 762 at 48.
36 At 48.
37 [2006] EWCA Crim 488 at 3.
38 At 3.
39 [2007] 1 Cr App R (S).

Appeal refused to interfere with sentences totalling 11 years' and 21 years' detention in a young offenders institution in the case of two defendants described as 'sexual slave traders'.

Forfeiture

5.21　Sections 60A and 60B set out forfeiture provisions for offences under ss57–59. The provisions apply to a land vehicle, ship or aircraft. This may be detained by a police or immigration officer pending decision on charge, resolution of proceedings or, on conviction, pending the court's decision on forfeiture.[40] On conviction under ss57–59, the court may order the forfeiture of any land vehicle, ship or aircraft used or intended to be used in connection with the offence if the convicted person, at the time the offence was committed, owned the vehicle or was a director, secretary or manager of a company which owned the vehicle. A land vehicle may also be forfeited if the convicted person was in possession of the vehicle under a hire-purchase agreement (or was director, secretary or manager of a company which was) or was driving the vehicle at the time of commission of the offence. In cases where the convicted person (or the relevant company) was in possession of a ship or aircraft under a hire-purchase agreement, or was a charterer or captain of a ship or aircraft, forfeiture may only be ordered where actual or constructive knowledge of the intention to use it in the course of an offence under ss57–59 can be established on the part of the owner or, if the owner is a company, on the part of a director, secretary or manager.[41] Further, the ship or aircraft must have minimum capacities.[42]

Other steps to deal with sex trafficking

5.22　In November 2008, a Home Office review *Tackling the demand for prostitution* recommended the introduction of a strict liability offence of paying for sex with someone who is controlled for another

---

40　Section 60B.

41　Section 60A as inserted by the Violent Crime Reduction Act 2006 s54 and Schedule 4.

42　Section 60A(7): 500 tons for an aircraft, 5,700 kgs for an aircraft. See further chapter 14.

person's gain[43] and also recommended amending the offences under the Sexual Offences Act 1985 to allow prosecution for first (rather than persistent) offences. The review also recommended an awareness campaign targeted at users of commercial sex and police powers to close for up to three months premises linked to sexual exploitation.

5.23 The offence goes beyond the recommendation in Convention CETS 197. The Report states: 'Under the new offence it will be irrelevant whether the sex buyer knew that the prostitute was controlled or not. It is argued that those who pay for sex will know that they could be paying for sex with a person who is controlled, and therefore they will think twice about what they are doing and their attitude towards those selling sex.' The recommended maximum penalty is £1,000. The proposed offence has the advantage of allowing freely concluded contracts for sex. Less clear is how exactly it will be enforced, ie how controlled prostitutes will be distinguished from others.

5.24 This measure was opposed by the English Collective of Prostitutes and others, who argued that licensing was more effective to ensure protection. At present, the law does not criminalise prostitution per se. The industry is criminalised in limited circumstances. Firstly, under s1 of the Street Offences Act 1959, it is an offence for a prostitute to loiter in a street or a public place for the purpose of prostitution. Street has a wide meaning, including doorways and entrances of premises abutting onto the street. The section does not cover trading one's sexual services off the street. As for the client, ss1, 2 and 4 of the Sexual Offences Act 1985 criminalise the offence commonly known as kerbcrawling ie where a person solicits another person (or different persons) for the purposes of prostitution (a) from a motor vehicle while it is in a street or public place; (b) in a street or public place. Both offences are triable summarily only. Soliciting by a prostitute carries with it a maximum penalty of a fine at level 2 or – on a repeat conviction – level 3. Soliciting by a client carries with it a maximum penalty of a fine at level 3. Off the street, it is an offence to keep or manage a brothel or to assist in doing so: ss33–36 of the Sexual Offences Act 1956. The Act does not define

---

43 The licensing system in the Netherlands was rejected on the grounds that it did not seem to have ended exploitation. The Swedish system of criminalising the buying of sex (regardless of knowledge of whether the prostitute had been trafficked or exploited) was rejected on the grounds that Sweden had more consensus on the issue and a smaller market (an estimated 1,500 people selling sex in Sweden with an estimated 80,000 in the UK).

Reproduced by permission of the Home Office.

what constitutes a brothel but guidance has been given in case-law. See *Kelly v Purvis*;[44] *Stevens v Christy*.[45] An arrangement with one woman and a receptionist who does not provide sexual services and does not control the woman, would not fall within the provisions. Some argue that publicising convictions for kerbcrawling would have the requisite deterrent effect.

44 [1983] 76 Cr App R 165.
45 (1987) 85 Cr App R 249.

Protection of children

Key points

- Transfer of a child for the purpose of exploitation amounts to trafficking, without the need to prove that the transfer is done using coercion, abduction, deception, abuse of power or exploitation of vulnerability or payment: UN Trafficking Protocol article 3(c) and Convention CETS 197 article 4.
- For sexual exploitation, this is reflected in national law under the Sexual Offences Act 2003 for children under 16 but not 18.
- For labour exploitation, unless the exploitation amounts to a breach of article 4, or concerns trafficking in human organs, the prosecution must at least show that the child, or a relevant adult, has been requested or induced to undertake any activity on the grounds that they are vulnerable (because young).
- Trafficked children may be unaccompanied, separated from their parents or carer, fostered or may even be in their family. There is evidence of a problem of children going missing from care who may be trafficked.
- Diagnostic indicators may be referred to but must not be substituted for an objective, individuated assessment.
- The guiding principle is child protection.
- The Convention on the Rights of the Child and its Optional Protocols ILO Convention 182 on the Worst Forms of Child Labour and the UNICEF guidelines on child trafficking all provide a framework.
- The best interests of the child must be a primary consideration in all decisions. A guardian must be appointed to identify and represent the best interests and to communicate with the child.

Definition of child trafficking

6.1   Children as labourers and as sexual objects are cheap and malleable. They are used in trafficking for the purposes of sexual exploitation but also for labour, domestic work, benefit fraud, begging and organ trafficking. A scoping study in 2007 found that the top source countries for children trafficked to the UK (with the numbers in brackets) were China (70); Nigeria (38); Vietnam (22); Afghanistan

(19); Eritrea (14); Romania (14); and Albania (14).[1] Eighty-five per cent of the children were between 15 and 17 years old. Many of the children trafficked or suspected to be trafficked to the UK enter the UK with a false passport or no passport at all.[2]

6.2   A child is generally regarded as not able to give informed consent. This principle is reflected in the relevant international instruments, in particular article 3(c) of the UN Trafficking Protocol[3] and article 4 of CETS 197.[4] Both make it clear that the consent of a child either to the transfer or to the exploitation is not a factor on which a trafficker can rely. As regards the transfer element of trafficking, this principle remains clear in national UK law. In the definitions in the Trafficking Protocol or in CETS 197, there is a requirement to show that the transfer was carried out by means of force, deception, abuse of vulnerability or the other means set out therein. In contrast, in UK law, this is not necessary for adults or children. The situation is less clear as regards the (intended) exploitation element of the offence. In cases of sexual exploitation, exploitation is defined by reference to 'a relevant offence'. This includes any relevant sexual conduct with a child under 16.[5] In respect of a child older than 16 but younger than 18, it includes relevant sexual offences and abuse of a position of trust.[6] There is still less clarity as regards the offence of trafficking for exploitation under the 2004 Act, although the 2004 Act was clearly intended to cover the exploitation of the vulnerability of a child and contains a provision which does this.[7] In the offences of trafficking both for sexual exploitation and for exploitation generally, a clause in each Act specifically reflecting the principles in article 3(c) of the Trafficking Protocol and article 4 of CETS 197 would have provided clarity.

6.3   The law and practice described in chapters 5 and 7 also applies to the trafficking of children. However, over and above that, child trafficking is dealt with through the application of child protection measures, trafficking being a form of child abuse.

---

1   Child Exploitation and Online Protection Centre (CEOP) Aarti Kapoor, *Scoping project into child trafficking in the UK*, 2007, p19. CEOP was launched in April 2006. The statistics do not of course mean that all children from those countries are trafficked, nor that trafficked children are all from those countries. These statistics are for information only and should not take the place of objective indicators.

2   Aarti Kapoor, 2007, at p21.

3   See 2.27.

4   See 3.16–3.17.

5   See 5.13–5.19.

6   See 5.14 in particular.

7   See 7.36.

6.4   Those special protection measures depend upon identification as a child and as a potential victim. Identification measures should be proactive. The efficacy of the measure depends crucially upon adequate communication between state agencies and between state and non-state actors. Such joined-up action is not always in evidence and needs to be particularly efficient where there are linguistic and cultural barriers to overcome as well as the need to communicate effectively with a child.

6.5   It follows from a conclusion that a child has been trafficked that their family or quasi-family environment has failed them in some way. Investigation into whether trafficking has occurred needs a careful analysis of the relationship between the child and the adult and of the position of the child in the group. Anyone who seeks to engage and draw out the child should be aware that the child may be psychologically dependant on their trafficker.

Coercion or deception does not need to be proved. However, here are some of the means by which control is exercised over children:

- Confiscation of the child's identity documents
- Threats of reporting the child to the authorities
- Violence, or threats of violence, towards the child
- Threats of violence towards members of the child's family
- Keeping the child socially isolated
- Keeping the child locked up
- Telling some children that they owe large sums of money and that they must work to pay this off
- Depriving the child of money
- Voodoo or witchcraft, which may be used to frighten children, for example, into thinking that if they tell anyone about the traffickers, they and their families will die[8]

Unaccompanied or separated children

6.6   Trafficked children may be with their family or they may be unaccompanied or separated. Unaccompanied children are children who have been separated from both parents and other relatives and are not being cared for by an adult who, by law or custom, is

8   *Safeguarding children* Department of Children, Schools and Families (2007).

responsible for doing so. Separated children are children who have been separated from both parents, or from their previous legal or customary caregiver, but not necessarily from other relatives. Children who have been trafficked may be with their family, unaccompanied or separated.

Fostered children

6.7   A private fostering arrangement is defined as an arrangement which is made privately, without any local authority involvement, for the care of a child who is under 16 (or under 18 if disabled) by someone other than a parent or close relative,[9] with the intention that it should last for 28 days or more.[10] There is a requirement to notify the local authority of a private fostering arrangement within 48 hours of the child's arrival. Section 8 (7A) of the Children Act 1989[11] requires local authorities to raise awareness within local communities of the notification requirement and to monitor. Local authorities have the duty to identify private fostering arrangements and to visit and assess the arrangement. The local authority is empowered to prohibit a carer from being a private foster carer if they are of the opinion that the carer is not a suitable person, the premises are not suitable or it would be prejudicial to the welfare of the child to continue in the arrangement.

Missing children

6.8   The CEOP report (note 1) at p48–50 and a report by ECPAT *Missing Out?* (2007) both identified a significant incidence of children going missing from local authority care. The risk of this occurring should be assessed by the local authority and steps taken to prevent it. Police should follow the guidance in *The management, recording and investigation of missing persons*,[12] in particular that every missing person's report should be assessed to identify the level of risk (high,

---

9   Grandparents, siblings, uncles or aunts by consanguinity or in-law, step-parent or someone with parental responsibility conferred under the 1989 Act.

10   Children Act 1989 s66. In Scotland the provisions are contained in the Foster Children (Scotland) Act 1984 and the Foster Children (Private Fostering) (Scotland) Regulations 1985.

11   As inserted by Children Act 2004 s44(7).

12   See   www.acpo.police.uk/asp/policies/Data/missing_persons_2005_ 24x02x05.pdf.

medium or low) to the missing person and a response made which is appropriate to that level of risk. The Department of Health have also issued good practice guidance on collaborative action.[13]

Diagnostic indicators

6.9   Diagnostic indicators can be used by an organisation or professionals to identify risk factors. The factors are neither a tick list nor an exclusive list. They are not a substitute for careful and objective consideration of the people and the facts. These diagnostic indicators are taken from the Department for Schools, Children and Families (DSCF). Some are more useful than others. Variations exist across different bodies, including Local Children Safeguarding Boards. They should be adapted to suit the particular service: for example, a GP is likely to need a different set of indicators to a border agency employee.

At port of entry[14]

The child, on arrival ...

- Has entered the country illegally
- Has no passport or other means of identification
- Has false documentation
- Possesses money and goods not accounted for
- Is malnourished
- Is unable to confirm the name and address of the person meeting them on arrival
- Has had their journey or visa arranged by someone other than themselves or their family
- Is accompanied by an adult who insists on remaining with the child at all times
- Is withdrawn and refuses to talk or appears afraid to talk to a person in authority
- Has a prepared story very similar to those that other children have given

---

13   *Children missing from home and care* (2002) available from www.dh.gov.uk/en/ Publicationsandstatistics/Lettersandcirculars/LocalAuthorityCirculars/ AllLocalAuthority/DH_4004872.

14   The Global Visa Regulations 2006, in force from 12 February 2006, require a visa to contain a photograph of the child plus details of who they are travelling with. Defects in this will be a strong indicator.

- Exhibits self-assurance, maturity and self-confidence not expected to be seen in a child of such age
- Does not appear to have money but does have a mobile phone
- Is unable, or reluctant to give details of accommodation or other personal details

The sponsor ...

- Has previously made multiple visa applications for other children and/or has acted as the guarantor for other children's visa applications
- Is known to have acted as the guarantor on the visa applications for other visitors who have not returned to their countries of origin on the expiry of those visas

The child, whilst resident in the UK ...

- Does not appear to have money but does have a mobile phone
- Receives unexplained/unidentified phone calls whilst in placement/temporary accommodation
- Possesses money and goods not accounted for
- Exhibits self assurance, maturity and self-confidence not expected to be seen in a child of such age
- Has a prepared story very similar to those other children have given
- Shows signs of physical or sexual abuse, and/or has contracted a sexually transmitted disease or has an unwanted pregnancy
- Has a history with missing links and unexplained moves
- Has gone missing from local authority care
- Is required to earn a minimum amount of money every day
- Works in various locations
- Has limited freedom of movement
- Appears to be missing for periods of time
- Is known to beg for money
- Performs excessive housework chores and rarely leaves the residence
- Is malnourished
- Is being cared for by adult(s) who are not his or her parents
- The quality of the relationship between the child and his or her adult carer(s) is not good
- Is one of a number of unrelated children found at one address
- Has not been registered with or attended a GP practice

- Has not been enrolled in school.
- Has to pay off an exorbitant debt, perhaps for travel costs, before being able to have control over his or her own earnings
- Is required to earn a minimum amount every day or hands over a large part of their earnings to another person
- Is excessively afraid of being deported

Child protection principles

6.10   Child protection principles are key and derive from international principles.

UN Convention on the Rights of the Child

6.11   These principles in turn derive from the United Nations Convention on the Rights of the Child (CRC).[15] The CRC should be read with the General Comments issued from time to time by the UN Committee on the Rights of the Child.[16] Near-universal[17] ratification gives the CRC particular weight. The CRC has two Optional Protocols to it: the Optional Protocol on the involvement of children in armed conflict; and the Optional Protocol on the sale of children, child prostitution and child pornography.[18] After a sustained campaign by children's rights organisations,[19] the UK government withdrew its reservation to the CRC in relation to children subject to immigration control with effect from 18 November 2008. It also indicated its intention to sign up to both Optional Protocols. This means CRC principles

15   Opened for signature, ratification and accession on 20 November 1989 and entry into force on 2 September 1990. Signed by the United Kingdom on 19 April 1990 and ratified on 16 December 1991. Full text and other relevant documentation available on www2.ohchr.org/English/bodies/crc.

16   See www.ohchr.org/english/bodies/crc/docs/GC General Comment 6, on the treatment of unaccompanied and separated children outside their country of origin is particularly relevant.

17   All states except Somalia and the US. The US position is now being reviewed.

18   Ratified by the UK on 9 February 2006.

19   See Opinion on the Reservation for Save the Children by Nicholas Blake QC and Sandhya Drew (2001) available at www.publications.parliament.uk/pa/it200102/itselect/itrights/132/13217.htm and Opinion for UNICEF UK and Save the Children UK by Sandhya Drew (2008) available from www.ecpat.org.uk/downloads/Legal_Opinion_on_UK_Immigration_Reservation_to_UNCRC.pdf.

should be fully applied to children subject to immigration control, including children who are trafficked. As to reliance in court, the CRC is an unincorporated treaty and does not have direct effect within national law.[20] This is less important than it might otherwise seem since it is well established that the CRC can be used in considering rights under the European Convention on Human Rights through the Human Rights Act 1998.[21]

Content of the UN Convention on the Rights of the Child

6.12   Key core principles of the CRC are:

- *Non-discrimination:* Non discrimination against children in the territory (article 2).
- *Best interests of the child:* The best interests of the child are a primary consideration in all actions concerning children, whether undertaken by public or private social welfare institutions, courts of law, administrative authorities or legislative bodies (article 3).
- *The right to life:* The right to life (article 6) which means that states parties shall ensure to the maximum extent possible the survival and development of the child.
- *Listening to the child:* Finally, article 12 provides that states parties shall assure to the child who is capable of forming his or her own views the right to express those views freely in all matters affecting the child, the views of the child being given due weight in accordance with the age and maturity of the child. For this purpose, the child shall in particular be provided the opportunity to be heard in any judicial or administrative proceedings affecting the child, either directly, or through a representative or an appropriate body, in a manner consistent with the procedural rules of national law.

Articles particularly relevant to trafficked children are the following.

- Articles 9 and 10 refer to family reunion. Article 9 provides that a child shall not be separated from his or her parents against their will, except where competent authorities subject to judicial review determine, in accordance with applicable law and procedures, that such separation is necessary for the best interests of the child.

---

20   See further Shaheed Fatima *Using international law in domestic courts,* Hart Publishing, 2005.

21   See *T and V v UK* (2000) EHRR 121;[1999] EHHR; *ID v Home Office* [2006] 1 WLR 1003; *SS v Secretary of State for the Home Department* [2007] EWHC 1654, 41.

Article 9(3) requires respect for the right of the child to maintain familial relations and in certain circumstances, tracing of their family. Article 10 requires that applications by a child or his or her parents to enter or leave a state for the purpose of family reunification shall be dealt with in a positive, humane and expeditious manner. Article 10(2) provides that where child and parent(s) live in different states, liberty of movement shall be facilitated so as to ensure contact.

- Article 11 requires states to take measures to combat the illicit transfer and non-return of children abroad and, to that end, the conclusion of bilateral or multilateral agreements or accession to existing agreements.

- Article 20 states that a child temporarily or permanently deprived of his or her family environment, or in whose own best interests cannot be allowed to remain in that environment, or in whose best interests cannot be allowed to remain in that environment, shall be entitled to special protection and assistance provided by the state.

- Article 22 provides that a child who is seeking refugee status or who is considered a refugee in accordance with applicable international or domestic law and procedures shall, whether unaccompanied or accompanied by his or her parents or any other person, receive appropriate protection and humanitarian assistance.

- Article 32 provides for protection of the right from economic exploitation and from performing any work that is likely to be hazardous or to interfere with the child's education, or to be harmful to the child's health or physical, mental, spiritual, moral or social development. As a means of progressive implementation of this article, states shall: (a) provide for a minimum age of employment; (b) provide for appropriate regulation of the hours and conditions of employment; (c) provide for appropriate penalties or other sanctions to ensure effective enforcement.

- Article 33 requires states to take all appropriate measures (legislative, administrative, social and educational) to protect children from the illicit use of narcotic drugs and psychotropic substances as defined in the relevant international treaties and to prevent the use of children in the illicit production and trafficking of such substances.

- Article 34 requires protection of the child from all forms of sexual exploitation and sexual abuse. This requires all appropriate national, bilateral and multilateral measures.

- Article 35 requires all appropriate national, bilateral and multilateral measures to prevent the abduction of, the sale of or traffic in children for any purpose or in any form.
- Article 36 requires states to protect the child against all other forms of exploitation prejudicial to any aspects of the child's welfare.
- Article 39 requires all appropriate measures to promote physical and psychological recovery and social reintegration of a child victim of, amongst other things, any form of neglect, exploitation or abuse. Such recovery or reintegration shall take place in an environment which fosters the health, self-respect and dignity of the child.

Implementation of the CRC is monitored by the Committee on the Rights of the Child, which also issues general comments.[22]

ILO Convention 182

6.13 The sale and trafficking of children is one of the worst forms of child labour which the International Labour Organization (ILO) identified as a priority for immediate elimination in its Convention 182.[23] The worst forms of labour described in the convention would certainly amount to labour exploitation. They include:

- the use, procuring or offering of a child for prostitution, for the production of pornography or for pornographic performances;[24]
- the use, procuring or offering of a child for illicit activities, in particular for the production and trafficking of drugs;[25] and
- work which by its nature or the circumstances in which it is carried out, is likely to harm the health, safety or morals of children.[26]

Article 6 required programmes of action to be designed and implemented at national level in consultation with employers' and workers' organisations. Article 7(2)(b) requires the state to identify and reach out to children at special risk. The state is required to

---

22 The committee may seek advice from UNICEF: article 45(a).
23 The full title is: Convention concerning the prohibition and immediate action for the elimination of the worst forms of child labour adopted by the Conference, 17 June 1999. Convention 182 was ratified by the UK on 22 March 2000.
24 Article 3(b).
25 Article 3(c).
26 Article 3(d).

designate the competent authority responsible for the implementation of the provisions giving effect to the convention. ILO-IPEC provides guidance on the elimination of child labour. In 2008, it published a five-book resource kit on *Combating trafficking in children for labour exploitation.*[27]

UNICEF Guidelines

6.14   UNICEF has issued guidelines and a reference guide on the Protection of Child Victims of Trafficking.[28] The reference guide contains extremely useful guidelines and checklists for professionals, including a Code of Conduct.[29]

European Convention on Human Rights

6.15   Although not specifically written to address child trafficking, the European Convention on Human Rights, given further effect in the UK by the Human Rights Act 1998, is also relevant,[30] in particular articles 3, 4 and 8.

National guidance

6.16   In 2007, the Department for Children, Schools and Families published *Safeguarding children who may have been trafficked.*[31] Similar guidance has been issued in Scotland: *Safeguarding children in Scotland who may have been trafficked.* This guidance on specific issues is intended to supplement the Department's general guidance (2006) *Working together to safeguard children.* The guidance is aimed at all state agencies (eg medical, police, youth offending, local authorities) who may encounter relevant children. It promotes a protective approach. It covers, but is not limited to, Local Safeguarding Children's Boards in England and Wales and Child Protection Committees in Scotland. Importantly, the guidance states that

27   Available from www.ilo.org/ipec. The guidance is useful for developed as well as developing countries.

28   See www.unicef.org/ceecis/UNICEF_child_trafficking_low.pdf.

29   See pp113–143.

30   See Sandhya Drew, *Children and the Human Rights Act,* Save the Children, 2000.

31   Published in 2007 by the Department for Children, Schools and Families. Available from www.dcsf.gov.uk or from 08456022260 ISBN 978-1-84478-974-0.

although the Border Agency may be part of the partnership, the nationality or immigration status of the child does not affect the agencies' statutory responsibilities under the 1989 or 2004 Acts.[32]

Identification as a child: Age disputes and age assessment

6.17 For the purposes of the CRC, 'child' means every human being below the age of 18 years unless under the law applicable to the child, majority is attained earlier. In the UK, any person below the age of 18 is therefore a child.[33] Identification as a child is the gateway to special protection. The Immigration Rules (HC395, as amended) define a child as 'a person under 18 years of age or who, in the absence of documentary evidence establishing age, appears to be that age'.

6.18 Ascertaining age through appearance is simple to state but complex in practice. In practice disputes on age frequently arise.[34] Children will frequently have been told by their traffickers to say that they are older than they really are. Equally, immigration officers often wrongly contend that a child is an adult. In such cases, reference should be made to the relevant guidance. The UNICEF guidelines on child trafficking provide at 3.1.2: 'Where the age of the victim is uncertain and there are reasons to believe that the victim is a child, the presumption shall be that the victim is a child. Pending verification of the victim's age, the victim will be treated as a child and will be accorded all special protection measures stipulated in these guidelines.' Article 10.2 of the European Convention against Trafficking requires a similar presumption that someone is a child where there are reasons to believe they are a child. Where the presumption is triggered, special protection measures should be taken pending age verification.[35] Internal guidance by UKBA also provides for the child to be given the benefit of any doubt.[36] With regard to evidence that the person is over 18 years of age, physical appearance and demeanour should strongly suggest that the person

---

32 See 7.6.

33 The age of sexual consent is 16.

34 Heaven Crawley, *When is a child not a child? Asylum, age disputes and the process of age assessment*, ILPA, May 2007 (www.ilpa.org).

35 Article 10.3.

36 See www.bia.homeoffice.gov.uk.

is over 18 years old.[37] Reasons to believe that the person is a child may include the following:

(a) evidence from the child;
(b) documents consistent with the assertion;
(c) evidence that the client is being transported to carry out an activity usually carried out by children;
(d) evidence of a different calendar system in the country of origin (eg Iran) to explain confusing statements;
(e) differing assessments by differing agencies;
(f) a medical opinion as to the client's age.

Visual assessment only by an immigration officer is not a reliable method: children who have been trafficked are likely to have had a less protected childhood than a child who has just left school and who has not worked full time. Medical methods of age assessment are: assessment of bone age, dental age assessment and the assessment of physical development (including puberty, height, weight and skin). Medical assessment is only accurate to within two years. Thus, age assessment is most difficult between the ages of 15 and 20.[38] Guidance published by the Royal College of Paediatrics and Child Health in 1999[39] stated at 5.6: 'Age determination is an inexact science and the margin of error can sometimes be as much as five years either side. Assessments of age measure maturity, not chronological age.' In 1996 the Royal College of Radiologists advised its members that x-rays should not be carried out for a purpose which was not clinical. Medical professional have also expressed concern about a likely lack of informed consent when carrying out x-rays on children in this context, since x-rays amount to an invasive procedure with no therapeutic gain. X-rays can only provide an indication of skeletal or developmental maturity from which conclusions about chronological age may be inferred. They do not assist at all in identification of level of vulnerability and need. For all these reasons, local authorities should carry out their own assessments rather than relying on the conclusions by the Border Agency. The Border Agency set up a working group of age assessment as of early 2008. Guidelines were set out in *R and B v London Borough of*

---

37   Association of Directors of Social Services (www.adss.or.uk).
38   Crawley, pp29–33.
39   Levenson and Sharma, *The health of refugee children, guidelines for paediatricians*, Royal College of Paediatrics and Child Health, November 1999.

Merton;[40] *R (T) v London Borough of Enfield:*[41] physical appearance and behaviour cannot be separated from questions of credibility (at 28); assessment of age can be determined informally, provided that minimum standards of inquiry and of fairness are adhered to (at 36); the decision-maker cannot determine age solely on the basis of the appearance of the applicant but must seek to elicit general background, including family history, education and activities in recent years. If there is a reason to doubt the applicant's statement as to his or her age, the decision-maker will have to make an assessment of the applicant's credibility, and will have to ask questions designed to test credibility (at 37); the social services department of a local authority cannot simply adopt a decision made by the Home Office. It must decide itself whether an applicant is a child and in need (at 39); a local authority is obliged to give adequate reasons for its decision that an applicant claiming to be a child is not a child (at 45); it is not necessary to obtain medical evidence (at 51); if an interpreter is required, he or she should be present throughout the interview (at 52); the decision-maker must explain to the applicant the purpose of the interview (at 55); procedural fairness requires the assessing officers to put to the child matters which they are minded to hold against him or her, so that there is an opportunity to correct any misunderstanding (at 55).

Action to be taken by adviser

6.19   If an adviser suspects that a child is being trafficked, they should contact the police based in a child abuse investigation unit or the local authority's social care unit. Alternatively, they can make an application to the court direct or obtain an injunction or an emergency child protection order. The local authority is required to set up a child protection plan and decide on a course of action within 24 hours. See the guidance given in *Working together to safeguard children* (2006).

Specific offences against children

6.20   As stated above, the general offences of trafficking for sexual exploitation (chapter 5) and for labour exploitation (chapter 7)

---

40   [2003] EWHC 1689 (Admin); [2003] 4 All ER 280.
41   [2004] EWHC 2297 (Admin).

FLOW CHART – REFERRAL*

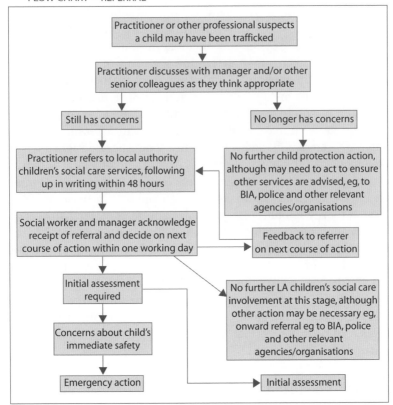

* At no stage should the adult purporting to be the child's parent, sponsor or carer be present at interviews with the child, or at meetings to discuss future actions.

include the trafficking of children. There are, in addition, specific offences against children. These are mainly contained in the Sexual Offences Act 2003, in particular paying for the sexual services of a child with a penalty from seven years to life; and causing, facilitating or controlling the sexual exploitation of a child in prostitution or pornography, for which the maximum sentence is 14 years. In Scotland, the offences are contained in ss9–12 of the Protection of Children and Prevention of Sexual Offences (Scotland) Act 2005. Sexual offences against children in the Sexual Offences Act 2003 have extraterritorial effect. The exact scope of this has been set out in chapter 5. In particular, there is no requirement for dual criminality – a British national may be prosecuted in the UK for offences abroad, even if the offence is not a crime in the country where the offence took place. However, the provisions are underused and there have been no prosecutions under s72 of the 2003 Act in the last three years, despite evidence of a continuing problem.[42] There has also been underuse and underenforcement of the requirements on sex offenders to notify the police if they plan to travel abroad for three days or more[43] and the power to issue a civil Foreign Travel Order[44] restricting the travel to six months for offenders who have committed a sexual offence against a child under 16.

Trafficking for labour exploitation

6.21 Cases will often concern defendants in a position of carer vis-à-vis the child. Arguments will therefore be raised as to whether the relationship, objectively viewed, is a relationship of exploitation or care. This is a difficult exercise.

Regina v Ernestina Quainoo, Samuel Quainoo

The following case, which concerned transfer into England in July 2004, was not charged as a labour trafficking offence, but concerned exploitation of a child. Following is the ruling of HHJ Lowen on Newton Hearing at Isleworth Crown Court, Regina v Ernestina Quainoo, Samuel Quainoo, 11 July 2008 on the defendants' conviction of assisting unlawful immigration under s25 of the Immigration Act 1971:

The application stated that [G] Quainoo was born in Ghana on 13 November 1990 and was, therefore, 14 years of age ... It was established that [G] was [GA] and was aged 17 or 18 when she entered the United Kingdom in July [2004] ... It was only when [G] came to the attention of Social Services in May 2006 that suspicions arose as to her true identity and the circumstances in which she came into the United Kingdom were investigated. She was then unwell and told Social Services that she was unhappy at home in the Quainoo home. The account she gave in a videotaped recorded interview, in essence, was to the effect that since her arrival in the United Kingdom, she had been mistreated by Mr and Mrs Quainoo; that she was regarded as being a servant of that family and had to look after their young child all day, each day, while the Quainoo

---

42 *Return to Sender* ECPAT UK (2008).
43 Sexual Offences Act 2003 s86.
44 Under Sexual Offences Act 2003 s114.

parents were both out of the house at work; they both had full-time jobs.

She said that she was required to cook the child's food, wash his clothes and was paid nothing, kept short of what she needed and that her freedom was restricted. She had no opportunity to befriend anyone, nor could she go to school or college. She just was used as a worker without pay. She was vulnerable, because she had to depend on the Quainoos as her identification into this country and on record in this country and her status here were, according to the authorities, a dependent – that of a dependent child and Mrs Quainoo's child at that.

The allegation against Mr and Mrs Quainoo is that they committed this offence of assisting the unlawful entry of [G] and that their purpose was to bring [G] to the United Kingdom to be a childminder and a house worker for their benefit and convenience and that she was retained in an entirely disadvantaged predicament of utter exploitation, subject entirely to their will; the culpability in such circumstances would, of course, be serious.

The courts dealing with offences of assisting unlawful immigration recognise that such offences may be committed in circumstances which may properly be regarded as less serious. For example, where assistance is given to a close relative who enters in order to join a separated family, or where there is a desperate need for a person to flee from oppression or harm.

In this case, Mr and Mrs Quainoo pleaded guilty on a basis which would, if true, substantially reduce their culpability. That basis was recorded in the document provided to the Court on the day that the guilty pleas were entered. Essentially, it was asserted that [G] had, prior to coming to the United Kingdom, been adopted in the sense that customary practice in Ghana would have sanctioned her inclusion into the Quainoo family as Mr and Mrs Quainoo's daughter. That she had, in Ghana, been treated as such for some time prior to her entry into the United Kingdom. That she had not been brought as a childminder, although she did from time to time care for the Quainoo's infant son. That it was [G]'s decision, in the United Kingdom, not to attend school or enter any education and that despite Mr and Mrs Quainoo's best efforts to encourage her to do so, that she could not work as she wished to, because of her age, according to the documents relied on for gaining entry into the United Kingdom and was such that she was too young to obtain any National Insurance number. That assertion is, of course, inconsistent with evidence of Mrs Quainoo given here today on oath that she at that stage already knew [G] to be 18.

...

I have been careful not to have regard to the complaints made by [G], which could not bear upon the narrow issue which really comes to this: for what purpose did these defendants arrange for [GA] to enter the United Kingdom?

I have kept in mind the need to distinguish evidence of [G's] unhappiness with the outcome from evidence as to the nature of the relationship at the time of entry. It is only the latter which could inform me of the status of [G] vis-à-vis Mr and Mrs Quainoo and I have kept in the forefront this question: was she in reality a servant or was she or may she have been regarded as a child of the family and treated as such, albeit an unhappy child whose own aspirations turned out to be disappointed by later events?

...

[G] was clear and precise at the time of her video interview and her evidence when cross-examined was largely consistent with that account. She conceded that she regarded herself as being part of the family when first brought to the United Kingdom, in the sense that she lived in the same house, watched the same television on occasions and was taken to the family general practitioner; she said that was about it. Of course, that is not determinative of the purpose which Mr and Mrs Quainoo had in mind when bringing her here.

I found Mrs Quainoo quite unable satisfactorily or convincingly to account for the reason why [G]'s date of birth had been given as 1990 in all the documents needed to show that she was a dependent child of 14, yet when issues arose as to why Mrs Quainoo had made no arrangements for that child to receive any form of school education, she relied on other assertions about [G]'s age and particularly that she believed [G], in fact, to be 18 years of age and, therefore, it would be inappropriate to try and place her in any kind of school.

I found Mrs Quainoo's evidence on matters of detail when cross-examined to be unconvincing and taken as a whole. In my judgment, I disbelieved her account of [G]'s relationship with her whilst in the United Kingdom. I disbelieved Mrs Quainoo's account of the true purpose for which the relevant documents were obtained and as to her status within the family.

I find the following relevant facts proved to the criminal standard: firstly that [G] had, by agreement between Mrs Quainoo and [G]'s natural mother, Mrs [AN], gone to work for Mrs Quainoo in Ghana as a childminder. An agreed wage had been paid initially; that wage was not paid when Mrs Quainoo undertook to provide for [G]'s education until she reached independence and, thereafter, Mrs Quainoo was to help [G] to find employment. Mrs Quainoo undertook to feed, clothe and house [G] in Ghana, whilst she in turn did childminding and chores. At the start of the relationship I have no doubt that the relationship was that of employer and employee.

Mrs Quainoo has asserted that a process akin to adoption took place but despite her high qualifications – and she is an educated and intelligent woman – she says that she was unaware that in Ghana, that process had no legal validity. There was no adoption of [G] as Mrs Quainoo's daughter so far as the law was concerned, even in Ghana.

Secondly, [G] had a friendship with Mrs Quainoo in Ghana and trusted her, that much I accept. She was an under-educated teenager and Mrs Quainoo had teaching qualifications, was a graduate and was in a totally different economic position to [G].

Thirdly, [G] complied with the deception necessary to ensure that she could enter the United Kingdom as Mrs Quainoo's child. She agreed to travel as such to the United Kingdom.

Next matter that I am satisfied has been established, was that whereas [G] was expectant of real opportunities to live a free and full life in the United Kingdom and to be integrated into the educational and employment progression, her role was regarded by Mr and Mrs Quainoo as strictly limited. I find that her status remained that of an employee. I find that throughout the period of her presence within the Quainoo household, she was treated as though she had the status of employee and nothing more than that, although she was accommodated within the household.

...

I accept that she was without financial means, without any independence and kept without regard for her need for friends and treated as an employee without any rights whatsoever. I accept she never was treated as a child who had become a daughter, as the Quainoos assert.

...

I am required to judge the purpose these defendants had when committing this offence and I have inferred from their conduct towards [GA] since her arrival in the United Kingdom, that the true purpose was to ensure a continuing employer/employee relationship and to enjoy childcare in a convenient way and at minimal cost and in reliance on the vulnerability of [G] as they exploited the illegality of the fabric of her life here; an illegality of their making and from which they derived the opportunity to abuse the trust [G] had placed in them.

In essence, I regard these defendants as having committed this offence out of self interest and for their own gain. There was, in my judgment, no compassionate motive involved whatsoever.

The judge imposed a sentence of 12 months' imprisonment suspended on Mrs Quainoo and a sentence of 18 months' imprisonment on Mr Quainoo.

The first conviction for labour trafficking

A more controversial case (arising out of the widely reported police raid in Slough) involved a 13-year-old Roma girl who was brought to the UK from Romania by adults (Reading Crown Court, 28 November 2008).[45] Her age was misrepresented and she was put to work selling the Big Issue. She worked in all weathers and was not properly clothed. The money she earned was taken from her. She gave video evidence to this effect which was used in court. The four defendants put forward what was essentially a defence of 'culture': that since they all sold the Big Issue and had all worked since they were children, putting the girl to work did not amount to labour exploitation. They were nevertheless convicted, in the first convictions under the Asylum and Immigration (Treatment of Claimants, etc) Act 2004. Their sentences ranged from one to three years for the offences under the 2004 Act. The case has aroused some controversy given the local hostility to the Roma and the evidence that selling the Big Issue was an activity undertaken by many adults in the group.

The 'best interests' principle

6.22   As soon as it is established that the person is a child, their best interests must be identified and implemented as a primary consideration by all arms of the state in relevant decisions.[46] This principle is further explained by the Committee on the Rights of the Child in its General Comment 6. Article 10 of Convention CETS 197 states that as soon as an unaccompanied child is identified as a victim, the state is required to provide for representation of the child by a legal guardian, organisation or authority which shall act in the best interests of the child; take the necessary steps to establish their identity and nationality; and make every effort to locate their family when this is in the best interests of the child.[47] A similar

---

45 An order made under the Contempt of Court Act 1981 prevents further identification of the child or child-identifying information about the adults.

46 Article 3, CRC. The formulation of the Children Act of 'paramount' consideration does not detract from the need for an individuated assessment although it means that where the child is a threat to the nation, this can be balanced against their best interest. This is, of course, a high threshold.

47 Convention CETS 197 article 10.4.

process is required by the UNICEF guidelines, which require the appoint-ment of a guardian to act throughout the whole process until a durable solution has been found.[48] Agencies whose interests conflict with that of the child cannot be eligible for guardianship.[49] The responsibilities of the guardian are:[50]

(1) To ensure that all decisions are taken in the child's best interests.

(2) To ensure that the child has appropriate care, accommodation, health care provisions, psycho-social support, education and language support.

(3) To ensure that the child has access to legal and other representation where necessary.

(4) To consult with, advise and keep the child victim informed of his or her rights.

(5) To contribute to the identification of a durable solution in the child's best interests.

(6) To keep the child informed of all the proceedings.

(7) To establish and maintain a link between the child and the various organisations which may provide services to the child.

(8) To assist the child in family tracing.

(9) To ensure that if repatriation or family reunification is possible, it is done in the best interests of the child.

(10) To ensure that the relevant paperwork is completed.

6.23   Regrettably, there is no sign of the government making provision for a guardian in trafficking cases.

6.24   The best interests must be identified through an individuated assessment.[51] This must be continually reviewed in light of information about the child's needs, their views and risks to the child.

Local authority duties towards children

6.25   The very fact that a child is identified as a possible victim of trafficking carries with it the risk that their current carers are not

---

48   *UNICEF Guidelines* p16.

49   Page 16.

50   *UNICEF Guidelines* 4.2 p17.

51   There is as yet no clear guidance at national level as to a framework for such guidance. In the different context of fieldwork, the UNHCR *Guidelines on formal determination of the best interests of the child* May 2006, are helpful.

providing them with suitable care. This triggers state duties with regard to care, which is led by local authorities through their children's services department exercising powers and duties under the 1989 and 2004 Children Acts. In addition to the overriding principle that the best interests of the child are paramount, local authorities in England and Wales have duties under ss17, 20 and 47 of the 1989 Children Act.[52] In Scotland, the corresponding duties are set out in ss22 and 25 of the Children (Scotland) Act 1995. Section 47 of the 1989 Act contains a duty to investigate cases where there is reasonable cause to suspect that a child who lives in the area is suffering or is likely to suffer significant harm (including neglect and including witnessing the ill treatment of another[53]) in order to determine whether the local authority should take any action to safeguard or promote the child's welfare. Under s17 the local authority has a general duty to safeguard and promote the welfare of children in need in their area. A child in need is defined as a child who will not achieve a reasonable standard of health or development or whose health or development will be impaired, without state services. There is a duty under s20 to accommodate a child in need, which is triggered when: (a) there is no person with parental responsibility; (b) the child is lost or abandoned; (c) the person who has been caring for him is prevented from providing him with suitable accommodation and care. Section 20 does not restrict the age of children supported under it to 16 years. Section 20(3) states: 'Every local authority shall provide accommodation for any child in need within their area who has reached the age of sixteen and whose welfare the authority consider is likely to be seriously prejudiced if they do not provide him with accommodation.'

6.26　　The practice developed in many authorities does not comply with this. Often children over 16 are supported under s17. In relation to accommodation, those under 16 are placed into foster care or residential care homes. Over 16s are placed in accommodation according to their needs and how independent they are. This type of accommodation is often semi-independent in shared houses, hostels or bed and breakfasts. In the case of over 16s (or sometimes over 15s in shared housing), most Local Authorities assign a social worker to every child to provide support for registering with education and

---

52　In Scotland, the relevant legislation in the Children (Scotland) Act 1995 and in Northern Ireland, the Children (Northern Ireland) Order 1995.

53　Section 31.

health services etc, and can contact the social worker at any time. There is a need to provide proper support for trafficked children, analogous to the quality of holistic support provided to women by the POPPY Project.

6.27   The Children Act 2004 was enacted in response to the recommendations by the Laming inquiry into the death of Victoria Climbie. By virtue of s11 (in England) and s28 (in Wales) of the Children Act 2004, certain public organisations are under a general duty to safeguard and promote the welfare of children. The scope of the duty is that the person or body must make arrangements for ensuring that their functions are discharged having regard to the need to safeguard and promote the welfare of children, and any services provided by another person pursuant to arrangements made by the person or body in the discharge of their functions are provided having regard to that need. Broadly, the organisations are local authorities, health authorities, the police and prison authorities. Specifically, the organisations under the duty are at present: local authorities (a children's services authority in England and a district council which is not such an authority); a strategic health authority; a special health authority, so far as exercising functions in relation to England; a Primary Care Trust, an NHS trust all or most of whose hospitals and facilities are situated in England, an NHS Foundation Trust; the police authority and chief officer of police for a police area in England; the British Transport Police Authority so far as exercising functions in relation to England; a local probation board for an area in England, a youth offending team for an area in England; the governor of a prison or secure training centre in England (or in the case of a contracted out prison or secure centre, its director); and any person to the extent that he is providing services under s11 of the Learning and Skills Act 2000. This will also include the UK Border Agency.[54]

Education

6.28   Local authorities in England, Wales and Scotland are under a legal obligation to ensure that education is available for all children of compulsory school age (ie up to 16). This duty applies regardless of the child's immigration status or rights of residence. The Education

54   Borders, Immigration and Citizenship Bill 2008, 2009.

and Inspections Act 2006 in England and Wales placed local authorities under a duty to make arrangements to identify children who are missing education. Children missing education are those of compulsory school age who are not on a school role and who are not receiving a suitable education otherwise (eg through home schooling). Statutory guidance is available at www.everychildmatters.gov.uk/ childrenmissingeducation, and in Scotland in the 'Children missing from education' section of *Safe and well: good practice in schools for keeping children safe and well.*

Privacy

6.29   Convention CETS 197 requires each party to protect the private life and identity of the victim.[55] The specific requirements are that personal data is to be stored and used in conformity with the conditions provided for in the Council of Europe Convention for the protection of individuals with regard to automatic processing of personal data (CETS No 108). States parties are also required to adopt measures to ensure, in particular, that the identity, or details allowing the identification, of a child victim of trafficking are not made publicly known, through the media or by any other means, except, in exceptional circumstances, in order to facilitate the tracing of family members or otherwise secure the well-being and protection of the child. Courts already have powers under the Contempt of Court Act 1981 to prevent reporting which would identify the child. That may include not identifying related adults.

Long-term solutions

6.30   The state is also required to identify a long-term solution for the child which may mean return to the sending state or which may mean settlement in the UK. This is dealt with in more detail in chapter 11.

---

55   Article 11.

CHAPTER 7

Trafficking for the purpose of exploitation

Key points

- Section 4 of the Asylum and Immigration (Treatment of Claimants etc) Act 2004 prohibits the arranging or facilitation of transfer into, within or out of the UK for the purpose of exploitation.
- This covers labour trafficking.
- It also covers organ trafficking.
- The definition in the 2004 Act covers abuse of vulnerability.
- The definitions and conventions of the International Labour Organization (ILO) should be referred to.
- The offence covers exploitation of or intention to exploit the vulnerability of children or those under a physical or mental disability. Arguably this does not truly reflect the principles in the UN Trafficking Protocol.

Introduction

7.1   A specific criminal prohibition on trafficking for the purposes of exploitation has only been in force since 1 December 2004. This is wide enough to cover labour exploitation. Since then, there has been only one prosecution. This is not because of a lack of labour trafficking or a lack of serious cases, some of which have been prosecuted as common law offences.

> On 5 February 2004, 23 Chinese workers died while cocklepicking in Morecambe Bay. Their gangmaster was convicted of manslaughter. The shellfish buyers were convicted of offences of assisting illegal immigration.

7.2   The lack of prosecutions may change shortly. On 18 November 2008, a number of arrests were made on a leek farm following a call from ex-employees and investigations (Operation Ruby). More than 60 Eastern European men and women aged between 15 and 67 were working in extremely poor conditions. Three people were arrested on charges of labour trafficking. Financial investigations continue and charges have yet to be brought.

7.3   Economists argue that labour trafficking occurs at the junction between the demand in the British economy for cheap flexible labour (even, and especially, during a recession) and the supply of labour, assisted by a reluctance on the part of immigration authorities to grant migrants a legitimate right to work. The UK Action Plan mentions a lack of information regarding the scale of the problem.[1]

7.4   The UN Protocols refer to trafficking for the purposes of sexual and of labour exploitation as if they were twin forms of trafficking. In practice, however, although the fundamental principles are the same, trafficking for the purposes of labour exploitation requires a significantly different approach than that used for trafficking for the purposes of sexual exploitation as regards strategies for its prevention, detection and elimination and as regards remedies for it. There is considerable debate on how to distinguish between extremely exploitative working conditions on the one hand and labour trafficking on the other. There is evidence that one category can shift into the other over time. There is, in addition, a degree of uncertainty in the definition.[2] Courts and public authorities continue to struggle with applying the definition of forced labour. Will only evidence of force suffice to prove forced labour? Do conditions which are particularly exploitative (eg failure to pay the minimum wage) give rise to a presumption (which will be rebuttable) that true consent has not been given? It is submitted that the difficulty arises through the fact that, while people will readily believe that prostitution is done unwillingly, they are far more reluctant to draw the same inference with labour.

7.5   Although national criminal law has been extended to cover trafficking for labour exploitation only relatively recently, labour trafficking has been addressed extensively in a number of conventions of the ILO. The ILO has also provided models of effective action. The law can be effectively enforced not only through the ordinary criminal courts but also through a system of labour inspection.[3] The ILO also pioneered the tripartite, or partnership, approach.

Criminal offence

7.6   The Sexual Offences Act 2003 only covered sex trafficking. There was therefore no specific prohibition on trafficking other than for sexual

---

1   See p5 of the Action Plan.
2   See also chapters 2 and 3.
3   See chapter 12.

services. The Asylum and Immigration (Treatment of Claimants etc) Act 2004 (AI(TC)A 2004, or 'the 2004 Act') created a criminal offence of trafficking people for exploitation. Exploitation is defined in the Act. It extends to all exploitation which is non-sexual. It thus includes exploitation for the purposes of forced labour, although it is not limited to exploitation of that kind. The section came into force on 1 December 2004.[4] It does not apply to offences committed before that date.

7.7   AI(TC)A 2004 s4[5] provides that a person commits an offence if he or she arranges or facilitates the arrival in, entry into,[6] travel within, or departure from the UK of an individual (the 'passenger') and (a) the person intends to exploit the passenger in the UK or elsewhere, or (b) the person believes that another person is likely to exploit the passenger in the UK or elsewhere (in the case of transfer into and within the UK) or elsewhere (in the case of transfer out of the UK).

> 4(1) A person commits an offence if he arranges or facilitates the arrival in the United Kingdom of an individual (the 'passenger') and–
>
> (a) he intends to exploit the passenger in the United Kingdom or elsewhere, or
> (b) he believes that another person is likely to exploit the passenger in the United Kingdom or elsewhere.
>
> (2) A person commits an offence if he arranges or facilitates travel within the United Kingdom by an individual (the 'passenger') in respect of whom he believes that an offence under subsection (1) may have been committed and–
>
> (a) he intends to exploit the passenger in the United Kingdom or elsewhere, or
> (b) he believes that another person is likely to exploit the passenger in the United Kingdom or elsewhere.

---

4   SI 2004/2999.
5   The offence reappeared in clauses 108 and 109 of the draft Immigration and Citizenship Bill 2008 (July 2008). There were some changes, which were essentially drafting changes. The bill was replaced by the Immigration Simplication Bill, a draft of which has not been published as of January 2009.
6   Inserted by s31(1) of the UK Borders Act 2007. Entry into force: 31 January 2008.

(3) A person commits an offence if he arranges or facilitates the departure from the United Kingdom of an individual (the 'passenger') and–

(a) he intends to exploit the passenger outside the United Kingdom, or
(b) he believes that another person is likely to exploit the passenger outside the United Kingdom.

(4) For the purposes of this section a person is exploited if (and only if)–

(a) he is the victim of behaviour that contravenes Article 4 of the Human Rights Convention (slavery and forced labour),
(b) he is encouraged, required or expected to do anything as a result of which he or another person would commit an offence under the Human Organ Transplants Act 1989 (c. 31) or the Human Organ Transplants (Northern Ireland) Order 1989 (SI 1989/2408 (N.I. 21)),
(c) he is subjected to force, threats or deception designed to induce him–
    (i)   to provide services of any kind,
    (ii) to provide another person with benefits of any kind, or
    (iii) to enable another person to acquire benefits of any kind, or
(d) he is requested or induced to undertake any activity, having been chosen as the subject of the request or inducement on the grounds that–
    (i)   he is mentally or physically ill or disabled, he is young or he has a family relationship with a person, and
    (ii) a person without the illness, disability, youth or family relationship would be likely to refuse the request or resist the inducement.

7.8   The offence has two constituent parts: the first relating to transfer, the second to exploitation or intention to exploit.

Transfer: arranging or facilitating arrival in, travel within or departure from the UK

7.9   Like the offence of trafficking for sexual exploitation in the Sexual Offences Act 2003, the offence is set out in three sections, dealing in turn with transfer into, within and out of the UK.

7.10   Facilitation bears its ordinary meaning of 'to make easier'. Thus the section will cover a range of actions through which a contribution is made to the transfer of the individual. Unlike the offence in the 2003 Act, the arrangement or facilitation of arrival, travel or departure does not have to be intentional. This is unlikely to be a significant difference since the relevant key intention is the intention to exploit.

7.11   More significantly, and unlike the definition in article 3 of the UN Protocol, the arrangement or facilitation does not have to be done 'by means of the threat or use of force or other forms of coercion, of abduction, of fraud, of deception, of the abuse of power or of a position of vulnerability or of the giving or receiving of payments or benefits to achieve the consent of a person having control over another person'. There is good reason for this. The UN Protocol is concerned with the definition of trafficking across a range of sending, transit and destination states. In contrast, the UK is a destination state. The primary concern (and the most readily available evidence) will be the exploitation for which the victim is intended.

7.12   The section is wide enough to cover the activities of a range of defendants along the supply chain, from the labour recruiter to the agent to the intended end user. This may include the initial request for labour, the supply of papers or other assistance. Importantly, the offence has extraterritorial effect since s4 applies to anything done whether inside or outside the UK.[7] All crimes along the chain can thus be prosecuted before a court in the UK.

7.13   The offence is not listed in Schedule 1 to the Serious Crimes Act 2007, but is likely to be considered as serious as the listed crimes. It is therefore an offence under the 2007 Act intentionally to encourage or assist an offence or to encourage or assist crime believing that an offence, or one or more offences, will be committed. To the extent that acts of encouragement are not caught by the 'facilitation' provision, they will be caught under the 2007 Act.

7.14   Common law inchoate offences may also be charged. These are conspiracy to commit an offence or attempt to commit the offence.

---

7   As substituted by s31 of the UK Borders Act 2007, with effect from 31 January 2008 (SI 2008/99), for the previously more limited extraterritorial effect, limited to arranging or facilitating outside the UK only if committed by a British citizen, a British overseas territories citizen, a British national (overseas), a British overseas citizen, a person who is a British subject under the British Nationality Act 198, a British protected person within the meaning of that Act or a body incorporated under the law of a part of the UK.

7.15   The concept of the abuse of vulnerability has shifted from being part of the definition of transfer (as it is in the UN Trafficking Protocol) to being part of the definition of exploitation. The UN Trafficking Protocol defines abuse of vulnerability in the transfer as 'any situation in which the person involved has no real and acceptable alternative but to submit to the abuse involved'. There is no reason why this definition cannot apply to the exploitation limb. In including abuse of vulnerability as a head of exploitation, the 2004 Act follows the approach taken in the European Union Framework Decision.

> ### Commission's Explanatory Memorandum to Article 1 of its proposed Framework Decision[8]
>
> As regards the elements qualifying a person for the purpose of labour exploitation as a criminal offence, [misuse of authority, influence or pressure or another form of abuse], which partly correspond to the United Nations Protocol, cover forms of taking advantage or exercising pressure when a person is trafficked. This objective is to ensure a comprehensive coverage of criminal conduct. This includes practices such as debt bondage in which the person has no choice but to submit to the pressure. It also includes the abuse of the vulnerability of persons, for instance of persons being mentally or physically disabled or of persons illegally remaining on the territory of a Member State who are often in a situation in which they have no choice, but to submit to the exploitation. These latter elements ensure also that the offence takes the specific situation of the victim into account and not only the conduct performed by the trafficker.

Intention to exploit

7.16   All three sections require intention to exploit the victim in the UK or elsewhere or belief that another person is likely to exploit the person in the UK or elsewhere. In addition, s4(2), which deals with trafficking within the UK, requires belief by the perpetrator that the victim may have been trafficked into the UK in breach of s4(1). This is an unnecessary extra hurdle to surmount and reveals a continued, and mistaken, focus on trafficking as primarily an immigration

---

8   http://eur-lex.europa.eu.

offence. Section 4(3), dealing with trafficking out of the UK, contains no such requirement.

7.17   Careful consideration should be given as to which offence or offences to charge. If there is doubt as to whether the requisite mental element (intention to exploit or belief that another will exploit) can be established at the time of the relevant arrangement or facilitation, ie on or before entry into the UK, then the offence of arranging or facilitating travel within the UK should also be considered.

Exploitation defined

7.18   Exploitation is defined in s4(4) as:

(a) behaviour which contravenes Article 4 of the European Convention on Human Rights;

(b) being encouraged, required or expected to do anything as a result of which the passenger or another person would commit an offence under the Human Organs Transplants Act 1989 or the Human Organ Transplants (Northern Ireland) Order 1989;

(c) where a person is subjected to force, threats or deception designed to induce him or her:

  (i)   to provide services of any kind;

  (ii) to provide another person with benefits of any kind; or

  (iii) to enable another person to acquire benefits of any kind; or

(d) where the person is requested or induced to undertake any activity, having been chosen as the subject of the request or inducement on the grounds that:

  (i)   the person is mentally or physically ill or disabled, is young or has a family relationship with a person; and

  (ii) a person without the illness, disability, youth or family relationship would be likely to refuse the request or resist the inducement.

7.19   Summary conviction carries a maximum penalty of 12 months' imprisonment and/or a fine not exceeding the statutory maximum. Conviction on indictment carries a maximum penalty of 14 years' imprisonment and/or a fine not exceeding the statutory maximum.

7.20   Each of the above categories of exploitation will be looked at in turn. There is no hierarchy of gravity among the different definitions. Exploitation is defined across four sections. The UN Protocol requires that 'exploitation shall include, *at a minimum*, the exploitation of the prostitution of others or other forms of sexual exploitation, forced labour or services, slavery or practices similar to slavery, servitude or the removal of organs'.[9] As regards forced labour or slavery or practices similar to slavery or servitude, the UK already has obligations to eliminate slavery, servitude or forced or compulsory labour under article 4 of the European Convention on Human Rights. The first section therefore simply refers to article 4. Removal of organs is prohibited in the second section. The third and fourth sections cover any trafficking not caught by the other sections. Parliamentary intention was to cover the definition in the UN Protocol and in article 4 and to comprehensively prohibit all forms of trafficking for (non-sexual) exploitation. This is reflected in the late addition as the bill went through parliament.[10] The interpretative notes to the Trafficking Protocol are relevant.[11]

Behaviour contravening article 4

7.21   The section is not happily drafted. Article 4 case-law involves cases brought by individuals against the state. In contrast, criminal prosecutions will involve cases brought by the state against alleged traffickers. However, the point of substance is that reference to article 4 is intended to be for substantive definition, ie that the behaviour must be of sufficient severity that it would amount to slavery, servitude or forced labour.

7.22   Article 4 provides:

1. No one shall be held in slavery or servitude.
2. No one shall be required to perform forced or compulsory labour.

Article 4(1) is non derogable, even in times of war or public emergency.[12] Derogation may be made from article 4(2) only in circumstances of war or other public emergency threatening the life of the nation and only to the extent strictly necessary. Article 4(3) contains some circumstances in which state inflicted labour does not amount to forced or compulsory labour or can be justified. It is of assistance in interpreting article 4(2). The exceptions are unlikely to be of relevance in human trafficking cases, since they concern state-imposed labour.

---

9   Emphasis added.
10   See para 7.36.
11   See chapter 2.
12   Article 15, ECHR.

7.23   In determining whether behaviour amounts to slavery, servitude or forced labour within the meaning of article 4 of the convention,[13] the courts must have regard to the jurisprudence of the European Court of Human Rights[14] as well as of national courts deciding cases under the Human Rights Act 1998. Further, the European Court has repeatedly referred to the body of ILO conventions, as part of the corpus of fundamental rights.[15]

ILO conventions

7.24   There are also ILO conventions requiring action to protect migrant workers and to address exploitation by recruitment agencies. However, in 1998, the ILO Declaration on Fundamental Principles and Rights at Work defined eight fundamental ILO conventions. Two of these are concerned with forced labour: Conventions 29 and 105, and one with child labour: Convention 182. According to the ILO Declaration on Fundamental Principles and Rights at Work, all ILO member states have an obligation, even if they have not ratified the ILO conventions in question, to respect, promote and realise the principle of the elimination of all forms of forced or compulsory labour. The ILO has a duty to assist states in this.

Slavery or servitude

7.25   The most serious conditions would amount to slavery or servitude. Slavery requires characteristics of ownership to be present. Servitude is wider. Articles 1 and 7 of the UN 1957 Supplementary Convention on the Abolition of Slavery, the Slave Trade and Institutions and Practices Similar to Slavery defined a person of servile status as someone subjected to:[16]

- Debt bondage
- Serfdom
- Any institution or practice regarding
    - the transfer of a woman on her marriage
    - the delivery of a child by his natural parents or guardian for labour

---

13 Article 4 of the Universal Declaration of Human Rights contains a similar prohibition.
14 See chapter 3.
15 See chapter 3.
16 See article 1.

What is anticipated is situations in which denial of the individual's freedom is not limited to denial of freedom of labour. The European Court of Human Rights in *Siliadin v France* 73316/01[17] upheld a complaint of servitude where a minor was brought to France for domestic work 15 hours a day, seven days a week, had her papers confiscated, was entirely dependent on the people she worked for, and was not permitted to leave the house. The court considered the UN 1957 Convention at 123–129 and held that with regard to servitude, it 'prohibits a particularly serious form of denial of freedom'. The court also referred to and adopted the conclusion of European Commission of Human Rights in the case of *Van Droogenbroeck v Belgium* 9 July 1980, Series B, Vol 44, p30, 78–80 that servitude comprises: 'in addition to the obligation to provide certain services to another ... the obligation to live on the other's property and the impossibility of changing his status'. Certain cases of domestic servants may therefore fall within the court's definition of servitude. Given the court's analysis, cases of serious abuse of domestic servants would be covered, although it will generally not be necessary to prove which part of article 4 applies.

Forced or compulsory labour

7.26   The meaning of forced labour should be taken from the relevant ILO conventions: The Forced Labour Convention 29(1930); The Abolition of Forced Labour Convention 105(1957); and the Worst Forms of Child Labour Labour Convention 182(1999) supplemented by ILO Recommendation 190.

Article 2(1) of Convention 29(1930) defines forced labour as: 'all work or service which is exacted from any person under the menace of any penalty and for which the said person has not offered himself voluntarily'. This definition excludes some forms of labour. Article 25: 'the illegal exaction of forced or compulsory labour shall be punishable as a penal offence, and it shall be an obligation on any Member ratifying this Convention to ensure that the penalties imposed by law are really adequate and are strictly enforced'.

7.27   The definition of forced labour in ILO Convention 29 is more specific than the term in article 4(2). The European Court of Human Rights has adopted it in *Van der Mussele* 8919/80, finding[18] no guidance in the travaux preparatoires of the convention and finding

17 See further chapter 3.
18 32–24.

clear evidence that article 4 was modelled on article 8 of the draft International Covenant on Civil and Political Rights and on ILO Convention 29. The court held that the ILO definition of forced or compulsory labour as 'all work or service which is exacted from any person under the menace of any penalty and for which the said person has not offered himself voluntarily' was a starting point for interpretation of article 4.[19] This involves considering, firstly, whether there exists in the circumstances of each case, the menace of a penalty; and secondly, even if the first condition is satisfied, whether the worker has offered himself or herself voluntarily.

'Exacted from any person under menace of a penalty'

7.28   However, forced labour under the ILO conventions does not require having to establish actual physical force. The ILO has made it clear that within the concept of labour which has been forced, the following are included: submission, vulnerability which is exploited, and financial debts which are disproportionately applied to the work. It should also be borne in mind that the case may involve initial deception and agreement to a different job.

ILO indicators of forced labour – (any one will suffice)[20]

(1) *Threats or actual physical harm to the worker.* This will encompass physical and sexual violence. It may itself be an assault.

(2) *Restriction of movement and confinement to the workplace or within a limited area.* This often happens in the case of domestic workers. This is likely also to amount to forced imprisonment.

(3) *Debt bondage* – where the worker works to pay off a debt or a loan, and is not paid adequately or at all for their services; the employer may provide food and accommodation at such inflated prices that the worker cannot escape the debt. Labour is demanded as a means of repayment of a loan, or of money given in advance. This most commonly occurs where a worker has paid money to the recruiter and is required to pay it off.

---

19   *Van der Mussele* 32.

20   See, ILO Special Action Programme to combat forced labour: *Human trafficking and forced labour exploitation, guidance for legislation and law enforcement* (2005).

This is of itself unlawful under UK law as a finder's fee.[21] It may also occur where work is underpaid and workers' accommodation is overcharged.

Status or condition arising from a pledge by a debtor of his or her personal services or of those of a person under his or her control as security for a debt, if the value of those services as reasonably assessed is not applied towards the liquidation of the debt or the length and nature of those services are not respectively limited and defined.[22]

(4) *Withholding of wages or excessive wage reductions* that violate previously made agreements.

(5) *Retention of passports and identity documents* so that the worker cannot leave or prove his or her identity and status.

(6) *Threat of denunciation to the authorities*, where the worker is in an irregular immigration status.

'And for which he has not offered himself voluntarily'

7.29   The ILO definition contains a requirement of lack of voluntariness, ie the labour must be work exacted under menace of a penalty *and* 'for which he has not offered himself voluntarily'. In *Van der Mussele*, the court held that notwithstanding actual consent, forced or compulsory labour may exist where a considerable and unreasonable imbalance exists between obligations undertaken by the worker in order to pursue an aim. This definition echoes the definition of debt bondage and courts should be willing to look beyond actual subjective consent to the objective terms and conditions of work.

7.30   The 'voluntariness' concept is not an issue where threats, restriction of movement, and deception are concerned, since the law will regard any submission to such methods as invalid. These are objective issues. The real issue arises where working conditions or remuneration are of a very low standard. Poor working conditions does not appear as an indicator in the ILO indicators of forced labour. Withholding of wages or excessive wage reductions does appear but not low wages per se. This is because 'the State or a particular employer cannot be held accountable for all external constraints or indirect coercion existing in practice'.[23] This may be

---

21 See 12.31.

22 Article 1a, UN Supplementary Convention on the Abolition of Slavery 1956.

23 *Human trafficking and forced labour exploitation*, Guidance for legislation and law enforcement [2005] International Labour Office, p22.

true in an international context with different standards applying. However, at national level, certain working conditions are set as a minimum. Working conditions falling below a minimum are good evidence from which to draw an inference that genuine consent has not been given, as the case below shows. The worse the conditions, the more readily will the inference be drawn. It is not unduly onerous on employers to honour that objective national standard in employment. The following case is an illustration of this principle.

A public interest petition was filed concerning the working conditions of construction workers on the 1984 Asiad Games Sports Complexes. The Supreme Court held that the term 'forced labour' should be read widely and rejected an argument that the term excluded work for which some payment had been made. The court held:

> It is obvious that ordinarily no one would willingly supply labour or service for another for less than the minimum wage, when he knows that under the law he is entitled to get a minimum wage for the labour or service provided by him. It may therefore be legitimately presumed that when a person provides labour or service against receipt of remuneration which is less than the minimum wage, he is acting under the force of some compulsion which drives him to work though he is paid less than what he is entitled under the law to receive ... It may be physical force which compels a person to provide labour or service to another or it may even be compulsion arising from hunger or poverty or want or destitution. Any factor which deprives a person of a choice of alternatives and compels him to adopt a particular course may properly be regarded as 'force' and if labour or service is compelled as a result of such 'force' it would be forced labour.

Indian Supreme Court in *People's Union for Democratic Rights and others v Union of India and others* [1983] 1 SCR 456

7.31   Thus, although the force (destitution) does not emanate from the employer, the employer has taken advantage of it to reduce payment to below the legal minimum.

The Committee of Experts' approach to the issue of voluntariness

While this is particular to the context of prison labour, it demonstrates a willingness to consider objective factors where there is a heightened risk of involuntariness.

The Committee has considered that, in the context of a captive labour force having no alternative access to the free labour market, the most reliable indicator of the voluntariness of labour is the work performed under conditions approximating a free labour relationship, which include wage levels (leaving room for deductions and attachments), social security and occupational safety and health. In addition, there may also be other factors that can be regarded as objective and measurable advantages which the prisoners could gain from the actual performance of the work and which be considered in determining whether consent was freely given and informed, such as the learning of new skills which could be deployed by prisoners when released, the offer of continuing work of the same type upon their release, or the opportunity to work cooperatively in a controlled environment enabling them to develop team skills. The Committee has indicated that all of these factors should be taken as a whole in determining whether consent was freely given and informed.

ILO Committee of Experts on the Application of Conventions and Recommendations (97th session, 2008) CEACR individual observation concerning Forced Labour Convention 1930 (No 29) United Kingdom (Ratification 1931) Ref: ILC 97 Report (III) 1A[24]

7.32   The issue of consent does not apply just at the time of entering into the agreement, since circumstances can change. A person's initial agreement to enter into a working relationship may be negatived by a change in the nature of the work or restrictions on leaving the employment.

7.33   Although under the ILO conventions, child labour is not necessarily forced labour, the wider wording of the 2004 Act will apply to any serious exploitation, actual or intended, of the vulnerability of a child.[25]

Trafficking in human organs

7.34   Relevant exploitation would also be committed where the victim is encouraged, required or expected to do anything as a result of which he or another person would commit an offence under the Human Organ Transplants Act 1989 or the Human Organ Transplants

24 See http://www.ilo.org/ilolex/gbe/ceacr2008.htm.
25 See further chapter 6.

(Northern Ireland) Order 1989. Sections 1 and 2 of the 1989 Act (and the 1989 Order in similar terms) prohibit commercial dealings in human organs which have been removed from a dead or a living person for transplant to another person (whether any of these matters have taken place in Great Britain or elsewhere) and transplants between persons who are not genetically related. The section is phrased so that coercion is not a necessary element.

Subjected to force, threats or deception designed to induce him (i) to provide services of any kind; (ii) to provide another person with benefits of any kind, or (iii) to enable another person to acquire benefits of any kind

7.35　This is a straightforward category. Relevant threats may be to take away the worker's passport or to denounce them to the immigration authorities or to harm them or their family in the UK or in the country of origin. The section is designed to cover all kinds of labour exacted under such threats, regardless of the exact contractual relationship and regardless of who benefits from the labour and how, and even if not amounting to a breach of article 4. The offence under this section, however, is not committed by the beneficiaries but by any person facilitating travel.

Requested or induced to undertake any activity, having been chosen as the subject of the request or inducement on the grounds that (i) he is mentally or physically ill or disabled, he is young or he has a family relationship with a person, and (ii) a person without the illness, disability, youth or family relationship would be likely to refuse the request or resist the inducement

7.36　Paragraph (d) is the widest category. It is intended to cover situations not covered by (c) where the request is made to Person A but Person B is intended to be exploited, for example where a parent is paid or threatened but no direct threat, request or inducement is made to the child. It focuses squarely on situations involving the exploitation of vulnerability.

> One must take care not to confuse the initial request, inducement or threat made to the parents – which, as stated, we do not consider to be strictly relevant to the question of whether the child is in fact exploited – with any subsequent request or inducement which may be made to the child himself, which may be relevant to the issue of whether the child is exploited, if subsection (4)(d) is relied on. The issue of force, threats or deception or of a request or inducement in

subsection 4(c) and (d) respectively is simply a means of determining when a person is exploited.

Lord Bassam of Brighton (Hansard, 18 May 2004)

We are satisfied that the ordinary meaning of the word 'inducement' is such that a person may be induced to do something notwithstanding his not being fully aware of what he is being induced to do. We therefore consider that subsection (4)(d) as drafted can apply in cases involving very young children, who may not be fully aware of the situation, of their actions, and of what it is they are being encouraged to do.

Lord Rooker (Hansard, 6 July 2004, Col 671)

The first conviction under the 2004 Act

The first conviction under this section occurred in October 2008.[26] The defendants, who were Romanian Roma, were convicted of trafficking a child into and within the UK, for exploitation (in that case putting the 13-year-old child to sell the Big Issue). This was a controversial prosecution resulting from police raids in Slough. The 'cultural' defence put forward failed but the sentences were relatively light: between one and three years.

Relevant evidence

7.37   It is the concept of force within the definition of forced labour which the courts and other relevant authorities are likely to find most difficult to understand in theory and to apply in practice. It is therefore important to remind the court of the exact definition and to put relevant guidance before the courts and any decision making body. In practice, few workers are led here in chains and it may be said that they have chosen to migrate. This is to ignore the reality for many of the transaction to which they are subjected. Free consent can be negated by:

(i)   disproportionate debt leading to debt bondage;

(ii) inability truly to consent because of physical or mental age;

(iii) deception or fraud;

(iv) force (coercion);

---

26   *R v Vasile, Stanciu, Vasile, Stocia* at Reading Crown Court, 14 November 2008. See 6.21. The cases are being appealed.

(v) exploitation of vulnerability leading to submission rather than consent (abuse of power).

7.38 This issue may be particularly difficult given that the more successful the investigation, the earlier the arrest and that in some cases the trafficker will be apprehended before the worker has done any work. In such cases, it is likely that the intelligence will have come from information on the networks used and from evidence of the treatment of other workers.

Short-term assistance and support

Key points

- Immediate assistance and support must be provided pursuant to the obligation under article 12 of the European Convention on Action against Human Trafficking.
- Where there are reasonable grounds for believing that an individual is the victim of trafficking, they will be granted a 45-day recovery and reflection period, which may be extended. Minimum support rights are granted from this point. The decision on whether there are reasonable grounds will be made by the UK Border Agency (UKBA). That decision will be subject to judicial review.
- Where a victim's stay is considered necessary either owing to their personal situation or their stay is necessary for the purpose of their co-operation with the authorities, a temporary, renewable one-year residence permit will be granted. This is granted under the UKBA discretionary leave policy.
- Where the client wishes to work, permit conditions should allow this.

8.1   As a result of its ratification on 17 December 2008 of the European Convention on Human Trafficking, the government has introduced measures relevant to the immediate or short-term support of those who may be victims of trafficking. These measures came into effect on 1 April 2009. These measures of support are accessed through identification as a victim by the United Kingdom Human Trafficking Centre (UKHTC) or the UKBA. Disputes over identification are likely to result in judicial review of decisions.

Elements of victim assistance and support

8.2   The relevant obligations under the convention are summarised here.[1] Article 12 of the CETS 197 (covered in greater detail in chapter 3) requires legislative or other measures to assist victims in recovery. The convention requires such assistance to include minimum standards of living, access to emergency medical treatment,

---

1   They are set out in full in chapter 3.

translation and interpreting services if needed, counselling, information on legal rights and services available, assistance in criminal proceedings against offenders and access to education for children. Article 13 requires provision of a recovery and reflection period, in cases where there are reasonable grounds to believe that the person concerned is a victim of trafficking. Article 14 requires a renewable residence permit to be issued to victims.

Criteria for assistance and support

8.3   The gateway to this assistance and support is initial identification by the state as a victim. CETS 197 (articles 10–13)[2] sets a low threshold, consistent with the protective intention of the provisions. All that is needed is 'reasonable grounds' (article 10(2)) to believe that a person has been a victim of trafficking in human beings. Reasonable grounds is not defined in the convention but has been considered often in national case law. It means simply that there is a set of circumstances which would give rise to a rational belief. Resolution of conflicts of fact or credibility issues have limited place at this initial stage. The short timescales[3] for decisions also suggest a low threshold. The Organization for Security and Cooperation in Europe (OSCE) goes further in its 2004 Handbook[4] and refers to the making of a presumption. About children, CETS 197 (article 10(3)) also provides that where the age of a victim is uncertain and there are reasons to believe that the victim is a child, the victim shall be presumed to be a child and shall be accorded special protection measures pending verification of their age.

8.4   The following lists identify key signs to assist staff in identifying victims or possible victims of sex trafficking. Note that these lists are far from exhaustive. They should not be treated as conditions which must be satisfied, but as the type of indicators which should alert the relevant front-line worker. They are neither exhaustive nor exclusive of other factors, but failure to act on them where present will render any decision vulnerable.

---

2   See 3.21.
3   See 8.6.
4   National Referral Mechanisms, OSCE, 2004, www.osce.org.

Key signs to assist staff in identifying victims / possible victims of trafficking

Home Office

The following should assist Officers in making a primary assessment of whether the individuals encountered are or may be potential victims of trafficking for sexual exploitation.

Consider whether there are signs of:

- Threat or actual physical harm to the individual
- Psychological abuse and intimidation
- Restriction on the individual's movement
- Debt bondage: provision of food, accommodation, travel expenses, clothing at very high prices

Consider the individual's physical/psychological symptoms of trafficking, for example:

- Fear
- Depression (lack of interest, hopelessness, suicidal)
- Anxiety (tense, restlessness, nervous, suddenly scared)
- Hostility (annoyed and irritated easily, temper outbursts)
- Or other physical and health symptoms including: fatigue, memory difficulties, headaches, abdominal and back pain

Consider whether:

- Wages are being withheld
- Travel documents have been retained or the individuals are in possession of false documents

Consider whether the individual:

- States he or she was threatened with being reported to the authorities because of their illegal status in the UK
- Mentions that he or she was deceived by the agent/trafficker, ie false promises, like well paid work, marriage or access to the education system
- Mentions that he or she was recruited through agents
- Shows unfamiliarity with the country
- Was asked or forced to provide sexual services
- Was subjected to crimes such as rape/abduction/kidnapping
- Had opportunity to escape controllers but never sought to take advantage of such opportunities
- Has few, if any, friends or family in the UK
- Claims to be older than their actual age – if Officers suspect that an individual may be a child (less than 18 years of age) they must contact Social Services immediately

National referral mechanism

8.5   CETS 197 requires the state to have in place 'competent authorities' with persons trained and qualified to prevent and combat trafficking in human beings and to identify and help victims, including children. CETS 197 (article 10.5 and article 35) also requires the various relevant agencies (police, immigration, customs and local authorities) to co-operate not only with each other but also with any organisations (for example, non governmental organisations) which are concerned with the provision of support. This requires a co-ordinated approach across all agencies, with specialist support sought where necessary. This is sometimes referred to as a National Referral Mechanism.

8.6   The function of a specialist co-ordinating agency has been assumed by the UK Human Trafficking Centre. The UKHTC is referred to as a Central Competent Authority, which does not reflect the term as it is used in CETS 197. The UKBA also has a function as a competent authority. These two bodies will between them determine the question of whether there are reasonable grounds to believe that a person is a victim of trafficking in human beings. The UKBA will take referrals from immigration officers. It is intended that all other referrals should go to and be determined by the UKHTC. How this will work in practice is as yet unclear. There is scope for confusion of roles. Children will not be dealt with separately, although there will be liaison with the relevant local authority. Given the particular issues arising in respect of the identification of children, this is less than satisfactory. However, the UKHTC has pioneered a partnership approach and is able to access specialist advice across sectors. If expert advice is sought and accepted, the process may function better than anticipated.

Home Office position

The exact form of a victim identification process and the options for which public body or bodies should make decisions on who qualifies as a victim has been the subject of extensive consultation, within and outside Government agencies. Two forms of competent authority have been subject to operational testing over recent months: one based in the UK Human Trafficking Centre; one based in the UK Border Agency. As there are immigration consequences for foreign nationals being found to be victims of trafficking, UKBA need to retain a decisive decision-making role on behalf of the Crown in those cases to ensure that the discretion of the Secretary of State on immigration matters is not fettered. As they have done previously, both agencies will continue to play a key role in identifying victims of trafficking, working closely with the police, local authorities, non-governmental organisations and any other public body likely to come into contact with victims.

Our plans to ratify the Convention will include a different national referral mechanism for children. This referral mechanism will recognise that Local Safeguarding Children's Boards (LSCBs) already consider the vulnerability of the child and are in a good position to consider whether the child has been trafficked or not. So, as part of national referral mechanism LSCBs will filter cases that get referred to a competent authority and it is therefore likely that the majority of those cases will be positively identified by the Competent Authority.

8.7   An adviser should therefore make a referral direct to the UKHTC as soon as possible. It may also be possible to access support directly through a relevant support body (eg POPPY project), who will then complete and pass on the referral form.[5] Where suitable, a request for counselling to the UKHTC or another body should be made at the same time. The counselling report may provide supportive evidence in the long-term, and will certainly prevent the client having to repeat their account unnecessarily.

First stage: recovery and reflection period

8.8   The first protection measure is a recovery and reflection period. The client may be present in the United Kingdom without authorisation. The scheme therefore provides for a period of grace in the first instance. The purpose of the recovery and reflection period is to allow the person time: (a) to recover from initial acute trauma; (b) to escape the influence of the alleged perpetrators of the trafficking; and (c) to take an informed decision about whether to assist the relevant authorities in relation to any investigation or prosecution arising in relation to the alleged trafficking. It is likely to be too early to take long-term decisions. A person who has been granted a

5   Referral form's were not available at the time of publication but will be available from www.ukhtc.org. Full details on the support arrangements had not been published.

recovery and reflection period will not be the subject of removal proceedings for so long as his or her recovery period remains valid.

8.9   This is a matter of administrative rather than statutory discretion. Where the UKBA has decided that there are reasonable grounds for believing that the individual is a victim of trafficking, they will be permitted to remain in the state for a period of 45 days. This will be extendable in some circumstances, for example, if an individual presents as having acute trauma and mental health difficulties. The UKBA expects this decision to be made on average within five days from referral. This is unrealistic. The experience of the POPPY Project[6] over the last six years indicates that an accurate assessment can take at least 30 days, to ensure that the woman feels safe enough to tell her story. A lack of trust of authority is likely to make any disclosures even slower. If this timetable is to be maintained, it should follow that a low threshold should be applied. The relevant (Home Office) Minister will issue, or cause to be issued, to a person who has been granted a recovery and reflection period a notice confirming the fact that the person has been granted permission to be present for 45 days.

8.10   The recovery and reflection period may be terminated, for example where the person has actively, voluntarily and on his or her own initiative renewed contact with the alleged perpetrators of the trafficking; secondly, where it is in the interests of national security or public policy (ordre public) to do so; or thirdly, where victim status is being claimed improperly. The power to terminate such a short period should, it is submitted, never be used. While identification of a safe house to a trafficker will result in accommodation being withdrawn, it should be understood that a range of mechanisms of control over victims may still have effect through fear of reprisals to self or family, Stockholm syndrome, or inducements to return. Retraction of claims should not be taken at face value without any further enquiry. The granting of a recovery and reflection period does not of itself create any right to reside in the state when the period in the notice has expired.

8.11   The decision on whether there are reasonable grounds will thus be made by the UKHTC. There is no appeal from either decision. The lack of a full merits appeal may be subject to challenge under

6   The author is grateful to Helen Atkins and her colleagues at the POPPY Project for some of the information in this chapter.

article 6. The decision will, however, be subject to judicial review on the usual grounds.

This can be on an expedited basis. If there is a strong case, support may be sought in the meantime, if need be by injunction. If necessary, an emergency application may be made to the local authority or to a victim support association[7] for basic support such as accommodation and subsistence.

Convention-compliant support

8.12   As set out above and fully in chapter 3, the convention requires minimum levels of support. These are the following.

Standards of living capable of ensuring their subsistence, through such measures as appropriate and secure accommodation, psychological and material assistance

8.13   The government will contract out this support to the third sector, which will be state funded. The outcome of a tendering process is expected in March 2009. Arrangements for support will change significantly as a result. The model for such support is the collaboration to date with the POPPY Project, consisting of an outreach team which has national scope and the direct service, based in London, which provides accommodation for victims of sex trafficking. POPPY also provided accommodation for women victims of labour trafficking in a 2008 pilot project. It is anticipated that the POPPY model will apply to victims of sex trafficking and trafficking for domestic servitude.

8.14   Any victims in administrative detention should of course be immediately released. At present 37 per cent of referrals to the POPPY Project are from women in custody. Where those women are on remand or have been convicted and sentenced, bail should be applied for pending representations on the charges and/or appeal against conviction.[8]

---

7   Such as the POPPY Project or the Salvation Army.
8   See further chapter 9.

The POPPY Project: A Model of Support

The POPPY Project can only provide accommodation and support to women aged over 18. In order to meet the government-defined criteria for assistance with the POPPY Project, women must have been:

- trafficked to the UK
- forced to work as a prostitute in the UK
- willing to consider co-operating with the authorities

The outreach team has the same criteria, and can provide support if the direct service is at capacity, offering crisis intervention, advocacy, and sign-posting by linking women with other agency support, and finding accommodation.

If POPPY is unable to accommodate a woman there are other ways that the project can help. There are very few services offering specialist support for women who have been trafficked in the UK. In order to develop immigration, psychological, physical health and education services, POPPY has developed partnerships with:

- hostels working with homeless people
- refuges for victims of domestic violence
- embassies and the IOM to assist return
- specialist legal advisers
- Therapeutic and psychological counselling through the Helen Bamber Foundation, women and Girls Network

Once accepted onto the project women are allocated a senior support worker and offered a range of specialist support services. These include:

- supported accommodation
- 24/7 access to support
- one-to-one key working
- access to emergency healthcare
- translation and interpretation
- provision of a weekly subsistence allowance
- regular health and needs assessments
- registration with a GP in order to receive any necessary medical treatment
- registration with a dentist
- access to therapy and counselling services
- access to leisure, education and English classes

- integration and/or re-settlement support including, where applicable, support with the voluntary return scheme
- education sessions covering areas such as equal opportunities, welfare benefits and healthy relationships
- help contacting family and friends
- support accessing legal advice, including information relating to immigration status and applications for asylum or safe return programmes
- liaison with police and immigration services
- regular risk assessments and safety planning

For more information about POPPY Accommodation and Support, or to make a referral, visit www.eaves4women.co.uk/POPPY_ project or call 020 7840 7129.

Access to emergency medical treatment and access to necessary medical treatment to others lawfully within its territory

8.15   The general rule for access to NHS treatment is that it is subject to an 'ordinary residence' test.[9] However, no charge is made, regardless of status, in respect of medical treatment at a hospital accident and emergency department, casualty department or dental or ophthalmic emergency department, nor for treatment of certain listed diseases, nor for sexually transmitted diseases or compulsory psychiatric treatment.[10] While overseas visitors are liable to be charged for other medical treatment, there are exempt categories. One exempt category is a person who the 'competent authorities' (for the purposes of the convention) consider there are reasonable grounds to believe is a victim and is within the reflection period or has been identified as a victim, or their (permanently co-habitiny) spouse, civil partner or child.[11] These regulations go beyond the minimum provided by

---

9   See eg *Shah v Barnet London Borough Council* [1983] 2 AC 309 and *A v Department of Health and West Middlesex University Hospital NHS Trust* [2008] EWHC 855 (Admin).

10   Regulation 3 of the National Health Service (Charges to Overseas Visitors) Regulations SI 1989/306.

11   Regulations 3 and 4 of the National Health Service (Charges to Overseas Visitors) Regulations 1989, as amended. In England, the amendment is by way of SI 2008/2251 and came into force on 6 October 2008. In Wales, it is by way of 2008/2364 and came into force on 1 October 2008. In Scotland, it is by way of 2008/290 and came into force on 6 October 2008.

Convention CETS 197 and do not require the patient to prove they are lawfully present.

Translation and interpretation services

8.16 These should be independent of the state, especially while the determination of status is ongoing. Any home office interpreters used at interviews should be checked to ensure they have no connections with traffickers. In cases of trafficking for sexual exploitation, interpreters of the same gender should be used.

Counselling and information, in particular as regards their legal rights and the services available to them, in a language that they can understand

8.17 Again, this should be independent. Assistance with applying to the Criminal Injuries Compensation Authority does not adequately comply with this duty. No guidance has yet been given by the Legal Services Commission on how applications for legal advice and assistance in trafficking cases are to be dealt with.

8.18 The information regarding rights should not be limited to a factual description but should include competent legal advice.

8.19 Advisers will need to consider ways of making their legal services linguistically accessible. Advisers should consider producing multi-linguistic leaflets and having essential sections of the website in plural languages. Where deemed important for better communication with the client, reliable interpreters should be used.[12]

Assistance to enable their rights and interests to be presented and considered at appropriate stages of criminal proceedings against offenders

8.20 The common law legal system does not provide for a partie civile allowing representation of victims' rights and interests in seeking compensation. The less satisfactory victim support system, allowing

12 See Appendix A – Resources.

for representation of victims' interests only through the prosecutor, is in place.[13]

Access to education for children

8.21   Child victims of trafficking must be given access to education.

8.22   Assistance to a victim must not be conditional on his or her willingness to act as a witness: article 12(6), Convention CETS 197.

Temporary residence permit

8.23   The European Convention requires the state to grant a residence permit.[14] In the case of the UK, the residence permit will be for one year, and renewable thereafter. The threshold for qualifying for a permit appears to be higher than the 'reasonable grounds test'. The impact assessment refers to a point where 'a competent authority has decided conclusively that an individual is a victim of trafficking'. The standard of proof is unclear. If conclusively means beyond a reasonable doubt, it is difficult to see how all the relevant investigation can be carried out in 45 days. There is also a risk of adverse conclusions drawn on such a standard being used by defendants at any subsequent trial for trafficking of the victim. This 45-day period is intended to be a period of recovery and reflection for the victim, not participation in intense investigation. It is also unlikely that a decision can be made at this early stage about whether the facts justify a prosecution. Therefore, it is more likely that the relevant standard is whether there is a prima facie case of trafficking, that this is not higher than the original threshold but has simply not been revealed to be incorrect. In such a case, a resident permit should be granted.

8.24   The convention CETS 197 requires states to issue a renewable residence permit either where the victim's stay is considered necessary owing to their personal situation or their stay is necessary for the purpose of their co-operation with the competent authorities in investigation or criminal proceedings, or both. In the UK, a permit can be applied for under either criterion. The permit will be generally issued under the discretionary leave policy in the first instance.

---

13   See further chapter 9.
14   See 3.24.

Following the reflection period, and once a competent authority has decided conclusively that an individual is a victim of trafficking, they may be eligible for a residence permit. The Convention provides that a residence permit should be granted where one or both of the following circumstances apply; a victim is co-operating with an investigation or criminal proceedings; or it is deemed necessary owing to 'their personal situation'. In respect of the second category, we judge that a combination of our existing obligations on asylum and human rights and our Discretionary Leave policy already cover situations where an individual's personal circumstances, such as their 'safety, health, family situation or some other factor' (para 184 of the Convention Explanatory Report) make it necessary for them to remain in the UK. Guidance to UKBA case owners would be amended to highlight the Convention to ensure that trafficking cases are considered under the relevant category. In addition we intend to extend Discretionary Leave to explicitly cover the first category as well. The Government has decided that where an individual is conclusively accepted as a victim of trafficking and qualifies for a residence permit it should be granted for a minimum of one year.[15]

8.25   Since the grant is discretionary, there is power to revoke the residence permit in certain circumstances, for example, if voluntary contact with the traffickers has been made, if the allegation of trafficking is fraudulent, or unfounded, or if it is in the interests of national security or public policy to revoke the order. As with revocation of the reflection period, this should be done very rarely given the traumatised state of many victims, and never without a full investigation. The criteria for renewal of the permit are similar to the criteria for initial grant of the permit. More controversial will be the issue of whether a permit can be revoked before its expiry if any investigation or prosecution has been concluded.

8.26   The rules are likely to make it clear that the grant of a temporary residence permit does not of itself create any right to long-term or permanent residence. As with the reflection period, where the holder has a pre-existing residence permit with an expiry date later than the expiry date of the temporary residence permit, the minister may, at the expiry of the recovery and reflection period, permit him or her to remain in the state for the remaining period of validity of the pre-existing permission.

---

15   See www.crimereduction.homeoffice.gov.uk/humantrafficking004.pdf.

8.27   The Impact Assessment anticipates a right to work being granted once the temporary residence permit has been granted. This is done by application to the Home Office.[16]

Obtaining other support

ESOL classes

8.28   In addition to the minimum rights required by the convention, clients may need classes in English as a second or other language (ESOL). The right to universal ESOL training up to Level 2 was removed in August 2007. However, provision continues. It can be obtained on application to the relevant local authority. It is also provided by some unions (eg GMB classes for sex workers, UNITE).

---

16 An asylum seeker can apply for permission to work if his or her claim has not been determined within a year. In practice this happens rarely. The Impact Assessment refers to income generated on support work schemes.

Victims in the criminal courts

> ## Key points
> - The client may be in the criminal courts as a defendant or as a victim.
> - Where applicable, reliance should be placed on the Crown Prosecution Service (CPS) Legal Guidance not to prosecute offences committed as a result of being a victim of trafficking.
> - CPS decisions on prosecution may be judicially reviewed.
> - Special measures may be taken to protect witnesses in court.
> - Further, long-term, protective measures may also be taken if there is a risk to safety.
> - Victims may not participate in criminal proceedings but compensation orders may be made.
> - Private prosecutions may be brought in the absence of state action.

9.1   Chapters 5, 6 and 7 considered the prohibitions in criminal law. Chapter 8 considered issues of identification and immediate support. This chapter considers how the rights and protection of victims can be asserted in criminal courts.

Victim as defendant

9.2   An individual who is present and/or working in breach of immigration law (a) may face criminal prosecution for criminal offences under the legislation; (b) may put their employer at risk of prosecution or civil liability; or (c) may be deported by the UK Border Agency (UKBA) under its administrative powers or on the recommendation of a judge after conviction in a criminal court. Thus, the client may not always be the prosecution witness in criminal proceedings, but a defendant. This section deals with representing defendants in criminal proceedings who may have been trafficked. The types of criminal proceedings in which this issue is most likely to arise are criminal proceedings involving immigration offences. However, the issue may arise in other offences.

Recognising the indicators

9.3   The issue may arise though the client raising the issue themselves. However, advisers should be alert to the fact that the client may not immediately self identify as a victim of trafficking. In those cases, the issue is whether the facts objectively can constitute trafficking, by reference to the indicators described in chapter 1. Where the issue arises, the adviser should collect the relevant evidence and if possible, consider referring the client to a specialist counsellor to elicit any further information. It is important to remember that the client may find it difficult to discuss the events and may be very fearful.

9.4   The first step is to seek discontinuance of the prosecution. In December 2007, the CPS published guidance which is published here in full. The guidance itself appears as part of the CPS Legal Guidance on Immigration Offences, Drugs Offences and Theft. There is no reason why the principles should not apply in proceedings involving drugs offences or theft, providing there is a sufficient nexus between having been trafficked and the commission of the offence. Thus, in a case involving drugs or an allegation of theft, if your client was coerced into carrying drugs through threats to her or to her family and brought into this country to carry out the offence, discontinuance of the prosecution should be sought. In many cases, establishing trafficking may involve establishing a defence of duress, but that will not always be the case. The CPS guidance sets out clearly what steps should be taken by a prosecutor with whom this issue has been raised.

9.5   In addition to discontinuance of the criminal proceedings against your client, consideration may be given to their acting as prosecution in criminal proceedings. In some cases, people involved in perpetration of the trafficking may be co-defendants in the same, or associated, criminal proceedings.

CPS Guidance[1]

Prosecution of defendants charged with immigration offences who might be trafficked victims

Victims of human trafficking may commit the following immigration offences whilst they are being coerced by another:

- using a false instrument under section 3 of the Forgery and Counterfeiting Act 1981;
- possession of a forged passport or documents under section 5 of the Forgery and Counterfeiting Act 1981;

---

1   See   www.cps.gov.uk/legal/h_to_k/human_trafficking_and_smuggling/#_ Prosecution.

- possession of a false identity document under section 25 Identity Cards Act 2006;
- failure to have a travel document at a leave or asylum interview under section 2 Asylum and Immigration (Treatment of Claimants) Act 2004.

When reviewing such a case, it may come to the notice of the prosecutor that the suspect is a 'credible' trafficked victim. For these purposes, 'credible' means that the investigating officers have reason to believe that the person has been trafficked.

In these circumstances, prosecutors must consider whether the public interest is best served in continuing the prosecution in respect of the immigration offence.

The following factors are relevant when deciding where the public interest lies:

- is the person a 'credible' trafficked victim;
- the role that the suspect has in the immigration offence;
- was the immigration offence a direct consequence of their trafficked situation;
- were violence, threats or coercion used on the trafficked victim to procure the commission of the offence;
- was the victim vulnerable or put in considerable fear.

Where information has come to light from other sources that a suspect might be the victim of trafficking, for example from a Non Government Organisation (NGO), the prosecutor should:

- contact the police officer or immigration officer investigating the immigration offences;
- ask the investigating officer to make enquiries and obtain information in connection with the claim that the suspect has been trafficked (this should be done by contacting the UK Human Trafficking Centre [UKHTC]);
- re-review the immigration case in light of any fresh information or evidence;
- if new evidence obtained supports the claim that the suspect has been trafficked **and** committed the immigration offences whilst they were coerced, give consideration to discontinuing the prosecution. Where there is clear evidence that the defendant has a credible defence of duress, the case should be discontinued on evidential grounds.

Information may be in the form of medical reports (psychiatrist reports) claiming post traumatic stress as a result of their trafficking experience. The prosecutor should take the same steps outlined above. Any such information should be copied to the investigating officer for his / her observations.

Guidance has been issued to police and immigration officers on identification of victims and what might constitute a credible trafficked victim. Further reports or statements obtained from the investigating officer and / or an officer from the UKHTC should be carefully reviewed. However, all decisions in the case remain the responsibility of the prosecutor.

Prosecution of young defendants charged with offences who might be trafficked victims

There may be instances where a youth faces criminal charges when he/she is a trafficked victim and the offences were committed when that person was in a coerced situation.

Recent cases have highlighted the following offences as those that are likely to be committed by child trafficked victims:

- theft (in organised 'pick pocketing' gangs), under section 1 Theft Act 1968;
- cultivation of cannabis plants, under section 6 Misuse of Drugs Act 1971.

Prosecutors should be alert to the possibility that in such circumstances, a young offender may actually be a victim of trafficking and have committed the offences under coercion.

Where there is clear evidence that the youth has a credible defence of duress, the case should be discontinued on evidential grounds. Where the information concerning coercion is less certain, further details should be sought from the police and youth offender teams, so that the public interest in continuing a prosecution can be considered carefully. Prosecutors should also be alert to the fact that an appropriate adult in interview could be the trafficker or a person allied to the trafficker.

Any youth who might be a trafficked victim should be afforded the protection of our child care legislation if there are concerns that they have been working under duress or if their well being has been threatened.

In these circumstances, the youth may well then become a victim or witness for a prosecution against those who have exploited them. The younger a child is, the more careful investigators and prosecutors have to be in deciding whether it is right to ask them to become involved in a criminal trial.

Prosecutors are reminded of the principles contained within the CPS policy statement on *'Children and Young People'* and in particular, our commitment to always consider what is best for children in criminal cases.

9.6   In *Regina v O*,[2] the Court of Appeal recommended that the CPS guidance be published in the criminal practitioner books Archbold and Blackstone's, in a case where the defendant's original defence team were unaware of the guidance. O was a 17-year-old Nigerian girl who had been trafficked into the UK for the purposes of sexual exploitation. Seeking to make her escape to France, she was arrested and charged under s25(1)(c) of the Identity Cards Act 2006, for possession of a Spanish ID card belonging to someone else. She was sentenced to eight months' imprisonment, despite her age and her reason for seeking to escape having been raised (belatedly) at the mitigation stage. On her unopposed appeal against conviction and sentence, the Court of Appeal quashed her conviction and sentence. The court was highly critical (referring to the circumstances as 'shameful') of the Crown Court Judge, the CPS and O's original defence team for failing to recognise that she was a minor (and thus should not have been tried in the Crown Court). The Court of Appeal admitted as fresh evidence a report from the POPPY Project which identified O as a victim of trafficking. The court was critical of the prosecutor for not having applied the code when the circumstances behind the defence were disclosed, and of the original defence team for not having sought an adjournment for an investigation into the possibility that she had been trafficked, even though a letter from the POPPY Project was in counsel's brief.

Reviewing a CPS decision

Amenability to review

9.7   Decisions by the CPS on prosecution are in principle subject to judicial review in the Administrative Courts. This includes both decisions to prosecute *R v DPP, ex p Kebilene*[3] and decisions not to prosecute: *R v DPP, ex p C;*[4] *Matalulu v DPP;*[5] *R (Da Silva) v DPP.*[6] Judicial review is, however, only available where there is no more suitable alternative remedy and so will be refused if the issue could be raised elsewhere. In the case of a decision not to prosecute, the issue of a private prosecution might be raised although the resources required for this make it an inaccessible alternative remedy for

2   [2008] EWCA Crim 2835, [2008] All ER (D) 07 (Sep).
3   [2000] 2 AC 326.
4   [1995] 1 Cr App R 136.
5   [2003] 4 LRC 712 at 733.
6   (2006) EWHC 3204.

many. In the case of a decision to prosecute, the courts have so far been reluctant to grant leave for judicial review where the issue can be raised by way of an application to stay proceedings as an abuse of process or in the trial itself: *Sharma v Browne-Antoine and others.*[7] This will in turn depend upon the stage which any investigation or prosecution has reached. If applicable, the guidance should therefore be raised as soon as possible. It can also be pointed out that a decision on the status of the client might lead to their appearing as a prosecution witness and therefore that judicial review is the most appropriate remedy.

Grounds of review

9.8 A judicial review will be granted of a decision where an error of law (illegality, irrationality, procedural impropriety) is established.[8] It will also include decisions where CPS policy (this would include the guidance above) has not been followed or properly applied: *R v DPP, ex p C*;[9] *R v DPP, ex p Manning*;[10] *R v Chief Constable of Kent, ex p B.*[11] It will also include a failure to understand and apply the law or irrational conclusion on the evidence: *R v DPP, ex p Jones (Timothy)*;[12] or failure to consider significant evidence: *R (on the application of Joseph) v DPP.*[13] A decision will also be unlawful if arrived at in bad faith, or as a result of corruption or fraud: *R v DPP, ex p Kebilene*;[14] *R v Panel on Takeovers and Mergers, ex p Fayed.*[15] Unlawfulness may also arise where there has been no proper consideration of the implications of proceedings, such as a decision in the civil courts (*R v DPP, ex p Treadaway*[16]) or a verdict of unlawful killing by an inquest jury: *R v DPP, ex p Manning*[17] and *R (on the application of Peter Dennis) v DPP.*[18] There is a also a duty to give reasons to interested parties, which would include the victim.

---

7 [2006] UKPC 57; [2007] 1 WLR 780 at 31.
8 See further Fordham, *Judicial review handbook*, 5th edn, Hart Publishing, 2008.
9 [1995] 1 Cr App R 136.
10 [2001] QB 330.
11 (1993) 93 Cr App R 416.
12 [2000] Crim LR 858.
13 [2001] Crim LR 489.
14 [2000] 2 AC 326.
15 [1992] BCC 524.
16 (1997) The Times, 31 October.
17 [2001] QB 330.
18 [2006] EWHC 3211.

9.9   The CPS guidance set out above would not apply where the criminal offence does not have the sufficient nexus with having been trafficked (even if the latter is established). In that case, it will be important to present a more general argument as to why protection of the trafficked victim overrides the need to prosecute a criminal offence. Evidence of a nexus, where it exists, should therefore be carefully presented. The circumstances may not provide grounds for discontinuance but may provide some mitigation if justified by the factual circumstances. This was illustrated in *Attorney-General's Reference Nos 129 and 132 of 2006/ R v Elisabeth Delgado-Fernandez and Godwin Zammit; R v Thanh Hue Thi*.[19] Miss Delgado-Fernandez, a former prostitute who agreed to work as a recruiting agent for Mr Zammit and was under his control, was given a lower sentence than he was. The Court of Appeal held that the judge was entitled to treat Miss Delgado-Fernandez more leniently than he did Mr Zammit, the crucial factors being that she was under his control and only received a modest share of the profits.

Witness protection for prosecution witnesses

9.10   If the client is giving evidence in criminal proceedings, in addition to the specific protection measures (reflection periods and residence permits) set out in chapter 8, a range of witness support and protection measures can be called upon where the witness fears that giving evidence against the defendants may lead to harm to themselves or to their family. These range from information leaflets in a variety of languages[20] to concrete measures for protection in court such as the giving of evidence by video link, behind a screen, voice distortion and press restrictions, pseudonyms or anonymity. The making of anonymity orders has now been put on a statutory basis by the Criminal Evidence (Witness Anonymity) Act 2008. The three conditions[21] are, first, that the measures are necessary to protect the safety of the witness or another person or in order to prevent real harm to the public interest; second that the measures are consistent with the defendant having a fair trial; and third that

19 [2005] EWCA Crim 3365.
20 See   www.victimsupport.org.uk/vs_england_wales/about_us/publications/ leaflet_translations.
21 Section 4.

the testimony is important and would not be given without the measure. Beyond the trial, there may be a need for witness protection for the witness and their family.

9.11   Special measures exist for the giving of evidence by witnesses in criminal proceedings who are eligible for such measures either because they are under the age of 17 at the time of the hearing or the quality of whose evidence is likely to be diminished by reason of circumstances relating to mental or physical disability[22] or where the quality of evidence given by a witness is likely to be diminished by reason of fear or distress on the part of the witness in connection with testifying in proceedings.[23] Firstly, the court must consider a number of factors, including the nature and alleged circumstances of the offence, the age and social background of the witness and any behaviour towards the witness on the part of the accused, their family or associates, or anyone who is a likely accused or witness.[24] The court must specifically consider the views of the witness.[25] The complainant in proceedings in respect of a sexual offence is eligible for special measures by virtue of the nature of the proceedings.[26] The court may consider this on application by a party or of its own motion.[27] If any witness is deemed eligible by the court, the court must next consider[28] whether any of the special measures, or a combination of them, would improve the quality of the evidence and against that must consider whether the measure 'might tend to inhibit ... evidence being effectively tested by a party to the proceedings'. The court may then make a specific measures direction, which has effect until the conclusion of proceedings. These may be:

- a screen to prevent the witness seeing the accused (although the witness must be visible to the judge, jury, legal representative and any interpreter);[29]
- the giving of evidence by live video link;[30]

22 Youth Justice and Criminal Evidence Act 1999 s16.
23 Sections 16 and 17.
24 Section 17(2).
25 Section 17(3).
26 Section 17(4).
27 Section 19.
28 Section 19.
29 Section 23.
30 Section 24.

- exclusion from the court of named persons (excluding the accused, lawyers or interpreter) in cases of a sexual offence or of possible intimidation;[31]
- video recording of evidence-in-chief[32] and in cross-examination (as with depositions or evidence taken pursuant to letters of request).[33]

A person charged with a sexual offence (as trafficking for the purpose of sexual exploitation is) or an offence under the Protection of Children Act 1978 may not personally cross-examine the complainant or a witness, including a witness who is charged with an offence.[34] In other cases, and at any stage, the court has the power to prevent cross-examination in person by an accused if it appears to the court that the quality of evidence is likely to be diminished by further cross-examination and would be improved by a direction.[35] The court must then allow cross-examination by a lawyer appointed by the accused or, failing that, by the court.[36]

9.12   The court also has the power to make a reporting direction[37] prohibiting any matter relating to any witness to be included in any publication during the lifetime of the witness if likely to lead members of the public to identify the individual as a witness in criminal proceedings. Prohibited identifying matter includes the witness's name, address, educational establishment, place of work and any still or moving picture. This power cannot be exercised by the court of its own motion. The court has to determine whether the witness is eligible and whether a reporting restriction would improve the quality of the evidence. As a sexual offence, the powers under the Sexual Offences (Amendment) Act 1992 as amended by the 1999 Act, Schedule 2 apply. This includes prohibiting publication of any name or other matter in connection with the proceedings before it which it has allowed to be withheld from the public. Witnesses are not required to reveal their address in open court. However, the courtroom is a public one and (subject to the use of screens) witnesses will have no anonymity in the court room itself. Proceedings

---

31 Section 25.
32 Section 27.
33 Section 28.
34 Sections 34–35.
35 Section 36.
36 Section 38.
37 Section 46. See also, in Scotland, the Vulnerable Witnesses (Scotland) Act 2004.

may be heard in private only if it is necessary in the interests of justice, and any concerns cannot be dealt with through the use of special measures. The application is made after the accused has been arraigned but before the jury has been sworn: which leaves the position uncertain until then. A witness may be referred to by a pseudonym. If an act of intimidation is committed by a person who knows or believes that the victim is involved in an investigation or proceedings while it is ongoing or within a year thereafter, it is presumed that there was an intention to interfere with the witness and an offence is committed under s51 of the Criminal Justice and Public Order Act 1994.

9.13   Thus far, the protection concerns proceedings. There may, however, be a need for longer-term protection of witnesses and their families. The Serious Organised Crime and Police Act 2005 places witness protection on a statutory footing. Where a protection provider (usually a chief police officer or the Director of the Serious Organised Crime Agency) considers that the safety of someone who was, is or might be a witness in legal proceedings (whether or not in the UK) is at risk, there is a statutory framework for a range of protective measures.[38] Protection across borders remains on a non-statutory basis and in some cases dependant on bilateral agreements.

Victim participation

9.14   Participation by victims is always balanced against the right of the accused to a fair trial. After conviction, a victim impact statement, written by the victim about the effects of the crime on them, is read out by the prosecuting lawyer after the verdict but before sentence. The victim should be given support in this process.

9.15   Other criminal legal systems provide for greater participation by victims than does the criminal legal system in the UK. In civil law systems such as France, victims may constitute a partie civile and initiate a claim for compensation in the criminal proceedings. This gives them a right to be separately represented at the criminal trial. Participation of victims is even greater under the Rome Statute of the International Criminal Court. In addition to protective steps (provided for by article 68(1)), victims have the right, where their personal interests are affected, to have their views and concerns presented and considered at appropriate stages and in a manner which is not prejudicial to or inconsistent with the fair trial rights of the accused

38 Serious Organised Crime and Police Act 2005 (in force 1 April 2006) ss82–94.

(article 68(3)). Victims are natural persons who have suffered harm as a result of the commission of a relevant crime.[39] The category may also include organisations or institutions which have sustained *direct* harm to any property dedicated to religion, education, art or science or charitable purposes, and to their historic monuments, hospitals and other places and objects for humanitarian purposes. Such victims may participate in a trial before the International Criminal Court if:

(1) they are a victim of a crime under the jurisdiction of the court;
(2) they have suffered any harm (injury or loss) as a result of the commission of a crime contained in charges before the court;
(3) their personal interests are affected (which falls to be judged on the particular issues arising at each stage before the court, for example if the court is considering a particular incident which harmed the victim).

The court has defined the personal interests of victims as including an interest to receive reparations but also an interest in being allowed to express their views and concerns, an interest in verifying particular facts and establishing the truth, an interest in protecting their dignity during the trial and ensuring their safety, and an interest in being recognised as victims in the case.[40] Where this test is satisfied, the victim should be entitled to express their views and concerns where necessary through statements, examination of witnesses or by filing written submissions. This participation must be consistent with a fair trial. If relevance is established, access may be given to confidential as well as to public documentation. The court may also allow victims to present evidence or to make submissions on the admissibility of evidence.

Private prosecutions

9.16　A victim may bring a private prosecution.[41] This usually occurs where the state has failed to act. The prosecution may be taken over

---

39　Rule 85.
40　Situation in the Democratic Republic of Congo, In the case of *The Prosecutor v Thomas Lubanga Dyilo* No ICC-01/04-01/06, 18 January 2008. Judges Fulford, Benito, Blattmann, 97–8 as amended by the Appeals Chamber, 11 July 2008 *The Prosecutor v Thomas Lubanga Dyilo* No. ICC-01/04-01/06 available at www.icc-cpi.int.
41　Prosecution of Offences Act 1985 s6(1).

by the Director of Public Prosecutions (DPP).[42] There is no duty on a private prosecutor to inform the DPP when initiating or during a prosecution. The substantive trafficking offences (set out in chapters 3, 4 and 5) do not require the consent of either DPP or the Attorney-General. Section 1(1) of the Protection of Children Act 1978 (taking, distributing, possessing, publishing indecent photographs of children) requires the consent of the DPP. In seeking consent, counsel's advice should be provided, together with relevant evidence. In some cases, the private prosecutor will want to approach the CPS for any evidence collected. Such evidence will generally be subject to an implied undertaking that they will only be used for the purposes of a prosecution (which may mean a prosecution by the person who gathered the material)[43] but it can be ordered to be disclosed for the purposes of a private prosecution or where the court is persuaded that the overall requirements of justice require it.[44]

---

42 Section 6(2).
43 *Taylor v Director of the Serious Fraud Office* 2 AC [1999] 177 at 197 per Kennedy LJ.
44 *R v Gregory Pawsey* [1989] Crim LR 152.

CHAPTER 10

Compensation

Key points

- Convention CETS 197 requires compensation to be paid.
- A victim of crime can apply to the convicting court for a compensation order to be paid by a convicted defendant.
- A claim may be made from the state fund administered by the Criminal Injuries Compensation Authority (CICA).
- A civil claim at common law may be brought in the ordinary courts or tribunals against the trafficker or the state.
- Transnational claims may also be made in appropriate circumstances.
- A claim may be brought against the state under the Human Rights Act 1998.
- A claim may be made to the European Court of Human Rights at Strasbourg but levels of compensation are low.

10.1   The UN Palermo Protocol article 6 and Convention CETS 197 article 15 both require provisions for compensation and redress. Despite this, the provisions for compensation for victims in the UK are hard to access and offer differing levels of compensation.

10.2   An individual may seek compensation for loss and damage which he or she has suffered. This may be financial or non-financial in nature. A claim can be pursued in a number of ways:

(1) a compensation order may be sought in criminal proceedings;
(2) compensation as a victim of crime from the state fund administered by the CICA;
(3) a civil claim against either the traffickers or, in some cases, the state;
(4) a claim under the Human Rights Act 1998.

This chapter will address how to make a claim for compensation to the CICA or in the ordinary courts. The chapter deals with issues of both sex trafficking and labour trafficking.

Compensation orders in criminal proceedings

10.3   A court may, on conviction, make a compensation order against the convicted person. This power is exercised under s130 of the Power of Criminal Courts (Sentencing) Act 2000, whereby a court which has convicted a person, or before which that person has been convicted,[1] may order the person to pay compensation for any personal injury, loss or damage resulting from the offence or any other offence which has been taken into consideration by the court in determining sentence. The power is additional to other sentencing, not a substitute for it. In *Inwood*,[2] Scarman LJ said (p73): 'Compensation orders were not introduced into our law to enable the convicted to buy themselves out of the penalties for crime. Compensation orders were introduced into our law as a convenient and rapid means of avoiding the expense of resort to civil litigation when the criminal clearly has means which would enable the compensation to be paid.' This principle was reiterated by Lord Taylor CJ in *A-G's Ref (No 5 of 1993)*.[3] The fact that a compensation order is being made should not, therefore, affect other sentencing such as the length of any term of imprisonment. However, s130(12) does require payment of compensation to take priority over payment of any fine. Where a court has the power to, but does not, make a compensation order, it shall give reasons, in passing sentence, for not so doing. Section 130(4) provides that compensation shall be of such amount as the court considers appropriate, having regard to any evidence and to any representations that are made by or on behalf of the accused or the prosecutor. A magistrates' court may not order more than £5,000 by way of compensation for any one offence and s131 provides a total limit where other offences are taken into consideration. There is no limit to the amount that the Crown Court may order. However, both courts must have regard to the offender's means. The victim is not separately represented on such a claim. Evidence, if necessary, is called by the prosecution.

10.4   The advantages of seeking a compensation order are that it is procedurally straightforward and non-payment may be punishable by imprisonment. However, it is unlikely to be a suitable remedy unless the defendant is worth the amount of the compensation or has assets. An example of when it may be used effectively is in prosecutions under the Gangmasters Licensing Act 2004 (see chapter 12).

10.5   It should be possible to call evidence on loss which ensures that loss is fully compensated. The judicial view is that compensation

---

1   As in the case of a Crown Court judge.
2   (1974) 60 Cr App R 70.
3   (1994) 15 Cr App R (S) 201.

orders are for straightforward cases only: in *Donovan*,[4] a car company had obtained £1,388 for loss of use of an undamaged car which had been stolen by the defendant. Eveleigh LJ stated: 'A compensation order is designed for the simple, straightforward case where the amount of the compensation can be readily and easily ascertained.' Since the calculation of loss of use was 'notoriously open to argument', the compensation order was quashed. However, this view would seem to be a judicial gloss on the statute and in *James*,[5] where a minimum sum was agreed, the Court of Appeal held that that sum could be awarded, notwithstanding the complexity, because such an order was the victim's sole chance to obtain compensation from the offender.

10.6   It is not necessary, for a compensation order to be made, that the offender would have civil liability for the loss: *Chappell*.[6] An award can be made for distress and anxiety (ie without the need to establish psychiatric injury which is medically recognised or nervous shock): *Bond v Chief Constable of Kent*[7]; *Godfrey*.[8] Nor do tort principles of causation apply, provided the injury results from the offence: *Rowlston v Kenny*[9]; *Thomson Holidays Ltd*.[10] However, damage or loss of some kind has to be established. Where the loss or damage is death, an order may be made in favour of anyone who incurred funeral expenses for the payment of those expenses: s130(9). A fixed sum for bereavement may be made in favour of a person who could claim bereavement damages[11] under the Fatal Accidents Act 1976 but only to the (fixed) level that they could be awarded under that Act: s130(10).

10.7   Payment is made into court by the offender and is then paid out to the victim. However, no payment will be made to the victim until the expiry of any appeal avenues or time limit for any such appeals. Furthermore, at any time until the offender has paid the money into court, the enforcing magistrates' court may discharge or reduce the

4   (1981) 3 Cr App R (S) 192.
5   [2003] Cr App R (S) 574.
6   (1984) 80 Cr App R 31.
7   [1983] 1 WLR 40.
8   (1994) 15 Cr App R (S) 536.
9   (1982) 4 Cr App R (S) 85.
10 [1974] QB 592.
11 Currently set at a fixed sum of £10,000.

order on the ground that the loss or damage has been held in civil proceedings to be less than it was taken to be for the purposes of the order, or that the offender's means are insufficient to satisfy both the compensation order and a confiscation order or that the offender's means have reduced unexpectedly.[12] Failure to comply with the order may be punished by imprisonment. Compensation may be ordered to be paid over a period, but such period should not be longer than three years (and less if the offender is not a UK citizen): *Bradburn*.[13]

10.8   The court may also make restitution orders and deprivation orders but they are unlikely to be relevant in trafficking cases and will not be dealt with in this book. If necessary, practitioners should refer to a criminal practitioner textbook.

Claims to the Criminal Injuries Compensation Authority

10.9   A claim may also be made to the CICA under the Criminal Injuries Compensation Scheme. Awards can be made under the scheme to victims of a violent crime. An award may be made whether or not there has been a criminal conviction. However, where there has been an acquittal or where no prosecution has been brought, it is important to set out a clear explanation about why this has happened. A claim may be made by the victim or by the victim's survivors if the victim has died. Application forms may be completed online or downloaded.[14]

10.10   The CICA was set up under the Criminal Injuries Compensation Act 1995. No award can be made in respect of injuries before 1 August 1964. Before 1996, awards were made on a tortious basis, that is to say based on what a claimant would have received in a civil claim for damages. With effect from April 1996, a tariff system was introduced, which allotted values under a tariff to each type of injury. The scheme was amended in April 2001 and again with effect from 3 November 2008. All applications on or after November 2008 are considered under the 2008 scheme.

---

12   Section 133.
13   (1973) 57 Cr App R 948.
14   Both at www.cica.gov.uk.

Personal injuries sustained in Great Britain and directly attributable to a relevant crime within the CICA scheme

10.11   Awards are made where the applicant has suffered personal injury as a result of having been the victim of a criminal injury, subject to conditions:

(a) The injuries must have been sustained in Great Britain (England, Scotland or Wales), but there are no citizenship or residence qualifying requirements. Secondary victims may be applicants. Thus, the family abroad of a victim of trafficking in Great Britain would qualify. There is a separate scheme for Northern Ireland.[15]

(b) The applicant must have been the victim of a violent crime or some other incident covered by the Scheme.[16] As stated above, it is not necessary for anyone to have been convicted, or even charged, with the offence. Cases have succeeded even where there has been an acquittal although this will depend on the supposed reason for the acquittal and the evidence before the criminal court. Where the assailant cannot be convicted by reason of age, sanity or diplomatic immunity, conduct may still be regarded as a criminal act.[17] However, in such a case, the applicant has to prove on the balance of probabilities that the act giving rise to the injury occurred.

(c) The injury meets a minimum level of severity, that is to say scratches or bruises which would in total attract an award at least £1,000.[18] Heads of damage are physical and mental injury and for past or future loss of earnings or special expenses caused by a violent crime.

Personal injury

10.12   For the purposes of the scheme, personal injury includes physical injury (including fatal injury), mental injury (that is, a medically

---

15   Details available from the Compensation Agency, Royston House, 34 Upper Queen Street, Belfast, BT1 6FD. Tel: 02890 249944.

16   Paragraph 8 lists a crime of violence (including arson, fire-raising or an act of poisoning), an offence of trespass on a railway, the (attempted) apprehension of an offender or (attempted) prevention of an offence or the giving of help to a constable.

17   CICA Scheme, para 10.

18   Before reductions.

recognised psychiatric or psychological illness) and disease. Mental disorder is disabling if it significantly impairs a person's functioning in some important part of his or her life: *R v CICAP ex p Bennett.* Paragraph 9 of the scheme gives a broad meaning to mental injury and disease (mental injury includes anxiety) provided there is supportive medical evidence. Mental injury flowing from physical injury may attract compensation. Mental injury not flowing from physical injury will only be compensated if the victim was put in reasonable fear of immediate physical harm to his or her own person or had a close relationship of love and affection with another person who suffered a criminal injury within the meaning of para 8, witnessed by the applicant to CICA. Involvement in the immediate aftermath is also sufficient to bring an applicant within the scheme. As regards a claim for mental injury arising out of a sexual offence, the applicant must have been the non-consenting victim.[19]

10.13   Financial losses can only be claimed if consequential on a relevant injury.

Crime of violence or other crime within the CICA scheme

10.14   What amounts to a crime of violence? The phrase is not a term of art.[20] The definition is fluid and will depend on all the factual circumstances. It is not limited to particular criminal offences. Most crimes of violence will involve the infliction or threat of force but some will not: per Lawton LJ in *R v Criminal Injuries Compensation Board, ex p Webb.*[21] The task of the panel is to decide whether the events that actually occurred were (a) a crime; and (b) a crime of violence.[22] A physical or sexual attack will usually qualify. Depending on the circumstances, so may the threat of either physical or sexual violence. However, the crime need not have been directed at the applicant, provided the applicant suffered injuries as a result of it. Thus, the scheme will plainly cover a sex worker who has been beaten but it may also cover a sex worker on whom violence has been threatened or another worker who has suffered mental injury seeing violence being inflicted on another worker.

---

19   See 10.16.
20   *R (August) v Criminal Injuries Compensation Appeals Panel* [2003] EWCA Civ 237.
21   [1987] 1 QB 74.
22   *R v Criminal Injuries Compensation Board, ex p Webb* [1987] 1 QB 74.

CICA award

In July 2007, an award was made in a case involving sex trafficking: an award was made to EM and MM, both victims of trafficking in the UK. MM was a young adult, trafficked for sexual exploitation. MM gave evidence in the criminal prosecution of her trafficker. She was granted humanitarian protection in the UK. MM was awarded £66,000 for sexual abuse and £40,000 for loss of earnings. Her younger sister, EM, who was a child when trafficked, was awarded £36,500, £20,000 of that being for loss of opportunity.

10.15   Where trafficking for labour is concerned, some care will have to be given to explaining how the crime was a crime of violence. The crime need not have been committed by the employer but may have been committed by the trafficker or other agent. Where there have been threats (whether to the worker or to their family) or coercion or actual violence, and as a result physical or mental injury has been caused, this should fall within the scheme. A trafficked worker may have suffered a physical injury at work. Where this is the result of an assault, it will fall within the usual principles. The position is less clear where the injury occurs as a result of negligence or recklessness, unless these are gross. If there have been inspections and prosecutions under the Health and Safety Executive (HSE) scheme, these should be referred to. Many serious cases risk falling outside the scheme.

10.16   Another sometimes troublesome concept often cited by CICA for the rejection of a claim is consent. In a claim arising out of a sexual offence, the victim must not have consented in fact. The CICA considers whether there has been consent in fact, not in law.[23] Thus, a child who cannot in law consent to sexual intercourse, may be found to have consented in fact and thus not be given an award. Real consent may negate what would otherwise be a crime under the scheme. Consent that is not real will not suffice. Nor will submission, which is not the same thing as consent. Where there is an assertion of vulnerability, the case officer and the panel must look beyond the issue of consent, since 'to ask whether [the victim] consented makes

---

23   CICA scheme, para 9(c).

no allowance for [her] vulnerability'. The panel should consider relative responsibility as between the victim and the offender: per Lord Woolf CJ in *R (on the application of JE) v The Criminal Injuries Compensation Appeals Panel.*[24]

Reduction or withholding of award

10.17   Even where a crime of violence, injury and causation is established, paragraphs 13–15 of the scheme provide for the reduction or withholding of an award which might otherwise be made. There are five grounds on which an award may be reduced or withheld, which are set out under para 13 of the 2008 Scheme:

(a) failure to take reasonable steps promptly to inform the police or other relevant authority of the matter;

(b) failure to co-operate in prosecution by the police or other authority;

(c) failure to give all reasonable assistance to the CICA or other body in connection with the application;

(d) conduct before, during or after the incident which makes it inappropriate that a full award or any award should be made;

(e) the applicant's character, as demonstrated by criminal convictions (excluding convictions spent at the date of application or death) or by other evidence available to the claims officer, which makes it inappropriate that a full award or any award be made.

These paragraphs have often been misinterpreted or misapplied by the CICA and consideration should always be given about whether a reduction or withholding of an award is justified in the particular circumstances of the case. The burden of proof is also on the applicant to satisfy the claims officer, and any reviewing officer, that an award should not be reconsidered, withheld or reduced. This often places a disproportionate burden to prove a negative.

Regulation 13(a)–(c)

10.18   Despite the wide wording of (a)–(c), delays by the victim which are due to fear or trauma are unlikely to prevent an award being made.

---

24   [2003] EWCA Civ 237 at 28–35. The case involved a 22-year-old with a learning impairment who had a sexual relationship with a 53-year-old convicted paedophile with whom he shared a cell.

Regulation 13(d) conduct before, during or after the incident which makes it inappropriate that a full award or any award should be made

10.19   Regulation 13(d) is supplemented by regulation 14 which provides for reduction/withholding of the award where the claims officer considers that excessive consumption of alcohol or use of illicit drugs contributed to the circumstances. This provision is very controversial since read literally it might result in reduction of an award by a trafficked woman who was a drug user.[25] However, the contributory link must be proved and it is arguable that this is a situation where it is for CICA to prove the link. Paragraph 15 applies the same principles to the character and conduct of a dead victim in respect of whose death a claim is being made.

10.20   In *R v CICB*[26], *ex p Gambles*,[27] Sedley J (as he then was) held that in order to reduce or withhold an award, it was for the Criminal Injuries Compensation Board (CICB) to establish a rational and proportionate nexus between the conduct of the applicant before and during (and in other cases after) the events, and in other cases his character too, before they can reduce or extinguish the award to which the applicant would otherwise be entitled. Sedley J held that the CICB had to ask itself three questions:

(1) Does the applicant's conduct make a full award inappropriate?
(2) If so, to what extent does the applicant's conduct impact on the appropriateness of the award?
(3) What award, if any, should the applicant consequently receive? *Gambles,* was however overruled by the Court of Appeal in *R v Criminal Injuries Compensation Board, ex p Cook*[28] that the CICA is not required to set out any particular sequence in its reasoning. However, the reasons should contain sufficient detail to enable the reader to know what conclusion has been reached on the principal important issue or issues.

---

25   In August 2008, the CICA denied that it was applying this principle in rape cases and accepted that it would be inappropriate to do so, since it was not possible to say that one caused the other.

26   The previous incarnation of the CICA.

27   [1994] PIQR P314.

28   [1996] 1 WLR 1037.

Paragraph 13(e) the applicant's character as shown by his criminal convictions (excluding convictions spent at the date of application or death) or by evidence available to the claims officer

10.21 Unlike cases where conduct is concerned, there need be no link between character and the injury suffered for an award to be reduced or withheld. The supposed rationale for this is that only deserving recipients should be awarded ex gratia public funds. Submissions that the character should be blameworthy or causally linked have been rejected. In the case of a claim in respect of a death, the award may be withheld on the grounds of either the character of the deceased or of the applicant: *R v CICB, ex p Cook*.[29]

10.22 In cases of trafficking, there may have been breach of immigration rules. Internal guidance[30] given by the authority for use by members of the authority and members of the panel provided that where an applicant enters legally or arrived illegally but subsequently has their immigration status made lawful, their immigration status is irrelevant. This principle would apply in cases where asylum had been granted or a resident permit had been issued. Where the entry or the stay is or becomes illegal (for example, because of overstaying or breach of conditions of entry), the guidance provides that the applicant may be considered as if they had been convicted and sentenced to six months as of the date of their appeal decision or date of application for compensation, whichever is later and the unlawful conduct principle would apply. Arguably, this approach is one which follows the principle under regulation 13(e) rather than 13(d) and thus arguably no contributory link is required. However, in cases of human trafficking, it is strongly arguable that the principle of adequate compensation should override the principle of upholding immigration law. It is also arguable that breach of immigration law is not an act which reflects adversely on either the character of the applicant or undermines public policy in the way that a criminal conviction does. In *The Queen on the application of Olga Andronati v Criminal Injuries Compensation Appeals Panel*,[31] a Ukrainian woman who had entered legally but overstayed her leave, was the victim of a gang rape by six men. Subsequent to the rape, she applied for and was granted asylum in Ireland. Being in the UK without leave was a criminal offence punishable by up to six months' imprisonment, and the CICA Panel withheld the award in its entirety. It was held at

29 [1996] 1 WLR 1037.
30 Quoted in *Andronati* below.
31 [2006] EWHC 1420 (Admin).

20–21 that the Panel had erred in failing to consider the relevance of the applicant's asylum claim:

> [C]ould she really have been expected to return to the Ukraine, where she was subsequently found to have a well-founded fear of persecution, simply because she could not lawfully remain in the United Kingdom … [T]he burden of proving the basis of her claim for asylum was, of course, on the claimant. But once the fact that she had been granted asylum had been raised, it is at least arguable that the Panel should have asked for more details about it.

Amount payable

10.23   Since 1996, the amount payable for an injury is determined by reference to a tariff. This made awards lower than they should be on ordinary principles. Where the Authority considers that the tariff does not provide for an injury which would qualify for at least the minimum amount, it may refer the matter to the Secretary of State (for the Home Office) together with a recommendation on the description of the injury and the amount for which it should qualify.[32] Compensation may be paid for loss of earnings,[33] special expenses such as the cost of National Health or where reasonable, private medical treatment for the injury (eg psychiatric treatment, counselling),[34] future costs of special expenses which can be determined by applying a multiplier to the annual ongoing cost of such expenses.[35]

10.24   Bereavement expenses are payable to a parent (natural or otherwise), child (natural or otherwise), spouse, civil partner or a former spouse or civil partner financially dependent on the deceased's earnings, or to a cohabitee of either gender who had been living with the deceased person for at least two years before the date of death.[36] Other than former spouses or civil partners, all of the above qualify for a standard amount of compensation which may be on level 10[37] (if there are or might be more than one qualifying claimant) or level 13[38] (if only one). This is payable by the fact of the death, without the

---

32   Scheme, para 28.
33   Scheme, paras 30–34.
34   Scheme, para 35.
35   Scheme, para 36.
36   Scheme, para 38.
37   Currently £5,500.
38   Currently £11,000.

need to prove a particular loss other than the death itself. A payment may also be made to reflect the loss of income from the claimant, termed dependency. The income must be from earnings, not from social security benefits received by the deceased in the UK or elsewhere.[39] There is no requirement that the earnings themselves must have been legal earnings, although issues might arise in respect of character and conduct. Compensation may also be awarded at a fixed annual level[40] for loss of parental services and any other payments which the claims officer considers reasonable.[41] An award can be made for a death resulting from an injury even where the deceased had been compensated for the injury, provided the total does not exceed £500,000.[42]

10.25 Awards other than tariff based awards, will be subject to deduction to take account of state benefits or insurance payments[43] and, in the case of claimants who are alive, pension payments.[44] All awards are subject to deduction of compensation received in other countries from similar funds and any awards paid by the court or compensation received as a result of a settlement.[45] Any amount ordered to be paid as compensation by a criminal court will also be ordered to be deducted.[46] The scheme provides[47] that where an applicant subsequently receives any other payment in respect of the same injury, but the award under the Scheme is not reduced accordingly, the applicant will be required to repay the amount. This will not apply where the other body, eg the High Court, has itself made a deduction to reflect the CICA award.

Procedure and practice

10.26 An application to the CICA should be made as soon as possible after the incident giving rise to the injury and must be received by the CICA within two years of the date of the incident. However, a claims officer may waive the time limit of two years where he or she considers it is practicable for the application to be considered and

---

39 Scheme, para 40.
40 Currently £5,000 (level 5).
41 Scheme, para 42.
42 Scheme, para 43.
43 Scheme, para 45.
44 Scheme, para 47.
45 Scheme, para 48.
46 Scheme, para 48.
47 Paragraph 49.

that by reason of the particular circumstances of the case, it would not have been reasonable to expect the applicant to have made an application within the two year period.[48] The burden of proof is on the applicant to make out a case for waiver of the time limits.[49]

10.27   In practice, there is often considerable delay by the claims assessment section in dealing with a claim. It is important therefore to monitor progress. Do not underestimate the importance of collecting the evidence rather than expecting the CICA to do so. Often, nothing is done by the CICA over a significant period of time. If possible, a supporting statement should be obtained from the investigating police officer, since the CICA will seek to contact them. A copy of the file should be requested. Any delays in reporting the crime should be addressed and explained. If there are problems in obtaining a prompt response from a police officer, contact the UKHTC to chase the matter up.

10.28   Any medical evidence such as hospital records or photographs should also be obtained as well as a supporting statement from the doctor. Paragraph 21 of the scheme requires the CICA to make arrangements for examination of the applicant by a medical practitioner or to reimburse the applicant's representatives if they arrange this and it is agreed that such an examination is necessary. This may involve reimbursement of reasonable contiguous legal fees: *C v (1) The Home Office; (2) The Criminal Injuries Compensation Authority*.[50] This principle is now reflected in Practice Direction CPD3L: where the CICA and the applicant agree that a specialist report (of whatever nature) is necessary, the expert will be jointly instructed and reasonable fees will be paid by CICA. Where either the need or the expert are not agreed, application should be made to the First-Tier Tribunal. An explanation should be set out and funding of the report requested. The CICA will seek permission to contact police, doctors, employers and other authorities, and providing statements up front reduces significant delays. Consideration should also be given to getting a report from a psychiatrist or psychologist.

10.29   Certain decisions by case officers may be challenged by an application for the decision to be reviewed by another case officer. These are decisions not to waive or extend time limits, not to re-open a case, to withhold an award, to make an award (including a reduced

48   This is a less flexible test than under The 2001 Scheme.
49   Scheme, para 19(1)(a).
50   [2004] EWCA Civ 234 per Sedley LJ.

award), to require repayment of an award and to withdraw an award.[51] This does not include decisions made on direction by the First-Tier Tribunal.[52] An application for a review must be made in writing, supported by reasons and received within 90 days of the decision being issued.[53]

10.30   Decisions which have not been reversed on review may be appealed within 90 days after the latest decision. Appeals are now made to and heard by the First-Tier Tribunal where previously they were heard by the Criminal Injuries Compensation Panel. This applies to all appeals heard after 3 November 2008, unless a serious injustice would occur – for example, where the procedure was less favourable in the circumstances. The First-Tier Tribunal was set up under the Tribunals, Courts and Enforcement Act 2007. The tribunal's procedure is set out in The Tribunal Procedure (First-tier Tribunal)(Social Entitlement Chamber) Rules 2008.[54] Rule 22 prescribes the form of the notice of appeal. The tribunal may make a decision without a hearing and in such a case, any party may apply for reconsideration at a hearing. In exceptional circumstances, an extension may be granted.[55]

10.31   It is important to collect all relevant evidence in advance of the hearing. This may involve ensuring that any relevant police officers who are able to confirm the applicant's account of events are aware of the hearing and attend with any relevant files. The tribunal has the power under Rule 16 to order witnesses to attend and to produce documents. Relevant disclosure should be sought from the CICA in advance of the hearing. Rule 5(3)(d) empowers the tribunal, under its case management powers, to require a party or another person to provide documents, information, evidence or submissions to the tribunal or another party. It is consistent with the overriding objectives[56] for this to be ordered to be done in advance of the hearing. The tribunal also has the power to make directions on its own initiative or on application by a party. On 2 June 2008, the CIC Panel issued Practice Direction CPD2 which required the CICA to have relevant evidence ready for appeals on eligibility within three months of the date of appeal. Where the direction is not complied

---

51   Scheme, para 58(1).
52   Scheme, para 58(2).
53   Scheme, para 59.
54   2008/2685.
55   Rule 27(4).
56   Rule 2.

with, the panel, according to the practice direction, might refuse to admit evidence and submissions from the CICA unless good cause was shown for the delay. This indicates a firm case management approach which aims to avoid delay. About the hearing itself, rule 30(2) provides that in a criminal injuries compensation case, the hearing must be held in private unless the appellant has consented for the hearing to be held in private and the tribunal considers that it is in the interests of justice for the heating to be held in public. The tribunal may meet the reasonable expenses of an applicant or any witness, or expenses incurred in connection with a medical inspection arranged by the tribunal.[57]

10.32   A party may seek reasons for a decision which finally disposes of all issues in the proceedings.[58] There is no appeal on the merits but the decision may be judicially reviewed on the usual grounds of illegality, irrationality and procedural impropriety. Under the 2007 Act, that judicial review is now carried out by the Upper Tribunal,[59] except in cases where a declaration of incompatibility under the Human Rights Act 1998 is sought. An appeal lies from the Upper Tribunal to the Court of Appeal on a point of law.

Making a claim for compensation in the ordinary courts

10.33   A claim for compensation may be made in the ordinary courts and the employment tribunal. Employment tribunal claims are dealt with in chapter 13. There are advantages to a claim in the ordinary courts. First, the litigator can choose from the greater range of common law causes of action in tort and contract and to claim the full range of heads of damage, including financial damages. Second, compensation is likely to be higher than from the CICA. If successful, costs are recoverable. Third, a wider range of defendants can be sued. The disadvantage is that such proceedings are likely to be more expensive. Whether it is worth bringing such a claim will also depend on the monetary value of the claim and on whether the defendant will be able to satisfy any judgment against them.

---

57   Rule 21.
58   Rule 34(3).
59   Part 1 of the 2007 Act and direction of the Lord Chief Justice specifying appeals under the scheme, for the purposes of section 18(6) of the 2007 Act.

Jurisdiction and transnational claims

10.34 Given the transnational nature of human trafficking, and depending on the identity of the defendant, questions of jurisdiction may arise. Generally, a claim may be filed against an individual or a company (including the head office of a multinational company) in their state of domicile or where the relevant exploitation took place. It may also be filed in the country of domicile of the worker. The adviser will need to consider which forum is likely to provide the swifter and more effective remedy. If the claimant can show why it would be more just for the matter to be tried in the UK,[60] and there is a sufficient connection, the courts will allow a claim to proceed, even where both parties are domiciled elsewhere. In such a case, the defendant can be served with proceedings even while on a visit to the UK: *Maharani Seethadevi Gaekwar of Baroda v Wildenstein*.[61] Determination of jurisdiction where both jurisdictions are within the European Community is regulated by the Jurisdiction and Judgments Regulation EU 44/2001. The broad rule is that a defendant domiciled in a member state must be sued in that state. There are a number of exceptions. Claims in contract may be brought in the courts for the place of performance. Claims over individual contracts of employment may also be brought in the courts for the place where the employee habitually carries out his work or in the courts for the place where the business which engaged the employee is or was situated. As regards employment issues, an employer is deemed to be domiciled in a member state where it operates any branch or agency. Generally, a corporation is deemed to be domiciled where it has its 'seat', central administration or place of business: article 60 of the Jurisdiction and Judgments Regulation EC 44/2001. A company's seat is its registered office or, if it does not have one, the place where it was incorporated. The 'principal place of business' of a company within article 60 is the place at the heart of its operations.[62] A civil claim against an EU-domiciled defendant which is based on the act giving rise to criminal proceedings should be brought in the same jurisdiction as the criminal proceedings:

---

60 See *Connelly v RTZ Corporation* [1996] QB 361; *Lubbe v Cape PLC* [2000] 1 WLR 1545.

61 [1972] 2 QB 283.

62 *King v Crown Energy Trading AG* [2003] EWHC 163 (Comm), (2003) The Times, 14 March.

article 5(4) reg 44/2001. It may be arguable that given the status of human trafficking cases, at least where serious breaches amounting to enslavement[63] are alleged, that a universal civil jurisdiction is conferred. The prospects of success of such an argument are uncertain, given *Jones v Kingdom of Saudi Arabia*,[64] and pending a decision from the Strasbourg court on Mr Jones' application. In most cases, such an argument will not be necessary. The location (the UK) of the actual or intended exploitation will provide a sufficient nexus to establish civil jurisdiction once the victims have arrived here.

The parties

10.35   The claim may be made against any person who commits a relevant tort, whether or not the relationship is directly governed by contract. This may include recruiters, agencies and end-users.

David et al v Signal International LLC

This claim was filed in the US District Court for the Eastern District of Louisiana on 10 March 2008. The plaintiffs are 12 individuals suing on behalf of over 500 Indian nationals who have filed suit in the US District Court for the Eastern District of Louisiana against Signal LLC, and its employees in respect of their recruitment from India and the Gulf under false promises to work in the United States.[65] The plaintiffs state that they were recruited in India in the aftermath of Hurricane Katrina to work in reconstruction under guestworker visas. They paid $20,000 per worker to recruiters and agents operating in India, the United Arab Emirates and the United States for recruitment, immigration and travel fees. On arrival, they were threatened with abuse of the legal process, physical restraint or other serious harm. They were required to live in guarded camps and when some workers spoke out, they were threatened with deportation and detained.

The defendants are the end user company and a network of agents and recruiters.

The plaintiffs are claiming damages for forced labour, human trafficking, fraud, racketeering and civil rights violations.

---

63   See chapter 2.
64   [2006] UKHL 26, [2007] 1 AC 270.
65   See www.splcenter.org.

Claim for damages against employers for assault, wrongful imprisonment and non-payment of wages for domestic worker

In December 1989, the High Court awarded Mrs Laxmi Swami, a migrant domestic worker, £300,000 for damages for assault, wrongful imprisonment and non-payment of wages by two sisters of the Emir of Kuwait. The two sisters spent six months of each year in Bayswater, bringing their servants with them. One of these, Mrs Laxmi Swami, was routinely beaten, had her eyes damaged when a bunch of keys were thrown at her, had two gold teeth yanked out and was falsely told that one of her four children had been killed in a motorbike accident. The princesses went out for the evening, often returning at 2 or 3 o'clock in the morning – Mrs Swami had to stand by the door awaiting their return. She slept for not more than two hours a night. Food was put in the dustbin and deliberately spoiled so that she could not eat it. In 1981, the princesses attempted to strangle her with an electric flex. Mrs Swami managed to escape to the Indian High Commission but was returned to her employers because she did not have her airfare home.[66]

Box A

Common law potential causes of action against private actors in a trafficking case (some of these torts are also criminal offences)

- Intentional infliction of emotional distress – intent to cause or reckless disregard of causing, emotional distress
- Tort of intimidation
- Assault – act intending to cause a harmful or offensive contact or reasonable imminent apprehension of such contact
- Battery – harmful or offensive contact without consent
- False imprisonment[67]
  - non-consensual intentional confinement of the victim
  - no lawful purpose

66 *Britain's Secret Slaves* Kalayaan, 1993, Bridget Anderson.
67 In a case in the US, a claim of false imprisonment succeeded where the victim had a key to the residence while her traffickers were abroad but was effectively imprisoned by the defendants' threats of arrest and her fear of them: *Deressa v Gobena* No 05 Civ 1334, 2006 US Dist LEXIS 8659 14–5.

- Fraudulent misrepresentation – a misrepresentation of which D was aware or reckless about the truth of, D intended to induce C's reliance, C reasonably relied on the misrepresentation, and suffered loss and damage
- Negligence
- Non-payment of wages
- Breach of contract (whether written or oral)

10.36   A claim may also be brought against a public authority (in which case consider bringing a claim under the Human Rights Act 1998 or a judicial review claim, as well as or instead of a common law claim). This may include public officials.

Box B

Claims against public officials and authorities (assuming they are not themselves traffickers, in which case the causes of action in Box A may be considered)

- Negligence
- Misfeasance in public office

10.37   Unlike in the United States (see the third box at para 10.35), there is no provision for class actions. There are three procedures which should be considered where a group has been trafficked for exploitation and/or exploited. A claimant may sue under Civil Procedure Rules 1998 (CPR) r19.6 as a representative of others who are not parties, where the non-parties have the same interest[68] in the claim as the representative claimant.[69] This does not require either the permission of the persons represented or of the court,[70] although

---

68   The representative party and the persons represented have the same interest where there is (a) a common interest; (b) a common grievance; and (c) a remedy beneficial to all: *Duke of Bedford v Ellis* [1901] AC1, followed in *Independiente Ltd v Music Trading On-Line (HK) Ltd* [2003] EWHC 470 (QB).

69   CPR r19.6.

70   *Independiente Ltd v Music Trading On-Line (HK) Ltd* [2003] EWHC 470 (QB); *Howells v Dominion Insurance Co Ltd* [2005] EWHC 552 (QB). The claim form should state, eg 'A, as representing herself and other women working in the brothel at X between [relevant dates]' or 'B, as representing himself and other Ukrainian workers recruited by X agency to work on Y farm'.

the court may direct that a person may not act as representative.[71] Those represented are not parties to the litigation, are not liable for costs and disclosure may only be ordered against them as non-parties.[72] Any judgment or order is binding on them but may not be enforced by them without the permission of the court.[73] Alternatively, a Group Litigation Order may be applied for either before or after commencement under CPR r19.11, where a number of claims gives rise to common, or related, issues of fact or law. The claims are managed through a central register. This order will be made only if the alternatives are not more suitable.[74] All litigants under the group order are parties and jointly liable for costs.[75] Lastly, separate claims may be consolidated under CPR r3.1(2)(g) after commencement, where issues of fact or law are closely connected. The order may be refused where there is insufficient overlap or the claims are at different stages.

Procedure

10.38 The standard of proof is the balance of probabilities. Any civil proceedings are likely to be stayed pending the resolution of criminal proceedings.

10.39 A claimant cannot recover twice for the same wrong. Thus, any damages received will be deducted from any CICA award and, vice versa, a court would take account of compensation awarded by the CICA or by the convicting criminal court.

Time limits

10.40 Time limits depend on the nature of the claim. A claim in negligence must be brought within three years from when the date of action accrues or from the date of knowledge, whichever is the later. Section 33 provides a discretion to extend this where it would be just and equitable to do so. This provision also applies to personal injuries

---

71 Rule 19.6(2). Any party may apply to the court for such an order.

72 *Ventouris v Mountain* [1990] 1 WLR 1370, QBD.

73 *Howells v Dominion Insurance Co Ltd* [2005] EWHC 552 (QB); *SmithKline Beecham Ltd PLC v Avery* [2007] EWHC 948 (QB); *Huntingdon Life Sciences Group PLC v Stop Huntingdon Animal Cruelty (SHAC)* [2007] EWHC 522 (QB).

74 PD 19B para 2.3.

75 On costs, see *Sayers v Merck SmithKline Beecham plc* [2001] EWCA Civ 2027; *Solutia UK Ltd v Griffiths* [2001] EWCA Civ 736.

which have been intentionally, rather than negligently, inflicted, such as through rape or sexual abuse or false imprisonment: *A v Hoare and other appeals*[76] approving *Letang v Cooper.*[77] The lead appeal in that case concerned a defendant who was imprisoned having been convicted of sexual assault and attempted rape of the claimant and who, 15 years later, won £7 million on the National Lottery. It was held that the claimant was entitled to seek exercise of the judicial discretion available under s33 of the Limitation Act 1980. It is therefore important to identify first what is the date of knowledge by the claimant of all relevant facts. If a claimant does not know until a certain date that the recruiter in her home country had sold her, then time would run from that date as against the recruiter.

Using the Human Rights Act 1998

10.41   Section 7 of the Human Rights Act 1998 establishes the right to sue a public authority where that public authority has acted or proposes to act in a way which is incompatible with a European Convention on Human Rights right. 'Act' includes a failure to act.[78] The term public authority is not defined in the 1998 Act but will plainly include government departments, local authorities including social services departments, the police and health authorities and courts and tribunals.[79] The position is less clear with a private sector body providing public services. The Act applies to any person certain of whose functions are functions of a public nature, but this will depend on the exact arrangements and relationship with the commissioning public authority.[80] Proceedings may only be brought by a victim, which is defined by reference to the jurisprudence of the Strasbourg Court.[81] This will include parents of a minor and

---

76   [2008] UKHL 6.

77   [1965] 1 QB 232.

78   But does not include a failure to introduce or make legislation.

79   Who are also bound by the duty under s3 to interpret legislation compatibly with convention rights.

80   *R (Heather) v Leonard Cheshire Foundation* [2001] EWHC Admin 429, [2002] 2 All ER 936; *R (Servite Houses) v Goldsmith* (2001) 33 HLR 35; *Poplar Housing and Regeneration Community Association Limited v Donoghue* [2001] EWCA Civ 595, [2002] QB 48; *R (Beer) v Hampshire Farmers Market Ltd* [2003] EWCA Civ 1056, [2004] 1 WLR 233; *YL v Birmingham City Council* [2007] UKHL 27, [2008] 1 AC 95.

81   Section 7(1)(b), (3)–(4) and (7).

surviving relatives[82] but not non-governmental organisations (NGOs). The test is therefore narrower than the test of standing in judicial review proceedings. The relevant convention rights in cases of human trafficking are likely to be articles 3, 4,[83] 6 and 14. A public authority has a statutory defence to a claim if it could not have acted differently under the relevant statute[84] or if it was acting so to give effect to the relevant legislation.[85] Claims under s7 of the Human Rights Act 1998 have to be brought within one year of the date on which the relevant act took place.[86] This time limit may be extended where the court considers it equitable to do so, but where another rule imposes a shorter time limit (such as the long stop of three months in judicial review), the shorter time limit prevails.[87]

10.42   Section 8 provides that in relation to any act (or proposed act) of a public authority which the court finds is (or would be) unlawful, it may grant such relief or remedy or make such order within its powers as it considers just and appropriate. A court may grant any remedy which it deems appropriate provided that it has jurisdiction to grant that remedy.[88] Thus, damages may only be awarded by a court which has power to make such an award, or order the payment of compensation, in civil proceedings.[89] Even then, no award may be made unless the court is satisfied that such an award is 'necessary to afford just satisfaction to the person in whose favour it is made'.[90] Further, the court must consider any other award made in relation to the act, and the consequences of any decision (of that or any other court) in respect of that act. The court must also take into account the jurisprudence of the Strasbourg court as regards remedies under article 41 of the European Convention. The UK courts have read the jurisprudence as requiring a different test to that which applies in common law cases in tort: *Anufrijeva v Southwark LBC*.[91] The court pointed to the greater importance of declarations and injunctions

---

82   *R (Holub) v Secretary of State for the Home Department* [2001] 1 WLR 1359.
83   For which see chapter 3 and chapter 7.
84   Section 6(2)(a).
85   Section 6(2)(b).
86   Section 7(5).
87   Section 7(5).
88   Section 8(11).
89   Section 8(2).
90   Section 8(3).
91   [2004] 2 WLR 603 at 49.

in human rights and constitutional cases.[92] They pointed out that the Strasbourg court does not automatically award monetary compensation and in some cases concludes that the finding itself affords 'just satisfaction'. However, the cases in which this has occurred are generally cases involving breaches of procedural right. This approach is unlikely to be applied in trafficking cases, where there will frequently be unpaid or underpaid work as well as psychological damage which passes the threshold set out in *Anufrijeva*. Leaving aside the question of the different priorities given to other remedies, the court in *Anufrijeva* held that where there is a comparable tort, guidance may be derived from case-law as well as from the Strasbourg court.[93] However, the overall test in an award of compensation for breach of convention rights is restitution in integrum. The applicant should, in so far as this is possible, be placed in the same position as if his Convention rights had not been infringed.[94] The approach is compensatory and exemplary damages are not awarded. If a decision of a public authority is being judicially reviewed in the Administrative Court, a claim for damages may be included. Where the claim is for maladministration, the claim should be brought in the Administrative Court. Consideration should always be given about whether it is appropriate to claim aggravated and/or exemplary damages.

92   53–54: 'Where an infringement of an individual's human rights has occurred, the concern will usually be to bring the infringement to an end and any question of compensation will be secondary, if any, importance'.

93   This approach to all claims under the Human Rights Act 1998 was recommended by the Law Commission but treated with caution by the Court: 49.

94   Para 59 of *Anufrijeva*.

Long-term solutions for individuals

Key points

- Long-term solutions may involve return and reintegration or reintegration in situ.
- In the medium term, residence permits may be renewed.
- Where the client is able or willing to return, the International Organization for Migration (IOM) return and resettlement programme should be considered.
- Where there is a real risk of re-trafficking, a claim may be made for asylum or humanitarian protection under article 3 or 4, or discretionary leave.
- Where there is a risk of retaliation because of evidence given, long-term witness protection should be arranged.
- Special considerations apply in the case of children, in particular the need for the child's best interests to be a primary consideration and for family tracing to be carried out safely and in appropriate cases.

11.1   Beyond obtaining immediate support and the resolution of criminal or civil proceedings, the adviser needs to consider how to advise and represent the client on their longer-term future in cases where they are subject to immigration decisions. This chapter deals with specific issues arising, in cases involving human trafficking, about solutions for the client's long-term future. The client may wish to return to their country of origin and resettle there. Alternatively, they may be unable or unwilling to do so. Different considerations again will apply where the client is a child. This chapter does not deal with detailed issues on immigration procedure.

Temporary residence permit

11.2   The temporary residence permit may be applied for in the medium term. As set out in chapters 3 and 8, the residence permit derives from obligations under European Convention CETS 197. It is a permit for one year and is renewable. There are two criteria for eligibility for the permit.

Co-operation with investigation or prosecution

11.3 The first is where a victim is co-operating with the investigation or criminal proceedings. The government proposes to extend its discretionary leave policy[1] to cover this situation.

The permit is deemed necessary owing to the client's 'personal situation'

11.4 As the Explanatory Note to Convention CETS 197 makes clear, this covers situations where an individual's personal circumstances, such as their 'safety, state of health, family situation or some other factor', make it necessary for them to remain in the UK. This will encompass the fact of having been trafficked in the past and the need for rehabilitation. It is not limited to those who establish a future risk. The government considers that its existing discretionary leave policy already covers such situations. The residence permit has been dealt with in chapter 8. The rest of this chapter considers longer term solutions.

The client wishes to return to his or her country of origin[2]

Assisted voluntary return for adults

11.5 Where the client wishes to return to the sending state, he or she may apply to take part in the Assisted Voluntary Return Programme run by the IOM.[3] Initial advice from the IOM is confidential. The IOM now offers a resettlement package tailored to the resettlement needs.

---

1 See www.ukba.homeoffice.gov.uk/sitecontent/documents/policyandlaw/asylumpolicyinstructions/apis/discretionaryleave.pdf.
2 It is of course possible that a person might have been a victim of trafficking and have no grounds to stay. However, the residence permit covers situations where stay is deemed necessary due to the personal situation. It is submitted that the most relevant factor here will be which course provides for the best rehabilitation: which is in turn dependent upon the victim's mental state and ties. These are likely to inform their own wishes.
3 See Appendix A – Resources.

Return of children

11.6   Where the client is a child, the state has a duty to make plans for the child's successful transition into adulthood. A simple voluntary return, even if those are the child's wishes, is not possible. Under the Convention on the Rights of the Child (CRC), and under UK Border Agency (UKBA) policy,[4] the state must satisfy itself that proper reception arrangements are in place, in light of the child's best interests and taking their views in account. The Foreign Office and International Social Services should be consulted for information on conditions in the destination country.

11.7   Where a child's family can be traced, that may be, in general cases, a powerful argument that it is in their best interests to return. However, in the case of a child who has been trafficked, the family may have been complicit. Detailed enquiries will have to be made by International Social Services as to whether the family can care for the child.

Extract from Committee on the Rights of the Child, General Comment 6 (2005):[5] Treatment of unaccompanied and separated children outside their country of origin

VII. FAMILY REUNIFICATION, RETURN AND OTHER FORMS OF DURABLE SOLUTIONS

(a) General

79.   The ultimate aim in addressing the fate of unaccompanied or separated children is to identify a durable solution that addresses all their protection needs, takes into account the child's view and, wherever possible, leads to overcoming the situation of a child being unaccompanied or separated. Efforts to find durable solutions for unaccompanied or separated children should be initiated and implemented without undue delay and, wherever possible, immediately upon the assessment of a child being unaccompanied or separated. Following a rights-based approach, the search for a durable solution commences with analysing the possibility of family reunification.

4   See www.ukba.homeoffice.gov.uk/sitecontent/documents/policyandlaw/asylumpolicyinstructions/.

5   CRC/GC/2005/6, 1 September 2005.

80. Tracing is an essential component of any search for a durable solution and should be prioritized except where the act of tracing, or the way in which tracing is conducted, would be contrary to the best interests of the child or jeopardize fundamental rights of those being traced. In any case, in conducting tracing activities, no reference should be made to the status of the child as an asylum-seeker or refugee. Subject to all of these conditions, such tracing efforts should also be continued during the asylum procedure. For all children who remain in the territory of the host State, whether on the basis of asylum, complementary forms of protection or due to other legal or factual obstacles to removal, a durable solution must be sought.

(b) Family reunification

81. In order to pay full respect to the obligation of States under article 9 of the Convention to ensure that a child shall not be separated from his or her parents against their will, all efforts should be made to return an unaccompanied or separated child to his or her parents except where further separation is necessary for the best interests of the child, taking full account of the right of the child to express his or her views (art. 12) (see also section IV (e), 'Right of the child to express his or her views freely'). While the considerations explicitly listed in article 9, paragraph 1, sentence 2, namely, cases involving abuse or neglect of the child by the parents, may prohibit reunification at any location, other best-interests considerations can provide an obstacle to reunification at specific locations only.

82. Family reunification in the country of origin is not in the best interests of the child and should therefore not be pursued where there is a 'reasonable risk' that such a return would lead to the violation of fundamental human rights of the child. Such risk is indisputably documented in the granting of refugee status or in a decision of the competent authorities on the applicability of non-refoulement obligations (including those deriving from article 3 of the Convention against Torture and Other Cruel, Inhuman or Degrading Treatment or Punishment and articles 6 and 7 of the International Covenant on Civil and Political Rights). Accordingly, the granting of refugee status constitutes a legally binding obstacle to return to the country of origin

and, consequently, to family reunification therein. Where the circumstances in the country of origin contain lower level risks and there is concern, for example, of the child being affected by the indiscriminate effects of generalized violence, such risks must be given full attention and balanced against other rights-based considerations, including the consequences of further separation. In this context, it must be recalled that the survival of the child is of paramount importance and a precondition for the enjoyment of any other rights.

83.   Whenever family reunification in the country of origin is not possible, irrespective of whether this is due to legal obstacles to return or whether the best-interests-based balancing test has decided against return, the obligations under article 9 and 10 of the Convention come into effect and should govern the host country's decisions on family reunification therein. In this context, States parties are particularly reminded that 'applications by a child or his or her parents to enter or leave a State party for the purpose of family reunification shall be dealt with by States parties in a positive, humane and expeditious manner' and 'shall entail no adverse consequences for the applicants and for the members of their family' (art. 10 (1)). Countries of origin must respect 'the right of the child and his or her parents to leave any country, including their own, and to enter their own country' (art. 10 (2)).

(c) Return to the country of origin

84.   Return to the country of origin is not an option if it would lead to a 'reasonable risk' that such return would result in the violation of fundamental human rights of the child, and in particular, if the principle of non-refoulement applies. Return to the country of origin shall in principle only be arranged if such return is in the best interests of the child. Such a determination shall, inter alia, take into account:

–   The safety, security and other conditions, including socio-economic conditions, awaiting the child upon return, including through home study, where appropriate, conducted by social network organizations;

–   The availability of care arrangements for that particular child;

–   The views of the child expressed in exercise of his or her right to do so under article 12 and those of the caretakers;

- The child's level of integration in the host country and the duration of absence from the home country;
- The child's right 'to preserve his or her identity, including nationality, name and family relations' (art. 8);
- The 'desirability of continuity in a child's upbringing and to the child's ethnic, religious, cultural and linguistic background' (art. 20).

85. In the absence of the availability of care provided by parents or members of the extended family, return to the country of origin should, in principle, not take place without advance secure and concrete arrangements of care and custodial responsibilities upon return to the country of origin.

86. Exceptionally, a return to the home country may be arranged, after careful balancing of the child's best interests and other considerations, if the latter are rights-based and override best interests of the child. Such may be the case in situations in which the child constitutes a serious risk to the security of the State or to the society. Non-rights-based arguments such as those relating to general migration control, cannot override best interests considerations.

87. In all cases return measures must be conducted in a safe, child-appropriate and gender-sensitive manner.

88. Countries of origin are also reminded in this context of their obligations pursuant to article 10 of the Convention and, in particular, to respect 'the right of the child and his or her parents to leave any country, including their own, and to enter their own country'.

...

(e) Intercountry adoption (art. 21)

91. States must have full respect for the preconditions provided under article 21 of the Convention as well as other relevant international instruments, including in particular the Hague Convention on Protection of Children and Cooperation in Respect of Inter-Country Adoption and its 1994 Recommendation Concerning the Application to Refugee and other Internationally Displaced Children when considering the adoption of unaccompanied and separated children. States should, in particular, observe the following:

- Adoption of unaccompanied or separated children should only be considered once it has been established that the child is in a position to be adopted. In practice, this means, inter alia, that efforts with regard to tracing and family reunification have failed, or that the parents have consented to the adoption. The consent of parents and the consent of other persons, institutions and authorities that are necessary for adoption must be free and informed. This supposes notably that such consent has not been induced by payment or compensation of any kind and has not been withdrawn;
- Unaccompanied or separated children must not be adopted in haste at the height of an emergency;
- Any adoption must be determined as being in the child's best interests and carried out in keeping with applicable national, international and customary law;
- The views of the child, depending upon his/her age and degree of maturity, should be sought and taken into account in all adoption procedures. This requirement implies that he/she has been counselled and duly informed of the consequences of adoption and of his/her consent to adoption, where such consent is required. Such consent must have been given freely and not induced by payment or compensation of any kind;
- Priority must be given to adoption by relatives in their country of residence. Where this is not an option, preference will be given to adoption within the community from which the child came or at least within his or her own culture;
- Adoption should not be considered:
  - Where there is reasonable hope of successful tracing and family reunification is in the child's best interests;
  - If it is contrary to the expressed wishes of the child or the parents;
  - Unless a reasonable time has passed during which all feasible steps to trace the parents or other surviving family members has been carried out. This period of time may vary with circumstances, in particular, those relating to the ability to conduct proper tracing; however, the process of tracing must be completed within a reasonable period of time;

> – Adoption in a country of asylum should not be taken up when there is the possibility of voluntary repatriation under conditions of safety and dignity in the near future.

Rehabilitation in the UK

11.8   The client, whether adult or child, may be unable or unwilling to return to their country of origin or in the case of a child, it may not be in their best interests to do so. The issue of stay in the UK beyond the remit of a residence permit[6] will therefore arise.

Adults

11.9   Convention CETS 197[7] requires states to establish repatriation and reintegration programmes. If that rehabilitation is best done in the UK, then the victim is entitled to rehabilitation in situ. The residence permit is for a fixed term of one year and subject to renewal. Since it is granted under the discretionary leave policy, a renewal may be applied for.

11.10   An application for asylum under the 1951 Convention on Refugees or for the grant of subsidiary protection in the form of humanitarian protection or discretionary leave may be applied for at any stage during the currency of the one-year residence permit, or indeed without such leave having been given. The criteria for the grant of asylum or humanitarian protection are set out in the Refugee or Person in Need of International Protection (Qualification) Regulations 2006,[8] implementing the Council Directive 2004/83/EC of 29 April 2004, on minimum standards for the qualification and status of third country nationals and stateless persons as refugees or as persons who otherwise need international protection. Article 3 of the regulations recognises that persecution or serious harm can be committed by any non-state actor if it can be demonstrated that the state or any party controlling the state or a substantial part of the

---

6   See 8.23–26.
7   Article 16.5. See, further, chapter 3.
8   SI 2006/2525.

state, including any international organisation, is unable or unwilling to provide protection against persecution or serious harm.

Asylum claim: on return, the client would suffer persecution as a member of a social group and is therefore a refugee

11.11   Refugee status confers rights to work, welfare, travel abroad, family reunion and the opportunity for expedited naturalisation. A person seeking asylum must show that they have a well-founded fear that on their return, they would suffer persecution for a convention reason. Past persecution is of itself not enough (since the fear, though real, must be well-founded) but it is good evidence on which to found a claim of future persecution. Severe or overt discrimination may have a cumulative effect and amount to persecution. Where the persecution comes from non-state actors, the question is whether the authorities would be able and willing to provide sufficient protection.[9] Convention reasons include race, religion, nationality, membership of a particular social group or political opinion. The social group must be defined by more than the fact or fear of persecution, because such a formulation is circular. However, this principle should not be read too broadly.[10] A group may be created of those who do not comply with a particular societal norm.[11] Women in Pakistan constitute a social group for the purposes of the 1951 Convention and 1967 Protocol on the Status of Refugees, because they share the immutable characteristic[12] of gender. Cohesiveness as a group is not a requirement of the convention. A similar argument could be raised in respect of children as a social group. Thus if they are subject to persecution from the state or are unprotected by the state from persecution by non-state actors, that amounts to persecution for a convention reason: *R v Immigration Appeal Tribunal, ex p Shah.*[13] It is

---

9   *Horvath v Secretary of State for the Home Department* [2001] 1 AC 489.

10   Care must be taken to limit this principle to its proper confines or it risks defeating otherwise valid claims. It is sometimes hard, in respect of a persecuted group, to be clear whether they are defined by the persecution of them or by the reason for the persecution of them. See the very clear analysis by Lord Steyn in *Shah* at 645B–G. In that case, Lord Steyn would have identified gender, suspicion of adultery and lack of protection as the characteristics of the group. See also per Lord Brown in *Fornah* at 468 E-469A.

11   *Shah* per Lord Hope 657G–658C who observes, the 'grouping' may be independent of will.

12   Ie one which an individual either cannot (including because it is a past fact) or is so fundamental to identity that they should not be required to change it.

13   [1999] 2 AC 629.

not necessary for all members of the social group to be persecuted.[14] Women who have been victims of sexual violence in the past, if that leads to a well-founded fear of persecution in the future, may similarly claim membership of a social group which is at once independent of and the cause of their current ill-treatment: per Baroness Hale in *Regina (Hoxha) v Special Adjudicator*.[15] It is important to carefully define the social group relied upon so that it amounts to a social group but also so as to be able to establish the risk of persecution against that group.[16] Thus, the focus should be on the vulnerability to be trafficked or re-trafficked or to suffer retribution or ostracism as a result, rather than the victim status itself.[17] Extreme expression of discriminatory treatment based on institutional inferiority is capable of amounting to persecution: *K v Secretary of State; Fornah v Secretary of State*[18] as may the past experience of having been trafficked: see per Hale at 463C–H. The Asylum and Immigration Tribunal has held that 'former victims of trafficking' and 'former victims of trafficking for sexual exploitation' are capable of being members of a particular social group, provided that group has a particular identity in the society in question: *SB (PSG – Protection Regulations – reg 6) Moldova CG*.[19]

Humanitarian protection

11.12 Under the directive and the regulations, a person is eligible for humanitarian protection if they are not a refugee but face a real risk of suffering 'serious harm' in the country of return, for example where there would be a breach of article 2, 3 or 4(1) of the European Convention on Human Rights on their return.

Discretionary leave to remain

11.13 Discretionary leave is granted for no longer than three years. Grant of discretionary leave carries with it the right to work and access to

---

14 *Shah* per Lord Hoffmann at 653G–654CD.

15 [2005] 1 WLR 1063 at 1074, 37.

16 See, again, *Shah* per Lord Hoffmann at 654B–G.

17 See the perceptive analysis by Lord Hoffmann in *Shah* at 654A–655A which may be applicable to cases where trafficking occurs in the context of armed conflict or a weak state. See more generally the UNHCR Guidelines on International Protection: Membership of a Particular Social Group 7 May 2002.

18 [2006] UKHL 46; [2007] 1 AC 412.

19 [2008] UKAIT 00002.

public funds. The period of discretionary leave is not actively reviewed during its currency, but it can be varied on grounds of conduct or change of circumstances in country of origin. The applicant will be considered for settlement after six years of discretionary leave.

Risk of re-trafficking as a breach of article 3 and/or 4

11.14   In addition, an application may be made for subsidiary protection in the form of humanitarian protection and under the Human Rights Act 1998 (and, if unsuccessful in the national courts, in Strasbourg under the European Convention on Human Rights). It is well established that where there is a real risk of torture or ill treatment in the state to which an applicant is being returned, the deporting state's responsibility is engaged: *Soering v UK.*[20] This principle applies to article 4(1), also a non-derogable article.

Return would breach the UK's obligations under Convention CETS 197

11.15   Section 33(6A) of the UK Borders Act 2007 (automatic deportation: exceptions), as amended by the Immigration and Nationality Act 2008, provides: '(6A) Exception 6 is where the Secretary of State thinks that the application of section 32(4) and (5) would contravene the United Kingdom's obligations under the Council of Europe Convention on Action against Trafficking in Human Beings (done at Warsaw on 16th May 2005)'. This will include obligations to rehabilitate.

Psychological damage if returned to sending state

11.16   There may be no sufficient evidence of objective risk of re-trafficking but the client may have a greater chance of psychological recovery[21] if rehabilitated in the UK. Application should be made for humanitarian or discretionary leave.

Civil proceedings in the UK

11.17   Involvement in proceedings only provides a ground for grant of the residence permit where the proceedings are criminal. Where the

---

20   7 July 1989 Series A, 161 paras 90–91.
21   For example, of psychological damage, see Zimmerman et al, *Stolen smiles: a summary report on the physical and psychological health consequences of women and children trafficked in Europe*, London School of Hygiene and Topical Medicine, 2006, www.lshtm.ac.uk.

proceedings are civil, an argument can be made that the claimant's continued presence is necessary for the proceedings: *R v Immigration Officer, ex p Quaquah.*[22] The success of any such argument will depend on the facts and the particular reasons why continued presence is necessary. In any era of internet communication, it will be important to spell out why the client needs to be in the jurisdiction in order to give instructions, evidence, etc or why it is undesirable that they be returned while civil proceedings are current, for example where there is a risk of intimidation. It is most likely any stay would be granted as discretionary leave, whether as a residence permit or under the general discretion.

Children

11.18   The previous policy of the UK Border Agency was to grant children discretionary leave until the age of 18 (now 17 and a half). Although this can no longer be relied on as a policy in all cases, in practice where there are serious questions about the circumstances of the child if returned, they will remain here. Again, General Comment 6 from the Committee on the Rights of the Child provides relevant guidance on steps to be taken where rehabilitation is in situ.

(d) Local integration

89.   Local integration is the primary option if return to the country of origin is impossible on either legal or factual grounds. Local integration must be based on a secure legal status (including residence status) and be governed by the Convention rights that are fully applicable to all children who remain in the country, irrespective of whether this is due to their recognition as a refugee, other legal obstacles to return, or whether the best-interests-based balancing test has decided against return.

90.   Once it has been determined that a separated or unaccompanied child will remain in the community, the relevant authorities should conduct an assessment of the child's situation and then, in consultation with the child and his or her guardian, determine the appropriate long-term arrangements within the local community and other necessary measures to facilitate such integration. The

---

22   CO/4738/98 15/12/1999.

long-term placement should be decided in the best interests of the child and, at this stage, institutional care should, wherever possible, serve only as a last resort. The separated or unaccompanied child should have the same access to rights (including to education, training, employment and health care) as enjoyed by national children. In ensuring that these rights are fully enjoyed by the unaccompanied or separated child, the host country may need to pay special attention to the extra measures required to address the child's vulnerable status, including, for example, through extra language training.[23]

Memoranda of understanding or diplomatic assurances

11.19   Where inter-state assurances are relied on to attempt to negate evidence of a risk on return, the court must not simply take them at face value but assess their credibility or weight in light of other evidence: *Saadi v Italy*.[24] It is therefore important to collect and put forward all relevant material on the extent of human trafficking in the relevant country and on whether the authorities in that country have record of taking adequate steps to prevent prohibit and to protect victims.[25]

---

23   CRC/GC/2005/6, 1 September 2005.

24   37201/06 at 148.

25   Relevant material may be obtained from Amnesty International, the UN Special Rapporteur on Human Trafficking and the US State Department.

CHAPTER 12

Labour inspection

Key points

- Labour inspection is an important part of preventing trafficking.
- Individual workers may report breaches of fundamental standards to the relevant inspection body anonymously.
- The licensing model of the Gangmaster Licensing Authority enables close supervision of employers and labour suppliers, but only in specific sectors.
- The HMRC Minimum Wages Unit allows HM Revenue and Customs (HMRC) to sue on behalf of workers for recovery of up to six years of the minimum wage.
- It remains unclear how protective of victims the licensing regime is.

General principles

12.1   In addition to criminalisation through the ordinary courts, the UK has a labour inspection framework. Inspection does not depend on an individual having to give evidence and confront the trafficker. In regulating labour suppliers and end-users of labour, it has a preventive function as an early warning system. The fines imposed can work to remove the profit element from trafficking and thus act as an effective deterrent. Withdrawal of a license is also effective. Both are backed up with custodial penalties under the main inspection regimes.

12.2   Central to the trafficking process is the relationship between the person who recruits, transport or transfers the worker and the person who engages the worker in exploitation. Recruiters can be working legally, semi-legally or entirely illegally. They can be opportunistic individuals or part of organised crime. Auxiliaries include those providing often false documentation and those providing transport. In many cases, it will be these persons rather than the end-user who are charged with a trafficking offence. The high levels of debt in which workers find themselves are often caused by disproportionate charges for recruitment, transfer and accommodation.

12.3   For these reasons, labour inspection of the workplace and associated areas is a key aspect of identification and elimination of human trafficking. However, an effective labour inspection system is dependent on having inspectors of a sufficient quality and number to ensure effective targeting and coverage. Its effectiveness is also dependent on good co-ordination between state bodies.

Operation Ruby – 18 November 2008

Two-hundred staff from nine state agencies – including East Midlands Foreign National Crime Team, Northamptonshire Police, UK Human Trafficking Centre, UK Borders Agency (UKBA), Serious Organised Crime Agency (SOCA) and Gangmasters Licensing Authority – were involved in arrests of a provider of labour services to farms in Northamptonshire. This was triggered by complaints from former workers.

Workers were recruited in Eastern Europe. On arrival, their passports were taken and most of the wages earned were withheld to pay for transport and housing costs.

At the time of the raid, A14 Vehicle Hire was operating under a conditional license from the Gangmasters Licensing Authority (GLA). The license was revoked with effect from 20 November 2008 after the joint raid and inspection.

12.4   The International Labour Organization (ILO) Constitution requires all member states to set up a system of labour inspections by the state and emphasises the need for a multi-agency approach and liaison with other bodies. Despite the existence, since 1947, of an ILO Labour Inspection Convention C81[1] covering inspection by industry and commerce and its Protocol P81[2] providing for extension to the services sector, the UK still has an underdeveloped, under-resourced and unco-ordinated system of labour inspection in place.

What about the workers?

12.5   The key question is the extent to which the inspection regime, as well as having a preventive effect through enforcement of minimum

---

1   Date of entry into force: 7 April 1950. The convention deals with labour inspection in industrial workplaces.
2   Which the UK has not ratified.

standards, protects the individual worker in inspected workplaces. It is essential that enquiries are made in all cases to establish whether the workers have been trafficked. It is also essential that workers, whether trafficked or not, are compensated for loss they have suffered as a result of the failure to comply with the relevant labour standards. If a worker is willing to give evidence or has left the employment, he or she may report the employer to the relevant agency.

Inspection bodies

12.6   There are a number of national inspection and enforcement bodies which regulate the labour market:

- Gangmasters Licensing Authority;
- HMRC Minimum Wage Compliance Unit;
- Health and Safety Executive;
- Employment Agency Standards Inspectorate (EASI); and
- Agricultural Wages Inspectorate.[3]

Gangmasters Licensing Authority

12.7   The most significant inspection body is the GLA, which was set up under the Gangmasters (Licensing) Act 2004.[4] The 2004 Act was passed[5] in response to the deaths of 23 Chinese[6] cocklepickers at Morecambe Bay during the night of 5 February 2004. The Act received royal assent on 8 July 2004 and came into force from 1 December 2004. The GLA began operations on 1 April 2006 and the licensing provisions in October and December 2006. It is the only labour inspection body with a licensing system.

12.8   The 2004 Act extends to England and Wales, Scotland and Northern Ireland. It makes provision for the licensing of activities involving the supply or use of workers in connection with agricultural

---

3   Not dealt with separately in this chapter.
4   Section 1 of the Act sets up the body.
5   It had previously been a private member's bill with slim hopes of success.
6   For a striking account of the working conditions of Chinese migrant workers in the UK, see Hsiao-Hung Pai, *Chinese whispers*, Penguin, 2008.

work, the gathering of wild creatures and wild plants, the harvesting of fish from fish farms, and certain processing and packaging. By s2, the functions of the authority are:

(a) to carry out the functions relating to licensing that are conferred on it by the Act;
(b) to ensure the carrying out of such inspection as it considers necessary of persons holding licenses under the Act;
(c) to keep under review generally the activities of persons acting as gangmasters;
(d) to supply information held by it to specified persons in accordance with the provisions of this Act; and
(e) to keep under review the operation of the Act.

Such other functions as may be prescribed in regulations made by the secretary of state.

12.9   Importantly, the Act, and thus the GLA, only regulates[7] certain sectors, which are: agricultural work; gathering shellfish and associated processing or packaging work, that is to say processing or packaging any produce derived from agricultural work or shellfish, or fish or products derived from shellfish. Agricultural work includes work in the following: dairy farming; the production for the purposes of any trade, business or other undertaking (whether carried on for profit or not) of consumable produce; the use of land as grazing, meadow or pasture land; the use of land as an orchard or as osier land or woodland or the use of land for market gardens or nursery grounds. Consumable produce means produce grown for sale, consumption or other use after severance from the land on which it is grown.

12.10   There have been calls, notably from the Trades Union Congress (TUC), UCAAT and UNITE, for the Act to apply to the care and cleaning and hospitality sectors and to the construction sector. Although s3(5) enables the secretary of state to make regulations to extend the Act to work comprising (a) the gathering of wild creatures, or wild plants, of a prescribed description and the processing and packaging of anything so gathered; and (b) the harvesting of fish from a fish farm. There is no power to extend the scope of the Act by regulation to any sector other than these two. Such extension would need to be done through primary legislation.

---

7   Section 3.

Who is a gangmaster

12.11   A person acts as a gangmaster if he supplies a worker to do work to which this Act applies for another person.[8] Where A supplies a worker to do work for another person, B, the precise contractual arrangements are not determinative. For the purposes of the Act it does not matter whether the worker works under a contract with A or is supplied to him by another person, whether the worker is supplied directly under arrangements between A and B or indirectly under arrangements involving one or more intermediaries, whether A supplies the worker himself or herself, or procures that the worker is supplied; whether the work is done under the control of A, B or an intermediary; whether the work done for B is for the purposes of a business carried on by him or her, or in connection with services provided by him or her to another person. The Act applies if A uses the worker to do work to which the Act applies in connection with services provided by him or her to another person. The Act also applies if A uses a worker to do any of the following work to which this Act applies for the purposes of a business carried out by him or her:

(a) harvesting or otherwise gathering agricultural produce following:
   (i) a sale, assignment or lease of produce to A; or
   (ii) the making of any other agreement with A where the sale, assignment, lease or other agreement was entered into for the purpose of enabling the harvesting or gathering to take place;
(b) gathering shellfish;
(c) processing or packaging agricultural produce harvested or gathered as mentioned in paragraph (a).

Agricultural produce means any produce derived from agriculture.[9] A is treated as using a worker to do work to which the Act applies if A makes arrangements under which the worker does the work (a) whether the worker works for A (or for another) or on his or her own account, and (b) whether or not A works under a contract (with A or another). Where regulations under s3(5)(b) extend the scope of work to which the Act applies, they may provide for the application of s3(5) and (6).

8   Section 4.
9   Section 4(5).

Licensing conditions and standards

12.12   Secondary legislation sets out the procedure for applying for a gangmaster's licence and prescribes conditions which will apply to the licences. In respect of inspections carried out on or after 6 April 2009, the *Gangmasters (Licensing Conditions) Rules 2009/307* apply.[10] Where there has been an inspection before 6 April 2009, the previous licence and conditions continue to apply. However, a licence holder must permit the GLA to inspect the business at any reasonable time. The licence must be renewed every 12 months. The GLA carries out an inspection for all new applicants and may conduct subsequent compliance inspections, which are based partly on risk assessment and are partly random. A licence is granted subject to the conditions set out in Schedule 2 of the regulations.[11] The GLA may grant a licence if it thinks fit[12] or subject to such additional conditions as it thinks fit.[13] The GLA has issued licensing standards, which comprise of the conditions under the regulations, together with other legal requirements. The licensing standards must be complied with in order to qualify for and retain a GLA licence. The GLA retains a residual discretion to add further conditions. The latest licensing standards are dated April 2009 and are available from www.gla.gov.uk. There are eight licensing standards.[14] The standards operate on a points system. A license may be awarded on conditions, or refused or revoked. Points are awarded for failure to meet a standard and 30 points or more result in failure. A critical standard is valued at 30 points.[15] Thus, failure to meet a critical standard will result in failure and immediate refusal or revocation of the license. In some cases, revocation will have immediate effect. This is generally related to substantive issues such as mistreatment of workers.[16] Where the

---

10   Revoking and replacing *The Gangmasters (Licensing Conditions) (No 2) Rules 2006/2373* and *The Gangmasters (Licensing Conditions) (No 2) Amendment Rules 2008/638* which applied to all inspections on or after 1 October 2006. Statutory Instrument *2006/2373* was preceded by SI *2006/660*. All the regulations were made under the negative resolution procedure.

11   Paragraphs 4–26.

12   *2004 Act*, s7(1).

13   *2004 Act*, s7(1) and GA Regulations, reg 4(3).

14   The licensing standards replace, following consultation, the version issued in October *2006*.

15   Other standards are each valued at eight points, save the requirement to notify the GLA of changes, which is valued at 16 points.

16   The standards make clear which these are.

relevant condition is the concern of another agency, the GLA may pass relevant information onto that agency.

TABLE OF LICENSING STANDARDS

Licensing Standard	Subject matter
Licensing Standard 1: Fit and proper person	• Licence holder[17] must be a fit and proper person [C][18] • Principal authority[19] must be competent, ie must understand the licensing requirement and management processes [C] • Any GLA additional licence conditions must be corrected within the time period [C] • Notification of GLA within 20 days of relevant changes
Licensing Standard 2: Pay and tax	• Payment of PAYE, NI and VAT [C] • Payment of at least the National Minimum Wage [C] • Proper records on wages, leave and benefits [C] • Provision of payslips [C]

Licensing Standard 3: Prevention of forced labour and mistreatment of workers	• There must be no physical and mental mistreatment of workers or threats to workers or others [C]
	• There must be no restricting a worker's movement, debt bondage or retaining ID documents [C]
	• This prohibits
	  – debts which prevent a worker from freely seeking other employment
	  – any detriment or threat to a worker as a result of the worker terminating the contract
	  – retention of identity papers (save to check entitlement to work in the UK and then only so long as necessary)
	  – force or coercion of a worker
	• If a worker is loaned money directly or indirectly by the licence holder to meet their travel or other expenses to take up a position, the worker cannot be required to repay a sum greater than the sum loaned and any agreement must be in writing
	• There must be no withholding of wages on basis of
	  – non payment by labour user
	  – failure by worker to prove they have worked during pay period [C]

---

17 This is used throughout the standards to include an applicant for a licence.

18 [C] indicates this is a critical standard.

19 This means the individual responsible for day-to-day management: 2009/307, reg 2. The standards set out details of what management processes are considered.

Licensing Standard	Subject matter
Licensing Standard 4: Accommodation	Where accommodation is let in connection with the contract of employment and accommodation is dependent upon continued employment or vice versa, the licence holder will be regarded as providing the accommodation, whether or not it is formally let by them. A licence holder will also be regarded as providing accommodation where they are associated with the landlord.[20]
	• Accommodation, where provided, must be safe and habitable [C] • Accommodation, where provided, must be licensed • If not otherwise provided, provision of suitable accommodation where worker lives away from their UK home with information on cost provided in advance[21] • Worker must be allowed to find suitable alternative accommodation if they choose, after 10 working days' notice
Licensing Standard 5: Working conditions	• Rest breaks • Maximum of 48 hours, subject to written agreement • Trade union membership must be permitted and not penalised • Gangmaster must not supply worker to replace a worker taking industrial action (this does not apply to unofficial strike action) • Respect for worker's confidentiality except as required by law (thus if a gangmaster is contributing to a blacklist this will contravene this standard) • Disciplinary and grievance procedures • Non-discrimination
Licensing Standard 6: Health and safety	Co-operation with the labour user to ensure: • Health and safety responsibility assigned and risk assessment carried out • Free health and safety training during working time • Provision of adequate personal protective equipment. Provision of PPE free to employees and to workers within the meaning of health and safety legislation. No deposits may be required for such PPE. Where the PPE is returnable and is not returned, the cost may be deduced from wages, provided that has been agreed in advance in writing

20   The forms of association are set out in the standards.
21   The standards make special provisions for workers under 18 years of age.

Licensing Standard	Subject matter
	• Adequate arrangements for washing and welfare facilities • Adequate arrangements for first aid and the monitoring of reportable incidents at work • Safe and legal transport to transport workers [C] • Planning and supervision of workers used to gather shellfish [C] • Sufficient fuel and adequate transport for shellfish collection [C] • Provision of lifejackets and life rafts for shellfish workers [C] • Maritime and Coastguard agency certification for any boat used [C] • Ensuring that workers possess and comply with any permit or licence for shellfish gathering [C]

Licensing Standard 7: Recruiting workers and contractual arrangements	• License holder must not charge a worker a fee for work-finding services nor make such services conditional of use of other services or on hiring or purchasing goods. Worker must be able to withdraw without incurring any detriment or penalty, subject to 5 days notice or 10 working days in respect of accommodation [C]
	• Worker must have entitlement to work in the UK (note this is not critical. This standard will not be failed if the employer makes out the statutory defence, ie that they have carried out a documents check and that the documents were apparently credible)
	• Before supplying a worker, licence holder must agree and provide relevant terms, including:
	  – type of work
	  – whether worker is supplied under contract of employment or contract for services
	  – undertaking to pay the worker for any work carried out regardless of whether the license holder has been paid
	  – length of notice
	  – pay and pay period
	  – right to holiday
	• Worker must be informed in writing of any fees relating to services which they have taken up. This should include amount or method of calculation, identity of person to whom fee payable, description of the goods or services to which the fee relates and the worker's right to withdraw from the arrangement

Licensing Standard	Subject matter

	• License holder must record, as soon as reasonably practicable:
	  – date terms agreed
	  – worker name, address and date of birth
	  – details of training, experience or qualifications
	  – name of relevant labour users
	  – details of contracts
	  – evidence of worker's consent to any payments made by the worker
	• Adequate agreements and records between license holder and labour user
	• Restrictions on charges to labour users which might act as disincentive to worker's entry into labour user's employment

Licensing Standard 8: Subcontracting and using other labour providers	• License holder must only sub-contract to, or use, GLA licensed-labour providers [C] • Adequate written or electronic records of dealing with other license holders. These must be kept for one year and on premises, or if elsewhere they must be readily accessible and capable of being delivered to GLA within 2 working days

Conditional licenses

12.13   The updated licensing standards contain a higher proportion of critical standards, in particular, in relation to loans or accommodation arrangements which may restrict a worker's freedom to leave the employment. This reflects an appreciation of the fact that elements of coercion or of the incurring of disproportionate debt may exist outside the workplace itself but be related to it. Licensing Standard 3 now includes the withholding of wages. This is intended to bring the standard in line with CETS 197.[22]

Reporting a gangmaster

12.14   A complaint about an existing licensee or about an unlicensed gangmaster may be made confidentially to the GLA.[23] A list of licensed gangmasters is available from the GLA online at www.gla. gov.uk.

---

22   GLA Impact Assessment.
23   See contact details in Appendix A – Resources.

Appeals by gangmasters

12.15   There is a right of appeal against any decision of the GLA:

- To refuse an application for a license
- To attach conditions to a license
- To revoke a license
- To refuse the transfer of a license

The Gangmasters (Appeals) Regulations SI 2006/662[24] provides for appeals in more detail. An appeal may be brought in respect of a full license or a provisional license. A license which is the subject of an appeal against modification or revocation continues to have effect pending determination of the appeal, unless the decision is one with immediate effect, such as failure of a standard which is critical.[25] If the appeal is withdrawn, the decision takes effect on the date it was scheduled to take effect, or on the sixth working day after promulgation of the decision, whichever is the later.[26] An appeal must be lodged no later than 20 working days after the date of the decision document (or ten days in the case of a decision which has immediate effect).[27] The appeal is heard at an oral hearing in front of an employment judge, unless the parties agree to written representations. If any worker is willing, they may be asked to give evidence. There is no further appeal against the decision. It is subject to judicial review by any person with sufficient standing.

Criminal offences

12.16   The licensing system is backed up by criminal sanctions. Section 12(1) of the 2004 Act provides that it is a criminal offence to operate as a gangmaster without a license. This does not including acting in breach of conditions of a license.[28] Section 12(2) is aimed at misuse or falsification of GLA documents. It is a criminal offence to possess a GLA license or other relevant document issued by the GLA which is intended to induce another person to wrongly believe that a relevant person is acting under a GLA license, where the document is false or improperly obtained (for example, obtained through false

---

24   Commencement 6 April 2006.
25   GA Regulations 2006, regs 5(3) and (4).
26   GA Regulations 2006, reg 5(5).
27   GA Regulations 2006, reg 6(1).
28   2004 Act, s12(1).

information)[29] and known or believed to be so, or relates to someone else.[30] Both offences under section 12 are punishable by a maximum of 10 years in prison or a fine. Both offences are lifestyle offences within the meaning of Schedule 2 of the Proceeds of Crime Act 2002.[31]

12.17   Section 13 of the 2004 Act creates a criminal offence of entering into an arrangement for the supply of labour or services with an unlicensed gangmaster.[32] A statutory defence is available to a person who has taken reasonable steps to satisfy themselves that the gangmaster was operating under the authority of a valid license and had no actual or constructive knowledge.[33] No regulations have yet prescribed what reasonable steps are, although there is the power to do so.[34] DEFRA have issued on reasonable steps.[35] The offence is summary only and is punishable by up to 51 weeks in England and Wales and up to six months in Scotland and Northern Ireland or by a fine.[36] There is a further criminal offence relating to obstruction of a GLA inspector.[37]

Powers of the inspectors

12.18   The inspectors have significant powers to enter premises and to make arrests. In practice, much of this work is currently done by police officers in joint operations where necessary. Section 14 gives enforcement officers powers of arrest: where the enforcement officer has reasonable grounds for suspecting that an offence has been committed, he or she may arrest without warrant anyone whom he or she has reasonable grounds for suspecting to be guilty of the offence, who is about to commit such an offence and anyone whom he or she has reasonable grounds for suspecting to be about to commit such an offence. Subsections (1) and (2) do not apply in Scotland. Section 16 sets out the powers of Compliance Officers. Section 17 provides for entry by warrant. A justice of the peace may

---

29   2004 Act, s12(5).
30   2004 Act, s12(2)(b) and (c).
31   See further para 14.5.
32   2004 Act, s13(1).
33   2004 Act, s13(2).
34   2004 Act, s13(3).
35   Available from www.gla.gov.uk.
36   2004 Act, s13(4).
37   See 12.18.

issue a warrant if satisfied by written information on oath that entry to a premises is necessary for the purpose of ascertaining whether there has been any contravention of s6 (unlicensed premises) and of one of the following:

(1) that admission has been refused or will be refused and that notice of intention to apply for a warrant has been given to the occupier of the premises;

(2) that an application for permission or the giving of notice would defeat the object of the entry;

(3) that the case is one of extreme urgency; or

(4) that the premises are unoccupied or the occupier is temporarily absent.

An officer entering premises by virtue of a warrant under this section may take with him or her when entering those premises such other persons and such other equipment as he or she considers necessary; carry out on those premises such inspections and examinations as he or she considers necessary for the purpose of ascertaining whether there has been any contravention of s6; and take possession of any book, document, data or record (in whatever form it is held) which is on the premises and retain it for as long as he or she considers it necessary for that purpose. The usual provisions apply as regards securing the premises on departure and leaving a relevant notice. Section 18 provides that a criminal offence is committed when an officer acting in pursuit of offences under this Act is obstructed. This includes the giving of false information. In England and Wales the maximum penalty on summary conviction is imprisonment for 51 weeks[38] or a fine or both; in Scotland or Northern Ireland it is imprisonment for six months or a fine or both.

12.19   Section 19 makes wide provision in relation to information exchange among state agencies. Such information sharing will be an important part of effective multi-agency working.

Effect on individual rights

12.20   In addition, contravention of or failure to comply with the 2004 Act or of the Rules on Licensing Conditions made under it by a license

---

38   Unless the office was committed before the commencement of s281(5) of the Criminal Justice Act 2003, in which case it is six months.

holder shall, so far as it causes damage, be actionable, without prejudice to any right of action or any defence which may exist apart from the Act and the Rules.[39] Rule 10 of the 2006 Rules also provides that even where a contractual term is prohibited or made unenforceable under the rules, first, the unenforceable term is severed from the contract and the contract continues in existence, and second, that a labour user is entitled to recover money paid pursuant to an unenforceable term. Workers themselves may also sue.

HMRC Minimum Wage Compliance Unit

12.21   The Minimum Wage Unit of HMRC enforces compliance with the National Minimum Wage Act 1998 and the National Minimum Wage Regulations 1999.[40]

12.22   The 1998 Act is intended to be comprehensive in its coverage. It applies to anyone who is a 'worker', that is to say who has agreed or works under a contract of employment or any other contract, oral or written.[41] The Act applies to agency workers insofar as they do not fall within that definition because of a lack of a contract with either the agency or the end-user.[42] The duty falls on whichever person is responsible for paying, or does pay, the worker.[43] The Act may, by regulation, be extended to other classes of individuals who are not otherwise workers.[44] On its website, the HMRC takes the view that workers must be 'legal', but this is nowhere set out in the 1998 Act.[45]

12.23   Enforcement is set out in the 1998 Act and 1999 Regulations. The Employment Act 2008[46] amends the 1998 Act to increase the penalties and to increase the powers of HMRC.

---

39   Reference in Act and r9, 2006 Rules.
40   SI 1999/584. Guidance on the operation of the Regulations is provided by the BERR at www.berr.gov.uk/employment/pay/national-minimum-wage/index. html.
41   Section 54(3).
42   Section 34.
43   Section 34(2).
44   Section 41.
45   See Law Commission report on this issue, expected March 2009.
46   Which received royal assent on 18 November 2008.

Powers of inspectors

12.24   Inspectors' powers are governed by s14 of the 1998 Act.[47] They may require production of relevant records, require an explanation of the records and additional information, and may enter any relevant premises in order to exercise any of those powers. An office can require a relevant person (eg employer, labour supplier or their agents) to attend to furnish the above explanation or information.[48] Section 12 of the 2008 Act gives HMRC officers the powers to apply for production orders and search warrants or to arrest a person suspected of committing an offence under s31.[49]

Civil enforcement

12.25   The previous system of enforcement and penalty notices is replaced by a new s19 providing for a single notice of underpayment[50] requiring the employer to pay the arrears named in the notice. The arrears period may be up to six years. The new s19A provides for a civil penalty of 50 per cent of the amount of underpayment, up to a maximum of £5,000.[51] Where an enforcement notice is not complied with in whole or in part, the HMRC may sue, on behalf of the worker, for unlawful deduction of wages or may commence other civil proceedings for breach of contract,[52] without prejudice to the worker's right to sue.[53]

Criminal offences

12.26   Section 31 creates a criminal offence where an employer refuses or wilfully neglects to pay a worker who qualifies for at least the minimum wage. The language of the statute means that this is not a strict liability offence. Criminal offences are also committed where

47   As amended by s10 of the 2008 Act.
48   Section 14(3).
49   The substantive powers are in s84 of the Finance Act 2007 and in Scotland the Criminal Law (Consolidation)(Scotland) Act 1995.
50   Section 9, 2008 Act. The employer may appeal to an employment tribunal against a notice of underpayment on grounds of compliance, error in the sum or error in the notice. If the appeal is successful, the notice has effect as rectified by the tribunal: s19C(8).
51   With a minimum of £100. The penalty may be suspended where criminal proceedings have been instituted under s31 of the 1998 Act.
52   Section 20(1).
53   Section 20(2).

records required to be kept[54] are not kept. Where an offence is committed due to an act or default of someone else (eg a manager does not keep records) that other person is also liable. In each case, there is a defence of due diligence and reasonable precautions.[55]

12.27   Intentional delay or obstruction of an enforcement officer or refusal or neglect to answer any question, furnish any information or produce any document when required to do so under s14(1) is also an offence.

12.28   The 2008 Act amends[56] mode of trial so that the trial can be heard in the Crown Court, which creates the prospect of an unlimited fine. Previously, the maximum fine was £5,000, which was the same amount as a civil penalty notice. This, and the cap, created little deterrent. Deliberate non-payment to HMRC of tax in the sum of £50,000 is punishable by a maximum of seven years in prison and an unlimited fine. Deliberate non-payment of minimum wages in the sum of £50,000 was previously punishable by a fine of £5,000 maximum. The increase was passed with the intention that 'the courts should be able to deal with the deliberate exploitation of the low-paid more strongly than at present'.[57]

Health and Safety Executive

12.29   Breaches of health and safety law and practice are dealt with by the Health and Safety Executive (HSE).[58] The HSE is responsible for monitoring all workplaces. The HSE enforces the Health and Safety at Work Act 1974, the Health and Safety Regulations and a number of sector-specific health and safety standards. As with other inspection bodies, there are powers of inspection and prosecution.

Employment Agency Standards Inspectorate

12.30   The Employment Agency Standards Inspectorate (EASI) is part of the Department for Business, Enterprise and Regulatory Reform

---

54   Section 9, 1998 Act.
55   Section 31(8).
56   Section 11.
47   Lord Jones, promoter of the Bill, Lords Hansard 13 March 2008, Column GC259.
58   See www.hse.gov.uk.

(BERR). EASI monitors compliance with the Employment Agency Act 1973 and the Conduct of Employment Agencies and Employment Business Regulations.[59] The 1973 Act applies to employment agencies[60] and to employment businesses[61] does not apply to an employment agency or business insofar as its activities consist of activities for which a license is required under the Gangmasters (Licensing) Act 2004.[62] Section 6 of the 1973 Act prohibits an agency[63] from requiring a fee from the work for finding them work. Breach of this restriction is a criminal offence.[64]

12.31   The 2003 Regulations set in detail the prohibition on direct and indirect charging for the finding of work.[65] Some bodies try to evade this through clauses providing for deductions from workers' wages for items such as transport, equipment, uniform and meals. These are not prohibited by the 2003 Regulations. The 2003 Regulations also prohibit[66] the bodies to which they apply from withholding or threatening to withhold a worker's pay on any of the following grounds:

(a) that the user has not paid the employment business;
(b) that the worker cannot produce a time sheet authenticated by the user;
(c) that the worker has not worked during a period other than that to which the payment relates;
(d) any other matter within the control of the employment business.

12.32   The standards are enforced in a number of ways. On application by the enforcement body, an employment tribunal may prohibit the agency or business from acting as such if satisfied that they are

---

59   SI 2003/3319.
60   Defined in s13(2) as the business (whether carried on for profit or whether or not in conjunction with other business) of providing services (by the provision of information or otherwise) for the purpose of finding persons employment with employers or of supplying employments with persons for employment by them.
61   Defined in s13(3) as the business of supplying persons in the employment of the person carrying on the business to act for, and under the control of, other persons in any capacity.
62   Section 27, 2004 Act.
63   Save in prescribed cases.
64   Section 6(2), now triable either way, see 12.32 below.
65   Except in very limited circumstances, ie stage and sport.
66   Reg 12.

unsuitable.[67] Breach of the 2003 Regulations is a criminal offence[68] which, as with the Minimum Wage Provisions, may now be tried on indictment, with a resultant unlimited fine.[69] Similar greater investigatory and prosecutory powers have been given to EASI. Failure to comply with the regulations is also actionable by an individual if loss or damage is caused as a result.[70]

67 Section 3A, 1973 Act.
68 Section 5(2), 1973 Act.
69 Section 15, Employment Act 2008, amending ss3B, 5(2) and 6(2) of the 1973 Act.
70 Reg 30, 2003 Regulations.

Representing migrant workers

Key points

- Protection of the fundamental labour rights of migrant workers is a key part of a preventive response to human trafficking.
- In practice this will involve identifying relevant persons and their agents and along the chain of recruitment, transfer and end-use.
- Such protection depends upon identification of fundamental employment rights in national law.
- A suitable legal framework for migrant workers rights in employment law is set out in the UN Convention on Migrant Workers which remains unratified by the UK.
- A substantial impediment to enforcement of some of the basic employment rights is the doctrine of illegality, preventing a court or tribunal from hearing a claim and often applied too widely.
- Advisers should be familiar with how to assist in applying for permission to work and other ways of regularising stay.

Generally

13.1   Not all migrant workers have been subjected to human trafficking. Not all migrant workers are even severely exploited. Not all trafficked people are migrants over national borders. However, a poorly regulated migrant labour market of workers vulnerable to exploitation is overwhelmingly the pool in which trafficking occurs. Human trafficking is one result of a state's failure to maintain consistent and high labour standards throughout its territory. This is as true of trafficking for the purposes of commercial sexual exploitation as it is of trafficking for the purposes of labour exploitation. It is commonly accepted that the policy aim is the prevention (as part of prevention of trafficking) of exploitation of such migrant workers. However, how this aim is to be achieved is the subject of radical divergence of approach. The economics of demand and supply have been such that efforts to achieve the aim solely through enforcement of immigration law have so far been ineffective. For this reason, it follows that proper protection of the fundamental labour rights of migrant workers is an essential element of prevention of human trafficking.[1] For sanctions against exploitative working to be successful, the state's administrative laws need to provide some security to the workers that their exposure of unacceptable working conditions will not result in immediate punishment in the form of expulsion. Chapter 10 addressed compensation for victims of trafficking. Chapter 12 concerned regulation through labour inspection. This chapter concerns enforcement of migrant workers' fundamental employment rights in the employment tribunals and civil courts.

Fundamental labour rights

13.2   In international human rights law, some labour rights have the character of fundamental and binding norms. These include the erga omnes principles[2] of equality and non-discrimination. They also include the ILO Core Labour Standards.[3] In its Advisory Opinion OC-18/03 of 17 September 2003, requested by the United Mexican States on *Juridical condition and rights of the undocumented migrants*, the Inter-American Court of Human Rights held that fundamental labour rights could not be dependent upon immigration status and were therefore enforceable in the courts (though the court also stressed that immigration enforcement action against the worker was also possible). The key passages from the opinion are set out in Table 13.1.

---

1   See eg Border and Immigration Agency, *Immigration, Asylum and Nationality Act 2006, comprehensive guidance for employers on preventing illegal working,* February 2008, states at p4: 'There is evidence that some of those who are working illegally are paid less than the minimum wage, do not pay tax, and may be doing dangerous work that breaks health and safety regulations. Employers who employ illegal migrant workers may do so because they want to avoid providing minimum standards, such as the National Minimum Wage and paid holidays. This is harmful to the workers involved and enables unscrupulous employers to gain an unfair advantage over legitimate competitors'. In *Secure Borders, Safe Haven* 5.2 the Government stated: 'Exploitation – whether of illegal or other workers – is harmful, not only for the victim, but also undermines our National Minimum Wage and labour standards. Both people trafficking and smuggling usually involve illegal working, and trafficking always involves exploitation. So successful action against illegal working and exploitation is not only desirable in itself, but will also reduce incentives for organised criminals to bring people to the UK.' The policy issue is whether this aim is achieved more effectively through immigration regulation or labour regulation.

2   Principles by which all states are bound, whether or not they have signed up to the relevant instrument.

3   See www.ilo.org.

Table 13.1

RELEVANT RIGHT	SOURCE OF THE RIGHT	EMPLOYMENT RELATIONSHIP REQUIRED
Within two months of start of employment, • to a statement of initial employment particulars; • an itemised pay statement including gross pay, deductions from gross pay and net pay; • the right not to be unfairly dismissed for asserting a statutory right	Part I, Employment Rights Act 1996	Employees, ie those working under a contract of service
• The right not to have unauthorised deductions made from wages	Part II, Employment Rights Act 1996	'Workers' within the meaning of Part II of the 1996 Act: 'those who have entered into, or work under, a contract of employment and any other contract whereby the individual undertakes to do or perform personally any work or services for another party to the contract whose status is not, by virtue of the contract, that of a client or customer of any profession or business undertaking carried on by the individual': ERA 1996 s230. Includes agency workers on the books of an employment agency.
• The right to a national minimum wage	National Minimum Wage Act 1998 and National Minimum Wage Regulations (NMW Regulations) 1999. £5.73 per hour. Apprentices: 18–21 year olds £4.77 17–18 year olds £3.53	Workers within the meaning of the 1998 Act, ie 'anyone working under a contract of employment or any other contract to perform personally any work or services, except to a professional client or business customer': s54(3). Includes agency workers and homeworkers: NMWA ss34 and 35. Excludes workers working as part of a family (sharing accommodation, food) eg au pairs: 1999 Regulations, reg 2(2)(a).
• The right to working time protection (it is not possible to contract out from this apart from with regards to a 48 hour week)	Working Time Regulations 1998/ 1833, implementing Directives 93/104/EC and 2000/43/EC (on protections of young workers) See non statutory guidance www.berr.gov.uk/employment/employment-legislation/employment-guidance/pag28978.html Special rules for young workers and night workers. Right not to work more than an average (over 17–26 weeks) of 48 hours per week including overtime.	Applies to workers, ie anyone working under a contract of employment or any other contract to perform personally any work or services, except to a professional client or business customer: 1998 Regs, reg 2(1). Temporary and agency workers are covered: reg 36. Domestic servants in private households are excluded from protection: reg 19.

Table 13.1 *Continued*

RELEVANT RIGHT	SOURCE OF THE RIGHT	EMPLOYMENT RELATIONSHIP REQUIRED
	May be opted out of only if worker freely consents. Worker may terminate the agreement at any time on notice of between seven days and three months. Right not to suffer detriment for refusing to enter into an opt-out or for bringing an opt-out to an end: ERA 1996 ss 45A and 101A. However, pro rata reduction in pay is likely to be lawful. Entitlement to a consecutive rest period of 11 consecutive hours. Exceptions for young workers and shift workers. 20 minutes (unpaid) break every six hours. There are numerous exceptions (set out in reg 21 of the 1998 Regulations), in particular of shift workers or where continuous work may be necessary eg work in hospitals or refuse collection or working on trains. Or where a foreseeable surge in activity eg postal services. However, there should be an equivalent period where convenient and, if not possible, sufficient protection to guarantee health and safety: reg 24.	
• The right to health and safety protection • Right not to be subjected to detriment or dismissal on grounds of responsibility for health and safety: s44 ERA	Health and Safety at Work Act 1974 Health and Safety Regulations under the Act in particular 1992/2793; 1992/2966; 1993/3004; 1999/3242	Workers
• The right to take part in trade union activities	Unlawful for an employer to subject a worker to a detriment for taking part in trade union activities or to offer them an inducement not to do so. Also unlawful for third parties to induce this: s150.	Worker: Trade Union and Labour Relations (Consolidation) Act 1992 s296
• The right not to suffer a detriment or dismissal for making a disclosure in the public interest	Part IVA, Employment Rights Act 1996	A worker, within the meaning of s230(3), ERA 1996: 'an individual who has entered into or works under (or, where the employment has ceased, worked under) – (a) a contract of employment, or (b) any other contract, whether express or implied and (if it is express) whether oral or in writing, whereby the individual undertakes to do or perform personally any work or services for another party to the contract whose status is not by virtue of the contract that of a client or customer of any profession or business undertaking carried on by the individual.' As further extended by s43K, Employment Rights Act 1996.
• Under Race Relations legislation, equality with other workers on grounds of nationality or national origins.		Employees, workers (persons who undertake to perform work personally), contract workers, who work under a contract to provide labour.

Inter-American Court of Human Rights, Advisory Opinion OC-18/03 of 17 September 2003, requested by the United Mexican States on Juridical Condition and Rights of the Undocumented Migrants

134–136 In this way, the migratory status of a person can never be a justification for depriving him of the enjoyment and exercise of his human rights, including those related to employment. On assuming an employment relationship, the migrant acquires rights as a worker, which must be recognized and guaranteed, irrespective of his regular or irregular status in the State of employment. These rights are a consequence of the employment relationship. It is important to clarify that the State and the individuals in a State are not obliged to offer employment to undocumented migrants. The State and individuals, such as employers, can abstain from establishing an employment relationship with migrants in an irregular situation. However, if undocumented migrants are engaged, they immediately become possessors of the labour rights corresponding to workers and may not be discriminated against because of their irregular situation. This is very important, because one of the principal problems that occurs in the context of immigration is that migrant workers who lack permission to work are engaged in unfavourable conditions compared to other workers.[4]

...

157 ... in the case of migrant workers, there are certain rights that assume a fundamental importance and yet are frequently violated, such as: the prohibition of obligatory or forced labour; the prohibition and abolition of child labour; special care for women workers, and the rights corresponding to: freedom of association and to organize and join a trade union, collective negotiation, fair wages for work performed, social security, judicial and administrative guarantees, a working day of reasonable length with adequate working conditions (safety and health), rest and compensation. The safeguard of these rights for migrants has great importance based on the principle of the inalienable nature

---

4   Inter-American Court of Human Rights, Advisory Opinion OC-18/03 of 17 September, 2003, requested by the United Mexican States on *Juridical condition and rights of the undocumented migrants* 134–136.

of such rights, which all workers possess, irrespective of their migratory status, and also the fundamental principle of human dignity embodied in Article 1 of the Universal Declaration, according to which '[a]ll human beings are born free and equal in dignity and rights. They are endowed with reason and conscience and should act towards one another in a spirit of brotherhood.'

...

159 On many occasions, undocumented migrant workers are not recognized the said labour rights. For example, many employers engage them to provide a specific service for less than the regular remuneration, dismiss them because they join unions, and threaten to deport them. Likewise, at times, undocumented migrant workers cannot even resort to the courts of justice to claim their rights owing to their irregular situation. This should not occur; because, even though an undocumented migrant worker could face deportation, he should always have the right to be represented before a competent body so that he is recognized all the labour rights he has acquired as a worker: section 159. The Inter-American Court also held that States could not suborn fundamental rights to their migration policies.[5]

The United Nations Convention on Migrant Workers

13.3   Key legal principles are also set out in the Convention on Migrant Workers, adopted in 1990, which drew on ILO Conventions 97, 143, 151 (recommendation on migrant workers), 29 (forced or compulsory labour) and 105 (forced labour). The convention came into force on 1 July 2003 but has not yet been signed or ratified by the UK. It sets out differing provisions based upon whether a worker is documented or undocumented.[6] Part III (articles 8–35) of the UN Convention applies to all migrant workers, whether documented or undocumented.

5   Sections 161–172 and see conclusions at pp113–114.
6   Article 5 defines documented as migrant workers who are authorised to enter, to stay and to engage in a remunerated activity; undocumented workers are those who are not. See further chapter 3.

Access to specific labour rights

13.4   This chapter is concerned with problems experienced by migrant workers in the migration for work. The migrant worker may have had a contract with a recruiter, an immigration consultant, a transport arranger, a labour supplier, the end user and their agents. Transport and accommodation may be provided at very high charges and demands made to be paid back out of wages. It may not always be clear who to sue. Suit may be brought in the ordinary courts relying on a contract or on a duty in tort.[7] This may be the case when money has been spent in reliance on a misrepresentation.

13.5   In many cases, however, the worker may wish simply to access basic labour rights such as wages for work done. These are set out in summary in Table 13.1. Access to these rights depends upon being able to prove a relevant employment relationship (as employee or worker) with the natural or legal person being sued. Many rights are restricted to those working under a contract of service even though much work is now done through subcontracting and use of agencies. This is despite the fact that s23 of the Employment Relations Act 1999 confers power to modify classes of employee to whom rights apply.

Labour rights

13.6   Fundamental labour rights in UK law need to be identified as they exist in UK law. Such rights will plainly include all the convention rights in Schedule 1 to the Human Rights Act 1998. They are likely also to include employment rights which cannot be contracted out of, ie mandatory minimum employment rights guaranteed by statute. Statutory minimum employment rights are set out in Table 13.1.

Who are employees?

13.7   As can be seen from Table 13.1, status as an employee gives rise to a range of rights. Courts have held that a relationship of employment must have the following two elements: control (ie the employer must exercise day-to-day control) and mutuality of obligation (there must be an obligation on the employer to provide the work and a

---

7   See chapter 10, which deals with compensation claims for human trafficking.

corresponding obligation on the employee to perform it). The two elements are a necessary but not always sufficient part of establishing that the client is an employee. *Dacas v Brook Street Bureau Ltd v another;*[8] *Muscat v Cable and Wireless.*[9]

Migrant domestic workers as employees

13.8   Advisers may be approached for advice by migrant domestic workers. These are a category of worker who enter the country accompanying a specific employer and who carry out work within a private household. Border Agency data shows that between 16,000 and 18,300 domestic visas are granted each year.[10] This domestic work may range from child care or other care work to cooking, driving, housekeeping or cleaning. Once in the country, and even under the domestic worker visa system, workers are vulnerable and subject to poor working conditions. Complaints received by Kalayaan have included: physical abuse, psychological abuse, sexual abuse, lack of own room or own bed, no regular meals or meal breaks, no time off and not being allowed out of the house.[11] Such treatment may amount to exploitation, to false imprisonment, assault or other torts.

13.9   Prior to 1998, immigration law did not specifically provide for such workers. They were not formally recognised as workers but were given leave to enter either as a visitor or as a member of the family they were working with or their passport was stamped 'to work with (the relevant family)'. This was not transferable. In 1998, a domestic worker visa was introduced, following campaigns by Kalayaan and others.[12] The relevant provisions are now to be

---

8   [2004] ICR 1437.

9   [2006] ICR 975.

10 Kalayaan and Oxfam *The new bonded labour?* 2008, p9. See www.kalayaan.org. uk. Kalayaan operates a registration system for migrant domestic workers. Of those who register, 80 per cent are women, mostly from developing countries in particular India, the Philippines, Sri Lanka and Indonesia. Employers of migrant domestic workers are mainly Middle Eastern, Indian or British. Kalayann reports that physical and psychological abuse are widespread.

11 Ibid, p13.

12 In June 2008, following a campaign by Kalayaan, UNITE and others, the government withdrew proposals to replace the current system with non-renewable six-month domestic assistant visas, which would not have been transferable from one employer to another.

found within Part 5 of the Immigration Rules: rr159A–159H.[13] (The Immigration Rules make separate provision for workers whom the Rules call 'private servants in a diplomatic household': see rr152–159 of the Immigration Rules.) Entry clearance must be applied for outside the country. Several conditions must be satisfied:

(1) The worker must have spent at least one year in the employment of the person with whom they are seeking leave to enter the UK, whether under the same roof or in a household which the employer uses on a regular basis.

(2) The worker is aged 18–65 inclusive.

(3) The person with whom the worker is seeking leave to enter must provide a written statement of the terms of employment of the worker[14] and a written undertaking that the worker will be able to maintain and accommodate herself without recourse to public funds (thus the employer must either feed and house the worker or provide a salary adequate for independent accommodation and for food).

The visa is renewable every year, provided the worker remains in continuous full-time employment in a private household. Domestic visas are given for either six months (if the employer is entering as a visitor) or 12 months (if the employer is planning to live for longer in the UK or to settle). The visa may be extended (see contacts for the list) provided that the worker has continued to be employed as a domestic worker in a private household and continues to be required for employment for the period of the extension sought as a domestic worker in a private household. If the employer has changed, details of the old and the new employers together with reasons for the change, should be provided and the details required for entry should be provided by the new employer. Extensions of the visa are given for 12 months. It is unlawful for the employer to hold the employee's passport without their consent. After five years continuously[15] in the

---

13 Accessible at www.ukba.homeoffice.gov.uk/policyandlaw/immigrationlaw/immigrationrules.

14 This must include at a minimum the name and address of the employer and employee, date on which employment started, duration of employment, notice period (minimum statutory entitlement being one week's notice after one month's employment and thereafter one week per year's employment), place of work, hours of work and days off each week, wage or salary (the statutory minimum being £5.52 per hour), method of payment, description of duties, annual leave entitlement (minimum four weeks' paid leave), arrangements for sick leave and sick pay.

15 Breaks of up to three months are allowed.

UK on a domestic worker visa, the worker may apply for indefinite leave to remain.

Agency workers: suing employment agencies and other auxiliaries

13.10 There are about 770,000 agency workers in the British workforce at any one time. Eight million workers in the European Union are temporary agency workers and the numbers are increasing. On 7 May 2008, the TUC (Trades Union Congress) published the report of its Commission on Vulnerable Employment.[16] It estimated that around 2 million workers in the UK were in vulnerable employment: defined as precarious work which places people at risk of continuing poverty and injustice resulting from an imbalance of power in the employer – worker relationship. It is estimated that agency workers form about 3.1 per cent of the UK workforce. The TUC found that 80 per cent of employers now subcontract parts of their business.[17]

13.11 Agency work involves a third party, an agency, which acts as an intermediary between the worker and the user company. Where an agency is involved, the duties usually assumed by an employer may be divided between the agency – which hires and pays – and the agency's client and end-user of the labour, for whom the individual works and who has day-to-day control. Accommodation may be provided by either. The labourer may be employed by the agency, the client, both or neither. Only employees have access to certain rights. As seen above, courts have been reluctant to imply an employment relationship between the user and the worker (in some respects, eg health and safety and equality law, the worker is protected as a contract worker). Because of their status, such workers often fall outside the scope of collective agreements.

Suing the agency

13.12 The agency may be sued in some circumstances: see Table 13.1. The agency is liable to any shortfall in the minimum wage.[18] The agency may also be sued under the Employment Agencies Act 1973 and the 2003 Regulations for charging impermissible fees and making or

---

16 Full report available to download from www.vulnerableworkers.org.uk.
17 Short report, p5.
18 National Minimum Wage Act 1998 s34 and 1999 Regulations reg 2.

seeking to make impermissible deductions and suing for recovery of pay. The agency worker is also protected.[19]

Suing the agency as employer for breaches of employment rights

13.13   In some cases, it is necessary to establish an employment relationship, eg for unfair dismissal rights. Polish workers recruited by an agency in Poland, who arranged their travel and accommodation, were held to be employees of the agency by an employment tribunal, despite a clause in the agreement denying such a relationship: *Consistent Group Limited v Kalwak and others*.[20] The workers were employees of the employment agency which supplied them to an end-user client even though it was the end-user rather than the agency who exercised control over the actual operation of their work.

Suing the end-user as employer for employment rights

13.14   The worker may wish to sue the end-user for conditions and treatment at work. Consideration should be given to whether an agency relationship has arisen. In some cases, the end-user may be the employer. However, a restrictive interpretation has been given by the Court of Appeal in *James v London Borough of Greenwich* in February 2008. The Court of Appeal held that Mrs James' work was adequately explained by the contract between Greenwich (the end-user) and the employment agency on the one hand and between Mrs James and the agency on the other.

13.15   It is necessary to establish an employment relationship with the end user because agency workers are often segregated into less favourable working terms and conditions. This is addressed by the Temporary (Agency) Workers Directive,[21] adopted by the European Parliament on 22 October 2008. The Directive gives agency workers the same basic employment rights as equivalent permanent employees of the client. These are defined[22] as working and employment conditions laid down by legislation, regulations, administrative provisions, collective agreements and/or other

---

19   Employment Rights Act 1996 s43K and Part IVA.
20   [2008] EWCA Civ 430. The case reached the Court of Appeal on other grounds.
21   The legal basis for the draft Directive is article 137(2) of the EC Treaty, which refers to the improvement of 'working conditions'.
22   Article 3.

binding general provisions in force in the user undertaking relating to: (a) the duration of working time, overtime, breaks, rest periods, nightwork, holidays and public holidays; (b) pay. These rights do not cover occupational benefits such as pension. The UK's Social Partners – deemed to be the CBI and the TUC – have agreed that agency workers will be given these rights after 12 weeks on an assignment. However, the UK will have until 2011 to implement the Directive.

Immigration status

13.16   Advisers may be asked to advise workers who have suffered breaches of their employment rights. As set out above, migrant workers who are here with the relevant permission under immigration law, have access to the full range of statutory and contractual employment rights, which are not based on citizenship or residency but on where the work is done.[23] The position is more complex in respect of work which is unauthorised. Migrants who are subject to immigration controls and who are here or who are working in breach of immigration rules, will have difficulty under the current law in enforcing their employment rights, even fundamental employment rights. It is important therefore to be clear about how the principles operate and the limits of their operation, as well as the exact nature of any breach of the immigration rules.

Unauthorised work

13.17   Work may be unauthorised in a variety of ways, as the following cases show: (a) someone who was granted limited leave to enter or to remain in the UK but who remained after their leave had expired, and who did not have a pending application for leave to be extended; (b) someone with a limited entitlement to work a certain numbers of hours per week who worked longer hours; (c) an asylum seeker working without permission; (d) someone who had entered clandestinely; (e) someone who was working in breach of the work permitted under their work permit.

13.18   Some of these problems are remediable and an adviser should therefore consider whether it is possible to regularise the client's

---

23 The work, however, must have a requisite link with the UK.

work or stay at least prospectively. Regularisation of stay is dealt with in part (for trafficked workers) in chapter 11. This chapter deals with regularisation of work.

Migrant workers who are entitled to be here: Countries whose citizens have the right to be and to work in the UK

13.19   Workers from the European Economic Area (EEA) are entitled to move freely within the EEA. In the case of the following countries, that also means the right to work: Austria, Belgium, Cyprus, Denmark, Finland, France, Germany, Greece, Iceland, Republic of Ireland, Italy, Liechtenstein, Luxembourg, Malta, the Netherlands, Norway, Spain and Sweden. By virtue of a separate treaty, Switzerland has full EEA rights. However, workers from some EEA countries have to register under the Workers Registration Scheme before they can work. These are workers from the following countries: Czech Republic, Estonia, Hungary, Lithuania, Poland, Slovakia, and Slovenia. Workers from Bulgaria and Romania generally have to meet the same criteria as non EEA nationals in order to take up work in the UK. However, they are able to set up a business and take self-employed work. All other non-citizen or non-resident workers need some form of permission to work in the UK.

Unauthorised working and the doctrine of illegality

13.20   Fundamental employment rights are not subject to a citizenship test and are not limited according to the immigration status of the claimant. The employment tribunal has territorial jurisdiction in cases where the employee's place of work is or would have been in the UK: *Lawson v SERCO*.[24] This is a statutory jurisdiction which has a protective intention. An even broader test applies to contract or tort claims in the ordinary courts. This is consistent with the approach under the Human Rights Act 1998 where claimants can make a claim regardless of their immigration status.

13.21   However, where work in the jurisdiction is unauthorised, immigration or other irregularities are raised by defendants to attempt to defeat a claim. This is despite the fact that upholding

24 [2006] IRLR HL.

employment rights and enforcing immigration law are separate.[25] The doctrine is often wrongly applied too widely. Advisers should be aware of its exact parameters. The doctrine expresses the public policy principle that a claimant ought not to benefit from their own unlawful conduct. Thus, for example, a contract which is unlawful, will not be enforced by the courts. The doctrine derives from the principle 'ex turpi causa non oritur actio'. According to *Winfield & Jolowicz,* 15th edn, p866, its true application is in contract alone. However, the courts have held that it does also apply in tort but that the exact scope of the doctrine varies according to whether the claim is a tortious claim or a contractual one. Unfair dismissal claims have been held to fall within the latter, since it is said such claims depend upon the existence of a contract of employment. The courts have not recognised or dealt with the category of statutory, non-derogable rights. There is a strong argument that a claim for breach of a statutory right does not involve relying on contractual rights. There is old authority against this: *Tomlinson v Dick Evans 'U' Drive Ltd*:[26] 'Unless he was a party to a contract of employment, the statute cannot and does not give him a right not to be unfairly dismissed, or to the right to receive a redundancy payment.'

13.22   Of course, where the worker has been trafficked and has the benefit of a residence permit, past illegality is unlikely to prevent a claim or create a list of deportation. The issue, however, has serious practical consequences for migrant workers who may have been exploited but not trafficked. Many are uncertain of their exact

---

25 A similar judicial debate is taking place in other jurisdictions. In *Hoffman Plastic Compounds Inc v National Labour Relations Board,* 535 US (2002) the US Supreme Court (with four dissents) quashed an award of backpay to Jose Castro, an unauthorised migrant worker who, with three others, had been sacked for trying to organise a union. It only emerged at the hearing before the NRLB that Mr Castro was not unauthorised to work. The Supreme Court referred to the policy of the relevant US legislation which, like the 2006 Act, required employment verification systems. The dissenting Opinion pointed out that denial of back pay for a 'gross violation of labor law' lowers the cost to the employer of an initial labour law violation (provided, of course, that the only victims are illegal aliens). The majority decision – with its effect that pay for work done cannot be claimed – has been criticised and distinguished on its facts. In *Rivera at al v NIBCO et al* 364 F.3d 1005, the US Court of Appeals for the Ninth Circuit upheld a ruling that in a Title VII (Equality) claim brought by 23 Latina and Southeast Asian women plaintiffs should not be required through the discovery process to give information at the liability stage about their immigration status. The court referred to the importance of enforcement of equality law through claims by individuals.

26 [1978] ICR 639 at 643A.

immigration status and fearful of the consequences of bringing their status to the attention of a court. It is not for the adviser to second-guess their decision on whether to bring a claim which risks doing this. This severely restricts the scope for claiming even basic employment rights such as unpaid wages, where issues of non payment of NI or tax arise or, even more importantly, questions of whether the employee was entitled to work in the UK.

13.23   In a 2005 paper to the TUC Legal Officers Group[27], the Law Commission appeared to acknowledge that employment contracts are significantly different to other contracts, since they are a gateway to non-derogable, statutory rights such as those under the National Minimum Wage Act 1998. The Law Commission asked whether or not in such cases, discretion on enforceability should be governed by statutory factors. However, the Law Commission's most recent consultation on illegality[28] does not suggest employment contracts are different and appears to favour criteria to be set out in case law. A more positive development has occurred in the European Parliament. The proposed directive providing for minimum standards on sanctions against employers of illegally staying third-country nationals[29] provides, in article 7, for backpayment of wages of at least the level of the minimum wage by the employer to unauthorised workers. Subject, therefore, to the prospect of change of the law, the following deals with how to address the question of illegality if it arises.

Claims in contract

13.24   Where the contract was illegal at the outset (for example, where the contract is to perform an illegal act or where the contract is prohibited by statute), the contract as a whole is unenforceable. Where the illegality arose during the performance of an otherwise lawful contract, this may not necessarily render the whole contract unenforceable: *Coral Leisure Group Ltd v Barnett*.[30] The EAT asked

---

27   See http://www.lawcom.gov.uk/docs/Illegal_transactions_pdf3.pdf.

28   See http://www.lawcom.gov.uk/docs/cp189.pdf.

29   COM(2007) 0249- C6-0143/2007- 2007/0094(COD). See http:///www.europarl.europa.eu/sides.

30   [1981] ICR 503. In that case, the employee alleged that during his employment, though not at the start of it, he had been asked to supply prostitutes to punters at casinos.

itself at 508B: 'can it really be that an employee who in the course of carrying out his duties knowingly breaks the law in one respect, is thereby automatically debarred forever from enforcing the rest of his contract of employment or of complaining of unfair dismissal?'. The courts may sever any illegality and allow enforcement of other rights. In *Blue Chip Trading Ltd v Helbawi*,[31] a student had permission to work part-time in term time and full-time during the vacation but not to pursue a career through a permanent full-time post. He brought and won a minimum wage claim. On appeal, Elias P held that while it was not possible to balance different policy objectives, it was possible to sever the lawful elements of the contract from the unlawful elements, since it was impossible 'sensibly to describe a potentially open ended employment contract as an entire and indivisible contract',[32] and thus the claimant could seek recovery of the minimum wage for the hours which he was not in breach of his limited permission to work. The same principle would apply in respect of periods when the worker was not authorised. This is a decision which, though limited in application, will be helpful in similar cases.

13.25   In assessing illegality in performance, in cases where the contract of employment is neither entered into for an illegal purpose nor prohibited by statute, the illegal performance of the contract will not render the contract unenforceable unless the employee knew of the facts which made the performance illegal and actively participated in the illegal performance: *Hall v Woolston Leisure Ltd* (CA).[33] To be unenforceable in contract, there must be a positive misrepresentation to the Inland Revenue (or other state agency) by the employee (not just the employer). Erroneous categorisation unaccompanied by false representations of fact is not enough. Misrepresentation by one or both parties as to the facts should be distinguished from an erroneous categorisation. There is no reason in public policy why the latter should render the employment contract unlawfully performed and therefore unenforceable. It is not sufficient to show that the employer's obligations were not complied with, and that the employee knew of the facts which lead to this. There must in addition be some misrepresentation to the relevant state agency if the contract is to be tainted by illegality of performance: *Enfield*

31 UKEAT/0397/08/LA.
32 At para 6.
33 [2001] ICR 99 at 110 F–H.

Technical Services Limited v Payne; BF Components Limited v Grace,[34] disapproving *Daymond v Enterprise South Devon.*[35]

13.26   The court in *Hall* also clarified the test under contract: p110 and held that the ET and EAT had erred in concluding that Mrs Hall would not have been able to enforce contractual aspect of her claim since, the contract not being illegal at its outset, knowledge and participation in the illegality would have to have been shown: per Mance LJ at 80, p123B–D. Knowledge alone does not suffice. In Mrs Hall's case, per Mance LJ, 'passive receipt of pay slips' would not have been sufficient. Mance LJ also doubted whether, had Mrs Hall been employed at the end of the tax year when a duty to file a tax return in respect of untaxed income, that would have affected her position. He observed: 'I say only that I should require persuasion that non-compliance with a duty under the taxes legislation to make her own tax return then should be viewed as impliedly prohibiting or affecting the enforceability of her contract of employment.'[36]

Claims in tort

13.27   The courts have held that a different test applies to tortious claims, which is: does the claim arise out of or is it so closely connected and inextricably bound up or linked with the illegal conduct of the claimant such that the tribunal should not permit the claimant to recover compensation, thus appearing to condone his or her conduct? Secondly, is there active participation by the employee in the illegal performance? While on their facts, the cases have tended to involve issues relating to the non-payment of tax or NI, the principles apply to questions of the right to work under the immigration rules. The courts have held that the tortious test applies to discrimination claims. It will also apply to personal injury claims.

13.28   In *Leighton v Michael*,[37] Miss Leighton, who worked in a fish and chip shop, did not have tax or NI deducted from her earnings. When she raised this with her employer, she was told that if she did not like it, she could leave. The Employment Appeal Tribunal (EAT) held (by a majority) that a claim of sex discrimination did not involve enforcing, relying upon or founding a claim on the contract of

34   [2008] EWCA Civ 393.

35   UKEAT/0005/07.

36   At p124 E–G.

37   [1995] ICR 1091.

employment with the effect that claims under the Sex Discrimination Act 1975 (but not of unfair dismissal) could be brought by Miss Leighton. The minority member held that it was not reasonable to expect Miss Leighton to have ceased her employment and that she should be able to bring her claim in any event. The decision in *Leighton* was criticised by another division of the EAT in *Johal v Adams*.[38] The EAT, with some force, criticised as illogical the distinction made between unfair dismissal and sex discrimination. However, *Leighton v Michael* was considered and approved in *Hall v Woolston Hall Leisure Ltd*.[39] Mrs Hall brought a claim of sex discrimination on grounds of pregnancy. The tribunal upheld her claim, holding that they had jurisdiction to do so under the principle in *Leighton* and awarded injury to feelings but declined to make an award for loss of earnings. Mrs Hall worked as a chef and on promotion received £250 in cash from her employer. Her pay slips, however, showed £250 as the gross pay, with a net sum of £186.65. Mrs Hall queried this with her employer who told her that 'that was how he did business'. The Court of Appeal held (at 20) that the Equal Treatment Directive 76/207 and in particular article 6, required the UK to give real and judicial protection to victims of sex discrimination at work and to provide a sanction with a real deterrent effect on the employer. Since the Directive itself did not provide for derogation, none could be made in national law. Turning to the common law, they addressed criticisms of *Leighton* that there was no sensible distinction to be made between claims for unfair dismissal and redundancy and claims for discrimination, since both were statutory claims dependent upon establishing an employment relationship. The Court of Appeal held that such a distinction could rightly be made. A claim of discrimination fell to be decided under tortious, not contractual, principles. Thus, the causal test applied, ie is the claimant's claim so closely connected or inextricably bound up with his own criminal or illegal conduct that the court could not permit him to recover without appearing to condone his conduct. They pointed out that some heads of damage might be recoverable while others might not be, ie that a claimant might be barred on grounds of illegality from pursuing a particular head of relief, rather than the whole of his or her claim.

13.29   Thus, the question of illegality will often depend upon a close reading of the facts and the particular characteristics of the worker

---

38 11 January 1996, unreported.
39 [2001] ICR 99.

in question and any finding on whether the worker was aware that it was not lawful for them to work.[40] The *Vakante* case[41] concerned a claim for race discrimination made by a Croatian who was seeking asylum. He did not seek Home Office permission to work pending determination of his asylum claim and so was not entitled to work and indeed committed a criminal offence under s24 of the Immigration Act 1971 when he did, since it was a condition of his leave that he did not work. On application for employment, he stated he did not need a work permit and the school did not check his work permit status. In July 2000, he was dismissed from the school where he had been working. On 18 June 2001 he received exceptional leave to remain and from that date was entitled to work. The ET held they had jurisdiction to hear the claim of race discrimination. The EAT drew a distinction between claims under the contract (including unfair dismissal) and claims in tort (including for personal injury and for discrimination). The EAT remitted the case to the tribunal for further consideration as to whether Mr Vakante was barred from bringing the claim. The Tribunal held that he was. A further appeal based upon Race Directive 2000/43 failed on the basis it was not in force at the relevant time.[42] Therefore, the Directive argument has not been ruled upon.

13.30   The subjective nature of the test to establish the knowledge and participation in any unlawfulness is illustrated by *Mrs Laong Wheeler v Quality Deep Limited t/a Thai Royale Restaurant*[43] Mrs Wheeler, was, in the words of the Court of Appeal, ' a foreign national working in this country in that [Thai] language with limited knowledge of the English language and of the tax and national insurance provisions of this country'. She brought a claim for unfair dismissal and failure to provide pay slips, contrary to s8 of the Employment Rights Act 1996. She had been employed as a cook at a Thai restaurant for four years. She alleged that her take home pay was £220 per week plus £40 per week benefits. The employer contended it was just over £155. During her employment, Mrs Wheeler was only given two payslips, neither of which recorded deductions for tax or NI, though they did have a tax reference and an NI Code. They showed a figure less than the sum she was in fact paid. The Court of Appeal overturned a finding

40   *Still v Minister of National Revenue* [1998] 1 FC 549 (Canada).
41   *The Governing Body of Addey and Stanhope School v V* [2003] ICR 290 and (n2) [2005] ICR 231.
42   *Vakante* [2004] EWCA Civ 1065. 2000/78 would also be relevant.
43   [2004] EWCA Civ 1085.

by the employment tribunal that Mrs Wheeler (and her English husband) had acquiesced in fraud on the Revenue, referring to her personal lack of knowledge of English language and tax system and to her continued requests for pay slips. In light of this case, there remains scope to minimise the impact of the illegality doctrine on the facts of a case, where any illegality has not been acquiesced in. Arguments based upon the right of access to the court under article 6[44] have been raised but have not to date succeeded.

Immigration, Asylum and Nationality Act 2006

13.31   For those workers whose employment commenced on or after 29 February 2008, the Immigration, Asylum and Nationality Act 2006 applies. This Act places a requirement on employers to carry out immigration checks to avoid the risk of having a civil or criminal penalty imposed upon them. The relevant provisions in the 2006 Act replaced ss8 and 8A of the little used[45] Asylum and Immigration Act 1996. The 2006 Act does not apply to employment which commenced before 29 February 2008, including employment which continued on or after that date: Immigration, Asylum and Nationality Act 2006 (Commencement of and Transitional and Saving Provisions) Order 2008,[46] article 5(1) and (2). In respect of that employment, the 1996 Act applies and the 2006 Act is of no effect: Article 5(2). The 2006 Act sets up a scheme of both civil penalties and criminal penalties.[47] The 2006 Act deals with unauthorised working entirely from the perspective of the employer. The employee is not a player in the legislative scheme, other than to provide documents proving entitlement to work.[48] However, it is important to be aware of the legislative scheme to challenge any related actions of the employer if unjustified.

13.32   Section 15 of the 2006 Act provides for a strict liability defence where a person employs an adult subject to immigration control if:

---

44 Setenios and in *Hall No* 27.
45 Between 1998 (the 1996 Act came into force on 27 January 1997) and October 2006, there were 65 prosecutions and only 24 convictions. The maximum penalty on conviction was a £5,000 fine.
46 SI 2008/310.
47 Sections 15–26.
48 The Home Office provides an employee checking service so the check can be done directly.

(a) the person has not been granted leave to enter or remain in the UK; or

(b) the person's leave to enter or remain in the UK:

    (i)   is invalid;

    (ii) has ceased to have effect (whether by reason of curtailment, revocation, cancellation, passage of time or otherwise); or

    (iii) is subject to a condition preventing him from accepting the employment.

Where contravention of the section occurs (after inspection visits by immigration), the employer is served with a penalty notice. The penalty notice must state why the employer is liable, the penalty amount[49] and the date by which the penalty must be paid.[50] The penalty notice may be challenged either by way of objection to the secretary of state[51] or appeal to a county court (or in Scotland, sheriff).[52] The grounds on which either challenge may be brought are the same, namely that there is no liability (because the worker is entitled or has permission to work in the UK), that (even if the worker was in breach of immigration law) the employer has an excuse under s15(3) from paying the penalty because he complied with any prescribed requirements, or that the amount of the penalty is too high. The employer has the burden of proof. On objection, the penalty may be increased by the secretary of state. The appeal may be brought within 28 days of the date of penalty or the decision after objection, but there is no requirement to object first.[53]

13.33   The penalty notice may not be challenged by an employer who knew of the breach of immigration law at any time during the period of employment.[54] In addition, an employer who knows that the employee is an adult subject to immigration control who does not have the relevant leave to remain or enter, whose leave to enter or remain is invalid or has expired, or who is subject to a condition preventing him from accepting the employment, may also

---

49 Maximum penalty for illegal employment of a person who is subject to immigration control: £10,000: Immigration (Employment of Adults Subject to Immigration Control) (Maximum Penalty) Order SI 2008/132.

50 Section 15(6). The section also requires the notice to explain procedures for objection and for enforcement.

51 Section 16.

52 Section 17.

53 Section 17(5).

54 Section 15(4).

be charged and convicted of the criminal offence under s21. Knowledge is treated as established within a body if a person who has responsibility for an aspect of the employment knows the fact and if an officer of a body (or the partner of a firm) is shown to have consented or connived at an offence, the officer[55] (or partner) is personally liable.[56] The criminal offence is punishable by up to 12 months' imprisonment.

13.34   Section 15(3) refers to prescribed requirements which are the basis for the statutory excuse. These requirements are prescribed in the Immigration (Restrictions on Employment) Order.[57] The order provides that an excuse is established where an employee provides a document which is set out in either List A or B appended to the order and if the employer takes specified steps to verify the authenticity of the documents. In the case of List A documents (broadly evidencing a right to work in the UK by virtue of being a UK, EEA or equivalent citizen or resident) this check need only be made prior to commencement of employment. In the case of List B documents (which broadly evidence a time-limited right to work), the documents must be produced and checked every 12 months in order to found a statutory excuse. The required steps are fully set out in the order and include: (a) checks on validity; (b) copy or copies retained; (c) checking of photograph if document contains one; (d) checking of date of birth as likely; (e) rightful ownership. The full List A and List B are appended in a schedule of the order, set out in the table below.

Immigration (Restrictions on Employment) Order

Articles 3 and 4

SCHEDULE

LIST A

1.   A passport showing that the holder, or a person named in the passport as the child of the holder, is a British citizen or a citizen of the United Kingdom and Colonies having the right of abode in the United Kingdom.

---

55 A director, manager or secretary, a person purporting to act as a director, manager or secretary or if the affairs of the body are managed by its members, a member.

56 Section 22.

57 SI 2007/3290.

2. A passport or national identity card showing that the holder, or a person named in the passport as the child of the holder, is a national of the European Economic Area or Switzerland.

3. A residence permit, registration certificate or document certifying or indicating permanent residence issued by the Home Office or the Border and Immigration Agency to a national of a European Economic Area country or Switzerland.

4. A permanent residence card issued by the Home Office or the Border and Immigration Agency to the family member of a national of a European Economic Area country or Switzerland.

5. A Biometric Immigration Document issued by the Border and Immigration Agency to the holder which indicates that the person named in it is allowed to stay indefinitely in the United Kingdom, or has no time limit on their stay in the United Kingdom.

6. A passport or other travel document endorsed to show that the holder is exempt from immigration control, is allowed to stay indefinitely in the United Kingdom, has the right of abode in the United Kingdom, or has no time limit on their stay in the United Kingdom.

7. An Immigration Status Document issued by the Home Office or the Border and Immigration Agency to the holder with an endorsement indicating that the person named in it is allowed to stay indefinitely in the United Kingdom or has no time limit on their stay in the United Kingdom, when produced in combination with an official document giving the person's permanent National Insurance Number and their name issued by a Government agency or a previous employer.

8. A full birth certificate issued in the United Kingdom which includes the name(s) of at least one of the holder's parents, when produced in combination with an official document giving the person's permanent National Insurance Number and their name issued by a Government agency or a previous employer.

9. A full adoption certificate issued in the United Kingdom which includes the name(s) of at least one of the holder's adoptive parents when produced in combination with an official document giving the person's permanent National Insurance Number and their name issued by a Government agency or a previous employer.

10. A birth certificate issued in the Channel Islands, the Isle of Man or Ireland, when produced in combination with an official document giving the person's permanent National Insurance Number and their name issued by a Government agency or a previous employer.

11. An adoption certificate issued in the Channel Islands, the Isle of Man or Ireland, when produced in combination with an official document giving the person's permanent National Insurance Number and their name issued by a Government agency or a previous employer.

12. A certificate of registration or naturalisation as a British citizen, when produced in combination with an official document giving the person's permanent National Insurance Number and their name issued by a Government agency or a previous employer.

13. A letter issued by the Home Office or the Border and Immigration Agency to the holder which indicates that the person named in it is allowed to stay indefinitely in the United Kingdom when produced in combination with an official document giving the person's permanent National Insurance Number and their name issued by a Government agency or a previous employer.

LIST B

1. A passport or travel document endorsed to show that the holder is allowed to stay in the United Kingdom and is allowed to do the type of work in question, provided that it does not require the issue of a work permit.

2. A Biometric Immigration Document issued by the Border and Immigration Agency to the holder which indicates that the person named in it can stay in the United Kingdom and is allowed to do the work in question.

3. A work permit or other approval to take employment issued by the Home Office or the Border and Immigration Agency when produced in combination with either a passport or another travel document endorsed to show the holder is allowed to stay in the United Kingdom and is allowed to do the work in question, or a letter issued by the Home Office or the Border and Immigration Agency to the holder or the employer or prospective employer confirming the same.

4. A certificate of application issued by the Home Office or the Border and Immigration Agency to or for a family member of a national of a European Economic Area country or Switzerland stating that the holder is permitted to take employment which is less than 6 months old when produced in combination with evidence of verification by the Border and Immigration Agency Employer Checking Service.

5. A residence card or document issued by the Home Office or the Border and Immigration Agency to a family member of a national of a European Economic Area country or Switzerland.

6. An Application Registration Card issued by the Home Office or the Border and Immigration Agency stating that the holder is permitted to take employment, when produced in combination with evidence of verification by the Border and Immigration Agency Employer Checking Service.

7. An Immigration Status Document issued by the Home Office or the Border and Immigration Agency to the holder with an endorsement indicating that the person named in it can stay in the United Kingdom, and is allowed to do the type of work in question, when produced in combination with an official document giving the person's permanent National Insurance Number and their name issued by a Government agency or a previous employer.

8. A letter issued by the Home Office or the Border and Immigration Agency to the holder or the employer or prospective employer, which indicates that the person named in it can stay in the United Kingdom and is allowed to do the work in question when produced in combination with an official document giving the person's permanent National Insurance Number and their name issued by a Government agency or a previous employer.

13.35   A dismissal by an employer as a result of a genuine, but mistaken, belief that the employee was not entitled to work in the UK would not entitle the employer to dismiss on grounds under s98(2)(d) of the Employment Rights Act 1996 (contravention of a duty or restriction imposed by or under an enactment): *Klusova v London Borough of Hounslow.*[58] A genuine but mistaken belief might,

---

58 [2007] EWCA Civ 1127.

however, be some other substantial reason within s98(1)(b). An unfair dismissal may be established where there is procedural unfairness or where dismissal has occurred in respect of a failure which could have been put right: *Kelly v University of Southampton*.[59]

Preventive action in sending states

13.36 In many cases, the deception of migrant workers begins in the sending state by promises which are not honoured. Preventive action can include action to regulate recruiters and agents in the sending state. This may include bilateral trade union agreements. The same Migration for Employment Convention (Revised) 1949 Convention No 97 assists on the issue of fraud and deception. The convention requires that where the State parties have a system of supervision or regulation, that they agree to require a document (a) to be delivered before departure or on arrival; (b) indicating conditions of work and pay; (c) general information on conditions in the destination state. Where the document is provided on arrival, it should state occupational category and conditions, in particular the minimum wage which will be paid.

59 [2008] ICR 357.

Eliminating the profit

Key points

- Upon criminal conviction of a trafficker in human beings, confiscation may be ordered of the proceeds of the crime. The human trafficking offences under the Sexual Offences Act 2003 and the Asylum and Immigration (Treatment of Claimants, etc) Act 2004 and offences under s12 of the Gangmasters (Licensing) Act 2004 are lifestyle offences. Conviction of a lifestyle offence gives rise to assumptions, extending back over a period of six years, that property acquired during that period was acquired as a result of general criminal conduct.

- If victims are seeking compensation from the trafficker rather than the state, victims' advisers and prosecutors need to give careful thought to the potential impact of any confiscation order on available assets.

- Upon conviction of a trafficker, forfeiture may be ordered of certain vehicles associated with the offence.

- Cash may also be seized and forfeited on application to a magistrates' court if the cash is recoverable property or is intended to be used in unlawful conduct. This may take the form of criminal or civil proceedings.

- Regardless of whether criminal proceedings have been brought, proceeds of crime may be recovered by the enforcement authority through civil recovery orders. This may occur where proceedings have failed or where they are delayed.

- The HMRC Criminal Taxes Unit has an important function in reducing or eliminating traffickers' profits.

Generally

14.1   Human trafficking is a commercial activity, the global annual profits of which are USD $31.7 million.[1] Effective disruption and elimination of the trade depends upon detection and elimination of the profits through assets recovery and confiscation. Despite this, and despite extensive powers to seize, forfeit, investigate and confiscate, the power to recover assets continues to be under-used.[2] The UK 2008

---

1   Patrick Belser, *Forced labour and human trafficking: estimating the profits*, working paper, Geneva, International Labour Office, 2005, p17.

2   Despite focus on this issue through a Government Asset Recovery Strategy as a result of which the 2002 Act was enacted: *Recovering the proceeds of crime* Performance and Innovation Unit, June 2000, CABI J00-5816/0006/D40.

Action Plan sets a target of £540,000 annually for what is described as 'cash seizures from trafficking criminals'. Actual figures have not been released.

14.2   Wide powers exist for asset recovery through forfeiture and confiscation upon conviction in a criminal court. Criminal offences of trafficking are deemed lifestyle offences in respect of which a series of assumptions may be made to facilitate confiscation. In addition, assets may be pursued through civil recovery orders or through use of taxation enforcement. The leading Acts are the Proceeds of Crime Act 2002 (POCA), the Serious Organised Crime and Police Act 2005 (SOCPA) and the Serious Crimes Act 2007. A number of different agencies have the standing to use asset recovery powers. In addition to the police, HMRC and the Serious Organised Crime Agency (SOCA) have a law enforcement function.

14.3   In theory, asset recovery by the state (which goes into the Consolidated Fund[3]) and compensation of victims are separate issues. However, asset recovery may have a direct or indirect bearing on victims' ability to recover compensation for loss and damage to them. This will depend upon whether the victims intend to seek compensation from the trafficker or the state, and if the former, on the extent of any assets.

Upon conviction of a criminal offence

14.4   The two main types of orders are confiscation and forfeiture.

Confiscation orders

14.5   A confiscation order[4] is an order made against the convicted person, ordering him or her to pay the amount of his or her benefit from crime. An order for confiscation follows a calculation of the value of proceeds from crime. Unlike a forfeiture order, a confiscation order is not directed towards a particular asset but against the person. Where a criminal has benefited financially from crime but no longer possesses the specific fruits of his crime, the person will be deprived of assets of equiva-lent value, if he or she has them. The object is to deprive the person, directly or indirectly, of what he or

3   Section 300.
4   Governed by Part 2 of POCA which merged the previous schemes under the Drug Trafficking Act 1994 for drug offences and under the Criminal Justice Act 1998 as amended by the Proceeds of Crime Act 1995 for other offences.

she has gained: *R v May*.[5] An order is made against the criminal for the amount identified as recoverable. It can only be made after conviction or committal for sentence.[6] Separate provision is made for confiscation in Scotland: (Part 3) ss92–155 and in Northern Ireland: (Part 4) ss156–239. An enquiry into whether a confiscation order must be held if the prosecution applies for one and may be held by the court of its own motion. The prosecution has a right of appeal against the decision.

14.6   The court must first decide whether the convicted person has a criminal lifestyle.[7] A conclusion of a criminal offence follows automatically[8] from a conviction for a lifestyle offence in Schedule 2. Schedule 2 to the Proceeds of Crime Act 2002 includes the following as lifestyle offences:

(1) the offences of trafficking for sexual exploitation contrary to ss57–59 of the Sexual Offences Act 2003;[9]
(2) the offences of trafficking for exploitation contrary to s4 of the Treatment of Claimants Act 2004;[10]
(3) offences under s12 of the Gangmasters (Licensing) Act 2004;[11]

and offences of attempting, conspiring or inciting the commission of any offence specified in the Schedule, or of aiding, abetting, counselling or procuring the commission of such an offence. Human trafficking is also a 'serious offence' within the meaning of the Serious Crime Act 2007.[12]

14.7   If the convicted person has a criminal lifestyle, the court must determine their benefit from their general criminal conduct.[13]

---

5 [2008] UKHL 28; [2008] 1 AC 1028.
6 Section 6, 2002 Act. Unless and until an order is made under s97 of the SOCPA 2005, magistrates' courts do not have the power to make confiscation orders.
7 Proceeds of Crime Act 2002, s75.
8 If the offence is not in Schedule 2, it is necessary to prove a course of conduct or an offence committed over at least six months unless benefit obtained is less than £5,000. Full details are set out in s75.
9 See further chapter 5.
10 See further chapter 6.
11 See further chapter 12.
12 Para 2 of Part 1 of Schedule 1 to the 2007 Act defines an offence under ss25, 25A or 25B under the Immigration Act 1971, offences under ss57–59 of the Sexual Offences Act 2003 and offences under s4 of the Asylum and Immigration (Treatment of Claimants, etc) Act 2004 as serious offences in England and Wales. Inchoate offences related to people trafficking are also serious offences, by virtue of para 14, Part 1, Schedule 1. The same applies to Northern Ireland by virtue of paras 18 and 30.
13 Section 6(4)(b).

General criminal conduct is all of the convicted person's conduct, regardless of when it occurred[14] or where it occurred, since it applies to conduct which constitutes an offence in England and Wales or which would constitute an offence if it occurred in England and Wales.[15] The High Court or Crown Court may order the defendant to provide information for the purposes of any question relevant to the determination of a confiscation hearing in the Crown Court following conviction: *Re O;*[16] *Re T.*[17] Where the defendant has been convicted of a lifestyle offence, the burden of proof shifts significantly as regards to the determination of benefit in that, in determining that benefit (the proof of which usually falls on the prosecution[18]), the court must make four assumptions.[19] The assumptions apply to the period beginning with six years before the date when proceedings for the lifestyle offence were started and to property wherever held.[20] They are that:

(i)   any property transferred to the convicted person during that period and at any date after conviction was obtained as a result of criminal conduct;[21] and

(ii)   at the earliest time they appear to have held it;[22]

(iii) any expenditure incurred during that period was incurred was met from property obtained as a result of their general criminal conduct;[23] and that

(iv) for the purpose of valuing any property obtained, they obtained it free of any other interests in it.[24]

An assumption will be disregarded if shown to be incorrect or if there would be a serious risk of injustice (eg inconsistency or miscalculation) in the making of the assumption.[25]

---

14   Section 76(2).

15   Section 76(1).

16   [1991] 2 QB 520.

17   [1996] 96 CrAppR 194.

18   Section 6(7).

19   Section 96.

20   For example, money transferred to Romania: *R v Craciun* [2007] EWCA Crim 727.

21   POCA s10(2).

22   POCA s10(3).

23   POCA s10(4).

24   POCA s10(5).

25   Section 96(6). *R v Jones* [2006] EWCA Crim 2061; [2007] 1 WLR 7. POCA s10(6). The serious injustice relates to the making of the assumption, not to its consequences: *R v Dore* [1997] 2 Cr App R (S) 152.

14.8   The last stage is identification of the recoverable sum. The recoverable amount is the same as the amount of a defendant's benefit,[26] unless the defendant proves[27] that the available amount is less than the benefit. Evidence of actual profit is also relevant. If a convicted person receives, but then passes on, some of the benefit, he or she is nonetheless liable for the whole amount. Provided a convicted person has joint control of property, the person is deemed to have 'obtained' any such property jointly held. The rationale of the confiscation regime is that the defendant is deprived of what he or she has gained or its equivalent. The defendant cannot, and should not, be deprived of what he or she has never obtained or its equivalent, because that would be a fine: *R v May* at 8. An order cannot be made for more than the convicted person's net worth.[28]

14.9   Having made the confiscation order, the court should impose a sentence of imprisonment in case of default. Bands of default sentence terms are set.[29] Once the sentence in default has been served, the convicted will continue to owe the amount due under the confiscation order, including interest.

Relationship with compensation of victims

14.10   Advocates for victims will be concerned to ensure that there are sufficient funds to satisfy any order for compensation made against the defendant.[30] The policy of the legislation is to preserve the victims right to compensation from the assets. Put otherwise, the clear intention of parliament is that the victim's claim should come before the state's.[31] In the absence of a risk to the victim's interests, however, for example where they have already been paid or where there are sufficient assets, there is no restriction on making orders both to confiscate and to compensate.[32] The most satisfactory way of

---

26   POCA s7(1).

27   POCA s7(2).

28   POCA s9.

29   See *R v Szraber* [199] 15 Cr App R (S) 821 for placing within a bind. Six months for between £5,000–10,000; 12 months for between £10,000–£20,000; 18 months for between £20,000–£50,000; two years for between £50,000–£100,000; three years for between £100,000–£250,000; five years for between £250,000–£1 million; ten years for an amount exceeding £1 million. Time actually served is half the term: Criminal Justice Act 2003, s258(2).

30   See chapter 10.

31   Per Kennedy LJ in *R v Mitchell and Mitchell* [2001] 2 Cr App R (S) 141 at 18.

32   *R v Nield* [2007] EWCA Crim 993.

proceeding will depend upon whether compensation is being sought through the making of a compensation order within the criminal proceedings or through the civil courts. Where the Crown Court makes a compensation order under s130 of the Powers of the Criminal Courts (Sentencing) Act 2000 as well as a confiscation order against the same person in the same proceedings, and the court believes there will be insufficient funds to satisfy orders, the court must earmark the amount identified as the shortfall in funds to be paid out as compensation out of the confiscation order: POCA, s13(5)–(6). The advantage to the victim is that this ensures enforcement under the confiscation provisions of sums due to victims.[33] The court may make the order before sentencing or may, on application by either party or of its own motion, postpone the order for up to two years from conviction or three months from disposal of any appeal, unless there are exceptional circumstances.[34] The amount ordered must be paid immediately and on application, up to 12 months later: POCA s11(1).

14.11   The position is less straightforward where the victim has brought or intends to bring civil proceedings against the convicted person in respect of the relevant conduct. If the court believes that any victim of the criminal conduct has at any time started or intends to start proceedings against the defendant in respect of loss, injury or damage sustained in connection with the conduct, it has a discretion not to make a confiscation order: POCA s6(6). The court must hold the relevant belief and has no jurisdiction to adjourn confiscation proceedings generally to protect victims' interests.[35] As with the power under s13, the purpose of the provision is to preserve the victim's right to compensation out of assets.[36] Since this provision merely allows the defendant to escape the immediate consequences of a confiscation order without any guarantee of compensation for the victim, victims would be well advised to seek a compensation order, and thus benefit from the earmarking under the confiscation order,[37] until any judgment in civil proceedings has been given.

---

33 This will be even more the case where a receiver has been appointed or a restraint order is in place: POCA ss48, 50 and 67.

34 Section 14(1)–(6).

35 *R v Hockey* [2007] EWCA Crim 1577.

36 See, under earlier legislation, *Borders (UK) Limited and ors v Commissioner of Police for the Metropolis and another* [2005] EWCA Civ 197.

37 See per Kennedy LJ in *R v Mitchell and Mitchell* [2001] 2 Cr App R (S) 141.

Forfeiture orders

14.12   An order for forfeiture involves identifying and forfeiting property which represents the proceeds of, or is in some other way connected with, the crime. It is not a means of stripping traffickers of their profits, but requires the identification of something tangible that can fairly be said to relate to the offence.[38] The order has the effect of transferring property rights to the state. Statutory provision is made for forfeiture powers in s60A–C[39] of the 2003 Act and in 5(4)–(5) of the 2004 Act. Sections 60A–60C of the 2003 Act applies to offences under s57–59. Section 5(4) of the 2004 Act applies to powers of forfeiture in s25C and 25D of the Immigration Act 1971 to the offence in s4 of the 2004 Act.

14.13   The powers are virtually identical in regards to forfeiture of land vehicles.[40] The court may order forfeiture of a vehicle used or intended to be used in connection with an offence where at the time of commission of the offence, the convicted person was driving it or owned[41] it (including possession under a hire-purchase agreement) or where the convicted person was a director, secretary or manager of a company which owned or possessed the vehicle under a hire-purchase agreement. The provisions do not authorise forfeiture where the offence was not committed by a director, secretary or manager of the company but where senior personnel (including a director, secretary or manager) knew of the trafficking. This is an unfortunate lacuna which misses an opportunity to encourage companies to ensure that their transportation is not used for the purposes of trafficking. The provisions differ slightly in regards to forfeiture of a ship or aircraft used or intended to be used in connection with the offence. In both cases, the court may order forfeiture where the convicted person owned, or was a director, secretary or manager of a company which owned, the ship or aircraft. Where the convicted person (or the company of which they were a director, secretary or manager) possessed the ship or aircraft under

---

38   For the limits of forfeiture, leading to the enactment of confiscation powers, see *Cuthbertson* [1981] AC 470.

39   As inserted by s54 of and Schedule 4 to the Violent Crime Reduction Act 2006, with effect from 12 February 2007.

40   The provisions in the Immigration Act 1971 Act refer to a vehicle. Section 60C(1) refers to a land vehicle, defined as 'any vehicle other than a ship or aircraft'.

41   Including jointly: s60C(2).

a hire-purchase agreement or was its charterer or captain, the court may only order forfeiture if certain additional conditions are satisfied. In the case of an offence under the 2004 Act, the further conditions are that the ship or aircraft carried more than 20 passengers[42] and that the person (or director, etc) who, at the time of the offence, owned the ship or aircraft, knew or ought to have known of the intention to use it in the course of commission of an offence. The provisions also apply up to a maximum size or weight of aircraft or ship.[43] The provisions under the 2003 Act[44] are identical save that there is no requirement for a minimum of 20 passengers. Representations may be made by anyone claiming to have an interest.[45]

14.14   The court also has the power to deprive an offender of property used for the purposes of crime, by virtue of section 143 of the Criminal Court (Sentencing) Act 2000. A court making such an order may order that the property be taken into possession of the Secretary of State for the Home Office (not the police) where the court considers that the offence related to immigration or asylum: Borders Act 2007 s25(1). This may have some applicability in trafficking cases.

14.15   Chapter 3 of the 2002 Act provides for the summary seizure of cash[46] by a customs officer or a constable or immigration officer[47] while lawfully on any premises if they have reasonable grounds for suspecting the existence on the premises of cash which (a) is recoverable property ie property obtained by unlawful conduct or is intended by any person for use in unlawful conduct; and (b) which is not less than a specified minimum amount.[48] Unlawful conduct is conduct within the United Kingdom which is criminal or conduct occurring outside the United Kingdom if criminal under the law of both jurisdictions.[49] Provided the reasonable suspicion is present,

---

42 Section 25C(9)–(11), 1971 Act as amended by s5(5) of the 2004 Act. SI 2004/2999, 2004/494.

43 Less than 500 tons for a ship, maximum weight for an aircraft of 5,700 kilogrammes: s25C(6) and (7).

44 Section 60(c).

45 Sections 60A(8) and 25C(8).

46 This includes cheques, bankers drafts, and bearers bonds and shares.

47 In relation to offences classed as immigration offences, of which s4 of the 2004 Act is one.

48 Currently £1,000.

49 POCA s241(2) .

a customs or police officer may search the suspected person and any articles they have with them and detain them so long as it is necessary to do so. These powers, since they are draconian, may be exercised only with the authorisation of a magistrates' or sheriff court, unless impracticable, in which case they must be authorised by a senior officer of the rank of police inspector or customs or immigration equivalent.[50] The cash seized may be held for 48 hours, extendable in the first instance up to three months by an order made by a magistrates' or a sheriff court, and up to two years from the date of the first order, only if there are reasonable grounds for suspecting that the cash is recoverable property and one of two conditions is satisfied: (i) it is justified pending further enquiries on its derivation; (ii) proceedings against any person for any offence with which the cash is connected have been started and have not been concluded.[51] Forfeiture may also be ordered of cash by a magistrates court or sheriff court if it is satisfied to the civil standard that the cash or part of it (i) is recoverable property; and (ii) is intended by any person for use in unlawful conduct. The application may be made to a magistrates court by the Commissioners of Customs and Excise or by a police constable. Where criminal proceedings have been brought, cash forfeiture proceedings will usually be adjourned until the conclusion of proceedings.

Restraint orders

14.16   A restraint order restrains the defendant from dealing with certain property.[52] It may be applied for before criminal charge. The application is made ex parte to a Crown Court judge. If a restraint order is in force, a constable or a customs officer may seize any realisable property to which it applies to prevent its removal from England and Wales. Restraint orders should be sought where possible since many offenders are willing to serve sentences in default, even where a compensation order is made.

Orders in civil proceedings

14.17   Recovery of the proceeds of crime does not depend upon a criminal conviction.

50   Section 290(2).
51   Section 295.
52   POCA s41.

Civil recovery orders

14.18 Part 5 of POCA introduced a new scheme for civil recovery of the proceeds of the unlawful conduct.[53] Such civil action can be taken by the enforcement authority in each jurisdiction. In England and Wales the enforcement authority is now the Serious Organised Crime Agency (SOCA).[54] There is provision for a victim to seek a declaration in respect of property – that they were deprived of the property and that at that time the property was not subject to civil recovery.[55] This is most common in cases involving theft or fraud. In trafficking cases, civil recovery is usually relevant to the effectiveness of state action rather than direct actions by victims, although it may have some application in cases where payment has been made for transport.

14.19 Civil proceedings may be brought in the Administrative Court (or Court of Session in Scotland) to recover property which is or represents, and is identified through tracing,[56] property obtained through unlawful conduct.[57] Property has a wide definition, but does not include financial advantage. Unlawful conduct is defined as conduct which is unlawful under the criminal law.[58] Civil recovery proceedings may be brought whether or not there has been criminal proceedings or a conviction and where a confiscation order has been quashed on appeal: *Singh v Director of the Assets Recovery Agency.*[59] The commission of a specific criminal offence or offences does not need to be proved in order for a recovery order to be made, but it is necessary to identify the matters which were alleged to constitute the kind of unlawful conduct by which the property which it was sought to recover was obtained. In order to be able to conclude, on a balance of probabilities, that the assets in question must have been acquired with the proceeds of unlawful conduct, it was insufficient simply to establish that the respondent to the application for a recovery order had a lifestyle which was inconsistent with any identified lawful

---

53 Section 240.
54 It may then be transferred: see Practice Direction – Proceeds of Crime. In Scotland, the enforcement authority is the Scottish Ministers, by virtue of s316.
55 Section 281.
56 Section 304.
57 Section 240(1)(b).
58 Section 241(1).
59 [2005] EWCA Civ 580; 1 WLR 3747. However, recovery will not be ordered of property subject to a confiscation order: POCA s308(9).

income: *Director of Assets Recovery Agency & Ors, R (on the application of) v Green & Ors* (Sullivan J).[60] This may depend upon the court's assessment of the reason put forward by the defendant: *The Director of the Assets Recovery Agency v Olupitan and Makinde* (Langley J).[61] Two separate tests apply to determine whether conduct is unlawful.[62] If conduct occurs in any part of the UK, it is unlawful if it is unlawful in that part of the UK.[63] If conduct occurs in another country it is only unlawful if it is unlawful both under the law of that country and would be unlawful under any part of UK law if committed in that part of the UK.[64] This enables, for example, recovery to be sought of a trafficker's proceeds abroad. Enforcement will depend upon international co-operation measures.

14.20   The court must decide on a balance of probabilities whether it has been proved that either any matters alleged to constitute unlawful conduct have occurred or that any person intended to use any cash in unlawful conduct. Thus, the unlawful conduct need not actually have happened. Property is obtained through unlawful conduct if it is obtained by or in return for the conduct.[65] Civil proceedings may be brought against any person whom the enforcement authority thinks holds recoverable property. The authority must identify at least in general terms the property which it seeks to recover. It may apply for an interim receiving order for the detention, custody or preservation of the property in question and for the appointment of an interim receiver. Such an order may be made if a good arguable case is established that the property is recoverable. Where the court is satisfied that any property is recoverable, it must make a recovery order.[66] The rights of innocent third parties are protected[67] if any provision in the order is incompatible with convention rights in the Human Rights Act 1998 or if the following four conditions are met:

(1) the person obtained the property in good faith;
(2) the person took steps in reliance on obtaining the property (reliance);

---

60 [2005] EWHC 3168.
61 [2007] EWHC 162 (QB).
62 Section 241.
63 Section 241(1).
64 Section 241(2).
65 Section 242.
66 Section 266.
67 Section 266(3)–(9).

(3) when the person took the steps, he or she had no notice (actual or constructive) that the property was recoverable; and

(4) if an order was made it would, because of the person's steps, be detrimental to him or her.

In addition, it must be established that it would not be just and equitable to make the order (having regard to the detriment of the individual and the interest of the enforcement authority in receiving the realised proceeds). The court must have regard to these last two factors but may also have regard to other matters. Once a recovery order has been made, a court-appointed trustee for civil recovery gives effect to it.[68]

Cross-jurisdictional recovery and international co-operation

14.21 Effective action to recover the proceeds of crime, whether in criminal or civil proceedings, is likely to span different jurisdictions. Where an order is made against assets in another jurisdiction, a receiver may be appointed in that jurisdiction[69] or the High Court may make an order against the defendant compelling the execution of a power of attorney abuse or order of repatriation.[70] Alternatively, international cooperation may be sought through a request made to the prosecuting authorities in the foreign state to freeze assets and realise proceeds.[71]

14.22 Proceeds transferred across borders may be traced across those borders. Equitable principles apply to the identification of recoverable property.[72] Thus, property may be traced into property which represents the original property[73] and may be identified even where mixed with other property,[74] as happens where it is used to increase funds held in a bank account or in part payment for the acquisition

---

68 Section 267.

69 POCA s84(1).

70 *DPP v Scarlett* [2001] 1 WLR 515.

71 POCA s74. The Proceeds of Crime Act 2002 (External Requests and Orders) Order 2005 SI 2005/3181 makes provision for the UK to provide international cooperation to other states, for example *Serious Fraud Officer v A* [2007] EWCA Crim 1927. In practice, assets that are traced abroad tend to remain abroad and be the subject of an inter-state asset sharing agreement.

72 Section 304(1).

73 Section 305.

74 Section 306.

of an asset, for the restoration or improvement of land or by a person holding a leasehold interest to acquire the freehold. However, as with equitable rules, the property may not be followed into the hands of someone who obtains the property in good faith, for value and without notice (actual or constructive) that it was recoverable property.

14.23   Interim property freezing orders and interim receivership orders may be sought to prevent transfer out of the jurisdiction.

Investigative orders

14.24   A range of orders may be obtained by SOCA to assist in investigations. They are:

(i)   Disclosure orders: the High Court or Crown Court may order the defendant to provide information for the purposes of any question relevant to the determination of a confiscation hearing in the Crown Court following conviction: *Re O*;[75] *Re T*.[76]

(ii)   Production Orders: such proceedings must be brought within 12 years of accrual from the date on which the cause of action accrued,[77] ie when the property is obtained through unlawful conduct or (in cases where it is indirectly so obtained) when it is obtained.[78] Similar provisions apply in Scotland[79] and Northern Ireland.[80] The order may be applied for on behalf of a foreign government: *R v Southwark Crown Court, ex p Customs and Excise*.[81]

(iii)   Account Monitoring Orders: Section 401: An account monitoring order may also be made.[82]

(iv)   Customer Information Orders: these require the provision, by a financial institution, of data relating to the account of a person, whether natural or legal, and whether UK resident or incorporated or not, whose account is with the institution.[83] Such an order

---

75   [1991] 2 QB 520.
76   [1996] 96 CrAppR 194.
77   Section 288(2).
78   Section 288(1).
79   Section 288(2).
80   Section 288(3).
81   [1990] 1 QB 650.
82   Sections 404–408.
83   Sections 397–403.

can only be made where the person whose data is required is subject to a confiscation investigation or a money laundering investigation or where property specified is subject to a civil recovery investigation and the person specified appears to hold the property.

Serious crime prevention orders

14.25   This order may be made by the Crown Court in respect of someone convicted of a serious offence[84] or by the High Court where it is satisfied that a person has been involved in serious crime (whether in England and Wales or elsewhere) and it has reasonable grounds to believe that making the order would protect the public by preventing, restricting or disrupting involvement by the person in serious crime in England and Wales.[85] The order may impose prohibitions, restrictions or requirements and any other appropriate terms and may relate to finances, property, premises and belongings.[86] It has effect for up to five years. People trafficking offences are serious offences by virtue of being set out in Schedule 1, para 2 of the Serious Crimes Act 2007.

Taxation

14.26   Where neither confiscation nor civil recovery are suitable, taxation powers can be deployed. HMRC have the power to tax any income, gains or profits which are chargeable to tax. HMRC now contain a specialist, effective, Criminal Taxes Unit. Despite the Unit's name, the power to tax arises without regard to the legality or illegality of the relevant activity, provided the activity is chargeable, and thus there is no need to establish criminal conduct.[87]

14.27   Part 6 of the Proceeds of Crime Act 2002 Act also provides for the exercise of general revenue functions by the now defunct Asset Recovery Agency. These powers are triggered where they have reasonable grounds to suspect that income or a gain arising to a

84   SCA 2007 s19(1) and (2).
85   SCA 2007 s1(1)
86   SCA 2007 ss1(3), 19(5), 5.
87   Cf s317 POCA.

person in respect of a chargeable period is chargeable to income tax or is a chargeable gain, or a company is chargeable to corporation tax on its profits arising in respect of a chargeable period, and in both cases that the income or gain arises or accrues as a result of criminal conduct (by the taxable person or by another and whether wholly or partly and whether directly or indirectly). Conduct is criminal if it would be criminal when committed in the United Kingdom.[88] The Serious Crime Act 2007 transferred these powers to the Serious Organised Crime Agency, together with the power to abolish Part 6 of the Act. Given the effectiveness of HMRC, it is unlikely that the powers under Part 6, with the additional requirement to suspect causation from criminal conduct, will be used. In any event, tax evasion is excluded from the definition of criminal conduct.[89] This means that HMRC, with their wide enforcement powers, have a significant role in eliminating or reducing the profits from trafficking.

88   POCA s326.
89   POCA s326(2).

Resources

Amnesty International

The Human Rights Action Centre
17-25 New Inn Yard
London EC2A 3EA
Tel: +44 (0) 20 7033 1500
Fax: +44 (0) 20 7033 1503
Textphone: +44 (0) 20 7033 1664
Email: sct@amnesty.org.uk
Individuals at risk:
0207 033 1572

Amnesty International Northern Ireland
397 Ormeau Road
Belfast
BT7 3GP
Tel: +44 (0) 28 9064 3000
Email: nireland@amnesty.org.uk

Amnesty International Scotland
9 Haymarket Terrace
Edinburgh EH12 5EZ
Tel: +44 (0) 844 800 9088
Fax: +44 (0) 131 313 7000
Email: scotland@amnesty.org.uk

Amnesty International Wales
Amnest Rhyngwladol Cymru
Temple Court
Cathedral Road
Heoly Gadeirlan
Caerdydd
Cardiff
CF11 9HA

Tel: +44 (0) 29 2078 6415
Fax: +44 (0) 29 2078 6416
Email: wales@amnesty.org.uk

Publishes useful country reports.

Anti-Slavery International

Thomas Clarkson House
The Stableyard
Broomgrove Road
London SW9 9TL
Tel: 0207 501 8290
Fax: 0207 738 4110
Email: antislavery@antislavery.org
www.antislavery.org

Campaigning group.

Base 75

75 Robertson Street
Glasgow G2 8QD,
United Kingdom
Tel: 0141 276 0737
http://www.gvaw.org.uk

Assistance in exiting street prostitution.

Child Exploitation and Online Protection Centre (CEOP)

33 Vauxhall Bridge Road
London SW1V 2WG
Tel: 0207 238 2320/2307
www.ceop.gov.uk

Children's Commissioner

11 MILLION
1 London Bridge
LONDON
SE1 9BG
General enquiries: 0844 800 9113
E-mail: info.request@11MILLION.org.uk
www. 11million.org.uk

Advocacy of children.

The Criminal Injuries Compensation Authority

Tay House
300 Bath Street
Glasgow G2 4LN
Tel: 0800 3583601 (8:30am–8pm Mon–Fri; 9am–1pm Sat)
Fax: 0141 331 2287
Ecophone text: 0141 331 5560
Website: www.cica.gov.uk

ECPAT UK

Grosvenor Gardens House
35-37 Grosvenor Gardens
London SW1W OBS
Tel: 0207 233 9887
www.ecpat.org.uk
Campaigning and advocacy.

Employment Agency Standards Inspectorate

Carries out routine inspections of agencies and investigates complaints about agency conduct.

Tel: 0845 955 5105 (Monday–Friday 9am–5pm)

European Commission

http://europa.eu.int/comm/index_en.htm

Foreign and Commonwealth Office

Tel: 0207 008 1500
For foreign diplomatic missions in London, see the London
Diplomatic List on www.fco.gov.uk

The Gangmasters Licensing Authority

PO Box 8538
Nottingham
NG8 9AF
Tel: 0845 602 5020
Email: enquiries@gla.gsi.gov.uk
www.gla.gov.uk

Inspection body. Has anonymous reporting line.

GMB union

National Office
22/24 Worple Road
London
SW19 4DD
Tel: 020 8947 3131
Fax: 020 8944 6552
Email: info@gmb.org.uk
Regional offices are listed at www.gmb.org.uk

Online application form available.

Health and Safety Executive

London only
Rose Court
2 Southwark Bridge
London
SE1 9HS
Fax: 020 7556 2102

Glasgow office
1st floor
Mercantile Chambers
53 Bothwell Street
Glasgow
G2 6TS
Fax: 0141 275 3100

The website has a full list of offices across the UK
Reporting an incident at work eg injury, dangerous occurrence or
work related disease Tel: 0845 300 99 23
www.hse.gov.uk

The Helen Bamber Foundation

5 Museum House
25 Museum Street
London WC1A 1JT

Fax: 020 7631 4493
www.helenbamber.org

Counselling and support services for, amongst others, victims of
trafficking Website has referral form which may be downloaded and
faxed.

Legal Services Commission

4 Abbey Orchard Street
London
SW1P 2BS
DX: 328 London
Tel: 0207 783 7000
http://www.legalservices.gov.uk/civil/forms asp

Provides funding in some circumstances.

HMRC

National Minimum Wage helpline: 0845 600 0678
Monday–Friday 9am–5pm
www.hmrc.gov.uk/leaflets/ssp.htm

To report an employer paying less than the National Minimum Wage.

International Labour Organization

4 route des Morillons
CH-1211 Genève 22
Switzerland
Switchboard: +41 (0) 22 799 6111
Fax:+41 (0) 22 798 8685
Website: http://www.ilo.org
E-mail: ilo@ilo.org

Specialist UN agency for the promotion of social justice and
internationally recognised human and labour rights.
Committee of experts considers and comments on country reports
annually.

International Organisation for Migration (IOM)

IOM (UK)
21 Westminster Palace Gardens, Artillery Row, London SW1P 1RR
Tel: +44 (0) 20 7233 0001 or 0800 783 2332
Fax: +44 (0) 20 7233 3001
www.iomlondon.org

Open 10am–1pm and 2pm–4:30pm, Monday to Friday. Branch
offices in Bristol, Glasgow and Liverpool.
All enquiries to IOM are treated confidentially and there is no need
for anyone to give their name in order to receive free advice.
Provides assisted voluntary return and monetary package for
reintegration.

International Social Services of the UK

ISS UK
Canterbury Court, Unit 1.11
1-3 Brixton Road
London
SW9 6DE
Telephone Advice Line: 020 7735 8941
Reception: 020 3176 0253
Fax: 020 7582 0696
Email: info@issuk.org.uk.
www.isssuk.org.uk.
Provides intercountry casework services, advice and information.

KALAYAAN

St. Francis Center
Pottery Lane
London W1 4NQ
Tel: 0207 243 2942

Specialist support to overseas domestic workers.

La Strada International

De Wittenstraat 25
1052 AK Amsterdam
The Netherlands
Tel: 00 31(0) 206881414
Fax: 00 31 (0) 206881013
Email: info@lastradaintemational.org
www. lastradainternational.org

The Medaille Trust

PO Box 119
Darlington
DL1 9BX
www.medaille.co.uk

Accommodation run by Catholic nuns for victims of sex trafficking.

Medical Foundation for the Care of Victims of Torture

111 Isledon Road
London N7 7JW
Tel: 020 7697 7777
www torturecare.org.uk

Missing People Helpline

0500 700700 after 07.30
www missingpeople.org.uk

This is a call centre number. 999 may be used in an emergency.

National Register of Public Service Interpreters Ltd

Saxon House
48 Southwark Street
London
SE1 1UN
Tel: 0207 940 3166
Email: nrpsi@iol.org.uk
www.nrpsi.co.uk

NSPCC Child Trafficking Advice and Information Line

Offers direct assistance to professionals and non-statutory services responsible for children.
NSPCC: 0800 107 7057

Organisation for Security and Cooperation in Europe (OSCE)

www.osce.org

Concerned with early warning, conflict prevention, crisis management and post conflict rehabilitation within its 55 participating states from Europe, Central Asia, the Caucasus and North America.
Has a Rapporteur on trafficking in persons.

POPPY Project

POPPY Project Duty Officer
Tel: 0207 735 2062 or 0771 730 6289 (24 hour).
www.eaves4women.co.uk/POPPY_Project

For full time accommodation or outreach support for victims of sex trafficking or trafficking for domestic servitude, subject to criteria.

RMT union

Unity House
39 Chalton Street
London NW1 1JD
Tel: 020 7387 4771
Fax: 020 7387 4123
Email: info@rmt.org uk

Union for workers in the transport sector.
To join, ask for the membership section or join online.

Salvation Army

101 Newington Causeway
London
SE1 6BN
Tel: 020 7367 4865
Fax: 020 7367 4712

Homelessness services across the country.

Trades Union Congress (TUC)

Congress House
Great Russell Street
London WC1B 3LS
Tel: 0207 636 4030
www.tuc.org.uk

Carries out policy work for the trade union movement. Practical support and membership enquiries should be directed to a relevant union.

UCATT

Construction and allied trades union

General office
177 Abbeville Road
London
SW4 9RL
Tel: 0207 622 2442
Fax: 0207 720 4081
Members' employment law advice line: 0800 262 467

UCATT Scotland
53 Morrison Street
Glasgow G5 8LB
Tel: 0141 420 2880
Fax: 0141 420 2881

UCATT Wales and South West
199 Newport Road
Cardiff
CF2 1AJ

Tel: 029 2049 8664
Fax: 029 2048 1166

Full list of offices and other information from www.ucatt.info.

United Nations Special Rapporteur on trafficking in persons (currently Ms Joy Ngozi Ezeilo)

c/o Office Of the High Commissioner for Human Rights
United Nations at Geneva
8-14 Avenue de la Paix
1211 Geneva 10
Switzerland
Fax: (+41 22) 917 9006
E-mail: urgent-action@ohcht.org (include in the subject box: Special Rapporteur on trafficking in persons)
www2.ohchr.org/english/issues/trafficking/index.htm

UNITE the union

The UK's largest union, covering a range of sectors

National offices
35 King Street
Covent Garden
London
WC2E 8JG
Tel: 020 7420 8900
Fax: 020 7420 8998

28 Theobald's Road
Holborn
London
WC1X 8TN
Tel: 020 7611 2500
Fax: 020 7611 2555

Membership enquiries to the regional office (the website contains a useful map listing regional and district offices).

UNITE Scotland
Transport House
290 Bath Street
Glasgow G2 4LD
Tel: 0141 404 1850
Fax: 0141 332 6157

UNITE Wales
1 Cathedral Road
Cardiff CF11 9SD
Tel: 02920 394 521
Fax: 02920 390 684

UNITE London and Eastern
'Woodberry'
218 Green Lanes
London N4 2HB
Tel: 020 8800 4281
Fax: 020 8802 8388

UNITE North-West
Transport House
Merchants Quay
Salford Quays
Salford M50 3SG
Tel: 0161 848 0909
Fax: 0161 872 6068

UNITE North West, Yorkshire and Humberside
Transport House
55 Call Lane
Leeds
West Yorkshire LS1 7BW
Tel: 0113 236 4830
Fax: 0113 236 4831

UNITE East Midlands
Unit 2
Pride Point Drive
Pride Park
Derby
DE24 8BX
Tel: 0133 254 8400 Fax: 013.32 548440

UNITE West Midlands
Transport House
9-17 Victoria Street
West Bromwich B70 8HX
Tel: 0121 553 6051
Fax: 0121 553 7846

UNITE South West
Transport House
Victoria Street
Bristol BS1 6AY
Tel: 0117 923 0555
Fax: 0117 923 0560

UNISON

Public sector union

1 Mabledon Place
London WC1H 9AJ
Tel: 0845 355 0845

Application forms and details of regional offices available at
www.unison.org.uk

United Kingdom Human Trafficking Centre

PO Box 4107
Sheffield
S1 9DQ
Tel: 0114 252 3891 (24 hour)
Fax: 0114 252 3806
www.ukhtc.org

Victim Support

Tel: 0845 303 0900 (9 00am–9 00pm Mon–Fri; 09.00am–7.00pm
Sat & Sun)
www.victimsupport.org.uk

Provides explanatory leaflets in a variety of languages.

Xtalk project

Runs a three month course of English for sex workers.
www.xtalkproject.net
For more information and the addresses of the classes
Tel: 0791 470 3372
www.iusw.org

Index

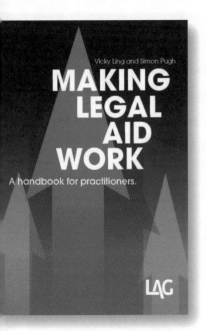

Making Legal Aid Work:

A handbook for practitioners

Vicky Ling and Simon Pugh

his is the ultimate quick reference guide to legal aid –
escribing the whole legal aid scheme in one conveniently
ized volume.

provides key information about all the types of public
unding, dealing with common queries which crop up
equently in practice. Taking a practical, hands-on
pproach it provides useful case-studies and checklists,
aking it indispensable to new caseworkers and trainees
s well as experienced practitioners.

978 1 903307 68 7 • 352pp • April 2009 • £40

lag.org.uk/books